Human**Resource** Management

Second Canadian Edition

Human **Resource** Management

Second Canadian Edition

R. Wayne Mondy, SPHR
McNeese State University

Robert M. Noe, SPHR
Texas A & M University - Commerce

Shane R. Premeaux
McNeese State University

Ronald A. Knowles
Algonquin College

Prentice
Hall

Toronto

Canadian Cataloguing in Publication Data

Main entry under title:

Human resource management

2nd Canadian ed.
Previous ed. written by Phillip Wright, R. Wayne Mondy, Robert M. Noe.
Includes index.
ISBN 0-13-014336-7

1. Personnel management. 2. Personnel management – Canada.
I. Mondy, R. Wayne, 1940– . II. Wright, Phillip Charles.
Human resource management.

HF5549.W75 2001   658.3   C00-930310-3

© 2001, 1996 Pearson Education Canada Inc., Toronto, Ontario

ISBN 0-13-014336-7

Vice President, Editorial Director: Michael Young
Acquisitions Editor: Mike Ryan
Marketing Manager: James Buchanan
Associate Editor: Lisa Marshall
Production Editor: Marisa D'Andrea
Copy Editor: Gilda Mekler
Production Coordinator: Janette Lush
Art Director: Mary Opper
Cover Design: Alex Li
Cover Image: © Bob Commander/SIS
Interior Design: Alex Li
Page Layout: Susan Thomas/Digital Zone

1 2 3 4 5   05 04 03 02 01

Printed and bound in Canada

Statistics Canada information is used with the permission of the Minister of Industry, as Minister responsible for Statistics Canada. Information on the availability of the wide range of data from Statistics Canada can be obtained from Statistics Canada's Regional Offices, its World Wide Web site at http://www.statcan.ca, and its toll-free access number 1-800-263-1136.

Prentice
Hall

BRIEF Contents

CONTENTS

Employee and Labour Relations   337

PREFACE

The world of human resource management has experienced major changes since the last edition of this book was published. The impact of global competition, the Internet, and rapid technological advances have accelerated trends in such areas as shared service centres, outsourcing, and just-in-time training. All business areas, including human resources, are being restructured in many organizations. Some observers have predicted that these changes will diminish the importance of human resource management. A more prevalent view of human resources, and one held by the authors, is that proper human resource management remains an organization's primary competitive edge. Increasingly, the managers of human resources are becoming strategic partners with top management, a testament to the increasing importance of human resources in organizations.

The second Canadian edition of *Human Resource Management* provides a realistic approach to the human resource management field. Even though the book is highly hands-on, it also provides thorough coverage of current human resource management theories and concepts. In fact, the interrelationship between the various human resource functions is a central theme that runs throughout the book. Each of the functions is described from the standpoint of its relationship to the strategic needs of organizations.

This book is written primarily for students studying human resource management for the first time. It puts them in touch with the real world through the use of numerous illustrations and company material showing how human resource management is practised in today's foremost organizations.

Features of this Book

We have included a number of features to make important human resource management concepts readable and understandable:

- **NEW** Learning Objectives and Summary are tied together. The summary at the end of the chapter is tied to the objectives at the beginning of the chapter.

SUMMARY

- **NEW** "A Global Perspective"
  Because of the impact of the global environment on human resource management, new major global topics have been added to each chapter under the heading of "A Global Perspective."

A GLOBAL PERSPECTIVE

- **NEW** "HR Trends and Innovations"

  Every chapter includes a section on "HR Trends and Innovations," which highlights the current trends in Human Resource Management.

TRENDS and INNOVATIONS

- **NEW** "HR Web Wisdom"
  Three or more Web sites per chapter, relating to topics highlighted in the chapter, are flagged in the "HR Web Wisdom" boxes appearing in the margin. One of the sites in each chapter refers to the Human Resources Development Canada Web site. Corresponding current Web addresses can be found in the Companion Web site at *http://www.pearsoned.ca/ mondy.* The Internet is a dynamic and evolving structure, and therefore users of these and other HR-related Web sites should frequently contact our Companion Web site where changes, improvements, and new resources are provided.

- A model (Figure 1-1 on page 3) has been developed as a vehicle for interrelating the many facets of HRM. We believe this overview is a valuable teaching and study device.

- Each key term is highlighted in bold type the first time it is defined or described. Key terms are defined in the margins and terms are highlighted in the index in bold with the page number for the definition.

- At least one vignette is provided at the beginning of each chapter to set the tone for a discussion of the major topics included within the chapter.

- A brief exercise, "HRM in Action," is included in the body of each chapter to permit students to make decisions concerning situations that could occur in the business world. Fifty percent of the incidents are new to this edition. Teaching notes are provided in the *Instructor's Resource Manual and CBC Video Guide.*

- Review questions appear at the end of each chapter to test students' understanding of the material presented in the chapter.

- A CBC video case appears at the end of each part of the textbook. Consisting of clips from the television program *Venture*, these video cases allow students to tie information contained in the text to actual business situations.

- A running case about the hypothetical Parma Cycle Co. also appears at the end of each part of the textbook. Each segment takes the story line one step further, so that students become aware of day-to-day HRM problems as they are managed within a familiar business situation.

- A comprehensive "HRM Incident" is provided at the end of each chapter. These exercises are designed to enhance class participation and group involvement. Teaching notes are included in the *Instructor's Resource Manual and CBC Video Guide.*

- Timely examples and material are used throughout the book to illustrate how a concept is actually used in practice.

By exposing students to the latest HR practices, we aim not only to stimulate interest in our discipline but to illustrate how textbook concepts come into actual play in well-managed organizations. Thus, we hope to make human resource management an essential part of every student's business education.

Supplements

These supplements are available for use with the second edition of *Human Resource Management:*

Companion Web Site:

This site contains Human Resource management Web links, Web resources, Internet exercises, and sample test questions for each chapter. Instructors will be interested in our online syllabus builder and the password-protected instructors' area containing electronic versions of key supplements and updates to the text. To obtain your password, please contact your Pearson Education Canada sales representative. See *http://www.pearsoned.ca/mondy* and explore! (ISBN: 0-13-014343-X)

Prentice Hall

COMPANION WEBSITE

Instructor's Resource Manual and CBC Video Guide:

This manual outlines the basic structure of each chapter and contains suggestions on how to use the text more effectively. It also includes suggested lecture outlines and answers to end-of-chapter questions, end-of-part case studies, and CBC video case study questions. (ISBN: 0-13-014337-5)

Test Item File:

The test item file contains over 1000 multiple choice and true/false questions with answers, level of difficulty, and relevant textbook pages listed for each question. (ISBN: 0-13-014338-3)

Pearson Education Canada Test Manager:

Using our new Test Manager program, the computerized test bank for Human Resource Management offers a comprehensive suite of tools for testing and assessment. Test Manager allows educators to easily create and distribute tests for their courses, either by printing and distributing through traditional methods or by on-line delivery via a Local Area Network (LAN) server. Test Manager has removed the guesswork from your next move by incorporating Screen Wizards that assist you with such tasks as managing question content, managing a portfolio of tests, testing students, and analyzing test results. In addition, this all-new testing package is backed with full technical support, comprehensive online help files, a guided tour, and complete written documentation. Available as a CD-ROM for Windows 95. (ISBN: 0-13-014339-1)

CBC/Pearson Education Canada Video Library:

Pearson Education Canada and the CBC have worked together to bring you the best and most comprehensive video package available in the higher education market, containing six segments from CBC *Venture* programs. Designed specifically to complement the textbook, this video library is an excellent tool for bringing students into contact with the world outside the classroom. (Please contact your Pearson Education Canada sales representative for details. These videos are subject to availability and terms negotiated upon adoption of the text.) (ISBN: 0-13-014342-1)

Electronic Transparencies:

More than 10 slides per chapter have been created in PowerPoint, complementing the chapter content and incorporating many figures and tables from the text. Lessons using these slides have been integrated into the *Instructor's Resource Manual.* (ISBN: 0-13-014330-8)

Acknowledgements

The assistance and the encouragement of many people are normally required in writing any book. Although it would be virtually impossible to list everyone who assisted in this project, we feel that certain people must be credited for the magnitude of their contribution: in particular, Phillip C. Wright for his groundbreaking work on the first Canadian edition and his continued support and advice.

We would also like to thank Sherry Torchinsky, Amber Wallace, and Lisa Marshall, all very competent and professional individuals, who were always available to ensure that our deadlines were met. As well, the support and encouragement of practising HRM professionals and managers from many parts of Canada have made this book possible.

We would also like to thank the reviewers of this book:

John Cavaliere, Sault College

Jane Guzar, Mohawk College

Linda Piper, Canadore College

Don Schepens, Grant MacEwan Community College

Robert Soroka, Dawson College

Larry Suffield, Lambton College

Ann Wylie, Niagara College

Ronald A. Knowles
R. Wayne Mondy
Robert M. Noe
Shane R. Premeaux
2001

This text has been approved by the Human Resources Professionals Association of Ontario and is listed as a recommended text in HRPAO's "Curriculum Summary".

CHAPTER

1

Human Resource Management: An Overview

CHAPTER OBJECTIVES

1. Identify the basic human resource management functions.

2. Identify who performs the human resource management tasks.

3. Explain the trend for the human resource manager to be a strategic partner.

4. Briefly describe the human resources implications of the growth in small business, technology, and the global economy.

5. Outline the employability skills required by human resource managers.

6. Distinguish among human resource executives, generalists, and specialists.

7. Describe the changes that occur in the human resource function as a firm grows larger and more complex.

8. Explain the nature of professionalization of human resources and the role of human resource associations.

9. Define ethics and relate ethics to human resource management.

As Harry Jones, vice president of human resources for Handwell, headquartered in Calgary, rose to leave the executive meeting, he realized that his job would be even busier than usual during the next six months. Handwell Enterprises produces high-tech components for both government and private industry, and greater production capacity is needed to meet industry demands. A decision had been made at the meeting to open a new plant in Duncan, British Columbia. Harry and the company's managers had analyzed a number of sites and had determined that Duncan most closely met their needs. When the plant is completed in a year, 500 new employees must be available and trained. In addition, 75 employees at the Calgary facility will be transferred to Duncan. It is Harry's responsibility to ensure that qualified new workers are hired and trained, and that the transferred workers are effectively integrated into the work force.

Edward Tan is the supervisor of 10 Green Owl convenience stores in Southern Ontario. As the Green Owl chain is relatively small (only 40 stores), it has no human resource department. Supervisors are in charge of all employment activities for their own stores. Edward must ensure that only the best people are recruited for positions as store managers and then must properly train them. If one of the managers fails to report for an assigned shift and Edward cannot find a replacement, he is expected to work the shift. It is Friday afternoon and Edward is hurriedly attempting to locate a replacement because one store manager just quit without giving notice.

Judy Lynley is the industrial relations manager for Axton Pneumotives, a small manufacturer of pumps located in Sussex, New Brunswick. The sixty-five machine operators in the firm belong to the International Association of Machinists and Aerospace Workers. Judy has been negotiating with union leaders for five weeks with little success. The union members have threatened to walk off the job if the contract is not resolved by midnight. However, if Judy's firm agrees to all the union's monetary demands, it will no longer be competitive in the industry.

arry, Edward and Judy all have one thing in common: they are deeply involved with some of the challenges and problems related to human resource management. Managing people in organizations has become more complex than ever before because of rapidly changing technology and increasingly complicated work environments. In the past, the company with access to the most capital or the latest technology had the best competitive advantage. "Today, companies that offer products with the highest quality are the ones with a leg up on the competition. But the only thing that will uphold a company's advantage tomorrow is the caliber of people in the organization."[1] According to the Canadian Council of Human Resources Associations (CCHRA), the only sustainable competitive advantage is the organization's ability to attract, retain, and apply the best human capabilities to the task at hand.[2] Increasingly, human resources are seen as a key element in improving competitiveness.

In this first chapter we begin to unravel the human resource challenge. We start with a discussion of the human resource management functions. Next, we address the issue of who performs the human resource management tasks and the role of human resource manager as a strategic partner. This is followed by a brief discussion of the human resource implications of the growth in small business, technology, and the global economy. We then outline the skills required by human resource managers. The distinction among human resource executives, generalists, and specialists; and the human resource function in organizations of different sizes are addressed next. Finally, we discuss professionalism and ethics in this dynamic discipline and describe the scope of the book.

Human Resource Management Functions

Human resource management (HRM): The utilization of a firm's human resources to achieve organizational objectives.

Human resource management (HRM) is the utilization of human resources to achieve organizational objectives. Consequently, all managers at every level must concern themselves with human resource management. Basically, managers get things done with and through the efforts of others. This requires effective human resource management.

Today's human resource problems and opportunities are enormous and appear to be expanding. Individuals dealing with human resource matters face a multitude of challenges, ranging from a constantly changing workforce to the ever-present scores of government regulations and a major technological revolution. Harry Jones, in the opening vignette, for example, must ensure that the new workforce is capable of being productive in a high-tech facility. Furthermore, global competition has caused organizations both large and small to be more conscious of cost and productivity. Because of the critical nature of human resource issues, these matters are receiving major attention from business owners and upper management.

People who are engaged in the management of human resources develop and work through an integrated human resource management system. As Figure 1-1 shows, six basic functional areas are associated with effective human resource management: human resource planning; human resource staffing; human resource development; compensation and benefits; safety and health; and employee and labour relations. A major report authored by the Canadian Council of Human Resources Associations (CCHRA) in partnership with Human Resources Canada confirmed that these areas, along with human resources information management and professional practices, constitute the core functions of human resource management.[3] A similar view is held by the Human Resources Professionals Association of Ontario and the Human Resources Institute of Alberta, Canada's two largest HRM associations, which both offer certification programs that closely parallel this classification.[4] Sound management practices are required for successful performance in each area. We discuss these functions next.

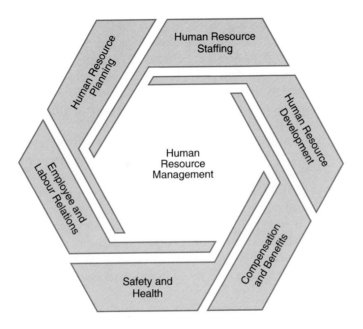

Figure 1-1

The Human Resource Management System

Human Resource Planning

An organization must have qualified individuals in specific jobs at specific places and times to accomplish its mission and goals. Obtaining such people involves human resource planning (HRP): the systematic process of reviewing and anticipating human resource requirements to ensure that the required numbers of employees, with the required skills, are available when needed. Successful HRP is vital if the organization is to accomplish its mission effectively. The planning process normally begins with an environmental assessment and the formulation of a strategic plan. Chapters 2 and 3 are devoted to these topics.

Staffing

The staffing function includes job analysis, recruitment and selection. Successful accomplishment of these three tasks is vital if the organization is to accomplish its mission effectively. *Job analysis* is an essential part of human resource planning and the topic of Chapter 4. Job analysis is the systematic process of determining the skills, duties, and knowledge required to perform jobs in an organization. It is a pervasive human resource technique that basically provides a summary of a job's duties and responsibilities, the job's relationship to other jobs, the knowledge and skills it requires, and the working conditions under which the job is performed.

Recruitment is the process of attracting qualified individuals and encouraging them to apply for work with the organization. *Selection* is the process through which the organization chooses, from a group of applicants, those individuals best suited both for open positions and for the company. Chapters 5 and 6 are devoted to these two topics.

Human Resource Development

Human resource development (HRD), discussed in Chapters 7, 8, 9, and 10, is the planned, continuous effort by management to improve employee competency levels and organizational performance. As such, HRD helps individuals, groups, and the entire organization become more effective. It is essential because people, technology, jobs, and organizations are always changing. Technology, in particular, is advancing at a staggering pace. Therefore, it is vital that employees be trained and developed to use this technology so as to attain the highest levels of productivity[5]. Harry Jones, in the opening vignette for example, must prepare 500 employees for their new assignments.

Large-scale or organizational-wide HRD programs are referred to as *organizational development* (OD). The purpose of OD is to alter the environment within the firm to enable employees to perform more productively.

Other aspects of HRD include training and development, career planning and development, and performance appraisal. Training helps employees acquire knowledge and skills needed for their present jobs. Development involves a longer-term focus that looks beyond today and today's job by preparing employees to keep pace with the organization as it changes and grows. The training and development process should begin when individuals join the firm and continue throughout their careers.

Career planning is an ongoing process in which an individual sets career goals and identifies the means to achieve them. *Career development* is a formal approach used by the organization to ensure that people with the proper qualifications and experience are available when needed. Individual careers and organizational needs are not separate and distinct. Organizations should assist employees in career planning so the needs of both can be satisfied.

Through *performance appraisal*, employees and teams are evaluated to determine how well they are performing their assigned tasks. Performance appraisal affords employees the opportunity to capitalize on their strengths and overcome identified deficiencies, thereby becoming more satisfied and productive employees.

HR professionals often use the term operative employees. **Operative employees** are all the workers in an organization except managers and professionals, such as engineers, accountants, or professional secretaries. Clerical workers, truck drivers, and waiters are examples of operative employees.

Operative employees:
All workers in a firm except managers and professionals.

Compensation and Benefits

The question of what constitutes a fair day's pay has plagued management, unions, and workers for a long time. A well-thought-out compensation system provides employees with adequate and equitable rewards for their contributions to meeting organizational goals. As used in this book, the term compensation includes all rewards that individuals receive as a result of their employment. The reward may be one or a combination of the following:

- **Pay:** The money that a person receives for performing a job
- **Benefits:** Additional financial rewards, other than base pay, such as paid vacations, sick leave, holidays, and medical insurance
- **Nonfinancial rewards:** Nonmonetary rewards, such as enjoyment of the work performed or a pleasant working environment

Although compensation includes all these rewards, the increasing importance of incentives and benefits warrants separate treatment. Many companies are cautiously experimenting with various incentive programs, in which small reductions in the increase in a worker's base pay are accompanied by large potential incentives based on team or area performance above an established norm. Ken Leach is president of Integrator Trump Systems Inc. of Bolton, Ontario. "Our people are disciplined and work hard," he says. "I want to reward their efforts with something on the table now. I want everyone who is here to retire here."[6] Smaller companies like Trump Systems and large corporations like IBM have had surprisingly good results with incentive programs, which are expected to expand dramatically in the future.[7] We discuss compensation in Chapter 11 and address benefits and other compensation issues in Chapter 12.

Safety and Health

Safety involves protecting employees from injuries caused by work-related accidents. Health refers to employees' freedom from illness and general physical and mental well being. These aspects of the job are important because employees who work in a safe environment and enjoy good health are more likely to be productive and yield long-term benefits to the organization. For this reason, progressive managers have long advocated and implemented adequate safety and health programs. Today, because of federal and provincial legislation, which reflects societal concerns, most organizations have become attentive to their employees' safety and health. Chapter 13 explores the topics of safety and health.

Employee and Labour Relations

In Canada, a business is required by law to recognize a union and bargain with it in good faith if the employees want the union to represent them. For the last fifteen years, the Canadian labour movement has managed to maintain a relatively constant percentage of union membership. According to the 1997 Directory of Labour Organizations in Canada, there were 15.1 million Canadian workers, 11.9 million of whom were eligible to join unions. Some four million workers, or 34 percent of all nonagricultural paid workers in Canada, are represented by a union in their workplace.[8]

But the labour relations field is changing and Canadian unions are at a crossroads. Worldwide competitive pressures are leading to new employer militancy and more aggressive bargaining. In addition, technology is being used to reduce costs and to increase productivity, a trend that has reduced the number of jobs in blue-collar occupations, where unions have traditionally been well represented. In the public sector too, budget cutting has decreased the number of employees eligible to join unions.

Changing social attitudes and fiercely competitive economic trends, combined with the highly technical nature of many new jobs, are likely to make it difficult for unions to maintain present membership levels. Furthermore, both unions and managers are under intense pressure to become more cooperative— a process that could undermine the union's traditional role.[9] Chapters 14, 15 and 16 are devoted to these types of employee and labour relations issues.

Human Resource Research and Information Management

Although human resource research and human resources information management are shown in Figure 1-1 as separate functions, they pervade all HRM functional areas. For instance, a study related to recruitment may suggest the type of worker most likely to succeed in that particular firm. Research on job safety may identify the causes of certain work-related accidents. The reasons for problems such as excessive absenteeism or too many grievances may not be readily apparent. Human resource research and information can shed light on their causes and provide keys to developing the most productive and satisfied workforce possible.

Interrelationship of HRM Functions

All HRM functional areas are highly interrelated. Management must recognize that decisions in one area will affect other areas. For instance, a firm that emphasizes recruiting top quality candidates but neglects to provide satisfactory compensation is wasting time, effort, and money. A firm's compensation system will be inadequate unless employees are provided a safe and healthy work environment. The interrelationships among the six HRM functional areas shown in Figure 1-1 will become more apparent as we address each functional topic throughout the book.

Who Performs the Human Resource Management Tasks?

All business units must operate under a strict budget in this competitive global environment and HR is no exception. Because of time and budgetary constraints, some company and HR executives have had to make difficult decisions regarding how traditional HR tasks are accomplished. Naturally, the six basic HR functional areas must be performed, but the person(s) or units accomplishing these functions are changing. While most organizations still have a traditional human resource manager, progressive organizations are increasingly finding it more efficient to rely on line managers, shared service centres and outsourcing to assist in the delivery of human resources. Some HR departments are getting smaller because other departments are now accomplishing certain functions. This shift permits HR managers to focus on more strategic and mission-oriented activities.

The Human Resource Manager

A **human resource manager** is an individual who normally acts in an advisory or staff capacity, working with other managers to help them deal with human resource matters. Traditionally, the human resource manager has been primarily responsible for coordinating the management of human resources to help the organization achieve its goals. As shown in the opening vignette for example, Harry Jones, as vice president of human resources, is in charge of selecting and recruiting 500 new employees in addition to facilitating the transfer of 75 employees from the Calgary facility.

Human resource manager: Individual who normally acts in an advisory (or staff) capacity when working with other (line) managers regarding human resource matters.

There is normally a shared responsibility between line managers and human resource professionals. The distinction between human resource management and the human resource manager is clearly illustrated by the following account:

> Bill Thieu, the production supervisor for Ajax Manufacturing, has just learned that one of his machine operators has resigned. He immediately calls Sandra Gianelli, the human resource manager, and says, "Sandra, I just had a Class A machine operator quit down here. Can you find some qualified people for me to interview?" "Sure Bill," Sandra replies. "I'll send two or three down to you within the week, and you can select the one that best fits your needs."

In this instance, both Bill and Sandra are concerned with accomplishing organizational goals, but from different perspectives. Sandra, as a human resource manager, identifies applicants who meet the criteria specified by Bill. Bill, however, will make the final decision as to who is hired because he is responsible for the machine operator's performance. His primary responsibility is production; hers is human resources. As a human resource manager, Sandra must constantly deal with the many problems related to human resources that Bill and the other managers face. Her job is to help them meet the human resource needs of the entire organization. In some firms, her function is also referred to as personnel, employee relations, or industrial relations.

A general trend is that HR personnel have begun to service an increasing number of employees. According to a report by the Canadian Council of Human Resources Associations (CCHRA), "HR professionals are at a crossroads—demands are greater and resources are fewer. Generally, more HR service is expected for fewer HR practitioners."[10] One study of 26 HR departments, for example, revealed that five years ago the average was one HR person servicing 60 employees; today the average is one to 90 employees. Respondents in the survey also expected this ratio to expand further to one to 100.[11]

Line Managers

Line managers, by the nature of their jobs, are involved with human resources. In a manufacturing firm, for example, the production manager meshes physical and human resources to produce goods in sufficient numbers and quality; the marketing manager works through sales representatives to sell the firm's products; and the finance manager obtains capital and manages investments to ensure sufficient operating funds. All three are involved in human resource management, but they are not human resource managers. They are line managers, people with formal authority and responsibility for achieving the firm's primary objectives. Line managers are responsible primarily for specific functional areas of the business such as production, finance and marketing. In contrast, the traditional human resource manager proposes and advises on human relations policies to be implemented by line managers. According to some experts, "The real human resource management game is played by the line manager. The human resource manager's role is to develop policies and programs—the rules of the game—and to function as a catalyst and energizer of the relationship between line management and employees."[12]

There is a growing trend for line managers to perform more of the basic HR functions. Managers are distributing core people processes such as employee relations and appraisals to front-line managers. When implemented, this may well reduce the size of the HR department. This trend has also allowed HR professionals to take on new responsibilities that add value to the firm—such as establishing an HR database to access benefits information, train employees, or track job postings.

Shared Service Centres

Shared service centre (SSC): A central place where routine, transaction-based activities that are dispersed throughout the organization are consolidated.

The concept of the **shared service centre (SSC)** is receiving increased consideration. These centres take routine, transaction-based activities that are dispersed throughout the organization and consolidate them in one place.[13] A major advantage is that HR managers can assume a more strategic role as they are freed from the more routine tasks. For example, a company with 20 strategic business units could consolidate routine HR tasks and perform them in one location. The increased volume makes the tasks more suitable for automation, which in turn would result in the need for fewer HR personnel.

Exploring with HR Web Wisdom

New to the second edition of *Human Resource Management* is *HR Web Wisdom*, which has Internet sources for at least three topics in each chapter. To ensure that the sources for each topic can be updated to provide the most current information, the Internet addresses for each are posted on the Prentice Hall Web site at: *http://www.pearsoned.ca/mondy*. One of the sites in each chapter relates to the home page of Human Resources Development Canada.

Outsourcing Firms

Outsourcing or contracting out is the process of transferring responsibility for an area of service and its objectives to an external provider.[14] The provision of HR through outside suppliers is increasingly becoming a basic part of operational services in companies. According to a study by the Conference Board of Canada, for example, 32 percent of companies surveyed outsourced their HR activities, and 55 percent planned to outsource even more.[15] Typically, outsourcing provides 'specialist' expertise in any number of HR areas such as recruitment, employment policy development, benefits administration, pension administration, training and development, retiree administration, and executive compensation administration. With outsourcing, a function such as training would be assigned to a firm outside the organization. Training tasks such as registration, scheduling, marketing, logistics, facilities management, instructor selection, course selection and development, and course evaluation would be contracted out. As one might expect, the key to outsourcing success is to determine which functions to outsource, the extent to which the function should be outsourced, and which functions to keep in-house.[16]

Major reasons for the increased popularity of HR outsourcing are[17]

- **Cost efficiencies.** First, organizations are concerned with streamlining costs and analyze closely the cost benefit of providing external versus internal HR services. For instance, such an analysis might reveal that it is less costly to **outsource** employee administration than it is to hire employees with this expertise, allowing HR departments to focus on management and employee development needs.

- **Limited resources and flexibility.** Many employers have limited in-house expertise to solve changing and complex HR issues. Statistics show, for example, that 98 percent of Canada's employers have less than 100 employees. Small and medium-sized firms are not likely to have the resources or the need to employ full-time HR experts. However, these organizations still have the same regulatory and legal problems faced by larger organizations. Outsourcing specific HR services provides flexibility and helps to bridge this gap. Services are accessed when the need arises.

- **Expertise.** Organizations that specialize in outsourcing tend to have access to up-to-date information, procedures, policies, and technology. This is especially true in the information technology area where outsourcing firms can provide access to Human Resource Information Systems (HRIS). These systems, which might otherwise be financially prohibitive,

Outsourcing: The process of transferring responsibility for an area of service and its objectives to an external provider.

HR Web Wisdom

http: www.pearsoned.ca/mondy

Outsourcing
Outsourcing solutions in human resources are reviewed.

HRM in *ACTION*

How Human Resource Management Is Practised

Sections entitled *HRM in Action* and *HRM Incident* are included in all chapters. These sections permit you to make decisions about situations that could occur in the real world. They are designed to stimulate discussion, test your creative skills and let you think through how you would react in typical human resource management situations. At the end of each chapter an *Experiential Exercise* gives you the opportunity to understand and respond to situations like those encountered in real life.

especially for smaller firms, can be tailored to provide a range of HR services, from manpower planning to benefits administration.

Companies that choose to outsource HR services must keep in mind that the external supplier will become a business partner. They must clearly define the roles and services being contracted out. Some organizations may initially resist the notion of outsourcing for reasons such as loss of control or eventual layoffs. However, the decision to outsource can often be beneficial to an organization and may allow HR management the opportunity to work on other activities, such as HR strategic planning, and alignment of HR strategies to corporate goals.

HR as a Strategic Partner

As previously mentioned, a trend may be developing whereby more companies will be outsourcing some HR tasks, placing other functions with shared service centres, or assigning the HR function to line managers. HRM, then, is moving away from being a transaction-based, paper-pushing, hiring/firing support activity. As the more routine and mundane tasks are removed from the responsibility of HR managers, these individuals will be able to focus their attention on issues of greater strategic importance to the organization. To succeed, HR executives must understand the complex organizational design and be able to determine the capabilities of the company's workforce, both today and in the future.[18] HR involvement in strategy is necessary to ensure that human resources support the firm's mission.

The human resource executive will increasingly become a strategic business partner and decision maker. A senior banking executive says: "I am now a strategic partner with line management and participate in business decisions which bring human resources perspectives to the general management of the company."[19] Being a strategic partner means understanding the company's business direction, what the product is and what it can do, who the typical customers are and how the company is positioned competitively in the marketplace.[20]

The future appears bright for HR managers willing to forge strategic partnerships with other business functional units. If these managers are to become strategic partners in their organizations, they must run their departments according to the same rigid criteria that apply to other units or divisions. They must be able to use data to forecast outcomes and to show how they add value to the company.[21]

Figure 1-2 provides a brief insight into why the profession is in flux.[22] Trends such as these have led many HR experts to conclude that the only certainty is continuous change.

Small Business

The small business sector is Canada's largest employer, accounting for over 50 percent of private sector employment and 43 percent of our economic output. Including the self-employed, more than 95 percent of the businesses in Canada have fewer than 20 employees. According to Industry Canada, new businesses account for more than half of all new jobs created, and about 50 percent of all new businesses start up from the home.[23]

There is no commonly agreed-on definition of what constitutes a small business. For example, Industry Canada has defined a small business as any firm

Figure 1-2

Some Outs and Ins of HR: Trends That Will Affect How Work Is Done in the Future

Source: *Adapted from Oren Harari, "Back to the Future of Work," Management Review 82 (September 1993): 35.*

OUT: Job titles such as "employee," "manager," "staff," and "professional"	**IN:** Everyone a business person, an "owner" of a complete business process, president of his or her job
OUT: Chain of command, reporting relationships, department, function, turf, sign-off, work as imposed-from-above tasks	**IN:** Self-management, responsiveness, proactivity, initiative, collaboration, egalitarianism, self-reliance, standards of excellence, personal responsibility, work as collection of self-initiated projects and teams
OUT: Stability, order, predictability, structure, better-safe-than-sorry	**IN:** Flux, disorder, ambiguity, risk, better -sorry-than-safe
OUT: Good citizenship—show up, be a good soldier, stay 9-to-5 in cubicle, don't make waves, wait for someone else to decide your fate, work in same organization for 30 years, retire with gold watch	**IN:** Make a difference—add value, challenge the process, work four hours or 18 hours per day, accept the job site as wherever the action is, learn from mistakes, develop career mobility and fluidity, work your tail off and be intensely loyal to Company X for one year or 10 years, and then move on to Company Y a better, more marketable person

HRM in *ACTION*

A Dying Job?

"Mr. Klass, I am really concerned with the outsourcing of training and benefits administration. It appears that my authority base is being depleted, and unless I am in charge of training it can't be done correctly. How can someone else provide the training services we need? Only we know what we need."

"Johnny, I understand that you are apprehensive about change, but you will decide what type of training is needed and will select who provides the training. Also, I understand there are several excellent training providers in the area. Another thing, Johnny, you are going to become my strategic partner just like the senior managers of production, finance, and marketing/sales. Your authority will expand, you will have input into the actual direction of the company in the future."

"I appreciate the pep talk, Mr. Klass, but as the importance and scope of what I actually do diminishes, so will my authority and my ability to develop human resources properly."

How should Mr. Klass respond?

with fewer than 100 paid employees in the manufacturing sector and fewer than 50 paid employees in all other sectors. Our major banks generally define a small business as one that has a loan authorization of less than $500,000. The Canadian Federation of Independent Business defines a small business as a firm that is independently owned and is not dominant in its field. From an HR point of view, a small business could be defined as one in which the owner–operator knows personally all key personnel. In most small businesses, this key group would ordinarily not exceed 20 employees. Regardless of the specific definition of a small business, this category certainly makes up the overwhelming majority of business establishments in this country. In fact, most self-employed entrepreneurs do not even have any employees working for them.

As shown in Figure 1-5, most small businesses do not have a formal HR unit. This means that the owner or in some cases, line managers may have to be involved in all six of the HR functions. If HR expertise is not available internally, it may also mean that key HR functions will have to be contracted out. Nevertheless, small businesses are ideal for implementing human resource initiatives because of their lack of bureaucracy and their ability to involve all individuals in the process of the business. Throughout this textbook we incorporate examples and case studies to reflect the HR issues and needs of the small business community.

Technology

The world has never before seen technological change as rapid as that occurring in the computer and telecommunications industries. One estimate is that a person may have to change his or her entire skill repertoire at least three or four times in a career.[24] The advances being made affect every area of a business including human resource management. For example, technology makes it feasible to provide *virtual* and *just-in-time training* for employees and the delivery of other HR services regardless of where employees are located or when they need them. This capability can potentially affect virtually every major HR task. The impact of technology on these practices is reinforced and exemplified throughout this book.

Human Resource Skills

What skills does a successful HR manager require? First and foremost, HR managers will need technical HR skills, which means, at the minimum, a working knowledge of the six HR functional categories. But in addition, HR professionals need generic skills—the general skills that employers look for when they hire any new recruits and that they seek to develop in their current employees. A widely used employability skills profile developed by the Conference Board of Canada is shown in Figure 1-3. Here the critical skills required of the Canadian workforce are grouped into three broad categories: [28]

1. **Academic skills.** Canadian employers need people who can communicate, think, and learn. According to the Canadian Council of Human Resources Associations, these three academic competencies are critical to the HR practitioner.

2. **Personal management skills.** Canadian employers need a person who can demonstrate positive attitudes and behaviours, responsibility, and adaptability/creativity.

3. **Teamwork skills.** Canadian employers need a person who can work with others.

The HRM In Action, HRM Incident, and Developing HRM Skills in each chapter of this book are designed to help you hone these three key employability skills.

Human Resource Executives, Generalists, and Specialists

Three key HR classifications are 1) executives, 2) generalists, and 3) specialists. An **executive** is a top-level manager who reports directly to the corporation's chief executive officer (CEO) or to the head of a major division. A **generalist,** who is often an executive, performs tasks in various human-resource-related areas. The generalist is involved in several or all of the six human resource management functions. A change is taking place in some companies. They are assigning a human resource generalist to each line organization and maintaining a smaller core of centralized staff. These individuals then serve the specific HR needs of the department.[29] A **specialist** may be a human resource executive, manager, or non-manager who is typically concerned with only one of the six functional areas of human resource management. Figure 1-4 helps clarify these distinctions.

Executive: A top-level manager who reports directly to a corporation's chief executive officer or the head of a major division.

Generalist: A person who performs tasks in a wide variety of human-resource-related areas.

Specialist: An individual who may be a human resource executive, a human resource manager, or a nonmanager and who is typically concerned with only one of the six functional areas of human resource management.

The vice president of industrial relations shown in Figure 1-4 specializes primarily in union-related matters. This person is both an executive and a specialist. The human resource vice president is both an executive and a generalist, having responsibility for a wide variety of functions. The manager of compensation and benefits is a specialist, as is the benefits analyst. Whereas an executive is identified by position level in the organization, generalists and specialists are distinguished by the breadth of responsibility of their positions.

In today's HR environment, a trend is developing for human resource professionals to be more generalists than specialists. The change does not suggest, however, that an HR professional is becoming a "jack of all trades and master of none." According to the CCHRA, the emergence of this generalist role means more training. Today's HR professional is expected to have a certain level of expertise in all the functional areas.[30] In addition, the HR professional must now be familiar with tasks that have been outsourced or placed with shared service centres.

The Human Resource Functions in Organizations of Various Sizes

The human resource function tends to change as firms grow and become more complex—and as the function achieves greater importance. Although the purpose of human resource management remains the same, the approach followed in accomplishing its objectives often changes.

As Figure 1-5 suggests, small businesses seldom have a formal human resource unit or HRM specialist, as other managers or the owner handle human resource functions. The main focus of their activities is generally on hiring and retaining capable employees. This does not mean human resources are less important than in a large firm. In fact, mistakes may be more damaging in small firms. For example, if the owner of a small business hires her first and only full-time salesperson, who promptly alienates the firm's customers, the business might actually fail. In a larger firm, such an error would likely be much less devastating.

In small firms, the HR person will be expected to handle most of the human resource activities. Even in a medium-sized firm there is little specialization (see Figure 1-6). A clerk may be available to handle correspondence, but the entire department may consist of one human resource manager or professional.

When the firm's human resource function becomes too complex for one person, separate sections are often created and placed under a human resource manager. These sections will typically perform tasks involving employment, training and development, compensation and benefits, safety and health, and labour relations, as depicted in Figure 1-7. Each human resource function may have a supervisor and staff reporting to the human resource manager. The HR manager works closely with top management in formulating corporate policy. This arrangement is the traditional HR model.

This traditional HR organizational structure of large-sized firms may begin to change as firms outsource, use shared service centres and evolve, leading to a more strategic and less operational HR role. But regardless of an organization's design, the six human resource functions must still be accomplished.

Figure 1-3

Employability Skills Profile: The Critical Skills Required for the Canadian Workplace

ACADEMIC SKILLS

Those skills which provide the basic foundation to get, keep and progress on a job and to achieve the best results.

Canadian employers need a person who can:

Communicate

- Understand and speak the languages in which business is conducted
- Listen to understand and learn
- Read, comprehend, and use written materials, including graphs, charts, and displays
- Write effectively in the languages in which business is conducted

Think

- Think critically and act logically to evaluate situations, solve problems, and make decisions
- Understand and solve problems involving mathematics and use the results
- Use technology, instruments, tools, and information systems effectively
- Access and apply specialized knowledge from various fields (e.g., skilled trades, technology, physical sciences, arts, and social sciences)

Learn

- Continue—for life—to learn and upgrade skills and competencies

PERSONAL MANAGEMENT SKILLS

The combination of skills, attitudes and behaviours required to get, keep and progress on a job and to achieve the best results.

Canadian employers need a person who can demonstrate:

Positive Attitudes and Behaviours

- Self-esteem and confidence
- Honesty, integrity, and personal ethics
- A positive attitude toward learning, growth, and personal health
- Initiative, energy, and persistence to get the job done

Responsibility

- The ability to set goals and priorities in work and personal life
- The ability to plan and manage time, money, and other resources to achieve goals
- Accountability for actions taken

Adaptability

- A positive attitude toward change
- Recognition of and respect for people's diversity and individual differences
- The ability to identify and suggest new ideas to get the job done: creativity

TEAMWORK SKILLS

Those skills needed to work with others on a job and to achieve the best results.

Canadian employers need a person who can:

Work with Others

- Understand and contribute to the organization's goals
- Understand and work within the culture of the group
- Plan and make decisions with others and support the outcomes
- Respect the thoughts and opinions of others in the group
- Exercise "give and take" to achieve group results
- Seek a team approach as appropriate
- Lead when appropriate, mobilizing the group for high performance

Source: Employability Skills Profile: *What are Employers Looking for? Brochure 1999 E/F (Ottawa: The Conference Board of Canada, 1999).*

Figure 1-4

Human Resource Executives,
Generalists, and Specialists

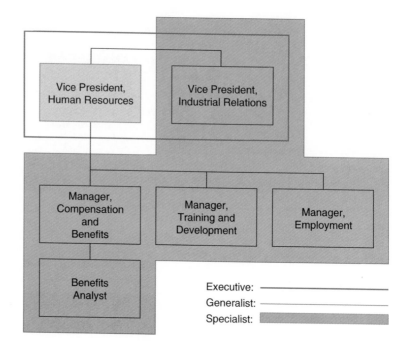

Figure 1-5

The Human Resource
Function in a Small Business

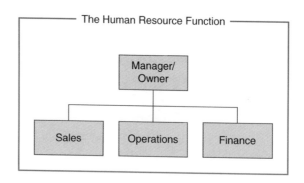

Figure 1-6

The Human Resource
Function in a Medium-Sized
Business

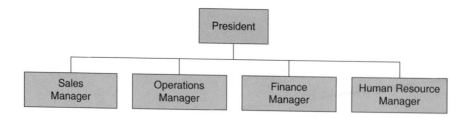

Figure 1-7

The Human Resource Functions in a Large Firm

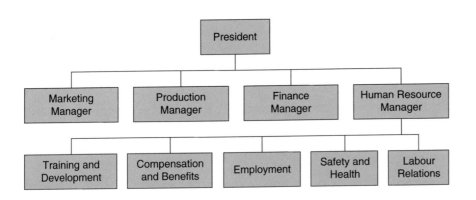

As we discuss in Chapters 3 and 7, the organizational mission and corporate culture also have a major effect in determining an appropriate HR organization. For example, the company depicted in Figure 1-8 has outsourced the training and development function and placed the benefits function with a shared service centre. Safety and health have been removed from HR and, because of their importance in this particular firm, report directly to the chief executive officer. Other HR tasks remain under the control of the HR manager.

HR Web Wisdom

http: www.pearsoned.ca/ mondy

HRDC–HR Links
Get started. Learn more about the mission and role of Human Resources Development Canada.

Figure 1-8

An Example of a New and Evolving HR Organization for Large Firms

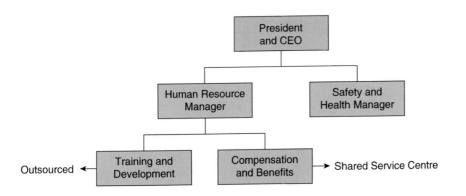

Professionalization of Human Resource Management

A **profession** is a vocation characterized by the existence of a common body of knowledge and a procedure for certifying members. Performance standards are established by members of the profession (self-regulation) rather than by outsiders. Most professions also have effective representative organizations that permit members to exchange ideas of mutual concern. These characteristics apply to the field of human resources. Among the more prominent national HR professional associations are the Canadian Council of Human Resources Associations (CCHRA), the Canadian Compensation Association, the Canadian Payroll Association, and the International Foundation of Employee Benefit Plans. Provincial HR professional organizations include, among others

Profession: A vocation whose practitioners share and use a common body of knowledge and recognize a procedure for certifying the practitioners.

- L'Association des professionals en ressources humaines de la province du Québec

- Human Resource Professionals Association of Ontario

- Human Resources Institute of Alberta

- British Columbia Human Resources Management Association

The Canadian Council of Human Resources Associations (CCHRA)

CCHRA
Learn more about the Canadian Council of Human Resources Associations (CCHRA) and related services and projects.

The Canadian Council of Human Resources Associations (CCHRA) is a collaborative effort of provincial and specialist human resources associations which currently represent the interests of more than 18 000 professionals across Canada. The origins of the CCHRA go back to 1992, when several provincial associations recognized the need to collaborate on national issues and share information. In 1994, the official constitution of the CCHRA was finalized by representatives from all across Canada. Two years later, Canada's first national human resources association was formally established. The mission of CCHRA is to

- establish national core standards for the human resources profession;

- foster communications among participating associations;

- be the recognized resource on equivalency for human resources qualifications across Canada; and

- provide a national and international collective voice on human resources issues.

One of the major responsibilities of the CCHRA is to foster national coordination and development of the Certified Human Resources Professional (CHRP) designation, which has been adopted by most provinces. This is a nationally recognized level of achievement within the field of human resources. It reflects a conviction that the professional practice of human resources management can safeguard the interest of the employers, the employee, and the general public.

The CHRP designation process is the responsibility of the cooperating provincial HR association. Currently, participating provinces manage and develop their own CHRP designation criteria. However, through an equivalency agreement, the CHRP designation is transferable between those provinces which recognize a CHRP designation. Thus, it is possible to transfer designation to a new province of residency. [31]

Canadian Compensation Association (CCA)

The Canadian Compensation Association (CCA), composed of some 1600 members, serves the information and training resource needs of compensation and benefits practitioners in Canada. Since 1985, CCA has been designing and presenting Canadian-specific educational seminars covering both the theoretical and practical aspects of the field.

The CCA offers the Certified Compensation Professional (CPP) program, a series of courses for compensation and benefits managers. The CCP designation is earned by passing nine examinations designed to measure mastery of the bodies of knowledge associated with the profession. Certification examinations are held after a two-day certification seminar, conducted in most major Canadian cities. Since 1985, more than 350 compensation and benefits professionals have earned this credential.

The CCA also offers a Benefits Certificate program to validate knowledge of benefits administration. Candidates must pass three benefits examinations. As with certification, both CCA members and nonmembers may earn the CCA Benefits Certificate. [32]

Canadian Payroll Association (CPA)

The Canadian Payroll Association (CPA) is a not-for-profit trade association. Since its inception in 1978, the CPA's role as the official representative of the Canadian payroll community has grown considerably. Currently, it provides leadership through advocacy and education to some 6000 members and their delegates in Canada and abroad.

The CPA Payroll Management Certificate Program was established to make payroll training more accessible in Canada. Since 1985, more than 14 000 students have registered in the Payroll Management Certificate Program (PMCP), considered by some employers a prerequisite for employment. Now a members-only program, PMCP continuing education is offered through the traditional correspondence study method, computer-based training (CBT) or classroom instruction at selected colleges and universities across Canada. There are three levels of designation: Introduction to Payroll (Level I), Intermediate Payroll (Level II), and Advanced Payroll (Level III).[33]

International Foundation of Employee Benefit Plans

The International Foundation of Employee Benefit Plans offers a certification program resulting in the designation Certified Employee Benefit Specialist (CEBS). The program consists of ten courses covering topics such as labour relations, group benefit and insurance plans, accounting, and investment analysis. Courses are offered through independent study, in study groups, or through classes offered at various locations nationwide.[34]

Ethics and Human Resource Management

The professionalization of human resource management has created the need for a uniform code of ethics. **Ethics** is the discipline dealing with what is good and bad, with right and wrong, or with moral duty and obligation. More companies in North America are stressing ethical conduct in business. One major reason for this change is that employees are better educated and well versed in the realities of the workplace. Apparently, the attitude has changed from "Should we be doing something in business ethics?" to "What should we be doing in business ethics?"[35]

Every day, people who work in human resources must make decisions that have ethical implications. Should a manager recommend against a woman

Ethics: The discipline dealing with what is good and bad, or right and wrong, or with moral duty and obligation.

applicant because she will be working exclusively with men? Should a very effective manager be fired because he or she violates certain company regulations? Can a manager share personal information about an employee gained accidentally? Such issues must be dealt with not from the standpoint of short-term benefit to the organization but on ethical social responsibility grounds.

Most professions have their own code of ethics or behaviour. A good example, from the Human Resources Institute of Alberta, is shown in Figure 1-9. In a growing number of companies as well, ethical codes have been established and communicated to all employees.[36]

Although few of the numerous codes that exist in our society conflict in principle, different codes may place greater or lesser emphasis on a particular aspect of ethics. And, of course, managers vary in the extent to which they apply their own codes under particular circumstances. It is vitally important that human resource managers are familiar with the ethical policies of their organization, isolate unacceptable practices and make every effort to act ethically themselves in dealing with others.

Figure 1-9

Human Resources Institute of Alberta – Code of Ethics

As a member of the Human Resources Institute of Alberta, I will commit myself to the principles outlined in the Code of Ethics. I will support and foster the society's code of ethical behaviour through a high standard of practice as a Human Resource Professional. As a Human Resources Professional I shall:

- Support, promote and apply the principles of human rights and dignity in the workplace, the profession and society;
- Treat information obtained in the course of business as confidential;
- Adhere to any statutory acts, regulations and by-laws which relate to the field of Human Resources;
- Either avoid or disclose a potential conflict of interest which might influence personal actions or judgments;
- Refrain from using a position of trust to receive special benefits, financial or material gain for myself, employees, employers, associates, other parties, or the Human Resources Institute of Alberta;
- Strive for individual growth and thus advance professional standards as a Human Resources Practitioner;
- Acknowledge the original developers of material and concepts that I may use in my professional practice, and observe all laws and restrictions of copyright;
- Strive to balance organizational and individual needs and interests in the practice of the profession; and
- Support other Human Resources Professionals in their adherence to this Code of Ethics.

Source: *Unanimously approved by the Board of Directors, Human Resources Institute of Alberta, May 12, 1990, Calgary, Alberta. http://www.hria.ab.ca/*

Scope of This Book

Effective human resource management is crucial to the success of every organization. To be effective, HR professionals and managers must understand and competently practise human resource management. We designed this human resource management book to provide you with the following:

- an insight into the evolving role of human resource management in today's organizations;

- an appreciation of the effect of environmental factors such as small business, technology and the new global economy;

- an understanding of human resource planning;

- an understanding of the staffing function, including job analysis, recruitment, and selection;

- an awareness of the role and importance of human resource development;

- an appreciation of how compensation and benefits programs are formulated and administered;

- an understanding of safety and health factors as they affect the firm's effectiveness and efficiency; and

- an opportunity to view employee and labour relations from both unionized and union-free standpoints.

Students often question whether the content of a book corresponds to the realities of the business world. In writing and revising this book, we have drawn heavily on the comments, observations, and experiences of human resource practitioners as well as our own extensive research efforts. We cite the human resource practices of leading business organizations to illustrate how theory can be applied in the real world. Our intent is to enable you to experience human resource management in action.

This book is organized into 16 chapters under seven parts, as shown in Figure 1-10; combined, they provide a comprehensive view of human resource management. As you read the book, we hope you will be stimulated to increase your knowledge of this rapidly changing, expanding, and challenging field.

Figure 1-10

Organization of this Book

I. INTRODUCTION

Chapter 1: Human Resource Management: An Overview

Chapter 2: The Environment of Human Resource Management

Chapter 3: Strategic Human Resource Planning

II. STAFFING

Chapter 4: Job Analysis

Chapter 5: Recruitment

Chapter 6: Selection

III. HUMAN RESOURCE DEVELOPMENT

Chapter 7: Organizational Change, Culture, and Development

Chapter 8: Training and Development

Chapter 9: Career Planning and Development

Chapter 10: Performance Appraisal

IV. COMPENSATION AND BENEFITS

Chapter 11: Compensation

Chapter 12: Benefits and Other Compensation Issues

V. SAFETY AND HEALTH

Chapter 13: A Safe and Healthy Work Environment

VI. EMPLOYEE AND LABOUR RELATIONS

Chapter 14: The Labour Union

Chapter 15: Collective Bargaining

Chapter 16: Internal Employee Relations

A GLOBAL PERSPECTIVE

The Global Economy

Canada is a trading nation. By the latter half of the 1990s, our exports were in the $300 billion range, representing about 43 percent of our gross domestic product. Every billion dollars in exports creates or sustains 11,000 jobs in Canada.[25] Although about 80 percent of our trade is with the United States, international corporations are becoming truly global, with business contacts in Hong Kong, Singapore, Japan, the United Kingdom, France, and Germany, to name only a few.

This interdependence of national economies has created a global marketplace, adding special challenges for human resource professionals. For example, international firms will need to decide either to adapt recruiting and compensation practices, or to maintain common HRM policies across all locations. While sometimes these decisions are partially answered by the strategy and structure decisions made by the organization, there still remains a great deal of latitude in the design of the final package of international human resource management practices.[26]

As firms broaden the scope of their activities, HRM practitioners will need additional skills to be able to advise on international taxation, develop international relocation and orientation programs, or arrange for translation. Even those who work only within their own country will need to acquire a broader perspective on their craft, along with the skills to administer more complex HR issues, as the task of helping various nationalities to work together has become one of the major challenges in the international HRM field.[27] We integrate key global issues confronting the HR manager throughout the textbook.

SUMMARY

1. **Identify the basic human resource management functions.**

   Six fundamental human resource management (HRM) functions are human resource planning; staffing; human resource development; compensation and benefits; safety and health; and employee and labour relations. In addition, the functions of human resource research and human resource information pervade these HRM fundamental responsibilities. All of these areas are highly interrelated: decisions in one area will affect other areas.

2. **Identify who performs the human resources management tasks.**

   Traditionally, the human resource manager has been primarily responsible for coordinating the management of human resources. A human resource manager normally acts in an advisory or staff capacity. Increasingly, progressive organizations are beginning to rely on line managers, shared service centres and outsourcing to assist in the delivery of human resources. This shift permits HR managers to focus on the more strategic value-added and mission-oriented activities of the organization.

3. **Explain the trend for the human resources manager to be a strategic partner.**

   The growing recognition of HR as a legitimate business unit has made it highly strategic in nature and increasingly critical to achieving corporate objectives. HR involvement in strategy is necessary to ensure that the HR functions support the firm's corporate mission. The human resource executive will increasingly become a strategic business partner and decision maker whose goal will be to add corporate value.

4. **Briefly describe the human resources implications of the growth in small business, technology and the global economy.**

   The growth in small business, rapid technological changes, and a fiercely competitive global economy are gradually changing the role and function of the traditional HR manager. Many of the basic functions of HR are being performed by other managers, relegated to shared service centres, or outsourced. Increasingly, HR managers must become generalists, partnering and taking on a more strategic role in the management and operation of companies.

5. **Outline the employability skills required by human resource managers.**

   HR managers need the fundamental HR skills, which means, at the minimum, a working knowledge of the six HR functional categories. But in addition, HR professionals need basic generic skills—the general academic, personal management, and teamwork skills that employers look for when they hire any new recruits and that they seek to develop in their current employees.

6. **Distinguish among executives, generalists, and specialists.**

   Executives are top-level managers who report directly to the corporation's chief executive officer or the head of a major division. Generalists, who are often executives, perform tasks in a wide variety of human resource-related areas. The generalist is involved in several or all of the human resource management functions. A specialist may be a human resource executive, manager, or nonmanager and is typically concerned with only one of the functional areas of human resource management.

7. **Describe the changes that occur in the human resource function as a firm grows larger and more complex.**

   Smaller businesses seldom have a formal human resource unit or HRM specialist. Even in some medium-sized firms there is little specialization. In these organizations, the HR person will be a generalist and expected to handle most of the human resource activities. Specialized tasks are likely to be contracted out. As a firm grows, the human resource function becomes too complex for one person; separate sections are often created and placed under a human resource manager. Each human resource function may even have a supervisor and staff reporting to the human resource manager.

   The traditional HR organizational structure of large-size firms is beginning to change as firms outsource, use shared service centres, and evolve. The organizational mission and corporate culture also have a major effect in determining an appropriate HR organization. But regardless of an organization's design and culture, the six human resource functions must still be accomplished.

8. **Explain the nature of professionalization of human resources and the role of human resource associations.**

   A profession is characterized by the existence of a common body of knowledge, and a procedure for certifying practitioners of this knowledge. Performance standards are established by members of the profession (self-regulation) rather than by outsiders. Most professions also have effective representative national and provincial organizations that permit members to exchange ideas of mutual concern. These characteristics apply to the field of human resources, and several well-known organizations such as the Canadian Council of Human Resources Associations (CCHRA) serve the profession.

9. **Define ethics and relate ethics to human resource management.**

   Ethics is the discipline dealing with what is good and bad, or right and wrong, or with moral duty and obligation. Individuals working with human resources must make ethical (or unethical) decisions every day. It is thus important that human resource managers are familiar with the ethical policies of their organization, isolate unacceptable practices and make every effort to act ethically themselves in dealing with others.

QUESTIONS FOR REVIEW

1. What human resource management functions must be performed regardless of the organization's size?

2. Who performs the human resource functions?

3. How should HR act as a strategic partner?

4. How has the growth in small business, technology and the global economy affected HR management?

5. What employability skills are required by HR professionals?

6. By definition and example, distinguish among human resource executives, generalists, and specialists.

7. How does the implementation of human resource functions change as a firm grows? Briefly describe each stage of development.

8. Define profession. Do you believe the field of human resource management is a profession? Explain your answer.

9. Define ethics. Why is ethics important to the field of human resource management?

DEVELOPING **HRM** SKILLS

An Experiential Exercise This is an exercise involving Jesse Heard, the Human Resource Manager at Parma Cycle Company, and his colleagues, the corporate planner and the comptroller. Parma Cycle Company is one of only three Canadian companies that manufacture complete bicycles. Most of its competitors import parts from other countries and assemble bicycles in Canada. Parma Cycle currently employs about 800 workers at wages well above the average level for that area. Most of these workers are machine operators and assemblers. Parma Cycle is experiencing severe difficulties competing with less expensive bicycles on the market, and the time has come for Parma to lower its costs.

Jesse Heard is faced with a dilemma. Many of the employees have been with the company for years; they are loyal and highly skilled. Jesse receives a call from Parma Cycle's president, Mr. Burgess, and is told to meet with the corporate planner and the comptroller to draft a plan that would move all but the most high-tech manufacturing to Mexico. Jesse realizes this move would result in the loss of 600 jobs.

HRM INCIDENT

The Hiring of a Friend's Daughter

Marcie Sweeney had recently graduated from university with a specialization in business administration. Marcie was quite bright, although her grades did not reflect her intelligence. She had thoroughly enjoyed school—dating, tennis, swimming, and similar stimulating academic events. When she graduated, she had not found a job. Her father was upset, and he took it on himself to see that Marcie became employed.

Allen Sweeney was executive vice president of a medium-sized manufacturing company. One of the people he contacted in seeking employment for his daughter was Bill Garbo, the president of another firm in the area from which his firm purchased many supplies. Bill told Allen to send Marcie to his office for an interview. She was surprised to learn, even before she left the office, that she had a job in the accounting department. Marcie may have been lazy but she certainly was not stupid. She realized that Bill had hired her in hopes of increased business from her father's company. Although Marcie's work was not challenging, it paid better than the other jobs in the accounting department.

It did not take long for her co-workers to discover why Marcie had been hired—she told them. When a difficult job was assigned to Marcie, she normally got one of the other employees to do it, implying that Mr. Garbo would be pleased with anyone who helped her out. She developed a pattern of coming in late, taking long lunch breaks, and leaving early. When the department manager attempted to reprimand her, Marcie would bring up her father's close relationship with the president. The department manager was at his limit when he asked for your help.

Questions

1. From an ethical standpoint, how would you evaluate the merits of Mr. Garbo's employing Marcie? Discuss.

2. Now that she is employed, what course would you follow to address her on-the-job behaviour?

3. Do you feel that a firm should have policies regarding practices such as hiring people like Marcie? Discuss.

CHAPTER

2

The Environment of Human Resource Management

CHAPTER OBJECTIVES

1. Identify the environmental factors that affect human resource management.

2. Distinguish between a proactive and a reactive response to the external environment.

3. Describe the issue of diversity and identify the diverse workforce that management now confronts.

4. Explain the importance of small business in today's work environment.

5. Define corporate culture and describe how it is developed and shaped.

When Wayne Simmons, vice president of human resources for Ranger Manufacturing, returned to his office from the weekly executive staff meeting, he was visibly disturbed. Ranger, a producer of high-quality telecommunications equipment, is headquartered in Winnipeg and has manufacturing plants in Saskatchewan, Alberta, and British Columbia. Wayne had just heard a rumour that an overseas firm had developed a new manufacturing process with the potential to cut costs substantially on products similar to those manufactured by the Longline Division. The Longline Division had been expanding rapidly, but Wayne knew that demand for Ranger's product was far from automatic. Customers might well switch to a cheaper product. Ranger might have to cut back production severely or even close the three plants in the Longline Division. These plants are located in areas of high unemployment, and plant closings would have a devastating effect on the economies of their respective communities. A few workers could be transferred to other locations but most would have to be laid off. Thus Wayne is now keenly aware of ways in which the external environment can affect Ranger's manufacturing operations.

Maggie Mitchell is an administrator at a non-profit agency, where her many duties include human resources. Government funding programs are drying up and two key private sponsors have just informed her that they won't be contributing this year. Money is already tight and it looks as if next year won't be any better. So she finds it hard to give raises for good work. Because funding is uncertain from one year to the next, staffers also worry about the security of their jobs, to the point that it sometimes interferes with their efficiency.

And, they have good reason to worry: she may even have to lay off a few of the full-time staff. She knows that adaptability is a key human resource

skill. But Maggie feels the stress; she is going to have to find some creative ways to get through these difficult times.[1]

In this chapter, we first identify the environmental factors that affect human resource management. Then we describe the means by which specific external environmental factors can influence human resource management and distinguish between a proactive and reactive response to the external environment. Next, we describe the diverse workforce that management now confronts and explain the importance of small business in today's work environment. In the final section we introduce the issue of corporate culture and human resource management in the global environment.

Environmental Factors Affecting Human Resource Management

Many interrelated factors affect human resource management (HRM). Such factors are part of either the firm's external environment or its internal environment (see Figure 2-1). The firm often has little, if any, control over how the external environment affects management of its human resources. For example, Maggie, in the opening caption, has very little control over private funding decisions or government funding policies. These factors impinge on the organization from outside its boundaries. Moreover, important factors within the firm itself, such as corporate culture, also affect how the firm manages its human resources.

Certain interrelationships tend to complicate the management of human resources. For instance, human resource professionals constantly work with people who represent all organizational levels and functional areas. To perform their tasks properly, they must recognize the different perspectives these individuals bring to human resource management.

Understanding the many interrelationships implied in Figure 2-1 is essential for the human resource professional to help other managers resolve issues and problems. For instance, a production manager may want to give a substantial pay raise to a particular employee. The human resource manager may know that this employee does an exceptional job; he or she should also be aware that granting the raise may affect pay practices in the production department and set a precedent for the entire firm. The human resource manager may have to explain to the production manager that such an action is not an isolated decision. They may have to consider alternative means of rewarding the employee for superior performance, without upsetting the organization's reward system. One solution may be for the human resource manager to encourage the employee to apply for a higher paying position that the employee is qualified to fill.

Figure 2-1

The Environments of
Human Resource
Management

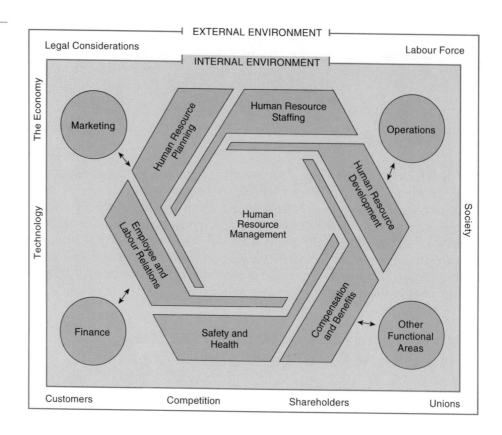

Whatever the case, the implications of a particular act must be considered
in light of its potential impact on a department and the entire organization.
Those involved in human resource management must see the big picture. The
basic HRM tasks always remain essentially the same. However, the manner in
which those tasks are accomplished may be altered substantially by factors in
the external environment. For example, in the opening vignette, Wayne
Simmons is aware that not only his work but several communities will be
affected by changes in the environment.

The External Environment

External environment:
The factors that affect a
firm's human resources
from outside the
organization's boundaries.

Factors that affect a firm's human resources from outside its boundaries make up
the **external environment**. External factors include the labour force, legal
considerations, society, unions, shareholders, competition, customers, technology, and the economy. Each factor, either separately or in combination with
others, can provide opportunities for human resource management and place
constraints on how human resource management tasks are accomplished.

The Labour Force

The labour force is a pool of individuals external to the firm from which the
organization obtains its workers. Because new employees are hired from out-

side the firm, the labour force is considered an external environmental factor. The **labour force** is composed of two groups (within the population 15 years of age and over): those employed and those unemployed (not employed and are looking for work). Note that, technically, people who are not actively looking for a job are not counted as part of the labour force. Thus, a full-time student, for example, would likely not be considered part of the labour force. In Canada, our total labour force, including those employed and unemployed, was about 16 million and our unemployment rate was in the 8 percent range in the latter part of the '90s. (See Figure 2-2.)

An employer's ability to find the right people for the job will depend, to a large degree, on labour force availability. Wage rates, too, will be influenced by the labour force. Information on the labour force —not just the basic numbers, but also trends—will help employers in their HR planning. For example, a 1999 labour study by Statistics Canada found that more men are choosing to work past the traditional retirement age of 65, usually on a part-time, contract, or self employed basis.[2] Maggie, in the opening vignette, may want to take advantage of this trend by developing a pool of seniors she could contract as she needs them.

An understanding of labour force dynamics can also help individuals plan their careers. Suppose, for example, that you are considering a career as a human resources specialist. How much would you expect to make? What are the chances you will find employment? Will your skills be in demand? The kinds of information shown in Figure 2-3 can help you make a decision.

The expectations, skills, and availability of the labour force are always changing, inevitably affecting employee characteristics in every organization. In turn, changes in the people within an organization affect the way management must

Labour force: A pool of individuals (population 15+) composed of two groups—those employed and those unemployed (not employed and currently looking for work).

Figure 2-2

Canada's Labour Force, 1999

	FEMALE	MALE	BOTH SEXES
Population, 15 years and over (thousands)	12 366	11 922	24 288
Labour force (thousands)	7 257	8 669	15 925
Participation rate (% in labour force)	58.7	72.7	65.6
Employed (thousands)	6 718	7 993	14 711
Employment rate (% of population employed)	54.3	67.0	60.6
Unemployed (thousands)	540	675	1 215
Unemployment rate (% of labour force unemployed)	7.4	7.8	7.6

Source: *Statistics Canada, "Labour force, employed and unemployed, numbers and rates": Statistics Canada Internet site (Jan. 2000): http://www.statcan.ca/english/Pgdb/People/Labour/labor07a.htm. Statistics Canada information is used with the permission of the Minister of Industry, as Minister responsible for Statisitics Canada.*

Figure 2-3

Specialists in Human
Resources

- 27 000 persons were employed in this occupation in 1996, an increase of 34.4% from 1986. Over the same period, employment in all occupations increased by 13.1%.
- 5% of workers in this occupation work part-time, well below the average of 19% for all occupations.
- 55% of persons working in this occupation are women, compared to an average of 45% for all occupations.
- The unemployment rate in this occupation averaged 3% from 1994 to 1996, well below the average of 6.7% for all occupations. These rates are among the lowest for professional occupations and for occupations in business, finance, and administration.
- Average earnings of year-round, full-time workers in this occupation in 1995 were $40 700, compared to an average of $35 700 for all occupations. These earnings levels are among the highest for occupations in business, finance and administration.
- Employment in these occupations is not very sensitive to overall economic conditions and is not seasonal.

LOOKING TO THE YEAR 2001

- Current labour market conditions for new entrants are good. Labour market conditions for new entrants will remain good through 2001
- Computerized human resource systems to maintain employee information will increase the skill needs of these professionals.
- Most of the increase in labour requirements through 2001 in this occupation will occur in the business services and other services sectors.

Source: This information is reproduced from Job Futures, a product of the Applied Research Branch, Human Resources Development Canada. Reproduced with the permission of the Minister of Public Works and Government Services Canada, 2000.

deal with its work force. Thus, changes in the country's labour force create dynamic situations within organizations. More on this topic will be discussed later in this chapter under the heading Managing the Diverse Workforce.

Legal Considerations

The legal environment for human resource management is a complex mix of laws and regulations involving not only federal and provincial legislation but also contract and common law.

Federal and Provincial Legislation

Specific details on how legislation affects HRM will be integrated into the appropriate chapters, but an overview will prove useful at this point. For simplicity, the federal and provincial legislative legal environment can be subdivided into two broad categories: human rights and employment standards.

Human rights An important part of our legislative framework is the Canadian Charter of Rights and Freedoms, 1982. Section 15, for example, outlines every citizen's rights before the law and provides the underpinnings for employment equity programs—legislation designed to promote equal employment opportunity for designated groups (women, minorities, aboriginal people, and the physically or mentally challenged). The charter also authorizes affirmative action programs designed to improve the lot of disadvantaged groups or individuals who may have suffered as a result of past discrimination.[3]

There are, in addition, a number of federal and provincial Acts that prohibit discrimination on certain fundamental characteristics or grounds. Federal human rights legislation affects federal employees, about 10 percent of the workforce. Two predominant pieces of federal legislation are the Canadian Human Rights Act and the Employment Equity Act:

- **Canadian Human Rights Act, 1978.** The Canadian Human Rights Act (CHRA) applies to the federal government and to federally regulated businesses such as banks, railways, airlines, and telecommunications companies. The CHRA forbids discrimination on the grounds of race, colour, religion, age, sex, sexual orientation, marital status or family status, and disability. The Canadian Human Rights Commission deals with initial complaints and resolves most cases. Unresolved situations are referred to the Canadian Human Rights Tribunal for action. If the Tribunal deems that discrimination has occurred, it decides on an appropriate remedy to prevent recurrence and to compensate the victim.[4]

- **Employment Equity Act, 1986.** Under the Employment Equity Act, federal employers, including Crown corporations or employers operating under federally regulated industries (with 100 or more employees) must provide an annual report. This report must describe workforce representation of the four designated groups: women, aboriginal peoples, members of visible minorities, and persons with disabilities. Compliance with the Act is monitored by the Canadian Human Rights Commission.

Many of the provinces have enacted legislation that reflect similar principles. Relevant provincial legislation includes

- Alberta's Individual Rights Protection Act
- British Columbia's Human Rights Act
- Nova Scotia's Human Rights Act
- Quebec's Charter of Rights and Freedoms
- Ontario's Human Rights Code.

Employment standards refers to the basic or minimum work-related obligations of employers. Legislation typically regulates such areas as minimum wage, employment of children, assurance of wage payments, leave provisions, termination notice, vacations and holidays, and hours of work. Federal employees are governed by a number of Acts including the Canada Labour Code, Fair Wages and Hours of Labour Act, the Holidays Act and the Wages Liability Act. Employment standards for the remaining 90 percent of employees are set by provincial legislation. For example, wages are governed by laws such as the Ontario Wages Act and Manitoba's Payment of Wages Act. Employment standards vary slightly from province to province but in general are similar to those set by federal legislation.

Contract and Common Law

The legal environment for human resources is further complicated by contract and common law. Contract law refers to individual and collective agreements and common law refers to judicial precedents that do not derive from specific pieces of legislation. How much notice, for example, must an employer provide before termination? The answer may be set out in a contract. If there is no contract, then common law applies. Under common law, "reasonable notice" depends on a number of factors, including the employee's age, position, salary, and length of service. Typically, employees are entitled to one month's notice for each year of service. But specific circumstances will also be considered.

Society

Legislation is an institutional expression of the values of society. But society may also exert pressure on human resource management in less formal ways. Individuals and special interest groups have found that they can effect change through their collective voices, votes, and other actions. For example, a 1999 KPMG business ethics survey found that an increasing number of Canadian executives see public demand for assurance of ethical practice in both the private and public sector as strong and increasing.[5] This influence is also obvious in the large number of regulatory laws that have been passed since the early 1960s. To remain acceptable to the general public, a firm must accomplish its purpose while complying with societal norms.

Social responsibility:
The implied, enforced, or felt obligation of managers, acting in their official capacities, to serve or protect the interests of groups other than themselves.

When a corporation behaves as if it has a conscience, it is said to be socially responsible. **Social responsibility** is an implied, enforced, or felt obligation of managers, acting in their official capacities, to serve or protect the interests of groups other than themselves. Many companies develop patterns of concern for moral and social issues. For example, in the opening vignette, Wayne Simmons was aware of and concerned about the impact that plant closure could have on communities. Companies can show social concern through their policy statements, their practices, and leadership over time. Open-door policies, grievance procedures, and employee benefit programs often stem as much from a desire to do what is right as from a concern for productivity and avoidance of strife.[6]

During the 1990s many corporations responded to societal demands and began to adopt a new corporate role as stakeholders in the community. They recognized their responsibilities not only to owners but also to other stakeholders such as employees, suppliers, customers, and the community. This desire to do what is right is now often contained in statements of company values, principles, and codes of conduct. In the KPMG business ethics survey, for example, 85 percent of the participating organizations had codes of conduct containing written statements of their values and principles.[7]

HR Web Wisdom
http: www.pearsoned.ca/ mondy

Acting with Integrity
Take a look at Nortel's "Community and Environment—Code of Business Conduct."

You may ask, Why should a business be concerned with stakeholders or the welfare of society if its goal is to make a profit and grow? Obviously, a business must make a profit over the long run if it is to survive; but if a firm does not satisfy society's needs, it will ultimately cease to exist. A firm operates by public consent to satisfy society's requirements. The organization is a member of the community in which it operates. Just as citizens work to improve the quality of life in their community, so too organizations must respect and work with other members of their community. For instance, within a firm's service area, there may be a high unemployment rate among a certain minority group. A policy of hiring not only qualified workers but also applicants who are capable of being trained may help to reduce unemployment for that minority group. In the long run, this approach will enhance the firm's image and thus may actually improve its profitability.

Unions

The wages, benefits, and working conditions of some four million Canadian employees reflect decisions made jointly by unions and management. A **union** is a group of employees who have joined together for the purpose of dealing with their employer. Unions are treated as an environmental factor because, essentially, they become a third party when they bargain with the company. In a unionized organization, the union rather than the individual employee negotiates an agreement with management.

Union: A group of employees who have joined together for the purpose of dealing collectively with their employer.

Unions, in Canada, exert a strong external influence even on nonunionized organizations. A management that does not want a union may take great care to provide satisfactory working conditions and competitive wages and benefits. Moreover, unions monitor broader trends in industry and in the economy, thus bringing broader demands and viewpoints into the firm.

As we discuss in Chapter 14, unions remain a powerful influence, with union membership in Canada accounting for about 34 percent of the nonagricultural work force. Nonetheless, union/management relations are in flux.[8] According to Dr. Reginald Bibby, in a study commissioned by the Work Research Foundation: "The mood of the country is one where freedom should be experienced in the workplace—where people and companies should be able to work when they are qualified to work, where individuals have a measure of freedom in joining unions and paying dues, and have input into how their dues are being used."[9] Furthermore, as new, more technical jobs require higher-level skills, the power and the influence of unions may very well decline. The emphasis will likely shift to human resource systems that deal directly with the individual worker and his or her needs.

Shareholders

The owners of a corporation are called **shareholders**. Because shareholders, or stockholders, have invested money in the firm, they may at times challenge programs considered by management to be beneficial to the organization. Managers may be forced to justify the merits of a particular program in terms of future projects, costs, revenues, and profits. For instance, $50 000 spent on implementing a management development program may require more justification than simply stating, "Managers should become more open and adaptive to the needs of employees." In many cases, shareholders are concerned with costs and revenues, not with the broader social implications. Management must be prepared to explain the merits of a particular program in terms of its economic as well as its social costs and benefits.

Shareholders: The owners of a corporation.

Competition

A firm may face intense competition in both its product and labour markets. Unless an organization is in the unusual position of monopolizing or dominating the market it serves, other firms will be producing similar products or services. A firm must maintain a supply of competent employees if it is to succeed, grow, and prosper. At the same time, other organizations are striving for that same objective. A firm's major task is to ensure that it obtains and retains a sufficient number of employees in various career fields to allow the firm to compete effectively. A bidding war often results when competitors attempt to fill certain critical positions in their firms. Because of the strategic nature of their needs, firms are sometimes forced to resort to unusual means to recruit and retain such employees. For example, because of the low unemployment rate and the demand for skilled technology workers in the late 1990s, some firms were paying bonuses of 25 to 30 percent of a person's annual salary to lure valued workers from their competitors.[10]

Customers

The people who actually use a firm's goods and services are also part of its external environment. Because sales are crucial to the firm's survival, management must ensure that its employment practices do not antagonize customers. Customers demand high-quality products and after-purchase service, and a firm's workforce should be capable of providing them. Sales are often lost or gained because of variances in product quality and follow-up service. These conditions relate directly to employees' skills, qualifications, and motivation.

Technology

The rate of technological change accelerated over the 1990s, and as a result, few firms operate today as they did even five years ago. More than 40 percent of Canadian households are now hooked up to the Internet and more than half of Canadian workers use computers on the job. New technologies, especially computer-based technologies (CBT) and advanced manufacturing technologies (AMT) have been widely adopted. By the latter half of the 1990s, more than 45 percent of establishments had adopted some form of CBT and 88 percent of manufacturing shipments were produced by some form of AMT.[11] Moreover, companies adopting new technologies experienced stronger growth in sales and market share than non-adapters.

Of major concern to human resource managers is the effect of technological changes on the workplace. Recruiting people with needed skills in high technology areas is often difficult. Thus, during the next decade, one of the most challenging areas in human resource management will be training employees to keep up with rapidly changing technology. According to Human Resources Development Canada, at least 43 percent of establishments now have formal employee participation programs in place—and this percentage is expected to increase dramatically.[12]

Technological change has also reinforced the trend toward a service economy and the increase in self-employed and contract workers. By the late 1990s, about three out of every four workers were employed in the service sector.

Between 1991 and 1996, the labour force in the service sector grew by 3.3 percent to almost 11 million, while the labour force in the goods-producing sector declined by 6 percent to about 4 million. The fastest growth (17 percent) occurred in the business services sector, where more than 26 percent of all individuals in this industry were self-employed.[13]

The Economy

The economy of the nation as a whole, and of its various geographic segments, is a major environmental factor affecting human resource management. In general, when the economy is booming, recruiting qualified workers is more difficult than in less prosperous times. This was the case in the late 1990s when some companies had to use employment bonuses to entice needed employees—especially in highly skilled occupations. On the other hand, during a downturn, more applicants are typically available.

To complicate this situation even further, one segment of the country may be experiencing a downturn, another a slow recovery, and another a boom. Such was the situation in the early 1990s: some of the western provinces were thriving, central Canada was gradually recovering, while Newfoundland was in the grip of a deep depression.

These kinds of situations within Canada are further exacerbated by far-reaching changes in the way business is being conducted worldwide. According to Industry Canada, a social, economic, and cultural revolution is transforming the world. Our society today is very different from the society of the developed world over the past century, based on mass production, manufacturing, and the exchange of tangible goods and products. Communications and information technologies have become the infrastructure for twenty-first-century society. This new global environment is based on the exchange of intangibles: ideas, information, knowledge, and intelligence. Today, Canadian HRM professionals must adjust to a new global economy driven by information and communications technologies[14]

The External Environment:
Proactive versus Reactive

Managers can approach changes in the external environment proactively or reactively. A **proactive response** involves taking action in anticipation of environmental changes. A **reactive response** involves simply dealing with environmental changes after they occur. For example, while pay equity legislation was weaving its way through various provincial legislatures, proactive companies were already designing programs to meet anticipated provisions. Those who waited until provincial laws went into effect to plan for required changes were being reactive.

Organizations exhibit varying degrees of proactive and reactive behaviour. In the case of equity legislation, some firms did only what the law required. Others went far beyond minimum compliance, allocating significant resources to create a more equitable work environment for employees. Those dealing with human resource management have discovered that a proactive attitude leads to performance improvement and reduces the level of damaging discrimination suits.[15]

Proactive response:
Taking action in anticipation of environmental changes.

Reactive response:
Simply reacting to environmental changes after they occur.

A firm may be either reactive or proactive in any matter, legal or otherwise. For example, reactive managers may demonstrate concern for employee welfare only after a union organizing attempt starts. Proactive managers try to spot early signs of discontent and correct the causes before matters get out of hand. Proactive managers prevent customer complaints rather than handle them.

Managing the Diverse Work Force

From McDonald's to Holiday Inn, Bell Canada to Canadian Tire, managers are learning not only to understand their kaleidoscopic work force, but also to manage in diverse work environments. At the same time as more businesses are expanding their operations overseas, many people are working in Canada alongside individuals whose cultures differ substantially from their own, and more ethnic minorities are entering the work force.[16] Managers must be knowledgeable about common group characteristics to manage diversity effectively. **Diversity** refers to any perceived difference among people: age, functional specialty, profession, sexual orientation, language, geographic origin, lifestyle, tenure with the organization, or position.

Diversity: Any perceived difference among people: age, functional specialty, profession, sexual orientation, geographic origin, lifestyle, tenure with the organization, or position.

Of key concern are the four groups designated under the Employment Equity Act: women, visible minority groups, aboriginals, and persons with disabilities. But to truly manage diversity also means considering such factors as age, bilingualism, work–family balance, and the contingent workforce.

As we enter the twenty-first century, labour market inequities still remain. Barriers to full participation include poor managerial attitudes, sexual harassment, poor communication, and lack of access for disabled people. In 1998, for example, the CHRC completed its first round of employment equity audits. Out of 36 audits completed, only two employers were found to be in complete compliance with the Equity Act. Attitude changes in the workplace will come only through a commitment by senior management and the development of policies on ethical behaviour and practice that are posted publicly and included in employee handbooks. According to Monica Armour, president of Transcultural Consultant Services of Toronto, major causes of disharmony are unequal promotions, unequal access to jobs, and racial and sexual innuendo. Accurate, precise job descriptions are the best protection for management when disputes with workers arise. As we discuss in Chapter 4, job descriptions, complete with a checklist of specific skills and duties, ensure that jobs are filled according to ability.[17]

HR Web Wisdom

http: www.pearsoned.ca/mondy

Diversity and Competitive Advantage
Diversity management presents new challenges that, if handled effectively, can enhance competitiveness.

The challenge for managers in the coming decades will be to recognize that different groups often think, act, learn, and communicate in different ways. Yet at the same time, the members of those groups are individuals with their own personal characteristics. Because each person, culture, and business situation is unique, there are no simple rules for managing diversity, but diversity experts say that employees need to develop patience, open-mindedness, acceptance, and cultural awareness.

Women in Business

Glass ceiling: A metaphor for an invisible or intangible barrier preventing women from rising to higher, more influential positions in organizations.

Women are gaining ground in the workforce. According to some experts the **glass ceiling**—the invisible or intangible barrier preventing women from rising to the top in organizations—is beginning to crack. Here are some indicators of the changes in the workforce since 1980:[18]

- More women in the workplace. The proportion of women aged 25 to 44 working full time was 73 percent in 1998, compared to just 59 percent in 1980.

- Women are better educated. Almost 20 percent of women between 25 and 44 years old had university degrees in 1998. In 1980 the rate was barely one in ten.

- Women are better paid than they were. Salaries for women are up slightly. The average woman aged 25 to 44 working full time made $30,500 in 1996—up from an inflation-adjusted $28,700 in 1980. Men's salaries actually decreased by 7 percent over this period.

- Longer tenure. Women between the ages of 25 and 44 now spend, on average, more than six years at each job. That's up from less than five years in 1980.

Experts generally agree that women have made strides towards employment equality. But still more progress needs to be made. For example, in 1996, women accounted for only 20 percent of senior management positions in Canada, up slightly from 17 percent in 1991.[19] In 1998, the average weekly earning for women was $567, compared to $739 per week for men. "The glass ceiling is still there, but it's more permeable than it was back in the 1980s," says Mary Thompson, a management professor at the University of Lethbridge.[20]

Aboriginals and Visible Minorities

Human resource managers must also take care to provide just and reasonable employment opportunities for aboriginals and visible minorities. Aboriginals are defined as those reporting North American Indian or Inuit ancestry, including Métis. This group constitutes about 4 percent of Canada's total population.[21]

The Employment Equity Act defines visible minorities as: "persons, other than Aboriginal peoples, who are non-Caucasian in race or non-white in colour." Under this Act, the following groups are designated by Statistics Canada as visible minorities: Chinese, South Asians, Blacks, Arabs and West Asians, Filipinos, Southeast Asians, Latin Americans, Japanese, Koreans, and Pacific islanders. In 1996, about 11 percent of Canada's population was classified as visible minority, up from 9 percent in 1991 and 6 percent in 1986. The 1996 Census also showed that about three out of every 10 individuals who were identified as visible minority were born in Canada; the rest were immigrants. Since the 1970s, the sources of immigration have changed greatly, with many more immigrants coming from non-European countries. Today, the largest visible minority group is Chinese constituting about 27 percent of the total visible minority population. Most visible minorities reside in Ontario (56 percent of all visible minorities, making up 16 percent of the province's total population) and British Columbia (21 percent of all visible minorities). As well, visible minorities are concentrated in large urban centres. For example, seven out of every ten visible minority persons in Canada lived in just three cities:

Toronto, Vancouver, and Montreal. Toronto alone housed about 42 percent of all visible minorities.[22]

People with Disabilities

According to one estimate, there are approximately 2.5 million disabled adults of working age in Canada (aged 15+), of whom 56 percent are in the workforce.[23] The World Health Organization and Statistics Canada define a disability as: "any restriction or lack (resulting from an impairment) of ability to perform an activity in a manner or within a range considered normal for a human being."[24] More common disabilities include limited hearing or sight, limited mobility, mental or emotional deficiencies, and various nerve disorders.

Studies indicate that disabled workers perform as well as other employees in terms of productivity, attendance, and average tenure.[25] In fact, in certain high-turnover occupations, disabled workers had lower turnover rates. Nevertheless, according to the Canadian Human Rights Commission (CHRC) people with disabilities rank as the most underrepresented minority group in the workplace. For example, although people with significant disabilities constitute about 7 percent of the general population, they hold less than 3 percent of the jobs in the federal workforce.

Although human rights legislation in Canada prohibits discrimination against qualified individuals with disabilities, a serious barrier to effective employment of disabled people is bias, or prejudice. Many people experience anxiety around workers with disabilities, especially if the disabilities are severe. Fellow workers may show pity or feel that a disabled worker is fragile. Some even show disgust. The manager can set the tone for proper treatment of workers with disabilities. If someone is unsure about how to act, or how much help to offer, the disabled person should be asked for guidance. Managers always must strive to treat employees with disabilities as they treat other employees, by holding them accountable for achievement.

French and English

French and English are Canada's two official languages. As such, human resources managers must be sensitive to Canada's cultural and language dualism. In 1996, there were about 60 percent of Canadians or 17 million persons who reported English as their mother tongue (anglophones); and 23.5 percent or about 6.7 million who reported French as their mother tongue (francophones). Mother tongue is defined as the first language learned at home in childhood and still understood by the individual at the time of the census. Although the numbers of francophones have been increasing, a major long-term trend has been the proportional or relative decline of francophones. For example, the proportion of francophones in the total population decreased from 29 percent in 1951 to less than 24 percent in 1996. According to Statistics Canada, this trend is the result of a growing number of immigrants (whose mother tongue was not French) and a declining fertility rate among francophones. A second key feature of the francophone population is its concentration in Quebec and New Brunswick. About 82 percent of those living in Quebec and 33 percent of those living in New Brunswick are francophones.[27]

Diversity in the Workplace[26]

"We're in the information age. These days there's really no excuse for not hiring people with disabilities—other than the fact that they can't get in the door," says Wenda Abel, executive director of Training Coordinating Group—Linkup Employment Services. The Internet has a huge potential for people with disabilities. It can connect people in so many different ways. "Maybe you live in a small town with one job counsellor who doesn't have a clue about disability; or you can't get out physically to interview; or you're a deaf person who uses sign language. There are all kinds of possibilities," says Keltie Creed, executive director of the Canadian Council on Rehabilitation and Work (CCRW).

The CCRW, in partnership with nine other direct service providers like the CNIB, have set up a national Web site to help people with disabilities to find jobs. The Virtual Employment Resource Centre is located at *www.worklink.com*. It is aimed at three groups: people with disabilities who are looking for work; employers in search of new employees; and those who work with people with disabilities, such as vocational and rehab counsellors. The service has interactive and static functions. People can dial in for counselling, chat in real time, or cruise the job listings, résumé bank, and information library.

Innovative projects like the Virtual Employment Resources Centre are ushering in a new era for people with disabilities, but most experts agree there is still a lot of work to be done. "If you look at the historical trends, all human rights movements have made big strides. People with disabilities are the last group to make their case," says Dave Shannon, a practising lawyer and human rights activist.

Work and Family

Increasingly, workers are finding it more difficult to balance their work and family lives. A 1999 study carried out for Health Canada found that 40 percent of working Canadians reported high levels of work–family conflict, up from 35.6 percent in 1991. According to this study, Canadians who have a hard time juggling their work and family lives are costing their employers at least $2. 7 billion a year in lost time.[28] In another study by the Conference Board, more than 50 percent of employers said employees in their organizations had turned down relocations because of a spouse's job and or concerns about children.[29] A few of the major causes of increased work stress include:

- **Career couples.** There has been a long-term trend among dual-earner families to having both partners working full-time year round.[30] The dual-career challenge is especially difficult in the international environment. According to a survey of 176 companies conducted by Price Waterhouse/Bennett Associates, nearly 57 percent of couples that move internationally are dual-career families. Fewer than 3 percent of the accompanying spouses are offered employment by the company sponsoring the move.[31]

- **Lone-parent families.** In 1996 there were about 1.1 million lone-parent families—up 19 percent from 1991 and 33 percent from 1986. In 1996, one in five children lived with a lone parent—up 19 percent from 1991. Of those children, 84 percent lived with the mother.[32]

- **The changing workplace.** Since 1975 almost half of the jobs created have been nonstandard and less secure: part-time, self-employed, telecommuting and home-based.

Changes in jobs have led to a new workplace dominated by information technologies. These changes affect almost every aspect of the workplace:[33]

- **The work space.** The traditional functions of business are no longer confined to one space. It is not uncommon, for example, for businesses to export key functions such as accounting and computer systems to geographic areas with lower-cost labour.

- **Work time.** The gap between private life and working life is closing. For example, one executive of a large computing firm, where 20 percent of the staff telecommute, reported that those staff were working 20 to 25 percent more hours.

- **The structure of employment.** A new pyramid is taking shape with design and technology specialists at the top and routine information processors at the bottom. Incomes are becoming polarized as middle managers are being displaced.

- **Job security.** Job cuts and downsizing in the nineties have undermined the motivation and loyalty both of those who left their jobs and of those who stayed.

These employment trends have increased work–family conflict. Proactive organizations are gradually instituting programs and policies in an attempt to reduce stress. For example, many companies have begun providing day care services for employees. More and more companies provide paid maternity leave (in addition to UI maternity benefits) and some offer paternity leave. Still other firms give time off for children's visits to doctors, which can be charged against the parents' sick leave or personal time. Some firms have revised their policies against nepotism to allow both partners to work for the same company. Other firms offer stress and career counselling and have developed polices to assist the spouse of an employee who is transferred. Firms are also beginning to offer more flexible benefit programs. Some companies are actually designing their buildings to help dual-career couples. One company, for example, specifically incorporated into its manufacturing plant a dry cleaner, a shoe-repair shop, and a cafeteria that prepares food employees can take home at night when they don't want to cook supper.[34]

HR Web Wisdom

http: www.pearsoned.ca/ mondy

HRDC — HR Links
The site includes various research papers on human resources issues.

Older Workers

The **baby boom**, that is those born between 1947 and 1966, totalled almost 10 million in 1996. Today, boomers, constituting about one-third of the population, are middle aged, and a time is approaching when Canada will have a larger proportion of older adults than ever before. In 1996, about 26 percent of the population was over the age of 50. By the year 2011, 33 percent of Canadians will be 50+. As the workforce grows older, the needs and interests of its members change. For example, a 1999 Statistics Canada study found that men over the age of 65 were increasingly likely to remain employed. Many chose self-employment while others preferred part-time work or flexible hours.[35] The greying of the workforce will require some adjustments. Some older workers will prefer less demanding full-time jobs and flexible work hours, others will choose retirement, and still others will favour part-time work. Many of these people have experience that can benefit a firm, but they may require retraining, coaching, and counselling as they move through the various stages of their careers.

Baby boom: Those born between 1947 and 1966.

Young Workers

Over the past few decades the labour market prospects for Canadian youth (aged 15–24), particularly for males, have become increasingly dim. For example, over the period 1980–1996, the average earnings (adjusted for inflation) of young males and females decreased by about 19 percent and 6 percent respectively. By 1998, the unemployment rate for young men was almost 17 percent (double the national average) and about 14 percent for young women. Although the employment rate for youth fell steadily over the 1990s, the good news is that a large portion (30 percent) of those not working spent more time in school. For example, John Watts is an accountant with PricewaterhouseCoopers in Vancouver. He remained in school and didn't enter the work force full-time until he was 26. John sums up the job market situation he faced in the late 1990s: "I think for young people in general, it's more difficult to get a full-time job than it used to be. You'll see a lot more people starting at 27 or 28 years old." Geoff Bowlby, a labour market specialist with Statistics Canada, describes the plight of Canadian youth and new

HRM in *ACTION*

Workplace Issue Laurie, who is 25, designed and is in charge of the Web site for a pharmaceutical company. The company is well known for an asthma drug. Laurie has suggested putting general information about asthma on the site as a way to draw in a bigger audience, but senior management is resisting. They would prefer to limit the site to company information and data from the annual report. Laurie believes this is boring to anyone except shareholders, but is shy about saying that bluntly since management are all about 20 years older than she is. [36]

How does a younger worker sway older colleagues?

workers: "Young workers because of their lack of seniority are first fired in bad times, and they are last hired because of their lack of experience." [37]

Proactive human resource managers must look for creative ways both to manage the new worker and to smooth out labour trends. For example, one company provides all its employees with a percentage of salary to use for career development and training. As another example, forward-thinking firms could make use of cooperative student employment. They could plan for employee sabbaticals so that during harder times, employees can retrain or retool. In this way the company will be ready for the next boom with trained and recharged employees.

Contingency Workers

Contingency workers:
Contract workers hired by companies to cope with unexpected or temporary challenges.

Throughout the 1990s many companies drastically reduced their full-time work force. After downsizing (a workplace issue discussed in the next chapter), thousands of full-time employees who lost their jobs were not rehired. Instead, many companies chose to employ **contingency workers**—contract workers hired by companies to cope with unexpected or temporary challenges. This workforce consists of part-timers, freelancers, subcontractors, people hired through employment agencies, and independent professionals. Contract workers are usually paid less than full-time employees and almost never receive benefits. Today contingency workers make up at least one-third of the workforce, and this form of employment is growing faster than any. In the past, these workers were almost all clerical staff. Now—due to a large extent to downsizing—professionals make up at least 20 percent of the total contingency workforce.[38]

The use of contingency workers, although more flexible and economical, is not without disadvantages. These workers tend to be less dependent on the firm and therefore less committed to its mission. Unless they are given extra training and closer supervision, they tend to exhibit high turnover and less corporate commitment. If managed properly, however, contingency employees can provide a firm with a body of well-trained, long-term employees that can be expanded or contracted as business conditions dictate.[39]

The Small Business

Every year, thousands of individuals, motivated by a desire to be their own boss, to earn a better income, and to realize their dreams, launch new business ventures. These individuals, often referred to as entrepreneurs, have been essential to the growth and vitality of the Canadian economy. Entrepreneurs are the soul of the new economy. They develop or recognize new products or business opportunities, secure the necessary start-up capital, and organize and operate the business. Most people who start their own businesses get a great deal of satisfaction from owning and managing them.

In 1998, nearly 2.5 million Canadians reported working at their own businesses, more than double the number 20 years earlier. Self-employed workers accounted for 16 percent of the total labour force, up from almost 12 percent during the late 1970s. Since 1990, self-employment on average has expanded by 4 percent per year, accounting for about 55 percent of the new jobs the economy has created. As we mentioned in Chapter 1, 95 percent of all businesses have fewer than 20 employees.[40]

Human resource professionals must be aware that the environment of managers in large and small businesses is often quite different. Managers in large firms may be separated from top management by numerous managerial layers. They may have difficulty seeing how they fit into the overall organization. They often know managers one or two layers above them but seldom those higher up. In some large companies, supervisors are restricted by many written guidelines, and they may feel more loyalty to their workers than to upper management.

Managers in small businesses often identify more closely with the goals of the firm. They can readily see how their efforts affect the firm's profits. In many instances, lower-level managers know the company executives personally. These supervisors know the organization's success is closely tied to their own effectiveness.

Corporate Culture

Corporate culture is the system of shared values, beliefs, and habits that interact with the formal organization structure to produce behavioural norms. Environmental factors, such as governmental action, workforce diversity, and global competition, often require a firm to change its culture and even make a clean break with the past. For example, the present culture of Bell Canada is distinctly different from the company's culture of just a few years ago when it virtually monopolized its industry. The gradual deregulation in the telecommunications industry has meant that the firm has had to deal with aggressive competitors and in doing so to develop a new modus operandi.

Our Canadian workforce reflects the increasing diversity of the country's population. To maximize the advantages of diversity—particularly the talents of aboriginals, persons with disabilities, visible minorities and women—companies are trying to create a culture in which each employee has the opportunity to contribute and to advance in the organization based on excellent performance. Human resource professionals know that critical factors, such as retention, motivation, and advancement, are highly dependent on the way employees react to their firm's culture.

Businesses are being forced to make many changes to stay competitive. A means of shaping corporate culture is through organizational development, a topic of Chapter 7. Companies must find ways to improve quality, increase speed of operations, and adopt a customer orientation. These changes are so fundamental that they must take root in a company's very essence; that is to say, in its *culture*. An organization's corporate culture is integral to fulfilling its mission and objectives; therefore, the factors that determine corporate culture are also crucial to the company's success.

Global competition is another key factor affecting corporate cultures. Competitive pressure from foreign firms, which few companies have escaped, can only be met by improving quality, pricing, and customer service. Because these critical factors are so dependent on a firm's culture, the culture itself must change if the firm is to survive, much less prosper.

Changes to a firm's culture should involve the whole organization. The chief executive officer should take a proactive role. The necessity of the change,

Corporate culture: The system of shared values, beliefs, and habits within an organization that interacts with the formal structure to produce behavioural norms.

Culture Change Strategy Questions and answers about culture change and human resources are addressed.

along with the goals sought, should be clearly communicated to all organizational members. They, too, should be involved either directly or indirectly.

Human Resource Management in the Global Environment

Global corporation:
An organization that has corporate units in a number of countries; the units are integrated to operate as one organization worldwide.

Our earlier discussion on environmental factors focused on organizations located and doing business mainly in Canada. The external environment confronting global enterprises is even more diverse and complex than that facing domestic firms. A **global corporation** (GC) has corporate units in a number of countries that are integrated to operate as one organization worldwide. Thus, as illustrated in Figure 2-4, global operations add another environmental layer to human resource management. Although the basic human resource management tasks remain essentially the same, the manner in which they are accomplished may be altered substantially by the global firm's external environment.

Obviously, human assets will play at least as large a role as advanced technology and economies of scale in competing in the global marketplace. Globally, HR professionals must manage human resources in an all-inclusive manner, thinking systematically and looking at the whole system.[41] Because the

Figure 2-4

Human Resource
Management in the Global
Environment

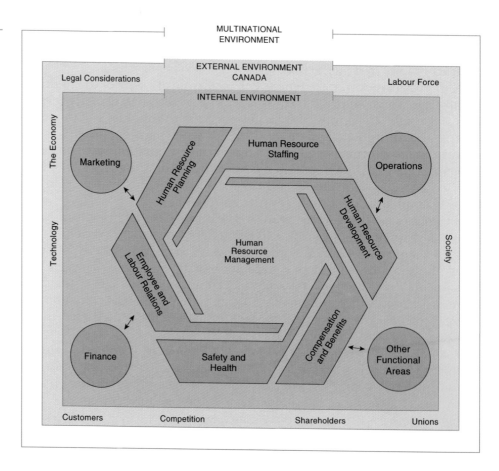

global environment is so complex, global HR managers must have unique abilities and skills. They should have "global experience outside the home country; global knowledge, attitudes, and perspectives toward international issues, events, and business; multicultural knowledge and expertise of national cultures; knowledge of working effectively and simultaneously with employees from different countries; cross-cultural interaction and communication skills, adaptation skills for living in foreign cultures, a willingness to modify [their] management style; and ... a catalyst-type personality for creating cultural synergy through practicing key skills and integrating national differences."[42]

A GLOBAL PERSPECTIVE

Global HR Experience: The Ticket to Success

Adapting to the global environment is essential to Canadian business as the worldwide marketplace expands and becomes more profitable. Exports alone represented about 43 percent of our gross domestic product in 1996. This figure is up from 29 percent in 1993. Global competition, air travel, satellite communication technology, the Internet, and wage differentials have made doing business abroad both necessary and feasible. Companies have responded by establishing more and more operations overseas. Unfortunately, while the number of Canadian employers working for Canadian firms overseas is expanding dramatically, there are few human resource professionals with a truly global perspective and effective global skills.

SUMMARY

1. Identify the environmental factors that affect human resource management.

Environmental factors, either separately or in combination, can provide opportunities for and place constraints on human resource management. These factors include: the labour force, legal considerations, society, unions, shareholders, competition, customers, technology, and the economy.

The labour force affects wage rates, as well as an employer's ability to find the right people for a particular occupational requirement. Federal and provincial human rights legislation and employment standards, in addition to contract and common law, set requirements for human resource managers.

Society may also exert pressure on human resource management in less formal ways. Individuals and special interest groups have found that they can effect change through their collective voices, votes, and other actions. A firm's wage levels, benefits, and working conditions reflect decisions made jointly by unions and management. Unions also exert a strong external influence even on nonunionized organizations. Because shareholders, or stockholders, have invested money in the firm, they may at times challenge programs considered by management to be beneficial to the organization. Competition will affect how a firm obtains and retains a sufficient number of employees in various career fields. Because sales are crucial to the firm's survival, management has the task of ensuring that its employment practices do not antagonize the customers it serves. Of major concern to those dealing with human resource management is the effect technological changes have had and will have on the work place. In particular, communications and information technologies have become driving industrial sectors. As a generalization, when the economy is booming, recruiting qualified workers is more difficult than in less prosperous times.

2. Distinguish between a proactive and a reactive response to the external environment.
Managers can approach changes in the external environment proactively or reactively. A proactive response involves taking action in anticipation of environmental changes. A reactive response involves simply reacting to environmental changes after they occur. A proactive attitude leads to better performance and reduces the chances of damaging legal actions.

3. Describe the issue of diversity and identify the diverse workforce that management now confronts.
Diversity refers to any perceived difference among people: age, functional specialty, profession, sexual orientation, language, geographic origin, lifestyle, tenure with the organization, or position. Managers must be knowledgeable about common group characteristics to manage diversity effectively. The challenge for managers is to recognize that different groups often think differently, act differently, learn differently, and communicate differently.

Because every person, culture, and business situation is unique, there are no simple rules for managing diversity, but employees need to develop patience, open-mindedness, acceptance, and cultural awareness.

Of key concern are four specific groups: women, visible minorities, aboriginals, and persons with disabilities. But diversity also involves such concerns as bilingualism, work–family balance, age, and the contingent workforce.

4. Explain the importance of small business in today's work environment.
In 1998, nearly 2.5 million Canadians reported working at their own businesses, more than double the number 20 years earlier. In Canada today, 95 percent of all businesses have fewer than 20 employees. Further, since 1990, small business has accounted for about 55 percent of all the new jobs.

5. Define corporate culture and describe how it is developed and shaped.
Corporate culture is the system of shared values, beliefs, and habits within an organization that interacts with the formal structure to produce behavioural norms. It is the pattern of basic assumptions, values, and artifacts shared by organizational members. Corporate culture can be influenced by environmental factors such as government action, workforce diversity, and global competition. Corporate culture can also be shaped internally through organizational development. In changing and developing a corporate culture, as much of the organization should be involved as possible, especially senior management.

QUESTIONS FOR REVIEW

1. What factors make up the external environment of human resource management? Briefly describe each of these factors.

2. Distinguish between a proactive and reactive response. Give an example of each.

3. Define diversity.

4. How is the composition of the Canadian labour force expected to change?

5. How important is small business to our economy?

6. Define corporate culture. What effect could it have on human resource management?

DEVELOPING **HRM** SKILLS

An Experiential Exercise

Jan Flack has just been promoted from assistant to the human resource director to assistant general manager. Although the general manager, Jerry Kozlowik, has mixed feelings about Jan, he did not directly oppose the promotion, but he did express his concerns to his immediate boss, Mr. Patel. Jerry's boss told him that he could handle her and that the company needed more female managers. Now, Jerry and Jan are about to have their first meeting since the promotion, which should prove very interesting.

If you like a little excitement, you will enjoy this exercise. It is obvious that Jerry and Jan will disagree on many aspects of supervision, and that diversity of opinions could lead to some interesting interactions. If you want to be in Jerry's shoes, or if you'd like to be Jan, volunteer quickly. Everyone else, observe carefully. Your instructor will provide the participants with additional information.

In any organization, decisions should be based on the best available information. The same is true with this simulation. Each decision period, your team will have the opportunity to purchase industry research that will aid you in the decision-making process. The surveys available are industry average quality, morale, grievances, and absenteeism; industry average and local comparable wage rates; average industry training, safety, and quality budgets; and the number of firms with employee participation programs.

HRM INCIDENT

The Environment

International Electronics Corp. (IEC) is an important part of the local economy. It is the largest employer in a rural community just north of Vancouver. It employs almost 10 percent of the local workforce; few alternative job opportunities are available in the area. Scott Tanaka, the human resource director at IEC, tells of a difficult decision he once had to make.

Everything was going along pretty well despite the economic recession, but I knew that sooner or later we would be affected. I got the word at a private meeting with the president, Mr. Deason, that we would have to cut the workforce by 30 percent on a crash basis. I was to get back to him within a week with a suggested plan. I knew that my plan would not be the final one, because the move was so major, but I knew that Mr. Deason was depending on me to provide at least a workable approach.

First, I thought about how the union would react. Certainly, workers would have to be let go in order of seniority. The union would try to protect as many jobs as possible. I also knew that all management actions during this period would be intensely scrutinized. We had to make sure we had our act together.

Then there was the impact on the surrounding community to consider. The local economy had not been in good shape recently. Aside from the effect on individual workers who were laid off, I knew our cutbacks would further depress the area's economy. I knew that a number of government officials and civic leaders would want to know how we were trying to minimize the harm done to the public in the area.

We really had to make the cuts, I believed. I had no choice because Mr. Deason had said we were going to do it. Also, I had recently read a news account that one of our competitors, in Calgary, had laid off several hundred workers in a cost-cutting move. To keep our sales from being further depressed, we had to keep our costs as low as those of our competitors. The market for electronics products is very competitive and a cost advantage of even 2 or 3 percent would allow competitors to take many of our customers.

Finally, a major reason for the cutbacks was to protect the interests of our shareholders. A few years ago a shareholder group disrupted our annual meeting to insist that IEC make certain environmental changes. In general, though, the shareholders seem to be more concerned with the return on their investment than with social responsibility. At our meeting, the president reminded me that, just like every other manager in the company, I should place the shareholders' interest foremost. I really was quite overwhelmed as I began to work up a personnel plan that would balance all the conflicting interests that I knew about.

Questions

1. List the elements in the company's environment that will affect Scott's suggested plan. How legitimate is the interest of each of these?

2. Is it true that Scott should be concerned first and foremost with protecting the interests of the shareholders? Discuss.

CHAPTER

3

Strategic Human Resource Planning

CHAPTER OBJECTIVES

1. Define strategic planning and describe the levels of strategic planning.

2. Explain the strategic planning process and identify the factors to be considered in strategy implementation.

3. Describe the human resource planning process.

4. Explain four common forecasting techniques and distinguish between requirements and availability forecasts.

5. Differentiate skills inventory from management inventory.

6. Distinguish between succession planning and succession development.

7. Identify what a firm can do when a surplus of workers exists.

8. Describe the concept of downsizing.

9. Define human resource information system (HRIS) and identify the features of an effective HRIS.

Mark Swann, the marketing director for Sharpco Manufacturing, commented at the weekly executive directors' meeting, "I have good news. We can get the large contract with Medord Corporation. All we have to do is complete the project in one year instead of two. I told them we could do it."

Linda Crane, vice president of strategic human resources, brought everyone back to reality by asserting, "As I understand it, our present workers do not have the expertise required to produce the quality that Medord's particular specifications require. Under the two-year project timetable, we planned to retrain our present workers gradually. With this new time schedule, we will have to go into the job market and recruit workers who are already experienced in this process. We may need to analyze this proposal further to see whether that is really what we want to do. Human resource costs will rise considerably if we attempt to complete the project in one year instead of two. Sure, Mark, we can do it, but with these constraints, will the project be cost effective?"

In this instance, Mark failed to consider the strategic nature of human resource planning in his projections. In today's fast-paced, competitive environment, failure to recognize the strategic nature of human resource planning will often destroy an otherwise well-thought-out plan.

The overall purpose of this chapter is to explain the role and nature of strategic planning within the context of human resources. We begin by defining strategic planning and explaining the levels of strategic planning. Next, we clarify the human resource planning process. Then, we examine some human resource forecasting techniques. Next, we discuss forecasting human resource requirements and availability and a firm's response to a surplus of workers. The issue of downsizing is then addressed. We devote the final section of the chapter to a discussion of the human resource information system and virtual human resources.

HR Web Wisdom

http: www.pearsoned.ca/ mondy

Strategic Planning
Gain a basic understanding of the concept and process of strategic planning.

HR and Strategic Planning

In Chapter 1, we stressed that HR executives are focusing their attention on how human resources can help the organization achieve its strategic objectives.[1] They now function as strategic partners with line executives in assuring that the organization achieves its mission. Thus, HR must be highly involved in the strategic planning process. Essentially, it is moving from a micro to a macro view of its mission.[2] **Strategic planning** is the process by which top management determines overall organizational purposes and objectives and how they are to be achieved.

When a firm's mission or purpose is clearly defined and its guiding principles understood, employees and managers are encouraged to put forth maximum effort in pursuing company objectives. Top management expects HR activities to be closely aligned to the mission to contribute to achieving these goals.[3] In the opening scenario, for example, because Mark had excluded HR from the strategic planning process he wanted to accept a contract that would not be profitable.

Strategic planning: The determination of overall organizational purposes and goals and how they are to be achieved.

The Levels of Strategic Planning

Strategic planning should be considered according to the organizational levels at which it occurs, particularly with the growth in recent decades of such complex organizations as Nortel, General Electric, Sun Microsystems and General Motors. Figure 3-1 illustrates the organizational levels of a typical complex corporation and the corresponding levels of strategic planning. Each level has its own distinctive characteristics and needs, calling for different methods and processes of formulating strategy. It is important to understand the differences in strategic planning at the corporate, business, and functional levels.

Corporate-level strategic planning is the process of defining the overall character and purpose of the organization, the businesses it will enter and leave, and the way its resources will be distributed among those businesses. This type of planning will determine what line of businesses the corporation should be in. Corporate-level strategy typically is concerned with the mix and utilization of business divisions called strategic business units (discussed later

Corporate-level strategic planning: The process of defining the overall character and purpose of the organization, the businesses it will enter and leave, and the way resources will be distributed among those businesses.

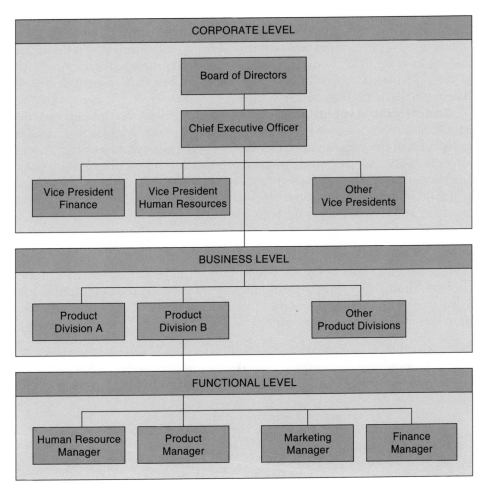

Figure 3-1

The Levels of Strategic
Planning

in the chapter). Planning at this level deals with the organization's course and determines the role of each business in the organization's grand strategy. It is primarily the responsibility of the organization's top executives, including the top HR executive.

Business-level strategic planning is the planning process concerned primarily with managing the interests and operations of a particular business. As many organizations have extensive interests in different businesses, top managers often have a difficult time organizing their varied activities. One way to deal with this problem is to create strategic business units.

A strategic business unit (SBU) is any part of a business organization that is treated separately for strategic planning purposes. It can be a single business or a collection of related businesses. The corporate-level strategy provides the general direction, and a business-level strategy provides the direction for each SBU. The business-level strategic plan is reviewed at the corporate level, changes are made if necessary, and the final strategic plan for the unit is approved. Each SBU has a unique corporate mission or purpose and product line; and its own competitors and markets.

Business-level strategic planning: The planning process concerned primarily with managing the interests and operations of a particular business.

Strategic business unit (SBU): Any part of a business organization that is treated separately for strategic planning purposes.

Some companies set up SBUs as separate profit centres, sometimes giving them virtual autonomy. Other companies have tight control over their SBUs, enforcing corporate policies and standards down to very low levels in the organization. In general, SBU business-level strategic planning is the responsibility of vice presidents or division heads. A human resource manager may be assigned to each strategic business unit.

Functional-level strategic planning is the process of determining policies and procedures for relatively narrow areas of activity that are critical to the success of the organization. Practically every large organization is divided into functional subdivisions, usually production, marketing, finance, and human resources. Each of these functional subdivisions is vital to the success of the organization. Functional-level strategic plans conform to both corporate-level and business-level strategic plans.

Functional-level strategic planning: The process of determining policies and procedures for relatively narrow areas of activity that are critical to the success of the organization.

The Strategic Planning Process

Strategic planning at all levels of the organization can be divided into four phases: (1) determining the organizational mission, (2) assessing the organization and its environment, (3) setting specific objectives or direction, and (4) determining strategies to accomplish those objectives (see Figure 3-2).[4] Examining each of

Figure 3-2

Formulating Strategy and Implementation

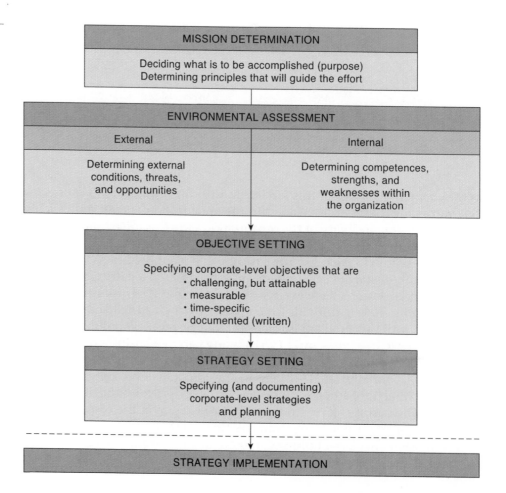

MISSION DETERMINATION

Deciding what is to be accomplished (purpose)
Determining principles that will guide the effort

ENVIRONMENTAL ASSESSMENT

External	Internal
Determining external conditions, threats, and opportunities	Determining competences, strengths, and weaknesses within the organization

OBJECTIVE SETTING

Specifying corporate-level objectives that are
• challenging, but attainable
• measurable
• time-specific
• documented (written)

STRATEGY SETTING

Specifying (and documenting) corporate-level strategies and planning

STRATEGY IMPLEMENTATION

these four phases, as well as the final step, implementation, reveals the importance of a systematic approach to strategic planning and implementation.

Determining Corporate Mission

An initial step or phase of the strategic planning process is to determine the corporate mission. The **corporate mission** is the sum total of the organization's ongoing purpose. Arriving at a mission statement should involve answering these questions: What are we in management attempting to do for whom? Should we maximize profit so that shareholders will receive higher dividends or so share price will increase? Alternatively, should we emphasize stability of earnings so that employees will remain secure?

Mission determination also requires deciding on the principles on which management decisions will be based. For example, to what extent will the corporation stress diversity, promotion from within, or a competitive compensation system? The answers to such questions tend to become embedded in a corporate culture and values and help determine the organizational mission.

Corporate mission:
The sum total of the organization's ongoing purpose.

HR Web Wisdom
http://www.pearsoned.ca/mondy

Mission Statements
Review the mission statements of some of Canada's fastest growing companies.

Assessing the Environment

Once the mission has been determined, the organization must be assessed for internal strengths and weaknesses, and threats and opportunities in the external environment. This has often been referred to as a **SWOT analysis**. Specific objectives can be established, and strategies can be developed for accomplishing those objectives. For example, a firm that has a highly skilled and motivated workforce would list that workforce as a strength. Likewise, a firm that has a diverse workforce in a global environment would likely see this diversity as a strength.

Making strategic plans involves information flows from both the internal and the external environment. From inside comes information about organizational competencies, strengths, and weaknesses. Scanning the external environment allows organizational strategists to identify threats and opportunities as well as constraints. In brief, the job in the planning phase is to develop strategies that take advantage of the company's strengths and minimize its weaknesses, allowing it to grasp opportunities and avoid threats. In the opening vignette, for example, Linda Crane was quick to point out to Mark Swann the company's internal weakness of an untrained workforce, which would necessitate going externally into the job market.

SWOT analysis: An organizational assessment of internal **S**trengths and **W**eaknesses, and external **T**hreats and **O**pportunities.

Setting Objectives

Explicitly stating objectives and directing all activities toward their attainment is a common element of strategic management. David Anderson of CANATOM NPM, a Profit 100 company, says: [5]

> One thing I've found very useful is to ensure that the company and the individual set goals and objectives. I talk about SMART objectives: **S**pecific, **M**easurable, **A**ttainable, **R**each in **T**ime. I always ask people to set objectives. And I find that if you can really get people to think about those things at day one, and put it in their own words, they come through.

Determining Strategy

Once objectives are established or direction is determined, strategies can be formulated. Many organizations limit their written strategic plans to financial budgets—and some do not even have budgets. Most authorities, however, advise putting strategies in writing. Whether or not strategies are written, the task of organizational strategists is to communicate clearly how the organization intends to accomplish its goals.

Implementing Strategy

Once the strategic planning is complete, the strategy must be implemented. Some people argue that implementation is the most difficult and most important part of strategic management. No matter how creative and well formulated the strategic plan, the organization will not benefit if the plan is incorrectly implemented. Strategy implementation involves several dimensions of the organization. It requires changes in the organization's behaviour; this can be brought about by changing one or more organizational dimensions, including management's leadership ability, organizational structure, information and control systems, technology, and human resources.

Leadership

A leader is able to get others to do what he or she wants them to do. Managers need strong leadership to influence organization members to adopt the behaviours needed for strategy implementation and, sometimes, to change their values and attitudes. Top-level managers may find it useful to build coalitions and persuade middle-level managers to buy in to the strategic plan. Involving managers and employees in formulating strategy makes implementation easier because they understand and are committed to the strategy they helped to design.

Organizational Structure

A company's organizational structure is typically illustrated by its organizational chart. This structure indicates individual managers' responsibilities and degrees of authority, as well as the jobs within departments. The structure also reflects the company's level of centralization and the types of departments that will be utilized.

Information and Control Systems

Information and control systems include reward systems, incentive, budgets for allocating resources, information systems, and the organization's rules, policies, and procedures. Managers and human resource professionals need to be proactive in securing this information to support implementation of the strategic plan. Managers and employees must be stimulated and rewarded for adhering to the new strategy and making it a success.

Technology

The knowledge, tools, and equipment used to accomplish an organization's assignments make up its technology. If an organization adopts a strategy of producing a new product, managers must often redesign jobs and construct new buildings and facilities. New technology may also be required for implementing a low-cost strategy if the technology can improve efficiency. As with other aspects of strategy implementation, the appropriate level of technology must be found for proper implementation of the strategic plan.

Human Resources

In certain situations, employees may simply be incompatible with a new strategy and they may have to be retrained or even replaced. The new strategy may foster resentment and resistance among both managers and employees, a matter that must be resolved quickly before it hinders strategy implementation. A proper balance of human resources must be developed to support strategy implementation.

The Human Resource Planning Process

The HR executive works with upper management to formulate corporate-level strategy. Once the corporate-level strategy has been agreed on, human resource planning can occur.

Human resource planning (HRP) is the process of systematically reviewing human resource requirements to ensure that the required number of employees, with the required skills, are available when they are needed.[6] The human resource planning process is illustrated in Figure 3-3. Note that strategic planning precedes human resource planning.

Linda Crane, in the opening vignette, was aware of her workforce's capabilities. She realized that the planned gradual training schedule would not work under the proposed contractual timetable. Human resource planning involves matching both the internal and external supply of people with job openings anticipated in the organization. This is becoming increasingly complex. Today, the labour pool is constantly changing as companies try to cope with rapid technological shifts and increasing globalization of the economy.[7]

Much of human resource planning normally begins after an organization's strategic plans have been formulated. For example, note in Figure 3-3 that human resource planning has two components: requirements and availability. Forecasting human resource requirements involves determining the number and type of employees needed, by skill level and location. These projections will reflect various factors, such as production plans and changes in productivity. In order to forecast availability, the human resource manager looks to both internal sources (present employees) and external sources (the labour market). When employee requirements and availability have been analyzed, the firm can determine whether it will have a surplus or a shortage of employees. Ways must be found to reduce the number of employees if a surplus is projected. Some of these methods include restricted hiring, reduced hours,

Human resource planning (HRP):
The process of systematically reviewing human resource requirements to ensure that the required number of employees, with the required skills, are available when they are needed.

Human Resource Planning
See an example of a human resource planning model and diagnostic.

Figure 3-3

The Human Resource
Planning Process

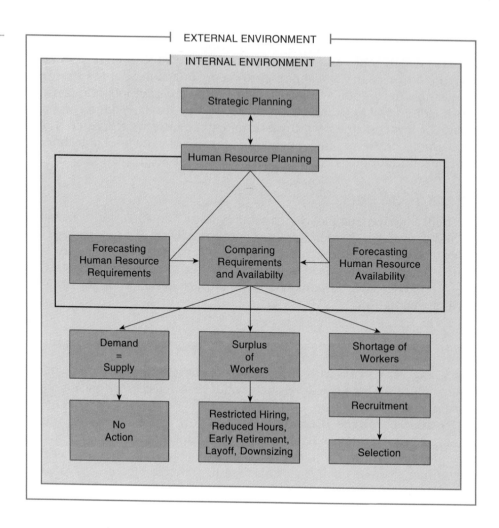

early retirements, and layoffs. If a shortage is forecast, the firm must obtain
the proper quantity and quality of workers from outside the organization.

Human Resource Forecasting

Forecasting Methods

Several techniques for forecasting human resource requirements and availability are currently used by those in the profession. Some are qualitative and
others are quantitative. Several of the better known methods are described in
this section.

Zero-base forecasting:
A method for estimating
future employment needs
using the organization's
current level of employment
as the starting point.

Zero-Base Forecasting

The **zero-base forecasting** approach uses the organization's current level
of employment as the starting point for determining future staffing needs.
Essentially the same procedure is used for human resource planning as for
zero-base budgeting, in which each budget must be justified each year. If an

employee retires, is fired, or leaves the firm for any other reason, the position is not automatically filled. Instead, an analysis is made to determine whether the firm can justify filling it. Equal concern is shown for creating new positions when they appear to be needed.

Bottom-up Approach

Human resource forecasting is often most effective when managers periodically project their human resource needs, comparing their current and anticipated levels, and give the human resource department adequate lead time to explore internal and external sources. Thus, some firms use what has been termed the **bottom-up approach** to employment forecasting. It is based on the reasoning that the manager in each unit is most knowledgeable about employment requirements. In the bottom-up approach, each successive level in the organization—starting with the lowest—forecasts its requirements, ultimately providing an aggregate forecast of employees needed.

Use of Predictor Variables

Another means of forecasting human resource requirements is to use past employment levels to predict future requirements. **Predictor variables** are factors known to have affected employment levels. One of the most useful predictors of employment levels is sales volume. Normally, there is a positive relationship between market demand for a product or service and the number of employees needed. The more a company produces, the more employees are required. In Figure 3-4, a firm's sales volume is depicted on the horizontal axis, and the number of employees actually required is shown on the vertical axis. In this illustration, as sales decrease, so does the number of employees needed. Using such a method, managers can approximate the number of employees required at different demand levels.

Simulation

Simulation is a technique for experimenting with a real-world situation through a mathematical model. The simulation model uses mathematical logic

Bottom-up approach:
A forecasting method beginning with the lowest organizational units and progressing upward through an organization ultimately to provide an aggregate forecast of employment needs.

Predictor variables:
Factors known to have an impact on a company's employment levels.

Simulation: A technique for experimenting with a real-world situation by means of a mathematical model that represents the actual situation.

HRM in *ACTION*

What, Me Justify?

"Cynthia, what do you mean by saying that I'm going to have to justify my need for the customer service position? One of my 10 employees in this job just quit, and I want a replacement now! We've had 10 customer service reps in my department for the two years that I've been here. If we've needed them in the past, certainly we will need them in the future."

This is the beginning of a conversation between Roberto Sanchez, a first-line supervisor with Call Centre Inc., and Cynthia Singh, its human resource manager.

How should Cynthia respond?

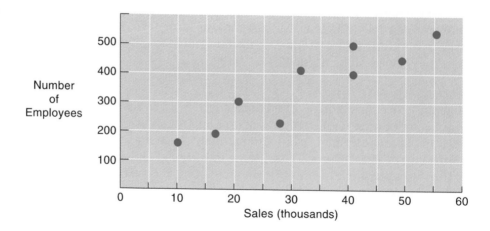

to predict what will occur. Simulation allows human resource managers to try out many "what if" scenarios without real-world consequences.

In human resource management, a simulation model might be developed to represent the interrelationships among employment levels and many other variables. The manager could then ask questions such as

- What would happen if we put 10 percent of the present workforce on overtime?

- What would happen if the plant had two shifts? Three shifts?

Forecasting Requirements

A **requirements forecast** is an estimate of the numbers and kinds of employees the organization will need at future dates to realize its stated goals. Before human resource requirements can be projected, demand for the firm's goods or services must first be forecast. This forecast is then converted into people requirements for the activities necessary to meet this demand. For example, manufacturing 1000 widgets each week might require 10 000 hours of work by assemblers during a 40-hour week. Dividing the 10,000 hours by the 40 hours in the workweek indicates that 250 assembly workers are needed. Similar calculations are performed for quality control checks, sales calls, and all the other jobs needed to produce and market the widgets.

Requirements forecast:
An estimate of the numbers and kinds of employees an organization will need at future dates to realize its stated objectives.

Forecasting Availability

Determining whether the firm will be able to secure employees with the necessary skills and from what sources is called an **availability forecast**. It helps to show whether the needed employees may be obtained from within the company (internal), from outside the organization (external), or from a combination of the two sources.

Availability forecast:
A process of determining whether a firm will be able to secure employees with the necessary skills from within the company, from outside the organization, or from a combination of the two sources.

Internal Sources of Supply

Many of the workers that will be needed for future positions may already work for the firm. If the firm is small, management probably knows all the workers sufficiently well to match their skills and aspirations with the company's needs. Suppose, for example, that a firm is creating a new sales position. Common knowledge in the company may be that Cecilia Garcia, a five-year employee, has both the skills and the desire to take over the new job. This unplanned process of matching people and positions may be sufficient for smaller firms. As organizations grow, however, the matching process becomes increasingly difficult. Both skills and management inventories are being used by organizations that take human resources seriously. Also, succession planning helps ensure an internal supply of highly qualified management personnel.

Skills inventories. A **skills inventory** is information maintained on the availability and preparedness of non-managerial employees to move either into higher level positions or laterally in the organization. A skills inventory generally includes

- Background and biographical data
- Work experience
- Specific skills and knowledge
- Licences or certifications held
- In-house training programs completed
- Previous performance appraisal evaluations
- Career goals

A properly designed and updated skills inventory system permits management to readily identify employees with particular skills and match them as well as possible to the changing needs of the company.

Management inventories. Some firms may maintain additional data for their managers, because managerial positions require a broader range of skills. A **management inventory** contains detailed information about each manager and is used to identify individuals who have the potential to move into higher level positions. It would likely include data such as the following:

- Work history and experience
- Educational background
- Assessment of strengths and weaknesses
- Developmental needs
- Promotion potential at present and with further development
- Current job performance
- Field of specialization
- Job preferences
- Geographic preferences
- Career goals and aspirations

Skills inventory: Information maintained on non-managerial employees in a company regarding their availability and preparedness to move either laterally or into higher level positions.

Management inventory: Detailed data regarding each manager in an organization; used in identifying individuals possessing the potential to move into higher level positions.

- Anticipated retirement date

- Personal history, including psychological assessments

Electronic management and skills inventories. Many companies now use intranets to help manage their people inventories and ease staff access to job availability and requirements. Employees maintain their electronic résumés through well-structured databases, which managers can search when they need people with specific skills.[8]

Succession Planning "I would say the most important HR issue facing us today is how do we bring in the talent required to ensure the continuity and, indeed, the growth of the company in the future," says David Anderson, executive vice president of CANATOM NPM.[9] During an economic downturn, the company chose not to hire trainees. But this lack of succession planning left the company with a shortage of junior people moving through on-the-job-training and thus a shortage in the steady supply of good managers. **Succession planning** is the process of ensuring that a qualified person will be available to assume a managerial position when the position becomes vacant whether through untimely death, resignation, termination, or orderly retirement.

Succession planning is particularly important for family-owned businesses. Family businesses are important to the Canadian economy. They account for over $1 trillion in sales each year and employ about 4.7 million people full-time and 1.3 million part-time. A 1999 study of more than 750 family companies sponsored by Deloitte & Touche found that more than half of the leaders planned to step down in the next decade, and most had no plan to deal with succession. That is "a recipe for disaster," said John Bowey, a family business specialist with Deloitte & Touche.[10]

The demographic, technological, and global changes that will confront management in this century make succession planning more important than ever. Organizations need to develop a profile of the types of people who can effectively lead and manage, both now and in the future.[11] At CANATOM NPM, for example, David Anderson and his team now review, twice a year, their succession plan for all key employees: "We identify the key skill areas that have to be covered for the company to function. Who is the key resource for that particular skill area and who is the individual's backup?"[12]

A key outcome of a management inventory is a succession plan. One example is shown in Figure 3-5. The chart shows a manager in the top box, with immediate subordinates in the lower boxes. Each position box shows a position title and the incumbent's name. The symbol * preceding the name identifies incumbents who will retire between 2001 and 2006, indicating that short-range planning is required. The symbol ** preceding the name identifies incumbents who will retire between 2007 and 2012, indicating that long-range planning is required. If the word *open* appears in the box, the position is unfilled. *Future* indicates that the position is anticipated but does not yet exist.

Additional information shown on the chart includes the following:

- **dev pgm:** Identifies the particular development program in which the employee participates.

Succession planning:
The process of ensuring that a qualified person will be available to assume a managerial position when it is vacant.

- **retire:** Indicates the month and year of the employee's planned retirement.

- **est prom:** Indicates the employee's estimated potential for promotion.

- **lrp:** Indicates the employee's long-range career potential with the company.

- **ppc:** Indicates the incumbent's current organizational level.

- **3 Development Needs:** Describes three priority development needs that have been identified.

- **Potential Positions:** Shows the title of each position to which the incumbent can potentially be promoted, along with codes that indicate an estimate of when the employee would be ready for promotion.

- **Possible Replacements:** Lists the names of up to 10 possible replacements for the incumbent, with codes indicating when the replacements would be ready for promotion to this position.

A recent concept related to succession planning is **succession development.** Succession development is the process of determining a comprehensive job profile of the key positions and then ensuring that key prospects are properly developed to match these qualifications. In succession planning, replacement candidates often do not know that they are being considered for a future position whereas in succession development, candidates are kept informed and encouraged to participate in their development process.[13]

Succession development: The process of determining a comprehensive job profile of the key positions and then ensuring that key prospects are properly developed to match these qualifications.

External Sources of Supply

Unless a firm is experiencing declining demand, it will eventually have to recruit some employees from outside the organization. As we discuss in Chapter 5, the "best" source of supply varies by industry, firm, and geographic location. Some organizations find that their best sources of potential employees are colleges and universities. Others get excellent results from vocational schools, competitors, or even unsolicited applications. Many firms now rely on the Internet.

As we have already discussed, forecasting can assist not only in identifying where potential employees may be found but also in predicting the types of individuals that will likely succeed in the organization. For example, a regional medical centre located far from any large metropolitan area reviewed its employment files of registered nurses. It discovered that nurses born and raised in small towns adapted better to the medical centre's environment than those who grew up in large cities. After studying these statistics, management modified its recruiting efforts.[14]

HR Web Wisdom

http: www.pearsoned.ca/ mondy

HRDC—HR Links
One source of on-line recruiting is HRDCs "Worklinks."

Surplus of Employees

A comparison of requirements and availability may indicate a worker surplus in the making; with this knowledge, restricted hiring, reduced hours, early retirements, and layoffs —topics revisited in Chapter 16—may be necessary. Downsizing, one result of worker surpluses, is treated as a separate topic.

Restricted Hiring

When a firm implements a restricted hiring policy, it reduces the workforce by not replacing employees who leave. New workers are hired only when the

Figure 3-5

Career Planning Inventory Organizational Review Chart

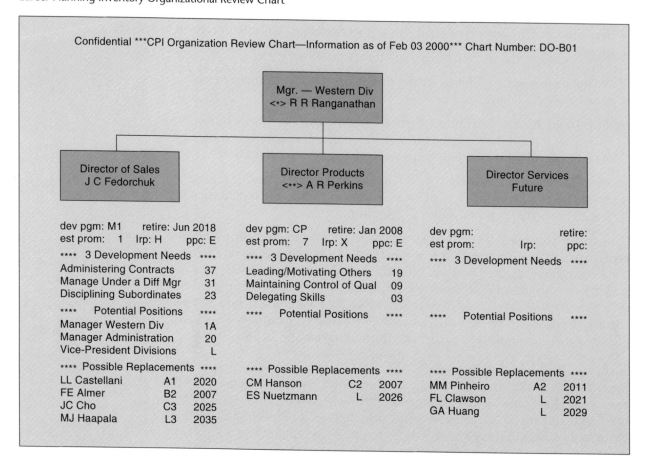

Confidential ***CPI Organization Review Chart—Information as of Feb 03 2000*** Chart Number: DO-B01

Mgr. — Western Div
<*> R R Ranganathan

Director of Sales J C Fedorchuk	Director Products <**> A R Perkins	Director Services Future

Director of Sales — J C Fedorchuk

dev pgm: M1   retire: Jun 2018
est prom: 1   lrp: H   ppc: E

**** 3 Development Needs ****
Administering Contracts   37
Manage Under a Diff Mgr   31
Disciplining Subordinates   23

**** Potential Positions ****
Manager Western Div   1A
Manager Administration   20
Vice-President Divisions   L

**** Possible Replacements ****
LL Castellani   A1   2020
FE Almer   B2   2007
JC Cho   C3   2025
MJ Haapala   L3   2035

Director Products — A R Perkins

dev pgm: CP   retire: Jan 2008
est prom: 7   lrp: X   ppc: E

**** 3 Development Needs ****
Leading/Motivating Others   19
Maintaining Control of Qual   09
Delegating Skills   03

**** Potential Positions ****

**** Possible Replacements ****
CM Hanson   C2   2007
ES Nuetzmann   L   2026

Director Services — Future

dev pgm: retire:
est prom: lrp: ppc:

**** 3 Development Needs ****

**** Potential Positions ****

**** Possible Replacements ****
MM Pinheiro   A2   2011
FL Clawson   L   2021
GA Huang   L   2029

overall performance of the organization may be affected if strategic jobs are not filled. For instance, if a quality control department that consisted of four inspectors lost one to a competitor, this individual probably would not be replaced. However, all four left, some of them would be replaced.

Reduced Hours

A company can respond to a reduced workload requirement by reducing the total number of hours employees work. Instead of continuing a 40-hour week, management may decide to cut each employee's time to 30 hours. This cutback normally applies only to hourly employees because management and other professionals typically are salaried (not paid on an hourly basis).

Early Retirement

Early retirement of some present employees is another way to reduce the number of workers. Some employees will be delighted to retire, but others will be somewhat reluctant. The latter may be willing to accept early retirement if the total retirement package is made sufficiently attractive.

Layoffs

At times, a firm has no choice but to lay off part of its workforce. A layoff is not the same as a firing, but it has the same basic effect—the worker is no longer employed. When the firm is unionized, layoff procedures are usually prescribed clearly by the labour–management agreement. Typically, workers with the least seniority are laid off first. If the firm is nonunionized, it may base layoff on a combination of factors, such as seniority and productivity level. When managers and other professionals are laid off, the decision is likely to be based on ability, although internal politics may be a factor.

Downsizing

Downsizing, also known as restructuring and *rightsizing*, is a one-time change in the organization and reduction in the number of people employed. Typically, both the organization and the number of people in the organization shrink. The trend among many organizations throughout the '90s was to cut staff and downsize. Managers were particularly hard hit. As a result, total full-time employment in Canada actually decreased between 1991 and 1996. Companies like The Bank of Montreal, the Thompson Group, Cara Operations, and CN Railways drastically reduced their full-time work force. For example, over the 1990s CN halved its workforce, from some 36 000 in the early 1990s to about 18 000.[15]

In some cases, downsizing was successful in improving profit. For example, in 1997 CN railways announced its highest operating profit ever at about $800 million on revenue of about 1.5 billion.[16] However, downsizing does not always turn a company around. A study by Mark Mentzer at the University of Saskatchewan, for example, concluded that profits don't usually grow when companies cut jobs.[17] The reason is that downsizing often does not solve the fundamental causes of the problems. Organizations have not developed appropriate strategies for growth; instead, they focus on reducing costs, which is merely attacking a symptom of the problem.[18]

One result of downsizing is that many layers are often pulled out of an organization, making advancement in the organization more difficult. In addition, when one firm downsizes, often others must follow if they are to be competitive. Such was the case in the financial services industry over the '90s. Thus, more and more individuals are finding themselves at a plateau in the same job until they retire. To reinvigorate demoralized workers, some firms are providing additional training, lateral moves, short sabbaticals, and compensation based on a person's contribution rather than his or her title.[19] Some firms are restoring their employees' enthusiasm by giving raises based on additional skills the workers acquire and use. We return to this topic in Chapter 9 when we deal with career planning and development.

Historically, firms have downsized in difficult times and rehired when times got better. But today, with firms competing globally, managers are rethinking their automatic rehiring strategies. For instance, CN recorded record profits in 1997 but rather than rehiring, continued to trim staff. In late 1998, Canadian National Railways announced it would further reduce its workforce by some 3000 people in its drive to make more profits. Paul Tellier, CN's chief executive, explained: "We are trying to become the most efficient railroad in North America."[20]

Downsizing: A one-time change in the organization and a resulting reduction in the number of people employed.

Virtual HR   Today's HR professionals use a word processing program to update the employee manual, a spreadsheet program to analyze the payroll, and a database to store employee evaluations and skills. Employees can use virtual HR to update or change their own data without talking with anyone in the human resource department. HR professionals perform pre-employment credit checks on job applicants.[22] As one human resource professional stated, "All human resources services will be available instantaneously on demand, at the place most convenient to the employee-anywhere in the world."[23] The ease of access and availability of human resource services to employees is analogous to banking with an automated teller machine. Additional virtual HR systems are being developed to further benefit the human resource manager in the areas of strategic planning, compensation, executive development, and succession studies.[24]

Downsizing often leads to the loss of employee trust. Workers who remain are suspicious of management, especially of the manager who had to deliver the news. They fear that they might be let go the next time, and often think, "I'd better take care of myself; the company won't." People who had been content with their jobs start looking around, especially if their present company does not provide them with the necessary development to keep up with industry trends. One of the main goals of HR in today's environment is to reestablish this lost worker trust.[21]

Human Resource Information Systems

Human resource information system (HRIS): Any organized approach to obtaining relevant and timely information on which to base human resource decisions.

A human resource information system (HRIS) is any organized approach for obtaining relevant and timely information on which to base human resource decisions. An effective system is crucial to sound human resource decision making; it typically employs computers and other sophisticated technologies to process data that reflect day-to-day operations of a company, organized in the form of information to facilitate the decision-making process.

An HRIS should be designed to provide information that is

- **Timely**—A manager needs up-to-date information.

- **Accurate**—A manager must be able to rely on the information.

- **Concise**—A manager can absorb only so much information at any one time.

- **Relevant**—A manager should receive only the information needed in a particular situation.

- **Complete**—A manager should have complete, not partial information.

The absence of even one of these characteristics reduces the effectiveness of an HRIS and complicates the decision-making process. Conversely, a system possessing all these characteristics enhances the ease and accuracy of the decision-making process. An effective system also produces several important reports and forecasts related to business operations:

- **Routine reports.** Business data summarized on a scheduled basis are referred to as routine reports. Weekly and monthly employment status reports may be sent to the general manager, whereas quarterly reports may be forwarded to top management.

- **Exception reports.** Exception reports highlight variations in operations that are serious enough to require management's attention. One type of exception report is the quality-exception report, completed when the number of product defects exceeds a predetermined maximum. The human resource manager may be interested in this type of information in order to identify additional training needs.

- **On-demand reports.** An on-demand report provides information in response to a specific request. The number of engineers with five years' work experience who speak fluent Spanish is an example of an on-demand report that the human resource manager could request from the database.[25]

- **Forecasts.** A forecast applies predictive models to specific situations. Managers need forecasts of the numbers and types of employees required to satisfy projected demand for the firm's product.

Firms realize that a properly developed HRIS can provide tremendous benefits to the organization. Figure 3-6 presents an overview of the human resource information system designed for one organization. Using many types of input data, the system makes available many types of output data that have far-reaching human resource planning and operational value. The HRIS ties together all human resource information into a system. Data from various input sources are integrated to provide the needed outputs. Information needed in the firm's human resource decision-making process is readily available when the system is properly designed. For instance, many firms are now studying historical trends to determine the best means of securing qualified applicants. In addition, complying with statutes and government regulations would be extremely difficult without the modern HRIS.

Figure 3-6

A Human Resource Information System

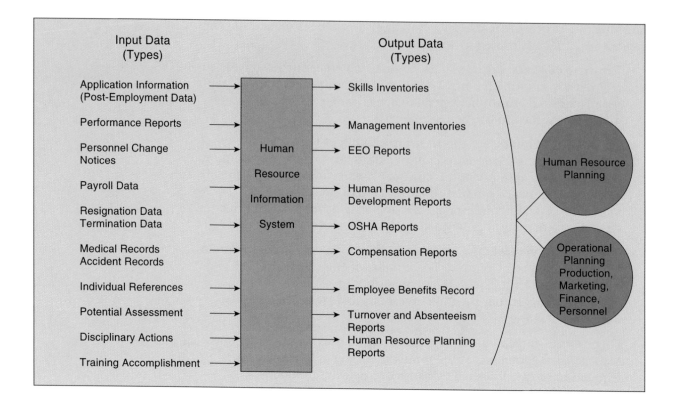

HRIS: Helping to Simplify Global HR Management

Human resource managers must follow trends toward globalization, and this requires them to use technological advancements in information technology.[26] An effective global human resource information system (GHRIS) is essential because of the complexity of managing a global labour force. A global HRIS is an organized approach for obtaining relevant and timely information on which to base human resource decisions. An ideal information system exists when users are supplied with all the information they need when they need it. Few companies have achieved this ideal, but new technology allows companies to cope more effectively with HR issues.[27]

Global HR may require activities such as cutting paycheques in various currencies; often, the regulations of multiple taxing agencies must be adhered to. Some HR practices must be consistent across the company, whereas others must change to accommodate local customs. Companies must often redesign their operations to keep up with global demands.[28] Regardless of the nature of the information system, information concerning the many relevant factors affecting human resources must be available in a timely fashion to ensure that the best human resource decisions are made. Departmental lines will continue to fade, and HR will be pulled in many directions. Successfully managing HR on a global level can be facilitated with a global human resource information system, taking advantage of new technology such as client/server computing, supernetworks, and groupware.[29]

According to Ralph W. Stevens, vice president of personnel and employee relations for Hamilton Oil Corporation, human resource professionals in each location must be experts on local laws, customs, salary structures, and so on. Through an effective GHRIS, Hamilton Oil's human resource management approach is becoming much more integrated. All of Hamilton Oil's human resource managers are linked electronically with a PC-based network. This system allows them to access a database of human resource statistics and other relevant material.[30]

Technology, in and of itself, cannot run a global human resources system. However, a state-of-the-art global human resource information system, properly implemented, can improve the effectiveness of an HR department by automating administrative tasks, reducing paperwork, simplifying work processes, and distributing better information to HR professionals and others who manage people in the global organization and each of its foreign operations.[31]

SUMMARY

1. Define strategic planning and describe the levels of strategic planning.

Strategic planning is the process by which senior management determines overall organizational purposes and objectives and how they are to be achieved. Corporate-level strategic planning is the process of defining the overall character and purpose of the organization, the businesses it will enter and leave, and how resources will be distributed among those businesses. The planning process concerned primarily with how to manage the operations is business-level strategic planning. The process of determining policies and procedures for relatively narrowly defined areas of activity is referred to as functional-level strategic planning.

2. Explain the strategic planning process and identify the factors to be considered in strategy implementation.

Strategic planning at all levels of the organization can be divided into four steps or phases: 1) determining the organizational mission, 2) assessing the organization and its environment, 3) setting specific objectives or direction, and 4) determining strategies to accomplish objectives. Major factors to be considered include leadership, organizational structure, information and control systems, technology, and human resources.

3. Describe the human resource planning process.

Human resource planning normally follows strategic planning. Human resource planning has two broad components: requirements and availability. When the requirements and availability of employees have been analyzed, the firm is in a position to determine whether there will be a surplus or shortage of employees. Ways must be found to reduce the number of employees if a surplus of workers is projected. If a shortage is forecast, the firm must rely on external recruitment and selection.

4. Explain four common forecasting techniques and distinguish between requirements and availability forecasts.

There are four common forecasting techniques. Zero-base forecasting uses the organization's current level of employment as the starting point for determining future staffing needs. The bottom-up approach is a forecasting method that proceeds upward in the

organization from small units to ultimately provide an aggregate forecast of employment needs. Predictor variables are other measures (such as sales) that have a relationship with human resource needs; managers can forecast human resource requirements based on requirements in the past at a given level of the predictor variable. Simulation is a technique used by HR professionals to answer questions about a real-world situation by experimenting with a mathematical model that mirrors it. A requirements forecast is an estimate of the numbers and kinds of employees the organization will need at future dates to realize its goals. Determining whether the firm will be able to secure employees with the necessary skills and from what sources is called availability forecasting.

5. Differentiate skills inventory from management inventory.

A skills inventory is information maintained on non-managerial employees regarding their availability and preparedness to move either upward or laterally in the organization. A management inventory contains detailed information about each manager and is used to identify individuals who have the potential to move into higher level positions.

6. Distinguish between succession planning and succession development.

Succession planning is the process of ensuring that a qualified person is available to assume a managerial position once the position is vacant. Succession development is the process of producing a comprehensive job profile of the key positions and then ensuring that key prospects are properly developed to match these qualifications.

7. Identify what a firm can do when a surplus of workers exists.

When a surplus of workers exists, a firm may implement one or more of the following major options: restricted hiring, reduced hours, early retirement, and layoffs.

8. Describe the concept of downsizing.

Downsizing, also known as restructuring and right-sizing, is essentially the reverse of company growth. It suggests a one-time change in the organization and the number of people who are employed by a firm. The purpose is to make the organization more efficient.

9. **Define human resource information system (HRIS) and identify the features of an effective HRIS.**

   A human resource information system (HRIS) is any organized approach for obtaining relevant and timely data on which to base human resource decisions. The information provided in an HRIS should be timely, accurate, concise, relevant, and complete.

QUESTIONS FOR REVIEW

1. Define strategic planning. What role does HR play in strategic planning?

2. List the levels of strategic planning. Give an example of each.

3. What are the steps or phases in the strategic planning process? Briefly describe each. What is SWOT analysis?

4. Describe the major factors for consideration in strategy implementation.

5. Describe the human resource planning process.

6. Identify and briefly describe four human resource forecasting techniques.

7. Distinguish between forecasting human resource requirements and availability. Use definitions and examples.

8. Distinguish between a management inventory and a skills inventory. What are the essential components of each?

9. Why is it important to have succession planning?

10. What actions could a firm take if it had a worker surplus?

11. Define and describe the purpose of downsizing. What are the career implications of downsizing?

12. What is the purpose of a human resource information system?

DEVELOPING **HRM** SKILLS

An Experiential Exercise

This exercise is designed to give you experience in dealing with some aspects of planning that a typical human resource manager faces. The old axiom "plan your work and work your plan" will probably have new meaning after this exercise.

You are the human resource manager at a large canning plant. Your plant produces several lines of canned food that are shipped to wholesale distributors nationwide. You are responsible for the human resource activities at the plant.

It is Monday morning, August 30. You have just returned from a week-long corporate executive meeting at the home office, attended by human resource managers from all the company's plants. You returned with notes and other materials concerning the company's goals and plans for the next six months. When you arrive at your office (an hour early), you find your in-basket full of notes, messages, and other correspondence.

Your instructor will provide you with additional information necessary to participate.

HRM INCIDENT

A Degree for Meter Readers?

Karen Feinstein was the HR recruiter for SaskGas Electric Company (SEC), a small supplier of natural gas and electricity for Moose Jaw, Saskatchewan, and the surrounding area. The company had expanded rapidly during the first half of the 1990s, and growth was expected to continue. In January 1998, SEC purchased the utilities system serving a neighbouring region. This expansion concerned Karen. The company workforce had increased by 30 percent the previous year, and Karen found it a struggle to recruit enough qualified job appicants. She knew that new expansion would intensify the problem.

Karen is particularly concerned about meter readers. The tasks involved in meter reading are relatively simple. A person drives to homes served by the company, finds the gas or electric meter, and records its current reading. If the meter has been tampered with, it is reported. Otherwise no decision making of any consequence is associated with the job. The reader performs no calculations. The pay is $10.00 per hour, high for unskilled work in the area. Even so, Karen has been having considerable difficulty keeping the 37 meter reader positions filled.

Karen was thinking about how to attract more job applicants when she received a call from the human resource director, Sam McCord. "Karen," Sam said, "I'm unhappy with the job specification calling for only a high school education for meter readers. In planning for the future, we need better educated people in the company. I've decided to change the education requirement for the meter reader job from a high school diploma to a college diploma."

"But, Sam," protested Karen, "the company is growing rapidly. If we are to have enough people to fill those jobs, we just can't insist on finding college graduates to perform such basic tasks. I don't see how we can meet our future needs for this job with such an unrealistic job qualification."

Sam terminated the conversation abruptly by saying, "No, I don't agree. We need to upgrade all the people in our organization. This is just part of a general effort to do that. Anyway, I cleared this with the president before I decided to do it."

Questions

1. Should there be a minimum education requirement for the meter reader job? Discuss.
2. What is your opinion of Sam's effort to upgrade the people in the organization?
3. What legal ramifications, if any, should Sam have considered?
4. Develop a skills inventory for a meter reader.

PART ONE CASE 1

Parma Cycle Company: An Overview

Parma Cycle Company of Delta, British Columbia, is the only company that manufactures complete bicycles in Canada. Most of Parma's competitors import parts from other countries and assemble bicycles here. Even Parma has finally begun to import many parts, mainly from Italy, Japan, and, more recently, Korea. By the late 1980s, Parma Cycle employed about 800 workers, most of them machine operators and assemblers. The area around Delta, like most regions of Canada, suffered from layoffs in the late 1980s. But conditions steadily improved during the mid-1990s, with unemployment falling below the national average of about 9.5 percent. Per capita income in Delta was above the national average in the late 1990s, making the region a high-cost place to produce. Although there had been temptations to move the facility to Mexico, the president had decided to stay in Canada for at least the next five years.

Bicycles are classified into eight types, including one-speed, low-priced multispeed, sport, touring and all-terrain. Parma Cycle makes only one-speed and low-priced multispeed bicycles, leaving the premium types to Schwinn, Panasonic, Peugeot, and a host of other competitors. Parma distributes bicycles under its own name through distributors to small retailers. However, most of the bicycles Parma manufactures are purchased by large national retailers and marketed under those retailers' house names. A few bicycles are exported to Europe and South America, but Parma finds it difficult to compete in the international market with Japanese and Italian manufacturers.

Parma Cycle Company, Inc., is a publicly held corporation, although 30 percent of its shares are controlled by a major recreational conglomerate corporation. There have been rumours of a takeover from time to time, but none ever materialized. Because of depressed earnings in the late 1980s, Parma's stock declined from $27 per share to $13 per share. Although interest rates fell after 1992, they increased again following the 1995 federal budget. The company found it costly, therefore, to raise funds to purchase new computerized milling machines that had been developed for bicycle manufacture. A high-performance racing cycle was planned for introduction in the late 1990s. But a research and development program aimed at cutting the cost of producing that bicycle was cancelled because of the high cost of financing.

Jesse Heard is the human resource director. He went to work at Parma Cycle in 1976. His first job was as a painter, when painting was done with a hand-held spray gun. He was later promoted to supervisor and worked in several departments at the plant. Parma encourages its supervisors to advance their education. Because the company paid for tuition fees, as well as books, Jesse had gone on to Simon Fraser University, receiving his bachelor's degree in personnel administration in 1986. Jesse was immediately promoted to a job in the human resource department and three years later became the human resource director.

In May 1994, the B.C. Human Rights Commission received a complaint about employment practices at Parma. It was alleged that while the proportion of women in the plant approached 75 percent, only eight percent of the Parma Cycle managers were female. There were only two female managers above the level of supervisor. Jesse Heard was advised of the complaint. He felt that the company was doing everything it should with regard to equal opportunity.

The company had an affirmative action program that encouraged managers to employ minority group members and women. In fact, Jesse's efforts to encourage the employment of women and minorities had provoked some managers to complain to the company president, his immediate superior.

In general, the working environment at

Figure I-1

Parma Cycle Company: Organizational Chart

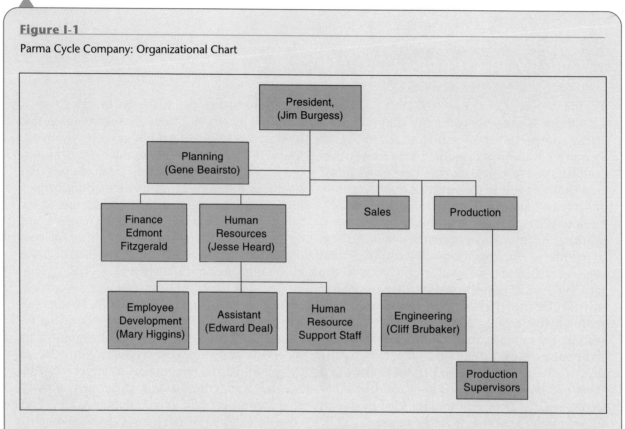

Parma Cycle is a good one. The company has a relatively flat organizational structure with few managerial levels, as shown in Figure I-1.

Most of Parma's workers are of European descent and are accustomed to working in a factory environment. Beginning in 1988, the company conducted periodic management training seminars in which managers were taught to be sensitive to workers and to cooperate with one another. The management philosophy was always one of decentralized authority. Managers, like Jesse Heard, were almost completely responsible for their own operations.

As a result of an aggressive safety program, there have been no fatal accidents at Parma during the last ten years. Work-related injuries remain well below the industry average. In 1990 the ventilation system in the factory was modernized. The lighting is good and the health and safety officer once remarked that the air was cleaner inside the factory than outside.

Gene Beairsto, the corporate planner, has said that he believes the company spends too much money on employee safety and working conditions and that this is a reason for Parma's declining profits. The company's mission has not changed since 1960, when it was stated as: "To enhance the wealth of the common shareholder through efficient production and aggressive marketing of bicycles while contributing to the well-being of our workers and to the stability of the Delta-area economy."

Parma's work force is represented by the International Association of Machinists and Aerospace Workers. Employee recruitment is done primarily through referrals from current workers. Selection is based on personal interviews, evaluation of job-related application forms, and, for certain jobs, a basic skills test conducted by the supervisor. The supervisor makes the final hiring decision. Workers must join the union before the end of a three-month probationary period. Over the years, the union has negotiated a wages and benefit package that is above average for the Delta area.

The Delta factory is laid out, coincidentally, like

a bicycle wheel, with component manufacturing departments representing the tire and spoke areas, and assembly being done in the centre of the factory, representing the hub. The factory work is neither especially difficult nor complicated. Technology for the bicycles Parma makes has changed very little over the years, and most of the jobs have become standardized.

Growing foreign competition, however, has necessitated an increased emphasis on productivity and a heightened concern for quality. Consequently, workers are encouraged to put forth additional effort, and production standards have been raised to the point where many employees complain of the faster work pace. The productivity improvement program was carried forward with the union's assistance. The union justified its participation on the basis of saving jobs. The last strike at Parma occurred in 1976.

Questions

1. Discuss the external environment of Parma Cycle Company and its effect on human resource management.

2. Is the internal environment at Parma Cycle a good one? Explain.

PART ONE CBC 🔵 VIDEO CASE

Downsizing

CBC Video Case Downsizing

Over the period from 1970 to the mid-1980s, North American companies believed that competitive advantage lay in size: the bigger the better. Middle management and corporate staff expanded rapidly as companies strove for continuous growth and expansion. The 1990s saw an almost complete about-face. Many companies woke up to find themselves overstaffed, overmanaged, less flexible, and less competitive. They were beginning to lose market share to foreign competitors and smaller firms.

One dominant response was to downsize. The most common strategy was a rapid, top-down across-the-board workforce reduction. Typically, the levels of organization were scaled down. During the 1990s, surveys revealed that more than half of Canadian employees were affected, directly or indirectly, by this trend. Often the downsizing effort went hand in hand with a heavy dose of technological change. Business expected an immediate increase in profitability and shareholder value.

In its aftermath, we now know that downsizing, on the whole, has led to dysfunctional corporate cultures, causing employees to behave inappropriately and to be unproductive. In fact, the 1990s saw the "productivity paradox"—a *decrease* in productivity despite downsizing and massive investments in technology. For the most part, downsizing has not stimulated investments in innovation and human capital. Few downsized companies have reported significant increases in profits and even fewer have seen enhanced productivity.

Particularly hard hit were middle managers—the very employees needed to revitalize a company and to bring it back to prosperity. Companies found it easier to remove middle managers: most were not protected by a union; nor did they require large severance packages as did senior managers. Besides, their productive output was hard to quantify. In 1991 there were about 1.4 million Canadians in management occupations. By the mid-1990s this number had decreased by about 15 percent. According to Eric Greenberg of the American Management Association (AMA), while middle managers made up about 8 percent of the workforce, they accounted for up to 20 percent of those who lost their jobs.

Most HR experts now agree that many companies went too far. The demise of job security poisoned the working atmosphere at all levels of corporate Canada, especially middle managers, and actually reduced productivity. For example, when Ontario shipbuilder Port Weller Dry Docks cut supervisors, says manager Ross Serianni, there weren't enough remaining supervisors to tell the workers what to do.

For many of those remaining in a downsized organization, it all added up to increased workload, distrust, and stress. A demoralized, disloyal, and dysfunctional workforce worried more about their own future than about company profitability. Loyalty, many feel, does not mean much any more, because anyone might be terminated. This mood has led to increased employee theft, lawsuits due to fraud, absenteeism, and stress-related injuries. Crime was made easier, as well, by reduced supervision, according to Norman Inkster, president of KPMG Investigation and Security Inc. And by the end of the 1990s, long-term disability stress claims were in the $350-million range. Calls for help increased steadily for corporate wellness experts such as Jack Santa-Barbara, CEO of CHC Working Well. The growth of employee assistance programs at CHC had risen by 50 percent since the late 1980s.

Today, companies and HR managers are trying to address the dark side of downsizing. Greenberg claims that the trend to downsize middle management is slowing down. He sees a more strategic focus on output rather than on pure employee cost cutting. Many companies, like Port Weller Dry Docks, are investing heavily in training and coaching. Their employees are learning how to work without as many supervisors and middle managers. Other firms are investing in corporate wellness programs to help employees deal with stress and changing organizational structures. Still others are embracing the concept of employability. If stable employment cannot be guaranteed, they argue, then companies have an obligation to help employees become more employable. This has led to increased spending on skills training and more emphasis on transferring employees to profitable areas. Corporate-sponsored career development centres are being opened to help both displaced and employed workers with tips on résumé writing, interviewing techniques, educational opportunities, and internal career openings.

Questions

1. Why do you think that so many companies downsized during the 1990s? What other options were available?

2. What is corporate culture? How does downsizing affect corporate culture?

3. How has downsizing affected the HR functions and the role of the human resource manager?

4. Briefly describe some proactive responses to downsizing.

5. As a human resource manager, set up a series of company guidelines to help the survivors of downsizing.

Video Resource: "Revenge of the Middle Manager," Venture 724 (October 12, 1999).

CHAPTER

4 Job Analysis

1. Define job analysis.

2. Discuss the reasons that job analysis is a basic human resource tool.

3. Describe the types of information required for job analysis.

4. Describe the various traditional and other job analysis methods.

5. Identify who conducts job analysis.

6. Describe the components of a well-designed job description.

7. Define job design and three key design concepts.

8. Explain four job evaluation methods.

"Mary, I'm having trouble figuring out what kind of machine operators you need," said John Anderson, the human resource director at Gulf Machineries. "I've sent four people for you to interview who seemed to meet the requirements outlined in the job description. You rejected all of them."

"To heck with the job description," replied Mary. "What I'm concerned with is finding someone who can do the job. The people you sent me couldn't do the job. Besides, I've never even seen the job description."

John took a copy of the job description to Mary and went over it point by point. They discovered that either the job description had never fit the job, or the job had changed a great deal since it was written. For example, the job description specified experience on an older model drill press, whereas the one in use was a new digital machine. Workers had to be more mathematically oriented to use the new machine effectively.

After hearing Mary describe the qualifications needed for the machine operator's job and explain the duties the operators perform, John said, "I think that now we can write an accurate description of the job, and using it as a guide, find the right kind of people. Let's work more closely so this kind of situation won't happen again."

The situation just described reflects a very common problem in human resource management: The job description did not adequately define the duties and skills needed to perform the job. Therefore, it became virtually impossible for John Anderson, the human resource director, to locate people with the required skills. Job analysis was critically needed to resolve the problem. As we stress throughout the remainder of this book, job analysis is a basic function of human resource management.

We begin the chapter by defining job analysis and explaining the reasons for conducting job analysis. Next, we review the types of information required for job analysis, discuss traditional and other job analysis methods, and describe who conducts job analysis. Then we explain the use of job analysis data in preparing job descriptions and job specifications. This is followed by an explanation of job design. In the final section we cover the controversial human resource issue of job evaluation.

Job Analysis: A Basic Human Resource Tool

In this rapidly changing work environment, the need for a sound job analysis system is critical.[1] New jobs are being created, and old jobs are being redesigned or eliminated. A job analysis conducted only a few years ago quite probably includes inaccurate data. Essentially, job analysis helps organizations address the fact of change.[2]

Job: A group of tasks that must be performed if an organization is to achieve its goals.

A **job** consists of a group of tasks that must be performed for an organization to achieve its goals. A job may require the services of one person, such as that of president, or the services of 75, as might be the case with data entry operators in a large firm.

Position: The tasks and responsibilities performed by one person; there is a position for every individual in an organization.

In a work group consisting of a supervisor, two senior clerks, and four word computer technicians, there are three jobs and seven positions. A **position** is the collection of tasks and responsibilities performed by one person; there is a position for every individual in an organization. For instance, a small company might have 25 jobs for its 75 employees, whereas in a large company 2000 jobs may exist for 50 000 employees. In some firms, as few as 10 jobs constitute 90 percent of a workforce.

Job analysis: The systematic process of determining the skills, duties, and knowledge required for performing specific jobs in an organization.

Job analysis is the systematic process of determining the skills, duties, and knowledge required for performing jobs in an organization.[3] It is an essential and pervasive human resource technique. The purpose of job analysis is to obtain answers to six important questions:

1. What physical and mental tasks does the worker accomplish?

2. When is the job to be completed?

3. Where is the job to be accomplished?

4. How does the worker do the job?

5. Why is the job done?

6. What qualifications are needed to perform the job?

Job analysis provides a summary of a job's duties and responsibilities, its relationship to other jobs, the knowledge and skills required, and the working conditions under which it is performed. The job analysis conducted by Mary and John in the opening vignette, for example, resulted in a different set of qualifications and duties for new machine operators. Job facts are gathered, analyzed, and recorded based on the job as it *is*, not as it *should* be. Determining what a job should be is a function often assigned to industrial engineers or methods analysts. Job analysis is conducted after the job has been designed, the worker has been trained, and the job is being performed.

Job analysis is performed on three occasions. First, when the organization is founded; second, when new jobs are created; and third, when jobs change significantly as a result of new technologies, methods, procedures, or systems. Job analysis is most often performed because of changes in the nature of jobs. Job analysis information is used to prepare both job descriptions and job specifications.

The **job description** is a document that provides information regarding the tasks, duties, responsibilities and competencies of the job. After John consulted with Mary regarding the new nature of the machine operator's job, he wrote a new job description that was accurate at that point in time. The minimum acceptable qualifications or competencies a person should possess to perform a particular job are normally contained in the **job specification**. We discuss both types of documents in greater detail later in the chapter.

Job description:
A document that provides information regarding the tasks, duties, responsibilities and competencies of the job.

Job specification:
A document that outlines the minimum acceptable qualifications or competencies a person should possess to perform a particular job.

Reasons for Conducting Job Analysis

As Figure 4-1 shows, data derived from job analysis affect virtually every aspect of human resource management. A major use of job analysis data is in the area of human resource planning. Merely knowing that the firm will need 1000 new employees to produce goods or services to satisfy sales demand is insufficient. Each job requires different knowledge, skills, and ability levels. Obviously, effective human resource planning must take these job requirements into consideration.

Employee recruitment and selection would be haphazard if the recruiter did not know the qualifications needed to perform the job. Lacking up-to-date job descriptions and specifications, a firm would have to recruit and select employees for jobs without having clear guidelines—an approach that could have disastrous consequences. Few firms would procure raw materials, supplies, or equipment blind. For example, when ordering personal computers, the purchasing department normally develops precise specifications. Surely the same logic should apply when searching for a firm's most valuable asset!

Job specifications also help to identify training and development needs. If the specification calls for a particular knowledge, skill, or ability that the incumbent does not have, training and/or development is probably in order. Such information should be used to help workers perform duties specified in their present job descriptions or to prepare them for promotion, not to judge them. Performance appraisals should be based solely on how well employees accomplish the duties specified in their job descriptions. A manager who evaluates an employee on other factors is wide open to allegations of discrimination.

Figure 4-1

Job Analysis: The Most Basic Human Resources Management Tool

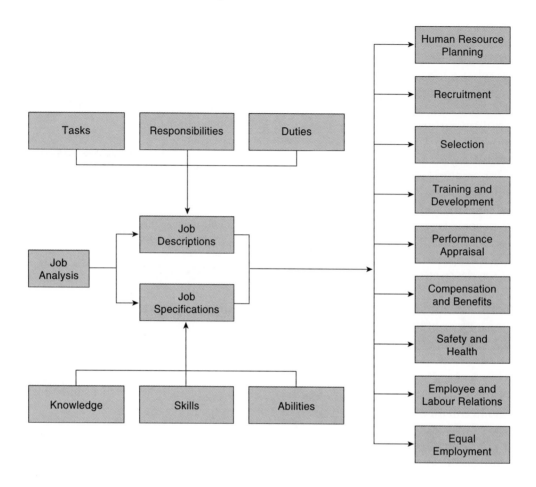

The relative value of a particular job to the company must be known before a dollar value can be placed on it. Relatively speaking, the more significant its duties and responsibilities, the more the job is worth. Jobs that require greater knowledge, skills, and abilities should be worth more to the firm. For example, the relative value of a job calling for a master's degree normally would be higher than that of a job that requires only a high school diploma.

Information derived from job analysis is also valuable in identifying safety and health considerations. For example, employers are required to state whether a job is hazardous. The job description/specification should reflect this condition. In addition, in certain hazardous jobs, workers may need specific information about the hazards to perform the jobs safely.

Job analysis information is also important to employee and labour relations. When employees are considered for promotion, transfer, or demotion, the job description provides a standard for comparison of talent. Regardless of whether the firm is unionized, information obtained through job analysis can often lead to more objective human resource decisions.

Finally, proper job analysis is important to demonstrate the legality of employment practices. Job analysis data are needed to defend, for example, decisions involving promotion, transfers, and demotions.

Thus far, we have described job analysis as it pertains to specific HRM functions. In practice, however, these functions are interrelated. Job analysis provides the basis for tying the functional areas together and the foundation for developing a sound human resource program. According to most human resources practitioners, job analysis is an integral component of any comprehensive human resource management strategy. In addition to determining and defining specific job functions, we need to establish links with other jobs within the unit and to determine the type of person who would likely be the best candidate for this position. We need to take the job analysis process "far beyond the traditional narrow-focused approaches of the past."[4]

TRENDS and INNOVATIONS

Job Analysis for Teams

Historically, companies established permanent jobs and filled these with people who best fit the job description.[5] The jobs were then maintained for years to come.[5] In some firms today, people are being hired and paid on a project basis. Better performance produces better income. Today, whenever someone asks "What is your job description?" the reply might well be "Whatever is required." This means that if a project has to be completed, individuals do what has to be done to complete the task.[6]

In a traditional organization, work was compartmentalized into jobs or positions, defined by functional and occupational domains. The result was disjointed execution, high unit cost, and uncompetitively long cycle times. With team design, there are no narrow jobs. Today, departments and functional domains have disappeared in some organizations and work is bundled into teams. The members of these teams have a far greater depth and breadth of skills than would have been required in traditional jobs. In addition, the teams often include employees from more than one company. This versatility allows an employee to take an entire business process from start to finish in one rapid, seamless flow. Formerly, there might have been 100 separate job classifications in a facility. With team design, there may be just 10 or fewer broadly defined roles on teams.[7]

Another dimension is added to job analysis when groups or teams are considered. The ability to work in teams is an important consideration. Recall that in Chapter 1 (Figure 1-2), teamwork was a key employability skill. Job analysis may determine how important it is for employees to be team players and work well in group situations. Other traits that might be discovered through job analysis include coordination skills and the ability to work in more than one system.[8]

Figure 4-2

Types of Data Collected in
Job Analysis*

1. **WORK ACTIVITIES**
   a. Work activities and processes
   b. Activity records (in film form, for example)
   c. Procedures used
   d. Personal responsibility

2. **WORKER-ORIENTED ACTIVITIES**
   a. Human behaviors, such as physical actions and communications on the job
   b. Elemental motions for methods analysis
   c. Personal job demands, such as energy expenditure

3. **MACHINES, TOOLS, EQUIPMENT, AND WORK AIDS USED**

4. **JOB-RELATED TANGIBLES AND INTANGIBLES**
   a. Knowledge dealt with or applied (as in accounting)

   b. Materials processed
   c. Products made or services performed

5. **WORK PERFORMANCE****
   a. Error analysis
   b. Work standards
   c. Work measurements, such as time taken for a task

6. **JOB CONTEXT**
   a. Work schedule
   b. Financial and nonfinancial incentives
   c. Physical working conditions
   d. Organizational and social contexts

7. **PERSONAL REQUIREMENTS FOR THE JOB**
   a. Personal attributes such as personality and interests
   b. Education and training required
   c. Work experience

* This information can be in the form of qualitative, verbal, narrative descriptions, or quantitative measurements of each item, such as error rates per unit of time or noise level.

** All job analysis systems do not develop the work performance aspects.

Source: *Reprinted by permission of Marvin D. Dunnette.*

Types of Job Analysis Information

Considerable information is needed for successful job analysis. The job analyst identifies the actual duties and responsibilities of the job and gathers the other types of data shown in Figure 4-2. Essential functions of the job are determined through this process. Note that work activities, worker-oriented activities, and the types of machines, tools, equipment, and work aids used in the job are all important. This information is used later to help determine the job skills needed. In addition, the job analyst looks at job-related tangibles and intangibles, such as the knowledge needed, the materials processed, and the goods made or services performed.

Some job analysis systems identify job standards. Work measurement studies may be needed to determine how long it takes to perform a task. With regard to job content, the analyst studies the work schedule, financial and non-financial incentives, and physical working conditions. Because many jobs are often performed in conjunction with others, organizational and social contexts are also noted. Finally, specific education, training, and work experience pertinent to the job are identified.

Job Analysis Methods

Traditional Methods

Job analysis has traditionally been conducted in a number of different ways because organizational needs and resources for conducting job analysis differ. Selection of a specific method should be based on the ways the information is to be used (job evaluation, pay increases, development, and so on) and the approach that is most feasible for a particular organization. We describe some of the most common traditional methods of job analysis in the following sections.

Questionnaires

Questionnaires are typically quick and economical to use. The job analyst may administer a structured questionnaire to employees, who identify the tasks they perform. This method is less useful if employees are not good with words. Also, some employees may tend to exaggerate the significance of their tasks, suggesting more responsibility than actually exists.

A portion of a job analysis questionnaire is presented in Figure 4-3. Although the entire questionnaire consists of twenty-five sections, only the first seven are shown here. These sections illustrate the depth of detail that can be collected using questionnaires.

Observation

When using the observation method, the job analyst usually watches the worker perform job tasks and records his or her observations. This method is used primarily to gather information on jobs emphasizing manual skills, such as those of a machine operator. It can also help the analyst identify interrelationships between physical and mental tasks. However, observation alone is usually an insufficient means of conducting job analysis, particularly when mental skills are dominant in a job. Observing a financial analyst at work would not reveal much about the requirements of the job.

Interviews

An understanding of the job may also be gained through interviewing both the employee and the supervisor. Usually the analyst interviews the employee first, helping the worker describe the duties performed. Then the analyst normally contacts the supervisor for additional information, to check the accuracy of the information obtained from the worker, and to clarify certain points.

Employee Recording

In some instances, job analysis information is gathered by having the employees describe their daily work activities in a diary or log. With this method, the problem of employees exaggerating job importance may have to be overcome.

Figure 4-3

Example of a Job Analysis
Questionnaire

The information from this questionnaire will be used to write a job description as well as to define hiring qualifications and special job characteristics. Answer as best you can, and don't worry about anyone "grading" your answers; the basic information about the job is what is important.

Your job title _____   Date _____

Name of person to whom you report

_____

Department _____   Shift _____
Your name _____   Phone ext. _____
How long have you been in this job?_____

1. Summarize in one or two sentences what your basic job function is. (What is the principal reason your job exists? What is your job designed to accomplish?)

   _____

2. Job responsibilities can be described in two ways:

What you do	**Why you do it**
(the duties people can watch you do)	(the effect or result you create)

A waiter/waitress, for example,
Places silverware, plates, glassware   *to present a ready and pleasing table*
                (DUTIES)   (RESULT)

List the major responsibilities of your job, including the approximate percentage of time spent on each. (It may be helpful to first list duties and then identify the results involved; or, if you prefer, list the major results expected of your job and then the duties required to accomplish each result.) Remember that sometimes two or three duties combine to produce the same result.

Duties	Results	% of time spent

(Add additional pages as necessary)

Rank in numerical order the responsibilities in order of importance to the organization:

Mark with a "D" the most difficult part of your job.

Mark with a "C" the responsibilities involving confidential data.

3. What formal course of instruction is required by law to perform this job?

   _____

   a) What formal courses of instruction might be helpful?

   _____

   b) What licensure or certification is required by law to perform this job?

   _____

4. What specific experiences or skills other than formal education do you feel a person must have in order to start this job today?

   _____

   a) Are there any jobs a person must have worked in before this job?

   _____

5. Given your answers to the above, how long do you feel it should take a qualified new person to perform this job competently?

   _____

Figure 4-3

(continued)

6. The way you perform your job affects other people in terms of quality and quantity of service received, as well as time and money gained or lost.

People you affect	*What would be the positive results of your good work on each type of person?*	*What typically might go wrong for each type of person if your job performance were poor? (Don't think of the rare catastrophe.)*

Customers

_____

Suppliers

_____

Senior managers

_____

Employees in your
own department

_____

Employees in other
departments

Example:

Suppliers	*Suppliers can plan their own production to meet our needs on time and at the right price*	*Our customers do not receive orders on time, as our suppliers were delayed.*

7. What part of your job entails the greatest chance for error?

_____
_____

   a. How often does this occur (daily, weekly, monthly)?

_____
_____

Source: *Adapted from R.J. Plachy,* Building a Fair Pay Program. *New York: American Management Association, pp. 87, 89.*

Even so, valuable understanding of highly specialized jobs, such as a recreation therapist, may be obtained in this way.

Other Job Analysis Methods

Over the years, many other attempts have been made to provide more systematic methods of conducting job analysis. We describe several of these approaches next.

Functional Job Analysis

Functional job analysis (FJA): A comprehensive job analysis approach that concentrates on the interactions among the work, the worker, and the organization.

Functional Job Analysis (FJA) is a comprehensive job analysis approach that concentrates on the interactions among the work, the worker, and the organization. This approach is a modification of the job analysis schedule. It is a worker-oriented method of describing jobs that identifies what a person actually does rather than his or her responsibilities.[9] The fundamental elements of FJA are these:

1. A major distinction is made between what gets done and what workers *do* to get things done. It is more important in job analysis to know the latter. For instance, a word processing operator doesn't keep the system running but performs a number of specific tasks to achieve this result.

2. Each job is defined by how individuals work with data, people, materials and/or equipment. *Only* those functions involved with data, people, materials and/or equipment are recorded.

3. These functions proceed from the simple to the complex. For example, the least complex form of data use might be comparing and the most complex could be synthesizing. It is assumed that if an upper-level function such as synthesizing is required, the related lower-level functions would also be required.

4. This analysis provides two measures of the job. First, relative complexity is measured—that is, the complexity of the interrelationship among data, people, materials and/or equipment. Second, there is a measure of proportional involvement. For example, 50 percent of a person's time may be spent in analyzing, 30 percent in supervising and 20 percent in operating.

Position Analysis Questionnaire

Position analysis questionnaire (PAQ): A structured job analysis questionnaire that uses a checklist approach to identify job elements.

The **position analysis questionnaire (PAQ)** is a structured job analysis questionnaire that uses a checklist approach to identify job elements. Advocates of the PAQ believe that its ability to identify job elements, behaviours required of job incumbents, and other job characteristics make its use applicable to analysis of virtually any type of job.

In one system, some 194 job descriptors relate to job-oriented elements. Each job descriptor is evaluated on a scale that measures extent of use, amount of time, importance of the job, possibility of occurrence, and applicability. With the aid of a computer program, each job is then scored relative to 32 job dimensions. The score derived represents a profile of the job, which can be compared with standard profiles to place the job into known job families; that is, jobs of a similar nature. The PAQ then identifies significant job behaviours and classifies jobs. Using the PAQ, job descriptions can be based on the relative importance and emphasis placed on various job elements.

The PAQ is completed by an employee or employees familiar with the job being studied—typically an experienced job incumbent or the immediate supervisor. The profiles and the job descriptions are then prepared by a job analyst.

Management Position Description Questionnaire

The **management position description questionnaire (MPDQ)** is a method of job analysis designed for management positions. In brief, it uses a checklist to analyze jobs. The MPDQ has been used to determine the training needs of individuals who are slated to move into managerial positions. It has also been used to evaluate and set compensation rates for managerial jobs and to assign the jobs to job families.

Management position description questionnaire (MPDQ): A form of job analysis designed for management positions that uses a checklist method to analyze jobs.

Occupational Measurement System[10]

Because of the many technological advances presently taking place, new and innovative job analysis methods are being developed.[11] The **occupational measurement system (OMS)** enables organizations to collect, store and analyze information pertinent to human resources by means of a computer database. The computer provides fast turnaround and more accurate job analysis, job descriptions, and evaluations. The computer also makes feasible the use of multiple regression statistical techniques that increase objectivity.

The OMS is designed to work with task-based information. Task-based job evaluation uses structured job analysis questionnaires as the basic input documents. These questionnaires are developed from a number of different sources, including a database of industry job tasks, the organization's job descriptions and job experts within the firm. The system includes a booklet with instructions and general information. The questionnaire contains items specifically tailored to the category of positions covered. Responses are given in data entry or optical scanning format. Sample items from a questionnaire are shown in Figure 4-4.

The OMS is an integrated computer software system specifically designed to process, to analyze, and to display task-based information. Typical reports generated by OMS are listed below.

Occupational measurement system (OMS): A system that enables organizations to collect, store, and analyze information pertinent to human resources by means of a computer database.

1. A functional and a detailed task-level job description. The job descriptions include the functions performed by each employee, job, or job classification, the specific tasks covered by those functions, and the amount of time spent on each function and task.

2. Skill and knowledge levels required to perform a function or a job as compared with those possessed by the incumbents and the differences between the two, if any, along with identified training needs.

3. Costs of production, both in terms of performance and supervision.

Combination of Methods

Usually an analyst does not use one job analysis method exclusively. A combination of methods is often more appropriate. In analyzing clerical and

Figure 4-4

A Job Analysis
Questionnaire

Instructions

Column 1	Expected job tasks for an office administrator are listed.
Column 2	Mark Y (yes) if the task is performed as part of your job duties, and N (no) if it is not part of your duties.
Column 3	Rate the relative time spent on performing the related task, on a scale of 1 (all of my time) to 10 (very little of my time), as shown on the scale below.
Column 4	Again using the scale, rate the relative time spent on supervising or coordinating the related task.

All of my time	moderate amount time	very little time
1 2 3	4 5 6 7	8 9 10

1. Job Task	2. Part of job duties: Yes (Y) or No (N)	3. Relative time spent performing task (on a scale of 1 to 10)	4. Relative time spent supervising or coordinating task (on a scale of 1 to 10)
Prepares time sheets			
Tracks employee attendance			
Develops office procedures			
Purchases office supplies			
Prepares travel arrangements			
Budgets office expenses			
Prepares labour cost analysis			
Prepares payroll			
Processes invoices			
Installs office software			
Operates office intranet system			
Plans and develops office electronic system			
Prepares company reports for internal and external distribution			
Provides office training			
Monitors office expenses			
Coordinates internal meetings			
Purchases office software			
Manages office e-mail			

administrative jobs, the analyst might use questionnaires supported by interviews and limited observation. In studying production jobs, interviews supplemented by extensive work observation may provide the necessary data. Basically, the analyst should employ the combination of techniques needed for accurate job descriptions/specifications.

Conducting Job Analysis

The person who conducts job analysis is interested in gathering data on what is involved in performing a particular job. Participants in job analysis should include, at a minimum, the employee and the employee's immediate supervisor. Large organizations may have one or more job analysts, but in small organizations line supervisors may be responsible for job analysis. Organizations that lack the technical expertise often use outside consultants to perform job analysis. Regardless of the approach taken, before conducting job analysis, the analyst should learn as much as possible about the job by reviewing organizational charts and talking with individuals acquainted with the jobs to be studied. Before beginning, the supervisor should introduce the analyst to the employees and explain the purpose of the job analysis. Although employee attitudes about the job are beyond the job analyst's control, the analyst must attempt to develop mutual trust and confidence with those whose jobs are being analyzed. Failure in this area will detract from an otherwise technically sound job analysis.

On completion of job analysis, two basic human resource documents—job descriptions and job specifications—can be prepared.

Job Description

Information obtained through job analysis is crucial to the development of job descriptions. Recall that previously we defined the job description as a document that outlines the tasks, duties, responsibilities, and working conditions pertaining to a job.

Job descriptions, then, must be both relevant and accurate.[12] They should provide concise statements of what employees are expected to do on the job and indicate exactly what employees do, how they do it, and the conditions under which the duties are performed.[13]

Among the items frequently included in a job description are:

- Major duties performed
- Percentage of time devoted to each duty
- Performance standards to be achieved
- Working conditions and possible hazards
- Number of employees performing the job and reporting relationships
- The machines, technology and equipment used on the job.

HR Web Wisdom
http: www.pearsoned.ca/ mondy

Job Descriptions
Learn how to write a job description.

As the contents of a job description may vary somewhat with the purpose for which it will be used, we now consider only those sections most commonly included.

Job Identification

The job identification section includes the job title, department, reporting relationship, and perhaps a job number or code. A good title will approximate closely the nature of the work content and will distinguish that job from others. Unfortunately, job titles are often misleading. An *executive secretary* in one organization may be little more than a highly paid clerk, whereas a person with the same title in another firm may have wide-ranging responsibilities. For example, one former student's first job after graduation was with a major tire and rubber company as an *assistant district service manager*. Because the primary duties of the job were to unload tires from trucks, check the tread wear and stack the tires in boxcars, a more appropriate title probably would have been *tire checker and stacker*.

One information source that assists in standardizing job titles is the *National Occupational Classification* (NOC).[14] The NOC includes standardized and comprehensive descriptions of job duties and related information for some 25 000 occupations in the Canadian labour market. These occupations are categorized into three levels: 26 major groups, 139 minor groups, and some 522 unit groups. This standardization permits employers in different industries and different parts of the country to more accurately match job requirements with worker skills.

As an example, the NOC definition for a Specialist in Human Resources would be numbered 1121. The two digits "11" refers to the major group "Professional Occupations in Business and Finance", the digit "2" identifies Human Resources and Business Services Professionals, while the last "1" pinpoints Specialist in Human Resources. This code, then, could identify any of the following major occupations:

- Business Agent, Labour Union

- Classification Officer

- Classification Specialist

- Compensation Research Analyst

- Conciliator

- Consultant, Human Resources

- Employee Relations Officer

- Employment Equity Officer

- Human Resources Research Officer

- Job Analyst

- Labour Relations Officer

- Mediator

- Union Representative

- Wage Analyst

All these jobs are filled by specialists in human resources who develop, implement, and evaluate human resource and labour relations policies, programs, and procedures, while advising managers and employees on personnel matters.

The NOC further defines "Specialists in Human Resources" as individuals who perform some or all of the following duties:

1. They develop, implement, and evaluate personnel and labour relations policies, programs, and procedures.

2. They advise managers and employees on the interpretation of personnel policies, benefit programs, and collective agreements.

3. They negotiate collective agreements on behalf of employers or workers and mediate labour disputes and grievances.

4. They research and prepare occupational classifications, job descriptions, and salary scales.

They also administer benefit, employment equity, and affirmative action programs, and maintain related records systems, while coordinating employee performance and appraisal programs. Finally, they may research employee benefit and health and safety practices and recommend changes or modifications to existing policies.

To perform as a specialist in human resources one should have:

1. a university degree or college diploma in a field related to personnel management, such as business administration, industrial relations, commerce, or psychology

or

2. a professional development program in personnel administration; and

3. some experience in a clerical or administrative position related to personnel administration.

The National Occupation Classification also lists several other occupations in the HRM field:

- Human Resources Managers—code 0112,

- Personnel and Recruitment Officers—code 1223,

- Personnel Clerks—code 1442,

- Professional Occupations in Business Services to Management—code 1122,

- Training Officers and Instructors—code 4131.

Job Futures is a two-part publication which uses the NOC and which provides HR information about the current world of work and projections for the future. It was developed by the Canadian Occupational Projection System (COPS) of the Applied Research Branch of Human Resources Development Canada (HRDC). Part I: Occupational Outlooks provides general information on 211 occupational groups covering all jobs in Canada. It also includes specific information on current labour market conditions and projections of how these conditions may change in the coming years. Part 2: Career Outlooks for Graduates provides general information on the educational and work experiences of recent graduates from trade and vocational schools, community colleges, and universities, and projections of job prospects in the next five years for graduates in these study areas. This source is a valuable career and HR planning resource and we encourage you to check it out.

HR Web Wisdom

http: www.pearsoned.ca/mondy

HRDC—HR Links
Visit the HRDC web site and check out the career prospects for "specialists in human resources" or other occupational groups of potential interest.

Date of the Job Analysis

The job analysis date is placed on the job description to aid in identifying job changes that would make the description obsolete. Some firms have found it

Figure 4-5

A Typical Job Description

Position Title: Administrative Support		Code:	Salary Grade:
Work Location:		Report To:	Function:

Basic Purpose/Accountabilities:
Responsible for providing and coordinating administrative support to assigned functional groups. Focus is on aligning contributions to department needs and company goals.

Primary Functions/Responsibilities:	Critical Skills/Leadership Criteria:
- Preparation of time sheets - Track employee attendance - Manage fixtures, furniture and equipment necessary to support the function - Process invoices, monitor expenditures - Coordinate and support meetings - Participate in planning process on projects - Type documentation to individuals external to company - Assist with presentation preparation and planning - Coordinate large scale documentation reproduction - External mailing/facsimile transmission - Coordinate central office supplies - Resource computer software applications - Coordinate work activities with other functions - Generate alternatives and make recommendations on improving area work process - Record retention/filing	CRITICAL SKILLS - Interpersonal skills/team player - Ability to influence others - Knowledge of business software applications - Confidentiality - Planning, organizing and time management - Written and oral communication - Customer orientation - Knowledge of operations and organization LEADERSHIP CRITERIA - Able to lead others - Engenders trust - Understands and uses functional expertise to contribute - Accepts ownership, is accountable and delivers on commitments - Oriented towards continuous learning

Quantitative Factors/Business Model Activities:	
Quantitative	Business Model

useful to place an expiration date on the document. This practice ensures periodic review of job content and minimizes the number of obsolete job descriptions.

Job Summary

The job summary provides a concise overview of the job. It is generally a short paragraph that states job content.

Duties Performed

The body of the job description delineates the major duties to be performed. Usually one sentence beginning with an action verb (such as receives, performs, establishes, or assembles) adequately explains each duty. Essential functions sometimes are shown in a separate section.

Job Specification

Recall that we defined job specification as a document containing the minimum acceptable qualifications or competencies that a person should possess to perform a particular job. According to Margaret Butteriss,[15] author of *Help*

Wanted, HR specialists often use the word **competencies** to refer to "requisite qualifications rather than specifying the means by which those qualifications were obtained." For example a degree or diploma in computer technology would not be considered a competency. This educational qualification is the means by which someone displays a competency such as ability "to apply visual basic to business simulations." Items typically included in the job specification are not only educational requirements, but competencies such as experience, personality traits, and technical abilities.

In practice, job specifications are often included as a major section of job descriptions. For instance, Figure 4-5 is an example of a job description for an administrative support position. Some of the critical skills or competencies needed for the job include interpersonal skills/team player, ability to influence others, and knowledge of software applications. This type of information is extremely valuable in the recruiting and selection process.

After jobs have been analyzed and the descriptions written, the results should be reviewed with the supervisor and the worker to ensure that they are accurate, clear, and understandable. The courtesy of reviewing results with employees also helps gain their acceptance. Because the job description and job specification are often combined into one form, we use the term job description in this book to include both documents.

> **Competencies:** Requisite skills and qualifications such as experience, personality traits, and technical abilities.

Job Design

Job design is the process of determining the specific tasks to be performed, the methods used in performing these tasks, and the way the job relates to other work in the organization. Three key concepts related to job design—job enrichment, job enlargement, and employee-centred work redesign—will be discussed next.

> **Job design:** A process of determining the specific tasks to be performed, the methods used in performing these tasks, and the way the job relates to other work in the organization.

Job Enrichment

In the past two decades, there has been considerable interest in and application of job enrichment in a wide variety of organizations. **Job enrichment**

> **Job enrichment:** The restructuring of the content and level of responsibility of a job to make it more challenging, meaningful, and interesting to a worker.

HRM in *ACTION*

What Kind of Person Do You Need?

"I can't determine what kind of computer programmer you need, André," said Bob Maracle, the human resource director. "Every applicant I sent down was proficient in FORTRAN and DOS, just like the job description stated."

"Get real, Bob," replied André. "We haven't required FORTRAN or DOS in years. The person I need has to be up-to-date on the latest network software. None of the people you sent me were qualified."

How would you respond?

consists of basic changes in the content and level of responsibility of a job so as to provide greater challenge to the worker. Job enrichment, then, is not promotion, but vertical expansion of responsibilities within a job that usually remains at the same level within the organization. The worker has the opportunity to derive a feeling of achievement, recognition, responsibility, and personal growth in performing the job. Although job enrichment programs are not always successful, they have improved job performance and worker satisfaction in many organizations.

Five principles should be followed when implementing job enrichment.[16]

1. Increasing job demands. The job should be changed in such a way as to increase the level of difficulty and responsibility.

2. Increasing the worker's accountability. More individual control and authority over the work should be allowed, with the manager retaining ultimate accountability.

3. Providing work scheduling freedom. Within limits, individual workers should be allowed to schedule their own work.

4. Providing feedback. Timely periodic reports on performance should be made directly to workers rather than through their supervisors.

5. Providing new learning experiences: Work situations should encourage opportunities for new experiences and personal growth.

Job Enlargement

Job enlargement: A change in the scope of a job so as to provide greater variety to the worker.

There is a clear distinction between job enrichment and job enlargement. **Job enlargement** involves changes in the scope of a job so as to provide greater variety to the worker. It provides a horizontal expansion of duties. For example, instead of knowing how to operate only one machine, a person learns to operate two or even three but is given no higher level of responsibility. On the other hand, job enrichment involves higher-level responsibilities; for instance, the worker may be given the additional responsibility of scheduling the three machines. Increased responsibility entails greater freedom to do the job; the worker makes more decisions and exercises more control over work.

Employee-Centred Work Redesign[17]

Employee-centred work redesign: A concept designed to link the mission of the company with the job satisfaction needs of employees.

A concept designed to link the mission of the company with the job satisfaction needs of employees is **employee-centred work redesign**. Employees are encouraged to become involved in redesigning their work to benefit both themselves and the organization. Workers can propose changes to make their jobs more satisfying, but they must also show how these changes better accomplish the goals of the entire unit. With this approach, the contribution of each employee is recognized, while at the same time, the focus remains on accomplishing the organizational mission.

Job Evaluation

Job evaluation is a technique or a process used to determine the relative value of one job in relation to every other job. The purpose of job evaluation is to eliminate internal inequities, especially those stemming from illogical pay structures. For example, a pay inequity exists if the mailroom supervisor earns more money than the accounting supervisor. More specifically, job evaluation has the potential to:

- describe the organization's job structure;

- bring equity and order to the relationships among jobs;

- develop a hierarchy of job value that can be used to create a pay structure; and

- achieve a consensus among managers and employees regarding jobs and pay within the firm.[18]

The human resource department is usually responsible for administering job evaluation programs. The job evaluation process, however, is typically conducted by a committee consisting of managers from different functional areas. A typical committee might include the human resource director as chairperson and the vice presidents for finance, production, and marketing. Including employee representatives is also wise, since results are more likely to be accepted.

Four job evaluation techniques are in general use: ranking, classification, factor comparison, and points rating, but there are innumerable variations of these methods.[19] A method is often modified to fit a particular work environment.

Ranking Method

The simplest of the four is the **ranking method**. In this method, the raters examine the description of each job being evaluated and arrange the jobs in order according to their value to the company. The initial tasks in this method—as with all the methods—are conducting job analysis and writing job descriptions.

Classification Method

The **classification method** involves defining a number of classes or grades to describe a group of jobs. In evaluating jobs by this method, the raters compare the job description with the class description. Class descriptions are prepared that reflect the differences of groups of jobs at various difficulty levels. The class description that most closely agrees with the job description determines the classification for that job. For example, in evaluating the job of word processing clerk, the description might include these duties:

1. Handle data entry of letters from prepared drafts

2. Address envelopes

3. Deliver completed correspondence to unit supervisor

Assuming that the remainder of the job description includes similar routine work, this job would most likely be placed in the classification called

Job evaluation: A technique or a process used to determine the relative value of one job in relation to every other job.

Ranking method: A job evaluation method in which the rater examines the description of each job being evaluated and arranges the jobs in order according to their value to the company.

Classification method: A job evaluation method in which classes or grades are defined to describe a group of jobs.

"clerk," rather than "administrative assistant," which might be the next highest classification. Clearly, defining grade descriptions for many diverse jobs is difficult. For this reason, some organizations have developed systems that combine classification with other methods of job evaluation.[20]

Factor Comparison Method

Factor comparison method: A job evaluation method in which raters make decisions on separate aspects, or factors, of the job, based on the assumption that there are five universal job factors.

The **factor comparison method** is somewhat more involved than the two previously discussed qualitative methods. In this method, raters need not keep the entire job in mind as they evaluate; instead, they make decisions on separate aspects, or factors, of the job. A basic underlying assumption is that there are five universal job factors:

- **Mental requirements,** such as intelligence, reasoning, and imagination
- **Skills,** such as facility in muscular coordination and training in the interpretation of sensory impressions
- **Physical requirements,** which involve sitting, standing, walking, lifting, and so on
- **Responsibilities,** which cover areas such as raw materials, money, records, and supervision.
- **Working conditions,** which reflect the environmental influences of noise, illumination, ventilation, hazards, and hours.

The committee first ranks each of the selected benchmark jobs on the relative degree of difficulty of each of the five factors. The committee also allocates the total pay rates for each job to each factor based on the importance of the respective factor to the job. This step is often difficult to explain satisfactorily to employees because the decision is highly subjective.

A job comparison scale, reflecting rankings and money allocations, is developed next (see Figure 4-6). All jobs shown in this chart, except for programmer analyst, are original benchmark jobs. The scale is then used to rate other jobs in the group being evaluated. The raters compare each job, factor by factor, with those appearing on the job comparison scale. Then they place the jobs on the chart in an appropriate position. For example, assume that the committee is evaluating the job of programmer analyst. The committee determines that this job has fewer mental requirements than that of systems analyst but more than those of programmer. The job would then be placed on the chart between these two jobs at a point agreed on by the committee. In this example, the committee evaluated the mental requirements factor at $3.80 (a point between the $4.00 and $3.40-values that had been allocated to the benchmark jobs of systems analyst and programmer, respectively). The committee repeats this procedure for the remaining four factors and then for all jobs to be evaluated. Adding the values of the five factors for each job yields the total value (wage) for the job.

The factor comparison method provides a systematic approach to job evaluation. However, at least two problems with it should be noted. The assumption that the five factors are universal has been questioned because certain factors may be more appropriate to some job groups than others. Also, while the steps are not overly complicated, they are somewhat detailed and may be difficult to explain to employees.

Point Method

In the **point method**, raters assign numerical values to specific job components, and the sum of these values provides a quantitative assessment of a job's relative worth.[21] Historically, some variation of the point plan has been the most popular option.

Point method: An approach to job evaluation in which numerical values are assigned to specific job components and the sum of these values provides a quantitative assessment of a job's relative worth.

The point method requires selection of job factors according to the nature of the specific group of jobs being evaluated. Because job factors vary from one group to another, a separate plan for each group of similar jobs (job clusters) is appropriate. Production jobs, clerical jobs, and sales jobs are examples of job clusters.

Figure 4-6
Job Comparison Scale

	MENTAL	SKILL	PHYSICAL	RESPONSIBILITY	WORKING CONDITIONS
$4.00	Systems Analyst (Programmer Analyst)			Systems Analyst	
3.80					
3.50	Programmer			Programmer	
		Data Entry Clerk Console Operator Programmer			
2.50	Console Operator	Systems Analyst			
2.00					
				Console Operator	
1.50	Data Entry Clerk			Data Entry Clerk	Data Entry Clerk Console Operator Systems Analyst Programmer
1.00			Data Entry Clerk Systems Analyst Programmer Console Operator		

Figure 4-7

Procedure for Establishing the Point Method of Job Evaluation

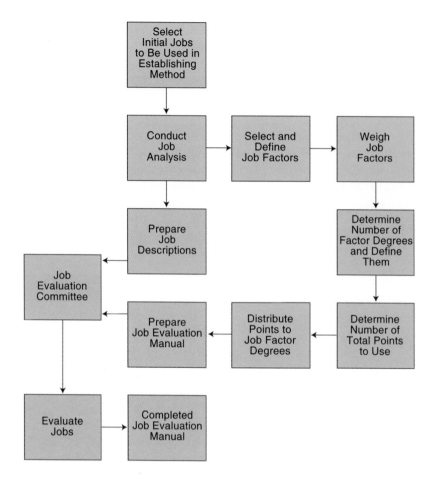

The procedure for establishing a point method is illustrated in Figure 4-7. After determining the group of jobs to be studied, analysts conduct job analysis and write job descriptions. The job evaluation committee will later use these descriptions as the basis for making evaluation decisions.

It should be noted that some consultants are moving away from job descriptions toward position analysis questionnaires (PAQ), as the formal job description takes too much time to write. The PAQ can be completed independently by both the employee and the manager; the results are then compared, discrepancies are discussed, and a final list of job duties, responsibilities, and authorities is compiled.

Next, the analysts select and define the factors to be used in measuring job value. These factors become the standards used for the evaluation of jobs. They can best be identified by people who are thoroughly familiar with the content of the jobs under consideration. Education, experience, job knowledge, mental effort, physical effort, responsibility, and working conditions are examples of factors. Each should be significant in helping to differentiate jobs. Factors that apply equally to all jobs obviously would not serve this purpose. As an example, in evaluating a company's clerical jobs, working conditions would not be an important differentiating value if all clerical workers had similar conditions. The number of factors used varies with the job cluster under consideration. It is strictly a subjective judgement. Different firms value jobs differently. For example, a relatively new organization in a fast-growing market will value job factors that relate to its growth in revenue and market share more than will a mature organization in a stable or declining market.[22]

The committee must establish factor weights according to their relative importance in the jobs to be evaluated. For example, if experience is considered quite important for a particular job cluster, this factor might be weighted as much as 35 percent. Physical effort (if used at all as a factor in an office cluster) would likely be low—perhaps less than 10 percent.

The next step is to determine the number of degrees for each job factor and define each degree. Degrees represent the number of distinct levels associated with a particular factor. The number of degrees needed for each factor depends on job requirements. If a particular cluster required virtually the same level of experience, for example, a smaller number of degrees would be appropriate compared to some clusters that required a broad range of experience.

The committee then determines the total number of points to be used in the plan. The number may vary, but 500 or 1000 points is typical. A smaller number of points (for example, 50) would not allow sufficient distinction among jobs, whereas a larger number (such as 50 000) would be unnecessarily cumbersome. The total number of points in a plan indicates the maximum points that any job could receive.

The next step is to distribute point values to job factor degrees; an example is shown in Figure 4-8.

Finally, a job evaluation manual is prepared. Although there is no standard format, the manual often contains an introductory section, factor and degree definitions, and job descriptions.

The job evaluation committee then evaluates jobs in each cluster by comparing each job description with the factors in the job evaluation manual. Point

Figure 4-8

An Example of the Point System (Using a Total of 500 Points)

JOB FACTOR	WEIGHT	DEGREE OF FACTOR				
		1	2	3	4	5
1. Education	50%	50	100	150	200	250
2. Responsibility	30%	30	70	110	150	
3. Physical Effort	12%	12	24	36	48	60
4. Working Conditions	8%	8	24	40		

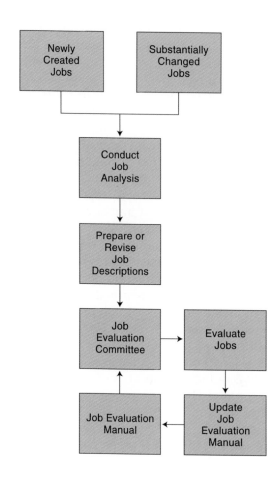

plans require time and effort to design. Historically, a redeeming feature of the method is that, once developed, the plan is useful over a long period of time.

The procedure for using an established point method is presented in Figure 4-9. As new jobs are created and the contents of old jobs changed substantially, job analysis must be conducted and job descriptions rewritten. The job evaluation committee evaluates the jobs and updates the manual. Only when job factors change, or for some reason the weights assigned become inappropriate, does the plan become obsolete.

It should be noted that not all organizations create their own job evaluation system. There are many validated programs for sale. Typically, a consulting firm would be contacted. A highly refined version of the point method is marketed in Canada by Hay Management Consultants. The Hay guide chart-profile method[23] contains only a few factors: know-how, problem solving, accountability, and, where appropriate, working conditions. Point values are assigned to these factors to determine the final point profile for any job.

Global Job Descriptions: The Domestic Blueprint Is Just Not Good Enough

According to one expert, as many as 20 percent of those sent on global assignments return prematurely. Many others endure global assignments but are ineffective in their jobs and social lives; marriage breakups are relatively common.[24] These types of failures can be traced directly to a selection process based on inaccurate job descriptions.

Determining the skills, duties, and knowledge required for performing global jobs is much more complex than making such determinations domestically. Whereas basic skills may be essentially the same for most domestic assignments, basic skills for an overseas assignment must often include foreign language skills, cultural adaptability, and the ability to cope with different work methods and procedures. For instance, research indicates that success in overseas work assignments depends on personal skills, people skills, and perceptual skills far beyond those needed to accomplish job-related tasks domestically. Personal skills are those techniques and attributes that facilitate mental and emotional well-being. They include means of finding solitude, such as meditation, prayer, and physical exercise routines, which tend to decrease the employee's stress level. An ability to manage time, to delegate, and to manage responsibilities are also essential personal skills.[25] In essence, a job description for a global position must take into account the need for knowledge that extends far beyond the job being accomplished in the domestic market.

The physical and mental tasks also carry much higher demands globally. The job to be completed often involves intangible issues such as transferring the domestic corporate culture overseas. One of the main areas in which job descriptions become complex is location considerations. When the job is to be completed overseas, job performance is often more difficult. Because the job is more complex, global job descriptions must be much more involved.

SUMMARY

1. **Define job analysis.**
   Job analysis is the systematic process of determining the skills, duties, and knowledge required for performing jobs in an organization.

2. **Discuss the reasons that job analysis is a basic human resource tool.**
   Without a properly conducted job analysis, a human resource manager's functions are difficult if not impossible to carry out. Job analysis data affects virtually every aspect of human resource management: human resource planning, recruitment, selection, job specifications, job descriptions, performance appraisal, compensation, safety and health, human resource research, employee and labour relations, and legal employment practices.

3. **Describe the types of information required for job analysis.**

The job analyst identifies the actual duties and responsibilities associated with the job. Work activities and worker-oriented activities are important, as well as knowledge of the types of machines, technology, equipment, and work aids used. The job analyst also looks for job-related tangibles and intangibles. Job analysis systems also identify the standards that are established for the job and job content. Specific education, training, and work experience pertinent to the job are also normally identified.

4. **Describe the various traditional and other job analysis methods.**

Traditional methods include a structured questionnaire on which employees identify the tasks they perform; the observation method, in which the job analyst watches the job being done and takes notes; interviews with the employee and the supervisor; and a diary or log kept by employees. More systematic methods include functional job analysis (FJA), a comprehensive approach that concentrates on the interactions among the work, the worker, and the organization; the position analysis questionnaire (PAQ), a structured document that uses a checklist to identify job elements; the management position description questionnaire (MPDQ), which also uses a checklist; and the occupational measurement system (OMS), a computer database used to collect, store, and analyze HR information. A combination of methods is often more appropriate than one method alone.

5. **Identify who conducts job analysis.**

At a minimum, the employee and the employee's immediate supervisor should participate in job analysis. Organizations that lack the technical expertise often use outside consultants to perform job analysis.

6. **Describe the components of a well-designed job description.**

While the contents of a job description will vary depending on the nature of the job, the organization, and the purpose, certain elements are common. Sections commonly include job identification, date, job summary, duties performed, and job specification. The job identification section includes the job title, department, reporting relationship, and a job number or code. A job analysis date helps indicate when the description has become obsolete. The job summary provides a concise overview. The body of the job description delineates the major duties and highlights essential job functions. A job specification sets out minimum qualifications or competencies, and typically includes educational requirements, experience, personality traits, and technical abilities.

7. **Define job design and three key design concepts.**

Job design is the process of determining the specific tasks to be performed, the methods used in performing the task, and how the job relates to other work in the organization. Job enrichment involves restructuring the content and level of responsibility of a job to make it more challenging, meaningful, and interesting to a worker. Job enlargement entails a change in the scope of a job so as to provide greater variety to the worker. Employee-centred work redesign links the mission of the company with employees' job satisfaction needs.

8. **Explain four job evaluation methods.**

In the ranking method, raters examine the description of each job being evaluated and arrange the jobs in order according to their perceived value to the company. In the classification method, a number of classes or grades are defined to describe a group of jobs. In the factor comparison method, raters make decisions on separate aspects, or factors, of the job. This method assumes the existence of five universal job factors: mental requirements; skills; physical requirements; responsibilities; and working conditions. In the point method, numerical values are assigned to specific job components; summing these values provides a quantitative assessment of a job's relative worth. The Hay Guide Chart-Profile Method is a highly refined version of the point method that uses the factors of know-how, problem solving, accountability, and additional compensable elements.

QUESTIONS FOR REVIEW

1. What is the distinction between a job and a position? Define job analysis.

2. Discuss what is meant by the statement, "Job analysis is a basic human resource management tool."

3. List and briefly describe the types of data that are typically gathered in conducting job analysis.

4. Describe the traditional methods of job analysis. Briefly explain the following terms:

   a. Functional job analysis

   b. Position analysis questionnaire

   c. Management position description questionnaire

   d. Occupational measurement system

5. What are the basic components of a job description? Briefly describe each.

6. Distinguish among job design, job enrichment, job enlargement and employee-centered work redesign.

7. Distinguish between the following job evaluation techniques:

   a. Ranking method

   b. Classification method

   c. Factor comparison method

   d. Point method

DEVELOPING **HRM** SKILLS

An Experiential Exercise

Developing and updating job descriptions is an integral part of the job of any human resource professional. Without properly designed job descriptions, performing some human resource management activities is extremely difficult. This exercise will permit you to gain a better appreciation of what is involved in preparing job descriptions, as job descriptions may vary even when the job analysis information is similar.

As the lone human resource specialist at Ottawa-based Shore Machine Works Ltd., you have been involved in job analysis planning for a new facility in Cambridge, Ontario. Most of the job analysis data have been gathered, and now it is time to prepare specific job descriptions. You have been given a stack of job analysis information sheets and assigned the task of writing job descriptions based on this information. When the production manager, Ed Kabadi, handed you the data sheet, he said, "I'd like you to do the first one, and then bring it to me and we'll go over it together."

The initial job description will be for the job of spot welder. Work activities primarily involve welding parts together. All parts consist of thin steel pieces weighing less than 1 kg. The preformed pieces to be welded together are taken from numbered bins surrounding the spot welder, placed in position on the machine, and welded. Relationship with other workers is fairly standard for a factory floor worker. Other machine operators running similar machines are within view, 5 to 12 m away. The crane operator moves the parts bins to this work station and away as required, placing them wherever specified by the operator. There is little time for social interaction on the job. Degree of supervision involved is fairly standard in this industry. The spot welder supervisor supervises twelve operators, all doing essentially the same job. Operators are expected to do their jobs with very little supervision, consulting the supervisor infrequently. Records and reports are not generated as part of this job. Skill and dexterity requirements are marginal. In order to meet the standard times, the worker must be able to take two parts from separate bins, place them together in the correct position and complete the part within 3.2 seconds. Working conditions are not ideal; the work station is relatively crowded, the operator is required to wear safety goggles, ambient temperature varies from 10°C to 28°C in summer. The noise level is about 60 decibels, safe but distracting, and the lighting is excellent.

Each participant will use the job description form and develop an appropriate job description. Several class members can participate. Instructors will provide the participants with any additional information necessary to complete the exercise.

HRM INCIDENT

A Job Well Done

As Professor Guy Allard toured the Mountjoy Tube Company plant in Magog, Quebec, he became more and more impressed with his young guide, Jim Murdoch. Jim was the assistant human resource director at Mountjoy Tube and was primarily responsible for job analysis. An industrial engineer was assigned full-time to the human resource department to assist Jim in job design. Professor Allard had been retained by the human resource director to study Mountjoy Tube's job analysis system and to make recommendations for improvements. He had gone through the files of job descriptions in the human resource office with Jim and found them, in general, to be complete and directly related to the jobs performed.

One of the first stops on the tour was the office of the weld mill supervisor, a 3-m by 3-m room out on the factory floor with glass windows on all sides. As Jim approached, the supervisor, Roger Duchesne, was outside his office.

"Hi, Jim," he said.

"Hello, Roger," said Jim. "This is Professor Allard. Could we look at your job descriptions and chat with you for a moment?"

"Sure, Jim," said Roger, opening the door. "Come on in and have a seat and I'll get them out." From their vantage point, the men in the office could see the workers in the weld mill area. As they reviewed each job description they observed every worker actually performing the work described. Roger Duchesne was familiar with each of the jobs. He was very knowledgeable about the job descriptions themselves, having contributed to the preparation or the revisions of each one.

"How are the job descriptions related to the performance evaluations here?" asked Professor Allard.

"Well," answered Roger, "I only evaluate the workers on the items in the job descriptions, which we came up with through careful job analysis. That way, I know I have to correct the job descriptions when something changes and they get too far out of whack with the job the guys are really doing. Jim's held training sessions for all us supervisors so that we understand how all this stuff ties in together: job analysis, job descriptions, and performance evaluations. I think it's a pretty good system."

Jim and Professor Allard went on to several other areas of the plant and found similar situations. Jim seemed to have a good relationship with each of the supervisors, as well as with the plant manager and the three midlevel managers they visited. As they headed back to the front office, Professor Allard was considering the comments he would soon make to the plant manager.

Questions

1. What desirable attributes of job analysis are evident at Mountjoy Tube Company?

2. What kind of report do you think Professor Allard should present to the plant manager?

3. Describe the relationship that might exist between the industrial engineer and the assistant human resource director regarding job analysis.

CHAPTER

5

Recruitment

CHAPTER OBJECTIVES

1. Define recruitment.

2. Identify alternatives that a firm might consider before resorting to outside recruitment.

3. Describe the recruitment process.

4. Describe how the external environment can affect the recruitment process.

5. Explain and describe internal recruitment methods.

6. Identify external sources of recruitment.

7. Identify external methods of recruitment.

8 Explain what needs to be accomplished to reduce discrimination.

Dorothy Bryant, the owner of a small company involved in the development of multimedia training systems, had obtained a large contract that necessitated the recruitment of two software design engineers. After considering various recruitment alternatives, Dorothy placed the following ad in a local newspaper with a circulation in excess of 100 000:

EMPLOYMENT OPPORTUNITY FOR SOFTWARE DESIGN ENGINEERS

2 positions available for software design engineers desiring career in growth industry.

Prefer recent university graduates with good appearance.

Apply today! Send your résumé, in confidence, to: D.A. Bryant
    X-Sell Software Development Ltd.,
    P.O. Box 1515
    Fredericton, N.B.
    E3B 5X6

More than 300 applications were received in the first week, and Dorothy was elated. However, when she reviewed the applicants, it appeared that few people possessed the desired qualifications for the job. To make matters worse, she received a call from the Human Rights Commission. It appeared that several potential applicants had complained about the way the ad was written.

D orothy learned, the hard way, the importance of proper recruiting practices. She obviously failed to include specific job requirements in her newspaper ad. As a result, an excessive number of unqualified people applied. Also, the road is paved for a potential legal problem because Dorothy uses a subjective criterion, *good appearance*, which was not job related. In addition, stating a preference for a recent university graduate may also prove to be ill-advised because of the age implication. Adding further to Dorothy's problem is the potential liability her ad creates for the firm by implying a career for employees. Her corporate lawyer will probably advise her to avoid any semblance of creating an implied contract for a candidate who is hired. The individual may later be discharged and then sue the company for breach of contract. Dorothy has found that preparing an effective, legally sound recruitment ad is not as simple as it once was.

Recruitment: The process of attracting individuals on a timely basis, in sufficient numbers, and with appropriate qualifications, and encouraging them to apply for jobs with an organization.

Recruitment is the process of attracting individuals on a timely basis, in sufficient numbers, and with appropriate qualifications, and encouraging them to apply for jobs with an organization. Finding the appropriate way of encouraging qualified candidates to apply for employment is extremely important when a firm needs to hire employees. Tapping productive sources of applicants and using suitable recruitment methods are essential for the greatest recruiting efficiency and effectiveness. Some firms, however, may prefer options other than recruitment. We begin the chapter by describing these alternatives. Next, we provide a framework of the recruitment process and outline external and internal environmental recruitment factors. We then present internal recruitment methods and external sources and methods of recruitment. In the final section we cover recruiting efforts specifically aimed at eliminating discrimination.

Alternatives to Recruitment

Even when human resource planning indicates a need for additional or replacement employees, a firm may decide against increasing the size of its workforce. Recruitment and selection costs are not insignificant when all the related expenses are considered: the search process, interviewing, agency fee payment, and relocation and processing of the new employee. Alternatives to recruitment commonly include outsourcing, use of contingent workers, employee leasing, and overtime.

Outsourcing

As defined in Chapter 1, outsourcing or subcontracting is the process of transferring responsibility for an area of service and its objectives to an external provider. Within the past few years, this practice has become widespread and increasingly a popular alternative involving virtually every functional area of business—including the human resource function. The decision to outsource functions may be made to avoid hiring additional employees or to implement reengineering programs and the subsequent downsizing of the firm. As with other alternatives, there is a downside to outsourcing. The primary obstacles seem to be twofold: cost issues and concern about loss of control.[1] To accommodate the current popularity of outsourcing, a number of organizations have been created. For example, IBM's Workforce Solutions WFS was a full-service human resource company that was spun off from its human resource operation.[2]

Contingent Workers

As we described in Chapter 2, contingent workers—also known as part-timers, temporaries, and independent contractors—make up the fastest growing segment of the Canadian economy. For example, in 1996 there were about 1.2 million persons working part-time throughout the year. This is almost double the number (680 000) who reported working on a part-time basis throughout the year in 1980. The comparable figure in 1970 was 351 000 persons.[3]

What accounts for the rapid growth of jobs for these workers? According to a Conference Board survey, over 80 percent of the companies responding indicated their number one reason was to achieve flexibility. Global competition and changing technology prevent employers from accurately forecasting their employment needs months in advance. To avoid hiring people one day and resorting to layoffs the next, firms look to a temporary workforce as a buffer.[4] Companies also want to control cost. The total cost of a permanent employee is generally estimated at 30 to 40 percent above the person's gross pay; this figure does not include, among other things, the costs of recruitment. To avoid some of these costs and to maintain flexibility as workloads vary, many organizations use part-time or temporary employees. Companies that provide temporary workers assist their clients in handling excess or special workloads. These companies assign their own employees to their customers and fulfill all the obligations normally associated with an employer. The client company avoids the expenses of recruitment, absenteeism and turnover, and employee benefits.

HR Web Wisdom
http: www.pearsoned.ca/mondy

Workplace Issues
This site covers various issues on the changing work place.

Employee Leasing

Another alternative to recruitment that is growing in popularity is employee leasing. Using this approach, a firm terminates some or most of its employees. A leasing company then hires them, usually at the same salary, and leases them back to the former employer, who becomes the client. The employees continue to work as before, with the client supervising their activities. The leasing company, however, assumes all responsibilities associated with being the employer.

A primary advantage of employee leasing to the client is being free from human resource administration, including payroll withholdings, employee benefits, pensions, medical, dental and disability insurance, educational allowances, and vacations.[5] The firm writes only one cheque per payroll period to cover wages, taxes, benefits, and an administrative fee to the leasing company that may range from 2 percent to 8 percent of payroll.

Leasing has advantages for employees, also. Because leasing companies provide workers for many companies, they often enjoy economies of scale that permit them to offer excellent, low-cost benefit programs. In addition, workers frequently have greater opportunities for job mobility. Some leasing firms operate throughout the nation, so if one spouse in a dual-career family is relocated, the leasing company may offer the other a job in the new location, too. Also, if a client organization suffers a downturn in business, the leasing company can transfer employees to another client, avoiding both layoff and loss of seniority.

A potential disadvantage to the client is erosion of employee loyalty, because workers receive pay and benefits from the leasing company. Regardless of any shortcomings, use of employee leasing is growing. By 2005, the industry in North America could involve almost $200 billion in revenues and more than 9 million employees.[6]

Overtime

Perhaps the most commonly used method of meeting short-term fluctuations in work volume is having permanent employees work overtime. For example, almost 2 million out of a total 11 million paid workers (17%) worked overtime in a typical week in the late 1990s. Over half (53%) were not paid or otherwise compensated for any of their overtime. The average number of overtime hours worked per week was 8.8 for those who were paid and 9.5 for those who were not compensated.[7] Overtime may help both employer and employees. The employer benefits by avoiding recruitment, selection, and training costs. Some employees gain from increased income during the overtime period.

There are potential problems with overtime, however. Many managers believe that when they work employees for unusually long periods of time, the company pays more and receives less in return. Employees may become fatigued and lack the energy to perform at a normal rate, especially when excessive overtime is required. Furthermore, as much as half the Canadian workforce does not get paid for overtime. Unpaid work can erode employee morale.

When overtime is paid, two other problems are possible. Employees may, consciously or not, pace themselves so that overtime will be assured. They may also become accustomed to the added income, and adjust their standard of living accordingly. Then, when overtime is no longer required and the paycheque shrinks, they may become disgruntled.

The Recruitment Process

As illustrated in Figure 5-1, when human resource planning indicates a need for employees, the firm may evaluate alternatives to recruitment. If these alternatives are found to be inappropriate, the recruitment process starts. Frequently, recruitment begins when a manager initiates an employee requisition. The **employee requisition** is a document that specifies job title, department, the date the employee is needed for work, and other details. A typical employee requisition appears in Figure 5-2. With this information, managers can refer to the appropriate job description to determine the qualifications the recruited

Employee requisition: A document that specifies job title, department, and the date by which an open job should be filled.

person needs. These qualifications, however, are becoming less clear-cut. For example, according to one HR expert: "Job descriptions aren't cleanly defined any longer....When you recruit and hire for task X, it won't be long before the employee will be asked to do A, B, C and D as well."[8] With such broad expectations from the company, the employee will obviously need a broader range of skills and abilities. More and more firms are dealing with this situation by hiring for attitude—striving to employ individuals who are motivated and adaptable and can work effectively in teams. For example, a 1995 study of Profit 100 entrepreneurs by Gene Luczkiw found that attitude was the most important characteristic in filling human resources requirements.[9] Hiring for organizational fit is discussed in Chapter 6.

The next step in the recruitment process is to determine whether qualified employees are available within the firm (the internal source) or must be recruited from external sources, such as colleges, universities, and other organizations. Because of the high cost of recruitment, organizations need to use the most productive recruitment sources and methods available.

Recruitment sources are the locations where qualified individuals can be found. **Recruitment methods** are the specific means by which potential employees can be attracted to the firm. When the sources of potential employ-

Recruitment sources:
Various locales in which qualified individuals are sought as potential employees.

Recruitment methods:
The specific means by which potential employees are attracted to an organization.

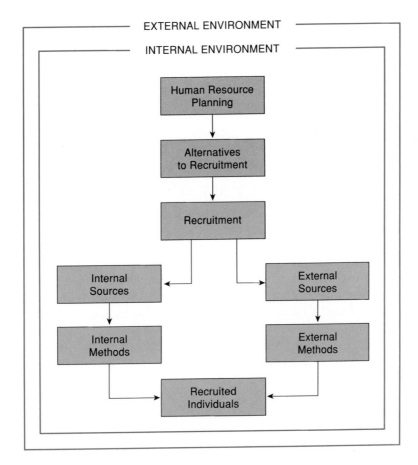

Figure 5-1
The Recruitment Process

Figure 5-2

An Employee Requisition

JOB NUMBER	JOB TITLE	DATE OF JOB VACANCY	DATE REPLACEMENT NEEDED	
PLEASE CHECK	☐ Permanent	☐ Temporary	☐ Part-Time	
	☐ Salary	☐ Hourly Wage	Job Class	
REASON FOR REQUEST: What management or employee action(s) caused the opening?				
BRIEF DESCRIPTION OF MINIMUM QUALIFICATIONS FOR THE JOB CANDIDATES:				
BRIEF DESCRIPTION OF JOB DUTIES				

LOCATION NAME	
DATE	MANAGER'S SIGNATURE

ees have been identified, appropriate methods for either internal or external recruitment are used to accomplish recruitment objectives.

External Environment of Recruitment

As with the other human resource functions, factors external to the organization can significantly affect the firm's recruitment activities. Of particular importance is the demand and supply of specific skills. If demand for a particular skill is high relative to supply, as was the case in some areas of the high-tech sector in the '90s, an extraordinary recruiting effort may be required. For example, in the late 1990s growth companies like Oasis Technology Ltd., needed highly skilled programmers. They were unable to find what they needed from Canadian sources, so they quickly expanded their HR search internationally to India and the Philippines.[10] When the unemployment rate in an organization's labour market is high, the firm's recruitment process may be simplified, as the number of unsolicited applicants is usually greater and the increased size of the labour pool provides a better opportunity for attracting qualified applicants. Conversely, as the unemployment rate drops, recruitment efforts must be increased and new sources explored.

Local labour market conditions are of primary importance in recruitment for most nonmanagerial, many supervisory, and even some middle-management positions. Filling top executive and professional positions however, often involves national or even international recruiting. For example, when the board of McCain Foods, the New Brunswick frozen-food processing giant, wished to appoint a new chief executive officer, they chose an experienced executive from Britain.[11] That a foreigner was chosen is not surprising, as McCain's products are sold around the globe.

Legal considerations also play a significant role in recruitment practices. Nondiscriminatory practices at this stage of first contact are also essential. We discuss this topic in more detail later in this chapter.

Internal Environmental Recruitment

An organization's promotion policy can also have a significant effect on recruitment. An organization can stress promotion from within its own ranks or fill positions from outside the organization. Depending on the circumstances, either approach may have merit.

Promotion from within (PFW) is the policy of filling vacancies above entry-level positions with current employees. When an organization emphasizes promotion from within, its workers have an incentive to strive for advancement. When employees see co-workers being promoted, they become more aware of their own opportunities, and morale often improves. Today's flatter organizational structures, with fewer levels of management, restrict upward mobility to a degree. However, the opportunity to move up in an organization will continue to serve as a motivating factor for some employees.

> **Promotion from within (PFW):** The policy of filling vacancies above entry-level positions with current employees.

Another advantage of internal recruitment is that the organization is usually well aware of its employees' capabilities. An employee's job performance may not, by itself, be a reliable criterion for promotion. Nevertheless, many of the employee's personal and job-related qualities will be known. The employee has a track record. The employee, too, knows the firm, its policies, and its people. Also, the company's investment in the individual may yield a higher return.

It is unlikely, however, that a firm can—or would even desire to—adhere rigidly to a practice of promotion from within. The vice president of human resources for a major automobile manufacturer offers this advice: "A strictly applied 'PFW' policy eventually leads to inbreeding, a lack of cross-fertilization, and a lack of creativity. A good goal, in my opinion, is to fill 80 percent of openings above entry-level positions from within." Frequently, new blood is needed to provide new ideas and innovation that must take place for firms to remain competitive.

Regulations related to the employment of relatives also may affect recruitment. While in some firms employees are encouraged to refer relatives and friends, in others this practice is discouraged. As well, certain working relationships among relatives are avoided. In many chartered accounting firms, for example, there has been a long-standing agreement that spouses should not work together if one needs to check the work of the other, a seemingly practical policy. As firms cannot legally discriminate on the basis of "marital status," however, these types of long-standing antinepotism rules may have to be reviewed (see Figure 5-3). Human resources professionals are well advised, therefore, to check

Figure 5-3

Employment: Prohibited Grounds of Discrimination

Prohibited Grounds	Federal	British Columbia	Alberta	Saskatchewan	Manitoba	Ontario	Quebec	New Brunswick	Prince Edward Island	Nova Scotia	Newfoundland	Northwest Territories	Yukon
Race or colour	●	●	●	●	●	●	●	●	●	●	●	●	●
Religion or creed	●	●	●	●	●	●	●	●	●	●	●	●	●
Age	●	(19-65)	(18+)	(18-64)	(18-65)	(18-65)	●	●	●	●	(19-65)	●	●
Sex (incl. pregnancy or childbirth)	●	●[1]	●	●	●[2]	●	●	●	●[1]	●	●[1]	●[1]	●
Marital Status	●	●	●	●	●	●	●[3]	●	●	●	●	●	●
Physical/mental handicap or disability	●	●	●	●	●	●	●	●	●	●	●	●	●
Sexual orientation	●[4]	●	●	●	●	●	●	●	●[1]	●	●[1]		●
National or ethnic origin (incl. linguistic background)	●			●[5]	●	●[6]	●	●				●[5]	
Family status	●	●	●	●	●	●	●[3]			●	●	●	
Dependence on alcohol or drug	●	●[1]	●[1]	●[1]	●[1]	●[1]	●	●[1,7]	●[1]	●[7]	●		
Ancestry or place of origin		●	●	●	●	●		●				●[5]	●
Political belief		●			●		●	●	●	●	●		●
Based on association					●	●		●	●	●			●
Pardoned conviction	●	●				●	●				●		
Record of criminal conviction		●					●			●			●
Source of income			●	●[8]		●		●		●	●		
Place of residence												●	
Assignment, attachment or seizure of pay												●	
Social condition/origin							●					●	
Language							●	●					●

Harassment on any of the prohibited grounds is considered a form of discrimination.

* Any limitation, exclusion, denial or preference may be permitted if a bona fide occupational requirement can be demonstrated.
1) complaints accepted based on policy
2) includes gender-determined characteristics
3) Quebec uses the term "civil status"
4) pursuant to a 1992 Ontario Court of Appeal decision, the Canadian Human Rights Commission now accepts complaints on the ground of sexual orientation
5) defined as nationality
6) Ontario's Code includes only "citizenship"
7) previous dependence only
8) defined as "receipt of public assistance"

This document is also available on computer diskette and as a sound recording to ensure it is accessible to people who are blind or vision impaired.

Threatening, intimidating or discriminating against someone who has filed a complaint, or hampering a complaint investigation, is a violation of provincial human rights codes, and at the federal level is a criminal offence.

No information on Nunavut was available at the time of publication. This chart is for quick reference only. For interpretation or further details, call the appropriate commission.

Source: Canadian Human Rights Commission. "Employment: Prohibited Grounds of Discrimination." Reproduced with permission of the Minister of Public Works and Government Services Canada, 1998.

carefully with the appropriate provincial and federal human rights legislation before implementing internal recruitment and promotional policies. Figure 5-3 combines data from all the human rights codes in Canada to show how jurisdictions vary in terms of prohibited grounds for discrimination.

Methods Used in Internal Recruitment

Management should be able to identify current employees who are capable of filling positions as they become available. Helpful tools used for internal recruitment include skills inventories, job posting, and bidding procedures. As we mentioned in Chapter 3, skills and management inventories permit organizations to determine whether current employees possess the qualifications for filling open positions. These inventories have proved to be extremely valuable to organizations when they are kept current. Inventories can be of tremendous value in locating talent internally and encouraging promotion from within.

Job posting is a procedure for informing employees that job openings exist. **Job bidding** is a technique that permits employees who believe they possess the required qualifications to apply for a posted job. Figure 5-4 shows the procedure a medium-sized firm might use. Some firms provide employees with an up-to-date computer list of job openings, or they may post openings on the company's intranet.

Regular use of job posting and bidding minimizes the common complaint that insiders never hear of a job opening until it has been filled. It reflects an openness that most employees generally value highly. A firm that offers freedom of choice and encourages career growth has a distinct advantage over firms that do not. However, an effective system takes considerable time and money. When bidders are unsuccessful, someone must explain to them why they were not chosen. If care has not been taken to ensure that the most qualified applicant is chosen, the system will lack credibility. Not even the best system can completely eliminate complaints.

Job posting: A procedure for informing employees that job openings exist.

Job bidding: A technique that permits employees who believe they possess the required qualifications to apply for a posted job.

Figure 5-4

Job Posting and Bidding Procedure

RESPONSIBILITY	ACTION REQUIRED
Human Resource Assistant	1. Upon receiving a Human Resource Requisition, send an e-mail or memo to each appropriate supervisor stating that a job opening exists. The message should include a job title, job number, pay grade, salary range, summary of the basic duties performed, and the essential qualifications required for the job (data to be taken from the job description/specification).
Supervisors	2. Ensure that the message is communicated to all within his or her section.
Interested Employees	3. Contact Human Resources

External Sources of Recruitment

At times, a firm must look beyond itself to find employees, particularly when expanding its workforce. External recruitment is needed to 1) fill entry-level jobs, 2) acquire skills not possessed by current employees, and (3) obtain employees with different backgrounds to provide new ideas. As Figure 5-5 shows, even when promotions are made internally, entry-level jobs must be filled from the outside. Thus, after the president of a firm retires, a series of internal promotions is made. Ultimately, however, the firm has to recruit externally to fill the entry-level position of salary analyst. If the president's position had been filled from the outside, the chain-reaction of promotions from within would not have occurred. Depending on the qualifications desired, employees may be attracted from a number of outside sources.

High Schools and Vocational Schools

Organizations concerned with recruiting clerical and other entry-level operative employees often depend heavily on high schools and vocational schools. Many of these schools have outstanding training programs for specific occupational skills, such as home appliance repair and small engine mechanics. Some companies work with schools to ensure a constant supply of trained individuals with specific job skills. In some areas, companies even lend employees to schools to assist in the training programs.

Community Colleges

Many community colleges are sensitive to the specific employment needs in their local labour markets, graduating highly sought-after students with marketable

Figure 5-5

Internal Promotion and External Recruitment

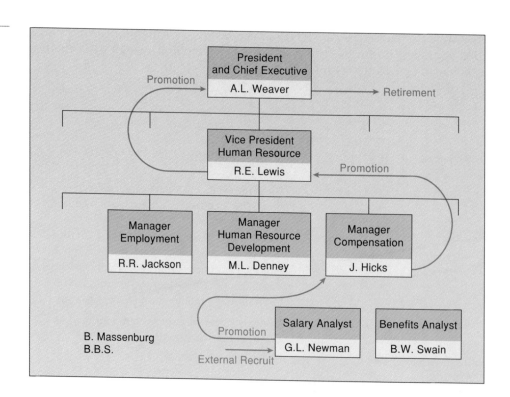

skills. In Canada, there is no "typical" community college. In some cases, colleges offer two-year (or shorter) programs designed specifically for the job market. In others, they offer vocational training plus preparation toward four-year university degree programs. Many community colleges also have excellent mid-management and postgraduate programs combined with training for specific fields such as international trade. In addition, career centres often provide a place for employers to contact students, thereby facilitating the recruitment process.

Universities

Universities represent a major source of potential professional, technical, and management employees for many organizations. Firms commonly send recruiters to campuses to interview prospective employees, although cost-reduction programs and labour market conditions have reduced this practice in recent years. Because on-campus recruitment is mutually beneficial, employers and university staff should develop and maintain close relationships. It is important that HR managers know the curricula and the quality of all learning institutions in their recruitment area.

Competitors and Other Firms

Competitors and other firms in the same industry or geographic area may be one of the most important source of recruits for positions in which recent experience is required. The fact that at least 5 percent of the working population, at any one time, is either actively seeking a new job or would be receptive to an offer emphasizes the importance of these sources.

The Unemployed

The unemployed often provide a valuable source of recruits. Qualified applicants join the unemployment rolls every day for various reasons. Companies may go out of business, cut back operations, or be merged with other firms, leaving qualified workers without jobs. Employees are also fired sometimes merely because of personality differences with their bosses. Not infrequently, employees become frustrated with their jobs and simply quit.

Older Individuals

Older workers, including those who are retired, may represent a valuable source of employees. Despite the stereotypes, evidence shows that older people can perform some jobs extremely well. When Kentucky Fried Chicken Corporation had difficulty recruiting younger workers, for example, it turned to older people and people with disabilities. Within six months, vacancies and turnover rates were dramatically reduced.

Management surveys indicate that most employers have high opinions of their older workers; they value them for many reasons, including their knowledge, skills, work ethic, loyalty, and literacy.[12] Unfortunately however, in Canada, this valuable resource is often wasted by discrimination against older workers. According to a report by Blossom Wigdor, chair of the National Advisory Council on Aging, some organizations have unwritten rules prohibiting the hiring of older workers, particularly when the job entails meeting the public.[13] Although the Canadian Human Rights Commission thus far has failed to include older workers on the list of groups protected by fair-hiring laws, HR professionals need to ensure that *ageism*, the conscious or unconscious discrimination against older people, is not tolerated. Indeed, in some companies, such as Kenworth of Canada, management has found that retraining older blue-collar workers is a good investment.[14]

Self-Employed Workers

Finally, the self-employed worker may also be a good potential recruit. As suggested previously, the self-employed make up the fastest growing employment category in Canada. All manner of skill and experience—technical, professional, administrative, or entrepreneurial—can be found among these individuals. Human resource managers will need to persuade these talented people to leave the freedom that self-employment affords, however, as many operate their own businesses in preference to working for someone else.[15]

There is the danger too, that working for a wage will become less attractive when the new employee is faced with the realities of corporate life. To cite but one example, when Ken Jensen, President of JCS Consulting Services Inc. of Maryhill, Ontario went to work for his major client after almost 15 years as a self-employed consultant, the arrangement lasted only three months. Mr. Jensen found corporate life too restrictive. He is now self-employed again and still works for his client (among others), but both parties have learned a valuable lesson about the psychology of the self-employed.[16]

Conventional External Methods of Recruitment

By examining recruitment sources, a firm determines the location of potential job applicants. It then seeks to attract these applicants by specific recruitment methods. Some conventional external methods of recruitment are discussed next.

Advertising

Advertising communicates the firm's employment needs to the public through media such as radio, newspaper, television, and industry publications. Advertisements should be written carefully, as Dorothy Bryant's experience in the opening vignette shows. Obviously, HR professionals should give prospective employees an accurate picture of both the job and the organization. Dorothy's ad did not provide a clear picture of the job or the job requirements, and was also flawed by subjective and improper criteria. The message also must indicate how an applicant is to respond: in person, by telephone, by fax, or by e-mail. Aside, however, from conveying this specific job information, the ad represents the organization to applicants and to the public. Human resource managers, then, must decide what corporate image they want to project.

Experience with various media will suggest the most appropriate advertising medium for specific types of jobs. One of the most common forms of advertising that provides broad coverage is the newspaper ad. In the late 1990s, a study by the Royal Bank, for example, found that this form of advertising accounted for about 50 percent of all new hires.[17] The drawback to help-wanted ads is that they invariably attract a large number of unqualified individuals, increasing the likelihood of making poor selection decisions.

On the other hand, the broad coverage makes a newspaper an ideal medium for creating awareness and for generating interest in the company as a whole, thus encouraging prospective candidates to seek information about the firm and other possible job opportunities. Examination of the Saturday edition of any major newspaper reveals the extensive use of advertising in recruiting practically every type of employee.

Certain media attract audiences that are more homogeneous in terms of employment skills, education, and orientation. Advertisements placed in publications like *The Globe and Mail* or the *National Post* relate primarily to managerial, professional, and technical positions. The readership is generally mobile and qualified for many of the positions advertised. By contrast, an advertisement placed in the *Vancouver Sun* or *Ottawa Citizen* would reach a more local market with a more varied skill base. Focusing on a specific labour pool, then, minimizes the likelihood of receiving unqualified applicants.

Virtually every professional group publishes a journal and there are many other widely read specialist publications. Advertising for a human resource executive position in *Canadian HR Reporter*, for example, would hit the target market because it is read almost exclusively by human resource professionals. Professional journals such as *Canadian Manager* are also widely used. Using journals, however, presents some problems. For one thing, they lack scheduling flexibility. Their deadlines may be weeks prior to the issue date, an obvious limitation when immediate staffing needs arise.

Other conventional media that can also be used include radio, billboards, and television. These methods are likely to be more expensive than newspapers or journals, but they have been used with success in specific situations. For instance, a regional medical centre used billboards successfully to attract registered nurses. One large manufacturing firm achieved considerable success in advertising for production trainees by means of spot advertisements on the radio. A large electronics firm used television to attract experienced engineers when it opened a new facility and needed more engineers immediately.

Employment Agencies

An **employment agency** is an organization that helps firms recruit employees and individuals locate jobs. These agencies perform many recruitment and selection functions that have proven quite beneficial to many organizations.

Employment agency: An organization that assists firms in recruiting employees and also aids individuals in their attempts to locate jobs.

Private employment agencies are used by firms to help fill virtually every type of position. However, they are best known for recruiting white-collar employees and offer an important service in bringing qualified applicants and open positions together. Occasional difficulties stem from a lack of industry standards, giving parts of the industry a bad reputation. However, a number of highly reputable, professionally managed employment agencies have operated successfully for decades. These agencies offer an important service by bringing qualified applicants together with potential employers.

Individuals should look for agencies where the fee is paid by the employer. One survey found employment agency fee schedules (charged to the employer) ranged from 25 to 35 percent of gross annual salary of the position to be filled.[18]

HR Web Wisdom

http: www.pearsoned.ca/ mondy

HRDC—HR Links
Looking for work? Have a look at HRDC's recruitment link.

Human Resources Development Canada

Human Resources Development Canada (HRDC) operates a large number of Canada Employment Centres (CECs) across Canada. Employers with jobs to fill can call in or e–mail "job orders" describing the nature of the job, basic duties, pay, location and any other relevant information. These orders are entered in an automated job bank.

Job seekers can access the HRDC job bank either at CEC offices, the Internet (via job banks) or through terminals placed in shopping malls and other public places. Applicants can be instructed to submit résumés, call, or visit the employer depending upon location and/or employer preference. The employer is responsible for screening and contacting the applicants for interviews. CECs also offer other services to both employees and employers. Job seekers who require additional information, counselling, or training, for example, can be helped, depending upon the results of a "service needs determination" performed by CEC staff. Then they may be eligible for counselling, retraining, or other assistance.

Company Recruiters

The most common use of recruiters is to work with technical and vocational schools, community colleges, and universities. The key contact for company recruiters on college and university campuses is often the director of student placement, who identifies qualified candidates, schedules interviews, and provides suitable interview rooms. This assistance enables organizations to use their own recruiters efficiently. Furthermore, the administrator is in an excellent position to find appropriately qualified students.

Résumé databases and the Internet (discussed later in this chapter), have already begun to alter the way postsecondary recruitment is approached. The database system allows recruiters to receive copies of students' résumés before they visit the campus. University and college recruitment becomes much more effective; recruiters can identify the most promising schools as well as specific students.[19]

An applicant should prepare carefully for the recruitment interview. In order to make a good impression, the prospect must do some research on the company. The school's placement service often has literature on the organization and its operations. In addition, an Internet or library search may yield information about the company's sales, number of employees, products, and other data. With these facts, prospects can engage the recruiter in conversation and ask relevant questions. Against other applicants with similar backgrounds and skills, an informed prospect always has a competitive advantage over those who are poorly prepared.

Special Events

Holding special events is a recruiting method that involves an effort by a single employer or group of employers to attract a large number of applicants for interviews. Job fairs, for example, are designed to bring together applicants and representatives of various companies. From an employer's viewpoint, a primary advantage of job fairs is the opportunity to meet a large number of candidates in a short time. More than a dozen commercial firms operate job fairs, but government agencies, charitable organizations, and business alliances also frequently sponsor them. As a recruitment method, job fairs offer the potential for a much lower cost per hire than traditional approaches.

Internships

An **internship** is a training method in which students divide their time between classes and working for an organization. One example is International Environmental Youth Corps (IEYC)—a program initiated by the federal Minister of the Environment in partnership with the Canadian environment industry. It is designed to place young Canadians in international internships within the environment sector. Graduates of Canadian colleges and universities who are under the age of 30 and would like to work in the environment industry are matched with Canadian companies and non-governmental organizations. In this arrangement, there is no obligation by the company to hire the student permanently or by the student to accept a permanent position with the firm following graduation.[20] An internship typically involves a temporary job for the summer months or a part-time job during the school year. In many instances, students alternate their schedules by working full-time one semester and studying full-time the next. During the internship, the student gets to view business practices firsthand. At the same time, the intern contributes to the firm by performing needed tasks. Through this relationship, a student can determine whether a company would be a desirable employer. Similarly, having a relatively lengthy period of time to observe the student's job performance, the firm can make a better judgment regarding the person's qualifications. In addition to other benefits, internships provide opportunities for students to bridge the gap from business theory to practice.

Internships also serve as an effective public relations tool, providing visibility for the company name and its products or service. Local communities have a favourable view of firms such as IBM Canada and Nortel Networks that offer internships.[21]

Internship: A training method whereby college or university students divide their time between attending classes and working for an orgazation.

Executive Search Firms

Executive search firms may be used to locate experienced professionals and executives when other sources prove inadequate. **Executive search firms** are organizations that search out the most qualified executive available for a specific position. They are generally retained by the companies needing specific types of individuals.

Throughout North America, executive search is a rapidly growing industry with estimated revenue in the range of $3 billion annually. More than 4 million potential candidates are contacted in order to place some 80 000 executives.[22] The executive search industry has evolved from a basic recruitment service to a highly sophisticated profession serving a greatly expanded role. Search firms now assist organizations in determining their human resource needs, establishing compensation packages, and revising organizational structures.

Most executive search firms differ from employment agencies and job advisory consultants in that they do not work for individuals. Search firms that work for corporations and governmental agencies are paid a retainer fee for each search, regardless of whether or not a suitable candidate is recruited. These firms often

Executive search firms: Organizations retained by a company to search for the most qualified executive available for a specific position.

develop a close relationship with their clients. They acquire an intimate knowledge of the organization, its culture, goals, structure, and the position to be filled. Retainer firms typically recruit executives for middle and upper level management positions or senior technical positions calling for salaries of over $60 000.

Contingency search firms, which grew out of the employment agency industry, focus on lower to middle management and some technical positions, with salaries from $30 000 to $70 000. Unlike retainer search firms, these organizations are paid only when a candidate is accepted.[23]

Professional Associations

In many functional business areas such as finance, marketing, accounting, and human resource, professional associations provide recruitment and placement services for their members. The Canadian Institute of Management, for example, operates a job referral service for members and employers.

Employee Referrals

Kee Transport, a Profit 100 company headquartered in Mississauga, Ontario, has an incentive program that pays its employees for every new driver they bring in.[24] Many organizations, especially small and medium-sized businesses, have found that their employees can play an important recruiting role by actively soliciting applications from their friends and associates. One recent study involving over 200 human resource executives indicated that employee referrals, along with college recruiting and executive search firms, produced the best employees for their organizations.[25] For example, at one high-tech company, hires from employee referrals rose from 15 percent to 52 percent within just a few years. This firm found that as referrals became their primary recruiting approach, the costs previously incurred from advertising and using placement agencies were significantly reduced. With a goal of not only attracting but also retaining employees, management found that this recruitment method also resulted in effective employee/employer bonding.[26]

Unsolicited Walk-in Applicants

The Royal Bank
Visit the Careers Directions site of the Royal Bank.

Purdy's Chocolates of Vancouver and Sherwood Village Spa in Mississauga are examples of firms that rely heavily on walk–ins as a principal source of hiring.[27] If an organization has the reputation of being a good place to work, it may be able to attract qualified prospects even without extensive recruitment efforts. Acting on their own initiative, well-qualified workers may seek out a specific company to apply for a job. Unsolicited applicants who apply because they are drawn by the firm's reputation often prove to be valuable employees.

Innovative External Methods of Recruitment

Technology has also affected recruitment. Newer methods include Internet recruiting, recruitment databases/automated applicant tracking systems, and virtual job fairs. In addition, sign-on bonuses are also being used.

Internet Recruiting

Print advertising will probably not be abandoned soon. However, advertising job openings on the Internet is becoming increasingly popular. Recruiters may search a number of electronic mail bulletin boards and use their own firm's Web site. A Web page can be put up inexpensively compared to print, which must be paid for by the word or column inch and the length of time the ad appears in a publication. Job postings on the Web site are easy to update and can be paid for with a flat fee for the site. Also, the firm may be able to attract otherwise inaccessible individuals. This includes, according to one executive, the passive job seekers—those who may be the best qualified but who are not currently looking for a job. In addition, firms may be able to attract the attention of candidates worldwide. One small software firm posted a listing for a software engineer on a worldwide electronic-mail bulletin board and received 200 résumés, some from as far away as Israel, Germany, and Hong Kong.[28] According to one survey of 150 executives, a full 40 percent reported that they are using the Internet to snare new recruits.[29] This response is somewhat surprising considering the newness of the approach.

Another study found that 67 percent of HR professionals now use the Internet as a recruitment tool. A majority of their firms began employing this alternative within the past year. However, although most respondents to this survey planned to continue using the Internet, they were only moderately satisfied with it as a recruitment method. The same study concluded that a relatively small number of positions are currently being filled through the Internet and that both newspaper advertisements and executive recruiters are usually more effective.[30] Nevertheless, expanded use of the Internet by employers and job seekers alike is a certainty. Candidates for employment, especially those with technical skills, will continue to explore the Web for job possibilities.

Impressive results using the Internet for recruiting are not achieved by simply posting jobs and waiting for applicants to e-mail résumés. For example, IBM Canada has created an extensive Web site that is both enticing and fruitful. It includes information on campus events, student programs, testimonials, upcoming events, and workplace issues and advice on how to construct an on-line résumé.[31]

A final caution about Internet recruiting: don't allow the Web site to become outdated. An incomplete page or obsolete Web address shows the firm in an unfavourable light.[32]

HR Web Wisdom

http: www.pearsoned.ca/ mondy

Links to jobs
Links are provided to some popular Web sites for employers and job seekers.

Recruitment Databases/Automated Applicant Tracking Systems

Computers have greatly facilitated many HRM functions, a trend that is sure to accelerate. Résumé databases have already begun to shape the way university and college recruitment is approached. By using a database system, recruiters can receive copies of students' résumés before they visit the campus. This makes college recruitment much more effective. Schools offering the most promising prospects can be determined as well as the specific students the recruiter wishes to interview.[34] Firms continue to seek ways to cut costs and universities strive to secure more jobs for their students.

Real-Time Recruitment

Relaxing on the deck of his beach hotel in Cancun, Mexico, Jack Hicks is job hunting using his personal digital assistant (PDA) linked by a satellite to various electronic professional job posting services. Hicks, a petroleum engineer based in Calgary, is enjoying a three-week vacation after a fairly long period of employment with a Saudi-based oil company. He is a professional contract employee working on a just-in-time basis rather than being a permanent employee of one firm. Just before completing each freelance assignment Hicks posts his résumé, compensation requirements, and availability date on the electronic bulletin board of his professional engineering organization. Very much like the various electronic professional job posting services, this bulletin board serves as a global link for employers and job seekers.

Guy Newman, vice president of Explore All Recovery, needs to assemble a joint U.S.–Canadian–Russian team of engineers to recover oil reserves from Siberian oil fields. Newman is seeking the remaining engineer needed for the team with specialized software capable of searching on-line databases for key words related to job experience and training. Once individuals with the needed specialties are isolated from databases of various bulletin boards and electronic job posting services, they are downloaded into Newman's desktop computer. Newman then reviews the various matches and identifies those who have the skills and experience needed, have reasonable compensation requirements, and are available immediately. Hicks's résumé is directly in line with Newman's needs and Newman knows Hicks's excellent reputation. In addition, Hicks has experience working in the inhospitable conditions of Siberia.

Newman e-mails Hicks indicating a strong interest in working with him on the upcoming Siberian project. The e-mail reaches Hicks, who is still relaxing in his lounge chair. Hicks is interested in the Siberian project, also having heard good things about Newman. Hicks uses his PDA to call Newman and leaves a voice-mail message indicating his strong interest. Newman e-mails Hicks an employment contract via his PDA. Newman and Hicks discuss the possibilities, using their visual/voice/data link capabilities. Several contractual changes are made and Hicks initials them on screen. Both Hicks and Newman sign the revised contract with their styluses, completing the deal. Newman goes back to work assembling the remaining team members while Hicks heads back to the beach.[33]

Databases operated by several independent networks continue to grow as some firms downsize and others become more aware of what computers can do. Résumé banks are available of individuals at all career levels in a wide variety of fields. Central databases can be accessed by corporate clients using their own personal computers. When a candidate's background matches an open position, the client may obtain a copy of the résumé to review. The process of matching candidates with positions dramatically reduces paperwork costs. For example, a job search through a national database firm may cost less than $1000. An executive search firm, on the other hand, normally charges about one-third of the candidate's first-year salary and bonus.[35] The cost and time efficiency of databases may make some recruiting methods obsolete, but they will not completely replace current systems. For example, searches for CEOs will always be politically sensitive and require special handling.

HR Web Wisdom

http: www.pearsoned.ca/ mondy

Cyber Fair Review
An example of an on-line virtual job fair is reviewed.

Virtual Job Fairs

In a **virtual job fair** students meet recruiters face-to-face in interviews conducted over special computers, which have lenses that transmit head-and-shoulder images of both parties. This "virtual" recruitment method is used by such companies as VIEWnet Inc. In its first Virtual Job Fair, recruiters at 20 major corporations, after reviewing 12 000 résumés, chose 1 000 students to interview for 300 jobs. The recruiters were able to visit all the schools virtually without having to leave their offices.[36]

Virtual job fair: A recruitment method in which students meet recruiters face-to-face in interviews conducted over special computers.

Sign-on Bonuses

As mentioned in Chapter 2, some firms are following the practice of the sports industry by offering sign-on bonuses to high-demand prospects. This strategy is especially prevalent in industries with severe shortages of highly skilled workers, such as information systems workers. As discussed in Chapter 12, lump-sum payments have broad appeal because they provide a way for companies to compensate employees (in this case, to recruit them) while controlling fixed pay rates.[37]

Figure 5-6

Currently Used Recruitment Methods

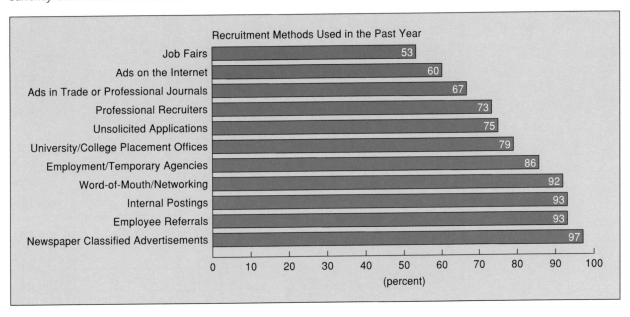

Recruitment Methods Used in the Past Year

Method	Percent
Job Fairs	53
Ads on the Internet	60
Ads in Trade or Professional Journals	67
Professional Recruiters	73
Unsolicited Applications	75
University/College Placement Offices	79
Employment/Temporary Agencies	86
Word-of-Mouth/Networking	92
Internal Postings	93
Employee Referrals	93
Newspaper Classified Advertisements	97

(percent)

Tailoring Recruitment Methods to Sources

As the preceding sections indicate, a number of recruitment methods are used by organizations to attract applicants. One North American survey of HR professionals revealed the extent to which these methods are currently used. Figure 5-6 shows that newspaper classified advertisements are used by virtually every firm included in the survey. Although ads on the Internet are used less frequently than all others except for job fairs, the rapid increase in use of the Internet will surely change these data—and rather quickly.

Each organization and each situation is unique, so the types and qualifications of workers needed to fill positions vary greatly. Thus, to be successful, recruitment must be tailored to the needs of each firm. In addition, recruitment sources and methods often vary according to the type of position being filled.

Figure 5-7 shows a matrix of the methods and sources of recruitment for an information systems manager. Managers must first identify the source (where prospective employees are) before choosing the methods (how to get them). Suppose, for example, that a large firm has an immediate need for an accounting manager with a minimum of five years' experience, and no one within the firm has these qualifications. It is most likely that such an individual is employed by another firm, very possibly a competitor, or is self-employed. After considering the recruitment source, the recruiter must then choose the method (or methods) of recruitment that offers the best prospects for attracting qualified

Figure 5-7

Methods and Sources of Recruitment for an Information Systems Manager

Source	Advertising	Private employment agencies	Public employment agencies	Recruiters	Special events	Internships	Executive search firms	Unsolicited applications	Professional associations	Employee referrals	Unsolicited applicants	Automated applicant tracking system	Resume databases
High schools													
Vocational schools													
Community colleges													
Colleges and universities													
Competitors and other firms	X	X					X		X				
Unemployed													
Self-employed													

candidates. Perhaps the job can be advertised in the classified section of *The Globe and Mail*, the *National Post*, or *CA Magazine*. Alternatively, an executive search firm may be used to locate qualified candidates. In addition, the recruiter may attend meetings of professional accounting associations. One or more of these methods will likely yield a pool of qualified applicants.

In another scenario, consider a firm's need for 20 entry-level machine operators whom the firm is willing to train. High schools and vocational schools or Canada Employment Centres (CEC) would probably be good recruitment sources. Methods of recruitment might include running newspaper ads, working through public employment agencies, sending recruiters to vocational schools, encouraging employee referrals, or contacting the local CEC.

The specific recruitment methods used will be affected by external environmental factors, including market supply and job requirements. Each organization should maintain employment records and conduct its own research to determine which recruitment sources and methods are most effective under various circumstances. Studies show that firms that conduct internal studies of recruitment effectiveness are significantly more profitable than those that do not.[38]

Eliminating Discrimination

In spite of human rights legislation, human resource practices that have an unequal effect on women, persons with disabilities, aboriginals, and minorities are deeply embedded in some organizations. A traditional recruitment method, such as employee referrals, for example, may perpetuate the effects of past discrimination, even after other discriminatory practices have been discontinued. The result, though not necessarily conscious, is a continuation of what has been labelled systemic discrimination.[39] Similarly, it may be discriminatory for a firm located near a First Nations reserve to insist on high school graduation for entry-level positions. Relatively few potential aboriginal applicants may have completed high school, although they could be quite capable of doing the job.[40] Or recruiters may overlook certain sources in the belief, based on entrenched stereotypes, that members of one sex would not be interested in, or competent at, certain jobs.

It must be remembered, as well, that the ethnic composition of society has changed radically. As we noted in Chapter 2, for example, about 11 percent of the Canadian population was classified as a visible minority in 1996, up from about 6 percent of the population in 1986. Our society is becoming increasingly diverse and multicultural. HRM professionals must be sure that all HR systems (recruitment, promotion, discipline, etc.), fall within the law.

As we discussed earlier in this chapter, the law varies depending upon where a firm operates. Everywhere in Canada it is illegal to consider race, religion, gender, disability, or marital status in making employment decisions such as hiring, firing, and promoting. On the other hand, one may, for example, discriminate on the basis of political belief in some provinces but not in other provinces (see Figure 5-3).[41]

Some groups are opposed to employment equity and charge that it results in so-called reverse discrimination. There is another side to the story, however. Because of past unequal opportunity, women, visible minority group members, aboriginals, and people with disabilities may not respond to traditional recruitment methods until specific action is taken to attract them. Unless special efforts are made, it is questionable whether they will ever be proportionally represented in the workforce. Therefore, any organization that adopts employment equity (either voluntarily or by mandate) should implement recruitment and other employment programs that make sure women, visible minorities, aboriginals and those with disabilities will be included in decision making. These programs should be carefully monitored to ensure their effectiveness.

The government of Canada has published specific guidelines to help employers achieve equality in the workplace. The guidelines cover grounds of discrimination such as sex, ancestry, colour, disability, marital status, or other non-bona-fide occupational requirements. Implementing equity and reporting the results is mandatory for organizations that fall under the Canada Labour Code (federal crown corporations, interprovincial transportation companies, communication agencies, and banks).[42] Other companies, too, may be well advised to follow the guidelines voluntarily.

To help HR managers initiate employment equity, a framework, shown in Figure 5-8, has been developed for reviewing and adjusting personnel systems.[43]

Figure 5-8

A Framework for Implementing Employment Equity

PHASE I: ORGANIZATIONAL READINESS

Step 1: Preparation

- Establish senior level commitment.
- Define mechanisms for consultation with employee representatives (e.g., bargaining agents).
- Identify communications resources.
- Assign senior staff and resources.
- Identify organizational values and attitudes and sources of support for or resistance to employment equity.

Step 2: Analysis

- Collect personnel information.
- Evaluate current work force information.
- Review formal and informal personnel policies and practices.
- Identify barriers to employment equity in policies and practices.

PHASE II: MANAGEMENT OF CHANGE

Step 3: Planning

- Establish goals and timetables.
- Design new or modified personnel systems and procedures.
- Develop special measures and reasonable accommodations.
- Determine monitoring and accountability mechanisms.

Step 4: Implementation

- Assign line management responsibility and accountability.
- Implement Employment Equity Plan of Action.
- Support plans with a communications strategy.

PHASE III: MAINTENANCE OF CHANGE

Step 5: Monitoring

- Establish feedback and problem-solving mechanisms.
- Carry out regular orientation and training programs for supervisors.
- Follow through in management performance evaluation.
- Reward achievements.
- Maintain and update personnel information.
- Make adjustments to program as required.

Source: Employment Equity: A Guide for Employers, *Human Resources Development Canada, 1994: 8–9. Reproduced with the permission of the Minister of Public Works and Government Services Canada, 2000.*

Designing an Employment Equity Program: Implications for Managers

Employment equity programs, whether legislated or voluntary, are a reality of our present day human resources environment.[44] Despite the recent swing to right-wing governments in provinces like Alberta and Ontario, there does still seem to be a general desire on the part of society to provide more equitable opportunities for everyone. Some strategies can help managers develop and implement employment equity programs.

Analysis

A critical prelude to any such program is an environmental scan to consider both internal and external influences. As illustrated in Figure 5-9, factors that must be considered include education/skills, demographics, and political, legal, social/cultural, economic, and technological implications. An examination of these elements will help determine what needs to be done, the potential effects on the organization, the most effective way to communicate the plan to workers and to ensure acceptance, and the potential benefits and disadvantages to the organization.

An important component of the environmental scan is workforce analysis, since the employment equity plan will be based on the data obtained. The analysis must, therefore, reflect as closely as possible the representation of designated groups within the current employee mix. Such a study is not a simple task, because many employees feel uncomfortable about disclosing personal information, particularly if they feel that it may be used against them in any way. It is imperative, therefore, to design the survey and to conduct the analysis in such a way as to secure the trust of employees.

Figure 5-9

An Environmental Analysis

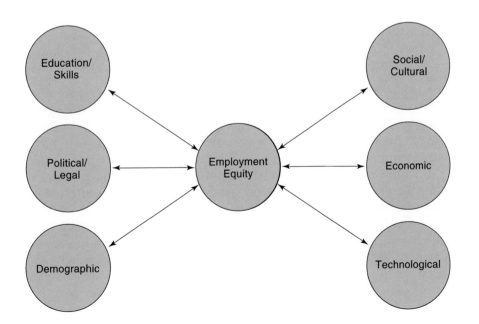

Implementation

Employment equity programs will have a better chance in an atmosphere that encourages flexibility, openness, and tolerance of differences. An open-minded approach is especially critical if it becomes necessary to modify job requirements or responsibilities to accommodate the special needs of a particular employee. Conflicts may arise from perceptions of reduced productivity or a backlash by workers from more traditional backgrounds.

There is, however, a spin-off benefit for the company. The creativity and problem-solving skills that workers and managers must use to successfully adapt the workplace for employment equity are precisely the qualities that can make them more effective in fulfilling their job responsibilities.

The development of partnerships with other community resources will also be helpful. It is neither possible nor practical for human resources managers (nor other managers for that matter) to acquire the knowledge and expertise required to modify jobs for individuals with varying needs and abilities. Community organizations and special interest groups can suggest ways to adapt jobs with technical aids or simple realignment of duties. They are also a valuable source of information about funding programs for wage and/or equipment subsidies, and can assist with staff training and sensitization.

Analysis of Recruitment Procedures

HR managers should analyze their recruitment procedures to make sure they are not discriminatory. For example, is overreliance on employee referral and unsolicited applicants perpetuating the composition of the organization's workforce?

It is helpful to develop a record of applicant flow, which includes personal and job-related data on each applicant. It indicates whether or not a job offer was extended and an explanation of the decision. Such records enable the HR professional or manager to analyze recruitment and selection practices and to take corrective action when necessary. This record will also be extremely useful if the firm's hiring practices are ever questioned. As well, recruiters should be trained to use objective, job-related standards.

Minority Members as Recruiters

Recruiters play a unique role in encouraging or discouraging visible minority groups, women, and people with disabilities to apply for jobs. Hiring qualified members of these groups as recruiters can be an effective way to broaden the range of applicants. If this is not feasible, another strategy is to have an operative employee or manager who is a member of a minority group accompany recruiters on visits to universities and colleges or participate in career days. Such employees should also be asked for input into recruitment planning and can serve effectively as referral sources.

The image of the company shown in help-wanted advertisements and brochures should be kept in mind as well. Pictures of ethnic minority members, women, and disabled employees—*not* in a section on employment equity, but used casually to illustrate other aspects of the company—give credibility to the message that a firm offers equal opportunity to everyone.

Only Able-Bodied Men?

Paul da Silva and Debra Coffee, two executives from competing firms, met at their annual professional conference. They were discussing the effect of recent human rights commission rulings on their firms. Paul said, "I don't think we will have any difficulty at our company. We don't employ any persons with disabilities but then all our production jobs require able-bodied men."

"Have you considered making reasonable accommodations for applicants with disabilities?" Debra asked. After thinking a moment, Paul replied, "I don't believe so, Debra. You see, our executive group is very pleased with the productivity in our plant. I really don't think they want to fix something that isn't broken."

Advertising

With few exceptions, jobs must be open to all individuals. Therefore, sex-segregated advertisements must not be used unless the applicant's sex is a bona fide occupational qualification. The burden of proof is on the employer to establish that the requirement is essential to successful performance of the job.

In one instance, for example, a public service agency needed orderlies to work with elderly male patients in their homes, where they would help the client with washing, toileting, etc. But the elderly men refused to allow women (mostly young women), to help them. The agency was in a dilemma. On the one hand, the human rights code prohibits gender discrimination; on the other, the clients were refusing the agency's services. The human rights commission was approached and permission was granted to advertise for male orderlies. Females could still appeal, however, if they thought the practice was discriminatory.

Working Together

To achieve long-term success, employment equity will need to become a more collaborative effort between all the parties involved. Government needs to streamline its administrative requirements and reduce bureaucracy. Educators should examine their programs to ensure they are appropriate for designated groups. The designated groups themselves must become proactive in helping to design programs that will aid their members and in researching ways to effectively accommodate them in employment without sacrificing company productivity. Finally, employers need to become more flexible and creative in integrating designated group members into their workplace.

If all interested parties work in partnership and demonstrate a collective will to make employment equity work, the ultimate success will some day be achieved: the program will no longer be needed.

A GLOBAL PERSPECTIVE

Understand the Global Workforce for Effective Worldwide Recruitment

Many of the recruitment methods used in Canada are also common practice in other countries. Even some alternatives to recruitment are identical. The use of temporary help, for example, is not foreign to Europe.[45] In fact, in Western Europe, the temporary help industry is larger than in North America. Cultures and employment laws vary from country to country. For example, although recruiting in the United Kingdom is much the same as in Canada, it is legal to discriminate on the basis of age.[46]

In other parts of Europe, however, hiring temporary help is much more highly regulated. In France, for example, the law requires that temporary employees be paid the same rate as full-time employees, plus a premium. Germany also is highly regulated, as temporary workers are considered to be permanent employees of the employment agency that employs them. Since younger workers in Japan are not as loyal to their employers as are their parents, a temporary employment sector is starting to develop. Japanese laws, however, are new and relatively inflexible. For example, they specify the kinds of work a temporary worker can perform and permission must be granted for any changes.[47]

A formidable task facing many multinational firms is the recruitment and development of a cadre of managers and executives who understand and can operate effectively in the global market environment. Many companies are attempting to provide suitable international experience for high-potential managers early in their careers, and are highlighting these international opportunities in recruiting university graduates. There is also an increase in external recruitment to fill management positions abroad.

Unfortunately, some firms seem to be unwilling to recruit and develop women as international managers. This reluctance is of particular concern because recent research suggests that women are more sensitive to cultural differences and, therefore, more able to work effectively with managers from other countries. To recruit effectively in the global marketplace, it is essential that human resource managers not ignore any portion of the labour pool.[48]

SUMMARY

1. Define recruitment.

Recruitment is the process of attracting individuals on a timely basis, in sufficient numbers, and with appropriate qualifications, and encouraging them to apply for jobs with an organization.

2. Identify alternatives that a firm might consider before resorting to outside recruitment.

Alternatives include outsourcing, contingent workers, employee leasing, and overtime.

3. Describe the recruitment process.

Frequently recruitment begins when a manager initiates an employee requisition. Next, management determines whether qualified employees are available within the firm (the internal source) or must be recruited externally from sources such as colleges, universities, and other firms. Once sources of potential employees are isolated, appropriate methods for either internal or external recruiting are used to accomplish recruitment goals.

4. Describe how the external environment can affect the recruitment process.

Supply and demand play a major role. If demand for a particular skill is high relative to supply, an extraordinary recruiting effort may be required. Local labour market conditions are important, especially for non-managerial positions. When the unemployment rate in an organization's labour market is high, it is easier to attract qualified applicants. As the unemployment rate drops, recruitment efforts must be increased and new sources explored. Legal considerations must also be kept in mind. Nondiscriminatory practices are essential.

5. Explain and describe internal recruitment methods.

An organization can rely on a policy of promotion from within. Skills and management inventories permit organizations to determine whether current employees possess the qualifications for filling open positions. Some firms inform employees that job openings exist through job posting and invite qualified employees to apply through job bidding. Openings may be supplied on a computer list or company intranet.

6. Identify external sources of recruitment.

External sources of recruitment include high schools and vocational schools, community colleges, universities, competitors and other firms, the unemployed, older individuals, and self-employed workers.

7. Identify external methods of recruitment.

External methods of recruitment include advertising, employment agencies, Human Resources Development Canada, recruiters, special events, internships, executive search firms, professional associations, employee referrals, unsolicited applicants, Internet recruiting, recruitment databases/automated applicant tracking systems, virtual job fairs, and sign-on bonuses. Recruitment sources and methods often vary according to environment, organization and the type of position being filled. Recruitment must be flexible and tailored to the needs of each firm.

8. Explain what needs to be accomplished to reduce discrimination.

Human resource practices that have an unequal effect on women, persons with disabilities, aboriginals, and minorities are deeply embedded in some organizations. HR professionals need to recognize that equity programs, whether legislated or voluntary, are a reality in the current environment. Long-term success in eliminating discrimination will require collaboration among all parties involved. To help HR managers initiate employment equity, a five-step framework is suggested, including preparation, analysis, planning, implementation; and monitoring.

QUESTIONS FOR REVIEW

1. What are some alternatives to recruitment?
2. Describe the basic components of the recruitment process.
3. List and discuss the various external and internal factors that may affect recruitment.
4. Describe the methods commonly used in internal recruitment. Briefly define each.
5. Discuss the reasons for an external recruitment program.
6. Briefly outline the sources for external recruitment.

7. Describe the various conventional and innovative methods of external recruitment.

8. How can a firm improve its recruiting efforts to eliminate discrimination?

DEVELOPING **HRM** SKILLS

An Experiential Exercise

Human resource managers are often responsible for preparing job descriptions. From these job descriptions, profiles of the types of people needed to fill various positions can be developed and recruitment efforts can be designed. The human resource manager must determine where the best applicants are located (recruitment sources) and how to entice them to join the organization (recruitment methods). This exercise is designed to provide an understanding of the relationship between recruitment sources and methods.

Participants will attempt to determine the most appropriate recruitment sources and methods for the job description that will be given to them. Your instructor will give you the additional information necessary to complete the exercise.

HRM INCIDENT

Right Idea, Wrong Plan

Robert Blair was human resource manager at Epler Manufacturing Company in Edmonton, Alberta. He was considering the need to recruit qualified women for Epler when Betty Quan walked into his office.

"Got a minute?" asked Betty. "I need to talk to you about next week's job fair at Fairview College."

"Sure," Robert replied, "but first, I need your advice about something. How can we get more women to apply for work here? We're running ads on the community service channel along with the classified ads in *The Edmonton Journal*. I think you and John have made recruiting trips to every community college within 200 miles. We've encouraged employee referral, too, and I still think that's our most reliable source of new workers. But we just aren't getting any female applicants."

From the president on down, the management at Epler claimed commitment to employment equity. According to Robert, the commitment went much deeper than posting the usual placards and filing an employment equity plan to qualify for the federal government contracts. Still, the percentage of female employees at Epler remained at only 30 percent. Epler paid competitive wages and had a good training program.

One need was for machine operator trainees. The machines were not difficult to operate and there was no educational requirement for the job. There were also several clerical and management trainee positions open.

Questions

1. Evaluate the current recruitment effort. How could Robert attain the firm's employment equity goal?

2. Map out an employment equity program for Epler Manufacturing Company.

CHAPTER

6

Selection

1. Define and briefly describe the need for employee selection.

2. Identify the environmental factors that affect the selection process.

3. Outline a general framework for the selection process.

4. Explain the importance of a preliminary employment interview.

5. Identify the basic information contained in a company application for employment form and an employment résumé.

6. Identify the various types of employment tests.

7. Describe the features of properly designed selection tests.

8. Identify the types of information that should be gained from the interview.

9. Describe the basic types of interviewing.

10. Describe the various methods of interviewing.

11. Explain the potential problems of interviewing.

12. Briefly explain the need for reference checks, physical examinations and notification of candidates.

Bill Jenkins is the owner/manager of Quality Printing Company. Because of an increase in business, shop employees have been working overtime for almost a month. Last week, Bill put an advertisement in the newspaper to hire a printer. Three people applied for the job. Bill considered Mark Ketchell the only one to be qualified. He called Mark's previous employer in Saskatoon, who responded, "Mark is a diligent, hardworking person. He is as honest as the day is long. He knows his trade, too." Bill also found that Mark had left Saskatoon after he was divorced a few months ago and that his work had deteriorated slightly prior to the divorce. The next day, Bill asked Mark to operate one of the printing presses. Mark did so competently, so he decided immediately to hire him.

Margaret Howard is the shipping supervisor

for Oshawa Warehousing, a major food distributor. One of Margaret's truck drivers just quit. She spoke to the human resource manager, Purvi Ragani, who said that she would begin the search right away. The next day an advertisement appeared in the local paper for the position. Purvi considered three of the 15 applicants to be qualified and called them in for an initial interview. The next morning Purvi called Margaret and said, "I have three drivers who look like they can do the job. When do you want me to set up an interview for you with them? I guess you'll want to give them a driving test at that time." Margaret interviewed the three drivers and gave them each a driving test and then called Purvi to state her choice. The next day the new driver reported to Margaret for work.

These incidents provide only a brief look at the all-important selection process. In the first case, Bill, as owner/manager of a small printing shop, handled the entire selection process himself. In the second case, Purvi, the human resource manager, was heavily involved in the selection process, but Margaret, the shipping supervisor, made the actual decision. Knowledge of the selection process was important in both of these situations— although for different reasons.

We begin this chapter by defining employee selection and outlining the need for it, as well as environmental factors that affect it. Then we describe the general framework for the selection process and the preliminary interview and review the application and résumé for employment. Next, we cover employment selection testing, including types of employment tests and characteristics of properly designed tests. In the ensuing sections, we discuss the employment interview, including interview planning, content, objectives, types, methods, and problematic issues. We then discuss reference and background checks, the selection decision, the possible need for physical examinations, and notification of candidates.

HR Web Wisdom

http: www.pearsoned.ca/ mondy

HRDC—HR Links
This site contains information on job screening techniques.

The Need for Employee Selection

Even if management has done everything else right—made realistic plans, designed a sound organizational structure, and implemented sound control systems—business goals cannot be attained without competent people. If too many mediocre or poor performers are hired, a firm cannot be successful for long. Thus an important HR function is **selection**: the process of choosing from a group of applicants the individual best suited for a particular position and organization.

Selection: The process of choosing from a group of applicants those individuals best suited for a particular position and organization.

Most managers admit that employee selection is one of their most difficult—and most important—business decisions.[1] As Peter Drucker has stated, "No other decisions are so long lasting in their consequences or so difficult to unmake. And yet, by and large, executives make poor promotion and staffing decisions. By all accounts, their batting average is no better than .333. At most, one-third of such decisions turn out right; one-third are minimally effective, and one-third are outright failures."[2] When hidden costs, such as loss of productivity and overtime for the remaining staff, are added, the cost of replacing a key employee approaches twice his or her annual salary.[3] Another estimate has valued replacement as high as $500 000 per hire. While these figures may appear to be excessive, it is important to consider the productivity difference between high and low performers—a differential estimated to be as high as three to one.[4] A firm that selects qualified employees, therefore, reaps substantial benefits, which are repeated every year the employee is on the payroll.

The goal of the selection process is to match people with jobs. If individuals are overqualified, underqualified, or for any reason do not *fit* into the job or into the organizational culture, they will be more likely to leave the firm. In global terms, the Canadian labour market is extremely mobile;[5] the percentage of those who leave their jobs can approach 20 percent in any given year. It appears that much of the movement is among the 18-24 age group, as "younger groups engage in more job-shopping with fewer constraints such as loss of significant pension credits . . ."[6]

Environmental Factors Affecting the Selection Process

A number of environmental factors affect the selection process, including legal considerations, time constraints, organizational hierarchy, the applicant pool, and the sector of employment.

Legal Considerations

As we outlined in Chapter 5, legislation and Human Rights Commission decisions have had a major effect on human resource management. Figure 6-1 identifies selection criteria that should be carefully avoided because of their discriminatory potential.

Time Constraints

The time available to make the selection decision, depending on the situation, can also influence the selection process. Margaret Howard needs a truck driver now; one just quit and someone must be found to drive the truck. Bill Jenkins may not feel as much time pressure because other employees have been covering the vacant position for nearly a month. Selecting a chief executive officer in a national search may take an entire year. In this case, considerable attention may have to be devoted to a careful study of résumés, intensive reference checking, and hours of interviews.

Organizational Hierarchy

Different approaches to selection are generally taken for filling positions at varying levels in the organization. For instance, consider the differences between hiring a top-level executive and a clerk. Extensive background checks and interviewing would be conducted to verify the experience and capabilities of the applicant for the executive position. On the other hand, an applicant for a clerical position would most likely only take a word processing test and perhaps have a short employment interview.

Applicant Pool

The number of qualified applicants for a particular job can also affect the selection process. The process can be truly selective only if there are several qualified applicants for a particular position. However, only a few applicants with the required skills may be available. The selection process then becomes a matter of choosing whoever is at hand. Expansion and contraction of the labour market also exerts considerable influence on availability and, thus, the selection process.

The number of people hired for a particular job compared to the individuals in the applicant pool is often expressed as a **selection ratio**:

$$\text{Selection ratio} \quad = \quad \frac{\text{Number of persons hired to fill a particular job}}{\text{Number of available applicants}}$$

A selection ratio of 1.00 indicates that there is only one qualified applicant for each position. An effective selection process is impossible in this situation. People who might otherwise be rejected are often hired. The lower the ratio falls below 1.00, the more alternatives the manager has in making a selection decision. For example, a selection ratio of 0.10 indicates that there are 10 qualified applicants for each position.

Selection ratio:
The number of people hired for a particular job compared to the total number of individuals in the applicant pool.

Sector of Employment

The sector of the economy in which individuals are to be employed—private, government, or not-for-profit—can also affect the selection process. Most businesses in the private sector are heavily profit-oriented. Prospective employees are screened for their potential contribution to profit goals. Conversely, in the public service, most hiring departments must establish a "statement of qualifications" for each job to be filled. In this case, the interview process would be primarily concerned with measuring each of the factors or characteristics outlined in the statement. Individuals being considered for positions in not-for-profit organizations (such as Scouts Canada, the YMCA, or a women's shelter) confront still a different situation. The salary level may not be competitive with private and governmental organizations. Therefore, a person who fills one of these positions must be not only qualified, but also dedicated to this type of work.

A General Framework for the Selection Process

Figure 6-2 illustrates a generalized selection process. It typically begins with the preliminary interview, after which obviously unqualified candidates are quickly rejected. Next, the firm's application for employment and/or applicant résumés will be reviewed in detail. Then, applicants will progress through a series of selection tests, the employment interview, and reference and background checks. In the final stages, the applicant may also be required to undergo a company physical examination.

Many firms use a probationary period to evaluate new employees' performance and suitability. This procedure may be either a substitute for certain

Figure 6.1

A Guide to Screening and Selection in Employment.

SUBJECT	AVOID ASKING	PREFERRED	COMMENT
Name	about name change whether it was changed by court order, marriage, or other reason maiden name Christian name		if needed for a reference, to check on previously held jobs or on educational credentials
Address	for addresses outside Canada	ask place and duration of current or recent addresses	
Age	for birth certificates, baptismal records, or about age in general age or birthdate	ask applicants if they have reached age (minimum or maximum) for work as defined by law	if precise age required for benefits plans or other legitimate purposes it can be determined after selection
Sex	Mr/Mrs/Miss/Ms males or females to fill in different or coded applications if male or female on applications about pregnancy, childbirth or childcare arrangements; includes asking if birth control is used or child bearing plans	can ask applicant if the attendance requirements or minimum service commitment can be met	any applicants can be addressed during interviews or in correspondence without using courtesy titles such as Mr/Mrs/Miss
Marital Status	whether applicant is single, married, divorced, engaged, separated, widowed or living common-law whether an applicant's spouse is subject to transfer about spouse's employment	ask whether there are any known circumstances that might prevent completion of a minimum service commitment, for example	if transfer or travel is part of the job, the applicant can be asked if this would cause a problem information on dependents for benefits can be determined after selection
Disability	for listing of all disabilities, limitations or health problems whether applicant drinks or uses drugs	ask if applicant has any condition that could affect ability to do the job	a disability is only relevant to job ability if it: – threatens the safety of property of others

Figure 6.1

A Guide to Screening and Selection in Employment. (*continued*)

SUBJECT	AVOID ASKING	PREFERRED	COMMENT
Disability (*continued*)	whether applicant has ever received psychiatric care or been hospitalized for emotional problems	ask if the applicant has any condition which should be considered in selection	– prevents the applicant from safe and adequate job performance even if reasonable efforts were made to accommodate the disability
Medical Information	if currently under physician's care name of family doctor if receiving counselling or therapy		medical exams should be preferably conducted after selection and only if an employee's condition is related to the job duties. Offers of employment can be made conditional on successful completion of a medical
Affiliations	for list of club or organizational memberships	membership in professional associations or occupational groups can be asked if a job requirement	applicants can decline to list any affiliation that might indicate a prohibited ground
Pardoned Conviction	whether an applicant has ever been convicted if an applicant has ever been arrested does applicant have a criminal record	if bonding is a job requirement ask if applicant is eligible	inquiries about criminal record/convictions— even those which have been pardoned—are discouraged unless related to job duties
References			the same restrictions that apply to questions asked of applicants apply when asking for employment references
Family Status	number of children or dependents about arrangements for child care	if the employer has a policy against the hiring of close relatives, an applicant can be asked about kinship to other employees	contacts for emergencies and/or details on dependents can be determined after selection
National or Ethnic Origin	about birthplace, nationality of ancestors, spouse or other relatives whether born in Canada if naturalized or landed immigrants for proof of citizenship	since those who are entitled to work in Canada must be citizens, landed immigrants or holders of valid work permits, applicants can be asked if they are legally entitled to work in Canada	documentation of eligibility to work (ie. papers, visas, etc.) can be requested after selection

<u>**Figure 6.1**</u>

A Guide to Screening and Selection in Employment. (*continued*)

SUBJECT	AVOID ASKING	PREFERRED	COMMENT
Military Service	about military service in other countries	inquiry about Canadian military service where employment preference is given to veterans, by law	
Language	mother tongue where language skills obtained	ask if applicant understands, writes or speaks languages which are required for job	testing or scoring applicants for language proficiency is not permitted unless fluency is job-related
Race or Colour	any inquiry which indicates race or colour, including colour of eyes, skin or hair colour		information required for security clearances or similar purposes can be obtained after selection
Photographs	for photo to be attached to application or sent to interviewer before interview		photos for security passes or company files can be taken after selection
Religion	about religious affiliation, church membership, frequency of church attendance if applicant will work a specific religious holiday for references from clergy or religious leader		employers are to reasonably accommodate religious needs of workers
Height and Weight			no inquiry unless there is evidence that they are bona fide occupational requirements

Source: *Reproduced with permission from the Canadian Human Rights Commission and the Minister of Supply and Services Canada, 1993.*

phases of the selection process or a check on its validity. The rationale is that people who do the job well during the probationary period are likely to do so over the long term. Joan Milne, President of Taylor Enterprises, a large Toronto-based association management firm, has stressed the importance of probation: ". . . at Taylor Enterprises we find that the probationary period is the best way to find out what a person is really like. Probationary periods are an essential part of the hiring process."[7]

Even in unionized firms, a new employee typically is not protected by the union–management agreement until after a certain probationary period of from

Figure 6-2

The Selection Process

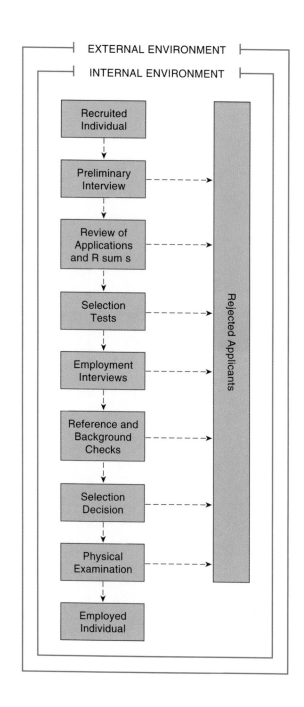

60 to 90 days. During that time, an employee may be terminated with little or no justification, although terminations at the very end of the probation period have been challenged. When the probationary period is over, however, firing a marginal employee may prove to be quite difficult. Firms with collective agreements must be especially careful to select the most productive workers. Once they come under the union–management agreement, its terms must be followed in changing the status of a worker.

Preliminary Interview

The selection process often begins with a preliminary interview, designed to screen out clearly unqualified applicants. At this stage, the interviewer asks a few straightforward questions. For instance, a position may require considerable work experience. If the interview fails to reveal relevant experience, any further discussion wastes both the firm's and the applicant's time.

A preliminary interview can have other benefits. A skilled interviewer, for example, may be able to steer the prospective employee to a more appropriate opening within the firm.

Applications of Employment

An early step in the selection process may be completing an application form. This step may come before or after the preliminary interview or, if preliminary interviews are not used, before or after the employment interview, depending upon whether or not a résumé has been submitted.

A well-designed and properly used application form can save time. Because essential information is included and presented in a standardized format, it can be more effective than résumés in reducing dozens of applicants to a few bona fide candidates. The specific type of information requested on an application for employment may vary from firm to firm, but sections are usually provided for name, address, telephone number, education, and work history. Two more items should be standard: a statement asking the applicant to certify that everything on the form is true and an authorization to check references.[8]

An employment application form must meet not only the firm's information needs but also human rights requirements. Potentially discriminatory questions about such factors as gender, race, age, and number of children living at home must not appear on the form. An example of a properly designed application form is shown in Figure 6-3. Some companies have terminals or an Internet site on which applicants can complete a job application form.

The information contained in a completed employment application is compared to the job description to determine whether or not a potential match exists between the firm's requirements and the applicant's qualifications. A few human resource departments have also established optical scanning programs that can handle the first-level application screening. These programs may also scan applications for other jobs the applicant may be qualified to fill. This comprehensive approach is not only more objective, but also less expensive than conventional screening systems.[9]

HR Web Wisdom

http: www.pearsoned.ca/ mondy

Résumé Tips
Here are some tips on preparing a better résumé and improving your work search.

Résumés

A **résumé** is a common tool for job applicants to present their education background, skills and competencies, work history, and qualifications. Even when résumés are not required by prospective employers, they are frequently submitted by job seekers. Although there are no hard and fast rules for designing résumés, some general guidelines can be followed, depending on the type and level of position sought. An example of a résumé submitted by a recent graduate

Résumé: A common method job applicants use to present their education background, skills and competencies, work history and qualifications.

Figure 6-3

An Application for
Employment

POSITION VACANCY APPLICATION

Position Vacancy Number _____   Position Title _____

Department/Faculty _____

Résumé attached   ☐ Yes   ☐ No

Are you currently working for The XYZ Corporation?   ☐ Yes   ☐ No

Have you previously worked for The XYZ Corporation?   ☐ Yes   ☐ No

PERSONAL DATA

Name _____
        Family Name   Given Names

Address _____
        Number and Street   City   Province   Postal Code

Telephone Number _____
        Home   Business

Are you legally entitled to work in Canada?   ☐ Yes   ☐ No

EDUCATION

Institution Attended	Grade, Degree, Diploma or Certificate Completed	Course or Area of Study
Elementary School		
Secondary School		
Community School		
University		
Post Graduate		

List any other special training or educational experience completed, for instance, certificates, apprenticeships, seminars, conferences:

_____
_____
_____

EMPLOYMENT HISTORY

List previous employment in order, beginning with present or last employer. Your present employer will not be contacted without your approval.

Employer _____   Started: Month/Year _____ Left: Month/Year _____

Address _____   Reason for Leaving _____

_____   Main Duties _____

Position _____ Salary _____   _____

Department _____   _____

Supervisor's Name and Title _____   _____

Supervisor's Business Telephone Number _____

May we contact the employer?   ☐ Yes ☐ No   *(Note: at least three similar sections would be included)*

GENERAL

Please detail any other relevant qualifications you have, for example, volunteer work experience, supervisory experience, promotions received, computer hardware and software knowledge, languages, equipment operated:

_____
_____
_____

Why have you applied for this position? Discuss some of your key reasons such as qualifications, experience, special interests, or opportunities. Are there any additional comments you wish to make to support your application?

_____
_____
_____

At what salary or rate of pay would you expect to start? $ _____

DECLARATION

I certify that the information provided in this application form is accurate and complete. I am aware that misrepresentation or falsification may result in rejection of my application or dismissal from employment.

Date _____   Signature _____

for a position in a public accounting firm is shown in Figure 6-4. As you see in this example, white space makes the résumé easier to read. The current and permanent addresses and telephone numbers of the applicant are prominently located. An objective statement is written to describe the type of opportunity desired. As most recent graduates are being hired for their potential value to a firm, education is a vital factor at this stage of their careers, and the applicant's education level is shown next. Work experience follows. This should be shown in reverse chronological order, with the most recent experience shown first.

Figure 6-4

Example of Résumé for an Entry–Level Position

HENRY DUPONT

Current Address:	Permanent Address:
15 Ridgewood Court	561 Springer Ave.
London, Ont.	Vancouver, BC
N6H 4N1	V5B 3R8
705-594-3869	604-876-5468

OBJECTIVE: To obtain an entry-level position in a Public Accounting firm.

EDUCATION: **Master of Business Administration**, December 1994
        University of Western Ontario
        Bachelor of Science in Business Administration, May 1992
        University of New Brunswick
        Concentration: Individual and Corporate Tax with emphasis on Management Information Systems
        Cumulative GPA: 3.7

HONOURS: Dean's List in Accounting and Finance
        Full Academic Scholarship
        President of Summer Conference Program

ACCOMPLISHMENTS: Conducted TQM seminars
        Successfully completed ISO-9000 courses
        Graduate-Assistant to the Associate Dean

EXPERIENCE: ASSISTANT ADMINISTRATOR

3/95 – Present   Touch of Class Foods Corporation
(full time)   Accounting Department
        • responsible for maintaining A/P and A/R ledgers
        • originated a responsive invoice program
        • prepared corporate tax returns and all schedules
        • oversaw intern program
        • initiated ISO-9000 Certifications in all areas of plant production

Summer 1993   **PERSONAL ASSISTANT**
Spring 1994   Mr. Charles Brandon
        Park Board of Trustees
        • Research and Development with City Sewer District
        • Assisted with general accounting procedures
        • Assisted with customer related issues
        • Assisted with the allocation of public funds

COMPUTER SKILLS: Microsoft Word, AmiPro, WordPerfect 5.1 - 6.1, Lotus 1 2 3, Microsoft Excel, Quattropro, Windows and Window Applications

AFFILIATIONS: ISO-9000 Certified Consultant
        TQM National Association

REFERENCES: Available upon request

Unwisely, many prospective employers spend little time reading résumés. In the few minutes some recruiters spend scanning a résumé, they have to determine the extent to which the applicant's qualifications meet the requirements of the job. It is imperative, therefore, that the résumé be concise. If the résumé is targeted to a specific job opening, it should reflect the skills and abilities of the applicant as they apply to the open position. A typical college or university graduate's résumé should be only one to two pages. The résumé should be neat, and grammatical errors must be avoided. A single error here can mean immediate rejection.

The experienced professional's résumé differs somewhat from that of a new graduate. For example, in lieu of an objective statement, a summary of several skills related to requirements of the open position would be more appropriate. Although education may still be an important factor, the candidate's experience should take priority and appear next. Rather than focusing on responsibilities in each previously-held position, the applicant should emphasize competencies and accomplishments. Self-improvement activities, rather than hobbies, should be included. This résumé may be longer than one page, while still being concise.[10]

Applicants must be careful that all the information is accurate. Résumé fraud is "being done regularly," according to Allen Beech, President of Drake Beam Morin of Canada Ltd., who reported that about 15 percent of the résumés he reviews were "in some way fraudulent."[11] But "one silly, stupid mistake can cost you the job. It is grounds for being fired . . . because you've intentionally lied," said David Sanderson-Kirby, vice-president of Sanderson Kirby and Associates, an executive career counselling firm.[12]

Employment Selection Tests

Selection tests are often used to assist in assessing an applicant's qualifications and potential for success. In Canada, few laws or regulations govern testing. In all jurisdictions, however, complaints can be made to the relevant Human Rights Commission if an applicant feels that a pre-employment test is written in such a way as to discriminate against job seekers because of country of origin, disability, or any of the other criteria listed in human rights legislation. In fact, "a major argument used successfully in the courts against testing was that the questions were biased in favour of white, middle-class Canadian-born candidates and discriminated against minorities and new immigrants."[13]

Evidence suggests that the use of tests is widespread, especially in the public sector and in medium-sized and large companies. Large organizations are likely to have trained specialists to run their testing programs.[14]

In addition to a physical examination (which we discuss further on), applicants can be asked to undergo a number of tests as a precondition of employment, including cognitive aptitude tests, job knowledge tests, personality tests, psychomotor abilities tests, work-sample tests, vocational interests tests, drug testing, and in some cases testing for AIDS.

Cognitive Aptitude Tests

Cognitive aptitude tests: Tests that measure an individual's ability to learn as well as to perform a job.

Cognitive aptitude tests measure an individual's ability to learn, as well as to perform a job. This type of test is particularly appropriate for making a selection

TRENDS and INNOVATIONS

Electronic Résumés

The RRSP season was just around the corner. Mackenzie Financial Corp. needed more finance professionals and they didn't have much time. Traditional recruiting would not be the solution. Placing an advertisement in a daily newspaper, for example, was time-consuming and expensive, costing Mackenzie anywhere from $6000 to $12 000 per ad. An outside recruitment agency was also out of the question. "This could easily set the company back as much as $17 000 per hire," recalled David Coward, manager of human resources at Mackenzie. He knew his eight-member human resource team needed a more effective and cost-efficient system of recruiting. Their answer was to turn to outsourcing and E-Cruiter.com for help.

E-Cruiter designed a customized career site for Mackenzie that allowed job seekers to apply on-line. In minutes the HR staff were able to cut and paste a job description onto the site and away it went across the world, that same day. Incoming applications were automatically scanned, sorted and ranked. Interviews could be scheduled with the click of a mouse. E-Cruiter automatically posted job openings to other Internet career sites such as Careermosaic and GlobeCareers. It also hosted the site, relieving Mackenzie of all kinds of technical issues. According to Coward, the results were almost immediate. The hiring cycle was reduced from 12 weeks to three—and what's more, the system saved thousands of dollars in recruitment costs. Evelyn Ledsham at E-Cruiter says that companies like Mackenzie usually see a return on their investment—ranging from $35 000 to $75 000—in two to six months.

Was this customized career site also better for job seekers? Just ask Bina Kadakia. She had sent out over 500 job applications with no positive response. Bina then clicked on to Mackenzie's site and in less than two weeks she had a contract job.

Source: Cindy Waxer, "Hired help sets sites on jobs," The Globe and Mail, October 28, 1999, T8.

from a group of inexperienced candidates. Job-related abilities may be classified as verbal, numerical, perceptual speed, spatial, and reasoning.

Job Knowledge Tests

Job knowledge tests are designed to measure a candidate's knowledge of job duties. Various kinds of tests are available commercially, but job analysis results may also be used to design a test specifically for any job. While such tests frequently involve written responses, they may be administered orally. Regardless of the format, they contain key questions that serve to distinguish experienced, skilled workers from the rest.

> **Job knowledge tests:** Tests designed to measure a candidate's knowledge of the duties of a job.

Personality Tests

Personality tests measure a person's motivation, flexibility, and ability to work in harmony with others. Some firms use these tests to classify personality types, such as introvert or extrovert. This information may help managers

> **Personality tests:** Tests that measure individual motivation, flexibility, and ability to work in harmony with others.

match people for teams, perhaps choosing a diverse group for creativity or a compatible group for a task-oriented team.[15] As selection tools, personality tests have been controversial because it is not clear that they measure what they are supposed to measure. Nevertheless, at least one recent study indicated that the use of personality tests was on the rise. Eighteen percent of the firms surveyed asked hourly workers to take a personality test and 22 percent of the firms ask managers to take one.[16]

Psychomotor Abilities Tests

Psychomotor abilities tests measure strength, coordination, and dexterity. The development of tests to determine these physical abilities has been accelerated by the growth in technology manufacturing. For example, some tasks are so delicate that magnifying lenses must be used. While standardized tests are not available to cover all physical competencies, it is feasible to measure those necessary for many routine production jobs and possibly some office jobs.

Work-Sample Tests

Work-sample tests require an applicant to perform a task or set of tasks representative of the job. Recent evidence suggests they are extremely valid, reduce test anxiety and are acceptable to applicants.

Vocational Interest Tests

Vocational interest tests indicate the occupation in which a person is most interested and is most likely to be satisfied. These tests compare the individual's interests with those of successful employees in a specific job. Although interest tests may have some application in employee selection, their primary use has been in counselling and vocational guidance.

Drug Testing

Few issues generate more controversy today than drug testing. Proponents of drug testing programs contend that they are necessary to ensure workplace safety, security, and productivity. They are also viewed as an accurate measure of drug use and as a means to deter it. Critics of drug testing argue just as vigorously that drug testing is an unjustifiable intrusion into an employee's private life.[17]

The entire issue of drug testing is a legal and ethical tangle that will take some time to sort out. For example, in the early 1990s, two prominent Canadian lawyers, Robert Solomon and Sydney Usprich, published a paper in *Business Quarterly* in which they tried to sort out the complicated legal and moral arguments surrounding employment drug testing (EDT). Even these experts were forced to admit that the question of EDT does not permit simplistic answers. Compounding the difficulty is the overriding problem of striking the proper balance between a worker's legitimate privacy rights and an employer's valid concerns for safety and efficiency in the workplace. Given the various legal issues and the lack of definitive precedents, it is difficult to formulate a policy that will not be challengeable on some level.[18]

Testing for Acquired Immune Deficiency Syndrome (AIDS)

In Canada, people with AIDS and those who test positive for the HIV virus cannot (in most cases) be denied employment as a result of this medical con-

Psychomotor abilities tests: Aptitude tests that measure strength, coordination, and dexterity.

Work-sample tests: Tests requiring the identification of a task or set of tasks that are representative of a particular job.

Vocational interest tests: A method of determining the occupation in which a person has the greatest interest and from which the person is most likely to receive satisfaction.

Mei's Dilemma[19]

Mei manages a unit at a large call centre in the financial services industry. Ian, one of the part-time customer service representatives, has recently learned he has AIDS. Several staffers, all of whom handle phone calls from customers, have told Mei they consider the workplace unsafe because of Ian's presence. One representative, Pat, has threatened to resign if Ian is not removed from the workplace. Employees are waiting to see what Mei will do.

As an HR manager, how would you advise Mei?

dition. Only in certain circumstances can the condition be taken into account, such as in some health care settings or in work requiring international travel where a foreign government might deny entry to HIV-positive employees. HIV testing, then, cannot be used as a selection tool except in these rare circumstances. HR professionals are well advised to solicit legal advice before attempting any such test.

Characteristics of Properly Designed Selection Tests

Properly designed selection tests are *standardized, objective, based on sound norms, reliable,* and *valid.*

Standardization refers to the uniformity of the procedures and conditions related to administering tests. If the performances of several applicants on the same test are to be compared fairly, all must take the test under conditions that are as close to identical as possible. For example, the content of instructions provided and the time allowed must be the same. The physical environment must also be similar. If one person takes a test in a noisy room and another takes it in a quiet environment, differences in test results are likely.

Objectivity in testing is achieved when everyone who is evaluating or scoring a test obtains the same results. Multiple-choice and true-false tests are said to be objective. The person taking the test either chooses the correct answer or does not. There is no room for normative judgment. Scoring true or false tests is a highly mechanical process, which lends itself to objective grading.

A **norm** provides a standard frame of reference for comparing an applicant's performance with that of others. Specifically, a norm reflects the distribution of many scores obtained by people similar to the applicant being tested. In theory, scores will tend to be distributed according to the normal probability curve shown in Figure 6-5. Standard deviations measure the amount of dispersion of the data. In a normalized test, approximately 68.3 percent of the scores will fall within one standard deviation from the mean. Individuals scoring in this range would be considered average. Individuals achieving scores outside the range of two standard deviations would probably be highly unsuccessful or highly successful, depending on the particular criterion used.

When a sufficient number of employees are performing the same or similar

Standardization: The degree of uniformity of the procedures and conditions related to administering a test.

Objectivity: The condition that is achieved when all individuals scoring a given test obtain the same results.

Norm: A distribution that provides a frame of reference for comparing an applicant's performance with that of others.

work, employers can standardize their own tests. Typically, this is not the case, and a national norm for a particular test must be used. A prospective employee takes the test, the score obtained is compared to the norm, and the significance of the test score is determined.

Reliability: The extent to which a selection test provides consistent results.

Validity: The extent to which a test measures what it purports to measure.

Reliability is the extent to which a selection test provides consistent results. Reliability data reveal the degree of confidence that can be placed in a test. If a test has low reliability, its validity as a predictor will also be low.

The basic requirement for a selection test is that it be valid.[23] **Validity** is the extent to which a test measures what it purports to measure. For example, if a selection test cannot indicate ability to perform the job, it has no value as a predictor.

Validity is commonly reported as a correlation coefficient, which summarizes the relationship between two variables. A coefficient of 0 shows no relationship, while a coefficient of either +1.0 or -1.0 indicates a perfect relationship—one positive and the other negative. If a test is designed to predict job performance and validity studies of the test indicate a high correlation coefficient, most prospective employees who score high on the test will probably later prove to be high performers. Naturally, no test will be 100 percent accurate, yet organizations strive for the highest feasible coefficient. The cumulative body of previous research indicates that tests yield correlation coefficients of 0.30 to 0.60, depending on the test and the job.[24]

Cutoff score: The score below which an applicant will not be considered for employment.

After a test has been shown to be valid, an appropriate cutoff score must be established. A **cutoff score** is the score below which an applicant will not be considered for employment. Cutoff scores will vary over time because they are directly related to the selection ratio. The more individuals apply for a job, the

Figure 6-5

A Normal Probability Curve

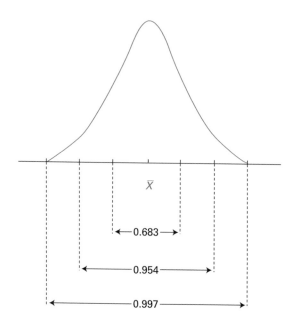

$\bar{X}$ = Mean or average score
68.3 percent of scores will be ± one standard deviation from the mean
95.4 percent of scores will be ± two standard deviations from the mean
99.7 percent of scores will be ± three standard deviations from the mean

more selective the firm can be and, therefore, the higher the cutoff scores. Cutoff scores should normally be set to reflect a reasonable expectation of acceptable proficiency.

Advantages and Disadvantages of Selection Tests

Advantages. Testing has remained an important selection tool because it is one of the most reliable and accurate means of choosing candidates from a pool of applicants.[22] As with all selection procedures, it is important to identify the essential functions of each job and to determine the skills needed to perform them. Thus, the most widely-used tests evaluate specific skills like keyboarding speed and accuracy. In fact, abilities testing can even help to select workers with the capability to perform safely a variety of physically demanding tasks.[23] Fortunately there is a wide range of tests available, allowing some companies to conduct a battery of skill, aptitude, and personality tests.[24]

Disadvantages. Job performance is related primarily to an individual's ability and motivation to do the job. Selection tests may predict an applicant's ability to do the job but they are less successful in indicating how much the applicant will want to perform it. For one reason or another, many employees never seem to reach their full potential. The factors related to success on the job are so numerous and complex that selection may always be more of an art than a science.

Another potential problem, related primarily to personality tests and interest inventories, has to do with applicants' honesty. An applicant may be strongly motivated to respond to questions untruthfully or to provide answers that he or she believes the interviewer expects. To prevent such behaviour, some tests have built-in lie detection scales, but intelligent people often detect them.

Yet another common problem is test anxiety. Applicants often become quite fearful when confronting yet another hurdle that might eliminate them from consideration. The test administrator's reassuring manner and a well-organized testing operation should serve to reduce this threat.

The dual problems of hiring the unqualified or less than qualified while rejecting qualified candidates will still exist regardless of the procedures followed. Managers can minimize such errors only through the use of well-developed tests administered by competent professionals. Even the best tests, however, are not perfect predictors. For these reasons, tests alone should never be used as the entire selection process; rather, test results should be considered in conjunction with other selection tools.

The Employment Interview

The **employment interview** is a job-related conversation in which the interviewer and applicant exchange information and expectations. It is especially significant because the applicants who reach this stage are considered to be the most promising candidates. Historically, interviews have not been valid predictors of success on the job. Most interviews have correlation coefficients in the 0.00 to 0.30 range.[25] Nevertheless, they continue to be the primary method used to evaluate applicants, used by virtually every company in Canada.

Employment interview:
A job oriented conversation in which an interviewer and an applicant exchange information and employment expectations.

Interview Planning

Interview planning is essential to effective employment interviews. The physical location of the interview should be both pleasant and private, providing for a minimum of interruptions. The interviewer should have a pleasant personality, empathy, and the ability to listen and communicate effectively. He or she should become familiar with the applicant's qualifications. As preparation for the interview, a job profile should be developed based on the job description. After job requirements have been listed, it is helpful to have an interview checklist that includes these types of information:

- comparison of a candidate's application and résumé with job requirements.

- list of specific questions related to the skills, education and experience sought.

- a brief plan to present the position, company, division, and department.

- pre-prepared questions about past applicant behaviour, not what future behaviour might be.

Content of the Interview

After establishing rapport with the applicant, the interviewer seeks additional job-related information to complement data provided by other selection tools. The interview can clarify certain points, reveal new information, and fill in data needed to make a sound selection decision. It is also important to inform the applicant about the company, the position, and job expectations of the candidate. Other areas typically covered include:

- **Occupational experience.** The interviewer will explore the candidate's demonstrated knowledge, skills, abilities, and willingness to handle responsibility. Although successful performance in one job does not guarantee success in another, it does provide an indication of the person's ability and willingness to work.

- **Academic achievement.** In the absence of significant work experience, a person's academic record takes on greater importance. Marks, however, should be considered in light of other factors. For example, involvement in work or extracurricular activities may have affected an applicant's grades.

- **Interpersonal skills.** An individual may possess important technical skills significant to accomplishing a job. However, a person who cannot work well with others is not likely to succeed on the job. This is especially true in today's world with increasing use of teams.

- **Personal qualities.** Personal qualities normally observed during the interview include physical appearance, speaking ability, vocabulary, poise, adaptability, and assertiveness. These attributes, as with all selection criteria, should be considered only if they are relevant to job performance.

- **Organizational fit.** A hiring criterion that is becoming much more prominent is organizational fit. Organizational fit is ill defined but refers to management's perception of the degree to which the prospective employee will fit in, for example, with the firm's culture or value system.[27]

Interviewee Objectives

Remember that interviewees also have expectations. These may be summarized as follows:[26]

- to be listened to and understood
- to have ample opportunity to present their qualifications
- to be treated fairly and with respect
- to gather information about the job and the company
- to make an informed decision concerning the desirability of the job

Types of Interviews

Interviews may be broadly classified as structured, unstructured, or behavioural description—which is a particular type of structured interview.

The unstructured (nondirective) interview. In the **unstructured** (nondirective) **interview**, the interviewer asks probing, open-ended questions. This type of interview is comprehensive, and the interviewer encourages the applicant to do much of the talking. The nondirective interview is often time-consuming and obtains different information from different candidates. The diversity adds to the potential legal woes. For example, unsuccessful applicants subjected to this interviewing approach may later claim in court that the reason for their failure to get the job was the employer's use of this information.

> **Unstructured interview:** A meeting with a job applicant during which the interviewer asks probing open-ended questions.

The structured (directive or patterned) interview. The **structured** (directive or patterned) **interview**. The structured interview consists of a series of job-related questions that are asked of each applicant for a particular job. Although interviews have historically been very poor predictors for making good selection decisions, the use of structured interviews does increase reliability and accuracy by reducing the subjectivity and inconsistency of unstructured interviews.

> **Structured interview:** A process in which an interviewer consistently presents the same series of job-related questions to each applicant for a particular job.

A structured job interview typically contains four types of questions:

- *Situational* questions, which pose a typical job situation to determine what the applicant did in a similar situation;
- *Job knowledge* questions, which probe the applicant's job-related knowledge. These questions may relate to basic educational skills or complex scientific or managerial skills.
- *Job-sample simulation* questions involving situations in which an applicant is likely to be required to perform a sample task from the job; and
- *Worker requirements* questions seeking to determine the applicant's willingness to conform to the requirements of the job. For example, the interviewer may ask whether the applicant is willing to perform repetitive work or move to another city.

Behaviour description interview: A structured interview that uses questions designed to probe an applicant's past behaviour in specific situations.

Behaviour description interview. The **behaviour description interview** is a structured interview that uses questions designed to probe the candidate's past behaviour in specific situations. It avoids making judgments about applicants' personalities and avoids hypothetical and self-evaluative questions. The situational behaviours are carefully selected for their relevance to job success. Questions are formed from the behaviours by asking applicants how they performed in the described situation. For example, a candidate for an engineering position might be asked, "Tell me about a time when you had to make an important decision without having all the information you needed." Benchmark or model answers derived from behaviours of successful employees are prepared for use in rating applicant responses.[28]

Methods of Interviewing

Interviews may be conducted in several ways. The level of the job to be filled and the labour market to be tapped determine the most appropriate approach. Three of the most popular formats are one-on-one, group, and board interviews. Some firms unwisely use the stress interview and others have experimented with videotaped and computer interviews.

In a typical employment interview, the applicant meets one-on-one with an interviewer. As the interview may be a highly emotional occasion for the applicant, meeting alone with the interviewer is often less threatening.

Group interview: A meeting in which several job applicants interact in the presence of one or more company representatives.

In a **group interview,** several applicants interact in the presence of one or more company representatives. This approach may provide useful insights into the candidates' interpersonal competence as they engage in group discussion. Another advantage of this technique is that it saves time for busy professionals and executives. Group interviews may be used in combination with other formats.

Board interview: A meeting in which one candidate is interviewed by several representatives of a company.

In a **board interview**, one candidate is interviewed by several representatives of the firm. Although a thorough examination of the applicant is likely, the interviewee's anxiety level is often quite high. In some cases—usually at the executive level—a board interview may even include the interviewee's spouse or family. Naturally, the amount of time devoted to a board interview will differ depending on the type and level of job.

Stress interview: A type of interview that intentionally creates anxiety to determine how a job applicant will react in certain types of situations.

Most interview sessions are designed to minimize the candidate's stress level. In contrast, the **stress interview** intentionally creates anxiety to determine how an applicant will react to stress on the job. The interviewer deliberately makes the candidate uncomfortable by asking blunt and sometimes discourteous questions. Many human resource professionals believe the stress interview to be not only inconsiderate but ineffective.

Some firms have also experimented with videotaped and computer interviews in an attempt to reduce selection costs—especially when a national search is required. However, most HR experts agree that the selection process is far too important to rely on these types of impersonal techniques.

Potential Problems with Interviewing

Since the interview is a form of test, it should be subject to the same validity requirements as any other step in the selection process. Few managers, however, are willing to pay the cost of validating interviews, which can be done only through extensive, long-term follow-up. There is significant evidence, however, that if two managers in a firm interview the same applicant at different times, the outcomes may differ.

In addition, the interview is perhaps more vulnerable to charges of discrimination than any other tool used in the selection process. In most cases, there is little or no documentation of the questions asked or of the answers received. The interviewer may ask irrelevant questions that would never appear on an application form. Some interviewers ask questions that are not job related or that reflect their personal biases.[29] Because there is no record of the interview, the dubious questions go unchallenged. Nevertheless, interviewing in this manner is risky and can lead to charges of discrimination. Since an interview is a test, all questions should be job related.

Figure 6-6 shows a number of potential problems that can threaten the success of employment interviews.

Reference and Background Checks

Reference checks include conversations with former employers or with people named by the applicant to verify information provided by the applicant and to gain additional insight. Personal reference checks may allow the firm to check the information furnished by the applicant and may provide further information. Applicants are often required to submit the names of several referees. An obvious flaw with this step in the selection process is that virtually everyone can name three or four people who will make favourable statements about him or her. Furthermore, personal references are likely to focus on the candidate's personal characteristics, not on objective, job-related data. For this reason, most organizations place more emphasis on investigations of previous employment.

Employment reference checks or background checks seek data from work-related referees (including previous employers), usually supplied by the applicant. The intensity of these background investigations depends on the level of responsibility inherent in the position to be filled. As with the personal reference, the main problem faced by an interviewer is obtaining an objective account of the applicant's work history. The reference check is best done only after a tentative hiring decision has been made, or after a short list of two or three candidates have been interviewed.

Today, most references are checked by phone, perhaps because of the perceived legal liability (although in fact, one is as responsible for untruthful spoken references as for written ones). Before checking references, the employer should ask the applicant for permission in writing, along with a signed statement not to hold referees liable for their opinions (note, though, that this latter requirement has not been tested extensively in Canadian courts). Then, the check should be made by two people, using an extension phone.

Reference checks:
Conversations with former employers or with people named by the applicant to verify the information provided by the applicant and to gain additional insight.

The Selection Decision

After obtaining and evaluating information about the finalists in a job selection process, the manager must take the most critical step of all: making the actual hiring decision. The final choice will be made from among those still in the

INAPPROPRIATE QUESTIONS

The responses generated by inappropriate questions create a legal liability for the employer. The most basic interviewing rule is, *Ask only job-related questions!*

PREMATURE JUDGEMENTS

Research suggests that interviewers often make judgments about candidates in the first few minutes of the interview, failing to consider a great deal of potentially valuable information.

INTERVIEWER DOMINATION

In successful interviews, relevant information flows both ways. Therefore, interviewers must learn to be good listeners as well as suppliers of information.

INCONSISTENT QUESTIONS

If interviewers ask all applicants essentially the same questions in the same sequence, all the applicants can be judged on the same basis. This enables better decisions to be made.

CENTRAL TENDENCY

When interviewers rate virtually all candidates as average, they fail to differentiate between strong and weak candidates.

HALO ERROR

When interviewers permit a single characteristic or a combination of a few characteristics to influence their overall impression of a person, the best applicant may not be selected.

CONTRAST EFFECTS

An error in judgment may occur when, for example, an interviewer meets with several poorly qualified applicants and then confronts a mediocre candidate. By comparison, the last applicant may appear to be better qualified than he or she actually is.

INTERVIEWER BIAS

Interviewers must understand and acknowledge their own prejudices and learn to deal with them. The only valid bias for an interviewer is to favour the best-qualified candidate for the open position.

LACK OF TRAINING

When the cost of making poor selection decisions is considered, the expense of training employees in interviewing skills can be easily justified.

BEHAVIOUR SAMPLE

Even if an interviewer spent a week with an applicant, the behaviour sample might be too small to judge the candidate's qualifications properly. In addition, the candidate's behaviour during an interview is seldom typical or natural.

NONVERBAL COMMUNICATION

Interviewers should make a conscious effort to view themselves as applicants do in order to avoid sending inappropriate or unintended nonverbal signals.

running after reference checks, selection tests, and interview information have been evaluated. The individual with the best overall qualifications may not be hired. Rather, the right person to hire is the one whose qualifications most closely conform to the requirements of the open position and the organization. If a firm is going to invest thousands of dollars to recruit, select, and train an employee, the manager must hire the most qualified available candidate for the position.

Human resource professionals may be involved in all phases leading up to the final employment decision. However, especially for higher level positions, the person who normally makes the final selection is the manager who will be responsible for the new employee's performance. The operating manager will review results of the selection methods used. All will not likely be weighted the same. But which data are most predictive of job success? In a survey of more than 200 HR executives, work samples, references/recommendations, unstructured interviews and structured interviews were rated as above average in their ability to predict employees' job performance.[30]

Physical Examination

After the decision has been made to extend a job offer, the next phase of the selection process can involve a physical examination. Physical examinations are performed only if the job requires a clearly determined level of physical effort, or if there is some physical attribute crucial to job performance, such as the ability to climb telephone poles. Even if the examination reveals a condition that would interfere with required tasks, the individual can be rejected only if reasonable accommodations cannot be made to allow the employee to perform the work. Rejections based on physical inability then, must be studied carefully to ensure that "reasonable accommodation" cannot be made.

Notifying Candidates

The selection process results should be made known to candidates—both successful and unsuccessful—as soon as possible. Any delay may result in the firm's losing a prime candidate, as top prospects often have other employment options. As a matter of courtesy and good public relations, unsuccessful candidates should also be promptly notified.

If currently employed by another firm, the successful candidate customarily gives between two and four weeks' notice. Even after this notice, the individual may need some personal time to prepare for the new job. This transition time is particularly important if the new job requires a move to another city. Thus, the amount of time before the individual can join the firm is often considerable—but necessary.

The firm may also want the individual to delay the date of employment. If, for example, the new employee's first assignment upon joining the firm is to attend a training school, the organization may request that the individual delay joining the firm until the school begins. This practice, which would only benefit the company, should not be abused, especially if it places an undue hardship on the individual.

Applicants may be rejected during any phase of the selection process. Research has indicated that most people can accept losing if they lose fairly.[31]

Problems occur when the selection process appears to be less than objective. It is therefore important for firms to develop and use rational selection tools.

When considerable time has been spent on the individual in the selection process, a company representative may sit down with the applicant and explain why another person was offered the job. Increasingly, however, time constraints may force the firm to write a rejection letter. However, such a letter can still be personalized. A personal touch will often reduce the stigma of rejection and the chance that the applicant will have negative feelings about the company. An impersonal letter is likely to have the opposite effect. The best an organization can do is to make selection decisions objectively and to hope that most individuals can, with time, accept the fact that they were not chosen.

A GLOBAL
PERSPECTIVE

Global Selection

Global staffing has been called the Achilles heel of international business. Inappropriate selections are often made that hamper the multinational operation. Although specific failure rates vary by country and company, as many as 40 percent of all expatriate assignments fail due to poor performance or the inability of the expatriate to adjust to the foreign environment. Less than one-third of expatriate failures are considered to be job related.

There are three primary reasons why North Americans who are sent overseas fail: 1) their families are misjudged, or are not even considered at the time of selection; 2) they are selected because of their domestic reputation; or 3) they lack adequate cross-cultural training. To overcome these obstacles, human resource managers should plan carefully to ensure that people chosen possess certain characteristics. Obviously, they must be technically qualified to do the job, but managers seem to pay too little attention to other criteria. For example, few firms administer tests to determine the relational/cross-cultural/interpersonal skills of their selectees.

The process of selecting a current employee for a foreign posting should involve broad measurement and evaluation of the candidate's expertise. Psychological tests, stress tests, evaluations by the candidate's superiors, subordinates, peers, and acquaintances, and professional evaluations from licensed psychologists can all aid in ascertaining the candidate's current level of interpersonal and cross-cultural skills. The candidate's spouse and children should undergo modified versions of the selection process, since family members confront slightly different challenges than do employees.

An international manager should know something about history, particularly in countries with traditional homogeneous cultures; understand the economic and sociological structures of various countries; and be interested in the host country and willing to learn and use the language, Above all, a manager should respect differing philosophical and ethical approaches to living and to business practice.

SUMMARY

1. Define and briefly describe the need for employee selection.

An important HR function is selection: the process of choosing from a group of applicants the individual best suited for a particular position and organization. The goal of the selection process is to match people with jobs. Business objectives cannot be attained without competent people. If too many mediocre or poor performers are hired, a firm cannot be successful for long. A firm that selects qualified employees, therefore, reaps substantial benefits, which are repeated every year the employee is on the payroll.

2. Identify the environmental factors that affect the selection process.

Legal considerations, time constraints, organizational hierarchy, the applicant pool, and the sector of employment affect the selection process.

3. Outline a general framework for the selection process.

The selection process typically begins with a preliminary interview. Next, the firm's application for employment and/or applicant résumés will be reviewed. Then applicants progress through a series of selection tests, an employment interview, and reference and background checks. A final selection is then made, following which the selected candidate may be required to undergo a company physical examination.

Many firms use a probationary period, which may be either a substitute for certain phases of the selection process, or a check on its validity.

4. Explain the importance of a preliminary employment interview.

The initial screening removes individuals who clearly do not fulfill the position requirements. A side benefit is that some candidates may be directed to more suitable openings in the firm.

5. Identify the basic information contained in a company application for employment form and an employment résumé.

A typical application form asks for name, address, telephone number, education, work history, certification that everything on the form is true, and an authorization to check references.

The contents and format of a résumé will depend on the nature of the job and the particular applicant. However most résumés contain employment expectations, education background, skills and competencies, work history, and qualifications. If the résumé is targeted to a specific opening, it should reflect skills and abilities relevant to the position. The résumé should be accurate, concise, neat, and grammatically correct. A single error can mean immediate rejection.

6. Identify the various types of employment tests.

Employment tests include cognitive aptitude tests, job knowledge tests, personality tests, psychomotor abilities tests, work-sample tests, vocational interests tests, drug tests, and in some cases testing for AIDS (only appropriate when relevant to the job).

7. Describe the features of properly designed selection tests.

Properly designed selection tests are standardized, objective, based on sound norms, reliable, and valid. Standardization refers to the uniformity of the procedures and conditions related to administering tests. Objectivity in testing is achieved when everyone scoring a test obtains the same results. A norm provides a frame of reference for comparing an applicant's performance with that of others. Reliability is the extent to which a selection test provides consistent results. Validity is the extent to which a test measures what it purports to measure.

8. Identify the types of information that should be gained from the interview.

The interview should provide additional information about the candidate's occupational experience, academic achievement and competencies, interpersonal skills, personal qualities, and organizational fit—the degree to which the prospective employee will fit in with the firm's culture or value system. The interviewer should also try to respond to the interviewee's expectations

9. Describe the basic types of interviewing.

An unstructured interview is one in which probing, open-ended questions are asked. A structured interview consists of a series of job-related questions that are asked of each applicant for a particular job. The behaviour description interview is a variant of the structured interview that uses questions designed to probe the candidate's past behaviour in specific situations.

10. Describe the various methods of interviewing.

In a typical employment interview, the applicant meets one-on-one with an interviewer. In a group interview, several applicants interact in the presence of one or more company representatives. In a board interview, one candidate is quizzed by several interviewers. A stress interview intentionally creates anxiety to determine how an applicant will react in certain types of environments. With increasing pressure to reduce costs, some firms have experimented with videotaped and computer interviews.

11. Explain the potential problems of interviewing.

Few managers, are willing to pay the cost of validating interviews. In addition, the interview is perhaps more vulnerable to charges of discrimination than any other tool used in the selection process. Thus, in practice, interviewing is risky and can lead to charges of discrimination and legal action. Since an interview is a test, all questions should be job related.

12. Briefly explain the need for reference checks, physical examinations, and notification of candidates.

Personal and employment reference checks verify the information provided by the applicant and give further insight. Background employment checks, in particular, may be helpful in determining whether the person's past work experience is related to the qualifications needed for the new position and in avoiding charges of negligent hiring.

After a candidate has been selected, a physical examination may be necessary if the job requires a clearly determined level of physical effort, or if there is some physical attribute crucial to job performance. However, the applicant can be rejected only if reasonable accommodations cannot be made that allow the employee to perform the work.

The selected candidate should be offered the position as soon as possible to ensure availability. As a matter of courtesy and good public relations, the unsuccessful candidates should also be promptly notified.

QUESTIONS FOR REVIEW

1. Why is selection important and what basic steps are normally followed in the selection process?

2. Identify and describe the various factors outside the control of the human resource manager that could affect the selection process.

3. What would be the selection ratio if there were 15 applicants to choose from and only one position to fill? Interpret the meaning of this selection ratio.

4. What is the general purpose of the preliminary interview?

5. What types of questions should be asked on an application form?

6. Prepare an employment résumé for yourself.

7. Identify and describe the various types of employment tests.

8. What are the characteristics of a properly designed selection test?

9. What information should be gained from the employment interview?

10. Describe the various types and methods of interviewing.

11. What are the potential problems of interviewing?

12. Briefly explain the need for reference checks, physical examinations, and notification of candidates.

An Experiential Exercise

As all managers recognize, many factors must be considered in selecting employees. In this exercise, George Nakash has just been promoted, but before he starts his new job, he must choose his replacement. George's firm has an employment equity program, but currently there are few women in management. George has some excellent employees to choose from, but there are many factors to consider before a decision can be made.

Senior managers have made it clear that they expect George to select someone who can perform as well as he has over the last six years. The majority of the people he worked with on the line have made it clear that they want Sam. The women on the line have indicated to everyone who will listen that it is time for a female supervisor in at least one division. But it is George's decision and he must select the best person, regardless of any criticism he may receive.

Sam Craik, employed by the company for 11 years, is one possible candidate. He wants this promotion, needs the higher pay, wants the respect and influence to be gained, and admires the nice office that George has now. Sam is recognized as one of the most technically capable individuals in the division. He is from the old school of thought: We get things done through discipline, and we don't put up with people allowing their personal problems to interfere with work.

Frieda Lott, an employee for seven years, is another candidate for promotion. She wants the job primarily because she can do good work and represent the women on the line. She believes she can deal effectively with the personal problems of others. She is recognized as technically capable and has an undergraduate degree in management.

Fred Rogov, an employee of the company for six years, is the final candidate. He believes he should get the promotion primarily because he can do the best job. Fred is very capable, but not quite as familiar with all the technical aspects of the job as Frieda or Sam. He has a degree in liberal arts, but he is taking business classes at night. Fred is also actively involved in the community and has held various civic offices. Four individuals will have roles in this exercise: one as George Nakash, the current supervisor, and three as the candidates for promotion. Instructors will provide the participants with additional information necessary to complete the exercise.

Business First

As production manager for Thompson Manufacturing, Jack Tozer has the final authority to approve the hiring of any new supervisors who work for him. The human resource manager performs the initial screening of all prospective supervisors and then sends the most likely candidates to Jack for interviews.

One day recently, Jack received a call from Pete Pedersen, the human resource manager: "Jack, I've just spoken to a young woman who may be just who you're looking for to fill that final line supervisor position. She has some good work experience and it appears as if her head is screwed on straight. She's here right now and available if you could possibly see her." Jack hesitated a moment before answering, "Gee, Pete," he said, "I'm certainly busy today but I'll try to squeeze her in. Send her on down."

A moment later Daisey Wong, the new applicant, arrived at Jack's office and introduced herself. "Come on in, Daisey," said Jack. "I'll be right with you after I make a few phone calls."

Fifteen minutes later Jack finished the calls and began talking with Daisey. Jack was quite impressed. After a few minutes Jack's door opened and a supervisor yelled, "We have a problem on line number 1 and need your help."

Jack stood up and said, "Excuse me a minute, Daisey." Ten minutes later Jack returned, and the conversation continued for ten more minutes before a series of phone calls again interrupted them.

The same pattern of interruptions continued for the next hour. Finally Daisey looked at her watch and said, "I'm sorry, Mr. Tozer, but I have to pick up my husband." "Sure thing, Daisey," Jack said as the phone rang again. "Call me later today."

Questions

1. What specific policies should a company follow to avoid interviews like this one?

2. Explain why Jack, not Pete, should make the selection.

PART TWO CASE 2

Parma Cycle Company: Workers for the New Plant

Gene Beairsto, the corporate planner at Parma Cycle Company, was ecstatic as he talked with the human resource director, Jesse Heard, that Tuesday morning in early 1996. He had just received word that the board of directors had approved the plan for Parma's new eastern plant, to be located in Digby, Nova Scotia.

"I really appreciate your help on this, Jesse," Gene said. "Without the research you did on the human resource needs for the new plant, I don't think that it would have been approved."

"We still have a long way to go," said Jesse. "There's no doubt that we can construct the building and install the machinery, but getting skilled workers in Digby may not be so easy."

"Well," said Gene, "the results of the labour survey that you did in the area last year indicate that we'll be able to get by. Anyway, some of the people here at Parma surely will agree to transfer."

"When is the new plant scheduled to open?" asked Jesse.

Gene replied, "The building will be finished in June, the machinery will be in by July, and the goal is to be in production by September."

"Gosh," said Jesse, "I'd better get to work."

A few minutes later, back in his office, Jesse considered what the future held at Parma Cycle. The company had been located in Delta, British Columbia since its founding. It had grown over the years to become the nation's third largest bicycle manufacturer. The decision to open the eastern plant had been made in hopes of cutting production costs, through lower wages, while improving quality. Although no one ever came right out and said it, it was assumed that the eastern plant would be nonunion. The elimination of union work rules was expected to be a benefit.

The Town of Digby had offered a 10-year exemption from all property taxes. This was a significant advantage because tax rates in the Delta area were extremely high. As well, there were generous financial incentives to be had from the government of Nova Scotia.

Jesse was pleased that he had been involved in the discussions from the time that the new plant had been first suggested. Even with all the advanced preparation he had done, he knew that the coming months would be extremely difficult for him and his staff.

As Jesse was thinking about all this, his assistant, Ed Deal, walked in with a bundle of papers. "Hi, Ed," said Jesse, "I'm glad you're here. The Digby plant is definitely on the way and you and I need to get our act together."

"That's great," said Ed. "It's quite a coincidence, too, because I was just going over this stack of job descriptions, identifying which ones might be eliminated as we scale back at this plant."

Jesse said, "Remember, Ed, we are not going to cut back very much here. Some jobs will be deleted and others added. But out of the 800 positions here, I'll bet that not more than 40 will actually be cut."

"So, what you are saying is that we basically have to staff the plant with people we hire from the Digby area?" Ed asked.

Jesse replied, "No, Ed, we will have some people here who are willing to transfer even though their jobs are not being eliminated. We will then replace them with others we hire in the Delta area. Most of the workers at Digby, though, will be recruited from that area."

"What about the management team?" asked Ed. "Well," said Jesse, "I think the boss already knows who the main people will be over there. They are managers we currently have on board plus a fellow we located at a defunct three-wheeler plant in Quebec."

"Who will be the human resource director down there?" asked Ed. "Well," replied Jesse, "I don't think I'm talking out of school by telling you that I plan to recommend you for the job."

After letting that soak in for a minute, Ed said, "It's no secret I was hoping for that. When will we know for sure?"

"There's really not much doubt," said Jesse,

"I'm so sure that I've decided to put you in charge of human resources for the whole project. During the next two weeks I'd like you to put together a comprehensive plan. I want a detailed report of the people we will need, including their qualifications. Secondly, we need more information about the labour supply around Digby. Finally, I'd like for you to come up with a general idea of who might be willing to transfer from this plant. They are really going to be the backbone of our workforce at Digby."

"Okay, Jesse, but I'll need a lot of help," said Ed as he gathered his papers and left. As Jesse watched Ed leave, he thought he noticed a certain snappiness about Ed's movements that had not been there before.

Questions

1. What procedures should be followed in determining the human resource needs at the new plant?

2. How might Jesse and Ed go about recruiting workers in Digby? What about managers?

PART TWO CBC 🍁 VIDEO CASE

Hiring Wars

Ramsey Hage, a graduate from the University of Ottawa, sent out about 200 résumés to Canadian firms. Only a few small start-up companies showed any interest. Most Canadian companies wanted two to three years' experience. But when he met recruiters from the American firm Lucent Technologies at a local job fair, things were different. Lucent flew him to New Jersey for intensive interviews and ultimately offered him a generous salary, a signing bonus, relocation pay, stock options, and help with the move. This was not an isolated case. One survey found that almost 80 percent of Canadian computer science and engineering students were willing to take jobs in the U.S.

By the end of the 1990s, Canada was evidencing a serious shortage of high tech and professional workers as many Canadians found jobs south of the border. The hot job market in the U.S.. had led American firms to redouble their recruiting efforts in Canada. The Conference Board of Canada warned that the brain drain of highly trained Canadians such as engineers, physicians, and nurses to the U.S. was a serious threat to Canada's economic future. This Canadian think tank estimated that about 100 000 Canadians, mostly on

temporary work visas, headed for the U.S. in 1997—up from about 17 000 in 1986—drawn by lower taxes, higher salaries, more growth opportunities, better exposure to leading technology, and a warmer climate.

Eric Kitchen works for Fast Lane Technologies Inc., a small Canadian company that moved from Ottawa to Halifax in the mid-1990s and established a partnership with Dalhousie University and Technical University of Nova Scotia. Fast Lane would have access to highly trained professionals, while university graduates would have a local job market. But by the end of the 1990s, the company found it difficult to compete with international recruiters: "Companies will literally go up to employees and say: 'How much are you making? I'll give you 10 percent more right off the bat.' Signing bonuses have gone out of whack."

American companies are reinventing the recruiting game. For example, Cisco Systems, in sunny San Jose, California, aims to hire 1000 new employees every quarter. Unlike many Canadian firms, Cisco has a selling mindset. The company is marketed as an upbeat place to work where suits and ties are a relic of the past. Jobs are posted on their Web site, along with a "friends" button that can get you a prescreening call. Cisco employees are offered bonuses and even free vacations for referrals.

According to John Roth, chief executive at Canada's Nortel Networks Corp, the brain drain is not limited to recent graduates and new entrants. The real issue, he says, is Canada's inability to recruit and keep good managers—the people necessary to run growth companies that will employ young people.

Roth believes that in the long run, students are influenced not so much by short-term promises and glitzy recruiting as by well-run companies with a future. A joint study by Personnel Systems and National Public Relations confirmed that the corporate work environment was one of the most important factors for Canadian students. A 1999 survey of the "35 Best Companies to Work For," by Hewitt Associates, concluded that attitude and corporate culture make the difference. Canada's best companies truly care about their employees, and prove it by offering such programs as flextime, paid sabbaticals, tuition, stock options, and flexible benefits.

A friendly environment was a major reason why James Cherry, one of Canada's top graduate students in 1999, resisted the lure of a job with IBM in Boston. Philsar Semiconductor, a small Canadian start-up company, offered not only a better-than-average salary and stock options, but an exciting work environment and recognition that people have a life outside work.

Some experts, like Roger Martin at the University of Toronto, warn that a long-term skill shortage is just beginning. As the population ages, companies will have to move from a "screening" to a "selling" mindset, putting as much effort into attracting recruits as they do into selling products. He predicts that twenty years from now, it may be *firms* that apply to potential *employees*.

Questions

1. Do you think aggressive U.S. recruiting of high-tech workers is temporary or the beginning of a broad trend? Discuss.

2. If you were an HR manager of a small Canadian high-tech company, how would you compete for new recruits?

3. Imagine you work in the HR department of a large company. Your boss asks you to prepare a proposal to show the company really cares about its employees. What programs would you recommend and why?

4. Why do Canadian graduates take employment positions in the U.S.?

Video Resource: "Hiring Wars," Venture 661 (September 23, 1997).

CHAPTER

7

Organizational Change, Culture, and Development

CHAPTER OBJECTIVES

1. Define human resource development.

2. Describe organizational change.

3. Define corporate culture and describe the factors that affect it.

4. Explain three broad types of organizational culture.

5. Define organization development and describe predominant organization development techniques.

6. Describe how managers can evaluate organization development (OD) programs.

During the past four years, the profits of International Motor Corporation have declined sharply. Teddy Katsaros, International's CEO, is especially concerned about the results of an attitude survey, which revealed that 60 percent of International's employees were dissatisfied with their jobs. Teddy thinks this malaise relates directly to excessive product recalls and employee turnover. In a recent board meeting he asserted, "We have increasing competition from both domestic and foreign corporations. If International is to survive and prosper, we need broad changes throughout the firm. The way things are going now, we may go under."

Throughout the 1990s, companies like International Motor Corporation have been forced to make a commitment to change. Effective managers have responded by investing heavily in **human resource development** (HRD)—the planned, continuous effort by management to improve employee competency and organizational performance. Three key issues in HRD are change management, organizational culture, and organizational development. We devote the first portion of this chapter to a discussion of organizational change. Next, we discuss corporate culture, including factors that create a culture; three broad types of cultures; and changing corporate cultures. The discussion then turns to organizational development (OD) methods, such as management by objectives and team building. In the final section we cover organizational development evaluation.

Human resource development:
A planned, continuous effort by management to improve employee competency and organizational performance.

Organizational Change

Organizational change involves moving from one condition or state to another—a process that may affect individuals, groups, or entire organizations. Today, ironically, change seems to be the only constant in modern business, whether it is the radical restructuring of a firm that trims a 4000-person headquarters down to 200 people[1] or the subtler changes to systems that occur at an ever-accelerating pace.

Everyone is affected by these changes, which can lead to conflict, stress and confusion. A major challenge for the modern human resource professional is to get employees and managers to understand and buy into the change process. Gordon Simpson, managing partner of The Mansis Development Corporation has noted, for example: "The workplace is changing dramatically and demands for the highest quality of product and service are increasing. To remain competitive in the face of these pressures, employee commitment is crucial."[2] In their role as change agents, human resource professionals must understand the change sequence or process, the accompanying difficulties, and the ways to reduce resistance to change.

Organizational change:
The movement from one condition or state to another—a process which is ongoing and systematic and which may affect individuals, groups, or entire organizations.

HR Web Wisdom
http: www.pearsoned.ca/mondy

Organizational Change
Current issues related to organizational change are reviewed.

The Change Process

Experts tell us that if change is to be implemented successfully, the process must be systematic. A major reason is to reduce the fear of the unknown. People feel more comfortable and are more likely to buy in when they know the four W's: *why, what, where,* and *when*. The impetus or driving force for change usually begins with a belief that the organization and its people can be made more productive and successful. Human resource development aimed at supporting change must also be recognized as an ongoing process, because both the organization's internal and external environments are dynamic, always impinging on the status quo. In the opening vignette, for example, Teddy felt the need to change because of competition.

One systematic approach to change is shown in Figure 7-1. To begin, the need for and belief in change are recognized by signals exerted from either the external environment or internal environment—factors we discussed in Chapter 2.

Once a need is recognized, HRD solutions or methods are developed. These should be flexible: capable of dealing with present requirements while adaptable

Figure 7-1

The Organizational Change Sequence

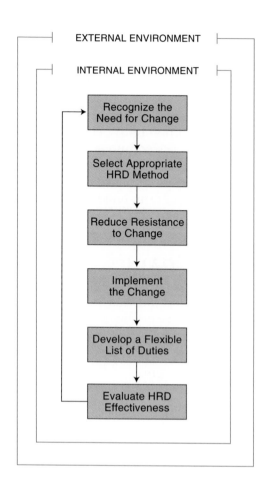

to further change. The solutions are then communicated, which reduces resistance to change, and implemented. Specific duties and responsibilities are then assigned. Finally, any effective HRD process must include evaluation of effectiveness or results. A primary measure of effectiveness is normally how the new program affects a firm's profitability or ability to meet objectives. Note that the process is continuous: after evaluation, the process begins again.

Understanding and Reducing Resistance

Reducing resistance to change is crucial to success. In part, resistance can be explained in terms of employee expectations and experiences. People often resist change when they feel their basic economic and social needs will not be met. For example, one of the most frightening prospects for many people is the threat of unemployment—understandable, given that most adults derive their primary income from work. Changes in organizations may also be seen as threatening a person's work status or disrupting established social groups and friendships. Because many social needs are satisfied on the job, any threat to these relationships may also be resisted.

Productivity and accuracy generally decline during periods of change. Instead of thinking about their work, employees are worrying about their survival or their loss of status. They may be absent more, either because of stress-induced illness or because they are looking for another job. Management must take action to minimize this potential loss of productivity. There are a number of approaches to reducing resistance to change.

Building Trust and Confidence

Bringing about a change in attitude requires trust and respect between the person attempting to implement the change and the individual(s) affected. Management builds trust by dealing with employees in an open and straightforward manner. Workers who are told that they need additional training, for example, will accept the idea much more readily if they have confidence in management. There is no shortcut to trust; it grows from a long period of fair dealing.

Open Communication

In some organizations, a great deal of information is unnecessarily treated as confidential, creating a climate of mistrust and fear. Effective managers work to open the communication channels as much as they reasonably can. Sharing information shows respect, gains trust, and allows managers to learn from employees in turn.

Employee Participation

In most cases, encouraging participation helps to overcome resistance. For example, Sylvia Lee, President of Lee Communications in Grand Centre, Alberta, has suggested that

> Involving people creates synergy, and synergy creates excitement. That's the productivity part. Not only do you get far better ideas from the group than you would from one person alone, but you also get the added bonus of "buy in." Here's the morale part—people who are part of the solution are part of the resolution. An employee who buys in to the decision because she helped reach it is going to get involved in implementing it. Synergy and buy in—there's nothing to beat the raw power of that combination.[3]

Caution and good judgment are in order, however. Management should not, for example, expect employees to participate in their own layoffs.[4]

Motivations

To achieve a balanced and productive working environment in an era of change, managers must work to assuage employees' fears of being unable to satisfy personal needs and at the same time accomplish organizational objectives. Managers must be convinced that it is, usually, their own actions, not the employees' inherent nature, that lead to hostility. Arthur Church, president and CEO of Champion Road Machinery Ltd. (based in Goderich, Ontario), summarizes this concept bluntly: "If anything goes wrong, 85 percent of the time it's management's fault."[5] Only when this philosophy is accepted can the effectiveness of human resource development programs be maximized. Managers need to address, then, the issue of corporate culture—the subject of the next section.

TRENDS and INNOVATIONS

Chief Knowledge Officer

In the new, technology-based economy, information abounds. Employees have access to all kinds of information via the Intranet, e-mail, company software, and so on. But the key issue in many companies today is not raw information, says Professor Joseph C. Paradi of the University of Toronto: "It's how do you go beyond these numbers?" How do you take vast sources of data and make sense out of them? This is the major concern of a growing corporate responsibility called knowledge management —the process of making practical use of information. As a result, a new corporate title, 'Chief Knowledge Officer' (CKO) is creeping into organizational charts.

The job of the CKO entails much more than just managing information. It's about building an infrastructure for employees to easily access and use the information. The job of the CKO is to establish a system in which employees can stickhandle through megabytes of information and somehow make sense of it.

Knowledge management is concerned with developing a strategy and process for disseminating knowledge. But a key stumbling block for the CKO is the company culture, says Professor Paradi: "In many organizations, there is a built-in tendency to hoard knowledge rather than share it." The key challenge for the CKO, then, is to develop a knowledge-sharing environment or culture—one in which employees value and are happy to share information.

Source: *An Advertising Supplement, "Knowledge-sharing culture is new corporate goal,"* The Globe and Mail, *September 17, 1999, C6.*

Corporate Culture

When beginning a new job, an employee may hear the comment, *This is the way we do things around here.* This bit of informal communication refers to something more formally known as corporate culture.[6] As we learned in Chapter 2, corporate culture is the system of shared values, beliefs, and habits that interact with the formal organization structure to produce behavioural norms. These patterns of standards, assumptions, values, and norms are shared by organizational members,[7] providing guidelines for employee behaviour.

Culture governs what the company stands for, what overall direction it takes, and how problems and opportunities are defined. It determines resource allocation, organizational structure, the systems in use, the people hired, the fit between jobs and people, and the required results and rewards.[8]

Today, businesses are constantly being forced to change to stay competitive. Managers keep searching for ways to improve quality, to increase speed of operations, and to adopt a customer orientation. These changes are so fundamental, they must take root in a company's very essence—in its culture.[9] The factors that determine corporate culture play a fundamental role in accomplishing an organization's mission and objectives and ultimate success.

HR Web Wisdom

http: www.pearsoned.ca/mondy

Culture Change Strategy
Questions and answers about culture change and human resources are addressed.

Factors That Influence Corporate Culture

The culture of an organization originates from senior management, stemming largely from what these executives do, rather than what they say. Other internal factors can also interact to shape the culture of a firm, including work group relationships, managers' and supervisors' leadership styles, organizational characteristics, and administrative processes (see Figure 7-2).

The Work Group

The characteristics of the immediate work group will affect one's perception of overall corporate culture. In particular, commitment to the mission of the work group—dedication and loyalty to group goals and objectives—influences cultural perceptions about the total organization. If the work groups are not serious about meeting their goals, it is difficult to develop a strong goal-oriented corporate culture. It is the group culture that determines (in large part) whether individual employees place their firm's best interests over short-term individual considerations, or whether they think, "I'm tired today, who cares if the damn bread is a little burned."[10] Social relationships within the group, such as

Figure 7-2

Factors That Influence Corporate Culture

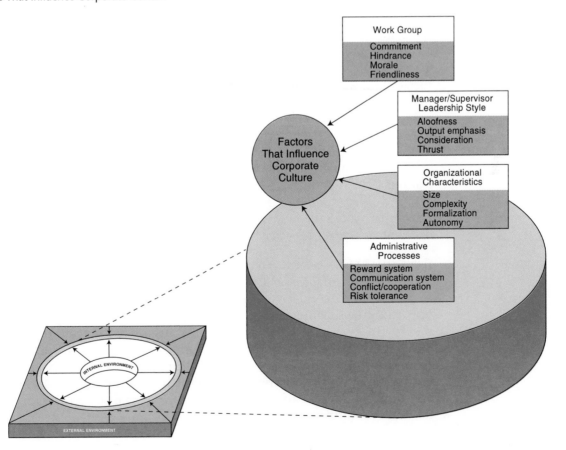

friendships, also affect the environment of group members and their perception of the corporate culture.

Manager/Supervisor Leadership Style

The leadership style of the immediate supervisor will have a considerable effect on culture—whether the manager is aloof and distant, for example, or always pushing for output. Group effectiveness is enhanced by a supervisor who is goal-directed, passionate, and considerate. In fact, it has been claimed that a leader's personality is correlated directly with a firm's strategic direction and level of success. Vision, as measured on a "Personality Index," also seems to be correlated with sales growth and profitability.[11]

Organizational Characteristics

Organizations vary in size and complexity. Large organizations tend to be more specialized and impersonal. Labour unions often find that large firms are easier to organize than smaller ones, because smaller firms tend to have a more closely knit social structure and to foster more informal relationships among employees and management. Complex organizations sometimes employ a greater number of professionals and specialists, which alters the general approach to problem solving.

Organizations also vary in the degree to which policies are written and in attempts to program behaviour through rules, procedures, and regulations. They can be distinguished, too, by the degree of decentralization of decision-making authority, which, in turn, affects management autonomy and employee freedom.

Toronto-based steel processor FedMet Inc., for example, had experienced a series of problems in the early 1990s as sales fell by 30 percent. A major turnaround was attributed to a change to a more decentralized, cooperative management style that led to lower product rejection rates, higher production volume, and an increase in the on-time delivery rate from 58 to 90 percent. Employees have stated they now look on their boss as a customer rather than as an employer.[12]

Although smaller businesses have been held up as examples of what organizations should be like (they're more flexible), large multinationals are not about to disappear. In fact, some authors suggest that increasing globalization is likely to play to the multinationals' strengths, as they can manufacture and distribute wherever they can discover or create demand. [13, 14]

Administrative Processes

Managers who can develop direct links between performance and rewards tend to create cultures conducive to achievement. Communication systems that are open and free-flowing tend to promote participation and creative environments. The general attitudes toward tolerance of conflict and risk handling also have considerable influence on teamwork, innovation, and creativity. From these and other factors, organization members develop a subjective impression of the organization and whether or not it is a good place to work. These impressions enhance or detract from performance, satisfaction, creativity, and commitment.

Types of Cultures

Management must be aware of the various types of corporate culture and why one particular culture may prove superior to another.[15] Some of the contrasting types of cultures are described below.

Permissive

Some Canadian businesses are culturally permissive, guided by the philosophy that organization members who are free to choose among alternatives make the soundest decisions. Managers who adopt this philosophy feel that when employees are asked to give up some of their individuality for the common good, the end result is often reinforcement of the status quo, resulting in stagnation and lack of creativity.

Autocratic

The opposite of the open and permissive culture is the closed, autocratic environment. It, too, may be characterized by high output goals. But such goals

---

HRM in ACTION

Corporate Culture— Before and After

Wayne, Yusuf, and Ryan were supervisors with a small chain of fifteen convenience stores in North Vancouver. Each had responsibility for five stores and reported directly to the company president, but they all worked as a team. Wayne coordinated the scheduling of clerks at all fifteen stores, Yusuf took care of inventory control and purchasing, while Ryan took responsibility for recruiting and hiring. Otherwise, they each did whatever needed to be done.

The situation changed markedly within a year, however, when the president, wishing to relieve himself of daily details, promoted Ryan to vice-president. Another supervisor, Phillip, was hired to manage Ryan's five stores. At first, everything went well, but soon Ryan, who was much more involved in store management than the president had been, told the three supervisors he wanted each of them to take care of their own five stores.

Wayne, Yusuf, and Phillip initially resisted Ryan's frequent orders and demands. After a few reprimands, though, the men decided to do as Ryan wanted. They rarely saw one another, and each took care of all aspects of store operations, as well as filling in for clerks who were late or sick. There were frequent problems, however, as Ryan accused the three supervisors of working against him and threatened them with dismissal if operations did not improve. Wayne, Yusuf, and Phillip saved him the trouble; they quit within days of one another. The president fired Ryan a few days later.

Explain the corporate culture that existed before and after Ryan's promotion to vice president.

are more likely to be imposed on the organization by dictatorial or even threatening leaders. The greater rigidity in this culture results from strict adherence to a formal chain of command, narrower spans of management, and stricter individual accountability. The emphasis is on the individual rather than on teamwork. The result is that employees often do only what they are told to do. An autocratic structure is necessary in some organizations—such as the armed forces, where the need to act instantly under fire requires a clear chain of command. It is not the most effective culture, however, for most organizations, especially not for those dealing with change.

Participative

Most attempts to alter organizational culture have been directed toward increasing participation in both planning and decision making. Major characteristics of this type of culture are shown in Figure 7-3. Two key characteristics are trust and open communication.

Involving more people in the decision-making process can improve productivity and morale. New ideas can be generated that encourage a more cooperative work effort. Employees who are involved in areas that matter to them will often respond to shared problems with innovative suggestions and unusually productive effort.

Group participation, however, may not be feasible when immediate decisions are required. In this situation, the manager may be forced to make a decision and issue directives. Thus, in some environments, it must be understood that the usual participative structures will have to be set aside from time to time. In addition, participation calls for some measure of self-discipline. Subordinates must learn to handle freedom and supervisors must learn to trust subordinates. Thus, the level of involvement in decision making depends largely on the abilities and the interests of both subordinates and managers.

Figure 7-3

Characteristics and Benefits of a Participative Culture

CHARACTERISTICS	BENEFITS
open communication	increased acceptance of management's ideas
consideration and supportiveness	increased cooperation between management and staff
leadership	reduced turnover
team problem solving	reduced absenteeism
worker autonomy	reduced complaints and grievances
information sharing	greater acceptance of changes
high output goals	improved attitudes toward the job and the organization

Changing the Corporate Culture

Environmental factors such as governmental action, workforce diversity, and global competition often necessitate a change in culture. In extreme cases, management may be required to make a complete break with the past. This process, called re-engineering (defined later), is an attempt to build the business, or parts of the business, as if nothing had existed before. In other words, management starts from the beginning to create entire new structures, work organizations, systems, and sometimes even a new workforce. This drastic action can destroy the existing organization, but often attempts are made to salvage the best parts of what existed before.[16]

Several problem areas inherent in counterproductive cultures:[17]

- **Stereotyping.** The most serious problem faced by women and minority managers related to frustrations in coping with gender and race stereotypes;

- **Discrimination and harassment.** Whether experiencing discrimination personally or witnessing it, managers reported that such incidents made them question whether or not they fit in with the firm;

- **Exclusion and isolation.** Women and minority managers indicate they are often excluded from social activities and left out of informal communication networks;

- **Work–family balance.** Women managers expressed the view that *playing the game* often requires compromising personal values and conforming to the expectations of others;

- **Career development.** In some organizations, opportunities for career progression still seem to be limited for women and minority managers.

These problem areas illustrate legitimate concerns that managers must consider in revamping their corporate cultures. For example, taken together, women and minorities represent a significant percentage of employees entering the workforce. If their talents are to be used to the fullest, corporate cultures of the future must reflect their needs. To take advantage of the diversity of the Canadian workforce, many managers are attempting to create cultures in which all employees can contribute and advance in the organization on the basis of ability. HR professionals know that critical factors such as retention, motivation, and advancement are highly dependent upon how employees react to their work culture.

In the final analysis, changing a firm's culture should be involve as much of the organization as possible, from the chief executive officer to the operative employees. The need to change, along with the outcomes being sought, should be communicated clearly to all members of the organization in a clearly understood process.

HR Web Wisdom
http: www.pearsoned.ca/mondy

HRDC—HR Links
Issues related to organizational development are addressed.

Organization Development

To survive and prosper in the highly competitive global environment of the next decade, organizations must be transformed into market-driven, innovative, and

Organization development (OD): An organization-wide application of behavioural science knowledge to the planned development and reinforcement of a firm's strategies, structures, and processes in order to improve effectiveness.

adaptive systems. In many firms, this urgent need is met through organization development, an HRD approach that involves everyone and everything in the organization. **Organization development (OD)** is an organization-wide application of behavioural science knowledge to the planned development and reinforcement of a firm's strategies, structures, and processes in order to improve effectiveness.[18]

While early OD applications focused on employee satisfaction, employee and organizational performance are now being emphasized as well. OD interventions provide an adaptive strategy for planning and implementing change and ensure the long-term reinforcement of change.

Organization development may involve changes in the firm's strategy, structure, and processes. In dealing with structure, the focus is on how people are grouped within the organization. The firm's processes include methods of communication and problem solving.[19] "Organizations must develop the capacity to learn effectively from past successes and failures and to apply the lessons to renewal."[20] As one Canadian author has suggested, businesses need to move toward "system learning," which "takes place when the organization develops the systematic processes to acquire, use and communicate organizational knowledge."[21]

Approaches to Organization Development

Survey Feedback

Survey feedback: A process of collecting data from an organizational unit through the use of a questionnaire or survey.

Survey feedback is a process of collecting data from an organizational unit through the use of a questionnaire or survey. A developing trend has been to combine survey feedback with other OD approaches, although it is a powerful approach in its own right.[22] Survey feedback involves a number of steps:

- Members of the organization, including top management, are involved in planning the survey.

- The survey instrument is administered to all members of the organizational unit.

- An OD consultant analyzes the data, tabulates results, suggests approaches to diagnosis, and trains participants in the feedback process.

- Data feedback begins at the top level of the organization and flows downward to groups reporting at successively lower levels.

- Feedback meetings provide an opportunity to discuss and to interpret data, to diagnose problem areas, and to develop action plans.[23]

Quality Circles

Quality circles: Employee groups that meet regularly with their supervisors to identify production problems and to recommend solutions.

Quality circles are employee groups that meet regularly with their supervisors to identify production problems and to recommend solutions. These recommendations are then presented to higher-level management for review. Approved solutions are implemented with employee participation.

In spite of numerous successful applications, however, the quality circle concept does not work well in many North American organizations. To implement a successful quality circle program, the firm must set clear goals and communicate both goals and results widely. Top management must support the program and create a climate conducive to participative management. A qualified manager must be selected to administer the program, and individual participants must receive quality circle training.

Management by Objectives

Management by objectives (MBO) is a management technique that emphasizes the setting of objectives by agreement of superior and subordinate. These objectives are then used as the primary basis for motivation, evaluation, and self-management. Objectives may be very specific operational targets, such as "a 30-percent increase in sales" or "production of 800 units per month," or may relate to personal growth or career development. As a management approach that encourages employers to anticipate and to plan, MBO directs efforts toward attainable goals, and discourages guessing, or making decisions based on hunches.

Since MBO emphasizes participative management, the approach becomes an important method of organization development that focuses on the achievement of individual and organizational goals. Individual participation in goal setting and the emphasis on self-control promote not only personal growth but also organizational success.

MBO can be used at all organizational levels. It is an interactive process that must be continually reviewed, modified, and updated. Senior management must initiate the MBO process by establishing long-range goals (see Figure 7-4) and must support the process. The president and vice president of human resources (superior and subordinate), for example, might jointly establish the firm's long-range goals in the HR area, along with intermediate and short-term objectives. At this point, president and vice president agree on the subordinate's performance objectives and action plans, which outline how the objectives will be achieved. The subordinate proceeds to work toward his or her goals. At the end of the appraisal period, both parties review the subordinate's performance and determine what can be done to overcome any problems or to enhance the employee's strengths. Goals then are established for the next period and the process is repeated. During this process, too, the vice president would be setting goals with the HR professionals and even support staff, so that MBO reaches throughout the organization.

From an organization development standpoint, MBO:

- provides an opportunity for development of managers and employees;
- increases the firm's ability to change;
- provides a more objective and tangible basis for performance appraisal and salary decisions;
- results in better overall management and higher performance levels;
- provides an effective overall planning system;
- forces managers to establish priorities and measurable targets or standards of performance;

Management by objectives (MBO):
A management technique that emphasizes the setting of objectives by agreement of superior and subordinate.

- clarifies specific roles, responsibilities, and authority;
- encourages joint participation in establishing objectives;
- promotes accountability;
- lets individuals know clearly what is expected of them,
- improves internal communication;
- helps identify promotable managers and employees; and
- increases employee motivation and commitment.

There are, however, potential problems in implementing MBO. Without the full support of senior management, the process is likely to fail. This commitment may be difficult to obtain, because implementing an MBO system often takes

Figure 7-4

The MBO Process

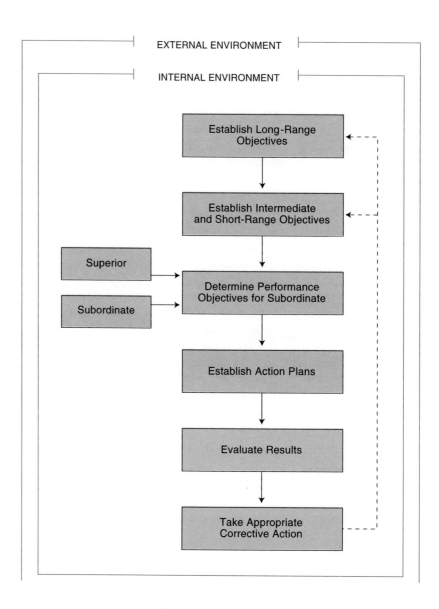

from three to five years. In addition, the long-term objectives on which MBO is based may be difficult to establish, as in many businesses there is a tendency to concentrate on short-term plans. The MBO system can also create a seemingly insurmountable amount of paperwork if it isn't closely monitored. Finally, some managers believe that MBO is excessively time consuming. The process forces them to think ahead and to determine how their goals and actions fit into the corporate strategy—not an easy task for many managers. We will return to this subject in Chapter 10 when we discuss the MBO evaluation method.

Job Enrichment

As defined in Chapter 4, job enrichment is the deliberate restructuring of a job to make it more challenging, meaningful, and interesting. This process emphasizes the accomplishment of significant tasks, so the employee gains a sense of achievement. Job enrichment takes an optimistic view of employee capabilities, presuming that individuals have the ability to perform more difficult and responsible tasks than they are currently performing. Furthermore, there is an assumption that most employees will respond favourably if challenged and that as a result, motivation and productivity will improve.

Job enrichment applied on a broad scale, therefore, becomes an important OD method, as the increased responsibility and challenge promotes continuous employee development. Thus, the nature of enriched jobs requires that employees keep their skills up to date.

Transactional Analysis[24]

Although not currently a popular OD intervention, **transactional analysis** (TA) was used for a number of years as a technique for teaching behavioural principles. TA considers each individual's three ego states—the Parent, the Adult, and the Child—in helping people understand interpersonal relations. TA provides a system for forming a mental image of the emotions and the thought processes used during interactions, whether in a social or in a business setting. Thus, employees begin to understand the emotions and needs of customers or fellow employees, while learning to respond appropriately to a wide variety of work-related situations.[25]

> **Transactional analysis:** An OD method that considers an individual's ego states in helping people understand interpersonal relations.

Quality of Work Life

Quality of work life (QWL) is the degree to which members of a work organization are able to satisfy their most important personal needs through organizational experiences. QWL programs include job redesign, the creation of autonomous work groups, and employee participation in decision making. A fundamental assumption is that QWL programs will increase job satisfaction and motivation, which in turn will lead to increased productivity.[26]

> **Quality of work life (QWL):** The degree to which members of a work organization are able to satisfy their most important personal needs through organizational experiences.

QWL programs are not short-term, quick-fix solutions. A successful program requires careful planning, The goals of a QWL program should be the joint responsibility of management and workers. Certain guidelines, however, may be helpful:

- Managers need to redefine "how we work in this organization."

- The willing participation of people at all levels of the organization must be solicited.

- A commitment from formal and informal leaders that goes beyond the rhetoric of endorsement and support must be demonstrated daily.

- Management must communicate and integrate strategic goals into the day-to-day business operations.

- New approaches and processes must be developed in most work situations, as business processes are never static, requiring constant adjustment or reengineering in response to changing internal and external environments.[27]

Research on QWL programs has found mixed results. Although many successes have been reported, it is often difficult to determine the variable responsible for production increases. HR managers need to recognize that most QWL programs remain experimental and that there is no conclusive formula to ensure success.[28]

Sensitivity Training

Sensitivity training:
An OD technique designed to make individuals more aware of themselves and of their effect on others.

Sensitivity training is an OD technique designed to make individuals more aware of themselves and of their effect on others. Different from traditional forms of training (which tend to stress the learning of a predetermined set of concepts),[29] sensitivity training features a group—often called a training group or T-group—in which there is no preestablished agenda or focus. The trainer's role is to serve as a facilitator in an unstructured environment where participants are encouraged to learn about themselves and others in the group. The objectives of sensitivity training are to enhance self-awareness, gain insight into one's own and others' behaviour, acquire the ability to analyze interpersonal behaviour, and improve group functioning.[30]

Ideally, when sensitivity training begins there is no agenda and no leader. Through dialogue people begin to learn about themselves and others. Participants are encouraged to look at themselves as others see them. Then, if they want to change, they can attempt to do so. Although the purpose of sensitivity training —to assist individuals to learn more about how they relate to other people—has not been questioned, the technique has been criticized. It is clear that sensitivity training often involves anxiety-provoking situations as participants often undergo severe emotional stress during training. In addition, some critics believe that it is one matter for participants to express true feelings in the psychological safety of the laboratory, but quite another to face their co-workers.[31] Information learned in a sensitivity group may prove to be irrelevant or even damaging, unless the participant returns to an organizational environment that supports the use of that knowledge. Individuals may be encouraged to be open and supportive in the T-group, but when they return to their jobs, they often revert to past behaviour patterns. Sensitivity training flourished in the 1970s, but is rarely used now.

Total Quality Management

Total quality management (TQM): A commitment on the part of everyone in an organization to excellence, with an emphasis on constant improvement achieved through teamwork and continuous upgrading.

Total quality management (TQM) is defined as a commitment on the part of everyone in an organization to excellence, with an emphasis on constant improvement achieved through teamwork and continuous upgrading. Many companies have 'total quality' programs that integrate all departments. Implied in the concept is a commitment to be the best and to provide the highest quality products and services, meeting or exceeding customer expectations. Managers make massive changes to stay competitive, constantly seeking ways to improve quality and to increase speed of operations, while adopting a customer orientation. These changes are so fundamental they must take root in a company's very essence, which means in its culture.

Thus, TQM often involves major cultural changes that require new ways of thinking and strong leadership at all levels. Individuals throughout the organization must be inspired to do their jobs differently. They must understand what needs to be done and why. Typically employees are made responsible for their own quality. This added responsibility requires re-organizing their jobs to give employees the authority to reject or rework products as they see fit.

Unfortunately, many TQM programs fail, despite the considerable amount of money spent, because the changes do not go deep enough. In some cases, senior executives do not get involved and there is no commitment to continued training. Old management structures are retained and the focus is on operations rather than thinking. This failure of imagination is easy to understand, since most managers are trained to look for simple solutions to immediate problems rather than dealing with complex, system-oriented concerns that take a major effort over time to produce results. TQM theory is often difficult to insert into long-standing corporate cultures, partly because it does not take into consideration managers' needs for high security and belonging. As well, in many companies, TQM results are not measured, and reward structures are not rearranged to encourage and to promote new behaviour, as employees often are excluded from the decision and power structures.[32]

Despite such difficulties in implementation, TQM can be a valid technique to keep and to improve market share by improving customer satisfaction. Instead of accepting the status quo, employees at all levels continually seek alternative methods or technologies that will improve existing processes. TQM provides a strategy for reducing the causes of poor quality, thereby increasing productivity.

TQM, then, is a process of continual quality improvement. In the short term, once every internal process is operating at or above a desired quality level, reliance on costly inspection practices can be reduced or eliminated. Attention can then be turned to monitoring the entire business to determine what sources of variation are still present. If variation can be eliminated, then production processes can be more precise, leading to fewer defects or errors, and improved quality.

Reengineering

When business problems occur, workers are often blamed, even though the real obstacle often lies in process design. Unfortunately, rather than looking for process problems, managers often focus on worker deficiencies, at least initially. If process is the problem, reengineering can substantially improve productivity.

Reengineering essentially requires the firm to rethink and redesign its entire business system from the ground up to become more competitive. **Reengineering** is "the fundamental rethinking and radical redesign of business processes to achieve dramatic improvements in critical, contemporary measures of performance, such as cost, quality, service, and speed."[33] Reengineering

Reengineering: The fundamental rethinking and radical redesign of business processes to achieve dramatic improvements in measures of performance, such as cost, quality, service, and speed.

organizes a company on the basis of process rather than by functional departments. Work is organized around outcomes rather than tasks or functions. Job designs, organizational structures, and management systems are emphasized. Reengineering should not be confused with downsizing (discussed in Chapter 3), even though a workforce reduction often results from this strategy.[34]

The term *process manager* is often used in the language of reengineering, A process manager, as distinct from a functional manager such as a production manager or a marketing manager, is responsible for all operations associated with a specific process.

Reengineering was a popular concept in the early to mid 1990s. Today its star has faded.[35] One study found that 85 percent of reengineering attempts failed.[36] Levi Strauss, for example, had a very disappointing and costly experience.[37] Nonetheless, like TQM, reengineering can be effective in certain instances. The use of reengineering at IBM to significantly change its benefit centre is a high profile example of success.[38]

Team Building and Self-Directed Teams

Many work situations make it imperative to subordinate individual autonomy in favour of cooperation within a group. Building effective teams has, therefore, become a business necessity. At the Alberta-Pacific Forest Industries Inc. mill near Boyle, Alberta, for example, maintenance workers were divided into self-directed work teams. Each team consisted of a planner, an area maintenance engineer, a team leader, and the required tradespeople. A production team consisted of a leader and a production specialist, plus appropriate trades. Together, the maintenance and the production teams formed a core that operated the wood room as a business unit. Eventually, they planned to have each core team run its area as a profit centre, taking full responsibility for own operations. [39]

Team building: A conscious effort to develop effective work groups throughout an organization.

Team building is the conscious effort to develop effective work groups, each composed of a small number of employees (usually five to seven) responsible for an entire work process or segment. Team members work together to improve their operation or product, plan and control their work, and handle day-to-day problems. They may even become involved in broader, company-wide issues, such as vendor quality, safety, and business planning.[40]

One major survey conducted by a human resources consulting firm found that 27 percent of the respondents currently used self-directed teams. Half the respondents predicted that the majority of their workforce would be organized in teams within the next five years.[41] The reason? In many cases, teams were found to be more productive, sometimes bringing gains of as much as 30 percent. In another survey, more than three-quarters of respondents (77 percent) reported increased in productivity. Seventy-two percent reported increases in quality and more than half felt that job satisfaction (65 percent), customer service (57 percent) and waste reduction (55 percent) had improved.

Advocating the use of teams years before they became commonplace, Douglas McGregor identified characteristics of effective management teams (see Figure 7-5). His version of an effective team emphasizes an informal organizational culture that is relatively free from tension. The team's decision-making process involves much discussion and broad participation. Communications are open, with an emphasis placed on listening to the views of others. Members feel free

Figure 7-5

Characteristics of Effective Teams

1. The atmosphere, which can be sensed in a few minutes of observation, tends to be informal, comfortable, and relaxed. There are no obvious tensions.

2. There is a lot of discussion in which virtually everyone participates, but it remains pertinent to the task of the group.

3. The task or the objective of the group is well understood and accepted by the members.

4. The members listen to each other! The discussion does not have the quality of jumping from one idea to another unrelated one. Every idea is given a hearing. People are not afraid of seeming foolish by expressing a creative thought, even if it seems fairly extreme.

5. There is disagreement. The group is comfortable with this and shows no signs of having to avoid conflict or to keep everything light and on a plane of sweetness. Disagreements are not suppressed or overridden by premature group action. Individuals who disagree do not appear to be trying to dominate the group or to express hostility. Their disagreement is an expression of a genuine difference of opinion, and they expect a hearing in order for a solution to be found.

6. Most decisions are reached by a kind of consensus in which it is clear that everybody is in general agreement and willing to go along.

7. Criticism is frequent, frank, and relatively comfortable. There is little evidence of personal attack, either open or hidden. The criticism has a constructive flavor in that it is oriented toward removing an obstacle that prevents the group from getting the job done.

8. People freely express their feelings as well as their ideas on both the problem and the group's operation. There is little pussyfooting; there are few hidden agendas. Everybody appears to know quite well how everybody else feels about any matter under discussion.

9. When action is taken, clear assignments are made and accepted.

10. The chairperson of the group does not dominate it, nor to the contrary, does the group defer unduly to him or her. In fact, the leadership shifts from time to time, depending on the circumstances. At various times, different members, because of their knowledge or experience, are in a position to act as "resources" for the group. The members utilize them in this fashion and they occupy leadership roles while they are thus being used. There is little evidence of a struggle for power as the group operates. The issue is not who controls but how to get the job done.

11. The group is conscious of its own operations. Frequently, it will stop to examine how well it is doing or what may be interfering with its operation. The problem may be a matter of procedure, or it may be that an individual's behavior is interfering with the accomplishment of the group's objectives. Whatever the problem, it is openly discussed until a solution is found.

Source: Adapted from Douglas McGregor, The Human Side of Management (New York: McGraw-Hill, 1960), 232-235. Reprinted by permission of the McGraw-Hill Book Company. All rights reserved.

to disagree but do so in an atmosphere of acceptance. The team pursues goals that its members understand and accept.

An example of effective teamwork can be found at the Shell Canada lubricants factory in Brockville, Ontario. Employing approximately 75 workers, this facility has about the same output as the two factories it replaced. Five integrated computer systems are used to pull together operations along with three self-managed teams called job families. Each operator must know all the jobs within the team and at least one job in each of the other two groups. Jobs are rotated about every 18 months. Each worker is expected to understand the entire business. As the hierarchical structures and the old command-and-control mentality have been discarded, staff absenteeism has fallen to about one-third the normal rate in manufacturing. While the Montreal and Toronto factories it replaced did almost no exporting, the Brockville plant is able to export to 44 countries.[43]

Effective work teams are goal-directed and focus on solving actual problems. The team-building process begins when the team leader defines a problem that requires organizational change (see Figure 7-6). The team then diagnoses the problem to determine the underlying causes, usually related to breakdowns in communication, inappropriate leadership styles, or deficiencies in organizational

Figure 7-6

The Team-Building Process

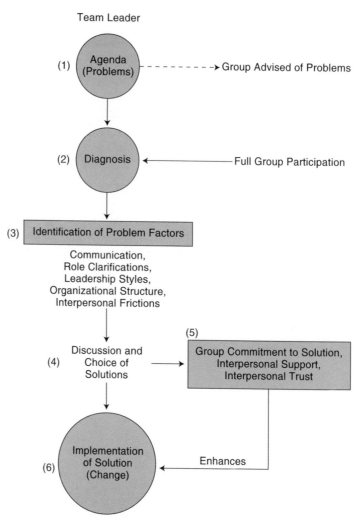

structure. Next team members consider alternative solutions and select the most appropriate. From their discussions, a commitment to the proposed course of action is likely to emerge. The interpersonal relations developed by team members also improve chances for implementing change. Team building, therefore, is a process by which participants and facilitators experience increasing levels of trust, openness, and willingness to explore core issues that affect the ability to work productively.[44]

Self-directed work teams are often difficult to build in a traditional work environment and there will always be resistance from those workers who are not able to adapt. A good example of ineffective teamwork is shown in the CBC video case referenced at the end of this section (Chapter 10). Psychological barriers that keep workers and managers in separate roles must be broken down, a process that can lead to conflict and fear on both sides. Teams bypass the usual routes of command and communication by drawing members from various parts of the company. Supervisors become coaches or facilitators. Teams need their own structure and tend to work best within well-entrenched quality programs such as continuous improvement, under which members look for ways to cut costs, save time, or improve the product. The company organization is flattened by streamlining layers of management, placing supervisors and functional team leaders on a management steering committee, and allowing workers to assume day-to-day decision-making responsibility. When teams do not work, it is often because of lack of management support. Note too, that old hierarchies can return once initial enthusiasm for the new order wears away.[45]

Evaluating Organization Development

When an OD intervention has been implemented, the question must be asked: *Did anything happen as a result of this experience?* All too often the answer is: *We don't know.* Evaluating organizational development programs is more difficult than determining whether or not an employee has learned to operate a particular piece of equipment. Nevertheless, managers need to know whether tangible benefits have resulted from an OD program (which probably cost considerable time and money) in order to plan for future changes or interventions.

One means of measuring program effectiveness is to assess changes in meeting performance criteria. Some of the factors to be measured might include 1) productivity, 2) absenteeism, 3) turnover, 4) accident rate, or 5) overtime costs. A lower turnover rate, for example, might mean that employees are more satisfied with their work and have chosen to remain with the firm. Lower production costs per unit suggests that workers may be paying more attention to their work. Although these data are useful, they probably will not provide the entire answer, as a variety of factors, both inside and outside the firm, can influence the workforce.

Effective managers do not wait for the program's completion to begin measuring results. Rather, evaluation is a continuous process using performance criteria to measure the effect of the change effort. Therefore, questionnaires should be administered periodically over an extended period of time.

Global Alliances

When a Canadian corporation expands operations to another country, an alliance is often formed with a company in the host country. Such collaboration makes it possible to share the costs and the risks of conducting business. Companies can share financial resources, technology, production facilities, marketing expertise, and of course, human resources.

Every effort is made to blend cultures and management styles of the partners as quickly as possible,[46] since long-term success requires a corporate culture that supports the goals of the one organization and deals effectively with the business environment. However a new culture is not easy to create. Ricky Chan, Deputy Chairman of Logic International Holdings Ltd., (an office furniture manufacturing and distribution group based in Hong Kong) made this observation:

> We have to remember that joint ventures have more than one parent. Constant attention is needed, therefore, as unlike shareholders, the joint venture partners are visible, powerful and capable of disagreeing about anything and everything. At the Board level, for example, there may be differences in priorities, direction and perhaps even in basic business values and ethics. At the functional management level, divided loyalty can be a problem, as staff assigned by the various partners look for signals from their parent company, rather than from the venture's general manager. [47]

Despite its disadvantages, the risk reduction, economies of scale, and the ability to meet or even block larger competition has led to the formation of joint ventures by the tens of thousands. Some operate relatively smoothly, others obviously fail, but ignoring the cultural aspects of the business can only lead to failure.[48] The likelihood of success for a joint venture seems to be directly proportional to the willingness of the major partners to assume active managerial responsibility, to share in key decisions, and to pay constant attention to maintaining a workable culture.

SUMMARY

1. **Define human resource development.**
   Human resource development (HRD) is the planned, continuous effort by management to improve employee competency levels and organizational performance.

2. **Describe organizational change.**
   Organizational change involves moving from one condition or state to another—a process that affects individuals, groups, and entire organizations. Organizational change must be viewed as ongoing and systematic. It usually begins with a recognition that improvement is needed, signalled by external or internal pressures. In their role as change agents, human resource professionals and managers must understand the change sequence as well as resistance and how to reduce it. Employee expectations and past experiences can lead to resistance, which can be reduced by building trust and confidence, open communication;, employee participation, and a clear statement of motivations.

3. **Define corporate culture and describe the factors that affect it.**
   Corporate culture is the system of shared values, beliefs, and habits within an organization that interacts with the formal structure to produce behavioural norms. Corporate culture develops from examples set by senior management, stemming largely from what they do, not what they say. Work group relationships, managers' and supervisors' leadership styles, organizational characteristics, and administrative processes also interact to shape the culture of a firm.

4. **Explain three broad types of organizational cultures.**
   Some Canadian businesses are culturally permissive, guided by the philosophy that organization members who are free to choose among alternatives make the soundest decisions. In contrast, a closed, autocratic culture is more rigid, with a formal chain of command, narrow spans of management, and strict individual accountability. In a participative culture, employees are involved and take ownership in the decision-making process, leading to improved productivity and morale. Despite its many benefits, this latter type of structure does not work in every situation.

5. **Define organization development and describe predominant organization development techniques.**
   Organization development (OD) applies behavioural science knowledge to an organization-wide effort aimed at improving effectiveness. Techniques include survey feedback, quality circles, management by objectives, job enrichment, transactional analysis, quality of work life, sensitivity training, total quality management, reengineering, and team building. Team building is generally considered one of the most effective OD techniques. Often techniques are combined.

6. **Describe how managers can evaluate organization development (OD) programs.**
   Managers need to know whether tangible benefits have resulted from an OD program. One indication is changes in performance measures such as productivity, absenteeism rate, turnover accident rates and overtime costs. Evaluation is a continuous process. Questionnaires should be administered periodically over an extended time.

QUESTIONS FOR REVIEW

1. Why is organizational change important? What are the steps in the organizational change sequence?

2. Why do many employees resist change? What can managers do to reduce resistance?

3. Define corporate culture. Explain the major factors that influence corporate culture.

4. Does a participative culture necessarily improve productivity? Defend your answer.

5. Briefly explain the differences between a permissive and autocratic culture.

6. Define each of the following terms:
   a. Organization development
   b. Quality circles

c. Management by objectives
d. Job enrichment
e. Quality of work life
f. Transactional analysis
g. Sensitivity training

h. Total quality management
i. Reengineering
j. Team building

7. How can organization development programs be evaluated?

DEVELOPING **HRM** SKILLS

An Experiential Exercise

In every organization, human resource professionals work with many individuals and groups. Cooperation is necessary if the tasks involved in human resource management are to be accomplished effectively. The Blue-Green exercise provides the opportunity to experience some of the interrelationships that occur in a structured setting, such as an organization or work group, and to examine the effect of teams on the work culture. Participants usually find the experience enlightening.

The Blue-Green exercise works best with groups of 12 to 40, and works equally well with people who have been working together for some time and with heterogeneous groups whose members barely know one another. Its impact, however, is probably greater for people required to work together.

The language used by the person conducting the exercise is extremely important, so listen carefully to the rules. The group will be divided into four subgroups of as nearly equal size as possible: Teams A-1, A-2, B-1, and B-2. Your instructor will give you additional necessary information.

HRM INCIDENT

Close to the Vest

Over the past few years, sales at Glenco Manufacturing had fallen, reflecting an industry-wide decline. During this time, Glenco had even been able to increase its share of the market slightly. Although forecasts indicated that demand for its products would improve in the future, Cecil Leung, the company president, believed that something needed to be done immediately to help the firm survive this temporary slump. As a first step, he employed a consulting firm to determine whether or not reorganization might be helpful.

A team of five consultants arrived at the firm. They told Mr. Leung that they first had to gain a thorough understanding of the current situation before they could make any recommendations. Mr. Leung assured them that the company was open to them. They could ask any questions that they thought were necessary.

The grapevine was full of rumours virtually from the day the consulting group arrived. One employee was heard to say, "If they shut down the company, I don't know if I could take care of my family." Another worker said, "If they move me away from my friends, I'm going to quit."

When workers questioned their supervisors, they received no explanations. No one had told the supervisors what was going on, either. The climate began to change to one of fear. Rather than being concerned about their daily work, employees worried about what was going to happen to the company and their jobs. As a result, productivity dropped drastically.

A month after the consultants departed, an informational memorandum was circulated throughout the company. It stated that the consultants had recommended a slight modification in the top levels of the organization to achieve greater efficiency. No one would be terminated. Any reductions would be the result of normal attrition. By this time, however, some of the most productive had already found other jobs and company operations were severely disrupted for several months.

Questions

1. Why did the employees assume the worst?

2. How could this difficulty have been avoided?

3. If you were on the consulting team, how would you suggest proceeding with the OD analysis?

CHAPTER

8

Training and Development

CHAPTER OBJECTIVES

1. Define training and development and learning organizations.

2. Describe the training and development process.

3. Identify the factors that influence training and development.

4. Explain training and development needs and objectives.

5. Identify the various training and development methods.

6. Define orientation and identify the purposes and stages of orientation.

7. Identify major challenges of implementing training and development programs.

8. Identify the methods by which training and development programs are evaluated.

Marian Lillie, an experienced accountant, had handled the administrative tasks for an automobile dealership for more than ten years. She was familiar with all aspects of the business. Two months ago, the dealership was sold to a young man who had graduated from a prominent university in British Columbia. Soon after he assumed control of the firm, he automated every conceivable administrative function. Marian was not consulted at any point in the process. She was, however, presented with a procedures manual when the project was completed. Later she was overheard telling a co-worker, "I know this new system is not going to work."

Howard Folz, a young university graduate with a major in Management Information Systems, was elated over a job offer from the region's largest employer. When he arrived for his first day of work, his supervisor, Amina Khan, took him on a tour of the office and factory. He was shown all the facilities, the firm's cafeteria, and finally his own work station. Amina's final remarks to him were, "We are delighted to have you with us, Howard. I will let you have your first assignment right after lunch. It's a simple system that involves two of our electronics groups utilizing fibre optics. I'll check with you in a few days to see how you're doing." As Amina left his work area, Howard was aghast. He wondered if he had just received all the initial training he would get.

It isn't difficult to imagine Marian Lillie's opposition to a system she doesn't understand. Her statement suggests she isn't likely to support the changes made without consulting her. Howard has a different, but equally serious problem. The university training he received in MIS was excellent, but he had learned very little about electronics, fibre optics, or his new employer's organization.

We devote the first portion of this chapter to defining and explaining the scope of training and development (T&D) and the learning organization. Next, we address elements of the T&D process, determining T&D needs, establishing objectives, and selecting T&D methods. In the final two sections of the chapter we discuss the orientation process and how T&D programs are implemented and evaluated.

Training and Development: Definition and Scope

Training is designed to permit learners to acquire knowledge and skills needed for their present jobs.[1] Showing a worker how to operate a lathe, or a supervisor how to schedule daily production, are examples of training. Training may be formal or informal. Formal training is planned and structured and takes place away from a person's usual workstation, perhaps in a classroom. Informal training, also called on-the-job training, happens, as the name suggests, in the course of the person's ongoing work. Strictly speaking, **development** differs from training. Development looks beyond the needs of the current job[2] to prepare employees to keep pace with the organization as it changes and grows. As we noted in the last chapter, HRD is often referred to as training and development.

In virtually every market, customers are demanding higher quality, lower costs, and faster cycle times. To meet these requirements, firms must continually improve their overall performance. Forward-thinking firms have become—or are striving to become—**learning organizations**—firms that value and encourage continuous performance-related human resources development. They view training as a strategic investment rather than an expense.

Training and development frequently improves workers' skills and boosts their motivation. This, in turn, leads to higher productivity and increased profitability. A study by Statistics Canada found that at least 53 percent of some 1400 growth firms offered their employees some form of training. According to Profit 100 surveys, more than 80 percent of Canada's fastest–growing companies invest heavily in employee training. In 1997, these Profit 100 companies spent an average of 2 percent of revenues on improving employee competencies—almost double the amount spent by Profit 100 companies at the beginning of the decade. This recent growth in training activity stems from the need to adapt to rapid environmental changes, to improve the quality of products and services, and to increase productivity.[3]

Yet many experts contend that Canadian managers are still not according training the importance it deserves. Indeed, in one Conference Board of Canada survey, training was not even included on the list of most pressing personnel management issues[4] (see Figure 8-1).

There are some indications of attitude change, however, as managers are becoming more aware of the profit-generating potential of a trained work force. Increasingly, employees are being viewed "as the root of competitive advantage."[5] Whereas in the past, training resources were mostly used for professionals,

Training: Activities designed to permit learners to acquire knowledge and skills needed for their present jobs.

Development: Learning that looks beyond the needs of the current job by preparing employees to keep pace with the organization as it changes and grows.

Learning organizations: Firms that recognize the critical importance of continuous performance-related human resource development and take appropriate action.

managers and executives, they are now distributed more equally across employment categories.[6] Selected training and development trends are shown in Figure 8-2. While no one can tell the future, managers need to look ahead in order to act proactively, particularly in rapidly changing areas such as training and development. Indeed, some of these prophecies are already coming true.

Figure 8-1

Most Pressing Management Issues (in rank order)

1. Personnel reshuffling due to restructuring or downsizing
2. Compensation or cost of labour
3. Industrial relations
4. Health care and other benefits
5. Pay and employment equity

Source: Reproduced with permission from the Conference Board of Canada.

Figure 8.2

Training and Development Trends

Managers involved with training and development should be aware of trends that may affect the way they perform:

- Skill requirements will continue to increase in response to rapid technological change. More complex equipment and processes will require more highly skilled workers.
- The Canadian workforce will become significantly better educated and more diverse.
- Corporate restructuring will continue to reshape businesses. Although large firms have historically provided most of the training, small firms offer the most promising future prospects for training.
- As outsourcing of training increases, training departments have shrunk. In the future, much of the training provided will be by independent consultants outside conventional training and development departments.
- The role of training departments will change significantly. Increasingly, these departments will act as brokers of learning services.
- Although traditional classroom delivery of training still predominates, advances in technology will revolutionize the way certain training is delivered.
- Training professionals will shift their focus from traditional training classes to flexible courses aimed more specifically at performance improvement.
- Integrated high-performance work systems will proliferate. Training will be integrated with actual work. Just-in-time and just-what's-needed training will be commonplace.
- More firms will strive to become learning organizations.
- Emphasis on human performance management will accelerate. The idea that people are a firm's most important asset will be put into action.[7]

The Training and Development Process

Major adjustments in the external and the internal environments necessitate corporate change. The general training and development process that helps facilitate this change is shown in Figure 8-3. Once the need for change is recognized, the process of determining training and development needs begins with two questions:

1. What are our training needs and objectives?

2. What do we want to accomplish through HRD activity?

T&D objectives might be as narrow as improving the supervisory ability of one manager, or as broad as honing the management skills of all first-line supervisors. After stating the objectives, management can determine appropriate methods for accomplishing them. T&D programs are implemented and then must be evaluated continuously to ensure that all activities are designed to further organizational objectives.

In some companies, training departments are being considered as profit centres rather than as overhead. A training department that is evaluated on results must function like a miniature business, charging internal departments as if they were outside clients.[8]

Factors Influencing Training and Development

Several of the most important influences on training and development are shown in Figure 8-4. How these factors are addressed often determines whether or not HRD objectives are achieved.

Management Support

First and most important, training and development programs must have top management's full support. This support must be real—not merely lip service—and must be communicated to the entire organization. In addition, all managers must demonstrate their commitment to the T&D process. According to one prominent director of corporate management development, "The primary responsibility for training and development lies with line managers, from the president and chair of the board on down. HRD management merely provides the technical expertise, plus blood, sweat and tears." All managers, then, must be convinced there will be a tangible payoff if resources are committed to training.[9] This means that some form of cost–benefit analysis (discussed later on in the chapter) should be made prior to implementing any T&D activity. Ideally, the training or development program should improve productivity, lower costs and/or increase profits. This step is too often omitted; according to a Conference Board of Canada study, only 5 percent of all training courses seem to be "subjected to a return on investment evaluation."[10]

Figure 8-3

The Training and
Development (T&D)
Process

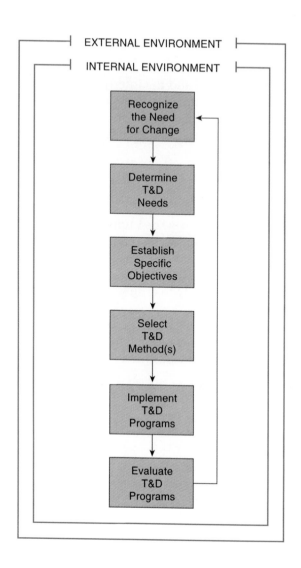

Figure 8-4

Factors Influencing Training
and Development

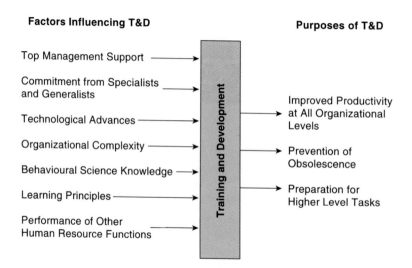

Learning and the Individual Employee

In recent years, increasingly rapid changes in products, systems, and methods have had a significant impact on job requirements. Thus, employees need to upgrade their skills constantly and to develop an attitude that permits them not only to adapt to change, but also to accept and even to seek change. All learning is to some degree a self-determined activity and leads to self-development. Moreover, people learn best when they are interested. Thus, an important role of the HRD manager is to help people set and reach their personal goals and to obtain the knowledge and the skills they need for present and future jobs. The HRD manager explains the type of training available, shows how to take advantage of various learning opportunities, and encourages learners to meet their goals.

The self-development concept leads to the philosophy that learning should be a life-long activity. Indeed, life-long learning is considered to be an important factor in an organization's ability to compete internationally.[11] Some general concepts are fundamentals to learning:

- Behaviour that is rewarded (reinforced) is more likely to recur.

- Reinforcement, to be most effective, must immediately follow the desired behaviour and be clearly connected with that behaviour.

- Learners progress in an area of learning only as far as they need to in order to achieve their purposes.

- Individuals are more likely to be enthusiastic about a learning situation if they themselves have participated in the planning and implementation of the project.

- What is learned is more likely to be available for use if it is learned in a situation much like that in which it is to be used and immediately preceding the time it is needed.

- The best time to learn is when the learning can be useful. Motivation is then at its strongest peak.

- Providing continuous feedback on the learner's progress enhances learning. By tracking an individual's progress, a learning curve can be prepared to reflect the trainee's progress over a period of time. Knowledge of results permits managers to establish realistic goals for future training.

- Practice may not make perfect but it does make better. Repetition of a task usually improves performance.

- For complex tasks, time should be allowed between training sessions for the learning to be assimilated.

Determining Training and Development Needs

Once the need for change is recognized, the next step is to determine specific training, education, and development needs. In today's highly competitive

Figure 8-5

Critical Training and
Development Challenges
for Major Employee Groups
(in rank order)

EXECUTIVE

1 Leadership
2 Strategic planning
3 Managing change

MANAGEMENT

1 Leadership
2 Managing change
3 Management & supervisory skills

**PROFESSIONAL &
TECHNICAL**

1 Technical knowledge & skills
2 Interpersonal skills
3 Quality & customer service

SALES & MARKETING

1 Sales & negotiation skills
2 Quality & customer service
3 Technical knowledge & skills

CLERICAL & OFFICE

1 Technical skills
2 Quality & customer service
3 Teamwork & team building

PRODUCTION

1 Technical skills
2 Quality & continuous improvement
3 Teamwork & team building

SERVICE

1 Quality & customer service
2 Technical skills
3 Quality & continuous improvement

TRADES

1 Technical skills
2 Trades upgrade
3 Quality & continuous improvement

business environment, it is a waste of resources to plunge into training programs because "other firms are doing it" or with a vague idea that some sort of training will solve all performance problems.[12] Training costs time and money. It should be undertaken only after a thorough performance analysis has identified real needs and only after exploring other interventions.[13]

A survey conducted by The Conference Board of Canada documented what executives considered the major training and development challenges for all types of employees. These are shown in Figure 8-5.[14]

Three types of analyses are required in order to determine T&D needs: organization analysis, task analysis, and person analysis.[15]

Organization analysis. Organization analysis examines the entire firm to determine where training and development should be conducted, studying structures, strategic goals, and plans. T&D should not be considered in isolation but as part of overall human resource planning. In fact, Keith Gilbert, vice-president of industrial relations (Ontario) for Molson Breweries has suggested that "a fundamental shift in the structure of organizations . . . is often necessary to sustain change."[16]

Task analysis. In conducting a task analysis, two primary factors should be determined: importance and proficiency. *Importance* relates to the relevance of specific tasks and behaviours in a particular job and the frequency with which they are performed. *Proficiency* is the employees' competence in performing these tasks. The appropriate data can be gleaned from job descriptions, performance appraisals, and interviews or surveys of supervisors and job incumbents.[17]

Person analysis. *Person analysis* focuses on the individual employee, dealing with two questions: *Who needs to be trained?* and *What kind of training is needed?* The first step in a person analysis is to compare employee performance with established standards. If the person's work is acceptable, training may not be needed. If the employee's performance is below standard, further investigation will be needed to identify the specific knowledge and skills required for satisfactory job performance.[18] Tests, role playing, and assessment centres may be helpful in conducting person analyses. The results from career planning programs may also be useful.

Establishing Training and Objectives

Clear, concise, and measurable T&D objectives must be formulated. Without them, it is impossible to design meaningful T&D programs and difficult to evaluate them. Figure 8-6 shows an example of an objectives and knowledge requirements statement adapted from a government publication.

Figure 8-6

Examples of Performance Objectives and Knowledge Requirements

BY SPENDING $XXX ON TRAINING EMPLOYEES TO USE THE NEW COMPUTER SYSTEM, THE XYZ CORPORATION WILL MEET THE FOLLOWING OBJECTIVES:

- 50 percent reduction in order processing time from receipt of order to shipping the product
- elimination of late penalties on accounts payable
- 100 percent of customer invoices mailed within 24 hours after shipment of product
- 50 percent reduction of accounts receivable
- 30 percent reduction in inventory
- elimination of back orders

KNOWLEDGE REQUIRED

- terminology
- system configuration
- interaction of hardware and software
- system start-up and shut-down procedures
- software packages (e.g. Windows 98, inventory, etc.)
- file set-up, accessing, and updating
- report generation

SKILLS REQUIRED

- keyboarding
- basic care of the system
- accessing appropriate software
- inputting and changing data
- report generation
- basic troubleshooting[19]

Figure 8-7

Training and Development Methods

METHOD	UTILIZED GENERALLY FOR			CONDUCTED PRIMARILY	
	Managers and Professionals	Operative Employees	All Employees	On-the-Job	Off-the-Job
Coaching			X	X	
Mentoring	X				X
Business Games			X		X
Case Study			X		X
Videotapes			X		X
In-basket Training			X		X
Internships	X			X	
Role Playing			X		X
Job Rotation			X	X	
Programmed Instruction			X		X
Computer-based Training			X		X
Cyberlearning:					
Internet/Intranet			X		X
Virtual Reality			X		X
Distance Learning and Videoconferencing			X		X
Classroom Programs			X		X
Corporate Universities			X		X
Community Colleges			X		X
On-the-job Training			X	X	
Apprenticeship Training		X		X	
Simulators			X		X
Vestibule Training		X			X

Training and Development Methods

When a person is working on a car, some tools are more helpful than others for certain tasks. The same logic applies to various training and development methods. Note the diverse methods shown in Figure 8-7. Note that T&D methods are used both on and off the job. Some methods are more applicable to managers and professionals and others to operative employees. However, the majority of T&D methods apply to all employees.

Coaching

Coaching is an on-the-job approach in which a manager provides one-to-one instruction. The coach (usually a senior manager) and the trainee (usually a less experienced management employee) jointly identify changes required

Coaching: An on-the-job approach in which a manager provides instruction on a one-to-one basis.

in particular areas of performance and then develop a plan to try out new behaviours.[20] The plan will outline on-the-job assignments, special projects, or even transfers that might help the junior manager gain the required skills and knowledge. The approach is to use opportunities available in the workplace as management development tools. Outside activities such as speaking engagements, conference attendance, and professional publishing also can be part of the plan. The key elements, however, are that development is planned, uses (mostly) workplace opportunities, and becomes part of a continual transfer of skills.[21] Thus, for this approach to be effective, the relationship between the coach and trainee must be based on mutual trust and confidence.

Mentoring

Mentoring is an approach to T&D in which the trainee is given the opportunity to learn on a one-to-one basis from more experienced organizational members. The mentor is usually an older, more experienced executive, located anywhere in the organization, who serves as a host, friend, confidant, and advisor to a new firm member. The relationship may be formally planned or it may develop informally; formal relationships, however, are most effective. Some research suggests a positive relationship between career prospects, higher incomes, and intensive mentoring.[22] Mentoring, then, is an important technique for improving the career prospects of all individuals within an organization.[23]

Mentoring: An on-the-job approach to training and development which the trainee is given the opportunity to learn on a one-to-one basis from more experienced organizational members.

Business Games

Simulations that represent actual business situations are referred to as **business games.** These simulations attempt to duplicate selected factors in a particular situation, which are then manipulated by the participants. Business games usually involve two or more hypothetical organizations competing in a given product market. The participants are assigned roles such as president, comptroller, or marketing vice president. They make decisions affecting price levels, production volumes, and inventory levels. Their decisions are normally manipulated by a computer program, so that the results simulate those of an actual business situation. Participants are able to see how their decisions affect other groups and vice versa. When a management trainee makes a bad decision that loses a million dollars (on screen), that trainee remembers the lesson learned—with no loss to the real company.

Business games: Simulations that represent actual business situations.

Case Study

The **case study** is a training method that asks trainees to solve real or simulated business problems. The trainee is expected to make decisions based on study of the information given in the case and, if an actual company is involved, on independent research of the company's environment. Typically, this method is used in the classroom with an instructor as facilitator.[24]

Case study: A training method that presents real or simulated business problems for trainees to solve.

Conference Method

The **widely used conference** (or discussion) **method** brings together individuals with common interests to discuss and attempt to solve problems. The group leader (often the supervisor) listens and keeps discussion on course,

Conference method: An instructional approach that brings together individuals with common interests to discuss and attempt to solve problems.

while encouraging group members to solve their own problems. Often trainees are solving real problems they may face in their everyday activities.

Videotapes

Videotapes continue to be a popular training tool, because they are flexible and inexpensive, which makes them especially appealing to small businesses that cannot afford more expensive approaches.

One application of videotapes is **behaviour modelling** — a technique of illustrating effective interpersonal skills and managerial behaviour in various situations. Behaviour modelling has been used successfully to train supervisors in such tasks as conducting performance appraisal reviews, correcting unacceptable performance, delegating work, improving safety habits, handling discrimination complaints, overcoming resistance to change, orienting new employees, and mediating between individuals or groups in conflict. [25]

Behaviour modelling: A training method that uses videotapes or live demonstrations to illustrate effective interpersonal skills or managerial functions.

In-Basket Training

In-basket training is a simulation in which the participant is given a number of typical memoranda, reports, and telephone messages. These papers, presented in no particular order, call for actions ranging from urgent to routine handling. The participant is required to act on the information, assigning priorities and making decisions.

In-basket training: A simulation in which the participant is given a number of typical memoranda, reports, and telephone messages.

Internships
Provided are examples of internship programs, which many believe are the bridge between academia and business.

Internships

Internships can also serve as an effective training method. As we discussed in Chapter 5, an internship program is a recruitment method whereby college or university students divide their time between attending classes and working for an organization.

From the employer's viewpoint, an internship provides an excellent means of viewing a potential permanent employee at work. Internships also provide advantages for students. The experience they obtain through working enables them to integrate theory learned in the classroom with the practice of management. At the same time, the interns' experience will help them determine whether or not the type of firm and the job appeals to them.

Role Playing

Role playing: A training method in which participants are required to respond to specific problems they may encounter in their jobs.

During a **role playing** exercise, participants are required to respond to specific problems they may encounter in their jobs. They learn by doing. Role playing is often used in management development. The technique is effective for teaching skills such as interviewing, grievance handling, performance appraisal, conference leadership, team problem solving, effective communication, or analysis of leadership styles. The Developing HRM Skills exercises in this book are an example of role playing.

Job Rotation

Job rotation: A training method that involves moving employees from one job to another to broaden their experience.

Job rotation involves moving employees from one job to another to broaden their experience, providing the breadth of knowledge often needed for performing higher level tasks. Rotational training programs help new employees understand a variety of jobs within their fields. There are, however, potential problems with this technique. New hires may be given such short assignments they feel more like visitors in a department than a part of the workforce. Since they often do not develop a high level of proficiency, they can lower the overall productivity of the work group. In addition, other employees may resent a fast-track employee rotating through their department who may in time become their boss.

Programmed Instruction (PI)

A teaching method that provides instruction without the intervention of an instructor is called **programmed instruction (PI).** Information is broken down into small portions, or frames. The learner reads each frame in sequence and responds to questions, receiving immediate feedback on response accuracy. If the answers are correct, the learner proceeds to the next frame. If incorrect, the learner repeats the frame. This approach provides immediate reinforcement and allows learners to proceed at their own pace. Programmed instruction material may be presented in a book or by more sophisticated, usually computerized, media.

Programmed instruction (PI): A teaching method that provides instruction without the intervention of an instructor.

Computer-Based Training

Computer-based training takes advantage of the speed, memory, and data manipulation capabilities of the computer. Increased speed of presentation and lessened dependence on an instructor are advantages. Computer-based training may also utilize multimedia. **Multimedia** enhances learning with audio, animation, graphics, and interactive video using the computer.

Technology is revolutionizing the way training and development programs can be delivered. One executive has stated, "It allows a human resources department to provide on-demand information that can be updated constantly and distributed nationally or globally."[26] Computer-based training is clearly more than a fad. In fact, the vast majority of large organizations use computers in training.[27] "A good example is Canadian Tire, with some 426 stores and 193 gasoline outlets serving communities nationwide, where continuous training for employees includes lessons on in-shop computers covering customer service procedures and technical updates on repairs.[28]

Computer-based training: A teaching method that takes advantage of the speed, memory, and data manipulation capabilities of the computer for greater flexibility of instruction.

Multimedia: A computer application that enhances learning with audio, animation, graphics, and interactive video using the computer.

Cyberlearning[29]

As we move rapidly toward just-in-time delivery of information, training and development professionals must have the expertise to develop strategies that optimize a firm's technological capabilities. *Cyberlearning* is a term used to identify these high-tech training methods, some of which are discussed next.

E-mail on the Internet may be used for distributing course material and sharing information. Interactive tutorials on the Internet and intranets also permit trainees to take courses on-line.

Intranets, proprietary electronic networks, permit delivery of programs that have been developed specifically for an organization's particular learning needs. To implement an intranet, an organization needs little more than a set

Intranets: Proprietary electronic networks that permit delivery of programs that have been developed specifically for an organization's particular learning needs.

Just-in-Time Training: An Example

Roy Levesque, a recent business school graduate, is in his first job as a district sales manager. He hasn't been in this position nearly long enough to feel confident in confronting one of his top sales reps, Glen Dikes. Glen has led the district in sales for the past eight years and is currently on track for a record year. Glen has a serious problem with alcohol abuse, however, and came to the office drunk for the third time this month.

Uncertain as to his next action, Roy turns to his personal computer and clicks on an icon that takes him to his firm's intranet program "Management Advisor/Drug and Alcohol Abuse/Confronting an Employee." This program, developed by the training department and several line managers, plays a video that describes the firm's policy on providing help to an employee with a substance abuse problem. It also details the steps of a confrontation interview.

The program then asks if the viewer would like to see an example of a confrontation interview. When Roy clicks on "yes," he sees a 10-minute tape of a confrontation interview showing the steps and points the manager should make, typical employee responses, and how a manager can deal with each.

Meanwhile, Dikes, suspecting that he may be fired, uses a company kiosk and clicks on the human resource icon. He reaches a program on "Employee Assistance/Drug Abuse & Alcohol/Telling Your Boss You Have a Problem." He then views a tape advising him how to inform his boss that he needs assistance for a personal problem and how to get help without being terminated.[31]

of networked PCs loaded with inexpensive browser software. Organizations may share a little of their intranet with outsiders but probably not all.[30] *Just-in-time training* becomes feasible with computers and the Internet or intranets.

Virtual Reality

Using virtual reality, trainees can view objects from a perspective otherwise impractical or impossible. For example, it is not feasible to turn a drill press on its side so it can be inspected from the bottom. A computer easily permits this type of manipulation.

Distance Learning and Videoconferencing

For the past decade, a number of firms in Canada have used videoconferencing and satellite classrooms for training. This approach to training is now interactive, offering much of the flexibility and spontaneity of a traditional classroom. At one IBM subsidiary, for example, highly sophisticated programs are offered over a satellite-based network. At each of the 44 sites on the system, a 25-inch monitor is used on a desk equipped with a student response unit connected to other classrooms and to the instructor. The student response unit has a voice-activated microphone, question and question-cancel buttons, and keypads that allow students to answer questions from the instructor. This technology can ensure consistent instruction, broaden access to training, and make it possible to train more people at lower costs per person.[32] It has proved its worth for remote locations with small numbers of learners, and offers particular benefits for multinational operations with far-flung operations, in which travel expenses can take an unacceptably large percentage of total training budgets.

Classroom Lecture

The traditional classroom lecture continues to be effective for certain types of employee training, as the lecturer may present a great deal of information in a relatively short time. Lectures are more effective when groups are small enough to permit discussion, when the lecturer is able to capture the imagination of the class, and when audiovisual equipment is used appropriately.

On-the-Job Training

On-the-job training (OJT) is an informal approach to training that permits an employee to learn job tasks by actually performing them. This form of training avoids the problem of transferring what has been learned to the job. Another benefit may be increased motivation, because it is clear to learners that they are acquiring the knowledge needed to perform their jobs. As the vice president of HR for a major Canadian retail company indicated, people "have a very low tolerance for sitting in classrooms learning out-dated theories. They want something useful, right now!"[33] However, the emphasis on production may detract from the learning process if trainees feel too much pressure to perform.

Both the manager and the trainee must recognize that OJT is a joint effort. To make OJT effective, the manager must create a climate of trust and open communication. The technique was successful for Recton Machine Works Ltd. in Sault Ste. Marie, Ontario, where an in-house job training strategy resulted in a 15 percent increase in production, allowing this 60-year-old company to expand.[34]

On-the-job training (OJT): An informal approach to training that permits an employee to learn job tasks by actually performing them.

Apprenticeship Training

Apprenticeship training is an integrated training and development technique that combines on-the-job training with classroom instruction. The job instruction component of apprenticeship is used to teach the requisite skills of a particular trade or occupation. Classroom instruction, which constitutes a relatively minor portion of the program (usually about 10–20 percent), teaches related theory and design concepts. For example, the four-year plumber program includes only three eight-week in-school sessions. In the classroom, plumber apprentices learn about such things as the physical properties of piping and other plumbing materials, industry codes, safety rules and operating procedures, trade tools and equipment, soldering techniques and the characteristics of various fittings and piping systems. On the job the trainees become familiar with relevant codes, regulations, and specifications and learn to install, service, and test systems and equipment.

Apprenticeship training: A combination of classroom instruction and on-the-job training.

HR Web Wisdom

http: www.pearsoned.ca/ mondy

HRDC — HR Links
Visit the "Sectoral Partnership Initiatives" link to learn more about apprenticeship programs in Canada.

The Canadian apprenticeship system includes more than 65 traditionally regulated occupations in four occupational sectors: construction (e.g., stone-mason, electrician, carpenter, plumber), motive power (motor vehicle mechanic, machinist), industrial (industrial mechanic, millwright) and service (baker, cook, hairstylist). In some of these regulated occupations, apprentices must earn a Certificate of Qualification by passing a provincial government examination. Apprentices who pass an interprovincial examination are awarded a Red Seal, indicating their qualifications are acceptable across the country.

All training must fit into a culture or it will not be effective, used, or accepted. Unfortunately, apprenticeship training never captured the imagination of the Canadian public, politicians, or educators.[35] With a few exceptions (mostly in the construction industry), apprenticeships have never fit into the mainstream North American culture. To make apprenticeships more acceptable as an alternative to college or university, the prestige of technical studies has to be raised and hands-on (cooperative) components made more meaningful. Students and parents must become convinced that apprenticeship leads to interesting careers and an acceptable standard of living. Advocates of apprenticeship can point to the successful example of Germany, where 65 percent of graduating engineers have previous apprenticeship training.[36]

Simulators

Simulators: Training devices of varying degrees of complexity that model the real world.

Simulators are training devices of varying degrees of complexity that model the real world. They range from simple paper mock-ups of mechanical devices to computerized simulations of total environments. Human resource development specialists may use simulated sales counters, automobiles, or airplanes.

Although simulator training lacks the immediacy and realism of on-the-job training, it is a useful way to give trainees preliminary experience of large, expensive equipment or dangerous environments. A prime example is in the training of airline pilots. A Brampton, Ontario company (Atlantic Aerospace Corp.), supplies aircraft maintenance simulator systems, both civilian and military, in Canada, Australia, the United States, and Saudi Arabia.[37] Space simulators allow astronauts to practise moving in an environment as close as possible to weightlessness. Sophisticated computer simulations let firefighters test strategy without burning real forests.

Vestibule Training

Vestibule training: Training that takes place away from the production area on equipment that closely resembles equipment used on the job.

Vestibule training takes place away from the production area on equipment that closely resembles equipment used on the job. For example, a group of lathes may be located in a training centre, where the trainees will be instructed in their use. This approach allows trainees to focus on learning the required skills without the stress of actual job performance, and also avoids disrupting production or customer service.

Orientation

Orientation: The guided adjustment of new employees, to the company, the job, and the work group.

After hiring, the initial T&D focus is on orientation. **Orientation**, a common type of formal training in Canadian organizations, is the guided adjustment of new employees, to the company, the job, and the work group. A well-planned orientation makes many of the other human resource management tasks easier. Companies recognize the benefits of orientation; according to a 1993 study conducted by the Canadian Labour Market and Productivity Centre, new employee orientation is the most widespread form of training in Canada, accounting for 20 percent of all training hours.[38]

A typical orientation program explains requirements for promotion and work rules. The mechanics of promotion, demotion, transfer, resignation, discharge, layoff, and retirement should be detailed in policy handbooks and given to each new employee. A summary of employee benefits is often provided.

Orientation is often the joint responsibility of the training staff and the line supervisor. As the new employee is concerned primarily with the job and with his or her supervisor, line involvement reduces anxiety about these factors, allowing the corporate message to be communicated more effectively. Successful orientation activities also tend to have a high degree of senior management involvement in program development and delivery.

Peers are also excellent information agents as they are usually more accessible to the newcomers than the boss. Peers also tend to have empathy for new people, experience within the organization, and the technical expertise to which new employees need access. Furthermore, close contact with peers helps new employees understand their co-workers' behavioural patterns, an important factor in effective job performance. There are, however, drawbacks to the peer orientation approach, sometimes called "following Nellie," or the "buddy system." Care must be taken to choose the right guide; otherwise the trainee may be exposed to bad work habits, safety procedures, and/or attitudes.

Purposes of Orientation

Orientation formats are unique to each firm. However, almost all emphasize the employment situation (job, department, and company), company policies and rules, compensation and benefits, corporate culture, team membership, employee development, and dealing with change and socialization.

The employment situation. A basic purpose, from the firm's viewpoint, is to have the new employee become productive as quickly as possible. Therefore, specific information about performing the job may be provided early on. Work becomes more meaningful and important to workers when they understand how it fits in with departmental and company goals.

Company policies and rules. Every job within an organization must be performed within the guidelines and constraints provided by policies and rules. Employees must understand these to have a smooth transition to the workplace. This information may be quite detailed, so it is often spelled out in an employee handbook.

Compensation and benefits. Employees have a special interest in the reward system. Information on pay and benefits is usually given during recruitment and selection, but a review is appropriate during orientation.

Corporate culture.　As discussed earlier in the book, the firm's culture—"how we do things around here"—covers everything from the way employees dress to the way they talk. New employees need to understand this culture, which can be communicated in a number of ways.

Team membership.　A new employee's ability and willingness to work in teams is most likely determined before he or she is hired. In orientation, the importance of becoming a valued member of the company team may be emphasized. Even though the individual is now and will always be important to organizations, many processes can be more effectively accomplished through teams. It is imperative that team spirit be instilled in each employee—and the sooner the better.

Employee development.　Employee development has become essentially a do-it-yourself process. However, some firms provide assistance in this area. Employees should know exactly what is expected of them and what is required by the firm for advancement in the job or for promotion. An individual's employment security is increasingly becoming dependent upon the ability to acquire a constantly changing range of needed knowledge and skills. Thus, employees should be kept aware of company-sponsored and external development programs and encouraged to take advantage of appropriate opportunities.

Dealing with change.　To survive in their jobs, employees at all levels must learn to deal effectively with change. To do so, they need to continually develop and expand their skills. This effort is advantageous for both the employee, who gains security, and the firm, which gains a more valuable performer.

Socialization.　To reduce the anxiety that new employees may experience, attempts should be made to integrate them into the informal organization. Although orientation programs are typically offered when an employee starts, they may also be useful at other times. As organizations change, different management styles may develop, communication methods may be altered, and the structure of the organization itself may take on a new form. Even the corporate culture may evolve into something different over time. Any of these changes may warrant reorientation. Without it, employees may find themselves in organizations they do not even recognize.

Stages in Effective Orientation

Typically, there are three major stages to an effective orientation program: a company overview, an introduction to the department, and follow-up.[39]

First, the HR department presents general information on matters that relate to all employees, such as a company overview, review of company policies and procedures, and salary levels. A checklist is often used to ensure that certain information is included (see Figure 8-8). It is also helpful for the new employee to know how his or her department fits into overall company operations. As well, orientation programs should provide information about how company products or services benefit society as a whole.

The employee's immediate supervisor is usually responsible for the second stage of orientation, although in some instances, the supervisor may delegate this task to a senior employee. This stage includes an overview of the department, a

Figure 8-8

New Employee Checklist

NEW EMPLOYEE CHECKLIST

Name ——————————— Employment Date ——————

Position Title ————————— Department ——————————

Pay Grade —— Appointment Type: PT —— FT —— Supervisor ——————

Probationary Period Ends ————————————————————

Five Month Performance Appraisal Due ——————————————————

Information Provided:

Orientation packet   By: ——————   Date ——————

I.D. card   By: ——————   Date ——————

Staff handbook   By: ——————   Date ——————

Grievance guide   By: ——————   Date ——————

Retirement information   By: ——————   Date ——————

Life insurance   By: ——————   Date ——————

Disability insurance   By: ——————   Date ——————

Supplementary health insurance By: ——————   Date ——————

I understand that an exit interview with a Human Resource Department representative is required of all terminating employees receiving benefits.

I have received the information checked above, understand my employment status, and have been fully informed about my insurance options and benefits.

I have chosen not to enrol in Supplementary health, Life, Disability insurance. (Circle those you are not enrolling in.)

————————————————————————   ————
Employee Signature   Date

————————————————————————   ————
Human Resource Representative   Date

Effective Date ————————————————

review of job requirements, a tour, a question and answer session, and introductions to other employees. In addition, safety needs to be stressed from the very first day on the job.[40] It is crucial that the supervisor clearly explain performance expectations and specific work rules. As well, the supervisor should try to ease the new hire into the informal work group as quickly as possible.

The new employee does not go through the orientation program only to be forgotten. Thus, the third stage involves an evaluation and follow-up by the human resource department in conjunction with the immediate supervisor. During the first week or so, the supervisor, with the assistance of human resource professionals, works with the new employee to clarify information and assure integration into the work group.

Figure 8-9

Sources of Training

	% Provided by In-House Staff Only	% Provided by Outside Suppliers Only	% Provided by Both
Salespeople	24	14	62
Professionals	12	19	70
Middle Managers	17	10	74
First-Line Supervisors	26	6	68
Senior Managers	11	20	69
Customer-Service People	37	6	57
Production Workers	51	5	45
Executives	9	31	60
Administrative Employees	27	14	59

Implementing Training and Development Programs

A well-conceived training program may fail if management can't convince the participants of its merits. Participants must believe the program will help them achieve their personal and professional goals. The credibility of HRD specialists, in turn, may depend on a series of successful programs.

A new program must be monitored carefully, and adjusted if necessary, especially during its initial phases. Training implies change, which some employees may resist vigorously. Others may simply wait, perhaps hoping that the program will fail. Participant feedback is vital so that the problems inevitable to any new program can be resolved before they undermine the program. Scheduling training for present employees may be particularly difficult because they already have specific full-time duties. Although it is the line manager's job to have positions covered while an employee is in training, the HRD manager must help with arrangements.

Records should be maintained on each employee's training program and performance both during training and on the job. This information is important not only in charting the individual employee's progress but also in measuring program effectiveness.[41] It can also be necessary to prove that supervisors have been trained properly—for example, when accidents are investigated.

Training conducted outside the organization also requires considerable coordination. As previously discussed, many business functions have been outsourced. This trend has included training and development for various types of employees. As shown in Figure 8-9, some training is likely to be provided by in-house staff only and some by outside suppliers only.

Evaluating Training and Development

Although billions of dollars a year are spent on employee training, there is no clear consensus within the training community on how to determine its value. Obviously, the credibility of T&D can be greatly enhanced by showing how the organization benefits from training programs. Thus, the HRD department must document its results in the form of memoranda to management and written reports.[42]

HRD professionals have taken several approaches to determining the worth of specific programs. These involve evaluations of 1) the participants' opinions of the program, 2) the extent to which participants have learned the material, 3) participants' ability to apply the new knowledge, 4) the extent to which training goals have been achieved, 5) return on investment, and 6) the practice and results of training in comparison to those of exemplary firms (benchmarking).

Participants' Opinions

Asking participants' opinions is an inexpensive approach that provides both immediate response and suggestions for improvements. Opinions, however, must be interpreted cautiously because they are subjective: they measure perceived learning rather than actual learning. For example, questionnaires filled out by recent participants in a three-day executive seminar in Bermuda are unlikely to be very critical. Even a seminar in a less exotic location can provide a welcome break from a hectic job, and this relief may lead to glowing evaluations. Furthermore, participants may not want to spoil the chances of others who might be chosen for future courses.

Extent of Learning

Tests of skill and knowledge may be used to determine what the participants have learned. For example, the same test could be administered before and after training. Employees could be assigned to an experimental group, which receives a particular training program, and a control group, which does not. Differences between the two groups on post-test results are attributed to the training.

Behavioural Change

While tests may indicate accurately what has been learned, they give little insight into whether the desired behavioural changes will take place. For example, a manager may learn about motivational techniques, but have difficulty applying the new knowledge. Consider the following scenario.

> Pat Sittel sat in the front row at a company-sponsored supervisory training seminar on empowering employees. As the lecturer made each point, Pat would nod her head in agreement. At the end of the two-day seminar, Pat demonstrated her understanding by writing an excellent essay on empowerment. Returning to her department, Pat tossed the essay onto her secretary's desk. "Ruth, stop working on those letters and get this typed up right away," she barked. "And then tell Ivan I want to see him. He didn't make out that last report the way I told him to." Although she

had understood the material presented in the seminar, Pat's failure to apply what she had learned didn't benefit the organization.

Behavioural change needs to be evaluated by the employee's supervisor. For example, Pat's manager might have been alerted to her overly intervening management style by the excessive overtime she put in. Measuring her overtime hours after training would give a partial objective measure of behavioural change; the supervisor might also get a more subjective impression of her management style by observing that morale in Pat's department was still low.

Accomplishment of Training and Development Objectives

Still another approach to evaluating T&D programs involves determining the extent to which stated objectives have been achieved. If the objective of an accident prevention program is to reduce the number and severity of accidents by 15 percent, for example, comparing accident rates before and after training provides a useful measurement of success. The problem is that many programs dealing with broader topics are more difficult to evaluate.

For example, suppose a group of executives was sent to a university for a one-week course in management and leadership development, and their performance actually improved after the course. This benefit might or might not be reflected in the overall performance level of the group, because other variables might distort the picture. Perhaps a mild recession has forced the layoff of several key employees; a competing firm has lured away one of the department's top engineers; or the company president has pressured the employment director to hire an incompetent relative. In any of these cases, the managers' new skills would not show up in an objective measure of department performance. While it is difficult to establish clear proof of the effect of training on performance it is important to try to obtain evidence of T&D's contributions to achieving organizational goals.[43]

Return on Investment (ROI)[44]

In return on investment evaluation, the training's monetary benefits are compared with its costs. The return on investment (ROI) may be calculated by first subtracting the costs from the total benefits of the training to produce the net benefits. Next, the net benefits are divided by the costs. An alternative method is to find the benefit/cost ratio (BCR). Here, you simply divide the total benefits by the cost. A literacy-skills training program at Magnavox provides an illustration:

> The training program produced benefits of $321 600 with a cost of $38 233. The BCR is 8.4. For every dollar invested, $8.40 was returned in the form of benefits. The net benefits are $283 367 ($321 600–$38 233). ROI is 741 percent ($283 367/$38 233 × 100). Using ROI, for every dollar invested in this training, there was a return of $7.41 in net benefits.

Usually, the benefits are the amount saved or gained in the year after training is completed. These benefits may continue but the effects may diminish over time. There are obviously difficulties in calculating either the ROI or the BCR—for example, it is difficult to determine how much of the benefits are due strictly to the training. However, estimates for other purposes are also imprecise.

Benchmarking[45]

Benchmarking uses exemplary practices of other organizations to evaluate and improve training and development programs. By some estimates, more than 70 percent of North American companies engage in some type of benchmarking. Most of this effort involves monitoring and measuring a firm's internal processes, such as operations, and then comparing the data with data from companies that excel in those areas. The use of benchmarking is expanding beyond core business operations and is being used by training functions. Because training programs for individual firms are unique, the training measures should be broad. For example, benchmarking questions often ask about the cost of training, the ratio of training staff to employees, and whether new or more traditional delivery systems are used. Information derived from these questions probably lacks the detail to permit specific improvements to the training curricula. However, a firm may recognize, for example, that another organization is able to deliver extensive training for relatively little cost. This information could then trigger the firm to follow up with interviews or site visits to determine whether that phenomenon represents a best practice. As training and development becomes more crucial to organizational success, determining model training practices and learning from them will become increasingly important.

In evaluating T&D programs, managers should strive for proof that the program is effective. Although such proof may be difficult to establish, the effect of training on performance should at least be estimated to show whether the training achieved its desired purpose.

Benchmarking: The use of exemplary practices of other organizations to evaluate and improve programs.

HR Web Wisdom

http: www.pearsoned.ca/mondy

Benchmarking
This site provides a number of benchmarking tools, techniques, surveys and studies.

HRM in *ACTION*

Is That Training Important?

Your boss has just returned from a conference. He has called all the supervisors into his office. "I want every employee in this place trained in CPR (cardiopulmonary resuscitation)," he says. Just this morning you got word of a big push to increase production for the upcoming seasonal surge in sales. You sure hope they get the CPR training done soon—you may need the treatment yourself. The boss has just asked you, "When do you want to schedule your people for the four hours of CPR training?"

How would you respond?

A GLOBAL PERSPECTIVE

Global Orientation

Because of the cost of global staffing and the staggering cost of failed expatriate assignments, employee orientation takes on increased importance in global operations.[46] For example, new employee orientation and training were critical priorities for both a joint venture between General Motors and Toyota and an alliance between Chrysler and Mitsubishi. In these two partnerships, millions of dollars were spent on orientation and training long before the manufacturing stage. The success of these global companies suggests that international alliances should expend as much effort preparing new employees to deal with the social context of their jobs (and to cope with the insecurities and frustrations of a new learning situation) as they do developing the technical skills that employees need to perform effectively.[47]

Orientation for global assignments must also incorporate cultural and linguistic elements. David Wheatley, director of DFW Consulting, a British firm, has suggested that "in order to be effective internationally, you have to not only be aware of different cultures, you must respect them and reconcile them."[48]

In the final analysis, international orientation should be a thoroughly planned process. Orientation plans must take into consideration technical, social and cultural factors as well as provisions for follow-up and evaluation. For example, Corning Inc. took the time to develop a thorough orientation plan. Two years after developing this comprehensive orientation system, the company showed a 69 percent reduction in voluntary turnover among new hires, an 8:1 benefit/cost ratio in the first year, and a 14:1 ratio annually thereafter.[49] Orientation programs should begin with an overview of the foreign country (including its history, culture and traditions), and the corporate values of partners—if necessary. Then, a description of the new venture, its organization, and management structure should be presented, followed by an introduction to the managers, departments, and co-workers.[50]

SUMMARY

1. Define training and development and learning organizations.

Training is designed to permit learners to acquire the knowledge and the skills needed for their present jobs. Development has a more long-term focus, involving learning that looks beyond today's job. Training and development is often referred to as human resource development. Learning organizations are firms that recognize the critical importance of continuous performance-related human resources development and take appropriate action.

2. Describe the training and development process.

Once the need for change is recognized and the factors that influence intervention are considered, the process of determining training and development needs begins. Essentially, two questions must be asked: *What are our training needs and objectives?* and *What do we want to accomplish through our T&D efforts?* The T&D process must be continuously evaluated to facilitate change and accomplish organizational objectives.

3. Identify the factors that influence training and development.

Training and development programs must have the full support of top management. All managers should be committed to and involved in the T&D process; they must be convinced that there will be a tangible payoff. Recent rapid changes in products, systems, and methods mean that employees need to upgrade their skills constantly and must not only adapt to but welcome change. An important role of the HRD manager is to help people set and reach their personal goals and to obtain the knowledge and the skills they need for present and future jobs.

4. Explain training and development needs and objectives.

Once the need for change is recognized by managers and employees, the next step is to determine specific training, education, and development needs. Three types of analyses are required: organization analysis, task analysis, and person analysis. Clear, concise, and measurable T&D objectives must be formulated next. Without goals, it is impossible to design and evaluate meaningful T&D programs.

5. Identify the various training and development methods.

Training and development methods include coaching, mentoring, business games, videotapes, in-basket training, internships, role playing, job rotation, programmed instruction, computer-based training, cyberlearning, classroom lectures, on-the-job training, apprenticeship training, simulators, and vestibule training.

6. Define orientation and identify the purposes and stages of orientation.

Orientation is the guided adjustment of new employees into the company, the job, and the work group. It acquaints employees with the employment situation, company policies and rules, compensation and benefits and corporate culture. Orientation may also cover employee development, dealing with change, and socialization. There are three typical stages in an effective orientation program: 1) general information about the organization, usually provided by the human resource department; 2) specific job training conducted by the employee's immediate supervisor; and 3) evaluation and follow-up conducted by the human resource department in conjunction with the immediate supervisor.

7. Identify major challenges of implementing training and development programs.

Management must believe in the net benefits of training and development. Participants must also believe a T&D program will help them achieve their personal and professional goals. T&D must be carefully monitored and modified. Records must be kept that chart the employees' progress and program effectiveness. Training also requires coordination, particularly when outside trainers are used.

8. Identify the methods by which training and development programs are evaluated.

Training and development programs are evaluated by several measures including participants' opinions, extent of learning, behavioural change, accomplishment of T&D objectives, return on investment (ROI), and benchmarking.

QUESTIONS FOR REVIEW

1. Distinguish between training, development, and the learning organization.

2. What are five training and development trends?

3. Describe the training and development process.

4. What types of analysis are required to determine T&D needs?

5. Explain five methods of training and development.

6. Define orientation and explain the reasons for employee orientation.

7. What are some of the major challenges of T&D programs?

8. Describe five methods of evaluating training and development programs.

DEVELOPING HRM SKILLS

An Experiential Exercise

Effective training cannot occur unless both content and methodology fit into the organization's culture.

Today will be a training day, with the training specialist from the main office attempting to train an unwilling supervisor. The specialist has almost completed this very difficult task and is looking forward to the last training session. All of the supervisors in this training session have risen through the ranks and have a definite dislike for university graduates. In addition, they all believe that they are experts on training in their areas. The training specialist wants to just get through this last briefing. As with the other supervisors, he'll show this supervisor the basics, and then go back to the main office where people are more receptive. As with the others, if no in-depth questions are asked, he'll provide no additional details. He really doubts if the main office expects much improvement anyway. This operation seems to be going okay as it is.

The supervisor involved in this training session is opposed to the training specialist trying to tell the supervisors how to train and resents being told that all supervisors must operate according to the methods of the company's new owner. This supervisor is scheduled to meet with the training specialist to learn how to train. It is rumoured that the specialist is some 24-year-old university graduate. According to the supervisor, "I was training my people before this hotshot was born. All of a sudden, we can't do anything right. I look forward to my private session. I'm going to reeducate the kid on training."

Two students will play roles in this exercise: one as the training specialist and the other as the supervisor. All students not playing roles should carefully observe the behaviour of both participants. The instructor will provide the participants with additional information necessary to complete the exercise.

Initiating a Training and Development Program?

As the initial training session began, John Robertson, the hospital administrator, spoke of the tremendous benefits he expected from the training and development program the hospital was starting. He also complimented Mariko Ohi, the human resource director, for her efforts in arranging the program. As he finished his five-minute talk, he said, "I'm not sure what Mariko has in store for you, but I know that training and development is important, and I'll expect each of you to put forth your best efforts to make it work." He then excused himself from the meeting and turned the program over to Mariko.

For several years Mariko had been trying to convince Mr. Robertson that the nurses could benefit from a training and development program. She believed that many problems within the hospital were related to knowledge upgrading. Reluctantly, Mr. Robertson had agreed to authorize funds to employ a consultant. Through management interviews and questionnaires completed by the supervisors, the consultant attempted to identify nursing training needs. In his final report, the consultant recommended twelve four-hour sessions emphasizing communication, skill upgrading, and motivation. Half the training would be done on company time and the other half on employee time (with no remuneration). Each session was to be repeated once so that nursing staff who missed it the first time could attend the second offering.

Mr. Robertson had signed the memo that Mariko had prepared, directing all nursing supervisors to support the training and development program. There was considerable grumbling, but all the nurses agreed to attend. As Mariko replaced Mr. Robertson at the podium, she could sense the lack of interest in the room.

Questions

1. Have any serious errors been made so far in the training program? What would you have done differently?

2. What advice do you have for Mariko at this point to help make the program effective?

CHAPTER

9

Career Planning and Development

CHAPTER OBJECTIVES

1. Define career planning and career development.

2. Describe career-related life stages.

3. Identify the career anchors that account for the way people select and prepare for a career.

4. Explain the importance of individual career planning and how a thorough self-assessment is crucial to career planning.

5. Define organizational career planning (OCP) and identify its objectives.

6. Describe the various types of career paths.

7. Explain plateauing.

8. Explain the concept of adding value to retain a present job.

9. Identify some of the methods of organizational career planning and development.

Mitch Allen and Thelma Gowen, both supervisors at Canadian Electronics of Hamilton, were in the employee lounge having a cup of coffee and discussing a point of mutual concern. Mitch said, "I'm beginning to get frustrated. When I joined Canadian four years ago, I really felt that I could make a career here. Now I'm not so sure. I spoke with the boss last week about where I might be in the next few years and all she kept saying was, "There are all kinds of possibilities." I need more than that.

I'd like to know what specific opportunities might be available if I continue to do a good job. I'm not sure if I want to spend my whole career here. I know we have cut out several management levels in the last couple of years. But there may be better chances for advancing my knowledge in other areas. This is a big company."

Thelma replied, "I'm having the same trouble. She told me, 'You are doing a great job and we want you to stay at Canadian.' I'd also like to know what other jobs are available if I get the proper training."

Obviously, Canadian Electronics has no career planning and development program. Mitch is frustrated, and Thelma wants to know what career avenues are available to her. Lacking this knowledge, they may decide not to remain with the company. Career planning and development are also important to the employer, because management must ensure that people with the necessary skills and experience will be available when needed.

In this chapter, we first discuss the concept of career planning and development. We then identify the major factors that affect career planning. Next, we address individual and organizational career planning. This is followed by a discussion of the various types of career paths. The concepts of adding value and plateauing are reviewed. Following this, we describe career development, career development responsibility, and the methods used in organizational career planning and development.

Career Planning and Development Defined

A **career** is a general course that a person chooses to pursue throughout his or her working life. **Career planning** is an ongoing process whereby an individual sets career goals and identifies the means to achieve them. The major focus of career planning should be the matching of personal goals with realistic work opportunities. Career planning should not concentrate only on advancement opportunities. Many traditional middle management positions have disappeared. Indeed, from a practical standpoint, there can never be enough high-level positions to make upward mobility a reality for everyone. At some point, therefore, career planning needs to focus on achieving personal successes that do not necessarily involve promotion.

One of the primary responsibilities of HR is to develop employees so they can accomplish organizational goals more effectively.[1] In **organizational career planning**, the organization identifies paths and activities for individual employees as they develop. Mitch and Thelma, in the opening vignette, were disgruntled because there was no evidence of any organizational career planning at Canadian Electronics. Organizational career planning is necessary to help ensure that an organization improves its ability to perform by identifying needed capabilities and the type of people required to perform in an ever-evolving business environment.[2]

Individual career plans and organizational human resource requirements cannot be considered in isolation from each other. A person whose individual career plan cannot be followed within an organization will probably leave the firm sooner or later—or, if forced to stay by lack of opportunities elsewhere, may become demoralized and less productive. Helping employees with career planning, therefore, meets the organization's needs as well as the individual's.

A **career path** is the job sequence one is likely to follow: for example, editorial assistant, production editor, managing editor or vice president. **Career development** is a formal human resource planning approach designed to ensure that people with the proper qualifications and experience are available

Career: A general course that a person chooses to pursue throughout his or her working life.

Career planning: An ongoing process whereby an individual sets career goals and identifies the means to achieve them.

Organizational career planning: The process of establishing career paths within a firm.

Career path: The job sequence one is likely to follow.

Career development: A formal human resource planning approach taken by an organization to ensure that people with the proper qualifications and experience are available when needed.

TRENDS and INNOVATIONS

A New Employment Contract

According to some HR experts, we have entered into a new era—a new employment contract—in which job security and loyalty to the organization, in the traditional sense, are dead.[3] Today fewer and fewer companies focus on offering real employment security. These companies do, however, offer career security through career planning and development. With such development, workers are offered opportunities to manage their complicated lives, deal with change, improve their skills and thus their employability in an ever-changing work environment. For example, CRS Robotics Corp., a Profit 100 company out of Burlington Ontario, offers its employees subsidized training even if not job related.[4] The responsibility rests on the employee to define what skills are most important to his or her career development. Under this new employment contract, employees owe the company their commitment while they are on board, and the company owes its workers the opportunity to learn new skills—but that's as far as the commitment goes.

According to Tom Pierson, manager of HR planning, staffing, and relocations at Hewlett-Packard (HP), not every firm buys into this new employment contract. HP rejects the employability doctrine outright, as just a rationalization for not being able to provide employment security. Hewlett-Packard has a corporate priority to offer employment security to its workers, avoiding layoffs and making every effort to keep employees on board, even during business downturns. HP "feels very strongly about employment security, and still cherishes careers with the company." Employment security is possible because of a commitment to career planning and development that prepares employees to contribute as the nature of work changes.[5]

Regardless of the company's employment philosophy, career planning and development are essential to ensure a qualified internal workforce, to decrease turnover and attrition rates, and to reduce the cost of retraining and educating new hires. A study by the Center for Creative Leadership, for example, indicated that companies with a greater emphasis on employee development enjoyed better retention rates and higher productivity levels. By contrast, even well-intentioned bosses may kill off their business by focusing on profit at the expense of people.[6]

HR Web Wisdom

http: www.pearsoned.ca/mondy

Career Planning
The steps in the career planning process are reviewed.

when needed. Career planning and development benefit both the individual and the organization.

Factors Affecting Career Planning

Several factors affect a person's view of a career. According to William Bridges, author of *JobShift*, the individual's place in the new economy is a product of the work environment, and the person's desires, abilities, temperament, and assets.[7] For today's worker and especially the newer entrants into the job market, the real prize is career security, which results from effective career planning.

Career security is the goal of developing a person's marketable skills and expertise, actions that help to ensure employment within a range of careers. Career security is different from job security. Job security implies long-term tenure in one job, often with one company, whereas career security results from a person's ability to perform within a career designation, often in more than one organization. Beyond the environmental and business conditions that shape the future of work (see Trends and Innovations Box) there are two major factors in career planning: career-related life stages and career anchors.

Career security: The development of marketable skills and expertise, actions that help to ensure employment within a range of careers.

Career–Related Life Stages

As people change constantly, they view their careers differently at various stages of their lives. Some of these changes result from the aging process, while others stem from opportunities for personal growth and increased status (see Figure 9-1).

The first stage, establishing identity, is typically reached between the ages of 10 and 20, when the individual explores career alternatives and begins to move into the adult world. Stage two (somewhere between the ages of 20 and 40) involves professional growth and becoming established in a career, including choosing an occupation and defining a career path. Self-maintenance and self-adjustment, characteristics of the third stage, generally last to age 50 and beyond. At this point, a person either accepts life as it is or attempts to make adjustments. Often career change and even divorce occur during this phase, because individuals seriously question the quality of their lives.

The final stage (mature) is sometimes seen as a time of diminishing physical and mental capabilities, during which a person may have lower aspirations and less motivation. In reality, although the older worker may be less able to perform intense physical work, most of the perceived problems associated with this final career stage are more imaginary than real.[8] This is a fortunate discovery, as

Figure 9-1

Life Stages

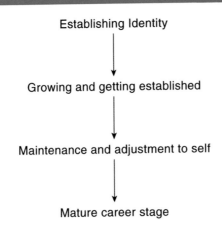

Source: *Adapted from James W. Walker,* Human Resource Planning. *(New York: McGraw-Hill Book Company, 1980). Used with permission of the McGraw-Hill Book Company.*

it is likely that in the future, many Canadians will be required to work into their 70s.[9] HR managers, then, will need to change entrenched attitudes that discriminate against older workers.

Career Anchors

Career anchor: Motives that account for the way people select and prepare for a career.

All of us have different aspirations, backgrounds, and experiences. Our personalities are moulded, to a certain extent, by the results of our interactions with our personal and work environments. The motives of today's workers in selecting and preparing for a career may be broad and complex. Such motives, or **career anchors,** include the following:[10]

1. **Managerial motivation.** The career goal of managers is to develop qualities of interpersonal, analytical, and emotional competence. These people are the traditional "careerists" who are motivated by organizational status and prestige and who aspire to climb the corporate ladder. People using this anchor want to manage people.

2. **Functional motivation.** The anchor for functional careerists is the continuous development of functional or technical talent. Many of these individuals do not seek managerial positions but look for more responsibility in their profession. For example, a young engineer may see himself down the road as a chief engineer.

3. **Security/income.** The anchor for security-conscious individuals is to stabilize their career situations, often by tying themselves to a particular organization or geographical location.

4. **Creativity.** Creative individuals tend to be entrepreneurial. They want to create or build something that is entirely their own. They have an entrepreneurial spirit, and want to be their own boss and work at their own pace.

5. **Autonomy and independence.** The career anchor for independent people is a desire to be free from organizational constraints. They value autonomy. In many cases these individuals are motivated by authenticity—they will not "hang up their personality" at the door, and they refuse to play the corporate game. You'll find many of these people starting up their own business.

6. **Technological competence.** A natural affinity for technology and a desire to work with technology whenever possible indicate technical competence.

7. **Lifestyle.** The motive or anchor for lifestylists is balance between work and family life. They expect their hard work to pay off by buying free time for play or other interests. They do not "live to work" but rather "work to live."

8. **Collegiality.** These workers value work relationships. They derive their identity from the work group or team. They are not happy working by themselves. The motive or anchor is a cohesive work environment.

Although each anchor has its own unique characteristics, they are not independent. In addition, most individuals share more than one trait. For example, a young lawyer may begin his or her career in a large legal firm; crave independence and lifestyle; and eventually start up a practice near a ski hill in a small town. In this case four career anchors come into play—functional competence, creativity, independence, and lifestyle. The point is that individuals must be aware, at various life stages, of what motives are most important to them in a work setting. Managers need to be flexible enough to provide alternative career paths and reward systems to attract and retain the best talent.

Career Planning

Through career planning—the process of planning a life's work—a person evaluates his or her own abilities and interests, considers alternative career opportunities, establishes career goals, and plans practical developmental activities. According to trend analyst Arnold Brown, more responsibility is shifting from employers to individuals: "People are being asked to take more control of their own careers and act like entrepreneurs."[11]

Flexibility in career planning is absolutely necessary in today's dynamic organizational environment. Workers must be ready to alter their career expectations and keep their options open in response to changes in the organization and the environment. For example, they might move sideways in the same organization to a more dynamic department, with no change in salary or title; leave the company for a more rewarding career elsewhere; remain in the same position and try to enhance their skills and explore new horizons; or move down to a job that may carry less weight but promises more growth.[12] Figure 9-2 presents guidelines to prepare for a new career path.

Individual Career Planning

Career planning begins with understanding oneself. One is then in a position to establish realistic career goals and to determine how to achieve these goals. Learning about oneself is referred to as **self-assessment**. Any characteristic that could affect one's future job performance should be considered. Realistic self-assessment may help a person avoid mistakes that could affect his or her entire career progression. Often (especially in times of high unemployment) an individual accepts a job without considering whether or not it matches his or her interests and abilities, an approach that can result in failure. Ideally, one should wait for a more suitable job, even if it carries a lower salary. If there is no choice but to accept a really unsuitable job, one should continue to look about for other options.

A thorough self-assessment helps to match an individual's specific qualities and goals with the right job or profession. Some useful tools include the strength/weakness balance sheet and the likes and dislikes survey.

Strength/Weakness Balance Sheet

A self-evaluation procedure that assists individuals in becoming aware of their strengths and weaknesses is called a **strength/weakness balance sheet**. Employees who understand their strengths can use them to maximum advantage,

Self-assessment:
The process of learning about oneself.

Self-Assessment
Individual self-assessment tools are presented.

Strength/weakness balance sheet:
A self-evaluation procedure that helps people become aware of their strengths and weaknesses.

Figure 9-2

Fourteen Steps on a New Career Path

1. **Accept the new values of the workplace by showing how you can help a company meet its bottom-line needs:** increasing profits, cutting costs, increasing productivity and efficiency, improving public relations, even getting new clients.

2. **Continually look for newer and better ways to be of more value to your employer.** Too many who did a good job 15 or 20 years ago are today doing the same thing and thinking that they are still doing a good job. Your company has changed; you need to change with it.

3. **Don't keep yourself stuck in an "information vacuum."** Today you can no longer afford to be unaware of what is happening to your company, industry, your community, your country, or, for that matter, the world.

4. **Don't be reactive.** Those who are successful today are those who prepare ahead of time, anticipate problems and opportunities, and get ready.

5. **Continually seek out a new education.** Expanded knowledge, increased information, and new skills are appearing at record pace. Those who are successful are those who find out what new skills and knowledge they need and who are taking the extra time and trouble to learn them. The others simply will not be competitive.

6. **Develop significant career and financial goals and detailed plans to reach them.** Otherwise, you are vulnerable.

7. **Avoid a state of denial.** When a person is in denial, he or she will ignore signs that something is wrong. Denial is one of the major reasons why people become immobilized and are not prepared for a problem or a change in the company.

8. **Prepare for survival in your present career and for taking the next job or career step.** Have you explored alternatives? Are your job search skills those of today, or are you using antiquated job search methods?

9. **Become motivated by your goals, not by anger, fear, or hopelessness.** In difficult and uncertain career situations, it is human nature to have strong feelings. The problem is that too many of us let those feelings guide our actions and our words.

10. **Market yourself aggressively.** Whether you have a job or are looking for a job, today's world demands that in order to survive and be successful, you must learn to market yourself; network with others, let others know the good work that you do, and don't burn your bridges by making unnecessary enemies. In particular, learn to market yourself within your present company.

11. **Improve your motivation and commitment.** Employers are no longer looking for those who are good enough, they are looking for those who are the most highly motivated. Demand and get the best out of yourself. Go to seminars and get counseling if there is a motivational block. Rejuvenate your enthusiasm and demonstrate it at work.

12. **Place your weaknesses and inadequacies in perspective;** do not allow them to loom so large in your mind that all you can see when you look in the mirror is failure. Remember that no one is without weaknesses, inadequacies, and mistakes.

13. **Realize that to survive and prosper in today's world, your primary job is to change yourself.** You are the one who has to keep up with your training and education. You are the one who has to learn new skills in networking. You are the one who has to develop a different perspective on your career and your employment.

14. **There's no reason HR professionals can't take advantage of the same professional counseling and guidance available to others.** Give yourself the edge and you can confidently move forward to define the career path you want.

Source: *Sander I. Marcus and Jotham G. Friedland, "Fourteen Steps on a New Career Path,"* HRMagazine *38 (March 1993): 55–56. Reprinted with the permission of* HR Magazine, *published by the Society for Human Resource Management, Alexandria, Virginia.*

while avoiding work situations emphasizing areas of weakness. Furthermore, by recognizing weaknesses, they are in a better position to overcome them.

To use a strength/weakness balance sheet, the individual lists strengths and weaknesses *as he or she perceives them*. This last phrase is important because of the importance of self-image to behaviour. Thus, a person who believes that he or she will make a poor first impression when meeting someone probably will make a poor impression. The perception of a weakness (or strength) often becomes a self-fulfilling prophecy.

Figure 9-3 shows an example of a strength/weakness balance sheet. Obviously Wayne (the person who wrote the sheet) did a lot of soul-searching

Figure 9-3

Strengths/Weaknesses Balance Sheet

STRENGTHS	WEAKNESSES
Work well with people.	Do not like constant supervision.
Like to be given a task and get it done in my own way.	Don't make friends very easily with individuals classified as my superiors.
Good manager of people.	Am extremely high-strung.
Hard worker.	Often say things without realizing consequences.
Lead by example.	Cannot stand to look busy when there is no work to be done.
People respect me as being fair and impartial.	Cannot stand to be inactive. Must be on the go constantly.
Tremendous amount of energy.	Cannot stand to sit at a desk all the time.
Function well in an active environment.	Basically a rebel at heart but have portrayed myself as just the opposite. My conservatism has gotten me jobs that I emotionally do not want.
Relatively open-minded.	
Feel comfortable in dealing with high-level businesspersons.	
Like to play politics. (This may be a weakness.)	Am sometimes nervous in an unfamiliar environment.
Get the job done when it is defined.	Make very few true friends.
Excellent at organizing other people's time.	Not a conformist but appear to be.
Can get the most out of people who are working for me.	Interest level hits peaks and valleys.
Have an outgoing personality—not shy.	Many people look on me as being unstable. Perhaps I am. Believe not.
Take care of those who take care of me. (This could be a weakness.)	Divorced.
Have a great amount of empathy.	Not a tremendous planner for short range. Long-range planning is better.
Work extremely well through other people. Get very close to few people.	Impatient—want to have things happen fast.
	Do not like details.
	Do not work well in an environment where I am the only party involved.

Source: *Wayne Sanders*

in making these evaluations. Typically, a person's weaknesses will outnumber strengths in the first few drafts. As the person repeats the process, however, some apparent weaknesses may eventually be recognized as strengths. Obtaining a clear understanding of one's strengths and weaknesses takes time. Typically, the process should take a minimum of one week. The balance sheet will not provide all the answers, but many people have gained a better understanding of themselves by completing one.

Other self-assessment methods are also available. One author has devised a personal analysis called DATA (for *Desires, Abilities, Temperament,* and *Assets*) which he suggests can be used to make realistic career choices. In his review of four books about career management, Ray Brillinger found that the writers agree on six essential points: [13]

1. The era of the single-employer (life long) career is past for almost everyone.

2. Virtually everyone must learn to practise self management—teams and networking have replaced the traditional boss.

3. Career planning must be proactive (attempting to forecast future events), not passive (waiting for an event to happen before acting).

4. Flexibility, adaptability, and life-long learning are keys to career success.

5. All jobs must be refined and redefined constantly.

6. Success is possible, but the methods have changed.

Likes and Dislikes Survey

An individual should also consider likes and dislikes as part of the self-assessment. A **likes and dislikes survey** helps people recognize restrictions they place on themselves. Some employees, for example, aren't willing to live in certain parts of the country; some aren't willing to travel more than a certain number of days per year. Such feelings limit the jobs that would be suitable for the person. Recognizing such self-imposed restrictions before the issue arises may reduce future career problems.

Some people would rather work within major organizations that sell well-known products. Others prefer smaller organizations, believing that the opportunities for advancement may be greater or that the work environment is more congenial. All such preferences that could influence job choice and performance should be listed in the likes and dislikes survey (see Figure 9-4).

Getting to know oneself is not a singular event. As people progress through life, their priorities change. People may think that they know themselves quite well at one stage of life and later begin to see themselves quite differently. Self-assessment, therefore, should be viewed as a continuous process.

Organizational Career Planning

Although the primary responsibility for career planning rests with the individual, organizational career planning identifies the paths and activities for individual employees.[14] Therefore, organizations must actively assist in the process. Organizational career planning must begin with a virtual redefinition of the way

Likes and dislikes survey:
A procedure that helps individuals recognize restrictions they place on themselves.

Figure 9-4

Likes and Dislikes Survey

LIKES	DISLIKES
Like to travel.	Do not want to work for a large firm.
Would like to live in the East.	Will not work in a large city.
Enjoy being my own boss.	Do not like to work behind a desk all day.
Would like to live in a medium-size city.	Do not like to wear suits all the time.
Enjoy watching football and baseball.	
Enjoy playing racquetball.	

Source: *Wayne Sanders*

work is done. The once stable, well-defined jobs of years past are now continually evolving, with the overall purpose of making the organization more adaptable in changing markets. Creativity, resourcefulness, flexibility, innovation, and adaptability are becoming much more important than the ability to perform a precisely specified job. Through effective organizational career planning, human resources will do better in developing a pool of men and women who can thrive in any number of organizational structures in the future.

The HR function should help redefine the concept of work by developing employees with multiple skills to fill broadly defined roles. Competence in a given job is less important than core competencies or the special skills that enable employees to be more productive. For example, the core competency at Walt Disney is the distinctive integration of creative, engineering, and marketing skills, which the company calls imagineering.[15] From the organization's viewpoint, career planning involves a conscious attempt to maximize a person's potential contributions. Consider your workers' aspirations and they will stay happier—a simple formula, but one often hard to execute.[16]

Career planning programs are vital in today's environment, in which traditional vertical mobility has all but disappeared. In most organizations, career planning programs are expected to achieve one or more of the following objectives:

- **More effective development of available talent.** Individuals are more likely to be committed to development that is part of a specific career plan.

- **Self-appraisal opportunities for employees considering new or nontraditional career paths.** Some excellent employers do not view traditional upward mobility as a career option since fewer and fewer promotion options are available. [17]

- **More efficient development of human resources within and among divisions and/or geographic locations.** Career paths should be developed that cut across divisions and geographic locations.

- **A demonstration of a tangible commitment to equity in employment.** It is often difficult to find qualified women and visible minorities to fill vacant positions. One means of overcoming this problem is to establish an effective career planning and development program.

- **Satisfaction of employees' personal development needs.** Individuals who see their personal development needs being met tend to be more satisfied with their jobs and with the organization.

- **Improvement of performance through on-the-job training experiences provided by horizontal and vertical career moves.** The job itself is the most important influence on career development. Each job can provide different challenges and experiences.

- **Increased employee loyalty and motivation, leading to decreased turnover.** Individuals who believe that management is interested in their careers will be more likely to remain with the organization.

- **A method of determining training and development needs.** If a person desires a certain career path and does not currently have the proper qualifications, a career plan will identify a training and development need.[18]

While all these objectives may be desirable, a successful career planning program depends on management's ability to meet those objectives considered most crucial to employee development and to the achievement of organizational goals.

HRM in *ACTION*

Legitimate Complaint?

"Fred, since you work in human resources, maybe you can explain why we hired Joanne Mendez," Dan Hakala asked of the human resource manager, Fred McGovern.

"What's the problem with Joanne, Dan?"

"Well, I went in to see Joanne and asked her to develop a career plan for me. I wanted to know how long it will take me to advance up the corporate ladder. She obviously doesn't know much about career planning."

"What did she do, Dan?" Fred asked.

"Well, instead of outlining a career plan, she said that I would need to first gain some self-insight. I've been here five years, and now she says I don't have enough self-insight, can you believe that? She wants me to do her job for her. In my opinion, someone should clean house in that department."

How would you respond?

Career Paths

Recall that a career path is the job sequence one is likely to follow. Historically, career paths have focused on upward mobility within a particular occupation and organization. Now, however, any one of five career paths may be developed: traditional, network, lateral skill, dual and transitory.

Types of Career Paths

Traditional or Vertical Career Path

The **traditional or vertical career path** is one wherein an employee progresses upward in the organization from one specific job to the next. The assumption is that each preceding job is essential preparation for the next, higher-level job. Therefore, an employee must move, step by step, from one job to the next to gain needed experience and preparation.

One of the biggest advantages of the traditional career path is that it is straightforward. The path is clearly laid out, and the employee knows the specific sequence of jobs through which he or she must progress. Today, however, the traditional approach has become harder to follow because of two broad changes in the workplace: on the one hand, a massive reduction in management positions and levels, due to mergers, downsizing, stagnation, and reengineering; and on the other hand, a decrease in paternalistic feelings toward employees, resulting in less job security and an erosion of employee loyalty. In addition, the work environment is changing so rapidly that new skills must be learned constantly. The certainties that characterized yesterday's business methods, then, have vanished in many industries. According to many experts, a predictable, secure career path will be open to only a very few employees.

Traditional or vertical career path: A vertical line of career progression from one specific job to the next.

Network or Spiral Career Path

The **network or spiral career path** contains both a vertical sequence of jobs and a series of horizontal opportunities. This approach recognizes the interchangeability of experience at certain levels and the need to broaden experience at one level before promotion to a higher level. The vertical and horizontal options lessen the probability of career blockage. One disadvantage of this type of career path is that it is more difficult to explain to employees the specific route their careers may take for a given line of work.

Network or spiral career path: A method of job progression that contains both vertical and horizontal opportunities.

Lateral Skill Path

Traditionally, a career path was viewed as moving upward to higher levels of management in the organization. The previous two career path methods include this possibility. But even when modern corporate structures mean no promotion is available, it does not follow that an individual has to remain in the same job for life. The **lateral skill path** allows for lateral moves within a firm that permit an employee to become revitalized and to find new challenges. A pay raise or promotion are not usually involved, but individuals can increase their value to the organization and themselves by gaining a broad range of experience.

Lateral skill path: A career path that allows for lateral moves within a firm to permit an employee to become revitalized and to find new challenges.

Dual Career Path

Dual career path: A career path that recognizes functional specialists should be allowed to contribute their expertise to a company without having to become managers.

As we move to a more technical and electronic work environment, the dual career path is becoming increasingly popular. [19] The **dual career path** recognizes that functional specialists such as engineers and technologists should be allowed to contribute their expertise to a company without having to become managers. For example, in leading organizations, such as Nortel Networks, dual career paths are established to encourage technical workers to remain in their field of expertise. Individuals are rewarded as they improve and hone their specialized technical knowledge. Compensation is comparable for technical and management jobs considered to be at a similar level.

The dual career path is becoming increasingly popular. In our highly technical world, specialized knowledge is often as important as managerial skill. Rather than creating poor managers out of competent technical specialists, the dual career path permits an organization to retain both highly skilled managers and highly skilled technical people. [19]

Transitory Career Path

Transitory career path: A career that adopts whatever occupation is available at the time.

According to David Foot and Daniel Stoffman in *Boom Bust & Echo*, "A worker who follows a **transitory career path** adopts whatever occupation is available at the time." [20] Typically, transitory workers do not hold a full-time job. These are the contingency workers we described in Chapter 2—the fastest growing part of our labour force. For example, an HR graduate might start out in the government as a temporary worker, then branch out as a home-based consultant, and later take a two-year overseas assignment as contract consultant for a multinational.

In the future the fastest-growing career paths will be the network and transitory paths. The contingency or transitory workforce will be made up of consultants, freelancers, subcontractors, and part-timers. Spiral or network workers will work in downsized, flatter organizations. They will make at least five lateral moves during their career. They will have to add value to their jobs and contend with the realities of plateauing.

Adding Value to Retain Present Job

According to HR practitioners like Barbara Moses, president of BBM Human Resource Consultants, the only job security in today's market is the extent to which an employee adds value to the organization. [21] The new attitude among many companies is this: "You will be employed by us as long you add value to the organization, and you are continuously responsible for finding ways to add value. In return, you have the right to demand interesting and important work, the freedom and resources to perform it well, pay that reflects your contribution, and the experience and training needed to be employable here or elsewhere." [22]

As an employee increases his or her value to an organization, the employee's value in the overall job market also increases. Job security has thus come to mean the ability and skill set to find another job—a concept that might be called enlightened self-interest. A person must discover what employers need and then develop the necessary skills to meet these needs. As one Avon executive stated, "Always be doing something that contributes significant, positive change to the organization. That's the ultimate job security." [23]

For many workers, the only tie that binds a worker to the company is a common commitment to success and growth.

Plateauing

People who aspire to move upward within their present organization may often be frustrated by **plateauing**. Plateauing, the state in which an employee's job functions and work content remain the same because of a lack of promotional opportunities with the firm, occurs at some point to almost every employee.[24] Plateauing in the 1990s became common because many organizations were downsizing and hierarchies were flattening, just as the baby-boom generation (those born between 1947 and 1966) began to reach its prime. In addition, women and minorities began competing for positions that once were not available to them.

Traditionally, for a large segment of the labour force, promotion has been an important measure of success. Thus, plateauing presents new organizational challenges if employees are to be kept productive and interested in their work. This problem can be approached in several ways. As mentioned previously, individuals can be moved laterally within the organization. Although status or pay may remain unchanged, the employee is given the opportunity to develop new skills. Managers who want to encourage lateral movement may also choose to use a skill-based pay system. Another approach is job enrichment, as we discussed in Chapter 4. Here, the challenges associated with the job are increased (without promotion), giving the work more meaning, leading to a greater sense of accomplishment. Exploratory career development, usually comprising short-term assignments in an area of potential interest, is yet another way of dealing with plateauing. These temporary transfers give an employee the opportunity to test ideas in another field without being committed to an actual move.

Plateauing: A career condition that occurs when an employee's job functions and work content remain the same because of a lack of promotional opportunities within a company.

Career Development

As we noted at the beginning of this chapter, career development is the formal approach taken by management to ensure that people with the proper qualifications and experience are available when needed. The goal is to enable a person to add value continuously, in order to satisfy organizational needs, both now and in the future. This process should involve everyone in the company.[25] Career development programs may be conducted in-house or by outside sources, such as professional organizations, colleges, or universities.

In-house programs are usually planned and implemented by a training and development unit within the firm's human resource department. Line managers often conduct program segments. Outside the company, organizations such as the Canadian Institute of Management and professional associations conduct conferences, seminars and other types of career development programs.

Certain principles should be observed when planning career development programs. First, the job itself has the greatest influence on career development. When each day presents a different challenge, what is learned on the job may be far more important than formally planned development activities. Second, the type of developmental skills needed should be determined by specific job demands. The skills necessary to become a first-line supervisor, for example, will likely differ from those needed for a promotion to middle management. Third, development will occur only when a person has not yet obtained all the skills demanded by his or her current job. Transferring an employee to a new job he or she is already fully capable of doing will produce little or no learning. Finally, the time required to develop the skills necessary for a planned goal can be reduced by identifying a rational sequence of job assignments.

Responsibility for Career Development

Many key individuals must work together if an organization is to have an effective career development program. Management must first make a commitment to support the program through policy decisions and by allocating sufficient resources. Human resource professionals are responsible for implementation, as they provide the necessary information, tools, guidance, and liaison with top management. The employee's immediate supervisor is responsible for providing support, advice, and feedback. The supervisor's attitude indicates to the employee the level of support for career development within the organization. Ultimately, however, the individual is responsible for developing his or her own career.[26]

Career Development Planning

Managers can assist individuals in career planning and development in numerous ways. Some current methods, most of which are used in various combinations, are listed here.

- **Superior/Subordinate Discussions.** The superior and subordinate jointly agree on career planning and development activities. The resources made available to achieve these objectives may support formal or informal development programs. Human resource professionals are often called on for assistance, as are psychologists and guidance counsellors.

- **Company Material.** Some firms provide material specifically developed to assist their employees in career planning and development. This material can be tailored to the firm's special needs.

- **Performance Appraisal System.** The firm's performance appraisal system can also be a valuable tool in career planning. Noting and discussing an employee's weaknesses and strengths can uncover development needs and suggest possible opportunities. If overcoming a particular weakness seems difficult or impossible, an alternative career path may be the solution.

- **Workshops.** Some organizations conduct workshops to help employees develop career paths. Employees define and match their specific career objectives with the needs of the organization.

A GLOBAL PERSPECTIVE

Culture Shock

It is estimated that 20 percent of the personnel sent abroad return prematurely; many others endure global assignments but are ineffective in their jobs, while their social lives can suffer to the point of marriage break-up. As a result, some consultants are advising their clients to hire a professional relocation services firm to help ease the problems of managers working abroad.[27]

The main reason for expatriate failure is culture shock, the feelings of anxiety regarding customs and security that can appear when an individual deals with a foreign society. Culture shock is often accompanied by medical and personal problems that can continue even after the employee returns home. In fact, one study found that many returned expatriates faulted their companies for not doing more 1) to prepare them for the shock of living in another culture; 2) to help their spouse find a job; or 3) to plan how the overseas assignment would fit into their career path.[28]

Prematurely returning employees are nearly always placed in positions with less decision-making ability and autonomy, lower pay, and fewer benefits. Worse, approximately one-quarter of all employees on overseas assignment do not have a position to return to. Others leave the company immediately, take demotions, or relocate. Many of these setbacks result from inadequate career planning, in that the overseas assignment is not regarded as part of an agreed-upon career path.

SUMMARY

1. Define career planning and career development.

Career planning is an ongoing process whereby an individual sets career goals and identifies the means to achieve them. Career development is a formal approach taken by the organization to ensure that people with the proper qualifications and experience are available when needed.

2. Describe career-related life stages.

Each person's career goes through stages that influence the person's knowledge of and preference for various occupations. People change constantly; thus, they view their careers differently at various stages of their lives. Some of these changes result from the aging process and others from opportunities for growth and status. The main stages of the career cycle include establishing identity, growing and getting established, maintenance and adjustment to self, and maturity.

3. Identify the career anchors that account for the way people select and prepare for a career.

The career anchors are managerial motivation, functional motivation, security/income, creativity, autonomy and independence, technological competence, lifestyle, and collegiality.

4. Explain the importance of individual career planning and how a thorough self-assessment is crucial to career planning.

Career planning is the ongoing process by which individuals plan their life's work. A person evaluates his or her own abilities and interests, considers alternative career opportunities, establishes career goals, and plans practical developmental activities. In career planning, more responsibility is shifting from employers to individuals. Individual career planning is an ongoing process that should be carried out in tandem with organizational planning.

Career planning begins with a thorough self-assessment to match an individual's specific qualities and goals with the right job or profession. A strength/weakness balance sheet can be helpful, as can a list of likes and dislikes.

5. Define organizational career planning (OCP) and identify its objectives.

The process of establishing career paths within a firm is referred to as organizational career planning. In most organizations, career planning programs are expected to achieve one or more of the following objectives: 1) more effective development of available talent; 2) self-appraisal opportunities for employees considering new or nontraditional career paths; 3) more efficient development of human resources within and among divisions and/or geographic locations; 4) a demonstration of a tangible commitment to equal employment opportunity and affirmative action; 5) satisfaction of employees' personal development needs; 6) improvement of performance through on-the-job training experiences provided by horizontal and vertical career moves; 7) increased employee loyalty and motivation, leading to decreased turnover; and 8) a method of determining training and development needs.

6. Describe the various types of career paths.

In the traditional or vertical career path, an employee progresses vertically upward in the organization from one specific job to the next. The network or spiral career path contains both a vertical sequence of jobs and a series of horizontal opportunities. The horizontal path is often composed of lateral moves within the firm that allow an employee to become revitalized and find new challenges. The dual career path recognizes that functional specialists can and should be allowed to continue to contribute their expertise to a company without having to become managers. A worker who follows a transitory career path adopts whatever occupation is available at the time—usually on a contract basis. In the future the fastest- growing career paths will be the network and transitory paths.

7. Explain plateauing.

Plateauing occurs when an employee's job functions and work content remain the same because of a lack of promotional opportunities within the firm. Several approaches may be used to deal with this problem, including lateral employment moves, job enrichment, and exploratory career development.

8. Explain the concept of adding value to retain a present job.

Regardless of the career path pursued, today's workers need to develop a plan whereby they are viewed as continually adding value to the organization. If employees cannot add value, the company does not need them, and much of the evolving work environment cannot use them either. Workers must anticipate and obtain the skills that will be needed for success in the future.

9. Identify some of the methods of organizational career planning and development.

Methods of organizational career planning and development include superior/subordinate discussions, company information material, performance appraisal system, and workshops.

QUESTIONS FOR REVIEW

1. Define the following terms:
   a. Career
   b. Career planning
   c. Organizational career planning
   d. Career path
   e. Career development.

2. Identify and discuss the basic career-related life stages that people pass through.

3. List and briefly define career anchors.

4. How should a strength/weakness balance sheet and a likes and dislikes survey be prepared?

5. What objectives are career planning programs expected to achieve?

6. What are the types of career paths? Briefly describe each.

7. Why is it important for an individual to constantly add value to the company?

8. Define plateauing.

9. Who is responsible for career development? Why?

10. Identify and describe some of the methods of organizational career planning and development.

DEVELOPING **HRM** SKILLS

An Experiential Exercise

Career planning and development is extremely important to many people. Workers want to know how they fit into the future of the organization. Employees who believe that they have a future with the company are often more productive than those who don't. This exercise is designed to assist in understanding what it takes for a human resource professional to progress through an organizational hierarchy. This progression depends partly on the individual's self-perceptions and perceptions of past experiences with the company. The exercise provides one method of individual career planning for the human resource manager described in the following scenario.

The individual being evaluated is 35 years old today and is put in a reflective mood by the birthday. At a career crossroads, this person looks back on 10 years of moderate success but realizes that few others in the organization of comparable age have more education or work experience. In fact, the company has several middle-and upper-level managers who are much older, often less intelligent, and who seem to spend an inordinate amount of time at the country club.

Assume that you are this person and have set your sights on an important human resource middle-management position in the next five to seven years, and a top management position with your organization in the next 10 to 15 years. You have figured out there are 20 factors that determine upward movement in your organization. You are now trying to decide which are most important for survival and success, and which are least important. This decision will determine whether you take the career path to organizational survival and success, or the path to career failure and stagnation.

Each student will be given a list of 20 factors. Rank the importance of each factor for your survival and success in the organization, with 1 being the most important factor, 2 the next most important, and so on.

Everyone in the class can participate in this exercise. Your instructor will give you additional information necessary to complete the exercise.

HRM INCIDENT

Decisions, Decisions

A nervous Derek Crow was ushered into the Levitt Corporation president's office by the secretary. In the office he encountered Alain Lebel, the human resource manager, and Peter Gorman, the vice-president. Derek was flattered when Peter stood to shake his hand.

"I'll make this short and sweet," Peter said. "You probably have heard that Alain plans to retire at the end of next year. In preparing for the staff changes, we would like to move you in as his assistant to get some cross-training experience."

Derek responded, "Why me, Mr. Gorman? I'm a purchasing coordinator. I've never even worked in the human resource area."

"Well," replied Peter, "we've been watching you carefully. I have personally reviewed your qualifications. From the company's standpoint, we know you can do the job. We need people who have been out in the company and can bring fresh perspectives to the human resource area." Peter instructed Derek to discuss the idea with Alain. Then he said he had to leave for another meeting. As he shook Derek's hand, he said, "We would like to coordinate your transition from the purchasing department to make it as smooth as possible for everyone, and I know you're involved in some priority projects over there. Alain will get back with me on a timeframe after you and he talk."

Derek was 32 and he had been with Levitt for seven years. His business administration degree, from the University of Victoria, had included a heavy concentration in the behavioural sciences. He thought this background probably was a factor in his selection. But Derek had worked only in purchasing. After three successful years as a buyer, he had been promoted to purchasing coordinator, with responsibility for supervising eight buyers and a small clerical staff.

He knew he was respected throughout the company. This was especially true in the production department, which had a great deal of interaction with purchasing. The production manager made no secret of his high regard for Derek. Derek also had taken time to get to know members of the finance and research department. In building these relationships, he had been seeking only to do his purchasing job better. He had had no idea that he would be considered for a job in the human resource department.

Questions

1. How should Derek respond to the new assignment? Discuss.

2. What are the main qualifications for a senior human resource manager? Discuss Derek's apparent qualifications for such a job.

3. If you were Derek, how would you decide if you wanted to accept the new job?

CHAPTER

10

Performance Appraisal

CHAPTER OBJECTIVES

1. Define performance appraisal and performance management.

2. Identify the uses of performance appraisal.

3. Describe the performance appraisal process.

4. Identify the aspects of a person's performance that an organization should evaluate.

5. Identify who may be responsible for performance appraisal.

6. Identify the various performance appraisal methods used.

7. List the problems that have been associated with performance appraisal.

8. Explain the characteristics of an effective appraisal system.

9. Explain how the appraisal interview should be conducted.

10. Describe assessment centres.

D oug, we simply must increase our productivity," exclaimed Marco Ghignoni, vice president of production for Block and Becker. "If we don't, the foreign competition is going to eat our lunch. It's not as if worker productivity has declined—or not much, anyway—but our people should be working together to improve it, and somehow they just don't seem to have the incentive to do it."

"I agree with you, Marco," said Doug Overbeck, vice president for human resources. "Part of the problem is this team stuff. Don't get me wrong, I'm convinced that our team approach in manufacturing is the right way to go. But it sure screws up the performance appraisal and reward systems. I mean, how are we supposed to evaluate team results and still somehow recognize who's really putting in something special and who's just going through the motions? All I know is, we better do something about it—and fast!"

Marco and Doug had begun to realize a need for identifying both team and individual performance. When a performance appraisal system is geared totally toward individual results, it is not surprising that employees show little interest in working in teams.[1] On the other hand, individual contributions must also be taken into account.

The overall purpose of this chapter is to emphasize the importance of performance appraisal as it relates to organizational effectiveness and its special implications for developing the firm's human resources. We begin this chapter by defining performance appraisal and its primary role in performance management. We then explain the uses and process of performance appraisal, what to evaluate, and responsibility for appraisal. We follow this with a discussion of the performance appraisal period, methods, and problems. Next, we describe the characteristics of an effective appraisal system, the appraisal interview, and assessment centres.

Performance Appraisal Defined

Performance appraisal (PA) is a system of review and evaluation of an individual's or team's job performance. Effective performance appraisal is a comprehensive employee review process—not just an event that occurs once a year. Accomplishments are assessed, feedback is provided, areas of improvement are identified, corrective plans are developed, and new personal goals are initiated.[2]

Conducting performance appraisals is often frustrating.[3,4] The negative aspects of the task tend to loom larger than the positive, and many managers, perceiving that employees dread appraisals, dislike them themselves But the task cannot be avoided. Performance appraisal is often linked to key organizational functions such as promotions, pay raises, terminations, transfers, admission to training programs, and areas with legal ramifications. Most organizations conclude there is a genuine need for evaluation, both from the point of view of the organization and of employees. Developing an effective performance appraisal system has been and will continue to be a high priority of human resource management

In well-run organizations, performance appraisal is a key element in the **performance management** system: that is, the process through which managers and employees work together to set expectations, review results, and reward performance. According to one study, firms that have effective performance management processes in place outperformed those without such systems on several critical measures including profits, cash flow, and stock market performance.[5]

Performance management has been described as an ongoing three-step process:[6]

1. **Performance planning,** by managers and employees, to determine performance expectations;

2. **Performance coaching/mentoring,** throughout the appraisal period;

3. **Performance appraisal/review:** a formal step that results in the individual and/or team evaluation.

Performance appraisal (PA): A formal system of periodic review and evaluation of an individual's or team job performance.

Performance management: The process of having managers and employees work together to set expectations, review results and reward performance.

Uses of Performance Appraisal

Although the primary goal of an appraisal system is normally to improve performance, appraisals are useful in several other areas.

Human resource planning. In assessing a firm's human resources, data must be available that describe the promotability and potential of all employees, especially key executives.

Recruitment and selection. Performance evaluation ratings may be helpful in predicting the performance of job applicants. For example, appraisal data may show that successful managers in a firm (identified through performance evaluations) exhibit certain behaviours when performing key tasks. These data may then provide benchmarks for evaluating applicant responses.

Training and development. A performance appraisal should point out an employee's specific needs for training and development. For instance, if Anne Jones's job requires skill in technical writing and she receives a marginal evaluation on this factor, she may need additional training in written communication.

Career planning and development. Performance appraisal data are essential in assessing an employee's strengths and weaknesses and in determining the person's potential. Managers may use such information to counsel employees and assist them in developing and implementing their career plans.

Compensation programs. Performance appraisal results provide a basis for rational decisions regarding pay adjustments. To encourage good performance, a firm should design and implement a fair performance appraisal system and then reward the most productive workers and teams accordingly.

Internal employee relations. Performance appraisal data are also frequently used for decisions in several areas of internal employee relations, including motivation, promotion, demotion, termination, layoff, and transfer. Keep in mind that self-esteem is essential for motivation. Therefore, appraisal systems must be designed and implemented in such a way as to maintain employees' self-esteem. Brutally frank descriptions of performance demotivate people.[7] On the other hand, ignoring deficiencies in a person's performance may hinder that individual's opportunity to improve and achieve his or her potential.

Assessment of employee potential. Some organizations attempt to assess employee potential as they appraise job performance. The best predictors of future behaviour are said to be past behaviours. However, an employee's past performance in a job may not accurately indicate future performance in a higher level or different position. For example, the best computer programmer may, if promoted, be a disaster as a data processing manager. Overemphasizing technical skills and ignoring other equally important skills are common errors in promotion decisions. Thus some firms separate the appraisal of performance,

which focuses on past behaviour, from the assessment of potential, which is future-oriented. These firms have established assessment centres, which we discuss in a later section.

The Performance Appraisal Process

This review process helps determine how well employees have accomplished the goals set for them, determines reasons for deficiencies, and prepares a plan to correct the problems. The discussion also results in establishing goals for the next evaluation period. Figure 10-1 shows a standard example of a review appraisal process.

The starting point in developing a performance appraisal process is to identify specific goals, keeping in mind the organization's internal and external environment. An appraisal system probably will not be able to serve every desired purpose effectively. Therefore, management should concentrate on the most important goals and ones that can realistically be achieved. For example, some firms may want to stress employee development; other organizations may want to focus on administrative decisions, such as pay adjustments. Too many performance appraisal systems fail because management expects too much from one method and does not determine specifically what it wants the system to accomplish.

After specific appraisal goals have been established, workers and teams must understand what is expected from them in their tasks. This understanding is greatly facilitated when the employees have had input into establishing goals. Next the work performed is examined and appraised. Lastly, the appraiser and the employee review work performance and evaluate it against established performance standards. This final step provides input into the establishment of new job expectations, as shown in Figure 10-1.

What to Evaluate

What aspect of a person's performance should an organization evaluate? In practice, the most common sets of appraisal criteria are traits, behaviours, task outcomes and skills and competencies.[8]

Traits

Employees are often evaluated on the basis of certain personal traits such as attitude, appearance, initiative, and so on. However, many of the traits commonly used are subjective and may be either unrelated to job performance or virtually impossible to define. In such cases, the result may be inaccurate evaluations and legal problems as well.

Behaviours

When an individual's task outcome is difficult to determine, a common procedure is to evaluate task-related behaviour. For example, a manager's leadership style might be evaluated. For people working in teams, it might be appropriate to evaluate cooperation and helping and encouraging others. For those

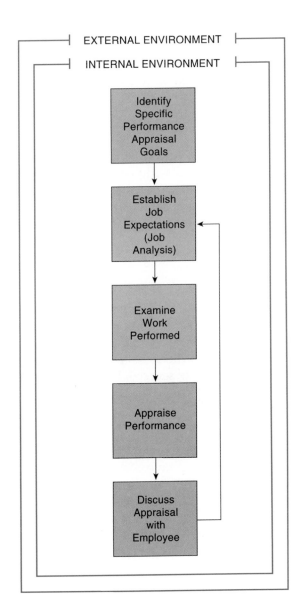

Figure 10-1

The Performance Appraisal Process

working with customers, helpful behaviour and customer service orientation might be evaluated.

Desired behaviours may be appropriate as evaluation criteria because of the belief that if recognized and rewarded, they will be repeated. In addition, firms pay people salaries for behaving in certain ways that produce results. People don't do traits; they do behaviours.[9]

Task Outcomes

Often employers will evaluate employees on the basis of whether or not the job or task was completed—that is, productivity. Managers must, however, take into consideration other factors.[10] For example, completion of results or output may not be within the control of the individual or team. Another problem might be a firm's failure to recognize the difference between quantity and quality of output. Overemphasizing productivity may result in such a frenzied work pace that mistakes are passed on to the customer.

Skills and Competencies

Most human resource experts now advise that individuals should be rewarded not only on the basis of productivity and goal achievement but also for their *demonstrated* advancement in skills and competencies. Note the difference between educational activities and achievements. Taking a course on Web page design, for example, would not be a demonstrated skill advancement. The skill advancement might be demonstrated by designing an effective Web page for the department.[11]

Responsibility for Appraisal

In most organizations, the human resource department is responsible for coordinating the design and implementation of performance appraisal programs. However, line managers also play a key role from beginning to end: it is usually they who are responsible for the actual appraisals, and they must directly participate in the program if it is to succeed. Who actually rates the employee? There are several possibilities.

Immediate Supervisor

Traditionally, an employee's immediate supervisor evaluates performance. This continues to be the most common choice, for several reasons. In the first place, the supervisor is usually in an excellent position to observe the employee's job performance. Furthermore, it is the supervisor who is responsible for managing a particular unit. When the task of evaluating subordinates is given to someone else, the supervisor's authority may be undermined. Finally, subordinate training and development is an important element in every manager's job, and appraisal programs and employee development are most often closely related.

On the negative side, the immediate supervisor may emphasize certain aspects of employee performance and neglect others. Also, managers have been known to manipulate evaluations to justify their decisions concerning pay increases and promotions. In project or matrix organizations, the functional supervisor may not have the opportunity to observe performance sufficiently to evaluate it.

Subordinates

Some firms have concluded that evaluation of managers by subordinates is feasible. They reason that subordinates are in an excellent position to view their superior's managerial effectiveness. Advocates of this approach believe that supervisors appraised in such a manner will become especially conscious of the work group's needs and will do a better job of managing. However, critics are concerned that the manager may be caught up in a popularity contest or that employees will be fearful of reprisal. If this approach has a chance for success, one thing is clear: anonymity of the evaluators must be guaranteed. Assuring this might be particularly difficult in a small department — especially if demographic data that could identify raters are included in the evaluation form.

Peers

Peer assessment is particularly useful for teams and groups. Since firms are increasingly being organized into groups and teams, peer assessment is becoming a popular appraisal indicator.[12] Peer appraisal has long had proponents who believed that such an approach is reliable if the work group is stable over a reasonably long period of time and performs tasks that require considerable interaction. Peer evaluation works best in a participative culture.

The rationale for evaluations conducted by team members includes the following:[13]

1. Team members know each other's performance better than anyone and can, therefore, evaluate performance more accurately.

2. Peer pressure is a powerful motivator for team members.

3. Members who recognize that peers within the team will be evaluating their work show increased commitment and productivity.

4. Peer review involves numerous opinions and is not dependent on one individual.

Problems with peer evaluations include the reluctance of people who work closely together, especially on teams, to criticize each other. Also, many team members will have little or no training in appraisal. Training in performance appraisal is obviously needed for team members as it is for anyone evaluating performance.

Self-Appraisal

Some experts reason that employees, if they understand the objectives they are expected to achieve and the standards by which they are to be evaluated, are in a good position to appraise their own performance.[14] Also, because employee development is self-development, employees who appraise their own performance may become more highly motivated. Self-appraisal, as a complement to other approaches, has great appeal to managers who are primarily concerned with employee participation and development. For compensation purposes, however, its value is considerably less.

Customer Appraisal

The buying behaviour of customers determines, in part, a firm's success. Therefore, some organizations believe it is important to obtain performance input from this critical source. For example, one study revealed that at least six award-winning companies used a customer appraisal approach because it demonstrated a commitment to the customer, held employees accountable, and fostered customer-focused change. Customer-related goals for executives

360 System
A state-of-the-art system for conducting 360-degree performance appraisals is presented.

360-degree feedback:
An increasingly popular appraisal method that involves input from multiple levels within the firm and external sources as well.

generally are of a broad, strategic nature such as to achieve a specified rating for overall quality for a given evaluation period. Targets for lower-level employees tend to be more specific—for example, to improve the rating for accurate delivery or reduce the number of dissatisfied customers by half. To make this approach work, employees should participate in setting goals and only outcomes within the employee's control should be rated.[15]

TRENDS and INNOVATIONS

360-Degree Feedback

The numerous approaches to appraisal are not mutually exclusive. In fact, **360-degree feedback**, or multirater evaluation, is an increasingly popular appraisal method that involves input from multiple levels within the firm and external sources as well. This method is used by a growing number of companies including General Electric, AT&T, and Digital Equipment.[16] In fact, 90 percent of Fortune 1000 companies use some form of multirater evaluation.[17]

360-Degree Feedback, unlike traditional approaches, focuses on skills needed across organizational boundaries. Also, by shifting the responsibility for evaluation from one person, many of the common appraisal errors can be reduced or eliminated. Having multiple raters also makes the process more legally defensible.

An appraisal system involving numerous evaluators will naturally take more time and, therefore, be more costly. A high degree of trust among participants and training in the appraisal system are needed regardless of how it is conducted. Nevertheless, the way firms are being organized and managed may require innovative alternatives to traditional top-down appraisals.

Performance Appraisal Period, Methods and Problems

Performance Appraisal Period

Formal performance evaluations are usually prepared at specific intervals. In most organizations, traditionally they are made either annually or semiannually. In the current business climate, however, it may be advisable for all firms to consider monitoring performance more often.[18] Changes occur so fast that employees need to look at objectives and their own role throughout the year to see if they need to be altered. A study by Hewitt Associates, for example, found that companies conducting multiple performance reviews had better results in terms of total shareholder return, return on equity, sales growth, and cash flow.[19]

The appraisal period may begin with each employee's date of hire, or all employees may be evaluated at the same time. In the interest of consistency, it may be advisable to perform evaluations on a calendar basis, not on anniversaries, since the latter makes comparisons among employees difficult.[20]

Performance Appraisal Methods

Managers may choose from among a number of appraisal methods, several of which are described below. The type of performance appraisal system used depends on its purpose. If the major emphasis is on selecting people for promotion, training, and merit pay increases, a traditional method such as rating scales may be appropriate. Collaborative methods may prove to be more appropriate for developing employees and helping them become more effective.

Rating Scales

A widely used appraisal method, which rates employees according to defined factors, is called the **rating scales method**. Using this approach, judgments about performance are recorded on a scale. The scale is divided into levels—normally five to seven in number—that are often defined by adjectives, such as outstanding, average, or unsatisfactory. Although an overall rating may be provided, generally more than one scale is used to measure more than one performance criterion. One reason for the popularity of the rating scales method is its simplicity, which permits many employees to be evaluated quickly.

Rating scales method: A widely used performance appraisal method that rates employees according to defined factors.

The factors chosen for evaluation are typically of two types: job-related and personal characteristics. Note that in Figure 10-2, job-related factors include quantity and quality of work, whereas personal factors include such attributes as dependability, initiative, adaptability, and cooperation. The rater (evaluator) completes the form by indicating the degree of each factor that is most descriptive of the employee and his or her performance.

Some firms provide space for the rater to comment on the evaluation given for each factor. This practice may be especially encouraged, or even required, when the rater gives either the highest or lowest rating. For instance, if an employee is rated unsatisfactory on initiative, the rater should provide written justification for this low evaluation. The purpose of this type of requirement is to avoid arbitrary and hastily made judgments.

As shown in Figure 10-2, each factor and each degree have been defined. In order to receive an exceptional rating for the factor *quality of work*, a person must consistently exceed the prescribed work requirements. The more precisely the various factors and degrees are defined, the better the rater can evaluate worker performance. Evaluation agreement throughout the organization is achieved when each rater interprets the factors and degrees in the same way. This ability may be acquired through training in performance appraisal.

Many rating scale performance appraisal forms also provide for an assessment of the employee's growth potential and advancement in core competencies. For example, the form shown in Figure 10-2 contains four categories relating to a person's potential for future growth and development. They range from *now at or near maximum performance in present job* to *no apparent limitations*. Although there are drawbacks in attempting to evaluate both past performance and future potential at the same time, this practice is often followed.

Computerized Rating Scales

HR tasks such as performance appraisal may seem too personal to relegate to machines. However, software programs are available to assist raters in this chore, which may be time-consuming and often unpleasant. For instance, a

Figure 10-2

Rating Scales Method of
Performance Appraisal

Employee's Name _____

Job Title _____

Department _____

Supervisor _____

Evaluation Period:
  From _____ to _____

Instructions for evaluation:
1. Consider only one factor at a time.
   Do not permit rating given for one
   factor to affect decision for others.
2. Consider performance for entire
   evaluation period. Avoid concentration on recent events or isolated
   incidents.
3. Remember that the average
   employee performs duties in a satisfactory manner. An above average
   or exceptional rating indicates that
   the employee has clearly distinguished himself or herself from the
   average employee.

EVALUATION FACTORS	Unsatisfactory. Does not meet requirements.	Below average. Needs improvement. Requirements occasionally not met.	Average. Consistently meets requirements.	Good. Frequently exceeds requirements.	Exceptional. Consistently exceeds requirements.
QUANTITY OF WORK: Consider the volume of work achieved. Is productivity at an acceptable level?					
QUALITY OF WORK: Consider accuracy, precision, neatness, and completeness in handling assigned duties.					
DEPENDABILITY: Consider degree to which employee can be relied on to meet work commitments.					
INITIATIVE: Consider self-reliance, resourcefulness, and willingness to accept responsibility.					
ADAPTABILITY: Consider ability to respond to changing requirements and conditions.					
COOPERATION: Consider ability to work for, and with, others. Are assignments, including overtime, willingly accepted?					

POTENTIAL FOR FUTURE GROWTH AND DEVELOPMENT:
☐ Now at or near maximum performance in present job.
☐ Now at or near maximum performance in this job, but has potential for improvement
   in another job, such as:
   _____
☐ Capable of progressing after further training and experience.
☐ No apparent limitations.

EMPLOYEE STATEMENT: I agree ☐   disagree ☐   with this evaluation
  Comments:
  _____
  _____

Employee	Date
Supervisor	Date
Reviewing Manager	Date

system might begin by notifying the supervisor when reviews for employees are scheduled. Computer systems can also assist in recording performance data relevant to employee performance throughout the rating period so they can easily be inserted in the final appraisal report. Based on information supplied by the rater, the program creates the text of the appraisal. For example, David's supervisor gives him a "3" (average on a graphic rating scale) for being competent in the factor *job knowledge* and a "4" (above average) for *supervision required*. The firm's performance appraisal procedure requires the rating supervisor to comment on each rating. Based on these ratings, the computer spits out, "David needs a minimal amount of supervision to fulfil his responsibilities. He demonstrates competency in the skills and knowledge required."[21]

Critical Incidents

The **critical incident method** requires that written records be kept of highly favourable and highly unfavourable work actions. When such an action affects the department's effectiveness significantly, either positively or negatively, the manager writes it down. It is called a critical incident. At the end of the appraisal period, the rater uses these records, along with other data, to evaluate employee performance. With this method, the appraisal is more likely to cover the entire evaluation period rather than focusing on the last few weeks or months.

Critical incident method: A performance appraisal technique that requires a written record of highly favourable and highly unfavourable employee work behaviour.

Essay

In the **essay method**, the rater simply writes a brief narrative describing the employee's performance. This method tends to focus on extreme behaviour in the employee's work rather than routine day-to-day performance. Ratings of this type depend heavily on the evaluator's writing ability. Some supervisors, because of their excellent writing skills, can make even a marginal worker sound like a top performer. Comparing essay evaluations might be difficult because no common criteria exist. However, some managers believe that the essay method is not only the simplest but also the best approach to employee evaluation.

Essay method: A performance appraisal method in which the rater writes a brief narrative describing an employee's performance.

Work Standards

The **work standards method** compares each employee's performance to a predetermined standard or expected level of output. Standards reflect the normal output of an average worker operating at a normal pace. Work standards may be applied to virtually all types of jobs, but they are most frequently used for production jobs. Several methods may be used in determining work standards, including time study and work sampling.

An obvious advantage of this method is objectivity. However, for employees to perceive that the standards are objective, they should understand clearly how the standards were set. The rationale for any changes to the standards must also be carefully explained.

Work standards method: A performance appraisal method that compares each employee's performance to a predetermined standard or expected level of output.

Ranking

In using the **ranking method**, the rater simply places all employees from a group in rank order of overall performance. For example, the best employee in the department is ranked highest, and the poorest is ranked lowest. A major difficulty occurs when individuals have performed at comparable levels.

Ranking method: A performance appraisal method in which the rater places all employees in a given group in rank order on the basis of their overall performance. Also, a job evaluation method in which the rater examines the description of each job being evaluated and arranges the jobs in order according to their value to the company.

Paired comparison:
A variation of the ranking method of performance appraisal in which the performance of each employee is compared with that of every other employee in the particular group.

Paired comparison is a variation of the ranking method in which the performance of each employee is compared with every other employee in the group. The comparison is often based on a single criterion, such as overall performance. The employee who receives the greatest number of favourable comparisons is ranked highest.

Some professionals in the field argue for using a comparative approach, such as ranking. For example, they feel that employees are promoted not because they achieve their objectives but rather because they achieve them better than others in their work group. Such decisions go beyond a single individual's performance and, therefore, should be considered on a broader basis.

Forced Distribution

Forced distribution method: An appraisal approach in which the rater is required to assign individuals in a work group to a limited number of levels similar to a normal frequency distribution.

In the **forced distribution method**, the rater is required to assign individuals in the work group to a limited number of levels similar to a normal frequency distribution. As an example, employees in the top 10 percent are placed in the highest group, the next 20 percent in the next group, the next 40 percent in the middle group, the next 20 percent in the second to lowest group, and the remaining 10 percent in the lowest category. This approach is based on the rather questionable assumption that all groups of employees will have the same distribution of excellent, average, and poor performers. If one department has done an outstanding job in selecting employees, the supervisor might be hard pressed to decide who should be placed in the lower categories.

Forced-Choice and Weighted Checklist Performance Reports

Forced-choice performance report:
A performance appraisal technique in which the rater is given a series of statements about an individual and indicates which items are most or least descriptive of the employee.

The **forced-choice performance report** requires that the appraiser choose from a series of statements those that are most or least descriptive of the employee. One difficulty with this method is that the descriptive statements may be virtually identical.

Weighted checklist performance report:
A performance appraisal technique in which the rater completes a form similar to a forced-choice performance report except that the various responses have been assigned different weights.

Using the **weighted checklist performance report**, the rater completes a form similar to the forced-choice performance report, but the various responses have been assigned different weights. The form includes questions related to the employee's behaviour, and the evaluator answers each question either positively or negatively. The evaluator is not aware of each question's weight, however.

As with forced-choice performance reports, the weighted checklist is expensive to design. Both methods strive for objectivity. However, since the evaluator does not know which items contribute most to successful performance, this approach is not useful for development.

Management by Objectives (MBO)

Management by objectives evaluation method: A method in which employees jointly establish measurable objectives with their superiors, who then give them latitude in how to achieve these objectives.

Employee input is central to using the MBO concept, potentially the most effective method of evaluating an employee's performance. Traditional appraisal methods often rely on personal traits, such as cooperation or dependability, and put the evaluator in the role of judge. The **management by objectives (MBO) evaluation method**, however, shifts the appraisal focus from the worker's personal traits to job performance, while the supervisor's role is transformed from umpire to counsellor and facilitator. Also, the employee's role changes from passive bystander to active participant.

Individuals jointly establish measurable objectives with their superiors, who then give them latitude in how to achieve these objectives. Jointly established goals allow the employee to be actively involved in the PA process. This ownership of objectives increases the likelihood they will be met.[22]

When MBO is used, the supervisor tends to keep communication channels open throughout the appraisal period. Then the employee and the supervisor meet for an appraisal interview, during which they formally review the extent to which objectives have been achieved and discuss the actions needed to solve remaining problems. This problem-solving discussion is likely to be the last in a series of conversations designed to assist the employee in progressing according to plan. Finally, objectives are established for the next evaluation period and the process is repeated. (See Figure 10-3.)

Figure 10-3

An Example of a Performance Appraisal Using MBO

NAME:		POSITION TITLE: PRODUCTION MANAGER	DEPARTMENT: MANUFACTURING
FUNCTIONS	**OBJECTIVES**	**RESULTS**	**PROBLEMS AND SOLUTIONS**
1. Select and train employees	A. All new employees prescreened and approved by HR Department	A. Hired one (1) person without aid of Personnel; released before 90-day probation ended.	A. Follow the rules.
	B. Training plan written for all new employees by 10/12/XX	B. Training plan written by 10/12/XX	B. None.
2. Supervise and coordinate work of employees	A. No more than three (3) grievances per month.	A. Averaged 4 per month.	A. Ask Labour Relations Manager to help analyze grievance pattern – eliminate problem areas by 6/1/XX.
	B. Employee productivity rate at 98 percent of standard.	B. Productivity at 96 percent	B. Work with Industrial Engineering to fine-tune systems.
3. Schedule production	A. No down time except for breakdown of major line.	A. No breakdowns.	A. None.
	B. No more than one (1) delay per week in shipping orders.	B. No delays.	B. None.
4. Maintain safe work practices	A. Discuss all accidents with Safety Director.	A. Discussed all but three (3) cases.	A. Reevaluate this objective and see if another approach would be more satisfactory by 3/1/XX.
	B. No lost-time accidents.	B. Three (3) lost-time accidents.	B. Investigate each accident and tie in with (A) above by 3/1/XX.

Problems in Performance Appraisal

Many performance appraisal methods have been severely criticized. The rating scales method seems to have received the greatest attention. In all fairness, many of the problems commonly mentioned are not inherent in the method; rather, they reflect improper usage. For example, raters may be inadequately trained or the appraisal criteria used may not be job related.

Lack of Objectivity

A potential weakness of traditional performance appraisal methods is that they lack objectivity. In the rating scales method, for example, commonly used factors such as attitude, loyalty, and personality are difficult to measure. In addition, these factors may have little to do with an employee's job performance.

Some subjectivity will always exist in appraisal methods. However, the use of job-related factors does increase objectivity. Employee appraisal based primarily on personal characteristics may place the evaluator—and the company—in untenable positions with the employee and equal employment opportunity guidelines. The firm would be hard pressed to show that these factors are job related.

Halo Error

Halo error: An error that occurs when an evaluator considers one factor to be of paramount importance and bases the employee's overall evaluation on the rating given for this particular factor.

Halo error occurs when the evaluator perceives one factor as having paramount importance and gives a good or bad overall rating to an employee based on this one factor. For example, Michael Wronski, accounting supervisor, placed a high value on neatness, which was a factor used in the company's performance appraisal system. As Michael was evaluating the performance of his senior accounting clerk, Paul Desjardins, he noted that Paul was not a very neat individual and gave him a low ranking on this factor. Also, consciously or unconsciously, Michael permitted the low ranking on neatness to carry over to other factors, giving Paul undeserved low ratings on all factors. Of course, if Paul had been very neat, the opposite could have occurred. Either way, the halo error does a disservice to the employee involved and to the organization.

Leniency/Strictness

Leniency: Giving undeserved high performance appraisal rating to an employee.

Giving undeserved high ratings is referred to as **leniency**. This behaviour is often motivated by a desire to avoid controversy over the appraisal. It is most prevalent when highly subjective (and difficult to defend) performance criteria are used, and the rater is required to discuss evaluation results with employees. One research study found that when managers know they are evaluating employees for administrative purposes, such as pay increases, they are likely to be more lenient than when evaluating performance to achieve employee development.[23]

Leniency may result in a number of organizational problems.[24]

1. When deficiencies are not recognized, organizations are denied accurate information regarding the effectiveness of their operations, potentially jeopardizing their success. Employees may not understand the need to improve their performance and the status quo will continue.

2. When appraisal data are used for determining merit pay, as is generally the case, leniency may lead to rapid depletion of the merit budget and

reduce the reward available for superior employees. Thus, the potential motivational effect of the merit pay program is reduced.

3. Finally, an organization will find it difficult to terminate a poorly performing employee if he or she has a record of satisfactory evaluations.

Being unduly critical of an employee's work performance is referred to as **strictness**. Although leniency is usually more prevalent than strictness, some managers apply an evaluation more rigorously than the company standard. This behaviour may be due to a lack of understanding of various evaluation factors. When one manager is overly strict on an entire unit, workers in that group suffer with regard to pay raises and promotion. Strictness applied to a particular individual has the potential for charges of discrimination.

One study revealed that more than 70 percent of responding managers

Strictness: Being unduly critical of an employee's work performance.

Figure 10-4

Reasons for Intentionally Inflating or Lowering Ratings

INFLATED RATINGS	LOWERED RATINGS
• The belief that accurate ratings would have a damaging effect on the subordinate's motivation and performance	• To scare better performance out of an employee
• The desire to improve an employee's eligibility for merit raises	• To punish a difficult or rebellious employee
• The desire to avoid airing the department's dirty laundry	• To encourage a problem employee to quit
• The wish to avoid creating a negative permanent record of poor performance that might hound the employee in the future	• To create a strong record to justify a planned firing
• The need to protect good performers whose performance was suffering because of personal problems	• To minimize the amount of the merit increase a subordinate receives
• The wish to reward employees displaying great effort even when results are relatively low	• To comply with an organization edict that discourages managers from giving high ratings
• The need to avoid confrontation with certain hard-to-manage employees	
• The desire to promote a poor or disliked employee up and out of the department	

Source: Clinton Longenecker and Dean Ludwig, "Ethical Dilemmas in Performance Appraisal Revisited," Journal of Business Ethics 9 (December 1990): 963. Reprinted by permission of Kluwer Academic Publishers.

believe that inflated and lowered ratings are intentionally given to subordinates. Figure 10-4 shows these managers' explanations for their rationale. The results suggest that the validity of many performance appraisal systems may be flawed. Evaluator training should be provided to emphasize the problems caused by rater errors.

Central Tendency

Central tendency:
A common error in performance appraisal that occurs when employees are incorrectly rated near the average or middle of a scale.

Central tendency is a common error that occurs when employees are incorrectly rated near the average or middle of the scale. Some rating scale systems require the evaluator to justify in writing extremely high or extremely low ratings. With such a system, the rater may avoid possible controversy or criticism by giving only average ratings.

Recent Behaviour Bias

Most employees know when they are scheduled for performance review. Although their actions may not be conscious, employees' behaviour often improves and productivity tends to rise several days or weeks before the scheduled evaluation. It is only natural for a rater to remember recent behaviour more clearly than actions from the more distant past. However, performance appraisals generally cover a specified period of time, and an individual's performance should be considered for the entire period.

Personal Bias

Supervisors who conduct performance appraisals may have personal biases related to employee characteristics: e.g., race, religion, gender, disability, or age. Policies prohibiting discrimination should be in place, therefore, and supervisors should be trained in appraisal techniques. As well, records should be kept that track appraisal results by various categories, so that patterns of discrimination can be spotted. Discrimination in appraisal can be based on many other factors. For example, mild-mannered people may be appraised more harshly because they are not likely to contest the results, while aggressive people are often given better appraisals to avoid strife.

HRM in ACTION

What Should I Do?

Janice is just completing her first year of service. It is time to prepare her annual performance appraisal. She has consistently done good work and has been a fine employee except for one morning last week. For some reason, Janice lost her temper and cursed a major client on the phone. Then she got up and went home without any explanation. You observed this episode but chose to say nothing about it. She has not mentioned the incident either, although she was back at work the next day. You have come to the attitude section on her performance appraisal.

How would you fill it in?

Judgmental Role of Evaluator

Supervisors conducting performance evaluations are at times accused of playing God with their employees. In some instances, supervisors control virtually every aspect of the process. Manipulating evaluations to justify their decisions about pay increases and promotions is one example of how supervisors may abuse the system. They make decisions about the ratings and often try to sell their version to the employees. The highly judgmental role of some evaluators often places employees on the defensive. Such relationships are hardly conducive to employee development, morale, and productivity.

Characteristics of an Effective Appraisal System

Although a perfect system does not exist, every system should include certain elements.[25]

Job-Related Criteria

The criteria used for appraising employee performance must be job related. More specifically, job information should be determined through job analysis. Subjective factors, such as initiative, enthusiasm, loyalty, and cooperation, are obviously important. Unless they can be clearly shown to be job related, however, they should not be used.

Performance Expectations

Managers and employees must agree on performance expectations in advance of the appraisal period. Evaluating employees using criteria that they know nothing about is not reasonable.

Performance expectations should consider not only productivity targets but also employee advancement in core competencies. For example, if a particular employee were required to learn French, the review should consider whether such knowledge has been demonstrated. Taking French-language training is not sufficient. In this example, the demonstrated ability to put the linguistic knowledge to practice is essential.[26]

Standardization

Employees in the same job category under the same supervisor should be appraised using the same evaluation instrument. Also important is that appraisals be conducted regularly for all employees and that they cover similar periods of time. Although annual evaluations are common, employees are evaluated more frequently by many successful firms. Feedback sessions and appraisal interviews should be regularly scheduled for all employees.

Another aspect of standardization is formal documentation. Employees should sign their evaluations. If the employee refuses to sign, the manager should document this behaviour. Records should also include a description of employee responsibilities, expected performance results, and the way these data will be viewed in making appraisal decisions.

Trained Appraisers

Responsibility for evaluating employee performance should be assigned to the individual or individuals who directly observe at least a representative sample of the worker's job performance. Usually, this person is the employee's immediate supervisor. However, as previously discussed, other approaches are gaining in popularity.[27]

Training in performance appraisal should be an ongoing process to ensure consistency. The training should cover how to rate employees and conduct appraisal interviews. Instructions should be rather detailed and stress the importance of making objective and unbiased ratings.

Open Communication

Most employees have a strong need to know how well they are performing. A good appraisal system provides highly desired feedback on a continuing basis. A worthwhile goal is to avoid surprises during the appraisal interview. Even though the interview presents an excellent opportunity for both parties to exchange ideas, it should never serve as a substitute for the day-to-day communication and coaching required by performance management.

Employee Access to Results

For the many appraisal systems that are designed to improve performance, withholding appraisal results would be unthinkable. Employees would be severely handicapped in their developmental efforts if denied access to this information. Also, employees' review of appraisal results allows them to detect any errors that may have been made. An employee may simply disagree with the evaluation and may want to challenge it. Employees who receive a substandard appraisal should be offered needed training and guidance. Supervisors must make an effort to salvage marginal employees. Individuals in this category should, however, be told the specific consequences if their performance does not reach an acceptable level.

Due Process

Ensuring due process is vital. If a formal policy does not exist, one should be developed to permit employees to appeal appraisal results they consider inaccurate or unfair. They must have a procedure for pursuing their grievances and having them addressed objectively.

Legality

Wrongful termination suits have increased greatly during the past decade. In Canada, firings must be made for "just cause." Poor performance is an example of just cause, but the employer must document the misconduct or shortcoming, describe what conduct is expected, provide a reasonable time for the employee to meet expectations, and issue a statement that failure to comply will result in termination. Hence, an appraisal system is essential to avoid what Malany Franklin, an employment law specialist with Borden and Elliot, describes as every employer's nightmare: the newly-terminated employee who spends "hours visiting the employment standards office, the human rights commission and a lawyer."[28]

The Appraisal Interview

Supervisors usually conduct a formal appraisal interview at the end of an employee's appraisal period. However, effective performance appraisal systems require more than this single interview. Instead, supervisors should maintain a continuous dialogue with employees, emphasizing their own responsibility for development and management's supportive role.

Objectives

In any event, a successful appraisal interview should be structured in a way that allows both the supervisor and the subordinate to view it as a problem-solving rather than a fault-finding session. The supervisor should consider three basic purposes when planning an appraisal interview:[29]

1. To review the employee's performance in terms of both productivity and core competencies.

2. To assist the employee in setting objectives—including the required measurement steps to measure these objectives—and personal development plans.

3. To suggest means for achieving established objectives and development needs, including support to be provided by the manager and firm.

Timing

The interview should be scheduled soon after the end of the appraisal period. Employees usually know when their interview should take place, and their anxiety tends to increase when it is delayed. Interviews with top performers are often pleasant experiences for all concerned. However, supervisors may be reluctant to meet face-to-face with poor performers. They tend to postpone these anxiety-provoking interviews.

The amount of time devoted to an appraisal interview varies considerably with company policy and the position of the evaluated employee. Although costs must be considered, there is merit in separating discussion of employee performance and development from discussion of pay increases. Many managers have learned that as soon as pay is mentioned it tends to dominate an interview. For this reason, pay discussions are commonly deferred for one to several weeks after the appraisal interview.[30]

Communication

Conducting an appraisal interview is often one of management's more difficult tasks. It requires tact and patience on the part of the supervisor. Praise should be provided when warranted, but it can have only limited value if not clearly deserved. Criticism is especially difficult to give. So-called constructive criticism is often not perceived that way by the employee. Yet it is difficult for a manager at any level to avoid criticism when conducting appraisal interviews. The supervisor should realize that all individuals have some deficiencies that may not be changed easily, if at all. Continued criticism may lead to frustration and have a damaging effect on employee development. Again, this possibility should not allow unacceptable employee behaviour to go unnoticed. However, discussions of sensitive issues should focus on the deficiency, not the person. Threats to the employee's self-esteem should be minimized whenever possible.

The entire performance appraisal process should be a positive experience for the employee. In practice, however, it often is not. Negative feelings can frequently be traced to the appraisal interview and the manner in which it was conducted by the supervisor. Ideally, employees will leave the interview feeling good about the supervisor, the company, the job, and themselves. The prospects for improved performance will be bleak if the employee's ego is deflated. Past behaviour cannot be changed, but future performance can. Specific plans for the employee's development should be clearly outlined and mutually agreed on.

Several suggestions for conducting appraisal interviews are provided in Figure 10-5.

Figure 10-5

Suggestions for Conducting Appraisal Interviews

1. Give the employee a few days' notice of the discussion and its purpose. Encourage the employee to give some preparatory thought to his or her job performance and development plans. In some cases, have employees read their written performance evaluation prior to the meeting.

2. Prepare notes and use the completed performance appraisal form as a discussion guide so that each important topic will be covered. Be ready to answer questions employees may ask about why you appraised them as you did. Encourage your employees to ask questions.

3. Be ready to suggest specific developmental activities suitable to each employee's needs. When there are specific performance problems, remember to "attack the problem, not the person."

4. Establish a friendly, helpful, and purposeful tone at the outset of the discussion. Recognize that it is not unusual for you and your employee to be nervous about the discussion, and use suitable techniques to put you both more at ease.

5. Assure your employee that everyone on the management team is being evaluated so that opportunities for improvement and development will not be overlooked and each person's performance will be fully recognized.

6. Make sure that the session is truly a discussion. Encourage employees to talk about how they feel they are doing on the job, how they might improve, and what developmental activities they might undertake. Often an employee's viewpoints on these matters will be quite close to your own.

7. When your appraisal differs from the employee's, discuss these differences. Sometimes employees have hidden reasons for performing in a certain manner or using certain methods. This is an opportunity to find out if such reasons exist.

8. These discussions should contain both constructive compliments and constructive criticism. Be sure to discuss the employee's strengths as well as weaknesses. Your employees should have clear pictures of how you view their performance when the discussions are concluded.

9. Occasionally the appraisal interview will uncover strong emotions. This is one of the values of regular appraisals; since they can bring out bothersome feelings, they can be dealt with honestly. The emotional dimension of managing is very important. Ignoring it can lead to poor performance. Deal with emotional issues when they arise because they block a person's ability to concentrate on other issues. Consult personnel for help when especially strong emotions are uncovered.

10. Make certain that your employees fully understand your appraisal of their performance. Sometimes it helps to have an employee orally summarize the appraisal as he or she understands it. If there are any misunderstandings, they can be cleared up on the spot. Ask questions to make sure you have been fully understood.

11. Discuss the future as well as the past. Plan with the employee specific changes in performance or specific developmental activities that will allow fuller use of potential. Ask what you can do to help.

12. End the discussion on a positive, future-improvement-oriented note. You and your employee are a team, working toward the development of everyone involved.

Source: Used with the permission of Cessna Aircraft Company.

Assessment Centres

Many appraisal systems evaluate an individual's past performance and at the same time attempt to assess his or her potential for advancement. However, some organizations have developed a separate approach for assessing potential. This process often takes place in what is appropriately referred to as an **assessment centre**.

Assessment centre:
An employee selection or appraisal approach that requires individuals to perform activities similar to those they might encounter in an actual job.

A GLOBAL PERSPECTIVE

Global Performance Appraisal: Factoring in Appropriate Employee Behaviours

A general management survey on perceptions of national management style was given to more than 700 managers representing diverse industries from North America, Indonesia, Malaysia, and Thailand. Results on survey items related to the design of performance appraisal systems revealed significant variances in management style. These differences suggest that North American performance appraisal principles may not transfer well across cultures.[31]

Yet an effective international system is essential for credible employee evaluations.[32] Valid performance appraisal is hard to achieve in Canada; evaluating overseas employees makes a normally complex problem extremely difficult.[33]

A strength in one culture might be considered a weakness in another. For example, the amount of time spent in personal conversation with a customer relates to cultural norms. What might be seen as wasting time on idle chatter in one country might be ordinary professional courtesy in another—and offensive curiosity in a third. In some cultures, managers are expected to make decisions, while employees expect to follow orders; in others, employees want to participate in decision making and authoritarian managers are seen as obsolete. The issue of appropriate performance standards also comes into question. An inflexible performance appraisal system can create a great deal of misunderstanding and even personal offence,[34] especially among foreign nationals working for a Canadian employer.

These problems may be avoided if HR professionals help managers to develop appraisal systems that enhance administrative decision making, as well as personal development. In addition, performance objectives for job assignments or tasks should be developed whenever possible. Third, managers must allow more time to achieve results in an overseas assignment. Finally, the objectives of the appraisal system should be flexible and responsive to potential markets and environmental contingencies.[35]

In an assessment centre, employees often perform activities similar to those they might encounter in an actual job. These simulated exercises are based on a thorough job analysis. The assessors usually observe the employees somewhere other than their normal workplace over a certain period of time. The assessors selected are typically experienced managers who both participate in the exercises and evaluate performances. Assessment centres are used increasingly to 1) identify employees who have higher level management potential, 2) select first-line supervisors, and 3) determine employee developmental needs.

An advantage of the assessment centre approach is the increased reliability and validity of the information provided. Assessment centres have been shown to be more successful than aptitude tests in predicting performance.

SUMMARY

1. **Define performance appraisal and performance management**
   Performance appraisal (PA) is a system of review and evaluation of an individual's or team's job performance. Performance management is the process of having managers and employees work together to set expectations, review results, and reward performance.

2. **Identify the uses of performance appraisal.**
   The primary goal of an appraisal system is normally to improve performance. Other uses include human resource planning, recruitment and selection, training and development, career planning and development, compensation programs, internal employee relations, and assessment of employee potential.

3. **Describe the performance appraisal process.**
   The steps in the performance appraisal process include identification of the specific performance appraisal goals, establishment of job expectations (job analysis), examination of work performed, appraisal, and discussion of appraisal with employee.

4. **Identify the aspects of a person's performance that an organization should evaluate.**
   An organization should evaluate traits, behaviours, task outcomes, and skill competencies.

5. **Identify who may be responsible for performance appraisal.**
   In most organizations, the human resource department is responsible for coordinating the design and implementation of performance appraisal programs. Immediate supervisors most often conduct the actual appraisal. Other people often involved include subordinates and peers. Self-appraisal and customer appraisal are also used. In 360-degree feedback, all these sources of appraisal are combined.

6. **Identify the various performance appraisal methods used.**
   Performance appraisal methods include rating scales, computer rating scales, critical incidents, essay, work standards, ranking, forced distribution, forced-choice, weighted checklist reports, and management by objectives.

7. **List the problems that have been associated with performance appraisal.**
   Problems associated with performance appraisals include lack of objectivity, halo error, leniency/strictness, central tendency, recent behaviour bias, personal bias, and the judgmental role of evaluators.

8. **Explain the characteristics of an effective appraisal system.**
   The criteria used for appraising employee performance should be job related. Managers must clearly explain their performance expectations to their employees in advance of the appraisal period. Performance expectations should consider not only productivity targets but also employee advancement in core competencies. Employees in the same job categories under a given supervisor should be appraised using the same evaluation instrument. Responsibility for evaluating employee performance should be assigned to the individual or individuals who directly observe at least a representative sample of the person's job performance. A good appraisal system provides highly desired feedback on a continuing basis. A formal procedure should be developed to permit employees to appeal appraisal results they consider inaccurate or

unfair. To avoid legal problems, the employer must document what conduct is expected, provide a reasonable time for the employee to meet expectations, and issue a statement that failure to comply will result in termination.

9. **Explain how the appraisal interview should be conducted.**

A successful appraisal interview should be structured in a way that allows both the supervisor and the subordinate to view it as a problem-solving rather than a fault-finding session. The interview should be scheduled soon after the end of the appraisal period. Discussions of sensitive issues should focus on the deficiency, not the person. The entire performance appraisal process should be a positive experience for the employee.

10. **Describe assessment centres.**

The assessment centre method is an appraisal approach that requires employees to participate in a series of activities similar to what they might be expected to do in an actual job. These situational activity exercises are developed as a result of thorough job analysis. The assessors observe the employees in a secluded environment, usually separate from the workplace, over a certain period of time.

QUESTIONS FOR REVIEW

1. Define performance appraisal and briefly discuss its basic purposes within the context of performance management.

2. What are the basic steps in the performance appraisal process?

3. What aspects of a person's performance should an organization evaluate?

4. Many different people can conduct performance appraisals. Briefly describe the various alternatives.

5. Briefly describe each of the following methods of performance appraisal:
   a. Rating scales
   b. Critical incidents
   c. Essay
   d. Work standards
   e. Ranking
   f. Forced distribution
   g. Forced-choice and weighted checklist performance reports
   h. Management by objectives

6. What are the various problems associated with performance appraisal? Briefly describe each.

7. What are the characteristics of an effective appraisal system?

8. Explain the process of conducting an effective appraisal interview.

9. Describe how an assessment centre could be used as a means of performance appraisal.

DEVELOPING HRM SKILLS

An Experiential Exercise

Some managers do not take PA as seriously as they should. This attitude is counterproductive, frequently lowering individual and group productivity.

Larry Cheechoo, supervisor of the electrical department, has a busy day scheduled, but he needs to squeeze in the last of his performance appraisals. They are due today, and he has only one more signature to get. Upon arriving for work he thinks, "I hate doing performance appraisals. It's the worst part of a supervisor's job. But, it does give me the chance to let my people know where they have to pull up their socks. The guy I'm appraising today has always exceeded his quotas, he is very helpful to those he likes, and he is excellent on the new computerized production setup; but if he wants to advance, he will need to change his behaviour. He seems to have problems working with the females on the line, and he doesn't seem to be very open-minded. Also, on September 23 he failed to secure his work area. This guy really has problems. Maybe our talk will do some good; either way I need to get this done. On the bright side, this is the last performance appraisal until next year."

Today is the day that Alex Martin gets his performance appraisal, and he is excited about it. Before the meeting with Larry, his supervisor, he thinks, "I've been very good on the new computerized setup, and very helpful to my friends on the line; this will help me get my promotion. I expect that the boss saved my performance appraisal for last to praise my performance and recommend me for that promotion that I've been deserving for some time. I've been passed over for promotion far too long, this has been a great year for me, and this will cap off a year of excellent performance."

When these two get together there will be a meeting of two quite different minds. In all likelihood, the meeting will be filled with disagreement, dissatisfaction, and maybe even hard feelings. This exercise will require one person to play the supervisor and another to be the evaluated employee. As only two can play, the rest should observe carefully. Instructors will provide the participants with additional information necessary to complete the exercise.

HRM INCIDENT

Objectives?

It was performance appraisal time again and Hans Funderburk knew that he would receive a low evaluation this time. Janet Stevens, Hans' boss, opened the appraisal interview with this comment, "The sales department had a good increase this quarter. Also, departmental expenses are down a good bit. But we have nowhere near accomplished the ambitious goals you and I set last quarter."

"I know," said Hans. "I thought we were going to make it, though. We would have, too, if we had received that big Sears order and if I could have gotten us on the Internet a little earlier in the quarter."

"I agree with you, Hans," said Janet. "Do you think we were just too ambitious or do you think there was some way we could have made the Sears sale and sped up the Web page design?"

"Yes," replied Hans, "we could have gotten the Sears order this quarter. I just made a couple of concessions to Sears and their purchasing manager tells me he can issue the order next week. The delay with the Internet was my responsibility; I thought I knew what I was doing, but it was a little more complicated than I expected."

The discussion continued for about 30 minutes longer. Hans discovered that Janet was going to mark him very high in all areas despite his failure to accomplish the goals that they had set.

Prior to the meeting, Janet had planned to suggest that the unattained goals for last period be set as the new goals for the coming quarter. After she and Hans had discussed matters, however, they both decided to establish new, somewhat higher goals. As he was about to leave the meeting, Hans said, "Janet, I feel good about these objectives, but I don't believe we have more than a 50 percent chance of accomplishing them."

"I believe you can do it," replied Janet. "If you knew for sure, though, the goals wouldn't be high enough."

"I see what you mean," said Hans, as he left the office.

Questions

1. What was wrong or right with Janet's appraisal of Hans's performance?
2. Should the new objectives be higher or lower than they are? Explain.

PART THREE CASE 3

Parma Cycle Company: Training the Work Force

As the date for the new plant opening drew near, Mary Higgins, director of employee development at Parma Cycle Company in Delta, B.C., grew increasingly nervous. With only six months to train the work force of the new Nova Scotia plant, Mary knew that there was little room for error.

Mary had already arranged to lease a building near the Digby factory site, and some of the machinery for the new plant was being installed in that building for training purposes. Most of the machinery was similar to that already being used at Parma, and Mary had selected trainers from among the supervisory staff at the Parma plant. One machine, however, a robotized frame assembler, was entirely new. The assembler was being purchased from a Japanese firm. Mary had sent two operators to train in the Japanese factory. They were both back.

Mary had made two trips to Digby. She had also retained a training consultant, a management professor from the University of New Brunswick. The training consultant had agreed to help Mary plan the training program and to evaluate the program as it went along. It was at the consultant's suggestion that Mary decided to use a combination of vestibule training and classroom lectures in developing a trained work force prior to factory start-up time. In the past, Parma Cycle had used on-the-job training almost exclusively, but she felt this approach wasn't feasible at the new plant.

As Mary was thinking about how short the time was, the phone rang. It was the human resource director, Jesse Heard, telling her that he was ready for their meeting. When she got to his office, she found him studying a training report she had prepared a few days earlier.

"Mary," said Jesse, "It looks like you have things well under control for the Digby plant. But I don't see anything here about training the employees who are going to be transferred over from this plant."

"Well," said Mary, "they have all been working in bicycle manufacture for quite a while. I thought it might not be necessary to have any formal training for them."

"That's true," said Jesse, "but most of them will be taking different jobs when they move to Digby."

"I'll get on it right away," said Mary.

"What are we going to do about supervisory training at the Digby plant?" asked Jesse.

Mary replied, "I think we'll use the same system we use here for the long haul. We'll bring our supervisors up through the ranks and have quarterly off-site seminars. To start, the supervisors who move from Delta can help train the others."

Jesse asked, "What do you think about bringing the supervisors hired in Digby up here for a few days to help them learn how we do things?"

"That's a good idea," said Mary. "We can pair them off with some of our better people."

"That won't help us with performance evaluations, Mary," said Jesse. "You know we're going to use a different system down there. We've decided to use management by objectives down to the supervisory level and a new three-item rating scale for the workers."

"I know that," answered Mary. "I had planned classroom training on that beginning the month after start-up at the Digby plant. I'm going to conduct those sessions myself. Because the performance scores will be used to allocate incentive bonuses, I want to make sure they are consistently assigned."

"Mary," said Jesse, "I'm really impressed with the way you are taking charge of this training effort. Just keep up the good work."

"Thank you, Jesse," said Mary. "I'll get back to you next week on the training I recommend for the workers who will transfer from Delta."

Questions

1. Describe how an untrained person hired in Digby could become a competent machine operator by the time the new plant opens.

2. Do you think Mary needed the training consultant? Why or why not?

3. What do you think of Mary's idea to have the supervisors for the new plant trained by those transferred from B.C.? Explain your answer.

PART THREE CBC ⊕ VIDEO CASE

The Trouble with Teams

The teamwork trend in business began with the automotive industry back in the early 1980s. At that time, North American car manufacturers were fighting for their lives against Japanese exports. "Many consultants and management people felt that the key to the Japanese success was a form of teamwork," says Wayne Lewchuk of McMaster University. The Japanese worked in small groups, taking turns doing different jobs. They gave their workers a voice in production, encouraging them to make productivity suggestions and take ownership of the production decisions. With this more democratic, egalitarian management style it seemed there was no business challenge a team couldn't tackle. The teamwork concept spread first through the auto sector then to other types of businesses. "North American businesses jumped on the team bandwagon," says Natalie Allen of the University of Western Ontario.

Today most well-managed companies use some form of teamwork. Quaker Canada is a good example. Plant workers switch jobs from packaging to quality testing. Teams have even taken over supervisory functions, doing their own scheduling and ordering of supplies. According to plant manager Scott Baker, getting the teams up and running required a huge effort. But Quaker Canada persisted. Three years later, the company had cut management staff by two-thirds and productivity was up .

Employees and management at Four Seasons Hotels—ranked as one of the 35 best Canadian companies to work for by Hewitt and Associates, in 1999—also sing the praises of the teamwork philosophy. Elizabeth Dexter, who manages a staff of 26, took a pay cut to come to Four Seasons. She liked the idea of being part of a team, and was also impressed with the company's reputation for valuing and truly listening its employees. To make sure that all employees buy into the teamwork culture and philosophy, all new employees go through four interviews before being hired, and then enter an intensive orientation process. It's expensive and time consuming, but it works for Four Seasons.

But not all companies report such success. While companies like Quaker Canada and Four Seasons Hotels remain committed to teams, some management gurus, such as management writer and consultant Peter Drucker and Harvard professor J. Richard Hackman, are jumping off the bandwagon.

Consider ESG Canada a successful startup company in Kingston, Ontario whose main product is a sound-monitoring system used in mines. The five equal partners have embraced the teamwork concept since the company's inception in the mid-1990s. With teamwork they believed that "...1 + 1 + 1 would equal 7 or even 8," recalls founding partner Cezar Trifu. All five have an equal say in decisions. But they are considering a change. "Sometimes it takes a lot of time and effort to get things accomplished. It's difficult to achieve consensus. It bogs us down," they say. For example, it took only one partner to block what might have turned into an important new partnership. Drucker would argue that small entrepreneurial companies like ESG need strong, decisive leadership more than they need democracy.

But small firms aren't the only ones having trouble making teams work. In fact, Lewchuk says that there is no proof that teams increase performance in the long run. In an MIT study of parts suppliers in Europe, the most productive, highest quality operations did not use teamwork. General Motors and Ford have found that teamwork has eroded management control. In some cases plants were not able to meet production targets and do the training needed for job rotation. "The reality is," says Lewchuk, "when workers are having team meetings and drinking coffee, they're not producing cars."

Hackman's research suggests that major

problems include lack of long-term commitment by senior management and an individualistic culture. "It is surprisingly common for successful innovations to be stopped by parent organizations," he says. Allen adds that social values lie at the root of teamwork problems: "Our society ranks stars above true team players. . . . What's it like to work in a group where the focus is supposed to be the *team's* productivity and the *team's* performance when your whole life and your career has been devoted to *your* promotion, *your* pay raise or *your* project?"

Questions

1. What organizational changes would you suggest to the partners at ESG?

2. Think about the last time you worked in a team. What went right? What went wrong? Why?

3. Why do you think teamwork has been successful at companies like the Four Seasons Hotels and Quaker Canada ?

4. Interview a manager from a local company that uses teamwork. List the pros and cons of working in teams in this company.

Video Resource: "The Trouble with Teams: Democracy in the Workplace," Venture 703 (March 9, 1999).

CHAPTER

11

Compensation

CHAPTER OBJECTIVES

1. Describe the various forms of compensation.

2. Explain the concept of compensation equity.

3. Identify the determinants of financial compensation.

4. Identify the principal organizational factors that should be considered in determining financial compensation.

5. Describe labour market factors that determine financial compensation.

6. Identify standard techniques for determining a job's relative worth.

7. Identify employee-related factors that are important in determining pay levels, structures, equity, and productivity.

8. Define job pricing and describe factors to be considered in job pricing.

Earl Lewis and his wife are full of excitement and anticipation as they leave their home for a shopping trip. Earl has just learned that his firm is implementing a new variable pay system and that his long record of high performance will finally pay off. He looks forward to the opportunity to increase his income so he can purchase some needed items for a new home.

Inez Scoggin's anxiety over scheduled chemotherapy for cancer is somewhat relieved. Her supervisor has assured her that a major portion of her drug costs will be covered by the firm's supplementary health insurance plan.

Trig Ekeland, executive director of the local YMCA, returns home dead tired from his job each evening no earlier than six o'clock. His salary is small compared to the salaries of many other local managers who have similar responsibilities. Yet Trig is an exceptionally happy person who believes that his work with youth, civic leaders, and other members of the community is extremely important and worthwhile.

A large manufacturing firm has employed Suzanne Abrahamson for eight years. Although her pay is not what she would like it to be, her job in the accounts payable department enables her to have contact with some of her best friends. She likes her supervisor and considers the overall working environment to be great. Suzanne would not trade jobs with anyone she knows.

Compensation and benefits are obviously important to Earl Lewis and Inez Scoggin, as they are to most employees. However, for Trig and Suzanne, other factors in a total compensation package also assume great importance. These components include a pleasant work environment and job satisfaction. Because it has many elements and a far-reaching impact on performance, compensation administration is one of management's most difficult and challenging human resource areas.

We begin this chapter with an overview of compensation and an explanation of compensation equity. Next, we discuss the components of the organization and the labour market as determinants of individual financial compensation. This is followed by a discussion of the job and the employee as determinants of financial compensation. The final section of this chapter is devoted to job pricing.

Compensation: An Overview

Compensation refers to all rewards earned by employees in return for their labour (see Figure 11-1). **Direct financial compensation** consists of pay received in the form of wages, salaries, bonuses, and commissions (Earl Lewis's new paycheque, for example). **Indirect financial compensation** (benefits) includes all financial rewards that are not included in direct compensation. Inez Scoggin's drug plan is an example. As illustrated in Figure 11-1, this form of compensation includes a wide variety of benefits.

Nonfinancial compensation, a topic we will return to in Chapter 12, is the personal satisfaction (nonmonetary) received from the job itself or from the psychological and/or physical environment of the job. Trig Ekeland and Suzanne Abrahamson, for example, are receiving important forms of nonfinancial compensation. Trig receives satisfaction from the work itself. Suzanne receives nonfinancial compensation from the environment of her job, particularly the contact it provides with friends.

To remain competitive, compensation systems must be developed to reward performance that relates directly to key business goals.[1] In determining effective rewards, however, the uniqueness of each employee must be considered. People have different needs or reasons for working. The most appropriate compensation package will meet these individual needs. When people are having difficulty providing food, shelter, and clothing for their families, for example, money may be the most important reward. Yet some people work long hours, receive little pay and still love their work. To a large degree, then, adequate or "fair" compensation is in the mind of the employee.

Compensation: The total of all rewards earned by employees in return for their labour.

Direct financial compensation: Pay that a person receives in the form of wages, salary, bonuses, and commissions.

Indirect financial compensation: All financial rewards that are not included in direct compensation.

Nonfinancial compensation: The personal satisfaction (nonmonetary) an employee receives from the job itself or from the psychological and/or physical environment in which the job is performed.

Compensation Equity

Management must create work environments that attract, motivate, and retain competent employees. As achieving these goals is accomplished largely through a firm's compensation system, managers must strive for compensation equity. **Workplace equity** refers to the perception that employees are being treated fairly. When chief executives are paid millions of dollars in one year and receive huge bonuses along with other benefits, for example, serious questions may arise within organizations as to what constitutes fairness.[2]

Workplace equity: The perception that employees are being treated fairly.

Figure 11-1

Components of a Total Compensation Program

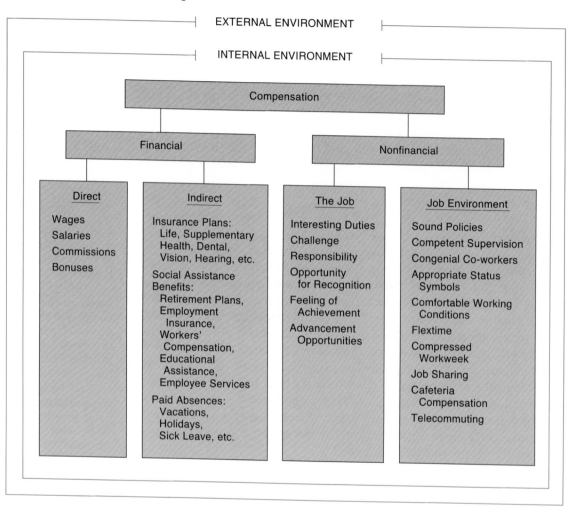

Building and maintaining equity has long been an organizational challenge. The difficulty arises largely because equity involves both external and internal considerations.[3] **External equity** exists when employees in a firm perceive that they are being rewarded fairly relative to those who perform similar jobs in other firms. Compensation surveys enable organizations to determine the level of external equity. **Internal equity** exists when employees in a firm perceive that they are being paid according to the relative value of their jobs within an organization. In this case, the job evaluation is a primary means for determining internal equity. Increasingly, equity is being considered within the context of a group or team. **Team equity** is achieved when groups or teams perceive that they are being rewarded in accordance with group performance. Determining the performance levels of teams is complicated because generally both the group and individual members must be appraised.

Perceived inequity or unfairness, either external or internal, can result in low morale and loss of effectiveness. For example, if employees feel they are being compensated unfairly, they may restrict their efforts or leave the firm, damaging the organization's overall performance.

Major Determinants of Individual Financial Compensation

Compensation theory has never been able to provide a completely satisfactory answer to the question of how to determine what an individual is worth on the job market. The issues are far too complex and individual. Establishing a fair and equitable compensation program—one that motivates employees and increases productive value—is an art as much as a science. A number of relevant factors are typically used to determine financial compensation (see Figure 11-2), including the organization, the labour market, the job, and the employee.[4]

The Organization as a Determinant of Financial Compensation

Compensation programs within organizations influence employee work attitudes and behaviour, and can enhance or undermine organizational performance.[5] The development of an effective and equitable compensation program, within a company, requires consideration of two major factors: compensation policies and ability to pay.

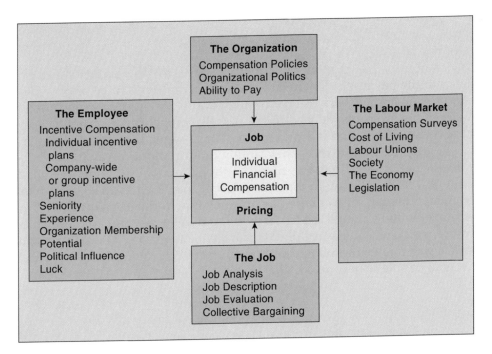

Figure 11-2

Primary Determinants of Individual Financial Compensation

Compensation Policies

Corporate culture has a major effect on an individual's wages and consequent behaviour. An organization often establishes, whether formally or informally, compensation policies that determine whether it will strive for an average wage position in the labour market, be a wage leader, or be a wage minimizer.

Market wage rate:
The average pay (or going rate) that most employers provide for the same job in a particular area or industry.

The **market wage rate**, or going rate, is the average pay among all employers for a given job in a particular area or industry. Many organizations have a policy that calls for paying the market wage rate. In such firms, management believes that it can attract qualified people and still keep wage costs low enough to maintain competitive prices for goods or services. Organizations that are wage leaders offer higher wages and salaries than competing firms. They believe that this strategy will enable them to attract high-quality, more productive employees, thus achieving lower *per unit* labour costs despite the higher wages. Still other firms have a policy or culture of wage minimization. They pay below the market wage rates either because of poor financial conditions or simply because they do not believe they require highly capable employees. This strategy, in its extreme, tends to result in unproductive, unmotivated workers, high turnover, and reduced customer service.

Compensation strategists recommend[8] that companies can strengthen and build a positive corporate compensation culture by

- developing and instituting a clear compensation policy;

- communicating to everyone the rationale for the corporate compensation policy;

- adhering consistently to the stated compensation policy;

- providing employees with objective and fair compensation surveys—both internal and external;

- emphasizing both internal and external equity.

Ability to Pay

An organization's assessment of its ability to pay is the second major factor in determining pay levels. Financially successful firms tend to be price leaders and provide higher-than-average compensation.[6] As most everyone knows, for example, firms entrenched in the fiercely competitive restaurant sector have consistently found it difficult to pay high wages. Most restaurants, as a result, are price minimizers—they simply cannot afford to pay high wages. Nonetheless, an organization's financial strength establishes only the upper limit of what it will pay. To arrive at a specific pay level, management must consider other factors—a major one of which is performance. One survey, for example, found a significant increase in the number of companies in which compensation schemes were linked to "quality performance."[7] Even in a restaurant, a staff member who increases the number of customers and thus sales is likely to be able to negotiate higher wages.

The Labour Market as a Determinant of Financial Compensation

Many employees judge the fairness of their compensation against the going wage rate within the labour market for their services. The **labour market** comprises all possible employees who are potentially available and qualified for a particular job. For managers or specialized professionals, the labour market recruitment area may be national or even international. Markets for unskilled or operative employees are usually more geographically localized. In this case, the going wage rate can vary considerably from one local labour market to another. Clerical jobs, for example, may carry an average annual salary of $29 000 per year in a large, urban community but only $18 000 or less in a small town. Compensation managers must be aware of these differences in order to compete successfully for employees. Major considerations will include compensation surveys, cost of living, labour unions, society and the consumer, the economy, and legislation.

Labour market:
All possible employees who are potentially available and qualified for a particular job.

Compensation Surveys

A **compensation survey** is a standard method of finding out what other firms are paying for specific jobs or job classes. Large organizations, in particular, routinely conduct compensation surveys to determine prevailing pay rates and benefits. These surveys not only determine the low, high, and average salaries for a given position, but also provide a sense of what competitors are paying.[8]

Prior to conducting a compensation survey, decisions are made to determine 1) the recruitment area of the survey, 2) the specific firms to be contacted, and 3) the jobs to include. The recruitment area is often defined based on employment records, which indicate, for example, where employees lived prior to employment with the company. The firms to be contacted are often from the same industry, but may also include others that compete for the same skills. Because obtaining data on all jobs may not be feasible, the human resource department often surveys only benchmark jobs. A **benchmark job** is one that is well known in the company and industry, one that represents the entire job structure, and one in which a large percentage of the workforce is employed. Often human resource professionals will rely on the *National Occupational Classification* system we described in Chapter 4.

One difficulty in conducting a compensation survey is determining which jobs are comparable. Since job titles may not adequately reflect the functions or requirements of the job, survey designers usually rely on job descriptions.

There are other methods of obtaining compensation data. Periodically, some professional organizations and private companies such as KPMG and Hay Management Consultants Ltd. conduct compensation surveys. The Society of Management Accountants, for example, publishes a yearly survey organized by province. As well, Statistics Canada issues a number of reports that detail salaries and wages.

Compensation survey:
A method of obtaining labour market data regarding what other firms are paying for specific jobs or job classes of jobs

Benchmark job: A well-known job, in which a large percentage of a company's workforce is employed, that represents the entire job structure.

HR Web Wisdom
http: www.pearsoned.ca/mondy

Occupational Outlooks
Choose an occupation and find out the full-time earnings expectations.

Cost of Living

The logic for using cost of living as a partial pay determinant is that if prices rise over a period of time and pay does not, *real pay* actually decreases. A pay increase must be roughly equivalent to the increased cost of living to maintain the level of real wages. For example, if an individual earns $24 000 during a year in which the average rate of inflation is five percent, a $100-per-month pay increase will be necessary merely to maintain that person's standard of living.

Labour Unions

The collective bargaining process between management and unions obviously has great potential impact on compensation decisions. The union, as we discuss in Chapters 14 and 15, affects company compensation policies in three important areas: 1) the standards used in making compensation decisions, 2) wage differentials, and 3) payment methods.

When a union uses comparable pay as a standard in making compensation demands, the employer must obtain accurate labour market data. When cost of living is emphasized, management may be pressured to include a **cost-of-living allowance (COLA)** as part of the payment package. This clause in a labour agreement means that wages automatically increase as the Statistics Canada cost-of-living index rises.

Cost-of-living allowance (COLA): An escalator clause in a labour agreement that automatically increases as the cost-of-living index rises.

Society and the Consumer

Compensation paid to employees affects a firm's prices for its goods or services. For this reason, consumers may also be interested in compensation decisions. Attempts to increase Canadian telephone rates[9] have generally met with consumer resistance, for example, as have increased insurance premiums.[10]

Businesses in a given labour market are also concerned with the pay practices of new firms locating in their area. In one instance, when the management of a large electronics firm announced plans to locate a branch plant in a relatively small community, it was confronted by local civic leaders. Their questions largely concerned the firm's wage and salary rates. Subtle pressure was applied to keep the company's salaries comparable to other wages in the community. The electronics firm agreed to begin operations with initial compensation at a lower level than it usually paid.

The Economy

The financial health of the economy also affects financial compensation decisions. A depressed economy generally increases the labour supply, serving to lower the average wage rate. Labour unions, government, and society are all less likely to press for pay increases in a depressed economy. Conversely, in most cases, the cost of living will rise in an expanding economy, exerting upward pressure on pay levels.

HR Web Wisdom
http: www.pearsoned.ca/ mondy

Employment Standards Legislation in Canada

This site sets out federal, provincial, and territorial employment legislative provisions.

Legislation[11]

Federal and provincial laws also affect compensation. Employment standards legislation sets out minimum compensation. In Canada, both the federal parliament and the provinces have the power to enact labour laws that regulate compensation. Federal powers are limited to specific industries (shown in Figure 11-3). With minor exceptions, provincial legislatures regulate most other aspects of commerce within their boundaries.

Figure 11-3

Hours of Work and Overtime Pay

JURISDICTION	STANDARD	MAXIMUM	OVERTIME PAID AFTER	EXCLUSIONS*
Federal	8 h/day 40 h/wk	48 h/wk	8 h/day; 40 h/wk 1½ times reg. pay	averaging allowed
Alberta	8 h/day 44 h/wk	Within a 12-h period/day	8 h/day; 44 h/wk 1½ times reg. pay	overtime agreements allowable
British Columbia	8 h/day 40 h/wk	— —	8 h/day; 40 h/wk 1½ times reg. pay 11 h/day; 48 h/wk 2 times reg. pay	
Manitoba	8 h/day 40 h/wk	8 h/day 40 h/wk	8 h/day; 40 h/wk 1½ times pay	professionals and some others
New Brunswick	—	—	44 h/wk 1½ times min. wage	—
Newfoundland	40 h/wk	—	40 h/wk 1½ times min. wage	professionals; students
Nova Scotia	48 h/wk	—	48 h/wk 1½ times min. wage	managerial and some others
Ontario	44 h/wk	8 h/day 48 h/wk	44 h/wk; 1½ times pay	managerial and some others
PEI	48 h/wk	—	48 h/wk; 1½ times pay	salespersons on commission and others
Quebec	44 h/wk	—	44 h/wk 1½ times pay	many: see Act
Saskatchewan	8 h/day 40 h/wk	44 h/wk	8 h/day; 40 h/wk 1½ times pay	managerial, professionals, and others

*Note: Exceptions tend to be extensive; the appropriate legislation should be consulted.

Source: Data obtained from Human Resources Development Canada, Employment Standards Legislation in Canada (1995-96). (Ottawa: Canada Communications Group, Minister of Supply and Services. DSS Cat. #631-781/1996 E.) and http://labour-travail.hrdc-drhc.gc.ca/policy/leg/e/stanf5-e2.html

Hours of Work and Overtime Pay

Provisions for hours of work and overtime vary across jurisdictions, as shown in Figure 11-3. There are two common concepts: the standard workday or workweek and the maximum hours that can be worked per week. Sometimes the law only provides that where the standard workday or workweek is exceeded, overtime must be paid—as is the case for New Brunswick. But some laws, in addition to standard hours of work, also provide a legal maximum number of hours per day or per week, in excess of which an employee is not permitted to work. Some jurisdictions also give employees the right to refuse overtime if they do not receive adequate notice or if they face a personal emergency.

Minimum Wages

Today, there is a variety of systems, depending on the jurisdiction. Most Canadians, however, are covered by the rates listed in Figure 11-4.

Figure 11-4

Minimum Wage Rates

JURISDICTION	HOURLY RATE	EFFECTIVE DATE
Federal	same as adult minimum wage rate in each provincial and territorial jurisdiction	December 18, 1996
Alberta	$5.90	October 1, 1999
British Columbia	$7.15	April 1, 1998
Manitoba	$6.00	April 1, 1999
New Brunswick	$5.50	July 1, 1996
Newfoundland[1]	$5.50	October 1, 1999
Northwest Territories[1]	$6.50/$7.00[2]	April 1, 1991
Nova Scotia	$5.70	October 1, 2000
Nunavut[1]	$7.00	April 1, 1999
Ontario	$6.85	January 1, 1995
Prince Edward Island	$5.40	September 1, 1997
Quebec	$6.90	October 1, 1998
Saskatchewan	$6.00	January 1, 1999
Yukon Territory	$7.20	October 1, 1998

[1] Sixteen years of age and over.
[2] For areas distant from the highway system.

Source: Adapted from Human Resources Development Canada, Employment Standards Legislation in Canada (1995-96). (Ottawa: Canada Communications Group, Minister of Supply and Services. DSS Cat. #631-781/1996 E.) and http://labour-travail.hrdc-drhc.gc.ca/policy/leg/e/stanf5-e2.html

Equal Pay for Equal Work (or for Work of Equal Value)

This topic has generated intense debate.[12] The intent of human rights legislation and/or employment standards legislation is to prohibit employers from paying less to women than to men who perform the same jobs or jobs of equal value. This concept allows for differences based on seniority, merit, or quantity of output. Most legislation (again, there are exceptions) allows individuals to initiate legal action or to complain before a tribunal or Employment Standards Officer. However, legislation varies widely by jurisdiction, and so individual Acts must be consulted. The Canadian Human Rights Act (federal) and provincial legislation apply these concepts to all organizations under their respective jurisdictions, in the private as well as the public sector. Labour Canada, for example, enforces a three-step process—education, monitoring, inspection—to ensure compliance in federally-regulated workplaces.

Pay Equity

Similar to equal pay for work of equal value, **pay equity** legislation seeks to correct systemic gender discrimination in compensation.[13] The purpose, then, is to change past practice, so that female-dominated jobs (e.g., librarian) are not paid less than male-dominated jobs (e.g., electrician) found to be of equal value.

In much of Canada, pay equity programs apply only to the public sector. The future status of pay equity will depend upon the political climate, or the social philosophy of the party in power, as successive governments amend the legislation.[14]

Pay equity: Legislation which seeks to redress systemic gender discrimination in compensation.

The Job as a Determinant of Financial Compensation

Individual jobs are a major determinant of financial compensation levels, as employees are paid for the value attached to duties, responsibilities, skills and other job-related factors like working conditions. The most common techniques for determining a job's relative worth include job analysis, job descriptions, and job evaluation. These were dealt with in Chapter 4. We suggest you might want to return to the section in Chapter 4 on job evaluation and refresh your memory. In addition to these factors, unions, when present in a firm, normally prefer to determine compensation through the process of collective bargaining—a topic we deal with in Chapter 15. But even in a unionized environment, specific job pay rates will still depend—to a large degree—on the functions and competencies of a specific position.

The Employee as a Determinant of Financial Compensation

In addition to the organization, the labour market, and the job, factors related to the employee are also essential in determining pay equity: individual incentive plans, company-wide and group incentive plans, seniority, experience, membership in the organization, and lastly, plain old fashioned luck!

Incentive Compensation

Top performers are attracted to firms that base their pay structure on performance. In particular, pay-for-performance appears to attract people with a strong work ethic[15] and people with a more entrepreneurial outlook.[16] A payment or compensation program that relates pay to productivity or performance is often referred to as **incentive compensation**. According to a 1998 Conference Board of Canada report, some 90 percent of all firms have some sort of incentive compensation program in place.[17] The basic purpose of all incentive programs is to improve employee productivity in order to gain a competitive advantage. To do this the firm must use various rewards and focus on the needs of the employee as well as the firm's business goals. Money can serve as an important motivator for those who value it—and many individuals do. However, a clear relationship must exist between performance and pay if money is to serve as an effective motivator. A number of major individual and group incentive compensation programs are briefly outlined below.

Incentive compensation: A payment program that relates pay to productivity.

Merit pay is a pay increase given to employees based on performance as indicated in the appraisal or evaluation. In some cases merit pay is simply added each year to an employee's base pay. Suppose, for example, an employee earning $30 000 per year receives a 6-percent merit raise for last year's performance. His or her new base income would become $31 800. This employee would continue to receive this 6-percent-higher salary even if future performance declined. This type of system is difficult to justify from the perspective of stimulating productivity.

Merit pay: Pay increase given to employees based on performance as indicated in the appraisal or evaluation.

A common type of merit pay is the **bonus or lump sum payment**. According to one study, for example, about 50 percent of Canadian firms have now instituted some form of lump sum or bonus pay system.[18] A bonus is a one-time incentive payment that is not added to the employee's base pay. Bonuses, then, are a variable form of compensation. They must be earned each year, allowing management to restrict fixed costs while providing constant financial incentive for improved performance.

Bonus (lump sum payment): A one-time incentive payment that is not added to the employees' base pay.

Piecework is a form of performance-based pay in which employees are paid for each unit they produce. There are several types of piecework plans depending on the job. A common example is the *straight piecework plan.* In this case, the piece rate —money earned per unit output—is normally calculated by dividing the job's hourly pay rate by a predetermined standard hourly output. For example, if the job's pay rate is $8.00 per hour and the standard output is 25 units per hour, then the piece rate would be $0.32. Thus, an employee who produced at the rate of 280 units per day would earn $89.60 in an eight-hour day. This employee would effectively receive $11.20 an hour ($89.60 /8). Most incentive plans in use today have a guaranteed base rate. In our example, it would be the $8 per hour rate.

Piecework: An incentive pay plan in which employees are paid for each unit produced.

One well-known potential problem with piecework plans is related to the output standard. Often, workers distrust the standards established by industrial engineers. They may also view with considerable skepticism any change to a standard, although change may be justified in the eyes of management. When individual output cannot be easily distinguished, group- and company-wide plans offer alternatives to individual incentive plans. These are discussed below.

Skill-based pay is a system that compensates employees on the basis of job-related skills and knowledge they possess, not for their job titles. It is a relatively new approach premised on the belief that more knowledgeable employees are more valuable to the firm and therefore should be rewarded accordingly.[19] The underlying purpose is to encourage employees to gain additional skills that will increase their value to the organization and improve its competitive position.

Skill-based pay: A system that compensates employees on the basis of their job-related skills and knowledge.

Competency-based pay is a compensation plan that rewards employees for their demonstrated expertise. Competencies include skills but also involve other factors such as motives, traits, values, attitudes, and self-concepts. Core competencies may be unique to each company, but one service firm identified these essential factors: [21]

Competency-based pay: A compensation plan that rewards employees for their demonstrated expertise.

- Team-centred—builds productive working relationships at levels within and outside the organization.

- Results-driven —is focused on achieving key objectives.

- Client-dedicated —works as a partner with internal and external clients.

TRENDS and INNOVATIONS

PROFIT 100[20]

How do PROFIT 100 companies reward their employees? Rick Spence, of *PROFIT* magazine says that PROFIT 100 companies engage in a riot of creative perks, benefits, and off-the-wall incentives. Here are just a few of his examples:

- **Aurora Microsystems.** All staff members had both salaries and incentive plans customized to their jobs. "We offer incentives to perform better, because these days just getting to keep your job isn't incentive enough," said Aurora president (1996–1997) Kevin Fitzgerald.

- **Akran Systems Ltd.** Financial incentives included bonuses to non-sales employees for referrals that resulted in sales, best monthly performance awards in different departments of the company, and "best employee suggestion" awards.

- **Datalog Technology Inc.** Employees were rewarded through profit sharing, share ownership for key personnel, higher than average pay scales and cash bonuses amounting to 20 percent of net profits.

- **CRS Robotics Corp**. Financial incentives included a share purchase plan, an incentive plan for new employees to buy in, profit–sharing, and above-average pay.

- **Fulcrum Technologies Inc.** Staff benefit from employee stock options, performance bonuses and above-average salaries.

- Innovative —generates and implements new ideas, products, services, and solutions to problems.

- Fast cycle —Displays a bias for action and decisiveness.

Profit sharing:
A compensation plan that distributes a predetermined percentage of the firm's profits to employees.

Profit sharing The incentive programs discussed above reward individual employees. There is also a number of company-wide incentive programs, of which profit-sharing is one of the most popular. During the 1990s, some 17 percent of fastest-growing companies in PROFIT 100 offered some sort of profit-sharing plans.[22] **Profit sharing** is a compensation plan that distributes a predetermined percentage of the firm's profits to employees. Many managers view this type of plan as a chance to integrate employee interests with those of the company. Profit-sharing plans can aid in recruitment, motivation, and employee retention, factors that relate directly to productivity.

There are several variations of profit sharing plans, but two basic kinds are widely used today—current profit sharing and deferred profit sharing.[23] Current plans provide payment to employees in cash or stock as soon as profits have been determined. Deferred plans involve placing company contributions in an irrevocable trust to be credited to the account of individual employees. The funds are normally invested in securities and become available to the employee (or his or her survivors) at retirement, termination, or death. These two plans may be combined, with part of the profit paid immediately and part deferred.

Incentive problems with profit sharing plans arise because the recipients seldom know precisely how they helped generate the profits, beyond just doing their jobs. If they do not know what they have done to deserve it, they may view it as an entitlement program. In fact the results may be just the opposite of what is desired.[24] However, profit sharing does tend to tie employees to the economic success of the firm, resulting in increased efficiency and lower costs. Most studies indicate that both employer and employee benefit, and profit-sharing plans are expected to spread.[25] According to a report prepared by Coopers & Lybrand, about 20 percent of small firms have implemented profit-sharing plans compared to only 5 percent five years ago.

Employee stock ownership plan (ESOP):
A company-wide incentive plan in which the company provides its employees with common stock.

Employee stock ownership plan (ESOP) An **employee stock ownership plan (ESOP)** is a contribution plan in which a firm makes a tax deductible contribution of stock shares or cash to a trust. Research indicates that when employees become owners, they increase their dedication to the firm, improve their work effort, reduce turnover, and generally bring a more harmonious atmosphere to the company.[26] About 26 percent of the PROFIT 100 fastest growing companies offered their employees some form of stock ownership incentive plan.[27] Although the potential advantages of ESOPs are impressive, critics point out the dangers of employees having all their eggs in one basket. Employees would be in a vulnerable position should their company fail.

Gain-sharing: Incentive plans that involve many or all employees in a common effort to achieve a firm's performance objectives.

Gain-Sharing plans are designed to bind employees to the firm's performance by providing an incentive payment based on improved company performance. Improved performance can take the form of increased productivity, increased customer satisfaction, lower costs, or better safety records.[28] Gain-sharing plans (also known as productivity incentives, team incentives, and performance-sharing incentives) generally refer to incentive plans that involve many or all employees in a common effort to achieve a firm's performance objectives.

There are many types of gain-sharing programs. One example is the so-called Scanlon plan. This program emphasizes employee empowerment and financial rewards to employees for savings in labour costs that result from their suggestions. These suggestions are evaluated by employee–management committees. Savings are calculated as a ratio of payroll costs to the sales value of what that payroll produces.[29]

Team-based compensation plans Nucor, a high-performing steel company, divides its production workers into work groups of 25 to 35 people and pays work group members a bonus based on their group's production over a certain predetermined standard. At Nucor, incentive packages like this led to a growth in sales of some 850 percent and a profit growth of some 1250 percent.[30] Tescor Energy Services, out of North York, Ontario, is another leading company that pays its employees a bonus for meeting team goals.[31]

Firms that, like Nucor, and Tescor Energy Services, are organized around teams appear to be growing in number, encouraging HR professionals to develop team-oriented compensation systems. Team-based pay plans must not only promote internal equity, but also encourage participation among team members in meeting predetermined objectives. The goal is to develop an environment in which people feel that "we're all in this together." Four key design features should be considered:

1. a direct and obvious link with the firm's strategic plan;

2. clearly defined, measurable team goals;

3. a system for allocating team-based incentives, either equally to all team members, or differentially in proportion to base pay; and

4. a method of separating team-based payment or incentives from base or regular salary.[32]

Seniority

The length of time an employee has been associated with the company, division, department, or job is referred to as **seniority**. While management generally prefers performance as the primary basis for compensation changes, collective labour agreements tend to favour seniority. Many union members believe that seniority provides a fair, objective basis for pay increases. There is also a widespread feeling that performance evaluation systems are too subjective, allowing management to reward favourite employees arbitrarily.

An acceptable compromise between performance and seniority might be to permit employees to receive pay increases to the midpoints of their pay grades on the basis of seniority. The rationale is that workers performing at an acceptable level should eventually receive the average wage or salary of their pay grades. Progression beyond the midpoint, however, should be based on performance. This practice would permit only outstanding performers to reach the maximum rate for the grade, reflecting the initial rationale for rate ranges.

Seniority: The length of time an employee has been associated with the company, division, department, or job.

Experience

Regardless of the nature of the task, on-the-job experience may greatly enhance a person's ability to perform, especially if progressively more sophisticated skills have been acquired in a successful work history. Individuals who express pride in their long tenure may be justified, but only if their experience has been of the right kind. A manager who has become increasingly autocratic over a 20-year career, for example, would not be valued in a progressively managed firm. Nevertheless, experience is often indispensable for gaining the insights necessary for performing many tasks.

Membership in the Organization

Some components of individual financial compensation are given to employees without regard for the particular job they perform or their level of productivity. These rewards are provided to all employees simply because they are members of the organization. For example, an average performer occupying a job in pay grade 1 may receive the same number of vacation days, the same amount of group life insurance, and the same reimbursement for educational expenses as a superior employee working in a job classified in pay grade 10. In fact, the worker in pay grade 1 may get more vacation time if he or she has been with the firm longer. Rewards based on organizational membership are intended to maintain a high degree of stability in the workforce and to recognize loyalty.

Luck

You've undoubtedly heard the expression, "It helps to be in the right place at the right time." There is more than a little truth in this statement as it relates to a person's compensation. Opportunities are continually presenting themselves in firms. Realistically, there is no way for managers to foresee many of the changes that occur. When asked to explain their most important reasons for success and effectiveness as managers, two chief executives responded candidly. One said, "Success is being at the right place at the right time and being recognized as having the ability to make timely decisions. It also depends on having good rapport with people, a good operating background, and the knowledge of how to develop people." The other replied, "My present position was attained by being in the right place at the right time with a history of getting the job done." Both executives recognize the significance of luck combined with the ability to perform. Their experiences lend support to the idea that luck works primarily for those who are effective.

Job Pricing

Job pricing: Placing a dollar value on the worth of a job.

Placing a dollar value on the worth of a job is called **job pricing**. As we have shown in Figure 11-2, primary considerations in pricing jobs are the organization's policies, the labour market, the job itself and the employee.

Firms often use pay grades and pay ranges in the job-pricing process. Firms may also choose to use broadbanding. In some cases they will employ a single-rate system because of the nature of the job.

Pay Grades

A **pay grade** is the grouping of similar jobs to simplify the job-pricing process. It is much more convenient for organizations to price 15 pay grades rather than 200 separate jobs. The simplicity of this approach is similar to the practice of a college or university in grouping grades of 90 to 100 into an A category, grades of 80 to 89 into a B category, and so on. A false implication of preciseness is also avoided.

Plotting jobs on a scatter diagram is often useful to managers in determining the appropriate number of pay grades for a company. In Figure 11-5, each dot on the scatter diagram represents one job as it relates to pay and evaluated points, which reflect its worth. When this procedure is used, a certain point spread will probably work satisfactorily (100 points was used in this illustration). Each dot represents one job but may involve dozens of positions. The large dot at the lower left represents the job of data entry clerk, which was evaluated at 75 points. The data entry clerk's hourly rate of $12.90 represents either the average wage currently being paid for the job or its market rate. This decision depends on how management wants to price its jobs.

A **wage curve** (or pay curve) is the fitting of plotted points to create a smooth progression between pay grades. The line that is drawn to minimize the distance between all dots and the line—a line of best fit—may be straight or curved. However, when the point system is used (normally considering only

Pay grade: Similar jobs grouped to simplify the job-pricing process.

Wage curve: The fitting of plotted points to create a smooth progression between pay grades (also know as *pay curve*).

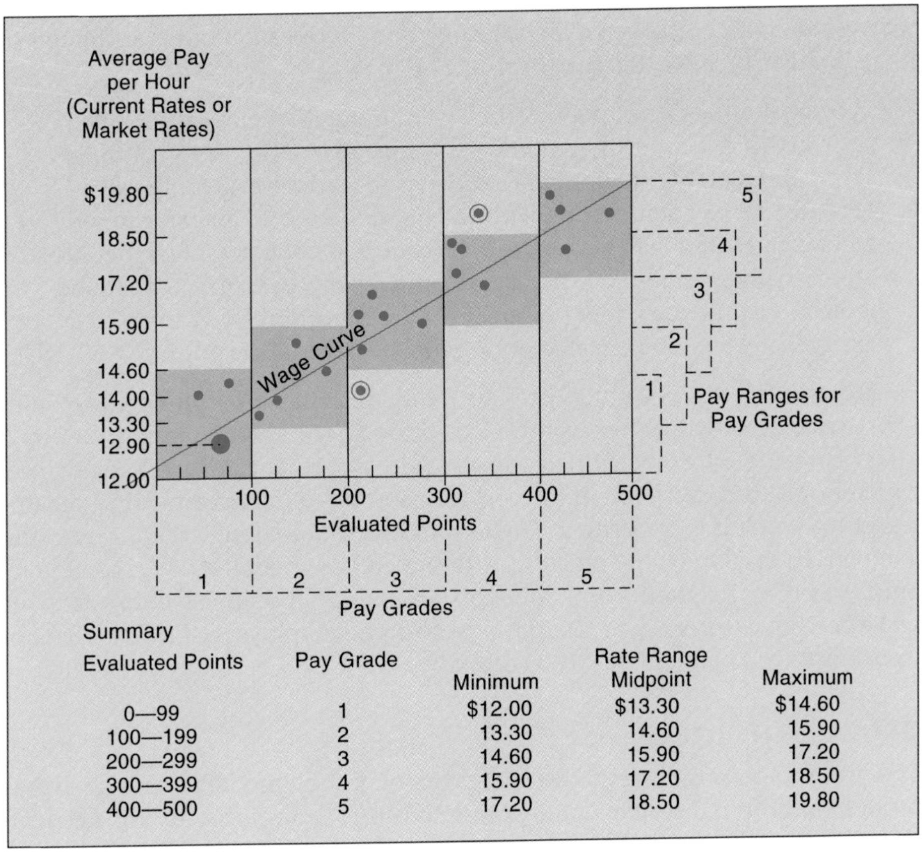

Figure 11-5

Scatter Diagram of Evaluated Jobs Illustrating the Wage Curve, Pay Grades, and Rating Ranges

Summary Evaluated Points	Pay Grade	Rate Range Minimum	Rate Range Midpoint	Rate Range Maximum
0—99	1	$12.00	$13.30	$14.60
100—199	2	13.30	14.60	15.90
200—299	3	14.60	15.90	17.20
300—399	4	15.90	17.20	18.50
400—500	5	17.20	18.50	19.80

one job cluster), a straight line is the usual result, as in Figure 11-5. This wage line can either be drawn freehand or be charted by using a statistical method.

Pay Ranges

After pay grades have been determined, the next decision is whether all individuals performing the same job will receive equal pay or whether pay ranges will be used. A **pay range** includes a minimum and maximum pay rate with enough variance between the two to allow for a significant pay difference. Pay ranges are generally preferred over single pay rates because they allow employees to be paid according to length of service and performance. Pay then serves as a positive incentive. When pay ranges are used, a method must be developed to advance individuals through the range.

Referring again to Figure 11-5, note that anyone can readily determine the minimum, midpoint, and maximum pay rates per hour for each of the five pay grades. For example, for pay grade 5, the minimum rate is $17.20, the midpoint is $18.50, and the maximum is $19.80. The minimum rate is often the rate that a person receives when joining the firm. The maximum pay rate represents the maximum that an employee can receive for that job, regardless of how well the job is performed. A person at the top of a pay grade will have to be promoted to a job in a higher pay grade to receive a pay increase unless either 1) an across-the-board adjustment is made, raising the entire pay range, or 2) the job is reevaluated and placed in a higher pay grade. This situation has caused numerous managers some anguish as they attempt to explain the pay system to an employee who is doing a tremendous job but is at the top of a pay grade. Consider this situation:

> Everyone in the department realized that Indira Khatami was the best secretary in the company. At times, she appeared to do the job of three secretaries. Bob Marshall, Indira's supervisor, was especially impressed. Recently, he had a discussion with the human resource manager to see what could be done to get a raise for Indira. After Bob described the situation, the human resource manager's only reply was, "Sorry, Bob. Indira is already at the top of her pay grade. There is nothing you can do except have her job upgraded or promote her to another position."

Situations such as Indira's present managers with a perplexing problem. Many would be inclined to make an exception to the system and give Indira a salary increase. However, this action would violate a traditional principle, which holds that every job in the organization has a maximum value, regardless of how well it is performed. The rationale is that making exceptions to the compensation plan would result in widespread pay inequities. We should recognize that many traditional concepts are being challenged today as firms make decisions necessary to retain top performing employees. If Indira Khatami were employed by a PROFIT 100 company, she would probably get a raise.

Broadbanding

The pressure on businesses to do things better, faster, and less expensively has brought all internal systems under close scrutiny. In response to this need, an approach termed broadbanding has been developed. **Broadbanding** is a technique that collapses many pay grades (salary grades) into a few wide bands to improve organizational effectiveness. Organizational downsizing and restructuring of jobs create broader job descriptions, with the result that employees perform more diverse tasks than they did previously. Moving an employee's job to a new band would occur only when there was a significant increase in accountability.[33] However, considerable advancement in pay is possible within each band. Figure 11-6 illustrates broadbanding as it relates to pay grades and rate ranges.

Broadbanding creates the basis for a simpler compensation system that de-emphasizes structure and control and places greater importance on judgment and flexible decision making. This is particularly important in firms with flat organizational structures that offer fewer promotional opportunities. According to some recent surveys, broadbanding improves a company's ability to

- Provide flexibility in the way work is performed
- Promote lateral development of employees
- Support business goals
- Develop employee skills and encourage a team focus
- Direct employee attention away from vertical promotional opportunities.[34]

However, broadbanding is not without pitfalls. Because each band consists of a broad range of jobs, the market value of these jobs may vary considerably. Unless carefully monitored, employees in jobs at the lower end of the band could progress to the top of the range and become overpaid.

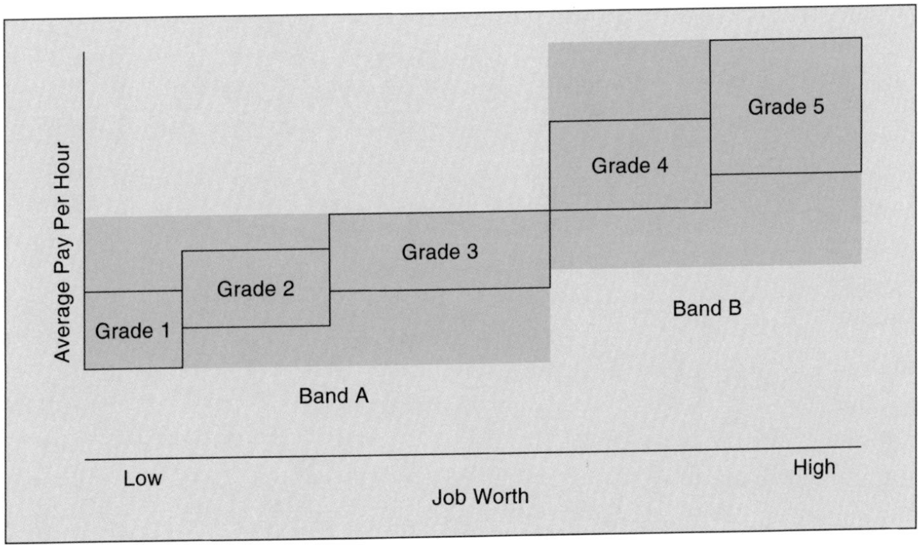

Broadbanding:
A compensation technique that collapses many pay grades (salary grades) into a few wide bands in order to improve organizational effectiveness.

Figure 11- 6

Broadbanding and its Relationship to Traditional Pay Grades and Ranges

Single-Rate System

Pay ranges are not appropriate for some workplace conditions such as assembly line operations. When all jobs within a unit are routine, with little opportunity for employees to vary their productivity, a single, or fixed-rate, system may be more appropriate. When single rates are used, everyone in the same job receives the same base pay, regardless of seniority or productivity. For example, this rate may correspond to the midpoint of a range determined by a compensation survey.

HRM in *ACTION*

A Compensation Problem

Gráinne Wosser, the data processing manager for a national insurance company, was perplexed as she spoke to Doron Horowitz, the human resource manager. Gráinne said, "I have trouble recruiting programmers and systems analysts. The data processing centre employs a total of 45 people, including 10 programmers and four systems analysts. During the past six months, 7 programmers and 3 systems analysts have quit. The people who left were experienced and competent. Their major reasons for leaving the company were better salaries and greater advancement opportunities elsewhere. Because of the shortage of experienced programmers and analysts, the replacements hired by the company have little prior experience. This situation has caused the data processing center to run continuously behind schedule."

How should Doron respond?

A GLOBAL PERSPECTIVE

Global Compensation: Don't Pay Too Much

Designing compensation programs for expatriates and local nationals is especially difficult. In Canada, most firms have a single policy that covers all employees. Firms that operate overseas, however, may have numerous standards, depending on the employee's situation. Allowances may be given for the number of children in a household, or an allowance may be provided for transportation if the employee lives a certain distance from the workplace, but not if accommodation is close by.

In some cases, base pay for workers outside the country may appear to be low at first glance. But the benefits package is often much better, when allowances for social conditions are considered.[35] For example, HR Education Development Ltd., a private-sector training company with business interests in Hong Kong, the Philippines and Guangzhou, China, has employed a number of young Canadian business graduates as trainers and consultants. While the base pay is only $800 Cdn. per month, trainers receive free lodging, maid service, a generous food allowance, medical insurance, and free return transportation. This package has an estimated value of $23 000 Cdn. When the opportunity of gaining international experience and making foreign contacts is added, this compensation arrangement can be attractive.[36]

Several questions arise, therefore, when considering compensation levels for global employees and alliances. In the case of alliances, should the partners' compensation systems be linked, or will they be synthesized into a common system? Will compensation rates be adjusted for local markets, or tied to similar jobs in the partner's home country? Often each partner in a venture has an established pay policy and those policies differ. At the very least, partners in these ventures need to reach an agreement on the broad objectives of a compensation program for employees.[37]

Global compensation programs should be designed to establish and to maintain a consistent relationship between the compensation of employees in all international alliances. The programs should also maintain compensation levels that are reasonable in relation to the practices of leading competitors. Failure to establish a uniform compensation policy can result in predictably adverse results, especially for employees doing the same jobs. Poorly designed compensation systems will inevitably lead to low morale, motivational problems, and less productive employees.[38] Despite these problems, the financial compensation provided to most expatriate managers appears to be satisfactory. According to a survey by Richard A. Guzzo, 80 percent of the respondents were satisfied with their financial rewards. The same respondents, however, were not pleased with their *nonfinancial* support, including proper preparation for overseas assignments and appropriate career path development.[39]

SUMMARY

1. **Describe the various forms of compensation.**
Compensation is the total of all rewards earned by employees in return for their labour service. Direct financial compensation consists of the pay a person receives in the form of wages, salaries, bonuses, and commissions. Indirect financial compensation (benefits) refers to all financial rewards that are not included in direct compensation. Nonfinancial compensation consists of the satisfaction a person receives from the job itself or from the psychological and/or physical work environment.

2. **Explain the concept of compensation equity.**
Workplace equity involves workers' perceptions that they are being treated fairly. Compensation equity involves a number of interrelated concepts. External equity exists when a firm's employees are paid comparably to workers who perform similar jobs in other firms. Internal equity exists when employees are paid according to the relative value of their jobs within an organization. Employee equity exists when individuals performing similar jobs for the same firm are paid according to factors unique to the employee, such as performance level or seniority. Team equity is achieved when more productive teams are rewarded more than less productive teams. Inequity or perceived unfairness in any of these categories or concepts can result in counterproductive morale problems.

3. **Identify the determinants of financial compensation.**
The organization, the labour market, the job, and the employee all have an impact on job pricing and the ultimate determination of an individual's financial compensation.

4. **Identify the principal organizational factors that should be considered in determining financial compensation.**
The development of an effective and equitable compensation program requires consideration of two major factors within a company: compensation policies and ability to pay. Compensation policies and programs within organizations influence employee work attitudes and behaviour, and can enhance or detract from organizational performance. Financially successful firms tend to be price leaders, providing higher-than-average compensation.

5. **Describe labour market factors that determine financial compensation.**
Many employees judge the fairness of their compensation against the going wage rate within the labour market for their services. Thus firms must consider prevailing market pay rates—in many cases through the use of compensation surveys and benchmarking. The cost of living must also be considered, since it affects the employee's real income. In a unionized bargaining environment, the collective bargaining process will likely affect the standards used in making compensation decisions, wage differentials, and payment methods. In some cases, society and consumer attitudes can affect compensation decisions. The economy also affects some pay decisions. Lastly, the amount of compensation a person receives can also be influenced by federal and provincial legislation.

6. **Identify standard techniques for identifying a job's relative worth.**
Individual jobs are a major determinant of financial compensation levels, as employees are paid for the value attached to duties, responsibilities, skills and other job-related factors like working conditions. Common techniques for determining a job's relative worth include job analysis, job descriptions, and job evaluation. In a unionized environment, compensation is heavily influenced by the process of collective bargaining. Normally, job descriptions, skill requirements and job evaluations are preferable alternatives to the use of job titles.

7. **Identify employee-related factors that are important in determining pay levels, structures, equity, and productivity.**
One major factor is incentive compensation. Individual incentive compensation programs include merit pay, piecework, skill-based pay, and competency-based pay. Company-wide or group incentive programs include profit sharing, employee stock ownership, gain sharing, and team-based compensation. Other employee considerations are seniority, experience, membership in the organization, and luck.

8. **Define job pricing and describe factors to be considered in job pricing.**
Placing a dollar value on the worth of a job is referred to as job pricing. Firms often use pay grades and pay ranges in the job-pricing process. A pay grade is the

grouping of similar jobs together to simplify the job-pricing process. A wage curve (or pay curve) is the fitting of plotted points to create a smooth progression between pay grades. A pay range includes a minimum and maximum pay rate with enough variance between the two to allow some significant pay difference. Broadbanding is a technique that collapses many pay grades (salary grades) into a few wide bands in order to improve organizational effectiveness. Pay ranges are not appropriate for some workplace conditions. When single rates are used, everyone in the same job receives the same base pay, regardless of seniority or productivity.

QUESTIONS FOR REVIEW

1. Explain the meaning of each of the following terms:
   a. Compensation
   b. Direct financial compensation
   c. Indirect financial compensation
   d. Nonfinancial compensation

2. Distinguish among workplace equity, external equity, and internal equity.

3. What are the primary determinants of individual financial compensation? Briefly describe each.

4. What major organizational factors should be considered as determinants of financial compensation?

5. What factors should be considered when the labour market is a determinant of financial compensation?

6. What are the major legal considerations involved in compensation?

7. Explain how the nature of the job can be a major determinant of financial compensation.

8. Briefly explain the meaning of each of the following:
   a. Merit pay
   b. Piecework
   c. Bonus
   d. Skill-based pay
   e. Competency-based pay
   f. Profit sharing
   g. Employee stock ownership plan
   h. Gain sharing

9. Describe the rationale and basic procedure for determining pay grades and pay ranges.

10. Why has broadbanding become an important compensation system?

DEVELOPING HRM SKILLS

An Experiential Exercise

Pay equity is likely to remain a key compensation issue, requiring some form of job analysis. The value of a job and workplace equity can be determined by a variety of factors—for example, skills and competencies, knowledge, effort, working conditions, and responsibilities—in addition to marketplace supply and demand. This exercise has been developed to impart an understanding and an appreciation for pay equity, based on two premises:

1. That it is possible to compare different jobs and to establish a pay relationship based on their value to the organization.

2. That the pay established by job market supply and demand can be inequitable and discriminatory, especially with regard to pay for women.

Everyone will be given a copy of Exhibit 1. Based on the premises outlined above, determine the following:

1. Which of the jobs would you consider *comparable*? Select a job from the second list and write it beside the job on the first list to which you feel it compares most closely.

2. What average monthly salary would you assign to each position?

After ten to fifteen minutes everyone will sign their Exhibits and turn them in. Then three participants with dissimilar comparisons will list their comparisons and salaries on the chalkboard or overhead and class discussion will begin.

HRM INCIDENT

It's Just Not Fair!

During a Saturday afternoon golf game with his friend Randy Dean, Harry Neil discovered that his department had hired a recent university grad as a systems analyst—at a starting salary almost as high as Harry's. Although Harry was good-natured, he was bewildered and upset. It had taken him five years to become a senior systems analyst and attain his current salary level at Trimark Data Systems. He had been generally pleased with the company and thoroughly enjoyed his job.

The following Monday morning, Harry confronted Dave Edwards, the human resource director, and asked if what he had heard was true. Dave apologetically admitted that it was and attempted to explain the company's situation: "Harry, the market for systems analysts is very tight, and for the company to attract qualified prospects, we have to offer a premium starting salary. We desperately needed another analyst, and this was the only way we could get one."

Harry asked Dave if his salary would be adjusted accordingly. Dave answered, "Your salary will be reevaluated at the regular time. You're doing a great job, though, and I'm sure the boss will recommend a raise." Harry thanked Dave for his time but left the office shaking his head and wondering about his future.

Questions

1. In terms of workplace equity, was Dave's explanation satisfactory? Discuss.
2. What action do you believe the company should have taken with regard to Harry?

CHAPTER 12

Benefits and Other Compensation Issues

CHAPTER OBJECTIVES

1. Define benefits and the need to communicate the benefits package.

2. Identify and describe the major legally required benefits.

3. Identify four major types or categories of voluntary benefits.

4. Explain the changing nature of benefits packages and the role of flexible compensation.

5. Explain the term nonfinancial compensation and the types of nonfinancial rewards.

6. Describe what companies are doing to improve workplace flexibility.

Jason Handelman, a college dropout, is a senior credit clerk at Ajax Manufacturing Company. A bright young man, Jason has been with Ajax for four years. He has received excellent performance ratings in each of the several positions he has held with the firm. During his last appraisal interview, however, Jason's supervisor implied that promotion to a higher level job would require additional formal education. Because Jason appeared to be receptive to the idea, his supervisor suggested that he check with the human resource manager to learn the details of Ajax's educational assistance policy. When Jason checked the specifics of the educational assistance program it was excellent, covering part of the tuition and the cost of required textbooks. Ajax's educational program and their other benefit programs were top notch, which was very important to Jason and his family.

Liz Polchies is a divorced mother of three elementary school children. She works as an illustrator for Busiform Company. Her normal working hours are from 8:00 a.m to 5:00 p.m., Monday through Friday. The children's school day begins at 9:00 a.m. and ends at 3:30 p.m. Liz has satisfactory child care arrangements after school. However, she faces an almost impossible task of transporting the children to school in the morning and arriving at her job on time. The school's principal permits the children to enter the building at 7:45 each morning to wait until classes begin, but Liz can't count on this practice to continue indefinitely. When Busiform management recently announced a new system of flexible working hours, Liz was delighted.

lthough these vignettes may seem to have little in common, both relate to the broad area of benefits, the theme of this chapter. Jason is investigating the possibility of continuing his education through his company's educational assistance program. Liz believes that the new flexible working hours will solve her difficult child care problem.

The overall purpose of this chapter is to explain and clarify the significance of benefits in a total compensation system. We begin with a discussion of benefits and explain why communication is an important element of the benefit plan design. Next we outline benefits that are legally required. This is followed by: a discussion of the various categories of voluntary benefits; an explanation of the changing nature of benefits packages; and the role of flexible compensation. We then outline how nonfinancial compensation stems from the job itself and the environment. We conclude this chapter with a brief discussion of the workplace flexibility concept and outline some of the major options.

Benefits
(Indirect Financial Compensation)

In most organizations, management recognizes the need to provide employees with insurance and other programs for their health, safety, security, and general welfare (see Figure 12-1). These programs, called **benefits**, include all financial rewards other than direct payment. Benefits cost the firm money, but employees usually receive them indirectly. For example, an organization may pay all or part of an annual supplemental health insurance premium for each employee. The employee does not receive this money, but obtains the benefit of extra health insurance coverage. This type of compensation has the advantage that premium rates are much lower for large groups of employees than for individual policies. In addition, many benefits are nontaxable to the employee and deductible as an expense by the employer, depending on the federal and/or provincial regulations.

Benefits: All financial rewards that generally are not paid directly to an employee.

Benefits are provided to employees because of their membership in the organization. For example, Jason, as an employee of Ajax Manufacturing, was entitled to receive educational benefits. Typically, benefits are not related to employee productivity and therefore, do not serve as motivation for improved performance. An attractive benefit package can, however, assist in the recruitment and the retention of a qualified workforce.

Most large firms offer benefits beyond those legally required. For example, a survey of work arrangements conducted by Statistics Canada for HRDC found that about 75 percent of large firms offered additional company pension, health, and dental plans. [1] Temporary, part-time workers and those working for smaller firms were far less likely to be entitled to supplemental pension, health, and dental plans, as shown in Figure 12-2. Creative benefits packages for these nontraditional types of employment will continue to be a major challenge for human resource professionals. Some of the less conventional types of benefits are also becoming common. For example, one survey of larger Canadian companies, by KPMG, indicated a marked increase in the number of benefits plans that help employees with stress or substance abuse problems, day care for children, and care of elderly relatives. [2]

Figure 12-1

Typical Benefits in a Total Compensation Program

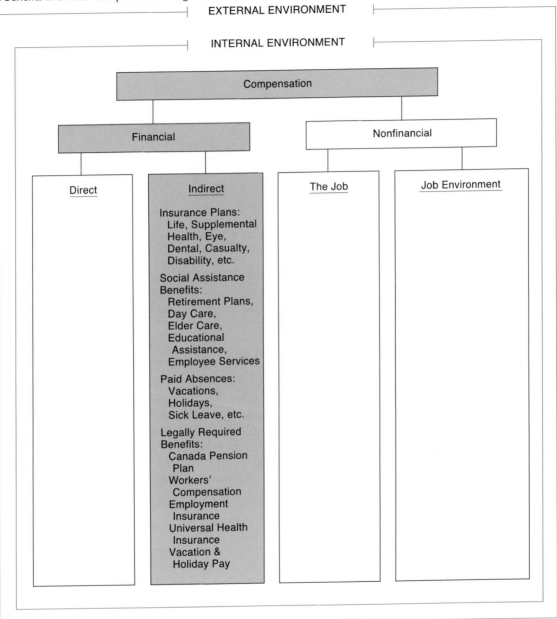

Communicating Information About the Benefits Package

Employee benefits can help to recruit and to retain a high-quality workforce. Effective management depends on an upward information flow from employees to know when benefit changes are needed. Program information must also

Figure 12-2

Job-Related Employee Benefits by Work Arrangement Characteristics

PERCENTAGE OF EMPLOYEES RECEIVING BENEFITS				
	Pension Plan Other Than CPP/QPP	Health Plan Other Than Provincial Health Care	Dental Plan	Paid Sick Leave
Full-time	58.4	68.1	64.3	65.7
Part-time	18.7	17.8	15.9	17.8
Permanent	55.5	64.4	60.0	62.2
Temporary	19.9	19.3	16.5	19.3
Firm size <20	12.8	22.1	19.7	29.2
Firm size >500	74.6	77.2	73.8	72.9
Union	81.1	82.8	75.9	77.0
Non-union	33.0	44.4	41.9	44.8

Source: Reproduced by permission of the Minister of Human Resources Development Canada, 2000.

be communicated downward. Regardless of the sophistication of a benefits program, money spent on benefits can be wasted if employees do not know what they are receiving. Managers must explain the rationale behind a new plan or changes to existing benefits. Otherwise, employees will likely accuse management of not being open about the full impact of the economic factors behind the change-over, especially if benefits will cost more. Employees may even resent payroll deductions, not realizing the greater contribution made by the employer and the range of benefits they receive.

Legally Required Benefits

HR Web Wisdom

http: www.pearsoned.ca/ mondy

HRDC–HR LINKS
Details on legally required benefits are provided.

Old Age Security Pension: A federally administered plan, designed to provide every Canadian, regardless of income, with a basic pension.

While most employee benefits are provided at the employer's discretion, or are negotiated by the employee's union, others are required by law. In Canada, major legally mandated benefits include Old Age Security Pension, Canada/Quebec Pension Plan, employment insurance, Workers' compensation, universal health insurance, vacation pay, and holiday pay.

Old Age Security Pension[3]

The **Old Age Security Pension** is a federally administered plan, designed to provide every Canadian, regardless of income, with a basic pension (which in 1999 amounted to $417.42 per month). This basic pension (referred to as "Old Age Security" by HRDC) can be increased through a "Guaranteed Income Supplement" for individuals and couples with limited incomes. For example, in 1999, the maximum monthly supplement for a married couple, both receiving the basic pension, was $323.12 each. A "Spouses Allowance" is also available for old age security pensioners or widows/widowers aged 60 to 64. The maximum spouse's allowance in 1999 was $817.57. Under certain conditions, this pension is payable anywhere in the world. So, as of 1999, you would not have to live in Canada as a condition for receiving your old age security pension.

The payments are adjusted for inflation and regarded as income, subject to income taxes like any other retirement income. The Income Tax Act also requires the repayment of Old Age Security Pension at the rate of 15 percent of net individual income above a threshold amount. The requirement to repay benefits begins at $53 215 and extends to $85 893, beyond which no old age security is remitted to the pensioner. What this means is that if your net income was $55 215, for example, you would have to remit $300. The remitted amounts are held by Revenue Canada as a credit for the pensioner.

Canada Pension Plan (CPP) and Quebec Pension Plan (QPP)[4]

The **Canada Pension Plan (CPP)** operates throughout Canada except for Quebec, which has its own similar program, the **Quebec Pension Plan (QPP)**. Both plans have been in existence since 1966 (revised in 1997). Which plan applies depends on workplace, not residence If you work in Quebec you pay into the QPP. If you work in any other province or territory you pay into the CPP. With few exceptions, everyone over the age of 18 pays into the CPP/QPP.

Canada Pension Plan (CPP) and **Quebec Pension Plan (QPP):** Legally required social insurance programs funded through contributions from employees, employers, and the self-employed.

There are three kinds of CPP/QPP benefits:

- retirement pension;

- disability benefits—which include pensions for disabled contributors and benefits for their dependent children; and

- survivor benefits—which include the death benefit, the surviving spouse's pension, and the children's benefit).

The plans are funded through employer and employee contributions. In 1999, both the employer and employee paid 3.5 percent of gross income between a minimum ($3500 in 1999) called the "Year's Basic Exemption" and a "Maximum Pensionable Earnings" ceiling ($37 400 in 1999). Individuals who earn less than $3 500 are not required to contribute. Those who earn more than $37 400 are not required or permitted to make additional contributions. Self-employed people must pay the entire premium or 7 percent (1999) of earnings between a set minimum and maximum. An example of the typical contributions and benefits (as of 1999) is shown in Figure 12-3.

Over the latter half of the 1990s, there was intense discussion about the long-term viability of this pension scheme. The main issue was that the CPP/QPP programs were supposed to be self-funding. Many experts argued that the contribution scheme would not be sufficient to fund the massive retirements forecast during the turn of the century and beyond. As a result, a federal-provincial agreement was reached in 1997 to accelerate contribution rate increases—from 7 percent in 1999 to 9.9 percent by 2003.

Figure 12-3a

Examples of Annual Contributions in 1999

Employment income ($)	Employee's contribution deducted at source ($)	Self-employed worker's contributions ($)
5 000	52.50	105.00
20 000	577.50	1155.00
37 400 +	1186.50	2373.00

Figure 12-3b

Examples of CPP/QPP Benefits (1999)

Type of benefit	Maximum CPP and QPP rate ($)
Retirement (age 65)	751.67
Disability	903.52
Survivors (65+)	451.00

Source: *Adapted from Human Resources Development Canada, "Maximum Canada Pension Plan Payment Rates": http://www.hrdc-drhc.gc.ca/isp/cpp/rates_e.shtml.*

Employment Insurance (EI)[5]

Employment insurance (EI): Temporary benefits paid to individuals by the federal government to workers who lose their jobs and are actively looking for but cannot find employment.

Under The Employment Insurance Act (1997), **employment insurance (EI)** benefits are provided to workers who lose their jobs and are actively searching for a new job. The Act also contains numerous special provisions such as the Family Income Supplement, a program for those who want to start their own business, and special help for employees who have been downsized. Added assistance is also available for those unable to work owing to illness, maternity, or caring for a newborn or newly adopted child.

In most cases individuals qualify for regular EI benefits if they lose their jobs and are actively looking for but cannot find work, provided that:

- They have paid into the Employment Insurance account; and

- They have worked the required number of insurable hours. The minimum insurable hours is based on the unemployment rate in the claimant's area of residence. To qualify, most people will need between 420 and 700 hours of work within the last 52 weeks, or since the start of their last claim, whichever is shorter.

There is one notable exception. Individuals filing a claim following their very first job will need at least 910 hours of work to qualify for benefits regardless of the unemployment rate.

The EI program provides financial benefits for a period of 14 to 45 weeks, depending on the claimant's past employment insurance contributions and the regional unemployment rate. In most cases, participants will receive 55 percent of their average weekly insured earnings to a maximum of $413 per week. Again there are exceptions to this general guideline. For example, under the Family Income Supplement Provision, claimants whose family income is under $25 921, are entitled to receive additional benefits.

HRDC administers the EI program, which is funded through employee premiums ($2.70 per $100 earnings) and employer premiums ($3.78 per $100 of employee earnings). Premiums are paid by all workers and all employers on every dollar earned up to the annual maximum insurable earnings of $39 000. As with most other sources of income in Canada, EI benefits are taxable.

Workers' Compensation

Workers' compensation refers to employee insurance resulting from workplace accidents or illness. Unlike most other countries, workers' compensation in Canada is a system of social insurance. Coverage is generally compulsory. For the most part, compensation programs for injured employees are administered by the provinces. Although benefits differ from province to province, in general, the various Workers' Compensation Acts provide for disability income, rehabilitation, and one-time payment for serious injuries such as the loss of an arm or a leg. Not only is there insurance available, but there are provincially run rehabilitation centres that focus on returning injured workers to the workplace. A typical centre might have four program areas: vocational assessment, prosthetics/orthotics, pain management, and work recovery. Often treatment is delivered by interdisciplinary teams, which may include physicians, nurses, physiotherapists, and occupational therapists.[6]

Workers' compensation: Legally entitled employee insurance and benefits resulting from workplace accidents or illness.

The cost of workers' compensation is borne by employers, who are assessed a rate per $100 of payroll, up to a maximum level of earnings. All employers are classified into rate groups according to primary business activity or industry (accounting, fish canning, electrical contractors, hairdressing salons, etc.). Each rate group is assigned a rate, based on the likelihood that accidents will occur.

Each rate group collectively pays the cost of all injuries within the rate group. However, to encourage safety consciousness, most provincial plans provide for rebates for employers with exceptionally safe workplaces and penalties for those with exceptionally unsafe workplaces.[7]

Each province administers its system through an appointed Workers' Compensation Board (WCB) responsible for setting benefit levels and for administering the various rehabilitation institutions. As well, there is an appeal procedure and an Appeals Board in each jurisdiction. Rate and duration of benefits vary from province to province, but are typically 75 percent of gross pay, or as much as 90 percent of after-tax earnings, during a period of total disability.

Like all benefit plans, workers' compensation has come under intense scrutiny during the last few years. Not only have claims for compensation become more expensive but entire new classifications of injury are becoming common. Claims for excessive stress and burnout, for example, were virtually unknown 20 years ago. The result has been a drain on WCB resources. HR professionals, therefore, need to monitor WCB systems on two fronts. First, they should work to ensure that internal environments (e.g., culture, safety systems, record keeping, rewards) minimize risk. Second, they should become active within their industry group or trade association in seeking to lower the overall accident rate—the subject of Chapter 13.

Universal Health Insurance

Universal health care:
A government-administered social insurance system in which all Canadians are unconditionally entitled to health services.

One of the fundamental principles that defines this country is the existence of a **universal health care** system. In fact, the health care sector is seen by most Canadians as, essentially, a public utility.[8] The provinces have jurisdiction over health care under a shared funding agreement with the federal government. Even though coverage may vary in each province, the basic services—for example, doctors' visits and hospitalization—have remained intact. In some jurisdictions, this health insurance in financed entirely through general revenues; in others, families and individuals pay a monthly premium, or employers may pay a payroll tax. For example, Newfoundland, Ontario, and Quebec levy a payroll tax to fund hospital and medical expenses.

The Canada Health Act (1984) was designed to enshrine the same level of health service for all Canadians. Under this Act, the federal government has transferred considerable amounts of money to the provinces each year to ensure equality. Since the late 1980s, however, these transfer payments have decreased substantially so that by the latter half of the 1990s, the federal government finances less than one-third of the cost of medicare,[9] and payments are scheduled to decrease still more. This shifting of costs from the federal to the provincial arena makes the maintenance of nation-wide standards difficult and confrontational. In fact, the governments of Alberta and Ontario have already suggested that for-profit (private) medical clinics might become necessary, an idea resisted vigorously by federal lawmakers. Although it is unlikely that universal health care will disappear, financial pressures will almost certainly lead to cutbacks that may change the "universal" nature of health care benefits in Canada.

From a human resources management viewpoint, cutbacks in universal health care programs may bring demands for additional employer-sponsored[10] supplemental health-care benefits—especially for the expanding temporary and part-time labour force. Unfortunately, faced with rising costs of dental care and many other supplemental benefits, many employers are poised to cut back.[11]

Vacation and Holiday Pay

Vacation and holiday pay: Yearly requirement of employers to provide every employee with paid time off for a vacation period and statutory holidays.

All provincial labour standards legislation, as well as the Canada Labour Code, have provisions for **vacation and holiday pay**. With few exceptions, in Canada, an annual vacation pay and holiday pay are the right of every employee. Employers are required to give every employee paid time off each year. Legislation varies slightly across jurisdictions, but the Canada Labour Code, which relates to federal employees, is typical. The basic entitlement is two weeks' vacation after one completed year of employment, increasing to three weeks after six consecutive years with the same employer. Where the vacation entitlement is two weeks, 4 percent of annual earnings must be paid; three weeks' vacation pay translates to 6 percent of earnings. [12]

Employees are also entitled by law to a number of statutory holidays. The number of public or statutory holidays varies by jurisdiction and province. For example, the Canada Labour Code (federal employees) provides for nine paid holidays per year: New Year's Day, Good Friday, Victoria Day, Canada Day, Labour Day, Thanksgiving Day, Remembrance Day, Christmas Day, and Boxing Day. Ontario allows for eight paid holidays and Nova Scotia for only five paid holidays. Work on any general holiday is not prohibited, but employees are normally paid $1^{1}/_{2}$ times regular wages. In some cases employers are allowed to give the employee another day off with pay.[13]

Voluntary Benefits

Managers in many organizations voluntarily provide numerous benefits. These voluntary benefits may be classified as 1) payment for time not worked, 2) health and security benefits, 3) employee services, and 4) severance pay. These benefits result from unilateral management decisions, from management contracts, or from union–management negotiations.

Payment for Time Not Worked

In providing payment for time not worked, employers recognize that employees need time away from the job for many purposes. Included in this category are paid vacations that exceed minimum labour standards, holidays other than those required by law, paid sick leave, and bereavement time. It is also common for organizations to provide payments to assist employees in performing civic duties. Most employees are also allowed to take some paid time off during work hours. Other benefits include rest periods, coffee breaks, clean-up time, and travel time.

Paid Vacations
Payment for time not worked serves important compensation goals. For example, paid vacations provide employees with an opportunity to rest and become rejuvenated (and, presumably, more productive), while encouraging them to remain with the firm. Typically, paid vacation time increases with seniority, with perhaps one week allowed after six months of service and two weeks after one year (the legal minimum), rising to four weeks a year after 10 years and five weeks a year after 15 years. Vacation time may also vary with organizational rank. For example, a senior executive, regardless of time with the firm, may be given one month's vacation.

Sick Leave
In many firms, each employee is allotted a certain number of paid sick leave days. Employees who are too sick to report to work continue to receive their pay up to the maximum number of days accumulated. As with vacation pay, the number of sick leave days can depend on seniority. Some sick leave programs have been severely criticized. At times they have been abused by individuals who falsely claim to be sick. To counter this practice, in some firms a doctor's statement is required after a set number of successive sick leave days.

Health and Security Benefits

Health and security benefits are often included as part of an employee's indirect financial compensation. Specific areas include supplemental health care, disability protection, dental and vision care, retirement benefits, share ownership, and life insurance.

Supplemental Health Care

Many employers provide coverage additional to the basic provincial or territorial health plan, often through a cost-sharing agreement with the employee. Semiprivate room coverage and drug payment plans are typical benefits. In organizations where employees are required to travel extensively, the employer often provides out-of-country health insurance to protect against sickness or accident in high-cost regions such as the United States.

These benefits vary widely from employer to employer. Increasingly, HR professionals are being called upon to manage these programs more effectively, even to the point of adopting American-style cost containment techniques that encourage the participation of all employees in deciding how to use limited health care resources more effectively.[14]

Disability Protection

Workers' compensation protects employees from job-related accidents and illnesses. In some firms, however, additional disability protection is provided that covers non-work-related accidents and illness. A sick leave policy may provide full salary for short-term health problems, after which a short-term disability plan may become operative. Long-term illness or disability activates a firm's long-term plan, which may provide from 50 to 66 percent of an employee's regular wages for periods from two years to life. Again, where they exist, the benefits range widely, depending upon the amount an employer is willing to spend and on the insurance company that provides the benefit.

Dental and Vision Care

For most companies in Canada, insurance premiums for extended benefits such as dental and eye care can account for up to 80 percent of insurance costs.[15] These plans are typically paid for by the employer, except for a deductible amount, which may amount to $25 to $50 per year.

Retirement Benefits

Private retirement plans provide income for employees who retire after reaching a certain age or after having served the firm for a specific period of time. Pension plans are vitally important to employees because the Old Age Pension and the Canada/Quebec Pension Plan were not designed to provide complete retirement income. Over the next 30 years, the Canadian population will be dominated by older people who are either retired or approaching retirement. Therefore, retirement financing will become a primary issue for individuals, employers, and governments.[16]

Registered pension plan: A private pension plan usually established by an employer on behalf of its employees, and recognized by Revenue Canada.

Most companies establish a **registered pension plan**: a private pension plan usually established by an employer on behalf of its employees, and recognized by Revenue Canada. There are two basic types of pension plans—

defined contribution pension plans and defined benefit pension plans.[17]

HR Web
Wisdom
http: www.pearsoned.ca/
mondy

**Retirement Information
and Resources**
Answers to frequently
asked questions, tax tips,
links, and a retirement
glossary are provided.

- *Defined contribution pension plan*. This type of plan defines the contribution made by the employee and the employer but does not define the pension income to be received at retirement. The amount will depend on the accumulated funds at retirement time.

- *Defined benefit pension plan*. This is a company-sponsored pension plan that guarantees a certain level of pension income at retirement, calculated according to a pre-determined formula. The employer agrees to provide a specific level of retirement income. An employee's seniority and position in the firm may determine the specific figure. A plan considered generous might provide a pension equivalent from 50 to 80 percent of an employee's final earnings.

In general, Canadians with a qualifying earned income are also entitled to establish their own personal **registered retirement savings plan (RRSP)**: a formal investment plan that allows an individual to accumulate savings and earning for retirement on a tax-sheltered basis.

An RRSP account can be opened at any major financial institution or investment dealer authorized to issue RRSPs. In general the annual RRSP deduction limit is equal to 18 percent of earned income from the previous year, to a yearly maximum of $13 500. This deduction limit is reduced by the yearly amount already contributed to any other registered pension or deferred profit sharing plan. For example, if an individual were to contribute $5 000 to a company plan, the RRSP deduction limit would be reduced to $8 500.

The goal of an RRSP is to allow the contributor to shelter earned income until retirement. The amount contributed to an RRSP is tax deductible. In addition, the investment interest earned, while in the RRSP account, is not taxed. The tax benefits derived from a RRSP contribution have made this investment about the most effective financial and tax-planning tool available. By the mid-1990s, for example, about 30 percent of all Canadian tax filers had contributed some $23 billion to RRSPs.

**Registered retirement
savings plan (RRSP):** a
formal investment plan that
allows an individual to
accumulate savings and
earning for retirement on a
tax-sheltered basis.

Share Ownership

As we mentioned in the last chapter, an employee share ownership plan (ESOP) is a program under which a firm makes a tax-deductible contribution of shares or cash to a trust. The firm then allocates the stock to the participating employees. When used as a retirement plan (sometimes referred to as a deferred profit-sharing plan), the plan pays retiring employees an amount based on the value of the shares at that time. If the firm's shares have fared well, this type of defined contribution plan will be satisfactory. Since share value may decline, however, the results may be disastrous, as was the case with Bramalea Ltd. Bramalea's ESOP gave employees the chance to buy shares at $18 each ($10 below market price). Five years later, these shares were worth less than 50 cents each.

Life Insurance

Group life insurance is a benefit commonly provided to protect the employee's family in the event of his or her death. Although the cost of group life insurance is relatively low, some plans call for the employee to pay part of the premium.

Coverage may be a flat amount (for instance, $20 000) or may be based on the employee's annual earnings. Typically, members of group plans do not have to show evidence of insurability. This provision is especially important to older employees and to those with health problems, who might find the cost of individual insurance to be prohibitive.

Some financial experts predict that insurance coverage may become a victim of economic cutbacks. Some smaller firms are having difficulty obtaining group insurance because insurers are reducing their use of small-client pools that combine small companies with similar risk profiles. This practice protects individual firms from a year in which one or two employees claim large settlements. However, insurance industry executives have become cautious because their profits are declining. Should pooling be discontinued, managers or owners of smaller firms will have to either withdraw this benefit or ask employees to pay a higher percentage of the premium.[18]

Employee Services

When managers at Crestor Energy Inc. of Alberta wanted to create a new corporate culture, they decided to add financial planning to the benefit package. Approximately 70 percent of the staff attended the four-hour evening sessions.[19] At Syncride Canada, as well, individual financial planning was viewed as a necessity. Every employee over 45 received one-on-one advice.[20]

Many organizations like Crestor and Syncride offer a variety of benefits, such as personal financial planning, that can be termed employee services. These benefits might also include company-subsidized lunches, financial assistance for employee-operated credit unions, legal and income tax aid, club memberships, athletic and recreational programs, discounts on company products, moving expenses, parking spaces, and tuition rebates. Employee assistance programs (EAPs), wellness programs, and physical fitness programs, all of which are discussed in Chapter 13, also represent important services that can enhance the employment relationship.

Several new types of benefits have been added to the traditional corporate plans. One example is subsidized day care. Here, the firm provides facilities for young children of employees at no cost or for a modest fee. This benefit is an effective recruitment aid that also helps to reduce absenteeism. The need for these programs has grown, as some 60 percent of all Canadian couples now are dual-income families.[21] The dual-income phenomenon, along with increases in the number of single parents, has also created demands for more flexibility in working hours and conditions (discussed later in this chapter). In an attempt to conserve energy and to relieve traffic congestion, for example, some firms transport workers to and from work. Participating employees pay a portion of the cost and ride in company vans or buses. Employees often find this service an attractive alternative to driving in heavy traffic. In other firms, company-subsidized cafeterias are provided. By offering these types of services, management hopes to gain increased productivity, less wasted time, increased employee morale and, in some instances, a healthier work force. In most cases, the payback is high in terms of employee relations.[22]

Severance Pay

As we discuss in Chapter 16, firms are required by law to provide employees with termination notice or pay in lieu of notice. The amount of notice or money will depend on the job, years of service, and the legal work jurisdiction. However, over and above statutory termination requirements, some firms also provide attractive severance benefits—sometimes referred to as a **"golden parachute" package**. The amount and conditions of severance benefits will depend on the position and length of service of the employee and the financial ability of the company. Golden parachute packages are usually negotiated by senior executives as a condition of employment. They argue that it takes a long time to find executive employment.[41]

"Golden parachute" package: Attractive severance benefits which exceed the company's legal requirements.

The Changing Nature of Benefit Packages

The payroll cost of benefits is substantial and rising. By the mid-1990s the cost of benefits in the private sector stood at about 35 percent of payroll. Benefits in the public sector were in the 45 percent range.[23] Moreover, the cost of specific benefits such as health and dental care rose sharply over the 1990s.[24] The cost of dental plans, for example, increased some 43 percent in the last decade.[25] Over the 1990s, employee health care costs increased by an estimated average of 20 percent per year because of additional claims and longer hospital stays (due in part to an aging population), more expensive technology, and higher prices. In addition, the federal government's extended drug patent protection law increased the cost of prescription drugs.

Until recently, most Canadians were unaware of the costs borne by employers. However, over the 1990s attitudes began to change, especially in provinces like Ontario and Quebec where new legislation made some benefits taxable. In response to rising costs, employers are now considering revising plans. Some are restricting the kinds of medical and dental expenses they will subsidize, or withdrawing family coverage.[26] Other companies are considering flexible plans, which provide a core of basic benefits, with additional options to be paid by the employee; or various cost-sharing schemes, including an employer-employee account to meet the cost of services not covered by the company plan.

In the future both employees and employers will need to reconsider the value of their benefits packages. Fundamental changes are likely to continue to occur in all aspects of nonfinancial compensation but the trend seems to be moving toward flexible compensation.[27]

Flexible Compensation (Cafeteria Compensation)

When management at 3M Canada Inc. decided to offer a cafeteria plan, two years were spent in the planning stage, with heavy input from employee focus groups. Called "Benelux," the benefits scheme was designed around a "core plus option" approach. Although the flex plan was effective in helping 3M keep benefits under control, the main purpose in establishing it was to provide for an increasingly wider range of employee needs and preferences.[28]

Flexible (cafeteria) **compensation plans**, like the one offered at 3M,

Flexible compensation plans: A method that allows employees to choose from among several alternatives in deciding how their financial compensation will be allocated.

permit employees to choose from among several alternatives in deciding how their financial compensation will be allocated. Usually, employees are given considerable latitude in determining how much they will take in the form of salary, life insurance, pension contributions, and other benefits. Choices in a current plan might include semiprivate hospital, supplemental accident, life insurance, and long-term disability benefits. Normally, each employee plan is costed separately, with the employee deciding how much of a benefits package he or she can afford.

Cafeteria plans increase flexibility by allowing each employee to determine what compensation package best satisfies his or her personal needs. For example, a 60-year-old man probably would not want to pay for subsidized day care as part of a benefits plan. Similarly, a young woman who jogs three miles every day might not place high value on a parking space near the firm's entrance. A number of possible compensation vehicles used in a cafeteria approach are shown in Figure 12-4.

Nonfinancial Compensation

Non-monetary incentives designed to stimulate productive work are called **nonfinancial compensation**. As employees receive sufficient pay to provide for basic necessities, their compensation interests tend to include factors in addition to money. They are inclined, for example, to desire rewards that satisfy higher-order needs, such as social, ego, and self-actualization needs. These needs may

Figure 12-4

Compensation Vehicles Used in a Cafeteria Compensation Approach

Accidental death, dismemberment insurance
Birthdays (vacation)
Bonus eligibility
Business and professional membership
Cash profit sharing
Club memberships
Commissions
Company-provided automobile
Company-provided housing
Company-provided or subsidized travel
Day care centres
Deferred bonus
Deferred compensation plan
Dental and eye care insurance
Discount on company products
Education costs
Educational activities (time off)
Free chequing account
Free or subsidized lunches
Group automobile insurance

Group homeowners' insurance
Group life insurance
Extended health care
Incentive growth fund
Interest-free loans
Long-term disability benefit
Matching educational donations
Nursing-home care
Drug plan
Personal accident insurance
Price discount plan
Recreation facilities
Resort facilities
Sabbatical leaves
Salary continuation
Savings plan
Scholarships for dependents
Severance pay
Sickness and accident insurance
Share bonus plan
Share purchase plan

HRM in *ACTION*

The Cost of Benefits

"Did you realize that the company spent over $170 000 on benefits last year?" asked Nancy Shelton, the comptroller. She was talking to Muhammad Rashid, the human resource manager. Nancy continued, "For a company our size, we sure spend a lot of money for what we get. Frankly, I think the employees couldn't care less about them. What do you think about going to a flexible benefits plan where employees pay only for what they want? We could save the company a lot of money and help out our employees at the same time."

If you were Muhammad, how would you respond?

---

be met through the job and/or the job environment. Figure 12-5 outlines the basic nonfinancial elements of the total compensation package.

The Job

As described in Chapter 4, a job consists of a group of tasks that must be performed for an organization to achieve its goals. The demise of the job as a way of organizing work has been predicted by some experts because of rapidly changing duties in a dynamic environment.[29] It is likely, however, that as long as tasks must be completed by humans, jobs—by whatever name—will exist. A major human resource management objective, then, is the matching of job requirements with employee abilities and aspirations. As jobs become more complex, this challenge is likely to become increasingly difficult.

Although the job design function is typically performed by other organizational units, the human resource manager is responsible (along with line managers) for recruiting, selecting, and placing individuals in jobs. A good case can also be made for the direct involvement of human resources professionals in job design. Offering the employee an interesting, fulfilling job can be an important part of nonfinancial compensation. In a number of organizations, therefore, there is an active job enrichment program (see Chapters 4 and 8).

Job characteristics are central to many theories of motivation, and a vital component of a total compensation program, as employees may receive important nonmonetary benefits by performing meaningful work. These intrinsic rewards are largely controlled by the organization, as management arranges required tasks into job content and, therefore, controls the job's indirect compensation possibilities. Selection and placement are also extremely important in this context, as a job that is challenging to one person may be boring to another. Failure to recognize individual differences often leads to major motivational problems.

Figure 12-5

Nonfinancial Elements of a Total Compensation Program

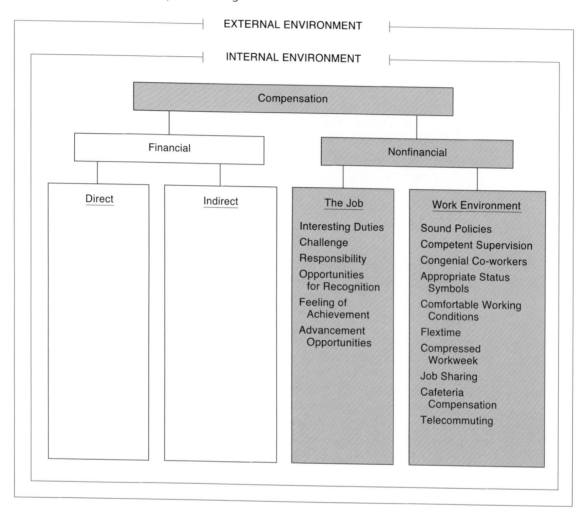

The Work Environment

The work environment is also an important aspect of nonfinancial compensation. We discussed the significance of a warm, supportive corporate culture in Chapter 8. A friendly environment means

- progressive policies that reflect management's sincere concern for employees as individuals

- competent and fair supervision

- congenial co-workers and compatible work groups

- organizational rewards that acknowledge the standing of the employee—often referred to as **status symbols**— such as titles or office size, location, and decor.

- comfortable working conditions.

Status symbols:
Organizational rewards that reflect the standing of the employee, such as titles or office size, location, and decor.

TRENDS and
INNOVATIONS

Congenial Work Environment at Cognos

Cognos Inc. in Ottawa is one of Canada's largest and fastest growing software manufacturers. Despite its rapid growth, the company still has the intimacy of a family business. The philosophy at Cognos is to invest in all its workers, not just the high fliers. One example of this inclusive corporate culture is Cognos's management skills program. It's aimed as much at managers-in-training as at senior managers. In fact, about 25 percent of all employees are involved in this program. Cognos also strives to build a culture that encourages learning while making it as informal as possible. For example, employees are encouraged to collaborate and to take part in online chat groups. Team retreats allow staff to get to know each other. According to Rod Brandvold, a Cognos vice president, "the best thing we can do as a company is to find ways to bring people together who wouldn't normally work together." [30]

Workplace Flexibility

Workplace flexibility entails a number of options designed to provide individuals with greater control over their jobs and work environment. Included in this category are flextime, the compressed workweek, job sharing, flexible compensation, telecommuting, regular part-time work, and modified retirement plans.

Workplace flexibility:
A form of nonfinancial compensation that entails a number of options, designed to provide individuals with greater control over their jobs and work environment.

Flextime

The practice of permitting employees to choose, within certain limitations, their own working hours, is called **flextime**. The percentage of Canadian employees on a flextime schedule increased from 17 percent in 1991 to almost 25 percent in 1995.[31] Warner-Lambert Canada, BC Hydro, and Ontario Hydro are just a few examples of organizations with formal flextime policies.[32]

Flextime: The practice of permitting employees to choose, within certain limitations, their own working hours.

Under a flextime system, employees work the same number of hours per day as they would on a standard schedule. However, they are permitted to work these hours within a *band width*, (defined as the maximum length of the workday) comprised of *core time* (that part of the day when all employees must be present) and *flexible time*—the period within which employees may vary their schedules (see Figure 12-6).

Perhaps flextime's most important feature is that employees are allowed to schedule their time to minimize conflicts between personal needs and job requirements, without being tempted to use sick leave. Flextime also permits employees to work at hours when they feel they can function best, catering to those who are early risers or those who prefer to work later in the day. Flextime is not, however, suitable for all types of organizations. For example, its use may be severely limited in assembly-line operations and in companies using multiple shifts.

HR Web Wisdom
http: www.pearsoned.ca/mondy

HRDC–HR Links
Provided are various studies on workplace flexibility and the changing nature of work.

Figure 12-6

Illustration of Flextime

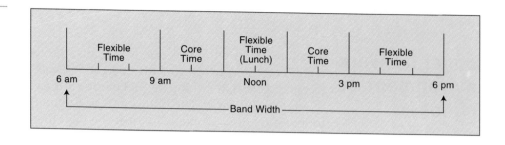

The Compressed Workweek

Compressed workweek:
Any arrangement of work hours that permits employees to fulfill their weekly work obligation in fewer days than the typical five-day workweek.

The **compressed workweek** is defined as any arrangement of work hours that permits employees to fulfill their weekly work obligation in fewer days than the typical five. A common compressed workweek is four 10-hour days. Under this arrangement, employees have reported greater job satisfaction and better use of leisure time for family life, personal business, and recreation.

In some instances, employers have experienced increased productivity along with reduced turnover and absenteeism. [33] Reduced absenteeism alone can increase productivity by 1 to 2 percent.[34] But in other firms, work scheduling and employee fatigue problems have been encountered, resulting in lower product quality and reduced customer service. As a result, in some organizations, the conventional five-day week has been reinstated.

Job Sharing

Job sharing: The filling of a job by two people who split the job duties in some agreed-on manner and are paid according to their relative contributions.

Job sharing is attractive to people who want to work fewer than 40 hours per week. This option allows two or more people to split the duties of one job in some agreed-on manner and to be paid according to their contributions. The employer pays for only one job, but gains the creativity of at least two employees. Although total financial compensation may be greater because of the additional benefits provided, this expense can be offset by increased productivity. Job sharing may be especially attractive to people who have substantial family responsibilities and to older workers who wish to retire gradually.

Telecommuting

Telecommuting: A work arrangement that allows employees to work at home or away from the office.

Telecommuting allows employees (sometimes called *teleworkers or telecommuters*) to work at home, or at a location away from the office. One survey of senior executives revealed that nearly two-thirds of North American companies now encourage telecommuting. More than 40 percent of the respondents to the survey had a formal telecommuting program in place.[35] According to HRDC, about 10 percent of all full-time permanent employees work, at least part of their week, from the home.[36] In Canada, telecommuting is forecast to grow by about 15 to 20 percent over the next few years to yield more than 700 000 telecommuter homes.[37]

Numerous advantages of telecommuting accrue to the company, the employee, and the community (see Figure 12-7). A major advantage of telecommuting is that it eliminates the need for office space. As one manager put it, "The expense of an employee is not just the person; it's also the fact that I pay

Figure 12-7

Advantages of Telecommuting

FOR THE COMPANY	FOR THE EMPLOYEE	FOR THE COMMUNITY
Helps attract new employees, especially those needing flexibility	Reduces transportation costs and commuting time	Decreases the environmental impact of commuting
Can increase retention rates	Allows personal control over working conditions	Conserves energy
Reduces sick time and absenteeism	Eliminates unplanned meetings or "drop ins"	Decreases traffic congestion
Increases productivity		Reduces the need for road repair
Increases employee job satisfaction	Provides more flexible child and elder care options	Takes pressure from public transportation
Maximizes office space	Increases privacy	
Decreases relocation costs	Reduces the stress of commuting	
Reduces overtime	Allows work to be done when one is most productive	
	Reduces clothing costs	
	Creates more time to spend with family	
	Enhances communications with supervisor	
	Provides the ability to work without interruption	

Source: *George M. Piskurich, "Making Telecommuting Work,"* Training & Development *50 (February 1996): 22.*

$90,000 a year for the office that person sits in."[38] Commuting distances are not a factor for teleworkers. Therefore, firms may hire the best available employees located virtually anywhere. In addition, telecommuting is advantageous to some disabled workers and workers with young children.

With all its advantages, telecommuting also has some potential pitfalls. For example, physical and emotional ties between employees and their firms may be weakened. Thus successful programs require a high degree of trust between employees and their supervisors. In addition to the way people are supervised, firms considering telecommuting also need to think about the following types of issues:

- Will compensation and benefits be affected? If so, how?

- Who will be responsible for workers injured at home?

- What about responsibility for purchasing and providing insurance coverage for equipment?

- How will taxes be affected by telecommuting?

- Will overtime be allowed?

- Will security be provided for the telecommuter's work? How?
- Will the firm have safety requirements for the home?

These questions seem to suggest that telecommuting poses insurmountable problems, but there aren't many examples of unsuccessful telecommuting. However, experience has provided two caveats. First, telecommuting should not be used as a means to reduce other standard benefits provided to employees. Second, telecommuting should not be implemented where the supervisor is opposed to the concept.[39]

Regular Part-Time Work

According to HRDC, part-time employees represent about 18 percent of the total paid (permanent) employees in Canada. The regular use of part-time workers has begun to gain momentum. This approach adds many highly qualified individuals to the labour market by permitting them to address both employment and family needs. For example, about 42 percent of part-time employees actually choose to work part-time for *personal* reasons.

One major problem with this concept has been that some employers have made extensive use of part-time people to avoid paying benefits. Whether or not this trend will continue is difficult to forecast. Only one province, Saskatchewan, has enacted legislation forcing employers to pay prorated benefits to part-time employees.[40]

Modified Retirement

Modified retirement: An option that permits older employees to work fewer than regular hours for a certain period before retirement.

Modified retirement is an option that permits older employees to work fewer than regular hours for a certain period before retirement. This option allows an employee to avoid an abrupt change in lifestyle and move more gracefully into retirement.

Global Compensation: Equity Issues

As executive talent is transferred across national borders, a host of human resource issues must be addressed and resolved. A major challenge facing human resources managers is the development of packages to reassure Canadian expatriates that benefits paid during a foreign posting will be fair in relation to what they would have received in Canada. The HR professional will have to ascertain, for example, whether or not the executive can be maintained on current supplementary health programs while on a foreign assignment. For example, health care costs in the United States are several times higher than in Canada. A Canadian executive who is transferred to the US would want to be reassured that health care benefits would be at least equal to those available under provincial health insurance.

Another challenge involves unravelling the complexities of the expatriate's retirement plans,[41] as there are a number of unique aspects of Canadian tax and pension systems. Thus retirement planning for expatriates must be careful and informed.[42] Typically, employees from the parent country receive a salary, a foreign premium of up to 50 percent, and relocation and living expense allowances. As well, their pay will likely be higher than pay for host-country nationals. This differential tends to create resentment in the host country, which may reduce cooperation. Many Canadians have found their standard of living and social class to be considerably higher in a foreign country than it had been at home. However, HR professionals should be aware that the corresponding drop in living standards when they return may create some difficulties.

An important incentive for Canadians to accept assignments in foreign countries is the opportunity to avoid high Canadian taxes, as often (but not always), all or a large part of income earned while residing in another country is tax exempt. HR managers should contact Revenue Canada before the employee leaves, however, as there are complex rules regarding foreign residency and tax-free status. Individuals are well advised to employ a tax accountant to help develop their own personal financial plan.

The successful management of employee benefits in a multinational corporation depends heavily on a corporate policy statement that outlines specific instructions for the development, approval, and administration of all benefit plans. Employee benefits covered by the policy statement should include any payment of company funds to employees other than base salary, such as pensions, medical and life insurance, vacations, and severance pay.[44] In drafting the policy statement, two general objectives must be met. First, the organization's overall welfare must be given primary consideration. Second, employee benefits must be competitive on the international level if a multinational corporation is to attract and retain dynamic, effective leaders and professionals.[45]

SUMMARY

1. Define benefits and the need to communicate the benefits package.

Benefits include all financial rewards that are not paid directly to the employee. Employee benefits can help to recruit and to retain a high-quality work force. Unless employees are made aware of the substantial costs involved, they tend to take their benefits for granted. Thus management must ensure a constant flow of benefits information both "up" and "down" the organization.

2. Identify and describe the major legally required benefits.

Legally required benefits include: the old age pension, Canada (CPP) or Quebec (QPP) pension plan, employment insurance, workers' compensation, universal health insurance, vacation pay, and holiday pay.

3. Identify four major types or categories of voluntary benefits.

Four major types of benefits provided include 1) payment for time not worked (such as vacation and holidays beyond the legal minimum, paid sick leave, and bereavement time, payments to assist employees in performing civic duties, coffee breaks, clean-up time, and travel time); 2) health and security benefits (such as supplemental health care, disability protection, dental and vision care, retirement benefits, supplemental unemployment benefits, and life insurance); 3) employee services (such as personal financial planning, company-subsidized lunches, financial assistance for employee-operated credit unions, legal and income tax aid, club memberships, athletic and recreational programs, discounts on company products, moving expenses, parking spaces, and tuition rebates, employee assistance programs, wellness programs, physical fitness programs, subsidized day care and cafeterias; and 4) severance pay over and above statutory requirements, such as "golden parachute" packages.

4. Explain the changing nature of benefits packages and the role of flexible compensation.

Due to escalating costs, employees and employers will need to reconsider the types and value of their benefits packages. The trend seems to favour flexible or cafeteria-style compensation plans, which permit employees to choose from among many alternatives, depending upon their needs and lifestyle. Unfortunately, rising benefit costs have forced many firms to shift a larger portion of the cost onto the employee. Small companies have been especially pressed, as some insurers now balk at pooling small-company risk.

5. Explain the term nonfinancial compensation and the types of nonfinancial rewards.

Non-monetary incentives designed to stimulate work are called nonfinancial compensation. Once employees are paid adequately to provide for basic necessities, they tend to want non-monetary rewards that will satisfy higher-order needs, such as social, ego, and self-actualization needs. These needs may be satisfied by the job itself and/or by the job environment. Progressive policies, good supervision, a congenial work group, appropriate recognition or status, comfortable working conditions, and workplace flexibility are all types of nonfinancial rewards.

6. Describe what companies are doing to improve workplace flexibility.

A major nonfinancial benefit can be the flexibility to choose working arrangements that suit the employee's personal needs. Permitting employees to choose, within certain limits, their own working hours is known as flextime. Any arrangement that permits employees to work full-time, but in fewer days than the typical five, is called a compressed workweek. In job sharing, at least two people split the duties of one job in some agreed-on manner and are paid according to their contributions. Telecommuting allows employees to do at least part of their work at home, usually on a computer. Flexibility can also be achieved through the use of part-time employment and modified retirement plans.

QUESTIONS FOR REVIEW

1. Define benefits. What are the general purposes of benefits?

2. Why is communication an important element of benefit plan design?

3. Which major benefits are required by law?

4. What are four basic categories of voluntary benefits? Give an example of each type.

5. What is a "golden parachute" package and when is it most likely to be used?

6. Briefly explain the changing nature of benefits. How have some managers responded?

7. Why are nonfinancial compensation considerations becoming so important? Under what circumstances can the job and the job environment provide nonfinancial compensation?

8. Distinguish between flextime and the compressed workweek. In what situations are the compressed work week and flextime not practical?

9. What is telecommuting and how can this option improve workplace flexibility?

DEVELOPING HRM SKILLS

An Experiential Exercise

Due to a downward trend in business and the resulting financial constraints over the last two years, Straight Manufacturing Company has been able to grant only cost-of-living increases to its employees. The firm has just signed a lucrative three-year contract, however, with a major automobile manufacturer. As a result, management has formed a salary review committee to award merit increases to deserving employees. Members of the salary review committee have only $13 500 of merit money, so deciding who will receive merit increases will be difficult. Louis Convoy, Sharon Kubiak, J. Ward Archer, Ed Wilson, C.J. Sass, and Dominic Passante have been recommended for raises.

Louis Convoy, financial analyst, has an undergraduate business degree and is currently working on an MBA. His previous work experience has allowed him to develop several outstanding financial contacts. Sharon Kubiak, HRM administrative assistant, began as a secretary and after three years with the organization was promoted to her present position. Because her first position was as secretary, her current salary is not at the range commensurate with her new position and responsibilities. J. Ward Archer, assistant plant manager, worked three years as a production supervisor after obtaining his undergraduate degree in business. He received an MBA from McGill two years ago. He is viewed by many as a successful fast tracker. Ed Wilson, production supervisor, has been with the organization for nine years; the last two years he has been a production supervisor. Last year he single-handedly prevented a wildcat strike. To become a member of management as a production supervisor, Ed took a pay cut in comparison to his union wages. C.J. Sass, director of computer services, has a doctoral degree in computer science and was hired away three years ago from the business school at a leading eastern university. Two-and-a-half years ago he introduced a corporation-wide Human Resource Information System that has refined the organization's internal recruiting and promotion policies. Dominic Passante, district sales manager, has been with the organization for 12 years. In his tenth year with the organization, Dominic was promoted to his current position. He has done a fine job.

Six students will serve on the salary review committee. While the committee would like to award significant merit increases to all those who have been recommended, there are limited funds available for raises. The committee must make a decision as to how the merit funds will be distributed. Your instructor will provide the participants with additional information necessary to complete the exercise.

HRM INCIDENT

A Benefits Package Designed for Whom?

Megan McGraw warmly greeted Kenneth Ogunlade, her next interviewee. Kenneth had an excellent academic record and appeared to be just the kind of person Megan's company, Beco Electric, was seeking. Megan was the postsecondary recruiter for Beco and had already interviewed six graduating students.

Based on the application form, Kenneth appeared to be the most promising candidate to be interviewed that day as he had an 87 percent average in his major field, industrial management. He was the vice president of the Student Government Association and activities chairman for the Business Society. The reference letters in Kenneth's file revealed that he was both very active socially and a rather intense and serious student. One of the letters, from Kenneth's employer the previous summer, expressed satisfaction with Kenneth's work habits.

Megan knew that discussion about compensation could be an important part of the recruiting interview, but she did not know which aspects of Beco's compensation and benefits program would appeal most to Kenneth. The company had an excellent profit-sharing plan, although 80 percent of profit distributions were deferred and included in each employee's retirement account. Health benefits were also good. The company's supplemental medical and dental plan paid almost 100 percent of costs. A company lunchroom provided meals at about 70 percent of outside prices, although few managers took advantage of this benefit. Employees were entitled to two weeks of paid vacation after the first year and three weeks after two years with the company. In addition, there were 12 paid holidays each year. Finally, the company encouraged advanced education, paying tuition and books in full, as well as allowing time off to attend classes during the day.

Questions

1. What aspects of Beco's compensation and benefits program are likely to appeal to Kenneth? Explain.

2. Is the total compensation package likely to be attractive to Kenneth? Explain.

3. If you were responsible for designing a flexible benefits package for Kenneth, what would it include? Why?

PART FOUR   CASE 4

Parma Cycle Company: The Pay Plan

At Parma Cycle Company in Delta, B.C., wage rates for hourly workers were established by a three-year labour-management agreement. The agreement provided for cost-of-living adjustments (COLA) based on changes in the Statistics Canada Consumer Price Index. Wage rates varied according to job class and by seniority within each class. For example, a machine operator with two to four years' seniority earned $10.75 per hour. With four to eight years' seniority the rate increased to $12.60 an hour. A company-paid benefit plan provided supplemental medical and dental care for employees. The company contributed 6.5 percent of wages to a retirement plan administered by the machinists' union.

Salaried workers at Parma Cycle were paid straight salaries based on a 40-hour workweek. For first- and second-level managers and clerical workers, work beyond 40 hours in any week was compensated on a pro rata basis. Above the second management level there was no additional compensation for work after 40 hours per week. COLA adjustments were made semiannually for all salaried employees.

Only in the sales department at Parma was any kind of incentive compensation program in effect. The sales representatives were paid a commission averaging about 2 percent of sales in addition to straight salary. The sales manager assigned the sales representatives to particular territories; they were given a choice of territories according to seniority. As older sales representatives left the company, some of the younger ones moved into the better sales areas. This shifting caused some of the more senior sales representatives to insist upon changes in territory to increase their sales potential. In a few cases they were accommodated, but no consistent policy was developed.

Parma Cycle Company was building a new plant in Digby, Nova Scotia. The new plant was to employ about 530 people, two-thirds the number working at the main plant in Delta, B.C.

Of course, the work force would be smaller than that at first. About two months before the new plant was scheduled to open, Jesse Heard, the human resource director, was asked to meet with the president to discuss the compensation policies to be followed in Digby. Jesse knew that Jim Burgess, the president, tended to take a personal hand in matters relating to pay, so he prepared thoroughly for their meeting.

Mr. Burgess had a reputation for getting right to the heart of the matter. "I'm worried about the pay differentials that we are going to have between this plant and the one in Digby," he began. "As I see it, some of the people down there won't be paid nearly as much as similar workers here."

"That's true," said Jesse. "That really is the main reason for the move to Digby. Without the union and with the low wage rates in that area, we will be able to pay just what the market requires. Most of the helpers and trainees will be available, we think, at minimum wage." "How will the pay classifications down there compare to those up here?" asked Mr. Burgess.

"Well," said Jesse, "up here we have 'workers' and 'machine operators' and the pay within classes is by seniority. Down there we plan to have helpers/trainees, grades 1 and 2, and machine operators, grades 1, 2, and 3. Seniority won't count. We will promote workers based on the recommendations of their supervisors and their performance evaluation scores."

"I liked the incentive plan when you told me about it before, Jesse," said Mr. Burgess. "Let's go over it again. As I understand it, we are going to take 30 percent of the cost savings and pay it out as semiannual bonuses." "Yes," said Jesse. "An individual's bonus will be a certain percentage of the gross wages paid during that period. But we will multiply that by the person's performance evaluation score." "Will the standard costs be the same as the ones we have here at the Delta plant?" asked Mr. Burgess. "Yes, they will," answered Jesse.

▼

Mr. Burgess continued, "The last time we talked I think you said that we would save money in Digby on the benefits package too."

"Yes," replied Jesse. "For one thing, the tradition in that area is for the company to pay the supplemental health insurance premium for a worker and for the worker to pay the portion applicable to any dependents. Also, we don't have a dental plan down there. Finally, I don't think that we will even have a retirement program for those workers, at least not for a few years." "I think I know the answer," said Mr. Burgess, "but what about the ones who transfer down from Delta?"

"They'll have the same benefits they have here," replied Jesse. "We will continue to cover them under the same insurance plan and guarantee that their wages will keep pace with those of similar workers here."

Questions

1. What are the pros and cons of paying workers on the basis of seniority?
2. How do cost-of-living adjustments work?
3. Is anything legally wrong with Parma's plan for paying salaried workers? Explain.
4. Are the pay and benefits differentials between the plants likely to create problems? Why or why not?

PART FOUR CBC ◉ VIDEO CASE

Retention: A Huge Issue

"I don't care if the company I work for knows I'm looking for another job," said a defiant job seeker at a local employment fair. "Maybe that will make them work harder at trying to keep me." Another job seeker commented that "It's naïve anymore to think that you're expected to stay with one employer forever." Years of brutal downsizing and heavy workloads have changed attitudes. Nadine Winter, an HR management consultant, summed up the mood of Canadian workers: "There is no sense of loyalty out there and there are plenty of opportunities to choose from."

By the end of the 1990s, things looked bright for Canada's job seekers. Unemployment was at an all-time low, job creation was expected to skyrocket, and the help wanted index was higher than it had been in years. At the same time, empowered workers had shucked corporate loyalty and were ready to change jobs if their needs weren't met. This meant a major challenge for companies. "Retention is a huge issue," said Peter Andrews, of In-Touch Survey Systems Inc.

Job turnover, or the percentage of employees voluntarily leaving a firm, was on the rise at many Canadian companies. At pharmaceutical company Janssen-Ortho Inc., for example, the yearly turnover rate had jumped from 4 percent to 9 percent. LGS Group Inc., a computer consulting firm. also woke up to find that their turnover rate had doubled from 15 percent to 30 percent. Planned expansion had to be curtailed. Replacing these employees is expensive. Not only are there recruitment and training costs, but also lost productivity. John Karr, a human resource specialist at Janssen-Ortho, estimated that the cost of replacing one employee could run anywhere from $25 000 to $150 000.

But why were employees leaving? Was it money? HR experts agree that competitive salaries are important. But according to Winter, "Organizations are making a huge mistake of thinking money is all that it takes. . . . Employees are suffocating from being overly supervised by their bosses. There is little investment in their training and development. There is inflexibility around how they work and when they work. Many employees feel they could do their job just as well from home—that they could telecommute." In short, employees want to know that their employer will listen and will care.

In a January 2000 survey by *The Globe and Mail*, HR professionals agreed that, while important, money was only the price of admission. Organizations had to learn to become an "employer of choice" —to create a work environment that is too good to leave.

After 16 years of faithful service, Cliff Hacking was looking for a caring company when he came to Canadian Tire Corporation. After five years, he says Canadian Tire has established a long-term culture that make him feel valued: "It's the kind of organization that treats people extremely well. It's fair and reasonable and the rules are well stated."

Labatt Breweries is another employer of choice. This company has had a "keep the staff strategy" for years and a turnover rate of only 2 percent. Peter Eduards, a Labatt's employee, says that the company "expects a lot but it gives a lot back to employees." According to Eduards, the three drivers of employee loyalty are management will, corporate culture, and the right attitude. Labatt's backs up its philosophy of caring with competitive salaries, programs like flextime and job sharing, and a casual work environment.

Ron Azzopardi works for Fantom Technologies Inc. Azzopardi, who owned his own business before joining Fantom, said that money was important to him but not as important as his well-being. He's committed to Fantom because the company values, including accountability and a casual work environment, are in sync with his own.

How can companies become employers of choice? The first step is to ask employees for feedback. Research at LGS showed that employees wanted challenging work. They wanted to feel valued and to know that they were progressing and learning new skills. The next step is to do something about it. LGS hired four full-time specialists to help staff manage their careers. Like most firms today, LGS cannot guarantee employment, but they can help staff improve their employability. Within nine months of initiating a retention plan, LGS cut turnover in half.

Questions

1. What organizational and labour market factors made employee retention a major issue in the late 1990s?

2. "We want to become an employer of choice," your boss suddenly announces. What procedure would you suggest and why?

3. Survey a local company. What do employees like about their jobs? What do they dislike? How would you improve the work environment at this company?

Video Resource: "Keeping them," Venture #682 (March 24, 1998).

CHAPTER

13

A Safe and Healthy Work Environment

CHAPTER OBJECTIVES

1. Explain why employers should be concerned about safety and health issues.
2. Explain the role of the HR professional in safety and health.
3. Outline and briefly explain occupational health and safety legislation.
4. Explain the major approaches to safety programs.
5. Explain the critical elements of an effective safety program.
6. Identify major workplace health and wellness issues.
7. Describe major holistic health and wellness programs.
8. Describe major specific or targeted health and wellness programs.

Dionne Moore, HR manager for Sather Manufacturing, was walking through the plant when her attention was caught by a group of employees clustered outside a door. They had backed out of a room where several chemicals were used in a critical manufacturing process. Dionne inspected the room, but couldn't find anything wrong, or even different from any other day. She was puzzled as to why the workers were reluctant to resume their tasks. They were adamant that conditions in the room were unhealthy. Dionne and the group's supervisor discussed the situation and wondered whether they should order the people to resume work, since the department was already behind schedule.

Chris Byrom, chief executive officer for Aztec Enterprises, is concerned about his vice president for marketing, 38-year-old Grant Weeks. The two had just returned from a short walk to the corporate attorney's office to discuss plans for an overseas joint venture. As they returned to Chris's office, Grant's face was flushed, he was breathing hard, and he had to take a chair to rest. His condition really alarmed Chris because he didn't think that such a brief bit of exercise should tire anyone, especially someone as apparently healthy as Grant. Chris knew that the firm couldn't afford to do without Grant's expertise even for a short time during their expansion plans.

Cheryl Weaver supervises 50 people in the administrative department of a large bank. Normally, she is a competent and conscientious manager with a reputation for doing the job right and on time. Until recently, Cheryl had been considered a strong candidate for vice president of administration. The situation has changed, however, because Cheryl is behaving differently. She can't seem to concentrate on her work and appears to be a victim of battle fatigue. "Oh, Cheryl," a co-worker advised, "you'll make it. You've always been so strong." But Cheryl shocked her associate when she responded, "I don't want to be told I'll make it on my own. I already know I can't."

D ionne, Chris, and Cheryl are each involved with one of the many critical areas related to employee health and safety. Dionne realizes that safety is a major concern in her organization and that she must strive constantly to maintain a safe and healthy work environment. Chris's experience has caused him to realize the serious ramifications of losing a key executive due to illness or death. Cheryl appears to be showing signs of burnout.

We begin this chapter by explaining why employers and HR professionals should be concerned about safety and health issues, and an overview of the Canadian safety legislation. In the next two sections, we discuss approaches to and critical elements of effective safety programs. We then identify key workplace health and wellness issues and review major holistic health and wellness programs. In the last section of this chapter we describe various employer programs targeted to specific illnesses or issues.

HR Web Wisdom

http: www.pearsoned.ca/ mondy

HRDC – HR Links
Provided are key links to occupational safety and health Web sites.

The Nature and Role of Safety and Health

An **accident** refers to an unplanned event that interrupts the completion of an activity, and that may or may not include injury or property damage. **Safety** involves protecting employees from injuries caused by work-related accidents. Safety issues are exemplified in the opening vignette. Several employees who work for Sather Manufacturing view as unsafe the use of chemicals in one phase of a critical manufacturing process. Dionne Moore and the group's supervisor now have a dilemma: If they ignore the workers' concerns, the group will continue to balk at working in what the group members consider to be an unsafe environment. If they force the group back to work, the company may be subject to legal action. On the other hand, if they address the employees' safety concerns, the company will probably have to modify the existing manufacturing process or reengineer the work environment for this phase. Either path will lead to further delays in the production schedule.

Health refers to employees' freedom from physical or emotional illness. As business and industry move toward flatter organizational structures with fewer employees, each one working harder, "fitness for work has become a paramount concern for human resource managers."[1] In the opening vignette, Grant is obviously not as well as one might expect a 38-year-old to be. Chris's concern is justified.

Accident: An unplanned event that interrupts the completion of an activity, and that may or may not include injury or property damage.

Safety: The protection of employees from injuries caused by work-related accidents.

Health: An employee's freedom from physical or emotional illness.

Figure 13-1

Workplace Accidents—
Billions in Losses and Many
Lives Ruined

ACTUAL EXAMPLES

- A 46-year-old truck driver was crushed against a concrete wall by a truck driven by one of his co-workers. He died instantly.

- A 16-year-old summer student was smothered under a pile of garbage at a waste treatment plant. His body was found by his father, a technician with the same company.

- A 26-year-old forklift driver at a hardware store fell from his seat and was crushed. He died before arriving at the hospital.

- Danielle was a brakeperson for a railway company in Eastern Quebec. As she went to uncouple a car, she fell beneath the wheels and lost her leg.

- A vending machine was not properly secured to a forklift. The vending machine slid off and crushed a 38-year old man instantly.

SELECTED STATISTICS

- Every year there are some 800 000 workplace accidents in Canada that result in lost work time.

- On average, a worker gets injured on the job every 9 seconds.

- Each year, about one in fifteen workers suffers an injury.

- Workplace accidents cost the country some $5 billion annually in compensation (direct costs) and a further $5 billion in indirect costs (such as days off, replacement workers' wages, and overtime).

- Each year some 16 million work days are lost due to accidents.

- One accident in three (with time loss) involves youth aged 15-29.

Sources: Canadian Centre for Occupational Health & Safety, "It might have happened to you," Article 24.9: http://www.ccohs.ca/NAOSH/ENGLISH/wk24-9en.htm; and "Compelling Statistics," Article 26.8: http://www.ccohs.ca/NAOSH/ENGLISH/w26-8en.htm

Job-related injuries and illnesses are more common than most people realize.[2] As shown in Figure 13-1, for example, workplace accidents are an expensive and painful reality. That is why safety and health issues have become a major concern of senior managers and human resource professionals. Employee accidents and illnesses lower productivity, effectiveness, employee morale, and quality of life.

Although line managers are primarily responsible for maintaining a safe and healthy work environment; human resource professionals provide staff expertise to help them deal with these issues. In addition, the human resource manager is frequently responsible for training, coordinating, and monitoring specific safety and health programs.

HR Web
Wisdom

http: www.pearsoned.ca/
mondy

Occupational Health and Safety Legislation
This site summarizes regulatory information from the thirteen jurisdictions in Canada (federal, provincial, and territorial).

Occupational Health and Safety (OHS) Legislation[3]

Through the various health and safety codes, governments attempt to provide safe working conditions for Canadians. There are two basic levels of safety legislation in Canada: federal and provincial. Federally, workplace health and

Figure 13-2

Jurisdiction of the Canada Labour Code

The Canada Labour Code covers the following areas:

- railways
- highway transport
- telephone and telegraph systems
- pipelines
- canals
- ferries, tunnels, and bridges
- shipping and shipping services
- radio and television broadcasting and cable systems
- airports
- banks
- grain elevators licensed by the Canadian Grain Commission, and certain feed mills and feed warehouses, flour mills, and grain seed cleaning plants
- federal public service ministries
- about 40 Crown corporations and agencies
- employment in the operation of ships, trains, and aircraft
- the exploration and development of petroleum on lands subject to federal jurisdiction.

Source: Adapted from A Guide to the Canada Labour Code: Occupational Safety and Health *(Ottawa: Labour Canada, 1992).*

safety falls under the Canada Labour Code. This legislation covers most inter-provincial and national industries (see Figure 13-2)—about 10 percent of all employees. As well, each province has occupational health and safety laws. Both regulations and enforcement vary by jurisdiction. HR practitioners and managers are encouraged to keep abreast of applicable legislation. A good place to start is the Internet (see Web Wisdom).

Most provincial occupational health and safety legislation covers the same basic elements: government responsibilities, employee rights and responsibilities, employer and supervisor responsibilities, joint health and safety committees (JHSC), and a workplace hazardous materials information system (WHMIS).

Government Responsibilities

General responsibilities of governments for occupational health and safety include:

- enforcement of occupational health and safety legislation
- workplace inspections
- dissemination of information
- promotion of training, education and research
- resolution of OHS disputes.

Employees' Rights and Responsibilities

Employees are responsible for:

- complying with OHS acts and regulations;
- using personal protective equipment and clothing as directed by the employer;
- reporting workplace hazards and dangers;
- working in the manner required by the employer and using prescribed safety equipment.

Employees have the right:

- to refuse unsafe work, provided certain procedures are followed (Figure 13-3 shows procedures for industries covered by the Canada Labour Code);
- to participate in workplace health and safety activities through a joint health and safety committee (JHSC) or as a worker health and safety representative;
- to be informed of actual and potential dangers in the workplace.

Employer Responsibilities

An employer must:

- establish and maintain a joint health and safety committee (see below), or cause workers to select at least one health and safety representative;
- take every reasonable precaution to ensure the workplace is safe;
- inform employees about any potential hazards and train them to safely use, handle, store, and dispose of hazardous substances and to handle emergencies;
- supply personal protective equipment and ensure that workers know how to use the equipment safely and properly;
- immediately report all critical injuries to the government department responsible for OHS;
- appoint a competent supervisor, who sets the standards for performance and ensures safe working conditions are always observed.

Supervisor Responsibilities

The supervisor must:

- ensure that workers use prescribed protective equipment devices;
- advise workers of potential and actual hazards;
- take every reasonable precaution in the circumstances for the protection of workers.

Figure 13-3

Procedures for Refusing
Dangerous Work under the
Canada Labour Code

Report to Employer

The employee must report his or her refusal immediately to his or her supervisor and to the safety and health representative or a member of the safety and health committee.

Investigation by Employer

The employer must then investigate the refusal in the presence of the employee and either a non-management member of the health and safety committee or the health and safety representative.

Continued Refusal

Where the employer decides that there is no danger, or takes steps to correct the danger and the employee has reasons to believe that a danger still exists, the employee may continue to refuse. Both the employer and the employee then must contact a safety officer appointed by the Ministry of Labour.

Reassignment of Employee and Task

Until the safety officer arrives, investigates and makes a decision, the employer cannot assign the work in question to another employee unless that other employee has been informed of the refusal. Meanwhile, the employee who refused to work may be asked by the employer to remain in a safe place nearby or may be assigned to reasonable alternative work.

Investigation and Decision by a Safety Officer

In the presence of the employer and the employee (or the employee's representative), the safety officer investigates the work refusal, decides whether a danger exists, and informs the employer and employee of this decision.

Result of Decision

If the safety officer decides that a danger *does* exist, he or she will issue a directive to the employer to correct the situation. The employee can continue to refuse the work until the employer complies with the directive.

If the safety officer decides that a danger *does not* exist, the employee no longer has the right to refuse under the protection of the Code. However, the employee may appeal the decision of the safety officer.

Appeals

Requests for a review of the decision of a safety officer may be made to the safety officer, requiring him or her to have the decision reviewed by the Canada Labour Relations Board or, for the public service, the Public Service Staff Relations Board. The request must be made in writing within seven days of receiving notification of the safety officer's decision.

Source: Canada Labour Code

Joint Health and Safety Committee (JHSC)

All Canadian jurisdictions call for either a **joint health and safety committee (JHSC)** or appointed representatives. Such representation is mandatory in some jurisdictions and subject to ministerial decision in others. The committee may

Joint health and safety committee (JHSC):
A committee required by law consisting of labour and management representatives who meet on a regular basis to deal with health and safety issues.

also be referred to by several other names, such as a health and safety committee or an occupational health committee. A joint health and safety committee is a forum for bringing the "internal responsibility" system into practice. The "internal responsibility" principle maintains that both employees and employers work together within their company to deal with occupational health and safety issues. As such, the committee consists of labour and management representatives who meet on a regular basis to deal with health and safety issues.

Certain types of workplaces may be exempt from the requirement to establish a JHSC depending on the size of work force, industry, accident record, or some combination of these factors. For example, in smaller companies with fewer than a specified number of employees, a health and safety representative is generally required.

Most Canadian health and safety legislation sets guidelines for organizing the committee, the structure of the committee, meeting frequency, and the roles and responsibilities of committee members. In particular, employers are responsible for the formation, structure and functioning of the committee. General duties and roles of health and safety committees are shown in Figure 13-4.

Workplace Hazardous Materials Information System (WHMIS)[4]

Workplace Hazardous Materials Information System (WHMIS): A national information system, required by law, designed to protect Canadian workers by providing safety and health information about hazardous materials.

Canadian workers have a legal and moral right to know how the materials they work with can affect their health or safety. The **Workplace Hazardous Materials Information System (WHMIS)** was created to help stop the injuries, illnesses, deaths, and medical costs resulting from exposure to hazardous materials. It is a national information system designed to protect Canadian workers by

Figure 13-4

Duties and Roles of Joint Health and Safety Committees

Generally, legislation in different jurisdictions across Canada require that health and safety committees or joint health and safety committees

- include both management and labour, with at least half of the members representing labour;
- meet regularly (some jurisdictions set a minimum of quarterly meetings, and others require monthly meetings);
- be co-chaired by a representative of management and a representative of labour
- be composed of employee representatives who are elected or selected by the workers or their union.
- act as an advisory body
- identify hazards and obtain information about them
- recommend corrective actions
- assist in resolving work refusal cases
- participate in accident investigations and workplace inspections
- make recommendations to the management regarding actions required to resolve health and safety concerns.

Source: Canadian Centre for Occupational Health and Safety, "OH & S Legislation in Canada – Basic Requirements,": http://www.ccohs.ca/oshanswers/legisl/responsi.html

providing safety and health information about hazardous materials. WHMIS became law through a series of complementary federal, provincial,and territorial legislation (October 31, 1988).

Workplace Responsibilities

The main components of WHMIS legislation are hazard identification and product classification, labelling, material safety data sheets, and worker training and education. Suppliers, employers, and workers all have defined responsibilities, which are specified in the Federal Hazardous Products Act and the Controlled Products Regulation, in addition to federal and provincial occupational safety and health legislation:

- Suppliers must clearly identify hazardous material and provide a material safety data sheet (MSDS).

- Employers must ensure products are labeled, a MSDS is available for employees, and establish employee education and training programs

- Workers must participate in training programs, apply safety practices, and inform their employers when labels are not visible or legible.

Enforcement

Safety officers with wide-ranging powers are appointed within the various provincial and federal jurisdictions. Generally, they can enter any workplace at any reasonable time and investigate, taking any necessary steps such as taking samples or photographs, conducting interviews, or making inspections. In addition, they have the power to order an employer not to disturb an area, to produce documents, to provide statements about health and safety conditions, and, most important, to correct unsafe working conditions. If the employer does not comply, the safety officer may recommend prosecution. For example, the Canada Labour Code provides for fines according to the seriousness of the offence (see, Figure 13-5). In addition, there are provisions for fines of up

---

HRM in ACTION

Safe or Not?

Stu is a long-term employee, who works hard, is well liked, and is very productive. Last week, in accordance with company policy, you gave a three-day suspension to the man who works beside him. The man was not wearing safety gear, although he had recently received a written notice for the same violation. As you come around the corner, you see Stu working without his safety glasses. He notices you and quickly puts them on. When you return to your desk, you check your records. You find that Stu was issued a notice for safety violation two weeks ago by another supervisor.

What action would you take?

Figure 13-5

Canada Labour Code
Offences and Maximum
Penalties

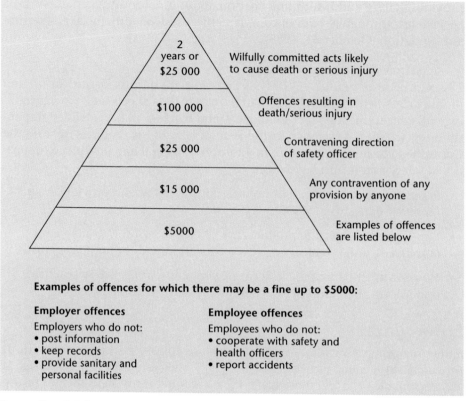

2 years or $25 000	Wilfully committed acts likely to cause death or serious injury
$100 000	Offences resulting in death/serious injury
$25 000	Contravening direction of safety officer
$15 000	Any contravention of any provision by anyone
$5000	Examples of offences are listed below

Examples of offences for which there may be a fine up to $5000:

Employer offences

Employers who do not:
• post information
• keep records
• provide sanitary and personal facilities

Employee offences

Employees who do not:
• cooperate with safety and health officers
• report accidents

Source: *Canada Labour Code*

to $1 million and up to two years' imprisonment for serious or repeated refusal to comply with WHMIS.

Approaches to Safety Programs

Safety programs may be designed to accomplish their purposes in two ways. The *first* approach is to create a psychological climate, a culture, that promotes a safe workplace, as accidents can be reduced when employees consciously think about safety. This attitude must permeate the firm's operations, so a strong company policy emphasizing safety and health is crucial. An organization's **occupational health and safety policy** is a workplace statement of principles and general rules that serve as guides for action. Senior management must be committed to ensuring that the policy is carried out with no exceptions. For example, a firm's policy might state: "It is the policy of the company that every employee be assigned to a safe and healthful place to work. We strongly desire accident prevention in all phases of our operations. Toward this end, the full cooperation of all employees will be required." For a more detailed example and discussion of a company policy statement, see Web Wisdom.

Occupational health and safety policy: A workplace statement of principles and general rules that serve as guides for action.

The implication of this policy is that workplace safety is everyone's job, from senior management to the lowest-level employee. Everyone should be encouraged to come up with solutions to safety problems.

The *second* approach is to develop and maintain a safe physical working environment. This is a proactive approach in which the environment is altered to prevent accidents. For example, safety devices might be installed on a machine to provide protection even if an operator is extremely tired, or is inattentive because of serious family problems. Every attempt is made to create a physical environment in which accidents are least likely to occur.

A Basic Occupational Health and Safety Program
Specific components of a health and safety program are provided.

Developing Safety Programs

Several organizational factors have to be in place to ensure the effective implementation of a safety program. Successful safety programs require commitment, leadership, and planning by managers; involvement or "buy-in" by all employees; an effective accident investigation program, trained supervisors and employees; and an effective evaluation system.

Management Rationale and Role

Progressive managers are investing an increasing amount of time, effort and money to promote a healthy and safe work environment. There are important reasons for this trend:[5]

- **Productivity** An effective safety program may boost morale and productivity, while simultaneously reducing costs. At work sites with excellent health and safety records, lost workday rates can run between 20 and 40 percent of the industry average.[6]

- **Profitability** Improved safety can reduce payouts related to rising workers' compensation costs.

- **Employee Relations** A good safety record is an effective vehicle for attracting and retaining employees.

- **Reduced Liability** An effective safety program can reduce corporate and executive liability if an employee is injured.

- **Marketing** A good safety record may improve competitiveness, as recruiting and winning contracts may become easier.

Every phase of human resource management is affected by workplace accident or injury. Consequences include personal loss, financial loss to injured employees, lost productivity, higher insurance premiums, possibility of fines and imprisonment, damaged employee relations, difficulties in recruiting, and increased turnover. Executives should also be strongly motivated to promote safety simply on grounds of human and social responsibility.

The critical role of management is made clear by legislation, which places the primary responsibility for employee safety on the shoulders of the employer.[7] The firm's managers, as the holders of authority, must take the lead in planning safety programs. Plans may be relatively simple, as for a small retail store,

Figure 13-6

Checklist: Health and Safety
Obligations for Executives

While it is not possible to provide an exhaustive list of all of the possible obligations under health and safety legislation, here are a number of suggestions that apply to all workplaces:

- Prepare a written health and safety policy, post the policy in a conspicuous place and distribute it to all workers.
- Ensure that all employees who receive the policy sign for it and that the written receipt is kept on file.
- Distribute the policy also to all employees, contractors and subcontractors.
- Where required, post copies of the relevant legislation (in Ontario for example, the *Occupational Health and Safety Act* must be posted).
- Put into place a program to implement the policy.
- Put into place a program to train all workers in workplace safety.
- Ensure that all individuals who do work for the company are properly trained even if they are not employed directly by the company.
- Document the instruction and training given to all workers.
- Put in writing all instructions necessary to protect health and safety; distribute them to all workers and secure a signed receipt from each that he or she has received the instruction.
- Ensure that a responsible person in the organization knows the applicable legislation and regulations and empower this person with the authority to enforce proper procedure.
- Ensure all orders are complied with and that they are immediately reported to someone in a position of authority within the company.
- Properly report all occupational accidents and illnesses.
- Ensure that all supervisors are properly trained and competent.
- Provide for regular inspection of the workplace for health and safety compliance and immediately correct all problems.
- Where required, ensure that a health and safety committee is in place and that the committee meets regularly and carries out its mandated function.
- Maintain all equipment in good condition, and ensure that safety devices such as guards are in place and functioning.
- Establish a safety system which includes regular supervision and inspection as well as internal reporting.
- Be aware of industry standards and ensure that the company does not fall below these standards.
- Put into place both remedial and contingency plans for emergencies, train all workers in proper emergency procedures and document this training.

Source: Reproduced with permission from *Canadian HR Reporter 8 (12), p. 15. © 1995 MPL Communications Inc.*

or more complex, as for a large automobile assembly plant. Figure 13-6 provides a basic checklist of steps management should take to fulfill that responsibility. For a detailed example and discussion of a company safety program, see Web Wisdom.

Workforce Involvement in Safety

In companies with effective safety programs, virtually everyone in the firm is involved. Participation by everyone helps to create positive attitudes, as employees tend to develop a sense of ownership toward the safety program. The development of a team concept whereby employees watch out for each other is a worthwhile goal. A method of advancing this philosophy is to form safety teams consistent with total quality management techniques.

In most cases, line managers are directly responsible for controlling conditions that cause accidents. As part of their responsibility then, they must set a proper example. If a supervisor fails to use safety devices, for example, subordinates may then feel these devices aren't really necessary. In many companies, one staff member coordinates the overall safety program. This individual, whose title might be safety director or safety engineer, educates line managers and employees about the merits of safety, while identifying and eliminating unsafe work conditions. Although this position may be advisory, a well-informed and assertive safety director may have considerable influence.

Employee feedback is essential. Good safety performance should be rewarded. Internal safety audits are a common tool, providing feedback and revealing problem areas. In addition, many organizations invite provincial or federal safety officers to review internal practices as part of an ongoing safety program.

Safety must begin with the hiring process, with an examination of the applicant's safety record, and continue through to orientation, training, and appraisal. Safety should become part of job design, maintenance, and work procedures, in a collaborative culture in which employees take personal responsibility for their own safety and the safety of their peers.[8]

Accident Investigation

Accidents can happen even in the most safety-conscious firms. Each accident, whether or not it results in an injury, should be carefully evaluated to determine the cause and to prevent recurrence. Ideally, an investigation and accident report is conducted by a team that includes an expert in accident causation, an employee representative, and the line manager. To prevent accidents, the supervisor must learn (through active participation in the safety program) why, how, and where accidents occur, and who is involved. As well, supervisors enhance their knowledge about accident prevention by helping to prepare accident reports.

HR Web Wisdom

http: www.pearsoned.ca/ mondy

Accidents in the Workforce
Guides to accident investigations, workplace inspections and due diligence are provided.

Training Supervisors and Employees

Health and safety training reduces accidents. Additionally, a company has a legal requirement to train its employees. In the event of an accident, an employer will likely be held responsible by a court unless it can be demonstrated that what lawyers call due diligence was exercised; that is, that the employer took all possible or practical precautions. In the event of an accident, management must be prepared to prove that an employee acted contrary to company policy, instruction, and training.[9] Otherwise, an employer might be fined for breaking health and safety regulations. Thus, it is not enough to work with supervisors and managers informally as the need arises; formal health and safety training is required.[10]

Experts recommend that safety training be an integral component of the employee's job training and career development, starting with orientation and continuing throughout an individual's career. The employer, through the supervisor, must take responsibility to ensure that safety training is relevant to both the employee and the organization. Training is likely to be most successful in those organizations where safety training is treated as a sound investment rather than a legislated obligation.[11] Employees must know the company's health and safety rules and policies.

In particular, safety must be emphasized during the training and orientation of new employees, not only because it is the company's legal responsibility but also because the early months of employment are often critical. Work injuries decrease substantially with length of service, a pattern that is consistent for both men and women.

Safety Program Evaluation

It would seem natural to assume that a safety program is succeeding if there is a reduction in the number and severity of accidents. In part, this is true.[12] However, accident frequency and severity rates, although informative, are not complete measures for evaluating the effectiveness of a health and safety program. For example, cases of occupational disease are usually underreported in these statistics. Moreover, the emphasis is usually on injury-producing accidents alone, not all accidents. Since accidents are rare events, especially in small organizations, the basis for comparison may be limited.

Rather than relying solely on injury rates, or after-the-event measures, it is desirable to use an audit as a before-the-fact measure of the effectiveness of an OHS program. An audit uses a checklist in which each safety element is subdivided into a series of questions. Each question is given a weighting factor depending on its importance. Records, observations, interviews, and questionnaires are used to evaluate performance for each sub-element. Audits determine if a company is following safety rules and policies. To generate improvements, evaluation results must also be transmitted upward to senior management and downward to line managers. A health and safety audit is a proactive approach. The assumption is that if a company is following the rules, a good safety record will follow.

Health and Wellness—Major Issues

There are a myriad of diseases, disorders, and illnesses that could be discussed under the topic of health and wellness, many of which are dealt with in the Web site referred to in Web Wisdom. We will focus here on a few of particular importance in the workplace.

Cumulative Trauma Disorders (CTD)

A **cumulative trauma disorder (CTD)** is an injury resulting from some trauma or stress to the body that occurs over a long period of time and that results in some physical or psychological malady. CTDs include a wide variety of problems, the most common of which are back pain, tennis elbow, tendonitis (an

Cumulative trauma disorder (CTD): An injury resulting from some trauma or stress to the body that occurs over a long period of time and that results in some physical or psychological malady.

inflammation of a tendon, a fibre connecting muscle to bone) and carpal tunnel syndrome (a condition affecting the hand and wrist causing numbness and pain). CTD usually results from repetitive motion, especially when work is done in an awkward posture, using some force, and without sufficient rest.

Today CTD is a primary concern of the safety specialist. One estimate, for example, found that more than 50 percent of all occupational illnesses reported were related to some sort of repetitive trauma. The growing frequency of repetitive motion problems is attributed to the increased use of computers and an aging population that is more vulnerable to such injuries. Safety and CTD issues related to teleworkers have become a particular concern of health and safety specialists, as discussed in the Trends & Innovations box.

HR Web Wisdom
http: www.pearsoned.ca/mondy

Health and Wellness
Numerous issues and topics related to health wellness are provided by the Canadian Centre for Occupational Health and Safety.

TRENDS and INNOVATIONS

Teleworking— The Legal Grey Area

A major area of health and safety concern occurs when a company has little control over the work environment. As we have already noted throughout this textbook, employees are increasingly working at home offices and using transient office worker space. Generally, health and safety legislation refers to all workers performing work for the employer, including teleworkers. But the issues of liability and compensation make telework a cloudy and controversial area. For example, what if an employee has an accident in the kitchen while on a break? How does an employee prove that a CTD was caused by company work?

To address issues that might not be fully covered in OHS legislation, the Canadian Centre for Occupational Health and Safety (CCOHS) has advised that the employer should have a written agreement with the teleworker that states:

- who supplies equipment;
- what type of access the employer and JHSC have to the teleworker's house for safety inspections;
- who is responsible for placing, maintaining, and storing equipment;
- what part of the residence constitutes the official "workplace";
- how to monitor the situation to ensure compliance with the law;
- that teleworkers are required to report any accident or injury to the supervisor immediately;
- how accidents or injuries are to be investigated;
- that employees who telework are subject to the same safety standards as other employees.

Source: Adapted from information provided by the Canadian Centre for Occupational Health and Safety (CCOHS), "Home Offices and the Telework Phenomenon," Internet site; http://www.ccohs.ca/naosh/english/w26-23en.htm (reprinted with the permission of the CCOHS).

Workplace Violence[13]

Workplace violence is any act in which a person is abused, threatened, intimidated, or assaulted in his or her employment and includes:

- threatening behaviour, such as shaking fists, destroying property or throwing objects;

- verbal or written threats: any expression of an intent to inflict harm;

- harassment: any behaviour that demeans, embarrasses, humiliates, annoys, alarms or verbally abuses a person and that is known or would be expected to be unwelcome. This includes words, gestures, intimidation, bullying, or other inappropriate activities;

- verbal abuse: swearing or insults;

- physical attacks: hitting, shoving, pushing, or kicking.

Stress

Stress is the body's nonspecific reaction to any demand made by the environment. Reactions to stress are highly individual; certain events may be quite stressful to one person but not to another. Moreover, the effect of stress is not always adverse. Mild stress, for example, may improve productivity, acting as a stimulus in developing creative ideas. Excessive stress, however, lowers productivity and innovation levels in the workplace. Figure 13-7 lists some of the behaviours exhibited by overstressed employees.

Although everyone lives with stress, severe and prolonged exposure can be harmful. In fact, stress can be as disruptive to an individual as an accident, resulting in attendance problems, excessive use of alcohol or other drugs, inadequate job performance, or overall poor health. There is increasing evidence, moreover, that severe, prolonged stress is related to heart disease, stroke, hypertension, cancer, emphysema, diabetes, and cirrhosis. Stress may even lead to suicide.

HR Web Wisdom
http: www.pearsoned.ca/ mondy

Stress Busters
This site provides offers thoughts for reducing work stress as well as stress-building concepts.

Figure 13-7

Signs of Stress

- Reduced clarity of judgment and effectiveness
- Rigid behaviour
- Complaints about poor health
- Strained relationships with others due to irritability
- Increasing excessive absence
- Emerging addictive behaviours (e.g., drugs, alcohol, smoking)
- Expressions of inadequacy and low self-esteem
- Apathy or anger on the job

Source: Michael Pesci, "Stress Management: Separating Myth from Reality." Personnel Administrator (January 1982) © 1982. Reprinted with the permission of HR Magazine, published by the Society for Human Resource Management, Alexandria, Virginia.

Figure 13-8
Stressful Jobs

The 12 jobs with the most stress are

1. Labourer	7. Manager/administrator
2. Secretary	8. Waitress/waiter
3. Inspector	9. Machine operator
4. Clinical lab technician	10. Farm owner
5. Office manager	11. Miner
6. Supervisor	12. Painter

Other high-stress jobs (in alphabetical order) are

Bank Teller	Nurse's aide
Clergy member	Plumber
Computer programmer	Police officer
Dental assistant	Practical nurse
Electrician	Public relations worker
Firefighter	Railroad switcher
Guard	Registered nurse
Hairdresser	Sales manager
Health aide	Sales representative
Health technician	Social worker
Machinist	Structural-metal worker
Meatcutter	Teacher's aide
Mechanic	Telephone operator
Musician	Warehouse worker

Some jobs are generally perceived as being more stressful than others. Stressful jobs are listed in Figure 13-8. A common factor among many of these jobs is the employee's lack of control over the work.

Burnout

One of the results of organizational and individual failure to deal with stress can be seen in the opening vignettes. Cheryl doesn't know exactly what has caused her run-down condition. She feels that she is at her wits' end and desperately needs assistance. Cheryl could be the victim of a stress-related phenomenon known as burnout. **Burnout** is a gradual state of fatigue or frustration that stems from devotion to a cause, way of life, or relationship that did not provide the expected reward. In essence, burnout is the perception that an individual is giving more than he or she is receiving, whether it is money, satisfaction, or praise. It is often associated with a midlife or mid-career crisis, but the condition can occur at different times to different people. Unrealistic expectations are often major contributors to burnout. When people strive excessively to achieve unattainable goals, they may experience a feeling of helplessness: the

Burnout: A gradual state of fatigue or frustration that stems from devotion to a cause, way of life, or relationship that did not provide the expected reward.

sense that no matter what they do they won't succeed. Thus, they lose their motivation to perform.

Those who work in the helping professions, such as teachers, nurses, counsellors, and social workers, seem to be especially susceptible to burnout, sometimes accelerated by job-related stress, whereas others may be vulnerable because of their upbringing, expectations, or personalities. Burnout is frequently associated with people who must work closely with others under tense conditions.

Alcohol and Drug Abuse

Alcoholism: A disease characterized by uncontrolled and compulsive drinking that interferes with normal living patterns.

Alcoholism is a disease characterized by uncontrolled and compulsive drinking that interferes with normal living patterns. Although difficult to quantify, it has been estimated that between 10 and 20 percent of Canadian employees are problem drinkers. Drinking-related problems cost employers between $1 billion and $3 billion yearly.[14] The problem, then, is enormous and it is not likely to disappear.

Although alcohol is a powerful drug, drugs are normally treated separately from alcohol because supervisors are less familiar with the signs and patterns of use of other drugs. All illegal drugs have some adverse affects. One study found, for example, that even occasional use of marijuana can impair eye–hand coordination up to 24 hours after ingestion.[15] Each year there are some 60 500 recorded drug offences. As with alcohol, drug abuse has also affected the workplace. According to one study, almost 70 percent of illicit drug users are employed. In some instances, problems associated with drug abusers may consume as much as 35 percent of a firm's profits.[16]

Chemically dependent employees exhibit behaviours that distinguish them from other workers. Employees using stimulants such as Benzedrine, Dexedrine, or cocaine can be extraordinarily restless or talkative, while those on depressants like morphine, Demerol, heroin, Amytal, Librium, and Valium can be irritable, nervous, confused, hostile, or depressed. Marijuana, hashish, and hallucinogens such as LSD speed up, slow down, or distort the senses, causing faulty judgment and poor coordination.

The action of a drug may vary depending upon factors such as:

- the person's frame of mind or emotional state;

- the familiarity or strangeness of the surroundings;

- the presence or absence of others, and the relationship with any companions;

- the quality and quantity of the drug;

- the method of taking the drug (e.g., oral, injection, sniffing);

- combination with other drugs;

- the physical size and condition of the person.

AIDS (Acquired Immune Deficiency Syndrome): A condition that undermines the body's immune system resulting in chronic, progressive illness and leaving infected people susceptible to a wide range of infections, cancers, and fatal diseases.

AIDS (Acquired Immune Deficiency Syndrome)[17]

The Human Immunodeficiency Virus (HIV) is the virus that causes **AIDS (Acquired Immune Deficiency Syndrome)**, a condition that undermines the

HR Web Wisdom

http: www.pearsoned.ca/mondy

THE AIDS FILE
Get all the facts: transmission, prevention, symptoms, statistics, and resources.

body's immune system, resulting in chronic, progressive illness and leaving infected people susceptible to a wide range of infections, cancers, and fatal diseases. HIV is transmitted through unprotected sexual intercourse, needle sharing, or contaminated blood products. It may also be transmitted by an infected mother to her infant during the pregnancy or delivery and through breastfeeding.

AIDS has become a worldwide epidemic. Since the first case was reported in Canada in 1982, some 43 000 positive HIV tests have been reported. AIDS has claimed almost 10 000 lives.

Medical researchers have determined that some individuals who are HIV positive are long-term nonprogressors; that is, they may never develop AIDS. Approximately 6 to 9 percent of people infected with HIV for more than 10 years are symptom-free. They show no signs of progressing to symptomatic infection and have a normal anticipated life span in the workplace. Only a few years ago, it was assumed that an individual with AIDS would have a short work life. Management should no longer make this assumption.[18]

Health and Wellness Programs

A formal company wellness program involves careful planning and a significant funding commitment. As with safety programs, a focus on employee wellness should reflect a company philosophy that emphasizes the value of human assets. Company health and wellness programs can be broken down into two categories. The first is company-wide holistic health and wellness programs, such as physical fitness and active living programs, employee assistance programs (EAP), and ergonomics. The second category is programs targeted to specific illnesses or issues, such as workplace violence, stress and burnout; substance abuse, or AIDS.

Major Holistic Health and Wellness Programs

Physical Fitness and Active Living Programs

From a management viewpoint, a fit workforce is desirable, as loss of productivity from coronary disease and other preventable health problems costs businesses billions of dollars annually, not including the costs of replacement and retraining. As well, company-sponsored fitness programs often reduce absenteeism, accidents, and sick pay.

Back and neck injuries, sprains, and strains are among the most common and costly problems in industry. For this reason, many wellness programs either began with a focus on physical fitness, or developed out of company-sponsored physical fitness programs. Although few organizations have fully staffed facilities, many Canadian firms have exercise programs designed to help keep their employees physically fit.

There has been a general movement away from defining "fitness" in narrow, "no pain, no gain" terms, however. Dr. Art Quinney, dean of physical education at The University of Alberta, has pointed out that "the old definition of fitness left many Canadians, including workers, at the sidelines. They saw fitness as being intimidating and unappealing."[19] Instead, some Canadian companies are now promoting *active living*: a way of life in which activity is valued as an important part of daily living. John Dimaurizio, director of human resources at Pratt-Whitney Canada's head office in Longueil, Quebec, describes the concept this way: "Active living in our workplace provides a recreational means for our employees and their families . . . to have fun. Our employees are happier on the job, more creative, and ultimately more productive."[20] A daily 40-minute walk, for example, will reduce anxiety levels by 14 percent.[21]

Employee Assistance Programs

Employee assistance program (EAP):
A comprehensive approach that many organizations have taken to deal with emotionally troubled employees.

An **employee assistance program (EAP)** is a comprehensive approach used by many organizations that deals with emotional problems arising from such issues as marital or family problems, job performance problems, stress, mental health issues, financial troubles, grief, alcohol and drug abuse, elder care, workplace violence, and even natural disasters, such as earthquakes, floods, and tornadoes.[22] A basic philosophy of EAP is to treat emotionally troubled employees with the same consideration given to employees with physical illnesses. Most EAP programs provide either for in-house professional counsellors or for referrals to an appropriate community social service agency. Typically, most or all of the costs are borne by the employer.

Advantages claimed for EAPs include increases in productivity and decreases in workers' compensation claims, absenteeism, and accident rates.[23] But an EAP will not succeed unless the employer is committed to promoting the program and educating employees and managers.[24] Supervisors, in particular, must be trained to recognize troubled employees and to be sensitive in referring them to the firm's EAP counsellors.[25]

Ergonomics

Ergonomics: The process of matching the job to the worker and the product to the user. It focuses on how work affects workers.

One specific safety and health approach that seems destined to become more common is the increased use of ergonomics. **Ergonomics** is the process of matching the job to the worker and the product to the user. Ergonomics attempts to adapt the machine or tool to the person rather than requiring the person to adjust to the machine. It focuses on how work affects workers. Ergonomic hazards refer to workplace conditions that pose the risk of injury to the musculoskeletal system. Such conditions may include temperature extremes, awkward postures that arise from improper work methods, and improperly designed workstations, tools, or equipment.[26]

In its broadest interpretation, ergonomics would include all attempts to structure work conditions so as to conserve energy, promote good posture, and allow workers to function without pain or impairment.

Specific or Targeted Health and Wellness Programs

Workplace Violence Prevention

Generally, firms in Canada have a legal commitment to protect their employees against violence. Only a few jurisdictions (British Columbia and Saskatchewan, for example) have specific workplace violence legislation. However, most other Canadian jurisdictions have a "general duty provision" in their Occupational Health & Safety legislation that requires employers to take all reasonable precautions to protect employees against violence in the workplace.

Within a firm, the most important component of any workplace violence prevention program is management commitment. Management commitment is best communicated in a written policy that:

- formally states zero tolerance for violent behaviour;

- shows that management is committed to dealing with incidents involving violence, harassment and other unacceptable behaviour;

- informs employees what specific behaviour (e.g., violence, intimidation, bullying, harassment) management considers inappropriate and unacceptable in the workplace;

- instructs employees on reporting procedures when incidents covered by the policy occur; and

- encourages employees to report such incidents.

Management of Stress and Burnout

While specific programs to prevent or relieve stress can be very helpful, properly designed general organizational programs have an important role to play in creating an environment—a corporate culture—that holds anxiety and tension to an acceptable level. The following list describes elements of such a culture.

- Employee inputs are sought and valued. Employees are given greater control over their work and participate in making decisions that affect them.

- Communication is emphasized. Employees know what is going on in the firm, what their particular roles are, and how well they are performing their jobs.

- Each person's role is defined, yet care is taken not to discourage risk takers and those who want to assume greater responsibility.

- Individuals are given the training and development they need to perform current and future jobs. Individuals are trained to work as effective team members and to develop an awareness of how they and their work relate to others.

- Employees are assisted in career planning. Equal consideration is given to achieving personal and organizational goals.

- Employee needs, both financial and nonfinancial, are met through an equitable reward system.

Managers should also watch for the following types of stress-related warning signals: 1) irritability, 2) forgetfulness, 3) frustration, 4) fatigue, 5) procrastination, 6) tension, or 7) increased alcohol or drug use.[27] Other symptoms might include recurring health problems, such as ulcers, back pain, or frequent headaches.

Substance Abuse Programs

Direct intervention programs are often developed to help supervisors deal with problem employees. The approach and the eventual treatment for both alcohol and drug abuse are quite similar. For this reason, alcohol and drug assistance are often combined under the label "substance abuse program." Such programs normally have four common features: policy statement, identification, intervention, and diagnosis and treatment.

Policy statement An important part of a company-wide policy toward substance abuse is to remove the stigma attached to the problem. Abuse must be viewed as an illness and any employee having this illness should receive the same consideration and offer of treatment that any sick or injured employee would. When such a policy is formulated, communicated, and supported by senior management, line supervisors not only know how to approach the problem, but their attitudes toward those with the disease will tend to be more supportive.

Identification Managers are not diagnosticians, and they may need professional advice. However, they should be aware that alcoholism/drug abuse is a possible cause of marked deterioration in job performance or absenteeism. For example, employees who drink excessively are sick, late, and absent three times as often as other workers.

Intervention Having identified a potential substance abuser, the employer/supervisor must meet with the employee. A major objective of this meeting is to establish that work performance has not been acceptable This is a critical stage. The employee must be made to acknowledge the reality of poor work performance. A second objective is to motivate the employee to accept professional counselling. The employee must be made aware of the seriousness of the situation and possible consequences should work performance not improve. Past transgressions should be clearly documented and levels of acceptable performance should be agreed upon in writing before the interview ends.

Diagnosis and treatment It must be stressed that the supervisor is not qualified to diagnose the employee's substance problem or suggest treatment measures. All diagnosis and treatment must be performed by qualified professionals. Although some in-house programs do exist, it is often more realistic to use outside rehabilitation sources. The employer's role at this stage is to maintain benefit and seniority rights, for although substance abusers are often able to follow outpatient treatment procedures, some will need hospitalization or other care during working hours. It is essential that an employer's policy account for such absences. The second task for the employer is to remain vigilant. For example, to recover completely from alcoholism requires a wrenching lifestyle change over a span of months or even years. It should not be assumed that a short-term conformance to work rules signals a complete recovery. In fact, some studies have suggested that nearly 50 percent of those treated for alcohol or drug abuse will relapse within one year.[28]

Obviously, an employee is free to refuse any suggestion or offer of help. In these situations, the manager has little alternative but to carry the disciplinary process through to dismissal. The key to this procedure is documentation, as it may have to be proven that all attempts to bring work performance to an acceptable level within a reasonable time have failed. If the worker is fired, the reason must be inadequate job performance. Alcoholism or refusal to accept treatment must never be stated as the reason for termination.

Workplace Policies on AIDS

All jurisdictions in Canada recognize HIV infection, HIV-related illness, and AIDS as a "disability" or "handicap" within the meaning of human rights statutes. What this means is that employers, under most circumstances, cannot legally discharge an employee who has contracted AIDS. However, since one AIDS occurrence may disrupt the workplace severely, HR professionals should ensure that proper policies are in place and that both management and employees are aware of the issues that surround this deadly condition. An AIDS program should include the following major components:[29]

- **Written Policy.** An HIV/AIDS policy that defines the company's position and practices is the foundation for the HIV/AIDS program. A good company policy sets the standards of behaviour expected of all employees, establishes compliance with all federal, provincial, and local laws, and lets all employees know where to go for assistance.

- **Manager/Labour Leader Training.** Managers need to know the laws that affect HIV/AIDS in the workplace. They need to know how to respond appropriately and compassionately; and they need specific information and strategies to reduce employee fear, work disruption, and customer concern. They also need to know the procedures to implement workplace safety precautions.

- **Employee and Family Education.** Facts and compassion are the focus of employee/family education. All employees and their families should know the policies of the workplace and where to get information. They should be informed of the relevant legislation and their legal rights.

Stress in the Global Marketplace

An international assignment can be a major stressor for expatriates. Expatriates are often under stress from the moment they learn of global assignments until well after returning home. Culture shock is the main stressor for those on international assignment. Even immigrants who return to their country of origin can experience culture shock, as business practices may have changed and their network of contacts may not exist.[30]

Stress arising from differences in business practices, standards, values, and behavioural norms is also inherent in international business. Such differences are particularly marked between developed countries and developing countries, especially when examining worker health, safety, and environmental issues.[31] One of the major concerns arising from the North American Free Trade Agreement, for example, is the perceived inadequacy of Mexican industrial safety standards.[32] Canadian expatriates may find it stressful to work in joint ventures they consider to be unsafe. Stress from any of these causes may lead to poor job performance, unhappy social lives, broken marriages, changes in sex drive, eating binges, substance abuse, homesickness, or bouts of depression, nervousness, anger, aggression, impatience with family members, and insomnia.

HR professionals must, therefore, work to limit relocation stress by preparing expatriates to deal with the norms, values, goals, and objectives of the host country.[33] Inappropriate preparation may result in failure and early return, an outcome costly both for the individual involved and for the organization. The average annual cost to send an employee overseas for one or two years is between $200 000 and $250 000. One executive estimates the cost (to the firm) of a failed expatriate assignment as three times the individual's salary, not including the price of lost productivity.

Stress prevention for expatriates starts with selection (see Chapter 6). Often, management chooses the most technically competent employees, even though the qualities that made them successful in Canada are different from those needed during an international assignment. Human resource professionals should help ensure that employees sent on global assignments have the personal, people, and perceptual skills needed to cope with the environment they will encounter.[34]

SUMMARY

1. Explain why employers should be concerned about safety and health issues.

Workplace accidents cost the country some $10 billion annually in direct and indirect costs. Employee accidents and illnesses lower productivity, effectiveness, employee morale, and quality of life. Thus aside from social and humanitarian reasons, safety and health issues have become a major economic concern of senior managers.

2. Explain the role of the HR professional in safety and health.

Although line managers are primarily responsible for maintaining a safe and healthy work environment, human resource professionals provide staff expertise to help them deal with these issues. In addition, the human resource manager is frequently responsible for training, coordinating, and monitoring specific safety and health programs.

3. Outline and briefly explain occupational safety legislation.

Federally, workplace health and safety falls under the Canada Labour Code. Each province and territory, as well, has enacted occupational health and safety legislation to deal with employees in the respective jurisdictions. Most jurisdictions contain common basic legal elements regarding government, employee, and supervisor/employer responsibilities. Most employers are also responsible for establishing joint health and safety committees and, if necessary, a workplace hazardous materials information system. In general, safety officers are appointed within the various jurisdictions to enforce the legislation.

4. Explain the major approaches to safety programs.

One approach is to create a psychological climate that promotes a safe workplace, as accidents can be reduced when employees consciously think about safety. This requires a strong occupational health and safety policy. A second approach is to develop and maintain a safe physical working environment. This is a proactive approach where the environment is altered to prevent accidents.

5. Explain the critical elements of an effective safety program.

Several organizational factors have to be in place to ensure the effective implementation of a safety pro-

gram. Successful safety programs require: commitment, leadership, and planning by managers; involvement or "buy-in" by all employees; an effective accident investigation program; trained supervisors and employees; and an effective evaluation system.

6. Identify major workplace health and wellness issues.

Major health and wellness issues include cumulative trauma disorders, workplace violence, stress and burnout, alcoholism and drugs, and AIDS.

7. Describe major holistic health and wellness programs.

Major holistic health and wellness programs include physical fitness and active living; employee assistance programs (EAP), and ergonomics. Progressive Canadian companies have expanded the concept of physical fitness to include active living: a way of life in which activity is valued as an important part of daily living. An employee assistance program (EAP) is a wellness approach that deals mainly with the emotional aspect of employee health. Most EAP programs are paid by the employer and provide either for in-house professional counsellors or for referrals to an appropriate community social service agency. Ergonomics programs attempt to structure work conditions so as to conserve energy, promote good posture, and allow workers to function without pain or impairment.

8. Describe major specific or targeted health and wellness programs.

Targeted health and wellness programs address one specific disorder or problem such as workplace violence, stress and burnout, substance abuse, or AIDS. Workplace violence prevention programs begin with a written policy that clearly spells out management's refusal to tolerate violence, as well as what behaviour is unacceptable and how violations should be dealt with. While specific programs to prevent or relieve stress can be very helpful, the work culture and properly designed organizational programs, can also help to reduce stress and burnout. Intervention programs for substance abuse usually include identification, intervention, and diagnosis and treatment. It is important to treat substance abuse problems as a disorder and to offer help. An AIDS program should include a written policy, management/labour leader training, and employee and family education. Both managers and employees must understand that an employee cannot normally be dismissed for AIDS/HIV, that infected employees rarely pose a risk to co-workers, and that some people with HIV may be able to continue to work indefinitely.

QUESTIONS FOR REVIEW

1. Why should management be concerned with health and safety issues?

2. Briefly explain Canada's health and safety legislation.

3. What are the duties and roles of a joint health and safety committee? Briefly describe the main components of and rationale for WHMIS legislation?

4. What are the two major approaches to safety programs? Briefly explain.

5. What are the critical elements of an effective safety program?

6. What are the major health and wellness issues?

7. What procedures should an employer implement to reduce the risk of liability related to accidents claimed by teleworkers?

8. What are some of the behaviours exhibited by overstressed employees?

9. What is AIDS and how is HIV transmitted?

10. Describe the major employer-sponsored holistic health and wellness programs.

11. Describe four health and wellness programs targeted to specific workplace illnesses or issues.

12. What are the major components of an effective workplace AIDS program?

DEVELOPING **HRM** SKILLS

An Experiential Exercise

At times, workers' personal problems may distract them from work and lead to unsafe behaviour. Dealing with one's personal problems is often difficult, and assisting employees in dealing with these issues can be taxing for managers. However, if the situation is undermining productivity or safety, it must be addressed. This exercise should provide a better understanding of how to handle a most difficult issue.

"I am going to do it and I am going to do it today. This has gone on long enough!," thought Simone Rosen, the data processing manager. "I can't put it off any longer. I realize that Walter has been with the company for 14 years, and with this department for 11 of those years, but this drinking thing is out of hand. Lately the problem is affecting other members of the work group. His friends are covering up pretty well for him, but that is causing their productivity to go down. Evidently Walter is not going to be able to work things out, and the situation will only get worse. We are going to meet today and resolve this matter one way or the other: he's dry or he's out! I'm not a villain, and I really want him to work things out, but this is causing the department problems."

Walter Hollingsworth, a programmer in the data processing department, was concerned. He thought, "I heard from a friend in the boss's office that I am going to get chewed out about my drinking. I have always gotten my work done, but I guess I've let things slip lately. I know I can lick this problem. I'm going to straighten myself out, and when I meet with the boss I'll admit that I drink too much sometimes; everybody does. Drinking has only recently affected my work. I'll do better in the future. I've been with the company for 14 years, and with this division for 11 of those years. One problem in all those years makes me a good risk. I can do it, and I deserve a chance. The boss should be compassionate."

Two students will participate. One will play Simone and one will play Walter. The rest of the class should observe carefully. The instructor will provide any additional information necessary to participate.

An Eye for an Eye

"Hey, here comes SN. Get those goggles on," warned Frank Farrish, a mechanical supervisor for Fastco, a large machinery maintenance company. At the warning, his five employees quickly donned their safety goggles and continued working. Joy Norris, the company safety officer (called SN by Frank, for Safety Nut), looked approvingly at Frank's crew. "Maybe," she thought, "I'm finally getting through to him."

It had been an uphill struggle for Joy. Not only was she one of the new breed—a professionally trained safety technician—but she was a woman working in the man's world of large machine maintenance. Still, when they found out she knew her job, the supervisors had gradually begun to accept her suggestions and now she was regarded as one of the boys. That is, everywhere except Frank's section. From the beginning, he had ridiculed both Joy and her ideas. He had coined the term "SN" and seen to it that none of his men accepted her programs. It was only after being threatened with dismissal by his boss, the district manager, that Frank had grudgingly issued safety goggles and allowed safety posters to be put up. Safety standards were still weak in Frank's section, but Joy had patience. Even he would come around sooner or later.

As Joy turned to head off to the next repair depot she heard the scream. Anyone who has ever seen a man after a splinter of steel has pierced his eye does not forget the sight easily.

One of Frank's men was writhing on the floor screaming hoarsely. Frank was dancing about in a panic, not knowing what to do.

"Bring a car in here fast!" snapped Joy. "You! Get the first aid kit—move! You two, help me get his hand away from his eye. He's only doing more damage!"

And so Joy calmed the injured employee, placed gauze over the eye and saw him carried, moaning, to a car for a quick ride to the hospital. On her return from the hospital, Joy found the district manager already in Frank's office. When he saw her, he said: "I think, Joy, that you should chair this meeting."

Questions

1. What is Joy's short-term task? How should she accomplish it?

2. What is her long-term task? How should she accomplish it?

3. Should safety officers have the authority to close operations or processes they deem to be unsafe?

PART FIVE CASE 5

Parma Cycle Company: Safety and Health at the New Plant

"I want the new plant to be a model of safety and health," said Jim Burgess, the president of Parma Cycle Company in Delta, B.C. "I do, too," said Jesse Heard, the human resource director, "but you have to be aware that it's going to cost a lot." "Remember now, Jesse," the president replied, "we're putting the plant in Digby, N.S. primarily to reduce costs. I believe that the main thing we can do for safety is to train our workers to be safety-oriented. That doesn't cost much."

"That's the main thing, I know," said Jesse, "but we'll also have to spend some money. There are several areas where safety can be improved by installing handrails. Also, a good number of the machines will come in without a chain-belt guard. We'll have to have those fabricated." "Well," said Jim, "let's just try to meet the government requirements on those kinds of things. I'd like to see a cost–benefit analysis of anything that goes beyond their standards." He was referring to Nova Scotia's Occupational Health and Safety Act (OHSA).

About that time, Cliff Brubaker, the chief engineer at Parma, who had also been summoned to the meeting, came in. After a few niceties, Cliff said, "Jim, making sure that all the machinery and the machine layouts meet OHSA requirements made engineering the new plant a lot more difficult. We won't be able to use our floor space nearly as efficiently at Digby as we do here in Delta. Also, the work flow is going to be less efficient because I had to separate machines to keep the area noise level below the maximum standard. Don't you think we could fudge a little on some of this? The Delta plant doesn't come close to meeting B.C.'s OHSA requirements, and we have only had one fine since I've been here."

"I don't think you can trade off personal safety against a few dollars of cost savings," Jesse said. "You remember when Clayton Braden lost his arm last year? The company came out okay on that because Clay didn't have us charged under OHSA. But what about Clay? How much was his arm worth?" "Don't get upset, Jesse," said Cliff. "I know what you mean and I really feel the same way. But we can go to extremes."

Jim Burgess spoke up, adding, "I don't think that meeting provincial safety standards is going to extremes. Besides, if companies like Parma Cycle don't take some initiative in protecting workers, we're going to see even more enforcement efforts in the future. I want to make sure that you both understand my position. Everything in the plant at Digby is to meet provincial requirements for health and safety as a minimum. If the requirements can be exceeded with no additional costs, I want to opt for maximum safety. If you have to spend extra money to improve safety or health at the Digby plant, I want to see a benefit–cost analysis on each item." "I think that's clear enough," said Jesse. "Me, too," said Cliff, "but I'll have to get back to you on a number of the modifications we had planned."

Questions

1. What do you think of Mr. Burgess's insistence on meeting provincial standards at the Digby plant?

2. Do you agree with Jesse that a firm should not "trade off personal safety against a few dollars of cost savings?"

PART FIVE CBC 🍁 VIDEO CASE

Absenteeism: A Costly Issue

Statistics Canada tells us that absenteeism costs the Canadian economy at least $10 billion per year. On average, each paid full-time worker loses almost eight days of work per year due to illness, disability, personal, and family responsibilities.

Were all these lost work days really necessary? Not according to Jeff Rosenthal, a senior manager at Toronto Hydro. "We were looking at, on any given day, about a hundred people not being here." Absenteeism, was costing the company about $5 million per year. Homewood Health Centre, a private psychiatric clinic in Guelph, Ontario, also had a hefty absenteeism problem. Janice Wall, who was in charge of Homewood's HR department, said her company was aiming for a $1.1 million cutback and the cost of absenteeism, at about $500 000, was an obvious target. Both companies suspected that employees were misusing time off. According to Rosenthal, employees seemed to believe they had a right to use their sick leave whether they were sick or not.

Both companies began attendance management, checking each employee's frequency, duration and patterns of absence. Attendance management is necessary, argues Michael Millman, a consultant with R.C. Whitney & Associates: "There are people that have tested the system and found that they do not need to come to work on a regular basis and when they don't come nothing ever happens."

Homewood went the high-tech route with tracking software from Kronos Computer Timing Systems Inc. Prime offenders were targeted for assistance or, if necessary, discipline. Hydro began with a massive awareness campaign to explain why the company cared so much. Then came the intimidating message: Everyone is important and needed. Absentees will be watched closely and, if warranted, termination will be an option.

Does attendance management work? Some experts, like Millman, think so: "A little pressure can go a long way if used sparingly." In the short term, Hydro corroborates this view: they reduced

absenteeism by 33 percent, representing a yearly saving of some $1.7 million. But other experts argue that the subtle—and in some cases not so subtle—intimidation of attendance management is not a long-term solution because it doesn't get at the root of the problem: work-family balance and motivation.

Marti Smye of Peopletech Inc. says that programs like Hydro's and Homewood's are based on the assumption that employees can't be trusted. She says a core cause of absenteeism is corporate abuse. As companies have reengineered, workloads have increased. "The burnout rate and stress have gone up incredibly. And so, people are taking time off and saying, 'I can't go to work today.'" In a 1999 Statistics Canada survey, half of Canadians between the ages of 25 and 44 said they did not have enough time with their family and friends. Smye argues that companies must consider workplace and personal needs.

The Canadian Imperial Bank of Commerce does not spell out a specific number of entitled sick days to avoid creating a sense of entitlement, says HR manager Judy Jaeger. Instead CIBC offers options such as job sharing, telecommuting, and compressed work weeks. It also has an employee assistance program to help employees cope. "Extensive studies have shown that work-family conflict increases absenteeism. So it isn't a big leap of faith to say that if we reduce work-family conflict we will reduce our absenteeism."

Kellie Siddle is a disability case manager at Marine Life. She has a stressful job and two preschoolers to look after. But to help with such work-family tradeoffs, the company offers an employee assistance program, flextime, on-site day care, a convenience store, and a fitness centre. At Marine Life there is little need to police staff. For employees like Kellie, absenteeism is low and productivity is high.

Everyone agrees that absenteeism is a key concern for Canadian business trying to compete for world markets. But is the answer incentive strategies or monitoring to prevent abuse? Some companies, like Homewood, are hedging their bets. In addition to computer monitoring, Homewood has introduced a fitness program and counselling services.

Questions

1. What are two major approaches to reducing absenteeism? What are the advantages and disadvantages of each?

2. "It clearly states in the Hydro agreement that we are given 18 days a year to use and if you have to use 18 days, there should be no reprisals," says Bruno Silan, president of Toronto Hydro's CUPE, Local One. If you were the HR manager at Toronto Hydro, how would you respond?

3. "The cost of absenteeism has skyrocketed," says your boss. "You're the HR expert. How do you suggest we get these costs under control?" Draft an absenteeism policy.

4. Visit two local companies. Explain the absenteeism policies of each.

Video Resource: "No Place to Hide," Venture #646 (June 15, 1997).

CHAPTER 14

The Labour Union

CHAPTER OBJECTIVES

1. Briefly describe the history and significance of the Canadian labour movement.

2. Identify key characteristics of the labour environment.

3. Outline basic elements of the union structure.

4. Explain why some employees voluntarily join unions while others tend to avoid joining a union.

5. Describe the three major management responses to union organizing.

6. Define collective bargaining and explain the certification process.

7. Explain the rationale for interest-based bargaining.

8. Describe major issues that will influence the future of labour–management relations.

Nicholas O'Sullivan, president of United Technologies, was disturbed and disappointed. He had just been informed by the Provincial Labour Relations Board that a majority of his employees had voted to have the union represent them. The past months had been difficult ones, with charges and countercharges being made by both management and labour. The vote had been close, with only a few votes tipping the scales in favour of labour.

He looked at the human resource manager, Marthanne Bello, and said, "I don't know what to do. The union will demand so much we can't possibly be competitive. I know they don't understand that we can't make our part-timers full-time employees. We don't fire people, but when we need to reduce the size of our workforce, part-timers give us the flexibility we need."

Marthanne replied, "Just because a union has won the right to be represented doesn't mean that union demands will be unreasonable, or that we have to accept all their terms. I believe that a reasonable contract can be negotiated. I know many of those guys and I am sure that we can work out a contract that will be fair to both sides."

Of course, Nicholas O'Sullivan does not have to concede to all the demands that the new union makes. What he must do, however, is enter into negotiations with the union in good faith and work out a collective agreement. Both sides will likely have to make compromises. If the union and management can learn to bargain in a professional manner, then United Technologies will be among the vast majority of firms that settle with their unions without strike action. As this is a first contract, the Labour Relations Board will be watching the negotiating process very closely to ensure that Nick O'Sullivan and the union negotiators behave according to the rules.

Organized labour: Workers belonging to a union.

Labour unions are an influential part of our work culture. As we noted in Chapter 1, some 4 million workers, or about 33 percent of all paid nonagricultural workers, are represented by a labour union in their workplace.[1] In Chapter 2 we defined a *union* as a group of employees who have joined together for the purpose of dealing collectively with their employer. Often the term union is used synonymously with labour union or trade union. **Organized labour**—that is, workers belonging to a union—and the gains made by the labour movement have improved the benefits and working conditions for Canadian workers.[2] Experts have found, for example: "It is indisputable that the efforts of organized labour have led to a decent standard of living and improved working conditions for millions of Canadian workers."[3]

We begin this chapter with a brief history of the Canadian labour movement and the legal traditions that underpin our labour relations system. Next, we describe several key common characteristics of the labour movement. We then describe the fundamental elements of the union structure, outline the three major forms of union representation, and provide major reasons why employees choose to join or not to join a union. This is followed by a discussion of management responses to union organizing. We then define collective bargaining and explain the certification process. Finally, we explore the major issues affecting the future of management–labour relations in Canada.

Brief History of the Canadian Labour Movement

Our present-day labour relations ideology and union structure are rooted deeply in the past. A brief history helps to clarify why both unions and management behave as they do and why the management/union relationship has traditionally been fractious and adversarial, characterized by conflict rather than cooperation.

As early as 1794, working people in Canada began to form groups, unions and associations designed to better their working conditions. But the Canadian labour movement grew slowly. By 1913, for example, less than 10 percent of Canada's labour force was unionized compared with more than 22 percent in Britain and Germany.[4] Throughout the early 1900s, employees who wished to organize were at the mercy of their employers, as large-scale immigration provided a cheap and willing pool of labour. During the formative years, extreme social and management resistance lead to bitter strikes and violence. Here are just a few examples. The Winnipeg General Strike of 1919 was effectively put down on "bloody Saturday" (June 21, 1919), when RCMP officers shot two and injured more than 30 in a crowd of strikers. Two thousand troops put down the 1923 plant occupation and strike at Sydney Steel. A Cape Breton miner was killed in 1925 in yet another labour dispute.[5] **Yellow-dog contracts** (signed employer–employee agreements prohibiting a worker from joining a union or engaging in union activities.), **blacklists** (lists of union sympathizers employers would not hire), and spies were used widely.

It was not until the 1930s, when progress in American labour legislation began to be copied, that unions in Canada gained a firm foothold. One important piece of U.S. legislation was the 1935 National Labor Relations Act (NLRA), commonly known as the Wagner Act. This U.S. Act prohibited a range of "unfair" management practices, such as interfering with an employee's right to join a union and refusing to bargain with a union.[6, 7] The basic principles of the Wagner Act were imported into Canada in 1944, under a famous Order-in-Council: **P.C. 1003**. This legislation defined the rights and obligations of both unions and employees, while implementing procedures for settling contract disputes.[8,9]

P.C. 1003, was followed, in 1946, by the so-called **Rand formula**—an arbitration ruling which established a Canadian legal precedent that still remains a pillar of Canadian labour relations. Justice Rand was called in to arbitrate a dispute at Ford Motor Company in Windsor, Ontario. He ruled that workers were not required to become members of the union but they were required to pay dues. His rationale for this ruling was to prevent non-union employees, who often enjoyed the same wages and benefits as union members, from getting a "free ride" without paying union dues.

Gradually, all provinces and territories began to develop their own distinct labour laws. Most provinces followed the Federal legislative principles of P.C. 1003, the subsequent (1948) Federal Industrial Relations Disputes and Investigations Act and the Canada Labour Code (1972) quite closely. In addition, most provincial legislation came to recognize the basic rights of every Canadian to join a union under the *Canadian Charter of Rights and Freedoms,* which was created as part of the 1982 repatriation of the *Canadian Constitution*. Over time, however, individual provinces have modified the federal legislation, gradually increasing the complexity and differences among jurisdictions.[10]

Key Characteristics of the Labour Environment

Today, except for those working under federal jurisdiction, labour relations has become primarily a provincial responsibility—often leading to legal nightmares and fractious relationships. Nonetheless, certain characteristics or principles are common to all jurisdictions in Canada: freedom of association; the existence of labour relations boards; specifically stated unfair labour practices; common broad objectives and philosophy and the right to strike—except for "essential" public sector jobs.

Freedom of Association

Under Section 2, Clause 2 (d), of the *Canadian Charter of Rights and Freedoms* (the *Charter*), every Canadian has the constitutional right to freedom of association.[11] With respect to labour issues, the courts have interpreted **freedom of association** to mean the right of all employees to choose the group, association, or

Yellow-dog contracts: Signed employer–employee agreements prohibiting a worker from joining a union or engaging in union activities.

Blacklists: Lists of union sympathizers employers would not hire.

P.C. 1003: An Order-in-Council (1944) that defined the rights and obligations of both unions and employees, while implementing procedures for settling contract disputes.

Rand formula: An arbitration ruling, named after Justice Rand, which dictated that all employees pay union dues, whether or not they become union members.

HRDC—HR Links
Provided is a review of the Canada Labour Code and provincial/federal "Your Legal Right" fact sheets.

Freedom of association: A legal term which in labour relations has come to mean the right of an employee to choose the group or association that will negotiate on his or her behalf with regard to wages and working conditions.

union that will negotiate on their behalf with regard to wages and working conditions. This basic right to join a union is also mirrored in the various provincial labour relations acts. For example, Section 5(1) of the Manitoba Relations Act states that every employee has the right:[12]

(a) to be a member of a union;

(b) to participate in the activities of that union; and

(c) to participate in the organization of a union.

There are some who believe that this right of association should also allow workers the right *not* to join a union. They advocate **right to work legislation,** which commonly refers to laws that prohibit unions from acting as the exclusive bargaining agent for a group of workers and that allow employees the "right" to work regardless of whether or not they are union members.

In the U.S., at least 21 states have enacted "right to work" laws. In these states, employees are not legally required to join a union. Understandably, this has led to a large decline in union membership (now only about 10 percent of U.S. nonagricultural workers belong to a union as opposed to 33 percent in Canada) and remains a major source of irritation between U.S. labour and management. Unions, both in Canada and the U.S., have interpreted this legislation as a legalized form of "union busting."

Canadian legislation has not, thus far, adopted this right to work principle. Since 1982, four major labour cases relating to freedom of association have been referred to the Supreme Court of Canada. The courts have consistently ruled that forced union membership is an infringement of an individual's rights under the Charter and provincial rights legislation. But they have further ruled that this infringement is legally justified for the protection of union security. Thus, in almost all situations, employees are required to be represented by the union and pay the required union dues. In rare cases where employees are allowed not to join the union—usually on conscientious or religious grounds—the employer is still required by law to deduct union dues and remit to the union under the Rand formula discussed above.[13]

Labour Relations Boards

Labour relations boards are independent tribunals that have the legal power to interpret and apply labour laws within their respective jurisdictions. They comprise government appointees, usually representing labour and management, with a neutral chairperson. Labour relations boards have wide-ranging authority to deal with labour law violations and unfair labour practices. In addition, they can make rulings on issues such as whether or not a union should be allowed into an organization, the appropriate size of a bargaining unit, and what employees should be in the unit. Labour relations board decisions have the same effect and authority as court orders. In most cases, they can even impose a first contract if it becomes apparent that either side is refusing to bargain in good faith. The use of labour relations boards, with their ability to be flexible, keeps a whole range of disputes from becoming bogged down in the courts. While they have

Right to work legislation: Laws that prohibit unions from acting as the exclusive bargaining agent for a group of workers and that allow employees the "right" to work regardless of whether or not they are union members.

HR Web Wisdom

http: www.pearsoned.ca/mondy

Workers, Unions and Choice
An analysis of the national industrial relations climate and key cases concerning workers' legal right to join or not to join a union are provided.

Labour relations boards: Independent tribunals with the legal power to interpret and apply labour laws within a jurisdiction.

been criticized on occasion for being too pro-management or too pro-labour, generally labour relations boards have acted in the best interests of both parties by providing more timely resolution to disputes and labour law violations.

Unfair Labour Practices

Unfair labour practices are specifically defined in the various jurisdictional labour codes. They prohibit both management and unions from interfering in the collective bargaining process. The following excerpts from the Canada Labour Code, (which applies to industries under federal jurisdiction) show the sorts of practices deemed unfair:[14]

- Section 94. (1): "No employer or person acting on behalf of an employer shall

    (a) participate in or interfere with the formation or administration of a trade union or the representation of employees by a trade union...."

- Section 94. (3): "No employer or person acting on behalf of an employer shall

    (a) refuse to employ...transfer, lay off...any person... because this person... (i) is or proposes to become...a member, officer, or representative of a trade union...."

- Section 95. "No trade union or person acting on behalf of a trade union shall

    (c) participate in or interfere with the formation or administration of an employers' organization."

Unfair labour practices: Practices defined in the various labour codes that prohibit both employers and unions from interfering in the collective bargaining process.

Broad Objectives and Common Philosophy

Several broad objectives characterize the Canadian labour movement as a whole: [15]

- to secure and, if possible, improve the living standards and economic status of its members;

- to enhance and, if possible, guarantee individual security against threats and contingencies that might result from market fluctuations, technological change, or management decisions;

- to influence power relations in the social system in ways that favour and do not threaten union gains and goals;

- to create mechanisms to guard against the use of arbitrary and capricious policies and practices in the workplace.

The underlying goal of the labour movement is to promote organizational democracy in an atmosphere of social dignity, while improving the economic and social situation of all individuals, especially those who work in lower-paying jobs. For example, consider the case of this single parent who destroyed her health working nights for minimum wage:

I get behind on bills and we eat a lot of cheap meals. My kids wear second-hand clothing and ride second-hand bikes. They take a lot of abuse from other kids because of it. . . We don't go out to movies or dinner or even to the Dairy Queen, it's just not in our budget.[16]

This is the type of person the labour movement would like to reach.

The Right to Strike

In the private sector, and in some public sector jobs, unions have the legal right to strike, which is embodied in jurisdictional legislation as we will discuss further in Chapter 15. However, in the public sector (both provincial and federal) some "essential" government workers—police and hospital workers, for example—cannot legally take strike action. Since collective bargaining rights in the public sector vary across jurisdictions, each jurisdiction has established its own list of essential groups or occupations. Nonetheless, any restrictions of this nature limit union bargaining power and are a major source of union frustration and militancy. As a result, despite decades of experience and the large numbers of employees involved (over 70 percent of public servants belong to a union), labour relations within the public sector remains one of the most contentious areas of union activity—a situation made even worse by budgetary constraints.

Union Structures

Over time, the labour movement has developed a complex structure of organizations, from local unions to the principal Canadian federation, the Canadian Labour Congress (CLC). Each level has its own officers and ways of managing its affairs.

The Local Union

Local union: The basic element in the structure of the Canadian labor movement.

Craft union: A union typically composed of members of a particular trade or skill.

Industrial union: A union that generally consists of all the workers in a particular industry. Type of work and skill level are not usually a condition of membership.

The basic element in the union structure is the **local union** (or simply, the local). To the individual union member, it is the most important level in the structure of organized labour.

There are two general types of local unions—craft and industrial— although in many cases the distinction has become rather blurred. A **craft union**, such as the Bricklayers Mason Independent Union of Canada, is typically composed of members of a particular trade or skill. Members usually acquire their job skills through an apprenticeship training program. An **industrial union**, such as United Auto Workers or the Canadian Union of Postal Workers, generally consists of all the workers in a particular industry. The type of work or level of skill are not usually a condition of membership in this type of union.

The local union's functions are many and varied. Through the local, the individual deals with the employer on a day-to-day basis. Administering the collective bargaining agreement and representing workers in handling grievances are two important activities. Other functions include keeping the membership informed about labour issues; promoting increased membership, maintaining effective contact with the national or federated union, and, when appropriate, negotiating with management at the local level.

The Independent Union

There are approximately 1000 local unions in Canada. About 300 labour unions are independent: that is, they are not affiliated with any national or federated union organization. Most independent unions have relatively few members. In total, independent unions represent less than 5 percent of the unionized workforce. Most locals tend to be affiliated with a national or federated union organization.

The National (or International) Union

Generally, local unions have the option to join or become a local chapter of a national or international association (if one exists). A **national union** refers to a Canadian parent organization composed of local unions, which it charters. An international union is a similar organization that crosses national borders; as the term is used in Canada, it refers to U.S.-based unions. The local union, however, is still responsible for the day-to-day issues that affect workers. This structure has sometimes been referred to as *bottom-up unionism*. The purpose of the national body is to improve bargaining strength and to provide coordination, policies and guidelines for all of the local groups. The local union—not the individual worker—holds membership in the national union. The national union is supported financially by each local union, whose contribution is based on its membership size. National unions that have no other affiliation account for about 20 percent of Canada's total union membership. Two examples of national unions are the Communications, Energy and Paperworkers Union of Canada (about 144 000 members) and the Industrial Wood and Allied Workers of Canada (about 43 000 members).

National union: A Canadian parent organization composed of local unions, which it charters.

The Union Federation

Most unions in Canada have chosen to join a federation. A **federation** is a union of unions representing the broad interest of the labour movement. There are numerous provincial, national, and international federations. The largest Canadian national federation is the Canadian Labour Congress (CLC) which represents some 2 million workers. About 40 percent of CLC members also belong to the American Federation of Labor and Congress of Industrial Organizations (AFL-CIO), the largest U.S. federation.

Federation: A union of unions representing the broad interest of the labour movement.

The CLC represents the interests of labour and its member national unions at the broadest level. The federation, for example, does not engage in collective bargaining. Its major purpose is to provide the channel by which member unions can cooperate to pursue common objectives and attempt to resolve internal issues faced by organized labour. According to the CLC, its major responsibilities are to: [17]

- promote decent wages and working conditions;
- lobby to improve health and safety laws;
- lobby for fair taxes and strong social programs;
- lobby for and develop job training and job creation programs;

- work for social equality and to end racism and discrimination;
- promote solidarity between workers in Canada and other countries.

The CLC is financed by its member national unions and is governed by a national convention, attended by some 2500 delegates, which meets every three years. The structure of the CLC, with its national, provincial, and local representation, is shown in Figure 14-1. Note that it is bound together by a series of committees and departments, many with regional representation. While this configuration may seem complex, it must be remembered that the Canadian labour movement is extremely diverse. It is a difficult balancing act to represent the incredible variety of international, national, regional, and local interest groups.

Shop Structures

In Canada, there are three major forms of union representation. A **closed shop** is one in which the employer can hire only union members. Closed shop agreements are common in the shipping and construction industries. When a collective agreement contains a **union shop** clause it means that all employees must become union members as a condition of employment. A third type of representation has been termed the **agency shop**. Sanctioned by the Rand formula discussed above, an agency shop requires all employees to pay dues but not necessarily to join the union. In practice, since they have

Closed shop: A form of union representation in which the employer can hire only union members.

Union shop: A form of union representation in which all employees must become union members as a condition of employment.

Agency shop: A form of union representation in which all employees are required to pay dues but not necessarily to join the union.

Figure 14-1

The Structure of the CLC-Affiliated Portion of the Canadian Labour Movement

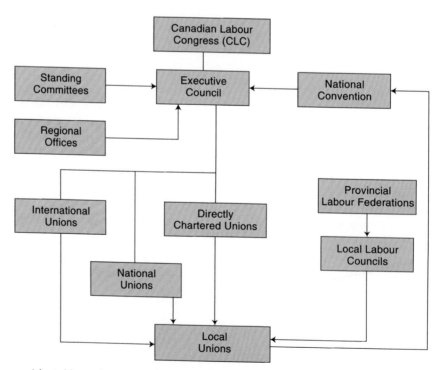

Source: *Adapted from John Crispo,* International Unionism *(Toronto:McGraw-Hill, 1967), p. 167; D.A. Peach and D. Kuechle,* The Practice of Industrial Relations. *(Toronto: McGraw Hill Ryerson, 1985), p. 10; Bureau of Labour Relations Canada,* Directory of Labour Relations in Canada: 1994–1995. *(Ottawa: Human Resources Development Canada), pp. xiii, xx.*

to pay dues anyway, most employees do join in order to have input (however small) into union activities.

It is difficult to determine exactly what portion of collective agreements falls into each of these three categories. According to Work Research Foundation, a small portion of collective agreements are closed shop, slightly more are union shops, and the largest proportion are agency shops.[18]

In the United States, there are proportionately fewer agency shops since they cannot legally exist in states that have "right to work" legislation.

Joining the Union

Individuals join unions for different reasons, which tend to change over time. These may involve job, personal, social, or political considerations. Some of the major reasons include dissatisfaction with management; a desire for improved compensation, job security, and managerial attitudes; need for a social outlet; opportunity for leadership; peer pressure; and the need for an alternative justice system.[18]

Some employees prefer, if possible, not to join a union. First, it costs money to be a union member. Typically, there is an initiation fee followed by dues that must be paid regularly. Second, many employees think that unions are unnecessary. They believe that they shouldn't have to depend on a third party to help satisfy their job-related needs. Third, just as there may be peer pressure in some firms to encourage employees to join the union, in other instances there may be as much pressure against union affiliation. A supportive corporate culture (discussed in Chapter 7) can also reduce the need for a union. If an organization has open communication and employee participation, a third party or union may not be needed as a representative or a protector.

Management Response to Union Organizing

When faced with an organizing initiative, management has three major choices. It can recognize and accept the union voluntarily; institute a policy of nonresistance; or try to resist. In any case, management must follow well-defined guidelines of acceptable behaviour.

Voluntary Recognition

In some instances management can voluntarily recognize a local union as the bargaining unit. In this case, referred to as **voluntary recognition**, there is no need for the local union to apply for certification with the labour relations board. Nonetheless, even when management does not oppose a bid to certify a union and does not seek recourse from a labour relations board, it must abide by certain rules. For example, management must not help form a union or in any way dominate a union. As well, if management voluntarily recognizes one union in lieu of another union (one perhaps more distasteful to the employer) that can prove it has majority support from the employees, then a labour relations board would rule the voluntary recognition invalid.

Voluntary recognition: A situation in which management does not oppose a bid to certify a union and does not seek recourse from a labour relations board.

Policy of Nonresistance

Resisting an attempt to organize a union is not always advantageous. Management must set aside personal feelings and make decisions in the firm's best interest. Unions can, in fact, offer certain benefits to firms. For example, the maritime and construction unions usually provide a ready source of labour from their hiring halls. A firm operating in one of these industries in an area that is strongly unionized may find it advantageous to accept a union in order to obtain qualified workers.

An additional factor is a realistic appraisal of the chances of successful resistance. Even when confident of success, management should consider the effect on morale and productivity of a drawn-out, bitter struggle against the employees' felt need to have a union. One study found, for example, that over the long term, a strategy of cooperation may be in a firm's best interest.[19] Some companies have virtually destroyed any chance of developing a cooperative work culture by resisting the establishment of a union too aggressively.

Resistance to Unions

Although there may be valid reasons for a firm to accept a union, a large percentage of executives would prefer that their companies do not become unionized. In fact, keeping organized labour out is a major goal for many organizations. Resistance to unions is based on many real and perceived disadvantages.

Costs

The compensation paid to union members is generally higher than that for nonunion workers. Moreover, unionization often entails additional labour costs arising from "the high cost of complex, payroll-padding work rules; work stoppages, strikes and slowdowns; lengthy negotiations and the grind of arbitration cases; and layoff by seniority."[20]

The working relationship between labour and management plays an important role in determining the extent of additional costs. Many unions are changing their attitudes, especially with regard to competitive cost issues. For example, some unions now acknowledge that inefficient work rules hurt their members as much as the employer. Costs have also been reduced as strikes become less common. In 1998 there were about 380 work stoppages, due mainly to striking workers.[21] The total number of workers involved in work stoppages accounted for only about 5 percent of all unionized employees. Today, approximately 90 percent of all union–management negotiations result in a signed agreement without a work stoppage. Despite these improved relations, it remains true that union members, in general, are more regulation-oriented and more highly paid than their nonunionized counterparts and thus, generally, employer costs are higher.[22]

Reduced Control over Operations

Typically, managers want to operate without restrictive work rules, which are seen to reduce their authority. There is a widespread perception that managers lose control in unionized workplaces. This belief was certainly true in the past, but changes have occurred on the part of both management and unions. The era when managers expect to have complete control over all aspects of their operation is fast coming to an end, at least in progressive firms. Cooperative management techniques and teamwork have been found to be much more effective. For their part, many union executives are beginning to realize that restrictive work rules do not work. Thus, some contracts are now being rewritten to allow management much more flexibility in the way work is allocated. But the issue of control is still unresolved in many workplaces.

Inability to Reward Superior Performance

Rewarding superior performance in a nonunion organization is, in theory, straightforward. By contrast, in a unionized organization, the compensation paid to each job classification is normally specified by the agreement and usually not based on performance. Although many new approaches are being developed, experience and seniority still appear to form the major criteria for determining pay.[23] With some exceptions, not enough advantage is taken of the opportunity to institute pay-for-performance, especially for employees who are not part of management.[24] On the whole, union negotiators are usually reluctant to agree to such schemes because of a desire to avoid favouritism— a work arrangement under which supervisors can reward their friends or the most subservient workers.

Collective Bargaining and the Certification Process

Collective bargaining is the process that includes organizing a bargaining unit, negotiating wages and conditions for employment, and enforcing the terms of the agreement for members of the bargaining group. The collective bargaining process, which we will address in more detail in the next chapter, begins when a group of employees decide to organize in order to negotiate a collective agreement with their employer. If a union does not exist, employees must form one or join an existing union. In some cases, recognition of a union as a bargaining agent may be acquired by the employer voluntarily agreeing to enter into a collective agreement.[25] However, in most cases a newly formed union must apply to its jurisdictional labour relations board and complete a process called certification, which we discuss below.

Until an organization representing workers is formally recognized or certified, it is usually called an association. Although associations can and do bargain with employers, they are not under the jurisdiction of labour relations boards.[26] Many associations, however, eventually become certified unions. The Nova Scotia Registered Nurses' Association, for example, evolved into a union after widespread and prolonged disagreements with hospital managers. According to labour codes, the key test as to whether an organization of employees may be considered a union is independence from the employer. Some professional employees, although they want the protection of a union, are uncomfortable with the term union, possibly because it has a working-class history. For this reason, professional groups may keep the name "association" even though they are legally certified as unions. In British Columbia alone, for example, there are about 75 certified teachers' "associations."

Collective bargaining: A process that includes organizing a bargaining unit, negotiating wages and conditions for employment, and enforcing the terms of the agreement for members of the bargaining group.

Certification: The formal process by which a union becomes recognized under labour law (within its jurisdiction) as the only bargaining agent (representative) for a group of employees known as a bargaining unit.

Certification means that a union is recognized under labour law as the only bargaining agent (representative) for a group of employees known as a bargaining unit. A bargaining unit may cover the employees in one plant or location, or it may include employees in two or more locations owned by the same employer. The unit may be large or small. Bargaining units, for example, have been known to represent fewer than ten employees.

The certification process requires that employees voluntarily sign membership cards, such as the sample shown in Figure 14-2, indicating they are paid members of a union. A small fee (normally one to five dollars) is all that is necessary for initial union membership in most jurisdictions.

The certification initiative can be taken either by employees or by professional union organizers on behalf of any union. Normally, before a union can be formed, a majority (more than 50 percent) of employees must voluntarily sign membership cards. However, the exact legal percentage of employees that must sign varies by jurisdiction. In New Brunswick, for example, if 60 percent or more sign cards, the labour relations board will normally certify a union without a separate vote. If between 50 and 59 percent sign up, the board has discretionary power in which a vote may or may not be taken.

In the beginning of an election campaign, the union organizers or supporters usually try to keep their objectives secret. If the tactic is successful, they reason that management will have less time to react. Once the attempt becomes known, however, union supporters promote their course more actively.

The manager's role during the campaign is crucial. Managers need to carefully avoid violating the law or engaging in unfair labour practices. Specifically, they should be aware of what can and cannot be done during the organizing campaign. Not only what is said by the manager but *how* it is said becomes very important. Human resource professionals can advise managers and supervisors in these matters. Throughout the campaign, HR professionals should also keep upper management informed about employee attitudes.

Figure 14-2

Sample of Union
Membership Card

Application for Membership in the XXYZZ Manufacturing Co. Employees' Union

I, the undersigned:

i) apply for membership in the above union and agree to abide by its Constitution and By-Laws

ii) hereby tender one dollar ($1.00) as payment for the initiation fee

iii) authorize the union to be my exclusive bargaining agent.

Signed...

On behalf of the above mentioned union, I hereby accept this application and acknowledge receipt of one dollar ($1.00) as payment of the initiation fee.

Signed... on behalf of the union.

Date... 20.......

Theoretically, both union and management are permitted to tell their stories without interference from the other side. At times, the campaign can become quite intense. In fact, some authors have referred to the organizing campaign as a "time of high drama."[27] Once union organizers feel they have sufficient numbers, an application is made to the appropriate labour relations board. The board will then notify management officially of the application and determine whether all the employees included on the proposed membership list are eligible. For example, managers (and sometimes supervisors) or employees who deal with confidential information may be ruled ineligible. In many Canadian jurisdictions, the time between initial application and the board decision is expedited (for example, in Alberta only about 12 days), so that management has little time to react.

Normally, management also has the option of appearing before the labour relations board to argue why certain employees should be excluded. The process of determining eligibility can be extremely important, especially if the vote is close. Loss of a few voting members has, on occasion, defeated attempts to organize. Having decided who is in the "unit" for election purposes, the labour relations board will either certify the union, order that a supervised vote be held, or refuse certification. The action taken depends upon the situation and the jurisdiction. Each case is reviewed separately.

Should a union be certified, management becomes legally required to negotiate a **collective agreement**, or contract, with the union outlining the compensation and working conditions of union members for a specified time period. Furthermore, management is required to *bargain in good faith*: that is, management must be able to show that it is sincerely trying to reach an agreement. Where an employer fails to do so, a union can submit a complaint to its labour relations board, charging bad faith bargaining. What happens next will depend on the jurisdiction. The board may order interest arbitration (discussed in the next chapter) for all or part of the contract, order the employer to reimburse the union for its additional costs, or even impose a "contract retroactive to the date at which, in the board's judgment, it should have started e.g., order back pay."[28]

Collective agreement: A union-management contract outlining the compensation and working conditions of union members for a specified time period.

Interest-based Bargaining

Historically, the employee–employer relationship has been adversarial. Management has often been perceived by employees as having the upper hand, and being in a position to take advantage. Unions evolved as the employee's principal protective agent. Their purpose was to bring about significant changes in employee labour conditions—at the expense of management. Tradition, along with the unwillingness of both parties to change, has led to acrimony, distrust and even violence. Conflict is heightened to an almost warlike state during strikes, lockouts, and negotiations.

Throughout the nineties, there was much debate about this traditional adversarial model. Today, the consensus is that confrontation is no longer productive, necessary, or appropriate. Unions and management must begin to adopt a more cooperative style. Close to two-thirds of Canadians now believe that labour–employer relations no longer need to be confrontational.[29] According to the Work Research Foundation, "adversarial labour relations won't survive global competition."[30] Executives like James Marchant, vice president, human resources, at Canadian Pacific Forest Products Ltd., have also called for a "shared vision."[31]

Unions and management are now just beginning to recognize the need for a more proactive, collaborative orientation toward building an effective working environment.[32] Both managers and employees are coming to the realization that all employees are legitimate stakeholders in the enterprise, and that the financial health of the employer is the only real security for everyone. Thus, progressive labour relations specialists are now promoting alternative collaborative techniques such as interest–based or relationship bargaining.[33] Other terms used in referring to this relatively new approach are mutual gains bargaining, win–win negotiation, and reasoned bargaining. **Interest-based bargaining** focuses on the mutual needs of the bargaining group rather than specifically entrenched positions. Conceptually, it is based on trust and a win–win environment. (See Figure 14-3 for a comparison with a traditional approach). The key point is that if cooperative labour-management relations are to work, both sides must commit themselves to cooperative unionism, often against formidable opposition. Management and unions must develop a common vision and then try to create an environment that fosters collaboration.

Interest-based bargaining: A negotiating process that focuses on the mutual needs of the bargaining group rather than specifically entrenched positions.

Figure 14-3

Interest-Based vs. Traditional Bargaining

INTEREST–BASED BARGAINING	TRADITIONAL BARGAINING
Cooperation and trust: based on an understanding of mutual interests	**Adversarial and mistrust:** based on position and power
Problem–solving: emphasis on win-win options	**Emotional:** based on ideology and subjectivity
Objective: based on data and information	**Positional:** A focus on specifically entrenched positions
Mutual interest: a focus on issues of concern to both parties	**Rigid:** A focus on specific entrenched position. Once the contract is signed, both parties are expected to live with it
Flexible: open to discussion of all options and an understanding that both parties can renegotiate	**Stationary:** The rules dictate the action
Innovation: Change the rules to meet the needs of the situation	**Confrontation:** a focus on exchange of demands. Emphasis on win–lose solutions

Source: Adapted from Human Resources Development Canada, "Workplace Innovations—Dialogue on Changes in the Workplace," http://labour-travail.hrdc-drhc.gc.ca/WIP/english/May95.pdf

The Future of Labour Unions

- **Union approval**. A majority of Canadians—58 percent—say they approve of labour unions. This approval level has remained steady since the early 1970s.

- **Mandatory membership.** Present law allows unions to require that all workers in a company join the union if the majority of workers have chosen that union. 42 percent of Canadians agreed that workers in this situation be required to become members of the union. In essence, the majority of Canadian believe that they should not be required to join a union.

- **Restrictions on bidding for jobs.** Currently, under the law, unions can restrict the bidding for some jobs to companies that have contracts with a particular union. Only 23 percent of Canadians feel that unions should be able to restrict bidding on jobs.

- **Union involvement in nonunion activities.** Compulsory union dues are used primarily for union business, such as collective bargaining. But a portion of union dues is often used for other purposes such as support of a political party. Some 80 percent of Canadians believe that contributions to support "nonunion" activities from union dues should be on a voluntary basis.

- **Dominant expectations.** More than 50 percent of Canadian believe that unions can contribute to the quality of their lives if unions focus on four factors:

    1. Helping to improve pay and working conditions;

    2. Support for problems at work;

    3. Increasing employee training opportunities; and

    4. A focus on labour–employer relations that is non-confrontational.

According to this study, most Canadians approve of unions in principle. In the future, unions will have to change the way they behave—especially regarding their present confrontational style—and the service they provide if the labour movement is gain the full support of Canadians.

Source: *Adapted from Reginald W. Bibby, "Canadians and Unions: A National Reading at the Turn of the New Century," Work Research Foundation: http://www.interlog.com/~wrf/gallup.htm*

HR Web Wisdom

http: www.pearsoned.ca/mondy

Labour Unions—Canadian Opinions
"Canadians and Unions— A National Reading at the Turn of the Century," a report prepared by Dr. Reginald W. Bibby for the Canadian Research Foundation.

The Future of the Canadian Labour Movement

The key issue for Canadian labour relations in the twenty-first century will be cooperation. Cooperative labour–management relationships are complex and controversial. Nonetheless, whatever changes emerge over the next few years,

> ... there will never be one formula or one plan for successful employee relations. The economic system is too complex and the markets demand different solutions to different problems, so likely, there will be both adversarial and co-operative employee relations systems in place for same time. This mix will always be in a state of fluctuation to meet the different circumstances of businesses, industries, and markets.[34]

Even so, new systems of work and labour–management cooperation such as interest-based bargaining, are emerging. But the scope of this trend and the extent to which it will be lasting are difficult to predict. There are no shortcuts. It will take a genuine commitment on the part of both labour and management to stay the course over a long period of time.[35]

While historically, unions have capitalized on employee dissatisfaction and insecurities, the threats to jobs and labour unions over the '90s did not seem to enhance this influence. Rapid changes in the economy and in world trade patterns, and the changing focus of work (more home-based workers and independent contractors, for example), combined with employer responses to even more competitive external environments (e.g., downsizing, introducing new technology, and contracting out) have posed enormous additional challenges for unions. The future of the Canadian labour movement will depend on the ability of unions to adapt to these changing market conditions: "The level of public support that labour unions will know in Canada in the new century will depend largely on the extent to which they are able to demonstrate the themes of freedom, flexibility, and functionality so pervasive in the culture—and expected of unions as well." [36]

Additionally, the future of the labour movement will depend on how unions deal with the plaguing issues of freedom of association, the injustices of compulsory unionism, and the use of union dues to support political parties. According to some experts, the reliance on compulsory unionism, political contributions and confrontation undermine the credibility of trade unions and collective bargaining in the long run. They further argue that "International and Canadian examples show that trade unions can flourish when they respect the rights of workers to exercise freedom of association."[37]

A final consideration is the growth of large international corporations—transnationals. As discussed in the Global Perspective Box, large corporations now have the power to shift their production to the country with lowest wage rates. How will unions and management in Canada respond to this external force? According to one labour expert:

> ... trade unions in this country have traditionally played a broad social role. They very often have filled in when government and society have let down the human side. We will be very cautious in supporting what is viewed as a corporate agenda driven by transnationals whose interests are in deregulation and privatization, not the social welfare of the citizens of this country.[38]

From a management perspective, progressive organizations are moving toward new collaborative systems such as interest-based bargaining. However,

HRM in *ACTION*

Help or Employer Interference?

Sandrine Lepage, one of the workers in the plant, has just come to see the human resource manager, Lonnie Miller, for advice. Apparently, an outside union organizer approached her yesterday and asked her to help with the union organizing effort. Sandrine wants some advice from Lonnie on how she should respond to the union request. Lonnie knows that there have been growing tensions lately and a lot of talk about unions. He has overheard what appear to be private conversations at coffee breaks and in the halls. Lonnie knows that if Sandrine starts working for a union, she will have a lot of influence. She seems to be a natural leader, and Lonnie thinks she is supervisory material.

How should Lonnie react to Sandrine's request?

many employers still cling to the "you're lucky to have a job" principle of labour relations. Despite growing recognition that unions should be involved much earlier in the corporate decision-making process, the adversarial approach is still very much in vogue. For example, according to Professor Morgan, a business strategist at the University of Windsor: "Labour now feels that it is a partner in modern corporation. And yet, when it comes to the time for divvying up the rewards, union members are not treated as partners at all, but as hired hands."[39] Professor Morgan and others predict continued labour strife well into the twenty-first century unless companies truly recognize unions as legitimate parties at the bargaining table.

U.S. Influence on the Canadian Labour Movement

The hundred years bounded by 1860 and 1960 saw very close ties between the Canadian and the American labour movements. But American influence declined rapidly from the 1960s on. A number of Canadian affiliates broke away from their American parents, establishing Canadian unions. By the mid-1990s, fewer than 30 percent of Canada's union members belonged to foreign-based organizations. Perhaps the best-known example of this trend came in the mid-1980s, when the Canadian section of the United Automobile Workers (UAW) established a separate organization, the Canadian Auto Workers Union (CAW).

This trend came about partly because of the perception that Canadian members were paying more into international coffers than they were receiving and partly because of arguments that Canadian unions could better support Canadian interests without interference from an international headquarters. U.S. right-to-work legislation also reduced the influence of American unions.

Today, unionism is much stronger in Canada than in the United States. Given the added competitive forces created by the various free trade agreements, with the resultant losses in unionized jobs, it is likely that the Canadian labour movement will continue to move away from international affiliations as Canadian unions strive to protect jobs at home.

Although unionism has been under pressure everywhere, nowhere else has it declined as in the U.S.[40] This shift has influenced some major internationals or transnationals to rethink their locations. For example, Mercedes-Benz chose to locate its production facilities not in Germany but in the United States, with its lower level of unionism.[41] In part, this company was trying to avoid Germany's strict unionized work regulations and high union wage rates. Some argue that these types of global decisions by transnationals will become a threat to unionism around the world as Canada and other countries are eventually to follow the pattern of the U.S. to compete for transnational jobs. [42]

SUMMARY

1. **Briefly describe the history and significance of the Canadian labour movement.**

   The history of the Canadian labour movement helps to clarify why the management/union relationship has traditionally been fractious and adversarial. It was not until after 1926, when progress in American labour legislation began to be copied, that unions in Canada gained a firm foothold. Order-in-Council P.C. 1003 spelled out rights and obligations for unions. The historic Rand formula dictated that all employees pay union dues, whether or not they become union members. This arbitration ruling encouraged employees to join unions. Today the federal government and all provinces and territories have labour laws. Labour relations is primarily a provincial responsibility. At first provincial laws mirrored federal legislation, but amendments have gradually increased the differences among jurisdictions.

2. **Identify key characteristics of the labour environment.**

   All jurisdictions in Canada guarantee freedom of association and define certain labour practices as unfair. All jurisdictions have labour relations boards. The labour movement shares the common basic goal of promoting organizational democracy in an atmosphere of social dignity, while improving the economic and social situation of all individuals, especially those who work in lower-paying jobs. Unions attempt to secure and enhance their members' living standards, to guarantee individual security, to exert social influence in favour of unions, and to create mechanisms that guard against arbitrary workplace policies. Canadian workers, except for those in "essential" public sector jobs, have the right to strike.

3. **Outline basic elements of the union structure.**

   The local union is the basic element in the structure of the Canadian labour movement. The local union deals with the employer on a day-to-day basis and administers the collective bargaining agreement. A craft union is typically composed of members of a particular trade or skill. An industrial union generally consists of all the workers in a particular industry. Some unions are independent (unaffiliated). Others join or become a local chapter of a national or international union (association). Most unions are members of a federation: a union of unions representing the broad interests of the labour movement. The Canadian Labour Congress (CLC) is the largest Canadian federation. In Canada, there are three major forms of union representation. In a closed shop, the employer can hire only union members. In a union shop, employees must become union members as a condition of employment. In an agency shop, employees are required to pay dues but not necessarily to join the union.

4. **Explain why some employees voluntarily join unions while others tend to avoid joining a union.**

   Employees may join a union because of dissatisfaction with management, a desire for improved compensation and working conditions, the need for a social outlet, an opportunity for leadership, peer pressure, or the need for an alternative justice system. Workers will tend to resist or avoid joining a union in organizations in which management communicates effectively and deals fairly with employee needs. Other reasons include dislike for any third-party intervention, the added expense of union dues, and peer pressure.

5. **Describe the three major management responses to union organizing.**

   Faced with a union organizing initiative, management can recognize and accept the union voluntarily; institute a policy of nonresistance; or can try to resist. In any case, management must follow well-defined guidelines of acceptable behaviour. Many executives would prefer that their companies not become unionized and attempt to resist union initiatives. The rationale includes increased costs (both real and perceived), reduced control over operations, and the inability to reward for superior performance.

6. **Define collective bargaining and explain the certification process.**

   Collective bargaining is a process that includes organizing a bargaining unit, negotiating wages and conditions for employment, and enforcing the terms of the agreement for members of the bargaining group. It begins when a group of employees decides to organize. Certification is the formal process by which a union becomes recognized under labour law as the only bargaining agent for a group of employees known as a bargaining unit. The certification process requires that employees (normally the majority) voluntarily sign membership cards. Once a union is certified by a labour board, management is legally required to negotiate a collective agreement.

7. Explain the rationale for interest-based bargaining.

Historically, the employee–employer relationship has been adversarial. Tradition, along with the unwillingness of both management and unions to change, has led to acrimony, distrust, and even violence. Today, the consensus is that confrontation is no longer productive, necessary, or appropriate. Both managers and employees are slowly realizing that all employees have a stake in the enterprise and that the health of the employer is the only real security for everyone. Thus, progressive labour relations specialists are now promoting techniques such as interest-based or relationship bargaining, focusing on the mutual needs of the bargaining group rather than entrenched positions.

8. Describe major issues that will influence the future of labour–management relations.

A key issue of Canadian labour relations in the twenty-first century will be cooperation. Although there appears to be a tendency toward cooperation, it is difficult to predict how lasting it will be. There will probably be both adversarial and co-operative employee relations systems in place for some time. Nevertheless, new systems of work and labour–management cooperation are gradually emerging. The future of the Canadian labour movement will also depend on the ability of unions to adapt to changing market conditions, the plaguing issue of freedom of association, the injustices of compulsory unionism, and the use of union dues to support political parties. The growth of transnationals, and the response from Canadian unions and management, will dramatically affect the labour movement.

QUESTIONS FOR REVIEW

1. Describe the key developments in the history of the Canadian labour movement in Canada.

2. Briefly explain the significance of Order-in-Council P.C. 1003 and the Rand formula.

3. Identify and briefly describe the key principles of labour law in all Canadian jurisdictions and the philosophy and goals of the labour movement.

4. Explain why the Canadian courts have not adopted the right to work principle.

5. How do labour relations in the public sector differ from those in the private sector?

6. Distinguish between an independent union, national union, and federation. Describe three major forms of union representation.

7. Why do some employees want to join a labour union while others prefer to avoid union representation?

8. When faced with a union organizing initiative, what are three major management choices?

9. What is collective bargaining? Briefly explain the certification process.

10. Why might adversarial labour relations be practised in Canada for the foreseeable future?

11. Explain the rationale for interest-based bargaining.

12. What key issues will influence the future of labour–management relations?

An Experiential Exercise

Union organizing activity is often met with mixed feelings by everyone affected. Management is usually opposed to such efforts. Beatriz Morrison, the production manager of the heavy motors division of MNP Corporation, knows that upper management does not care much for unions. They believe this unionizing effort is not good for anybody involved with this company and that the union wants to turn the employees against them. Upper management also believes that a union will destroy the company's competitive edge, something that they feel has happened in many other firms. The firm must do everything possible to circumvent this union organizing effort, but it must do so in line with Labour Relations Board guidelines.

Beatriz thought, "I've got to meet with Ray Olynyk, the supervisor over in Section 4, today. He is a little too eager about stopping the union. We don't want this union, but we also don't want the Labour Relations Board breathing down our necks. Even indirect threats can get us into trouble. Ray must understand the ground rules. Obviously, we don't want this union, but no supervisor can threaten loss of jobs or benefits, or fire anybody. I'm going to tell Ray that if his employees ask his opinion, he can set out the pros and cons, but he must be careful."

One student will play the production manager and another will play the supervisor. The rest should observe carefully. The instructor will provide the participants with additional information.

Maybe I Will and Maybe I Won't

Yesterday Steve Harding was offered a job as an operator trainee with Gem Manufacturing. He had recently graduated from Milford High School in a small town in Northern Manitoba. Steve had no college aspirations, so upon graduation, he moved to Calgary to look for a job.

Steve's immediate supervisor spent only a short time with him and then turned him over to Gaylord Rader, an experienced operator, for training. After they had talked for a short time, Gaylord asked, "Have you given any thought to joining our union? You'll like our members."

Steve had not considered this. Moreover, he had never associated with union members, and his parents had never been members either. At Milford High his teachers had not talked much about unions. The fact that this union operated under the Rand formula meant nothing to him. Steve replied, "I don't know. Maybe. Maybe not."

The day progressed much the same way, with several people asking Steve virtually the same question. They were all friendly, but there seemed to be a barrier that separated Steve from the other workers. One worker looked Steve right in the eyes and said, "You're going to join, aren't you?" Steve still did not know, but he was beginning to lean in that direction.

After the buzzer rang to end the shift, Steve went to the washroom. Just as he entered, David Clements, the union steward, also walked in. After they exchanged greetings, David said, "I hear that you're not sure about wanting to join our union. You and everyone else reaps the benefits of the work we've done in the past. It doesn't seem fair for you to be rewarded for what others have done, if you're not willing to do a bit yourself. Tell you what, why don't you join us down at the union hall tonight for our beer bust? We'll discuss it more then."

Steve nodded and finished cleaning up. "That might be fun," he thought.

Questions

1. What are the reasons why Steve might want or not want to join the union?

2. How are the other workers likely to react toward Steve if he chooses not to join? Discuss.

3. If he decides not to join the union, will he have to pay union dues?

CHAPTER

15

Collective Bargaining

CHAPTER OBJECTIVES

1. Discuss the effect of external environmental factors on the collective bargaining process.

2. Identify the various types of union–management relationships that affect the collective bargaining process.

3. Describe the collective bargaining structure and process.

4. Describe what both labour and management do as they prepare for negotiations.

5. Explain the process of negotiating.

6. Identify and describe union and management ways to overcome breakdowns in negotiations.

7. Describe what is involved in ratifying and administering a collective agreement.

8. Discuss the future of collective bargaining.

Barbara Washington, the chief union negotiator for MBI Inc. was meeting with company representatives on a new contract. Both the union team and management had been preparing for this encounter for a long time. Barbara's deep concern was whether or not union members would support a strike vote if one were called. Sales for the industry were generally down because of imports. In fact, there had even been some layoffs at competing firms. The union members' attitude, she thought, could be described as "Get what you can for us, but don't rock the boat." She hoped, however, that skilful negotiating could win concessions from management.

In the first session, Barbara's team presented its demands to management. The team had determined that pay was the main issue, and demanded a 10-percent increase spread over three years. Management countered by saying that since sales were down it could not afford to provide any pay raises. After much heated discussion, both sides agreed to reevaluate their positions and meet again in two days. Barbara met with her negotiating team in private, and it was decided to decrease the salary demand slightly. The team felt that the least they could accept was an eight-percent raise.

At the next meeting, Barbara presented the revised demands to management. They were not well received. Liam Thompson, the director of industrial relations, began by saying, "We cannot afford a pay increase in this contract, but we will make every attempt to ensure that no layoffs occur. Increasing wages at this time will virtually guarantee a reduction in the work force."

Barbara's confidence collapsed. She knew that there was no way that the general membership was willing to accept layoffs and that a strike vote would be virtually impossible to obtain. She asked for a recess to review the new proposal.

Barbara's experience is common for unionized businesses in Canada. Although there is some movement toward a more cooperative approach to negotiating labour contracts, in the main, union and management negotiators still rely on an adversarial approach. Canadians, on average, spend more time out of work because of strikes and lockouts than workers in any of the other major industrial (G7) countries. This traditional "win–lose" technique pits management against labour, so that each side is concerned mainly with its own interests.

We devote the first portion of the chapter to the external and internal environmental factors affecting the collective bargaining process. This is followed by a review of the various union–management relationships, a description of the collective bargaining structure and process, and an explanation of how labour and management prepare for negotiations. Next, we address key bargaining issues, the process of negotiating, and overcoming breakdowns in negotiations. Then we discuss ratification and administration of a collective agreement. A section on the future of collective bargaining concludes this chapter.

The Collective Bargaining Environment

Recall that we defined collective bargaining as a process that includes the organizing of a bargaining unit, negotiating wages and conditions for employment, and enforcing the terms of the agreement for members of the bargaining group. The collective bargaining process is fundamental to management–labour relations in Canada, affecting about one-third of all Canadian workers.

In 1999, for example, at least 250 collective agreements affected the working conditions and livelihood of some 400 000 workers.[1] The results of these collective agreements were determined by both external and internal environmental factors.

External Factors

External environmental factors are conditions over which the bargaining unit or company have little control. The 1990s saw several prevalent changes:[2]

- Competitive business-led initiatives toward "lean production" and resulting pressures to restructure, downsize, and contract out.;

- A renewed competitive emphasis on product quality and improved distribution channels;

HR Web Wisdom

http: www.pearsoned.ca/ mondy

Worker Representation and Protection in the New Economy
A review and analysis is provided of the present state of collective bargaining.

- A focus on internal cost strategies;
- Increased international competition and globalization of production;
- The ability of newly industrialized countries to secure major portions of production capacity—particularly in the heavily unionized manufacturing sector;
- A movement toward labour-saving technology;
- Deregulation in such areas as transportation, communications, and finance;
- Continued public demands for municipal, provincial, and federal governments to downsize and reduce expenditures;
- Growth in entrepreneurship and the small business sector.

These external environmental factors had a dramatic impact on the Canadian labour movement, the traditional employer–employee relationship and the resulting collective bargaining process.

Longer contracts. Contracts gradually became longer, in an attempt to establish a more secure workplace and business environment. In 1991 the average contract lasted about 18 months. By 1997, the average contract duration had increased dramatically to 36 months. Longer contracts led to a lower volume of collective negotiation: in 1996, the Workplace Information Directorate of HRDC reported about 350 settlements (covering about 775 000 workers)—the lowest since it began collecting information in 1978.[3]

Union uncertainty and fragmentation. Unions became uncertain how best to represent current and future workers in evolving workplaces. Union responses to business-led strategy, such as lean production and workplace reorganization, became polarized and fragmented. According to HRDC, some unions chose to resist management initiatives, others passively cooperated, and still others developed a cooperative strategy.[4]

Erosion of union bargaining power. Downsizing, technological and organizational change, and the drive toward the "high performance workplace" occurred "with little or no consultation with unions, and certainly with little or no willingness to respond to issues of key interest to workers."[5] The erosion of union power was reflected in a gradual decrease in the number of strikes and lockouts—decreasing from some 600 per year in the early 1990s to about 300 per year by the later half of the 90s.[6]

Reduction in union jobs and wages. Lean production and the shift of corporate functions to outside suppliers led to the gradual conversion of stable, unionized jobs into more precarious, low-paying jobs with small employers in fiercely competitive markets. According to the Conference Board of Canada, over the 1990s, nonunionized staff earned higher wage increases than unionized staff. By the late 1990s unionized wage settlements averaged about 1.5 percent; non unionized wage increases were in the 3-percent range.[7]

Increased inequality of wages. According to the OECD Outlook, by the mid-1990s about 24 percent of all Canadians were employed in low-paying jobs (defined as earnings less than two-thirds of the average wage)—the highest proportion of any advanced country outside of the U.S.[8] The gradual shift to a nonunionized workforce increased the inequality of pay among workers. In addition, the largest nonunion pay increases reflected market demands. According to the Conference Board of Canada, companies attempted to maintain or reduce overall salary expenses and at the same time reward star performers. Skilled, professional, and management employees received higher increases at the expense of unskilled jobs.[9]

Mounting worker insecurity and stress. Workers who remained after the restructuring, downsizing and layoffs were working longer hours and experiencing marked increases in stress. By the end of the decade, almost one in five employees were working more than 50 hours per week. Many working Canadians—particularly in dual income families—reported increased stress levels and struggled to balance their work and family life.[10]

HRDC—HR Links
This site provides information and publications on innovative workplace practices over the '90s.

Innovative or adaptive workplace practices. Over the 1990s, there were strong social and economic pressures for management and especially unions to develop innovative practices in their collective agreements.[11] Examples are highlighted in the Trends & Innovations box.

Internal Factors

In addition to the external environment, collective bargaining is also affected by internal factors—forces or behaviour that can be controlled by a bargaining unit or company. Within this context, there are several possible types of union–management relationships:

1. **Conflict.** Each challenges the other's actions and motivation; cooperation is nonexistent; uncompromising attitudes and union militancy are the norm.

2. **Armed truce.** Each views the other as antagonistic, but tries to avoid head-on conflict; bargaining obligations and contract provisions are strictly interpreted.

3. **Power bargaining.** Management accepts the union; each side tries to gain advantage from the other.

4. **Accommodation.** Each tolerates the other in a "live and let live" atmosphere and attempts to reduce conflict without eliminating it.

5. **Cooperation.** Each side accepts the other, and both work together to resolve human resource and production problems as they occur.

6. **Collusion.** Both "cooperate" to the point of adversely affecting the legitimate interests of employees, other businesses in the industry, and the public. This relationship may involve conniving to control markets, supplies, and prices illegally and/or unethically.[12]

The internal environment and the quality of union–management relations can vary over time. The first three types of relationships are generally unsatisfactory, collusion is unacceptable, and cooperation has been rare in the past.

TRENDS and INNOVATIONS

Innovative and Adaptive Workplace Practices

During the years 1995 and 1996, Human Resources Development Canada (HRDC) reported more than 600 settlements in large bargaining units (at least 500 employees) across Canada. Almost 70 percent of these bargaining units reported more than one innovative or adaptive practice. A vast majority of agreements (more than 80 percent) included adaptive changes in compensation and working conditions. Here are just a few examples of the current trend toward innovative practices in collective agreements reported by HRDC.

Gain sharing The International Brotherhood of Electrical Workers (IBEW) and the BC Gas Utility Ltd. negotiated an employee gain-sharing program. This fostered teamwork and provided the opportunity for both employees and the employer to benefit from worker contributions.

Bonuses Harbour Castle Westin and its union settlement included a performance bonus based on employee attendance records, hotel's quarterly financial objective, guest satisfaction study scores and employees' department safety record. The Alberta Wheat Pool and Grain Services union negotiated a performance enhancement program providing for lump-sum bonuses based on the achievement of a specified return on investment.

Performance incentives The United Steelworkers of America negotiated an income-sharing plan designed to reward employees during periods of profitability. The Communications, Energy and Paperworkers Union agreed to develop an incentive plan based on rewarding performance in achieving specified business objectives, including environmental, health, and safety objectives.

Hours of work The Professional Association of Medical Technologies agreed to implement a four-day week (32 hours), with prorated benefits such as vacation entitlements and sick leave. This provision added flexibility for workers not wanting to work the traditional five-day week and reduced the number of potential layoffs. The Canadian Auto Workers (CAW) agreed to a system of time off in lieu of overtime pay. Auto makers benefited from reduced overtime expenses and workers benefited from the need for additional employees.

Training The Communications, Energy and Paperworkers Union of Canada negotiated a training program for laid-off workers. The International Association of Machinists and Aerospace Workers (IAMAW) negotiated payment of training premiums for workers who delivered on-the-job training. In addition, premiums or incentives were paid for recognized skill-related certificates.

Source: Human Resources Development Canada, "Workplace Innovations Overview—1996," 5: http://labour-travail.hrdc-drhc.gc.ca/wip/publications.html-ssi; and "Workplace Innovations—Dialogue on Changes in the Workplace," 1995, 1: http://labour-travail.hrdc-drhc.gc.ca/WIP/english/June96.pdf

But there are some signs this relationship is changing. Typically, Canadian union–management relationships have been characterized by some form of accommodation—as was the case for MBI Inc. in the opening vignette. However, as we have noted, a trend toward cooperation has grown as joint economic survival has become all-important.

The Collective Bargaining Process

The term *collective bargaining* is frequently prefaced with terms such as companywide, industrywide, or multiemployer, which serve to specify more precisely the structure of collective bargaining. **Companywide bargaining** refers to collective negotiations that takes place between a company with many plants and (typically) a single union representing employees of a particular craft or skill. The terms and conditions negotiated are generally uniform throughout the company. **Industrywide bargaining** refers to negotiations that cover an entire industry, while **multiemployer bargaining** takes place between a union and a group or association of employers (hence the term *association bargaining*). Most contract bargaining is carried out under the companywide structure, as was the case in the opening vignette. Multiemployer or industrywide bargaining is rare.

Even though collective bargaining is widely practised, there is no standard format of what to do or how to do it. In fact, diversity is probably the most prominent characteristic. The collective bargaining process, in general, is shown in Figure 15-1. Depending on the relationship between the parties, bargaining may be relatively simple or may entail a long, tense struggle. Success, for both sides, requires good communication skills. The following tips can lead to successful collective bargaining for managers and unions:

1. **Prepare.** Don't underestimate the importance of the first preparatory, non-adversarial meeting between labour and management representatives. Use this opportunity to set the ground rules for future sessions.

2. **Document.** Carefully document each meeting because accurate, well-organized notes can be quite useful in initial, and subsequent, contract negotiations.

3. **Research.** Within the bounds of law and propriety, develop a personal profile of each member of the committee who will take part in the collective process.

4. **Collaborate.** Accept negotiators as peers; never underestimate them.

5. **Communicate.** Maintain strong communications with individuals who are most affected by the contract and who best know the issues being discussed.

As shown in Figure 15-1, the first step in the collective bargaining process is preparing for negotiations. This step is often extensive and ongoing for both union and management. After the issues to be negotiated have been determined, the two sides confer to reach a mutually acceptable contract. Although breakdowns in negotiations can occur, both labour and management have

Companywide bargaining: Collective negotiations that takes place between a company with many plants and (typically) a single union representing employees of a particular craft or skill.

Industrywide bargaining: Collective negotiations that cover an entire industry.

Multiemployer bargaining: Collective negotiations that take place between a union and a group or association of employers.

tools and arguments that can be used to convince the other side to accept their views. Eventually management and the union reach an agreement that defines the rules of work for the duration of the contract. The final two steps are formalizing the agreement, usually by a ratification vote by the union membership, and administering it.

Note that an important part of collective bargaining is the actual administration of the agreement over the term of the contract. As well, note the feedback loop from Administration back to Preparing for Negotiation. Collective bargaining is a continuous and dynamic process, and preparation for the next round of negotiations often begins the moment a contract is signed.

In today's changing environment, human resource managers can play an important role in the bargaining process in both nonunionized and unionized workplaces. In a nonunionized organization, the HR professional usually

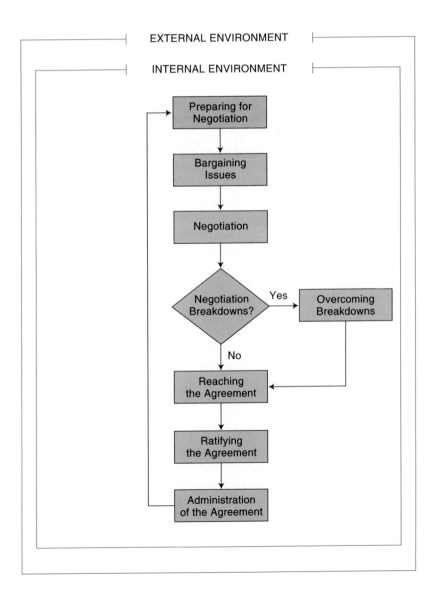

Figure 15-1

The Collective Bargaining Process

deals with employees individually and salary is the major issue. But the HR professional can take on a broader role. For example, innovative and responsive policies can be initiated with varying degrees of worker involvement. Such programs might include employee empowerment, quality initiatives, gain sharing, profit sharing or self-directed teams.

When a firm is unionized, the human resource manager's role tends to change significantly. The human resource manager must deal with a union organizational structure consisting of union stewards and business agents, rather than with individual employees. The human resource manager will most likely administer the contract and therefore should play an integral role in resolving contractual issues. According to one veteran negotiator, a capable human resource manager is the ideal person to negotiate the contract.[13]

Collective Bargaining Provisions
Provided is a selective list of collective bargaining provisions.

Because the role of first-line supervisors is crucial, the human resource manager must maintain close contact with them before, during, and after collective bargaining. First-line supervisors administer the contract on a day-to-day basis and know whether or not it is working well. A knowledgeable human resource manager can limit animosity and avoid the "stick-it-to-'em" mentality. Human resource managers who play an active role in collective bargaining, then, can help to make the process operate more smoothly, both during and after negotiations.

Preparing for Negotiations

Prior to beginning negotiations, both the management and the union team must prepare positions and accomplish certain tasks. During this stage, the psychological aspects of collective bargaining become evident. The psychological challenge is to approach an often adversarial process in a constructive manner. It is "a situation that is fundamental to law, politics, business, and government, because out of the clash of ideas, points of view, and interests come agreement, consensus and justice."[14]

Those involved in the collective bargaining process will be matching wits, will experience victory as well as defeat, and will almost always resolve their differences, resulting in a contract. The role of those who meet at the bargaining table involves the mobilization and the management of aggression. Thus, their personalities have a direct effect on what can be accomplished and how quickly agreement can be reached. Problems can be compounded by differences in experience and educational backgrounds. Finally, the longer, more involved, and intense the bargaining sessions are, the greater the emotional strain on the participants.'

Prior to the first bargaining session, the negotiators should study the culture, climate, history, present economic state, and wage and benefits structure of the organization and of similar organizations. Since a typical labour agreement now lasts about three years, negotiators should devise a contract that is usable both now and in the future. This consideration is important for both management and labour, but in fact both sides often discover during the term of an agreement that contract provisions need to be added, deleted, or modified. Because it is extremely difficult to amend a signed contract, these items usually become proposals to be addressed in the next round of negotiations.

There can be a "reopener" provision in a contract, however, that allows either side to reopen negotiations at a specified time or under special conditions, prior to the end of the contract. For example, the faculty at the University of New Brunswick (UBE) ratified a contract that paid wages to plus or minus 2 percent of the average pay in 14 other Canadian universities. There was a reopener clause, however, so that if another provincial government were to cut university wages substantially, UNB's faculty could negotiate another pay arrangement.

Bargaining issues may encompass anything that affects the workplace: wages, hours, duties, work schedules, lunch and rest periods, safety. . . . In fact any item or activity that is not prohibited by criminal or civil law can be negotiated. Some contracts, for example, even contain provisions about the price of meals in the company cafeteria. A listing of major collective bargaining provisions is provided in Figure 15-2.

Contracts must also meet certain provisions set out in the applicable federal or jurisdictional Industrial or Labour Relations Act. While the acts vary somewhat, many of the requirements are similar. Typically, every collective agreement must recognize the union and the employer as exclusive bargaining agents. That is, no individual represented by a union can make special deals. Every agreement must contain a clause prohibiting strikes and lockouts while the contract is in force, and there are rules regarding the length and the starting date of contracts. As well, every collective agreement usually provides for binding arbitration, should the parties wish to prevent a strike.[15]

A responsive union must continually gather information about membership needs and attitudes. This is typically the responsibility of the **union steward**—an employee elected by union members in his or her work area who represents their interests. The union steward is normally in the best position to collect this information, funneling information up through the union's chain of command to where the data are compiled and analyzed. In most cases stewards are not paid for their union work.

The many interrelated tasks that management must accomplish are presented in Figure 15-3. In this example, management allows approximately six months to prepare for negotiations. All aspects of the current contract are considered, including flaws that should be corrected. Management should listen carefully to first-line supervisors, as they are affected directly by any error made while negotiating the contract. An alert first-line supervisor may also have a sense of likely union demands. Managers may also periodically seek information about employee attitudes. Surveys can be administered to workers, for example, to determine feelings toward jobs and the job environment.

Another step in preparing for negotiations is to identify various positions that both union and management will take as the negotiations progress. Usually each side takes an initial extreme position, representing the preferred outcome. Both sides will likely determine absolute limits on each demand or offer: a point beyond which they will not make concessions to keep negotiations going. Both sides also prepare fallback positions based on combinations of issues. These preparations should be detailed because clear minds do not always prevail during the heat of negotiations.

Finally, selecting the bargaining team is a major consideration. The composition of the management team usually depends on the type and size of the

Union steward:
An employee elected by union members in his or her work area who, on a volunteer basis, represents their interests.

Figure 15 -2

Major Collective Bargaining
Provisions

MAJOR PROVISIONS	EXAMPLES
Union security	• Contracting-out • Supervisors not to perform bargaining unit work • Labour–management committee
Employee security	• Sexual harassment • Disabled workers • Job sharing
Seniority	• Seniority on transfer • Bumping • Severance pay
Hours	• Scheduling (e.g. flextime and compressed) • Paid meal period • Overtime
Pay guarantees	• Wage incentive plans • Cost of living allowances • Shift premiums
Vacations	• Graduated vacation pay • Vacation bonus • Vacation carryover
Maternity/adoption leave	• Seniority during maternity leave • Employer supplements • Number of weeks granted
Other leave	• Educational leave • Bereavement leave • Union business
Industrial safety	• Health and safety committee—powers • Hours of work • Smoking control
Employee benefits	• Weekly sick pay • Dental plan • Group life insurance
Part-time workers	• Hours of work • Vacation • Sick leave
Pensions	• Benefit levels • Age/service requirements • Cost-of-living adjustment

Source: Adapted from Human Resources Development Canada, "Provisions coded on the CAIRS database." http://labour-travail.hrdc-drhc.gc.ca/doc/wid-dimt/eng/workcond.cfm

Figure 15-3

An Example of Company Preparations for Negotiations

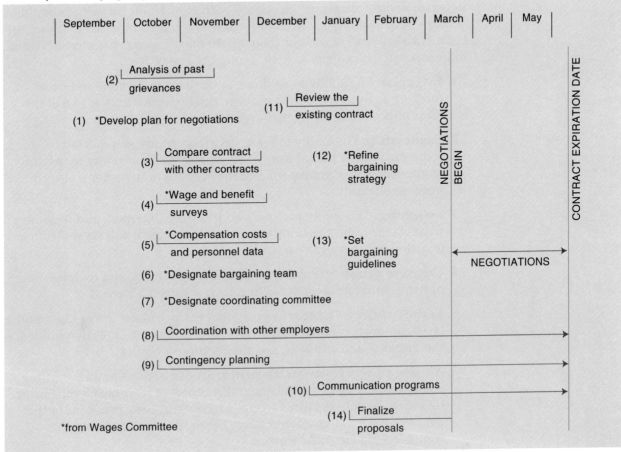

Source: *Adapted from Ronald L. Miller, "Preparations for Negotiations," Personal Journal, 57 (January 1978), p. 38. Reprinted with permission.*

organization. Normally bargaining is conducted by labour relations specialists, with the advice and assistance of operating managers. Sometimes, senior executives are involved directly, particularly in smaller firms. Larger companies use staff specialists (a human resource manager or industrial relations executive), managers of principal operating divisions, and, in some cases, an outside consultant or labour attorney. It is essential, however, that the human resource manager become actively involved in the collective bargaining process. The CEO should not be directly involved in negotiations. Someone on the management side needs to give final approval. As well, there may be times when "thinking" or "cooling off" time is needed. The obligation to consult the CEO can give negotiators from both sides an opportunity to take a break from negotiations.

The responsibility for conducting negotiations for the union is usually entrusted to union officers. At the local level, the negotiating committee will normally be supplemented by rank-and-file members elected specifically for this purpose. In addition, a national union may often send a representative to act in an advisory capacity, or even to participate directly in the bargaining sessions. The real task of the union negotiating team is to develop and obtain solutions to the problems raised by the union's membership. The union's chief negotiator must, therefore, be chosen with care. Upon his or her shoulders rests the responsibility for what ultimately is accepted or rejected in the contract. The ideal chief negotiator should have the following characteristics (these same characteristics apply to management negotiators):

1. **Integrity.** The ability to sit down at the bargaining table and convey integrity to others—both by manner and by reputation—is one of the most important assets a chief negotiator can possess.

2. **Leadership.** The ability to make decisions, sometimes quickly, sometimes under the pressure of events, is vital. The ability to inspire confidence and to get the full benefit from his or her team is also an important quality.

3. **Listening.** The ability to listen and to absorb, interpret, and remember what occurs in negotiations is important, because it will suggest courses of action or avenues to explore.

4. **Creative mind.** The ability to surround a problem, and to devise four or five alternative approaches to getting it solved is needed.

5. **Verbal ability.** The effective negotiator is articulate. She or he should be in thorough command of those verbal persuasion skills that influence the thinking, the attitudes, and the decisions of others.

6. **Ability to work well with people.** A negotiator should have the ability to meet and communicate with others at their own level. She or he should be able to talk as an equal to the company president or the employer's legal counsel, and adapt her or his style to a committee composed of blue collar workers.[16]

All other members of the team are entrusted with supporting roles that help the chief negotiator function at top efficiency. Below we provide guidelines for a five-member team. This comes from a labour organization, but could be a useful model for assembling any negotiating team.[17]

Second member of the team usually sits beside the chief negotiator to her or his right. She or he functions as a second pair of eyes and ears and helps the chief negotiator to formulate strategy.

Third member may be assigned the responsibility of reading and interpreting management's actions. She or he will observe body language closely and attempt to put it into the context and perspective of opportunity.

Fourth member may be responsible for taking notes on what is agreed to, what was discussed during caucus, what counterproposals management may have made, etc. Accurate notes that reflect the union's intent are valuable, and records should be transcribed from these notes and kept from year to year as reference.

Fifth member may be responsible only for recording statements made by management that might be used against them in a public relations sense. Any intemperate remark made in the heat of debate by management which might be used to unify the membership or to play on public opinion would be recorded by this individual.

The number of individuals who make up the negotiating team is not as important as the dedication and the competence with which they confront their tasks—and the degree of unity and support they receive from the general membership. In a three-member negotiating team, for example, all five functions might still be performed, but two team members double up on their assignments. In general, three to five people is an ideal size.

Negotiating the Agreement

There is no way to ensure speedy negotiation of agreements satisfactory to both parties. At best, the parties can attempt to create an atmosphere that will lend itself to steady progress. For example, the two negotiating teams usually meet at a neutral site, such as a hotel. It is important that a favourable relationship be established early in order to avoid eleventh-hour bargaining. It is equally important that union and management negotiators strive to develop and to maintain communication. Traditional collective bargaining is a problem-solving activity, so good communication is essential. Lastly, negotiations should be conducted in the privacy of the conference room, not through the news media. If the negotiators feel that publicity is necessary, joint releases to the media may avoid unnecessary conflict.

The negotiating phase of collective bargaining begins with each side presenting its initial demands. Because a collective bargaining settlement can be expensive for a firm, the cost of various proposals should be estimated as accurately as possible. The term *negotiating* suggests a certain amount of give-and-take, the purpose of which is to lower the other side's expectations. The union will bargain to upgrade their members' economic and working conditions. The employer will negotiate to maintain or enhance profitability. One of the most costly components of any collective bargaining agreement is a wage increase provision.

An example of the negotiation of a wage increase is shown in Figure 15-4. In this example, labour initially demands an increase of $0.40 per hour. Management counters with an offer of only $0.10 per hour. Both labour and management—as expected—reject each other's demands. Plan B calls for labour to lower its demand to an increase of $0.30 per hour. Management counters with its own Plan B, an offer of $0.20. The positions in Plan B are feasible to both sides, as both proposed wage increases are in the bargaining zone: the range of possible outcomes acceptable to both management and labour—in this case, an increase of between $0.20 and $0.30 per hour. The exact amount will be determined by the power of the bargaining unit and the skills of the negotiators.

Even though one party may appear to possess the greater power, negotiators often take care to keep the other side from losing face. They recognize that the balance of power may shift rapidly. Generally, neither side expects to have all its initial demands met. Demands that the union does not expect to receive

Figure 15-4

An Example of Negotiating a Wage Increase

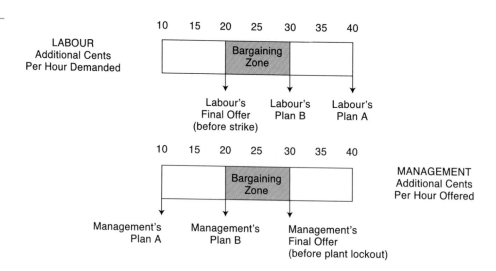

Beachhead demands:
Demands that the union does not expect management to meet when they are first made.

Positional bargaining:
A traditional approach to bargaining in which management and labour begin with opposite positions.

when they are first made are known as **beachhead demands**. For example, in the opening vignette the labour union's beachhead demand was a wage increase of 10 percent.

We have now described the traditional (and still the most common) approach to bargaining. This approach has been termed **positional bargaining**, in which management and labour begin with opposite positions.

Breakdowns in Negotiations

At times negotiations break down, even though both labour and management may want to finalize a contract. This impasse does not necessarily mean a strike. A series of possible options follows:

Conciliation[18]

In most jurisdictions in Canada, a legal strike may take place only after the expiry of a collective agreement and after both parties pass through a process called **conciliation:** a formal, non-binding, labour dispute resolution process—compulsory in most jurisdictions—in which a government-appointed third party (conciliator) is called upon to help reach a workable agreement. Appointed by the minister of labour (in the relevant jurisdiction) at the request of either party, the conciliator has no legal power to resolve the dispute. He or she tries to keep the negotiations going as long as possible to avert a strike. If these negotiations fail, the conciliator reports the breakdown to the minister. Only then (usually after another specified period of time), can strike action begin.

Conciliation: A formal, non-binding, labour dispute resolution process—compulsory in most jurisdictions—in which a government-appointed third party (conciliator) is called upon to help reach a workable agreement.

The first premise in any collective bargaining situation is that management and labour should attempt to resolve their differences by themselves. If an impasse is reached, governments have concluded that it is in the public interest that a neutral person should attempt to assist them. The mechanics of obtaining a conciliation officer are straightforward. Once the union and management have met and an impasse in negotiations has been reached, either of the parties may apply to the minister of labour requesting an appointment. The only requisite conditions are that union and management must have met and that proper notice must be given to the other party.

Once appointed, the conciliation officer contacts both union and management to establish a time and a place for a meeting. The conciliation officer's role is to not to make judgments on the positions taken by either side, but to assist the union and management in settling their own differences. The officer may make suggestions to either or both sides, but such suggestions are not binding and can be either accepted or ignored. Once the parties have reviewed the matters in dispute with the conciliation officer, the usual practice is for the officer to meet separately with both sides. At this stage, the officer will be probing to see if the formal positions held earlier are flexible and also to try to obtain insight into each side's major bargaining goals.

If the conciliation officer concludes that a settlement cannot be reached, he or she prepares a report for the minister. The minister then either forms a conciliation board, or, as is the usual practice, issues a **no-board report** if there is no hope for a settlement. A set number of days after the issuance of the no-board report, (the exact time lapse depending on the jurisdiction), the union is in a legal strike position and management is in a position to legally lock out the employees.

No-board report: A report by the minister of labour stating that a settlement cannot be reached through conciliation.

Mediation[19]

Once the collective bargaining dispute has passed through the conciliation stage without resolution, time begins to run down to the point where a lawful strike or lockout may take place. In theory, the interval after the issuance of a no-board report is intended to give the parties an opportunity to meet and negotiate before a legal strike or lockout takes place. While the union and management may meet and bargain on their own, a mechanism called mediation has been established to provide assistance during this period. Mediators fill a gap left by conciliation boards, which are seldom used today.

Mediation is a voluntary, non-binding process in which two parties contract a neutral third party (mediator) to actively help in a dispute resolution. Both parties must agree on the process. They may ask the minister to appoint a mediator or may agree on one themselves. Like a conciliator, a mediator has no power to force either side into making concessions Mediators normally become directly involved in the negotiation procedure, however, and are thus more proactive than conciliators. The mediation process is usually quite intense, as mediators can make suggestions, help with contract wording and use their personalities and reputation to put pressure on either or both parties. As a general rule, a mediator will continue to be available to both sides as long as the dispute lasts. Thus, a mediator may have a number of meetings extending over a long period, even while a strike or lockout continues.

Mediation: A voluntary, non-binding process in which two parties contract a neutral third party to actively help in a dispute resolution.

A common tactic for a mediator is to meet separately with the management and labour sides, sometimes carrying messages, sometimes making suggestions. Only when the mediator feels that progress can be made are the two sides brought together. The mediator will often use time pressure as a lever to persuade both union and management to modify their positions. Another common strategy is to try to reduce the differences bit by bit, so that a settlement can eventually be reached. Unlike conciliation, mediation often involves trying to wear down the negotiators physically and mentally by continuous meetings around the clock, in the hope that one or both will break, or at least compromise significantly.[20]

If a mediator succeeds in producing an agreement, it is usually put into writing as a memorandum of settlement. The general terms are set out and the bargaining committee returns to the local and presents the terms of the memorandum to members at a ratification meeting.

Arbitration

Arbitration: A process in which a dispute is submitted to an impartial third party for a binding decision.

A third method of dispute resolution is **arbitration**, a process in which a dispute is submitted to an impartial third party who basically acts a judge. An arbitrator's decisions are binding, that is, both sides are legally bound to the decision. There are two types of union–management disputes: rights disputes and contract (interest) disputes. Those that involve employee disputes concerning the interpretation and application of the provisions of an *existing* contract are referred to as **rights arbitration**. This type of arbitration is mainly used in settling grievances, which we discuss below. To avoid strikes or lockouts during the term of a collective agreement, both federal and provincial legislation in most provinces dictates that all contracts have a clause allowing the parties to submit any unresolved grievances to arbitration. This process enables both sides to make their case before a single arbitrator or a board of three arbitrators.

Rights arbitration: The imposition of a third-party (arbitrator) binding decision for disputes involving the interpretation and application of an existing contract.

Contract (interest) arbitration: The imposition of a third-party (arbitrator) binding decision involving disputes over the terms of a proposed collective bargaining agreement.

The other type of arbitration, **contract (interest) arbitration**, involves disputes over the terms of proposed collective bargaining agreements. Contract arbitration is not common in the private sector. Unions and employers rarely agree to submit the basic terms of a contract (such as wages, hours, and working conditions) to a neutral party for disposition. They prefer to rely on collective bargaining and the threat of economic pressure (such as strikes and lockouts) to decide these issues. However, since these tools are not available for contracts involving "essential" professionals in the public sector, it is common to refer contracts to an arbitrator if a conciliator cannot break an impasse. The terms of the arbitrator's award are final and binding upon both sides.

The general practice for parties appearing before an arbitrator is to make their presentations in a written brief, supplemented by additional oral arguments. The arbitrator normally has authority to make a decision that falls somewhere between the two parties' submissions. On occasion, the parties may choose the final offer selection method," in which the arbitrator is limited to choosing the position of either the employer or the union. If, for example, the union wanted an 8-percent wage increase and the employer was offering 4 percent, the arbitrator could award either 8 percent or 4 percent, but not 6 percent. Final offer selection may cover an entire collective agreement, or may be done item by item only for issues on which the parties cannot agree.

Strategies for Overcoming Negotiation Breakdowns

Union Strategies

There are times when a union believes that it must exert extreme pressure to get management to agree to its bargaining demands. Strikes and boycotts are the primary means a union may use to overcome breakdowns in negotiations.

Strikes

When union members refuse to work in order to exert pressure on management in negotiations, their action is referred to as a **strike**. A strike halts production, resulting in lost customers and revenue, which the union hopes will force management to submit to its terms. The timing of a strike is important in determining its effectiveness. Often a good time for a union is when business is thriving or expanding. Conversely, a union might gain little from a strike if a firm's sales are poor, or if a large inventory has been built up.

Strike: An action by union members who refuse to work in order to exert pressure on management in negotiations.

Contrary to the stereotype, unions use the strike only as a last resort. Strikes are extremely expensive—not only for the employer, but also for the union and its members. For example, a union's treasury is often depleted by payment of strike benefits to its members. At the same time, since these benefits are far below normal paycheques, members suffer a drop in standard of living. Sometimes during negotiations (especially at the beginning) the union may want to strengthen its negotiating position by taking a strike vote. This vote does not necessarily mean that there will *be* a strike, only that the union leaders now have the authority to call one *if* negotiations reach an impasse. A favourable strike vote can add a sense of urgency to efforts to reach an agreement.

Successful passage of a strike vote has additional implications for union members. Virtually every union's constitution contains a clause requiring the members to support and participate in a strike if one is called. Union members can be fined for failure to comply. Thus, union members place themselves in jeopardy if they cross a picket line without the consent of the union. As well, in some jurisdictions, it is illegal for union members to return to work while their union is on strike. For these reasons more subtle measures, such as "sickouts" (in which large numbers of employees call in sick) and work slowdowns have been used successfully by union members to bring pressure on the company without the impact of a strike on the membership.

Having decided on strike action, the union executive should establish an appropriate committee structure.[21] Several essential committees are generally needed, and others may be added to deal with the circumstances of the particular strike. Typical committees include the following:

1. **The Strike Action Committee**, composed of four to six people, is responsible for the overall leadership of the strike and for the coordination of the various committee activities.

2. **The Finance Committee** is responsible for proposing a strike action budget, keeping accurate records of all expenditures, and paying strike benefits to all eligible members.

3. **The Strike Services Committee** organizes toilets, picket line materials, shelter, vehicles, food supplies, and other essential services, including social events.

4. **The Publicity Committee** generates, manages, and controls all internal and external publicity materials and public relations.

5. **The Picket Line Committee** organizes and controls picket-line activity. A union does not have the right to prevent access to an employer's property. In practice, picket lines often have slowed entry because of the intense emotion generated during a strike. However, when police action is required to restrict picket activity, the union invariably receives bad publicity, so picket lines must be managed carefully.

It is imperative that a chairperson be appointed for every committee; that concise minutes be kept at every committee meeting; that the committees meet often, but as briefly as possible; that reports be made to the strike organizer; and, most important, that for every aspect of the operation one individual be responsible.

Although a strike sometimes appears a long time away, the first strike day can arrive quite suddenly! Depending on the size of union membership, the executive should appoint a strike organizer with the authority to make on-the-spot decisions during the strike. In larger unions it is advisable not to appoint the president to the position of strike organizer. The president, as the union's chief spokesperson, must remain free from this heavy organizing burden and from potentially controversial issues. However, in smaller unions, several tasks may have to be assumed by the same person. It is vital that the strike organizer stay in constant close contact with the executive or, in an emergency, with the president of the union. The job of the strike organizer is to make the strike work, but not to make union policy. It is very important that the roles be clearly defined in advance and that friction does not develop.

It is also important that the relationship between the negotiation team and the executive be clearly defined. The former negotiates not only the agreement, but also the end to the strike. It is a good idea to have at least one executive member on the negotiation team, but ideally not the president. The executive must, however, remain in charge.

The union executive should ensure that it has immediate knowledgeable legal advice available throughout the strike. Legal counsel should be informed as soon as possible about the likelihood of a strike and about any anticipated legal complications. Legal counsel should be consulted to ensure that all the legal steps necessary for a strike have been followed by the union prior to strike action.

Boycotts

Boycott: Refusal by union members to use or buy the firm's products.

The boycott is another of labour's weapons to get management to agree to its demands. A **boycott** involves an agreement by union members to refuse to use or buy the firm's products. A boycott exerts economic pressure on management, and the effect often lasts much longer than that of a strike. Once shoppers change buying habits, their behaviour will likely continue long after the boycott has ended. At times, significant pressures can be exerted on a business when union members, their families, and friends refuse to purchase the firm's products and encourage the public not to patronize the firm. This approach is especially effective when the products are sold at retail outlets and are easily identifiable by brand name. For example, in its dispute with the Irving Co. at its paper mill in Saint John, the Canadian Paperworkers Union attempted to organize a provincewide boycott of all Irving-owned gas stations and lumber stores.[22]

Management Strategies

Prestrike Preparation

Management, too, needs to be well prepared and organized to deal with a strike. Planning should begin as soon as a strike begins to seem like a possibility. Although planning must take into account the nature of the enterprise, the sector, the union, and the legal context; in general, planning would include prestrike preparation, maintaining operations during the strike, and poststrike follow-up. Part of these discussions could include considerations of alternatives to the strike, such as binding arbitration.

Prestrike preparations would also encompass communications (internal and external), the establishment of a management strike committee, and the preparation of a strike manual (or an update of an existing manual). Many of the issues also require legal advice. For example, where does the union have a right to set up its picket line? Good communication is central to management response to a strike, since managers have many questions to address. For example, How will management ensure that the picketing is peaceful? How will employees (other than those in the bargaining unit) gain access to the premises? Will any members of the bargaining unit who do not wish to strike be allowed to work? [23]

Lockout

Management may also use various strategies to encourage unions to return to the bargaining table. One form of action, somewhat analogous to a strike, is called a **lockout**—the deliberate withholding of work by an employer. During a lockout, management keeps employees out of the workplace and may run the operation with management personnel and/or temporary replacements—in those jurisdictions where replacement workers are legal. Unable to work, the employees do not get paid. In the mid-1990s, the National Hockey League owners used this tactic. Even though the players had agreed to keep playing while negotiations were underway, management locked them out in an effort to speed up the bargaining process and to ensure that the players would not be in a position to strike during the playoffs.[24]

Although the lockout is used infrequently, fear of a lockout may bring labour back to the bargaining table. A lockout is particularly effective when management is dealing with a weak union, when the union treasury is depleted, or when the business has excessive inventories. As with strike action, then, the timing of a lockout can be very important.

Another alternative available to management—if legal in the company's jurisdiction—is to place management and/or nonunion workers in the striking workers' jobs. This tactic can be quite effective, if the firm is not labour

Lockout: The deliberate withholding of work by an employer.

intensive and if maintenance demands are not high (as they are at a petroleum refinery or a chemical plant). When replacement personnel are used, management will try to continue production and, in rare cases, attempt to show how production actually increases with the use of nonunion employees. Using replacement workers (called *scabs* by union members) is illegal in British Columbia and Quebec. Even where the practice is legal, using replacement workers risks inviting violence and creates bitterness among employees, which may adversely affect the firm's performance long after the strike has ended.

Ratification and Administration

Ratifying the Agreement

As we noted in the last chapter, fewer than 10 percent of all collective agreements, in Canada, result in a strike or work stoppage. Typically, agreement is reached before the current contract expires. After the negotiators have reached a tentative agreement on all contract terms, they prepare a written statement, complete with the effective start and termination dates. The approval process for management is often easier than for labour. The president or CEO can usually make a decision on the part of the company. Any difficulty that might have stood in the way of obtaining approval has probably already been resolved through discussions with senior management.

Ratification vote: A vote by union membership to accept or to reject a proposed collective agreement—which, normally, does not become final unless a majority of the union members approve.

However, the approval process is more complex for the union. Until a majority of members approve, the proposed agreement is not final. While not required by law in all jurisdictions, most unions hold a **ratification vote**, at which the membership votes to accept or to reject the proposed collective agreement. At times, union members reject the proposal and a new round of negotiations must begin. In recent years, approximately 10 percent of all tentative agreements have been rejected when presented to the union membership. Many of these rejections might not have occurred if union negotiators had communicated more effectively with their membership, or if management had been more aware of employee needs and perceptions.

Administration of the Agreement

Negotiating, as it relates to the total collective bargaining process, may be likened to the tip of an iceberg. It is the visible phase, the part that makes the news. The larger and perhaps more important part is contract or agreement administration, consisting of ongoing activities seldom viewed by the public. The agreement establishes the union–management relationship for the duration of the contract. Usually, neither party can unilaterally change the contract's language until the expiration date. The main problem encountered in contract administration, therefore, is uniform day-to-day interpretation and application of the contract's terms. Ideally, the aim of both management and the union is to make the agreement work to the benefit of everyone—often not an easy task.

Both management and labour are responsible for explaining and implementing the agreement. This process should begin with meetings or training sessions, not only to point out significant features, but also to provide a clause-by-clause analysis of the contract. First-line supervisors and union stewards, in particular, need to know their responsibilities and what to do when disagreements arise. The human resource manager plays a key role in this day-to-day administration. He or she gives advice on matters of discipline, works to resolve grievances, and helps first-line supervisors establish good working relationships within the terms of the agreement.

Grievance Resolution

When management and labour ratify a contract, both sides undertake to abide by their agreement. In the workplace, however, there may be times when employees feel their rights have been violated, or the terms of the contract have not been followed. These real or perceived wrongs may result from an individual supervisor's decision or action, or from the way a clause in the contract has been interpreted. The vehicle used to address these concerns is called a **grievance**, defined as "a formal dispute between an employee (or the union) and management involving the interpretation, application, or an alleged violation of the collective agreement."[25] Most collective agreements limit grievances to matters covered in the contract.

A clearly defined grievance procedure—which we discuss in Chapter 16—benefits both employees and management. Individual employees can have their concerns dealt with in an orderly fashion. Supervisors can no longer ignore valid complaints or fire people as troublemakers. Similarly, from the employer's viewpoint, grievances act "as a communications device, letting the employer know fairly quickly just what matters . . . are sources of discontent."[26]

As we noted above, if a settlement cannot be reached, a rights arbitration process, is initiated.[27] Most collective agreements outline the process for choosing arbitrators and the manner in which arbitrators will handle grievances—which we deal with in the next chapter. Although the decision of a grievance (rights) arbitrator is final and binding on both sides, there is, nonetheless, a limited right of appeal to the courts, if the decision allegedly violates the law. Because of the high costs and the amount of time involved in pursuing a grievance

Grievance: A formal dispute between an employee (or the union) and management involving the interpretation, application, or an alleged violation of the collective agreement.

HRM in ACTION

Can He Be Fired?

"I think I might have messed up this morning," said the maintenance supervisor, George LaChaine, to Doug Williams, the industrial relations manager. "One of the technicians in my section wasn't doing the job exactly according to specs, so I blew up and fired him. Five minutes later the union steward was in the office. She said something like situations such as this are covered in our contract and that I was violating it. I had never spoken to the technician before about that particular offence, and the steward said the contract called for both oral and written warnings before termination."

How would you respond?

through to arbitration, both unions and employers are motivated to solve their disagreements before this stage. Thus, it has been estimated that no more than 2 percent of grievances go before an arbitrator.[28]

The Future of Collective Bargaining

Throughout the 1990s management gradually wrested the power advantage from unions in collective bargaining—a situation that is not expected to change in the near future. Market factors such as restructuring, downsizing, globalization, and labour-saving technology reduced the traditional antagonistic power of unions to command huge wage gains and benefit packages. Indicators of the shift in bargaining power from unions to employers included a trend to lower wage increases for unionized employees, a decreasing number of strikes and days lost due to labour disputes, longer contracts, and the increased labour acceptance of outsourcing and contracting out.

Market factors also contributed to fundamental changes in the nature of work. Part-time and contract work expanded as the number of permanent, full-time jobs shrank; core workers worked longer hours and suffered stress; small businesses became a larger part of the job market; employment became less secure; and wages were polarized. Can the current union organization evolve to deal with these new workplace realities, or will it need to change completely? Governments, labour, and business all face major challenges related to collective bargaining:

- **Cooperation.** Labour and management need to shed their traditional adversarial style and adapt to a new cooperative, participative bargaining relationship. [29]

- **Flexibility and creativity.** Unions and management need to collectively agree on innovative programs that satisfy the needs of employees and employers, such as gain sharing, profit sharing and flextime.

- **Fragmented labour market.** A key issue for the labour movement will be to find ways to maintain access to collective bargaining while employment is shifting from large firms and the public sector to service sector jobs, smaller employers, self-employment, part-time and contract workers.

- **Restructuring.** Governments, unions, and management need to deal harmoniously with the restructuring fallout and the realities of the new workplace, such as career transitions, job losses, worker insecurity, workplace stress, and contracting out.

- **Polarity.** Governments, unions, and employers need to deal with the festering issue of wage polarity: the marked increase in wage differentials between low-skilled and high-skilled jobs. Some argue that labour will take on an increased focus and militancy as the "voice of the working class and the disadvantaged." Others argue for more government intervention, while still others put their faith in the long-term forces of the free market to correct labour inequities.

A **GLOBAL** PERSPECTIVE

Canada and United States—Different Laws Reflect Different Cultures[30]

In the late 1990s, the local economy in Hilton, Alberta ground to a halt when 700 workers in this small town walked off the job at Welwood of Canada Inc. Welwood is the Canadian subsidiary of the U.S.-based Champion International Corp., which operates pulp and sawmill plants on both sides of the border. According to Peter Lanosky, Welwood's human resources manager, this strike would not have happened if the company had been located in the United States, where labour disputes tend to get solved much more quickly. The issue at Welwood was a "flexible" work practices program in which workers were being asked to switch jobs when necessary. This kind of arrangement has long been in place in the U.S. plants.

Over the nineties, a new era for Canadian business was signalled by the signing of such international agreements as NAFTA with the U.S. and Mexico in 1994, and agreements with Chile and Israel in 1996. Today, Canada is a trading nation that must forge networks of business relationships around the world, particularly in the U.S., to ensure economic survival. Some one-third of all jobs now depend on international trade. Exports are in the $300 million range and represent almost 45 percent of our gross national product. About 80 percent of our exports go to the U.S. The labour dispute at Welwood highlights the need to understand how our labour relation systems and culture differ from those of our major trading partner.

Despite the general decline in the power of Canadian unions over the 1990s, a common complaint among both Canadian companies and American companies operating in Canada is that labour relations are far more combative in Canada. For example, historically, the average workdays lost due to strikes and lockouts have been about five times as high in Canada as in the U.S. Some argue that this leads to the tendency for Canadian companies to set up shop south of the border and discourages foreign capital investment. According to Professor Richard Chaykowski, a Queens University professor, there is little doubt that international investors see Canada as a country where labour relations are problematic. U.S. labour laws are much less supportive of unions, collective bargaining, and the right to strike (see Figure 15-5). This goes a long way in explaining the militancy of Canadian labour unions and why only about 10 percent of U.S. workers are unionized as opposed to 33 percent of Canadian workers.

But the difference between the two countries is more than legal. Businesses in both countries should recognize that labour laws in Canada and the U.S. reflect two distinct social and cultural environments. Canadian workers' rights have been pushed into the mainstream consciousness while the rights of the worker in the U.S. have been put on the back burner. In the U.S., competitive supremacy has taken precedence over social equity. This distinct social-political difference partly explains why unions such as the Canadian Auto Workers (CAW) split with the

▼

American-dominated United Auto Workers (UAW). According to Buzz Hargrove of the CAW, Canadians are less likely to bend to what he called the "corporate agenda." Historically, Canadians have been more concerned with the social issues of wage inequality and job security. For example, a study, by Richard Freeman of Harvard University, estimated that a dramatic increase in wage inequality and the number of working poor in the U.S. was largely due to declining unionization.[31] According to Freeman, Canada's stronger—or more combative—unions' better labour standards and income support programs have resulted in lower wage inequality and relatively fewer highly contingent and precarious jobs than in the U.S.

So far, Canadians have been willing to pay the price of strikes such as those at Welwood in an effort to protect their distinct culture and social fabric. The major issue for business is to understand that both American and Canadian labour relations and culture differ and try to work harmoniously within this framework.

Figure 15-5

Collective Bargaining: A Comparison

CANADA	UNITED STATES
Working days lost: 292 work days lost each year, on average, per 1000 employees (1986–1995)	Working days lost: 62 work days lost each year, on average, per 1000 employees (1986–1995)
Union membership: 33% of non-agricultural workforce	Union membership: 10% of non-agricultural workforce
Wages of unionized workers: $19/hr. (Can.)	Wages of unionized workers: $23/hr. (U.S.)
Wages of nonunionized workers: $16/hr. (Can.)	Wages of non-unionized workers: $18/hr. (U.S.)
Eleven distinct labour law systems and a federal system that applies to the territories.	A national system of labour laws.
Majority of provinces allow temporary replacements; Quebec and British Columbia do not.	Temporary replacements are allowed.
Permanent replacement workers are universally prohibited.	Economic strikers may be permanently replaced except for those who strike over unfair labour practices.
Generally a union vote is required before strike action.	A strike vote is not required by law, but most unions call a vote.
Most jurisdictions require government mediation/conciliation prior to strike action.	Government mediation/conciliation is voluntary.
In almost all cases, deduction of dues is required from union and non-union members of a bargaining unit.	21 states have "right to work" laws, which prohibit unions from collecting dues from those who choose not to join the union.

Source: Adapted from Mark MacKinnon, "Canada leads G7 in time lost to strikes" and "Trouble in Alberta Mill Town Highlights Cross-Border Differences," The Globe and Mail (April 5, 1999): B4.

SUMMARY

1. **Discuss the effect of external environmental factors on the collective bargaining process.**

   Influential external forces have included competitive business-led initiatives toward "lean production," product quality, and improved distribution channels; cost reduction; international competition and globalization of production; a movement toward labour-saving technology; deregulation; downsizing and cost cutting in the public sector; and the growth in small business. These external environmental factors have led to longer contracts, union uncertainty and fragmentation, erosion of union bargaining power, reduction in union jobs and wages, polarization of wages, mounting worker insecurity and stress, and gradual growth in innovative or adaptive workplace practices.

2. **Identify the various types of union–management relationships that affect the collective bargaining process.**

   Possible union–management relationships include conflict, armed truce, power bargaining, accommodation, cooperation, and collusion. Typically, Canadian union–management relationships have been characterized by some form of accommodation. However, cooperation is a growing trend as joint economic survival has become all-important.

3. **Describe the collective bargaining structure and process.**

   The structure of collective bargaining can be companywide, industrywide or multiemployer. Most contract bargaining is companywide. Depending on union–management relations encountered, the collective bargaining process may be relatively simple, or it may be a long, tense struggle. Success, for both sides, requires preparation, documentation, research, collaboration and communication. The first step in the collective bargaining process is preparing for negotiations. After the issues to be negotiated have been determined, the two sides negotiate to reach a mutually acceptable contract. Union and management must also be prepared for a breakdown in negotiations. The final step is for the agreement to be formalized by management and the union, usually involving a union ratification vote.

4. **Describe what both labour and management do as they prepare for negotiations.**

   Before beginning negotiations, both the management and the union team must prepare their respective positions. During this stage, the psychological aspects of collective bargaining become evident. The personalities of the bargaining team have a direct effect on what can be accomplished and how quickly agreement can be reached. Negotiators should devise a contract that is usable both now and in the future. Contracts must also meet all legal requirements. A union must continually gather information about membership needs and attitudes, which is normally the responsibility of the union steward. Management must also gather information, research, listen carefully to first-line supervisors, and, if possible, seek information about employee attitudes. Usually each side takes an extreme initial position, representing the preferred outcome. Both sides must also prepare fallback positions based on combinations of issues. These preparations by management and unions should be detailed. Selecting the bargaining team is important for both management and unions. Union officers usually conduct negotiations for the union; at the local level, the negotiating committee will normally be supplemented by elected rank-and-file members. Both management and union will have a chief negotiator.

5. **Explain the process of negotiating.**

   Speedy negotiation of an agreement satisfactory to both parties is not always possible. The negotiating phase of collective bargaining begins with each side presenting its initial demands. The traditional (and still the most common) approach to bargaining is positional bargaining, in which management and labour begin with opposite positions. Generally, neither side expects to have all its initial demands met. The most contentious issue is normally wage increases.

6. **Identify and describe union and management ways to overcome breakdowns in negotiations.**

   A union–management impasse does not necessarily mean a strike. Traditional preventive actions include conciliation, mediation, and arbitration. Conciliation and mediation are formal, non-binding, labour-dispute resolution processes in which a government-appointed third party tries to help reach a workable agreement. Mediators play a more active role than conciliators. In contrast, an arbitrator's decision is final and binding. A union may try to pressure management to resolve the dispute through strikes (withdrawal of labour) and boycotts (a refusal to buy the firm's products). Unions use the strike only as a last resort. More subtle measures, such as "sickouts" and work slowdowns have been used successfully. Prestrike preparations are an important management strategy. The deliberate withholding of work, a lockout, is another form of management strategy. Although the lockout is used infrequently, fear of a lockout may bring labour back to the bargaining table. Another management alternative is to place management and/or nonunion workers in the striking workers' jobs. Even when this practice is legal, it risks inviting violence and creates bitterness.

7. Describe what is involved in ratifying and administering a collective agreement.
After the negotiators have reached a tentative settlement, both management and the union must approve or ratify the agreement. The approval process for management is often easier than for labour. Most unions hold a ratification vote among the membership. If union members reject the proposal, a new round of negotiations must begin. Once ratified, a contract must be administered. The main problem encountered in contract administration is uniform day-to-day interpretation and application of the contract's terms. Management and the union should begin by explaining the terms of the agreement. First-line supervisors and union stewards, in particular, need to know their responsibilities and what to do when disagreements arise. The human resource manager

plays a key role in this day-to-day administration. If employees feel their rights have been violated, or the terms of the contract have not been followed, they can launch a grievance: a formal dispute between an employee (or the union) and management. A clearly defined grievance procedure benefits both employees and management. Most collective agreements limit grievances to matters covered in the contract. The final stage of a grievance is normally rights arbitration. Because pursuing a grievance is costly and time-consuming, both unions and employers are motivated to solve their disagreements.

8. Discuss the future of collective bargaining.
Management has gradually wrested the power advantage from unions in collective bargaining—a situation that is not expected to change in the near future. Market factors such as restructuring, downsizing, globalization, and labour-saving technology have reduced the traditional power of unions. Fundamental changes in the workplace include expansion of part-time and contract work as permanent, full-time positions have decreased; longer hours and more stress for remaining core workers; a shift to small businesses; rising employment insecurity; and polarization of wages. Government, labour and business face the challenge of achieving cooperation, flexibility, and creativity in collective bargaining, and of dealing with the fragmented labour market, restructuring, and wage polarity.

QUESTIONS FOR REVIEW

1. Discuss the impact of recent external environmental factors on the collective bargaining process.

2. What are the various types of union–management relationships that affect the collective bargaining process?

3. Discuss the basic steps involved in the collective bargaining process and how management and labour prepare for negotiations.

4. Identify five major collective bargaining provisions and give an example of each.

5. What personality characteristics would you look for in selecting a chief negotiator?

6. Outline the committee structure a union might set up in the event of a strike.

7. What are the typical bargaining issues?

8. Briefly discuss the primary ways by which breakdowns in negotiations can be overcome.

9. Briefly explain the meaning of the following terms:
   a. rights arbitration
   b. contract (interest) arbitration,
   c. strike
   d. lockout
   e. boycott

10. What are the key issues involved in the ratification and administration of a labour agreement?

11. Explain the major issues affecting the future of collective bargaining.

DEVELOPING **HRM** SKILLS

An Experiential Exercise

A major part of the human resource manager's job is to advise all levels of management on human resource matters. The human resource manager's knowledge and experience are often required in dealing with union matters, especially in handling situations that may affect future negotiations. This exercise provides additional insight into the importance of handling employee problems properly.

The human resource manager, Gregory Menchew, works very closely with all the managers and employees in an attempt to settle problems before they become critical. Today, one of the union stewards, Eugene Shum, called for an appointment and said he had a complaint. The manager agreed to talk to Eugene, but first he wants to talk to the supervisor, Stan Bradley. That way Gregory can get both sides of the story. Gregory really hopes this is not a major problem, since the company and the union will begin negotiations soon for a new contract.

Stan Bradley has been with the company for 12 years, the last four as a supervisor. He is a very safety-conscious supervisor with a reputation for strictly enforcing the rules. In Stan's opinion this safety-consciousness is the reason there has not been a single lost-time accident in the division since he became the supervisor. There is a rule in the plant, well known to everyone, that every intersection is a four-way stop for forklift trucks. According to the collective agreement, even minor safety violations justify a three-day suspension and a written warning. Stan saw a forklift truck, with Charlie Fox at the wheel, come around a corner at a high speed and not stop at an intersection. Virtually no one except Charlie and Stan was at the plant, but Stan suspended Charlie for three days and placed a written warning in his personnel folder.

Eugene Shum was elected union steward last year. There have been few grievances since the election, and therefore Eugene has done little as union steward. A couple of workers have brought complaints, but management was found to be correct in each case and workers were told so. Eugene likes being the union steward and believes that it might be tough to be reelected unless he can make a "show." In Eugene's opinion, Charlie Fox was improperly suspended for three days. Eugene has found his reelection platform.

Three individuals will participate in this exercise: one to serve as the human resource manager, one to serve as the supervisor, and another to play the role of union steward. The instructor will provide the participants with additional information necessary to complete the exercise.

HRM INCIDENT

Strategy

"They want what?" the mayor exclaimed.

"Like I said," the town clerk replied, "17 percent over two years."

"There is no way that the taxpayers will accept a settlement anywhere near that," reiterated the mayor. "I don't care if the garbage doesn't get collected for a century. We can't go more than 8 percent over the next two years."

The town clerk looked worried. "How much loss of service do you think the public will accept? Suppose they do go on strike? I'm the one who always gets the complaints. Then there's the health problem with rats running all over the place! Remember over in Neibringtown, when that little kid was bitten? There was a hell of an outcry."

The mayor agreed: "Garbage collectors always have strong bargaining power, but, if I don't fight this, I'll be voted out in the next election. I say we offer six percent over 18 months. Then we can go either way—six percent over 12 months or eight percent over two years."

"I wonder if we have any other options?" worried the town clerk.

"Well, we could threaten not to hire any more union personnel and to job out the collection service to private contractors if the union wasn't cooperative," mused the mayor.

"That's a good idea!" The town clerk sounded enthusiastic. "Also, we can mount a newspaper advertising campaign to get the public behind us. If we play on the fear of massive tax increases, the garbage collectors won't have much public sympathy."

"What about asking the union to guarantee garbage collection for old people during a strike? If they refuse, they'll look bad in the public eye; if they accept, we are rid of a major problem. Most people can bring their trash to a central collection point. Not all old people can," chuckled the mayor. "We can't lose on that issue!"

"Okay, then," said the town clerk. "It looks like we have the beginning of a bargaining strategy here. Actually, I feel better now. I think we're in a rather strong position."

Questions

1. Discuss the plight of public sector unions faced with the reality of a limited tax base and public pressure to lower taxes.

2. Is the town clerk right? Is the town in a good bargaining position? Explain your answer.

3. What strengths does the union have in its position?

4. If you were a labour relations consultant, would you agree with the present strategy? What alternatives, if any, would you propose?

CHAPTER

16

Internal Employee Relations

CHAPTER OBJECTIVES

1. Define internal employee relations.

2. Define discipline and disciplinary action. Describe the disciplinary action process.

3. Discuss two key approaches to discipline; and the key issues involved in administering discipline.

4. Briefly explain the grievance handling process in union and nonunion organizations.

5. Explain how managers deal with terminations and layoffs.

6. Describe three major alternatives to termination or layoff.

7. Briefly outline three key HR issues related to termination/layoff.

8. Describe the internal relations issues related to promotion, resignation, and retirement.

Gary Halmes, the production supervisor for Manitoba Manufacturing, was mad at the world when he arrived at work. The automobile mechanic had not repaired his car on time the day before, so he had been forced to take a taxi to work this morning. No one was safe around Gary today, and it was not the time for Phillip Meiros, a member of Local 264, to report for work late. Without hesitation, Gary said, "You know our company can't tolerate this type of behaviour. I don't want to see you around here anymore. You're fired." Just as quickly, Phillip replied, "You're way off base. Our contract calls for three warnings for tardiness. My steward will hear about this."

Matthew Morton, a 10-year employee at Ketro Productions, arrived at the human resource manager's office to turn in his letter of resignation. Matt was very upset with his supervisor, John Higgins. When the human resource manager, Kersti Yamada, asked what was wrong, Matt replied, "Yesterday, I made a mistake and set my machine up wrong. It was the first time in years that I'd done that. My boss chewed me out in front of my friends. I wouldn't take that from the president, much less a two-bit supervisor!"

These scenarios represent only two of the many situations that human resource managers confront when dealing with internal employee relations. Gary Halmes has just been reminded that his power to fire a worker has limits. Matthew Morton's resignation might have been avoided if his supervisor had not shown poor judgment and disciplined him in front of his friends.

In this chapter, we first define internal employee relations. Next, we discuss the reasons for disciplinary action, the discipline process, approaches to discipline, and administration of discipline. We then describe the grievance handling process for union and non-union employees. Next, we discuss the issues of termination and layoffs, followed by a review of three alternative options: early retirement, demotions, and transfers. This is followed by a discussion of three key termination/layoff issues: wrongful dismissal, outplacement, and caring for those employees who remain in the organization. Lastly we describe internal relations issues related to promotion, resignation and retirement.

Internal Employee Relations Defined

Internal employee relations: Those human resource management activities associated with the movement of employees within the organization.

Most employees do not remain in the same job within an organization for their entire career. They move upward, laterally, downward, and out in response to both internal and external opportunities. In order to ensure that individuals with the proper skills and experience are available at all levels, therefore, concerted efforts are required to maintain good internal employee relations. **Internal employee relations** consist of human resource management activities associated with the movement of employees within the organization, including promotion, transfer, demotion, resignation, discharge, layoff, and retirement. Discipline and disciplinary action are also crucial aspects of internal employee relations.

Disciplinary Action Process

Discipline: The state of employee self-control and orderly conduct.

Disciplinary action: The invoking of a consequence against an employee who fails to meet established standards or comply with organizational rules.

Discipline is the state of employee self-control and orderly conduct and indicates the extent of genuine teamwork within an organization. **Disciplinary action** invokes a consequence against an employee who fails to meet established standards or comply with organizational rules. Effective disciplinary action addresses the employee's wrongful behaviour, not the employee as a person. Incorrectly administered disciplinary action is destructive to both the employee and the organization. Thus, disciplinary action should not be applied haphazardly. In the opening caption, for example, both Gary Halmes and John Higgins were haphazard in their application of discipline, with the result that two problematic employee relations situations developed.

Discipline is dynamic and ongoing. Because one person's actions can affect the whole work group, the proper application of discipline fosters acceptable behaviour by other group members. Conversely, unjustified or improperly administered discipline can have a detrimental effect on everyone. The disciplinary action process is shown in Figure 16-1. As with all aspects of human resource management, disciplinary policies and actions are affected by the external environment. Changes in technology, for example, may render a rule inappropriate or may necessitate new rules. Laws and government regulations that affect company policies and rules are also changing constantly. The various Occupational Safety and Health Acts, for example, have encouraged many firms to establish stricter safety standards. Unions are another external factor. Specific punishments for rule violations are subject to collective bargaining.

Changes in the firm's internal environment can also alter the disciplinary process. Through organizational development, the firm may alter its culture, thus changing how first-line supervisors handle discipline. A management stance of treating employees as mature human beings would affect the process significantly (see the later section on discipline without punishment). The disciplinary action process deals largely with infractions of rules. Rules are specific guides to behaviour on the job. Rules may relate to general conduct in the workplace, to interactions with peers and supervisors, to specific requirements of job tasks, and to safe behaviour.

Once management has established rules, they must communicate them to employees. People cannot obey rules they are unaware of. When an employee violates a rule, corrective action may be necessary. The purpose of disciplinary action is not to chastise the violator but to alter behaviour detrimental to

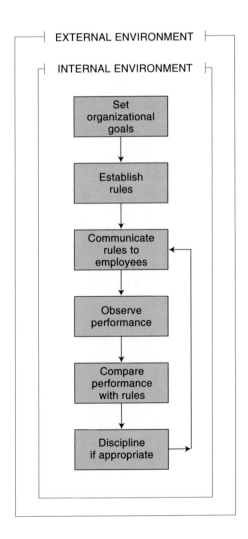

Figure 16-1

The Disciplinary Action Process

organizational objectives. Discipline is useless unless employees clearly realize exactly what behaviours were unacceptable and understand what is expected from them in the future. Additionally, note how the process shown in Figure 16-1 includes feedback from the point of taking appropriate disciplinary action to communicating rules to employees.

Approaches to Disciplinary Action

Several disciplinary frameworks have been developed. We discuss two: progressive disciplinary action and discipline without punishment.

Progressive Disciplinary Action

Progressive disciplinary action is intended to ensure that the minimum consequence appropriate to the offence is imposed, as determined by a series of questions about the severity of the offence. As illustrated in Figure 16-2, the manager must ask these questions in sequence to determine the proper disciplinary action. This step-by-step disciplinary method is often called *just cause* discipline. To begin with, the manager must determine whether the improper behaviour is severe enough to warrant disciplinary action. Having answered *yes*, the manager next considers whether the violation warrants more than a verbal warning.[1] For a first minor infraction, probably a verbal warning will suffice. In fact, several verbal warnings might be given for repeated minor offences before the manager decides that a violation warrants more than a verbal warning. The manager follows the same procedure for each level of the progressive disciplinary process, not considering termination until each lower-level question has been answered *yes*. A more severe violation might warrant a higher-level response. For example, assaulting a supervisor or another worker might justify immediate termination.

Maintaining proper documentation is extremely important; otherwise, there is no legal basis for terminating an employee. Even at the verbal warning stage, each infraction must be documented and placed in the employee's personnel file. Verbal warnings are generally recorded in memo format and are not signed by the employee. The employee must be shown the paperwork for any more serious offences and asked to sign. Of course, he or she has the right to refuse; therefore, a witness should always be present during a disciplinary interview.

Discipline Without Punishment

The progressive discipline system, explained above, is based on the idea that consequences will cause people to modify their behaviour. The **discipline without punishment system**, in contrast, is based on the concept that management does not *control* behaviour. It is the employee's responsibility to behave according to established work rules and procedures. In this approach, employees are encouraged to resolve issues in their own and their employer's best interest. The concept, then, places responsibility for behaviour and the subsequent consequences on the employee, conveying the message, "in this firm we hire adults; we expect them to behave as adults."

Progressive disciplinary action: An approach to discipline designed to ensure that the minimum consequence appropriate to the offence is imposed.

Discipline without punishment: An approach in which employees are encouraged to resolve issues in their own and their employer's best interest.

Figure 16-2

The Progressive Disciplinary Approach

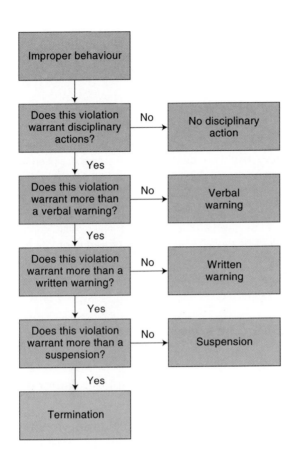

The system revolves around a series of documented steps:

1. **First step:** An interview (not a warning), during which the problem is discussed and the employee is counselled. There are no threats or warnings, but a commitment to behave as requested is sought.

2. **Second step:** If the unwarranted behaviour is repeated, the supervisor counsels the employee again; this time a memo summarizing the conversation and the employee's commitment to changed behaviour is placed in the employee's personnel file. At this stage, the counselling may or may not require a witness.

3. **Third step:** On the third repetition, the employee is asked to take three or four days' leave, with pay.[2] This is not a holiday. The individual will be given a series of questions to answer on return to work. Depending on the situation, the questions can be quite pointed: for example, "Do you realize that the next infraction will mean immediate dismissal?" or, "Will you confirm that you will follow company rules on the issue in question in the future?" On return from leave, the employee is counselled again, this time almost certainly in the presence of an employer and an employee representative. The employee's decision to change behaviour is

Figure 16-3

Recommended Disciplinary Procedures

- All employees should be given a copy of the employer's rules on disciplinary procedures. The procedures should specify which employees they cover and what disciplinary actions may be taken, and should allow matters to be dealt with quickly.
- Employees should be told of complaints against them and given an opportunity to state their case. They should have the right to be accompanied by a union representative or fellow employee of their choice.
- Disciplinary action should not be taken until the case has been fully investigated. Immediate superiors should not have the power to dismiss without reference to senior management, and, except for gross misconduct, no employee should be dismissed for a first breach of discipline.
- Employees should be given an explanation for any penalty imposed, and they should have a right of appeal, with specified procedures to be followed.
- When disciplinary action other than summary dismissal is needed, supervisors should give a formal/verbal warning in the case of minor offenses, or a written warning in more serious cases.

Source: "Code on Discipline Procedure" Industrial Management 7 (August 1977), p. 7. Used with permission.

documented and placed on file. The employee and/or the witnesses sign the document.

4. Fourth step: If there is yet another rule infringement, there is no alternative but to terminate the employee, but this drastic action will be based on decisions made by the employee.

Administration of Disciplinary Action

As might be expected, discipline (no matter what system is used) is not a pleasant supervisory task. Many managers avoid taking action, for a number of reasons:

1. **Lack of training:** The supervisor may not have the knowledge and skill necessary to handle disciplinary problems.

2. **Fear:** The supervisor may be concerned that top management will not support a disciplinary action.

3. **The only one:** The supervisor may think "No one else is disciplining employees, so why should I?"

4. **Guilt:** The supervisor may think: "How can I discipline someone if I've done the same thing?"

5. **Loss of friendship:** The supervisor may believe that disciplinary action will damage friendship with an employee or the employee's associates.

6. **Time loss:** The supervisor may begrudge the time that is required to administer and explain discipline.

7. **Loss of temper:** The supervisor may be afraid of losing his or her temper when talking to an employee about a rule violation.

8. **Rationalization:** The supervisor may think, "The employee knows it was a wrong thing to do, so why do we need to talk about it?"[3]

To assist management in administering discipline properly, a *Code on Discipline Procedure* should be prepared. An example is shown in Figure 16-3. The code should stress communication of rules, telling the employee of the complaint, conducting a full investigation, and giving the employee an opportunity to tell his or her side of the story. These actions are recommended no matter what disciplinary system is in place.

Grievance Handling Under a Collective Bargaining Agreement

If employees in an organization are represented by a union, workers who believe they have been disciplined or dealt with unjustly can appeal through the grievance and arbitration procedures of the collective bargaining agreement, as we referred to in the last chapter. Obviously, Phillip Meiros, in the opening vignette, knew that the collective bargaining agreement negotiated by the union required three warnings for tardiness, and therefore he could not be fired for being late one time. Gary Halmes, the production supervisor, was wrong in not following the collective bargaining agreement and Phillip let him know it.

Despite its defects, the grievance procedure has been described as one of the great accomplishments of the industrial relations movement. [4] The grievance system encourages and facilitates the settlement of disputes between labour and management. A grievance procedure permits employees to express

---

HRM in ACTION

An Exception to the Rule?

As Mike Bowen, a first-line supervisor for Kwik Corporation, entered the office of Sarah Findley, human resource director, he was obviously disturbed and wanted help. Mike started the conversation by saying, "Kevin Smith, one of my employees, violated company policy today by failing to wear his safety glasses on a very dangerous job. The company policy states that any employee who does not follow the safety guidelines will receive a written reprimand on the first offence and will be terminated on the second violation. Kevin has already received one reprimand and has just committed his second violation. However, he has been one of my best workers over five years, and letting him go could have a really negative impact on productivity."

What advice should Sarah provide?

complaints without jeopardizing their jobs. It also assists management in seeking out the underlying causes and solutions to employee complaints.

The Grievance Procedure

All labour agreements include some form of grievance procedure. As we noted near the end of Chapter 15, a grievance is a formal complaint outlining an employee's dissatisfaction or feeling of personal injustice relating to some aspect of his or her employment. A grievance under a collective bargaining agreement is normally restricted to violations of the terms and conditions of the agreement, but grievances may also arise from other circumstances:

- a violation of law;
- a violation of the intent of the parties as stipulated during contract negotiations;
- a violation of company rules;
- a change in working conditions or past company practices;
- a violation of health and/or safety standards.[5]

Grievance procedures are varied, reflecting differences in organizational or decision-making structures or the size of a work unit or company. Three common principles guide effective grievance administration:

1. Grievances should be heard promptly.

2. Procedures and forms for airing grievances must be easy to use and well understood by employees and their supervisors.

3. Direct and timely avenues of appeal from rulings of line supervision must exist.[6]

The multiple-step grievance procedure shown in Figure 16-4 is the most common type. In the informal complaint step, the employee usually presents the grievance orally and informally to the immediate supervisor. A union steward may be present. This step offers the greatest potential for improved labour relations and a large majority of grievances are settled here. If the issue remains unresolved, the first formal step begins when a written grievance is submitted to the supervisor by the union steward. The grievance is dated and signed by the employee and the union steward. It describes the events as perceived by the employee, cites the contract provision that allegedly was violated, and indicates what settlement is desired. At this point the supervisor must answer the complaint in writing, either accepting or rejecting the grievance.

If the issue is still unresolved, a meeting is held between the second-level manager (the supervisor's direct superior) or an HR manager and higher union officials, perhaps even a grievance committee or chief steward. Should the grievance not be settled at this meeting, it is appealed to the third formal step. Typically, this step involves the firm's top labour representative (such as the vice president of industrial relations) and high-level union officials. At times, depending on the severity of the grievance, the president may represent the firm. A grievance that remains unresolved at the conclusion of the third formal

Figure 16-4

An Example of a Multiple-Step Grievance Procedure

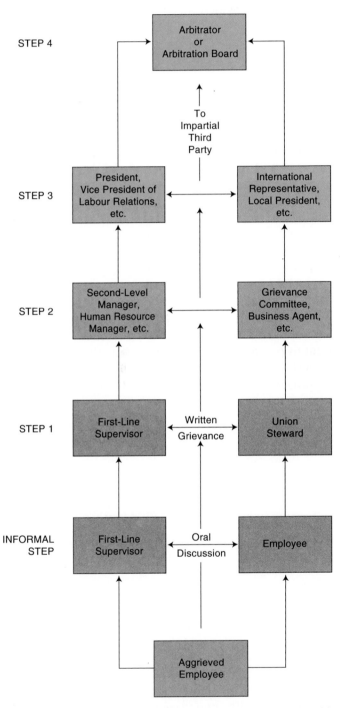

Source: Robert W. Eckles et al., Essentials of Management for First-Line Supervision *(New York: John Wiley & Sons, 1974), p. 529. Reprinted by permission of John Wiley & Sons, Inc.*

step may go to arbitration, if provided for in the agreement and if the union decides to persevere.

HR Web Wisdom

http: www.pearsoned.ca/ mondy

HRDC—HR Links

Provided is information on mediation and arbitration, as well as links to providers of mediation and arbitration services.

Just cause: A reasonable and legal response by management to an employee's conduct.

Arbitration

The final step in most grievance procedures is arbitration, a process whereby the dispute is submitted to an arbitrator, or a three-person arbitration board, for resolution. There has been a gradual trend toward single arbitrators. Three-person boards are more expensive and take up to two-and-a-half months longer to hand down a decision than a single arbitrator.[7] Arbitrators deal with such varied issues as warnings and suspensions, loss of seniority rights, fines, loss of fringe benefits, and demotion.

Should the grievance concern discipline or discharge, the concept of showing **just cause**—a reasonable and legal response to an employee's conduct— must be thoroughly understood by both parties. From the union's point of view, proceeding to arbitration without a well-documented and convincing case can be demoralizing, expensive, and embarrassing. From the employer's point of view, it is equally important to always be prepared for possible grievances. Managers should realize that, in many jurisdictions. any disciplinary action that affects a unionized employee may ultimately be taken to arbitration, even if this remedy is not specified in the labour agreement. Thus, many employers are careful to prepare records that will constitute proof of disciplinary action and the just causes for it. A written warning format usually follows the "progressive" approach and will vary. However, the following information is normally included:

1. statement of facts concerning the offence;

2. identification of the rule that was violated;

3. statement of what resulted or could have resulted because of the violation;

4. identification of any previous similar violations by the same individual;

5. statement of possible future consequences should the violation occur again;

6. signature and date.

It is important to document verbal reprimands because they may be the first step that ultimately leads to arbitration. An example of a written warning is shown in Figure 16-5.

The arbitrator has the power to review management's decision, but will intervene only when it is clear that the employer has acted in an arbitrary and unreasonable manner. Jurisdictional labour relations acts give arbitrators the right to uphold, repeal, or modify penalties imposed by management. The labour contract itself can also place limitations on an arbitrator's action. Collective agreements can specifically set out the penalties for a given infraction. An arbitrator is, however, obligated to take statutes into account, even if it means having to treat the language of the collective agreement as invalid.

In a unionized setting, if either the union or management decide in favour

Figure 16-5

An Example of a Written Warning

DATE:	August 1, 2000
TO:	Shane Boudreaux
FROM:	Wayne Sanders
SUBJECT:	Written Warning

We are quite concerned because today you were 30 minutes late to work and offered no justification for this. According to our records, a similar offence occurred on July 25, 2000. At that time you were informed that failure to report to work on time is unacceptable. I am therefore notifying you in writing that you must report to work on time. You will be suspended from work without pay for three days if you are late again without explanation.

Please sign this form to indicate that you have read and understand this warning. Signing is not an indication of agreement.

_____

Name

_____

Date

of arbitration, the union and the company must select an arbitrator or board. Most agreements specify the selection method; some even include a list of potential arbitrators. When choosing an arbitrator, both management and labour will study the candidates' previous decisions in an attempt to detect any biases. Obviously, neither party wants to select an arbitrator who might tend to favour the other's position.[8] If a selection method is not specified, or if either the employer or the union cannot agree on an arbitrator or board, then normally the minister of labour (in the relevant jurisdiction) will be asked to make the appointment.

Arbitrators must possess exceptional patience and judgment to render a fair and impartial decision because of the variety of factors to be considered, which include

- the nature of the offence;
- due process and procedural correctness;
- the griever's past record;
- length of service with the company;
- knowledge of the rules;
- warnings;
- the consistency of rule enforcement;
- any discriminatory treatment.

After the arbitrator or board has been selected, a hearing is held. The issue is presented to the arbitrator(s) in a document that summarizes the question(s) to be decided. At the hearing, each side presents its case. Since arbitration is an adversarial process, the arbitrator may conduct the hearing much like a courtroom proceeding. Witnesses, cross-examination, transcripts, and legal counsel may all be used. Other hearings may be conducted less formally. Instead of an official transcript, which may require the presence of a court stenographer, for example, the arbitrator's notes may be sufficient. The parties may also submit, or be asked to submit, formal written statements. After the hearing, the arbitrator or arbitrators study the material and testimony, reaching a decision as soon as possible, generally within 30 to 60 days. The decision is usually accompanied by a written opinion giving reasons for the decision.

Should either management or labour be unhappy with the decision, there is little chance for appeal. The courts will generally enforce an arbitrator's decision unless 1) the arbitrator's decision is shown to be unreasonable or capricious in that it did not address the issues; 2) the arbitrator exceeded his or her authority; or 3) the award or decision violated the law.

Weaknesses of Arbitration

Arbitration has achieved a certain degree of success in resolving grievances. The process is not, however, without weaknesses. First, both sides lose control by agreeing to allow a third party to decide for them. Some practitioners also claim that arbitration is losing its effectiveness because of the length of time between the first step of the grievance procedure and final settlement. In some cases, 100-250 days may elapse before a decision is made.[9] By the time it is finally settled, the reason for the initial filing of the grievance may even be forgotten. Others object to the cost of arbitration—over $25 000 for a three-day hearing[10]—which has been rising at an alarming rate. For all these reasons, most unions and management consider arbitration to be the solution of last resort. Research suggests that in three out of four cases, mediation resolves grievances without the need for arbitration.[11]

Grievance Handling in Nonunion Organizations

In the past, few firms without unions have had formalized grievance procedures. The situation is changing, however, as more and more managers see the advantages of establishing formal grievance procedures and encourage employees to use them.[12] While the step-by step procedure for handling union grievances is common practice, the means of resolving complaints in nonunion firms vary. A well-designed grievance procedure ensures that the employee has ample opportunity to make complaints without fear of reprisal. If the system is to work, everyone must be well-informed about the program and convinced that management wants it to be used. Most employees hesitate to formalize their complaints and must be urged to avail themselves of the process.[13]

Typically, an employee initiates a complaint with his or her immediate supervisor. If the complaint involves the supervisor, however, the individual should be permitted to proceed directly to an employee relations specialist or to a manager at the next level. The grievance ultimately may be taken to the organization's top executive for a final decision. One large engineering, con-

HR Web Wisdom

http: www.pearsoned.ca/ mondy

Dispute Resolution
This site provides information and discussion on various alternative dispute resolution approaches.

struction, and maintenance company, for example, has a unique dispute resolution program. Whenever workers feel they need to resolve a dispute, they may choose one or all four of the following options: open-door policy, conference, mediation, or arbitration. "We wanted to give our employees several ports of entry to lodge a complaint if they wanted to," said the manager of employee relations.[14]

TRENDS and INNOVATIONS

Alternative Dispute Resolution

As the number of employment-related lawsuits has increased dramatically, companies look for ways to protect themselves against the costs and uncertainties of the judicial system. **Alternative dispute resolution (ADR)** is a procedure in which the employee and the company agree ahead of time that any problems will be addressed by an agreed-on means. The main concept behind the ADR is that the traditional approach of presenting a dispute to a judge is not always best. Alternative means include an ombudsperson, mediation, conciliation, or even mini-trials. ADR may be used to settle such varied complaints as being fired without cause, sexual harassment, or discrimination. Alcoa, Brown & Root, Fairchild Aircraft, Levi Strauss, and McGraw-Hill are some of the companies that have implemented an ADR program.[15] When ADR is used, there is typically a stepped procedure. The first step might be a facilitated interaction between the complaining employee and the supervisor involved, followed by a review with a senior manager or a review board. Then mediation would be attempted, followed finally by arbitration.[16]

A promising form of ADR is the Grievance Mediation approach, which has been recommended by the Preventive Mediation Program of the Federal Mediation and Conciliation Service.[17] The premise of this approach is that the principles of mediation can be applied to grievances. The federal government has found this approach to be less formal, less costly and more effective than arbitration. Grievance mediation includes four basic steps:

1. After the last step of the grievance, the parties are given the option of choosing mediation rather than arbitration.

2. Both parties must request mediation in writing.

3. The mediator must further confirm that both parties want mediation.

4. The mediator proceeds to assist both parties, but if no solution can be reached, then both parties may choose arbitration. Nothing said or done in the grievance mediation may be brought up during the subsequent arbitration.

Alternative Dispute Resolution: A procedure agreed to ahead of time by the employee and the company for resolving any problems that may arise.

Termination

Termination—firing or dismissing an employee—is one of the most severe penalties that management can impose and should therefore be very carefully considered. The termination experience is traumatic for the employee, leading to feelings of failure, fear, disappointment, and, inevitably, anger. Firing is also difficult for the person who makes the decision. The realization that termination may affect not only the employee but often an entire family increases the trauma. Not knowing how the terminated employee will react may also create considerable anxiety for the manager who must do the firing.

There is a distinct psychology that surrounds termination.[18] The fired employee may experience a series of emotions in quick succession: initial shock (even if he or she knew or suspected), anger, the feeling that there must have been a mistake, possible identity collapse and/or ego disintegration. Then wild swings in mood may follow, perhaps culminating in depression. The restoration in self-confidence can take some time. Concurrently, the manager may experience feelings of self-pity (*Why me?*), followed by guilt (*Could I have done better for this person?*) and sympathy (*How will the employee survive?*). There may also be a private desire to retain the employee, or, conversely, a tendency to blame the employee for "doing this" to the manager.

Thus the manager must prepare for the termination interview in order to remain in complete control. The termination interview should always be conducted before a witness and in an environment where the manager has a psychological advantage, for example, the company boardroom. Some managers avoid using their own offices for this purpose, as they do not want employees to associate routine calls to the office with the possibility of dismissal. The environment should be calm, formal, polite, and unemotional. No matter what the fired employee says or does, the manager must keep control over his or her emotions. The employee should be told of the decision and given (documented) reasons, even though this may not be required by law. An official letter of termination should be provided. It should be made clear that the decision is final. There should be no debate.

Managers must also be security conscious. Depending on the circumstances, an employee should not even be allowed to return to the workplace unescorted, as some employees have done considerable damage in their desire to seek revenge. Passwords, locks, and combinations, therefore, may have to be changed immediately. Employees have often been known to destroy or steal important documents and company secrets. In addition, if a dismissed employee seems to be particularly angry, management should not give the person ready access to his or her peers. Relations with other employees can be undermined by "badmouthing" and perhaps outright lies about the situation.

Most experts strongly advise that the terminated employee be treated with dignity and respect. Managers, for example, should avoid blaming the employee. By taking away the blame (and thus most of the emotion) surrounding the firing decision, it is possible to help the employee deal constructively with the situation. Another practical reason for treating terminated employees with dignity and respect is that in the event of a wrongful dismissal suit, management practices will be scrutinized carefully by the courts. Although some employees may still sue, their case will be weakened if an employer has a reputation for fair and generous treatment. As with layoffs, some managers hire outplacement specialists (see page 405), to help the dismissed individual find a new job. Time can be allowed to check with a lawyer, or secretarial and photocopying services can be offered. It must be remembered that the person who is fired may someday be in a position to influence a major customer or to affect the business in some significant way. If both the company and the employee can come away from this situation as amicably as possible and with mutual respect intact, that will be in the best interests of everyone involved.

Layoffs

Often, when business is slow, a firm has no choice but to lay off workers. In the case of a layoff, the company temporarily terminates an employee and provides the individual with a specific recall to work date. If no recall to work date is given, then in almost all cases the worker is considered to have been terminated.

Layoff: A temporary job termination accompanied by a specific recall to work date.

Although being laid off is not the same as dismissal, the effect is similar: the worker loses his or her job. Being laid off can have extreme psychological consequences. One electrical engineer who was laid off after nearly 30 years with Xerox said: "Losing my job was the most shocking experience I've ever had in my life. I almost think it's worse than the death of a loved one, because at least we learn about death as we grow up. No one in my age group ever learned about being laid off."[19]

As with termination, layoffs should be conducted in a manner that preserves individual dignity. Throughout the 1990s, CBC laid off its staff as part of that corporation's seemingly never-ending cutbacks. Even though one network manager claimed, "We are doing this in as humane a fashion as we can," a senior CBC-TV producer was told she was "a redundant producer component." In the bitter words of Harry Rasky, an award-winning producer: "Civility is a beautiful Canadian quality. We understand it's important to treat people properly. That didn't happen in this case."[20] Care should be taken, therefore, in how the news is communicated to those affected and in how outsiders learn of the layoffs. Otherwise, a difficult HR situation will be made worse by bad publicity and bitterness.

Layoff and Recall Procedures

When the firm has a union, the layoff procedures are usually written into the collective agreement. This agreement takes into consideration the employee's legal rights. Seniority is often the criterion for layoffs, with the most junior employees laid off first and the most senior laid-off employees recalled first. The collective agreement may also have a **bumping procedure**. When senior-level positions are eliminated, the people occupying them have the right to "bump" or replace workers from lower-level positions, assuming that they have the proper qualifications for the lower-level jobs and more seniority than the incumbents. When extensive bumping occurs, the composition of the workforce is altered, sometimes affecting productivity.

Bumping procedure: The process (usually based on seniority) by which employees occupying senior positions have the right to "bump" or replace workers from lower-level positions.

In a nonunionized workplace, jurisdictional labour laws come into force. In most cases, these laws do not require the employer to give written notice or other advance warning. Normally, there is no requirement even to tell employees why they are being laid off.[21] However, whether the firm has a union or not, carefully constructed layoff/recall procedures should be developed.[22,23] Employees should understand when they are hired how the recall system will work in the event of a layoff. In the case of a nonunionized firm, where employees have no collective agreement to rely on, it is even more important that management establish procedures. Again, seniority could be an integral part of the process, but, frequently, other factors such as employee productivity can be considered. When productivity is a criterion, management must be careful to ensure that the decision *is* made on the basis of productivity, not favouritism.

Alternatives to Termination and Layoff

Prior to terminating or laying off an employee, management is well advised to consider all the alternatives. Three of the most popular options are early retirement, demotions, and transfers.

Early Retirement

Sometimes employees will be offered early retirement before reaching the organization's normal length-of-service requirement. Often retirement pay is reduced for each year the retirement date is advanced. Early retirement can be a win—win for both management and employees. It can satisfy the firm's immediate need to cut costs and an employee's need to retire with dignity. As a result, early retirement packages have been used extensively as an alternative to terminations or layoffs, especially in large scaled restructuring and downsizing. However, in a large percentage of downsized companies, management has not been happy with the results.[24] Research indicates that successful large scale early retirement programs need to be carefully planned. HR managers must first consider a number of factors. For example, a firm can be left with fewer and less-experienced employees who are nonetheless required to perform the same amount of work. The longer-term result can be overworked, demoralized employees and reduced customer service. Care must also be taken not to demoralize staff between 30 and 49 who are unable to leave. Early retirement also means that a firm can quickly lose its most experienced staff, which could seriously harm long-term growth.

Demotion

Demotion: The process of moving a worker to a lower-level position, which typically involves a reduction in pay.

Another alternative, used especially for long-term employees, is **demotion:** the process of moving a worker to a lower-level position, which typically involves a reduction in pay. Emotions often run high when an individual is demoted. The demoted person may feel betrayed, embarrassed, angry, and disappointed, resulting in further productivity decreases. Demotion, then, should be used with planning and caution. One means of reducing the trauma associated with demotions is to establish a probationary period for newly promoted workers, during which they try out the new job. Should the person not be suitable, the move back to the old job may not be as disappointing as it would have been had the promotion seemed permanent. If demotion is chosen over termination or layoff, efforts must be made to preserve the individual's self-esteem. For example, the person may be asked how he or she would like to handle announcing the demotion. Every effort should be made to project a positive image of the worker's value to the company.

In a unionized organization, the process of demotion is usually stipulated in the collective agreement. Should a decision be made to demote someone for unsatisfactory performance, the union is usually notified and given the specific reasons for the demotion. Often the demotion will be challenged through the formal grievance procedure. Documentation is necessary, therefore, for the demotion to be upheld.

Transfers

Rather than layoff or termination, some firms will also consider transfer. A **transfer** is the lateral movement of an employee within an organization, which may be initiated by the firm or by an employee. This lateral movement does not imply that a person is being promoted or demoted. Transfers serve several purposes. First, managers often find it necessary to reorganize. In order to fill positions created by reorganization, employee moves not entailing promotion may be necessary. The same is true when an office or a department is closed. Rather than terminating valued employees, managers may transfer them to other areas.

Another reason for using transfers is to make positions available in the primary promotion channel. Typically, companies are organized into a hierarchical structure resembling a pyramid. Each succeeding promotion is more difficult to obtain because fewer positions exist. At times, very productive but unpromotable employees occupy a position that blocks other qualified colleagues' opportunities for promotion. Faced with career stagnation, the most capable future managers may seek employment elsewhere. In order to keep promotion channels open and retain valued employees, management may decide to transfer employees who are unpromotable but productive at their present levels.

Transfers may also be used to satisfy employees' personal needs or career plans. The reasons for wanting a transfer are numerous. For example, an individual may need to work closer to home to care for aging parents. He or she may dislike a long commute. Factors such as these may be so important that employees will resign if a transfer is not approved.

Before approval, a transfer request should be analyzed to determine the best interests of both firm and individual. Transfers may be disruptive, for example, if a qualified replacement isn't available to take the vacated position. Management should establish transfer policies and procedures so that employees will be informed in advance as to when a transfer request is likely to be approved and under what conditions. For example, if the transfer is for personal reasons, some firms do not pay moving costs.

Transfer: The lateral movement of an employee within an organization.

Termination and Layoff—Key Issues

Three key termination or layoff issues that HR professionals must concern themselves with are wrongful dismissal, outplacement, and caring for those who remain after employees have left the firm.

Wrongful Dismissal

If an employee is protected by a collective agreement, the remedy for wrongful dismissal is normally through the grievance process. The employer must show there was just cause for termination.

At-will employees: Nonunionized workers whose employment depends almost entirely on the continued goodwill of the employer.

The rights of those employees not represented by a union—which includes a growing percentage of the Canadian workforce—has become a major HR issue. These nonunion employees have come to be known as **at-will employees**; which means that their employment depends almost entirely on the continued goodwill of the employer. Most *at-will* employees are hired for a job on the basis of an "indefinite term," that is, there is no stipulated termination date of the employment contract. If an employee is terminated without just cause, the employee is entitled to either reasonable notice or compensation instead of notice, as a result of past decisions made by the courts under *common law*, or the body of legal precedents that has built up over the years. [25,26] These common law decisions also take into consideration the jurisdiction's labour laws, which usually stipulate some basic or minimum recompense for terminated employees depending on the length of employment. For example, in one province, a terminated employee is entitled to vacation pay owed, in addition to a notice period or the equivalent termination pay.[27] See, for example, Figure 16-6.

Figure 16-6

Notice of Termination

How much notice of termination is an employee entitled to? The answer varies by jurisdiction; the following minimums are set out in the Ontario Employment Standards Act.

HOW LONG WITH THE EMPLOYER	NOTICE PERIOD OR TERMINATION PAY
Less than 3 months	0
3 months, but under 1 year	1 week
1 year, but under 3 years	2 weeks
3 years, but under 4 years	3 weeks
4 years, but under 5 years	4 weeks
5 years, but under 6 years	5 weeks
6 years, but under 7 years	6 weeks
7 years, but under 8 years	7 weeks
8 years or more	8 weeks

Source: Ontario Ministry of Labour, Employment Standards Fact Sheet, "Termination of Employment," http://www.gov.on.ca/LAB/es/terminae.htm

Any employer can legally terminate an employee without reason or notice. When faced with a perceived wrongful dismissal, an unsatisfied nonunion employee has only one recourse: to sue for damages through the court system. In court, the employer must then prove that just cause exists. If an employee is found to have been wrongfully dismissed—that is, there is no just cause—the typical damages are limited to 1) loss of wages or salary for a period of time the court considers to be reasonable notice of termination; and 2) any other monies that might have been paid, such as bonuses, profit-sharing income, medical or insurance plan benefits, pension fund contribution, and vacation pay. In short, the court will attempt to place the employee in the financial position he or she would have been in if reasonable notice had been given. This means that punitive damages and damages for mental stress have been awarded only in rare cases.[28] Throughout this process, it is in the best interest of the dismissed employee not to remain idle. Any legal damages will take into consideration evidence of an honest attempt to find alternative employment and reasonable expenses connected with a job search can be claimed as part of the legal action.[29]

Many employers are now beginning to hire employees on the basis of a fixed-term contract. That is, employee and employer agree on a specific time period for employment. Under this arrangement, once the contract ends, the employer has no further obligations. Technically, the employer would not be responsible for paying any further compensation such as termination pay. The main issue that has arisen recently is the situation in which an employee has been working under a series of consecutive renewed fixed-term contracts. Some employers have been using the renewed fixed-contract arrangement and thus planning to avoid any termination compensation or liability. In situations such as this, common law applies, and the courts have used the "smell test."[30] If a fixed contract is consistently extended, so that in practice the pattern of employment resembles an indefinite contract relationship, then the employee is entitled to termination compensation as though it were an indefinite contract. What this means is that employers considering fixed contracts must be able to prove that the employee fully understood and agreed to the fixed term conditions of the contract.

Outplacement

Many organizations have established a systematic means of helping laid off or terminated employees to locate jobs through outplacement.[31,32] **Outplacement** is the process of helping laid-off or terminated employees find employment elsewhere. Other terms used to describe outplacement are *relocation* and *career counselling*. The use of outplacement began at the executive level, but has recently become popular for mid- and lower-level employees, particularly in a takeover or mass restructuring. Outplacement, although costly, can reduce liabilities, both because a former employee who gets a new job quickly cannot claim a major loss of revenue and because an employee who feels he or she was treated fairly is less likely to sue.

Through outplacement, management tries to soften the blow of displacement. Some firms now want an outplacement counsellor to be present at the dismissal to control expressions of anger and to foster hope and optimism. Other services provided through outplacement are aptitude testing and transition centres; individual counselling, including aptitude testing and assistance

Outplacement: The process of helping laid-off or terminated employees find employment elsewhere.

in résumé preparation; job fairs; complete access to office equipment such as computers, fax machines, Internet, and photocopiers; and free postage for mailing application letters and résumés.[33]

Whatever the cause, termination should be conducted in a way that preserves the employee's dignity as much as possible. This is important not only on ethical but on practical grounds. Although chances of re-employment depend upon the fired employee's level and the industry, remember that few people remain unemployed forever. The person who is terminated or laid off may someday be in a position to influence a major customer or to affect the business in some significant way. No manager wants disgruntled, angry employees to seek revenge for past wrongs. Partly because of such fears, companies are investing more heavily in EAP and outplacement programs. Morris Berchard, executive vice-president of Warren Shepell, one of the largest EAP providers in Canada, quotes one of his clients: "We are having to cut back so much, we want to give our employees something to help them through these difficult times."[34]

Caring for Those Who Remain

One of the most neglected facets of HR management is the care of those remaining in the firm after other employees have been terminated or laid off. Forced separation dramatically affects those left behind—both managers and operatives. First, there are feelings of shock and dismay, followed by relief (*It wasn't me!*) and perhaps feelings of sympathy or of self-righteousness (*He deserved it, damn him!*). Depending on the relationship with the fired individual, there can be feelings of anger at the employer or manager. Remaining workers may become demoralized, overworked, confused, and anxious about their own jobs. Their trust has to be regained, as the memory of seeing their peers forced out of the organization can last for years.

Promotion

Promotion: The movement of an employee to a higher-level position in the organization.

Promotion is the movement of an employee to a higher-level position in the organization. An individual who obtains a promotion normally receives additional financial rewards and the ego enhancement associated with achievement and accomplishment. Most employees feel good about being promoted. But for every individual who gains a promotion, there are likely others who were not selected. An employee's promotion, therefore, may even result in a short-term decline in productivity, or in some instances the resignation of unsuccessful candidates.

Most labour market studies suggest that in the foreseeable future, promotions will not be as commonplace as in the past.[35] In many firms, the number of levels and middle management positions have declined, leaving fewer promotional opportunities. Consequently, managers must look for other ways to reward employees. As we noted in Chapter 9, network and transitory career paths are becoming more common. If trends continue, many employees are apt to shun the traditional internal promotion, leave the firm, and follow a transitory career path. Other employees who retain their jobs are likely to experience a spiral or network path. These workers, employed in downsized, flatter organizations, are expected to make at least five lateral moves during their careers.

Firms will be encouraged to design jobs that offer opportunities to learn new skills, providing some variation in job tasks.[36]

Resignation

Even when management is strongly committed to making the environment a good place to work, employees still resign. In fact, according one career transition expert, "managers . . . would be well advised to realize people who are now 18 may well change jobs six to eight times before they are 40 and, today, five years with a company is a reasonable career target."[37]

A certain amount of turnover is healthy for an organization and is often necessary to afford employees who stay the opportunity to fulfil career objectives. When turnover becomes excessive, however, the problem must be faced. The most qualified employees are often the ones who resign, because they are more mobile. If too many of a firm's highly qualified and competent workers are leaving, a means must be found to reverse the trend.

Analyzing Resignations

A frequently given reason for resignation is to obtain better salary and/or benefits. Research, however, has shown that even when employees mention pay as a reason for resigning, they often have other, deeper reasons for deciding to leave. Management should continuously identify the causes and correct them as quickly as possible.

Exit interviews and/or post-exit questionnaires are standard methods for determining why employees leave a particular firm.[38] In one survey, more than 90 percent of respondents indicated their companies had some form of exit interview program.[39] Typically, the exit interview is the firm's last contact with the employee and encourages the employee to divulge reasons for resigning. A human resource professional usually conducts this interview, as an employee is not as likely to respond as freely during an interview with the supervisor; reasoning that he or she may need a letter of recommendation from that supervisor in the future. The typical exit interview might consist of

- establishing rapport;
- exploring the purpose of the interview;
- exploring attitudes regarding the old job;
- discussing reasons for leaving;
- comparing the old and the new jobs;
- asking for recommended changes.[40]

Note that the interviewer is focusing on job-related factors while probing for the real reasons that the person is leaving. (Figure 16-7 gives an example of appropriate questions.) Over a period of time, properly conducted exit interviews can provide considerable insight into why employees resign. Patterns are often identified that uncover weaknesses in the firm's human resource management system, allowing corrective action to be taken.

The post-exit questionnaire is sent to former employees several weeks after they leave the organization. Usually, they have already started work at their new company. The questionnaire is structured to draw out the real reason the employee resigned. Ample blank space is also provided so that former employees can express their feelings about their former job and organization. One strength of this approach is that the individuals are no longer with the firm and may respond more freely to the questions. A weakness is that the interviewer is not present to interpret and to probe for the real reasons for leaving.

Notice of Resignation

In most firms, at least two weeks' notice is requested of departing employees. A month's notice may be required, however, from professional and managerial staff. Where notice is expected, this policy should be communicated to all employees. A surprise, immediate resignation may not only affect morale (as other employees wonder why), but make continuing operations difficult.

Retirement

Most long-term employees leave an organization by retiring. Retirement plans may be based on a certain age, or a certain number of years with the firm, or

Figure 16-7

Questions for an Exit Interview

1. Let's begin by your outlining briefly some of the duties of your job.

2. Of the duties you just outlined, tell me three or four that are crucial to the performance of your job.

3. Tell me about some of the duties you liked the most and what you liked about performing those duties.

4. Now, tell me about some of the duties you liked least and what you did not like about performing those duties.

5. Suppose you describe the amount of variety in your job.

6. Let's talk a little bit now about the amount of work assigned to you. For example, was the amount assigned not enough at times, perhaps too much at times, or was it fairly stable and even overall?

7. Suppose you give me an example of an incident that occurred on your job that was especially satisfying to you. What about an incident that was a little less satisfying?

8. Let's talk now about the extent to which you feel you were given the opportunity to use your educational background, skills, and abilities on your job.

9. Tell me how you would assess the quality of training on your job.

10. Suppose you describe the promotional opportunities open to you in your job.

Source: *Wanda R. Embrey, R. Wayne Mondy, and Robert M. Noe, "Exit Interview: A Tool for Personnel Development." Reprinted from* Personnel Administrator *(May 1979). Reprinted by permission of* HRMagazine *(formerly* Personnel Administrator*) published by the Society for Human Resource Management, Alexandria, Virginia.*

A GLOBAL
PERSPECTIVE

Responding to Crisis in a Global Setting

Any group of employees (domestic or expatriate) will have crises from time to time. Good employee relations are created when HR professionals acknowledge their problems and offer appropriate help or advice. Responses may range from sending a condolence card or ensuring that other employees know where to visit a sick colleague to spending considerable time finding the appropriate support network to resolve a serious family crisis. More extensive counselling may be part of an EAP, as we described in Chapter 13.

The role of the company can be much larger, however, when employees confront a crisis in a foreign country. According to one vice president of a major corporation "for an expatriate employee thousands of miles away from home, the company is the family. . . . Whenever something goes wrong, and it will, he or she will naturally turn to the company for help." The key to maintaining good employee relations is for the HR professional to be able to help when an expatriate employee is in difficulty. Global human resource professionals have been called on to assist expatriates with a wide range of difficult problems including medical emergencies, natural disasters, revolutions, and other international crises.[44]

Medical emergencies occur fairly frequently. Ralph W. Stevens, vice president of personnel and employee relations for Hamilton Oil Corporation, recalls the case of a high-ranking technical manager who suffered a stroke while on business in Korea, where the company maintains no office. Stevens managed to find a first-rate physician, set the employee up in a well-regarded hospital, and transfer sufficient funds to cover the medical bills, while comforting the manager's frantic family![45]

Various contingency plans, including means and methods to evacuate workers if necessary, should be in place if a firm operates in politically volatile areas. Similarly, HR professionals should be prepared to deal with natural disasters, such as earthquakes and hurricanes, as well as personal disaster. Nothing is more difficult than the death of an expatriate employee abroad. The HR professional may even have to coordinate the transport of a coffin from an international site while giving solace to a grieving family.[46] The ultimate test of management's concern for employees comes in times of crisis.

both. Upon retirement, some former employees receive a pension each month for the remainder of their lives. Some experts are sounding warnings, however, that future retirees will not be able to expect the same benefit levels as previous generations. In fact, it may be necessary for many Canadians to work, at least part-time, well into their seventies.[41] Indeed, it has been pointed out that complete retirement at 65 is a relatively recent phenomenon and that the retirement age of 65 is not based on any particular logic or supportable reason.[42]

Retirement Planning

Strong emotions often accompany retirement. As retirement approaches, the individual may be haunted by questions: *Do I have enough money? What will I do? Will I be able to adjust?* Just as a well-planned orientation program eases the transition of a new employee into the organization, so a company-sponsored retirement planning program eases the transition of long-term employees from work to leisure,[43] or to some other paid or volunteer activity.

Often, management invests time, staff, and money to provide useful information to those approaching retirement. Typically, this information relates to finances, housing, relocation, family relations, attitude adjustment, and legal affairs. In some firms, the focus is on adapting the employee to retirement living by considering both the social and the psychological implications of retirement. Retired individuals are often brought to meetings to speak and to answer questions about retirement life and managing lifestyle change. Such assistance can help smooth this major transition in an individual's life.

SUMMARY

1. Define internal employee relations.

Internal employee relations consists of those human resource management activities associated with the movement of employees within the organization. This HR function is important to ensure that individuals with the proper skills and experience are available at all levels when the need arises.

2. Define discipline and disciplinary action. Describe the disciplinary action process.

Discipline is the state of employee self-control and orderly conduct and indicates the extent of genuine teamwork within an organization. Disciplinary action invokes a consequence against an employee who fails to meet established standards or comply with organizational rules. Effective disciplinary action addresses the employee's wrongful behaviour, not the employee as a person. The disciplinary action process is based on rules and can be described by six steps: 1) set organizational goals; 2) establish rules; 3) communicate rules; 4) observe performance; 5) compare performance with rules; and 6) discipline if appropriate. The process should include feedback.

3. Discuss two key approaches to discipline and the key issues involved in administering discipline.

Two approaches to discipline are progressive disciplinary action and discipline without punishment. Progressive disciplinary action (also called *just cause* discipline) is a step-by-step method that imposes the minimum consequence appropriate to the offence. Discipline without punishment is an approach in which employees are encouraged to resolve issues in their own and the employer's best interest. This concept places responsibility for behaviour and its consequences on the employee. This system also entails a series of documented steps. Many managers avoid taking disciplinary action because of lack of training, fear, guilt, fear of loss of friendship, time requirements, fear of losing control, and rationalization. A written code can provide a useful framework for management in administering discipline.

4. Briefly explain the grievance process in union and nonunion organizations.

Union employees who believe they have been disciplined or dealt with unjustly can appeal through the grievance and arbitration procedures of the collective bargaining agreement. In most cases, a grievance that remains unresolved goes to arbitration, at which point an employer must document just cause for its actions. There is little chance to appeal an arbitrated decision. Arbitration has achieved a certain degree of success in resolving grievances but it is slow and costly and takes control away from the principals. In the past, few firms without unions had formalized grievance procedures. The situation is changing, as more and more managers see the advantages of establishing formal grievance procedures and encourage employees to use them.

5. Explain how managers deal with termination and layoffs.

The termination or layoff experience is traumatic for the employee and management. Thus a manager should prepare for a termination interview and be security conscious. The terminated employee must be treated with dignity and respect. Because of the emotional and legal complexities, increasingly, managers are hiring outplacement specialists. When the firm has a union, termination/layoff procedures are usually written into the collective agreement. Seniority is often the criterion for layoffs. In a nonunionized workplace, jurisdictional labour laws come into force.

6. Describe three major alternatives to termination or layoff.

Three common alternatives to termination or layoff are early retirement, demotion, and transfer. Carefully planned, early retirement can benefit both management and employees. Demotion, used mostly with long-term employees, should be done with care to preserve the individual's self-esteem. Transfers are considered when managers find it necessary to reorganize, to make positions available in the primary promotion channel, and to satisfy employee's personal needs or career plans. Management should establish transfer policies and procedures and make employees aware of them in advance.

7. Briefly outline three key HR issues related to termination/layoff.

Three key issues are wrongful dismissal, outplacement, and caring for those who remain after employees have left the firm. If an employee is protected by a collective agreement, the remedy for wrongful dismissal is through the grievance process. The rights of nonunionized or at-will employees have become a major HR issue. In most cases, if an at-will employee is terminated without just cause, the employee is legally entitled to either reasonable notice or compensation instead of notice. Fixed-term contracts avoid such obligations, but courts may sometimes find that a de facto indefinite-term contract exists. The only recourse for a nonunion employee who believes he or she was wrongfully dismissed is to sue through the court system. Outplacement—helping laid off or terminated employees locate jobs—can soften the blow for the employee, reduce the employer's legal risk, and reduce the risk that a disgruntled former employee will seek revenge. Remaining employees may be demoralized, anxious, angry, and overworked. The firm must work to regain their trust. EAP programs can be helpful.

8. Describe the internal relations issues related to promotion, resignation, and retirement.

In the foreseeable future, promotions will not be as easily available as in the past. Consequently, managers must look for other ways to reward employees. If trends continue, many employees will follow a transitory or a spiral career path. Even when management is strongly committed to making the environment a good place to work, employees still resign. In most firms, at least two weeks' resignation notice is requested. Often the most qualified employees are the ones who resign. Thus exit interviews and/or post-exit questionnaires can be useful in helping HR professionals learn how to keep valued employees. Most long-term employees leave an organization by retiring. Some experts caution that future retirees will not be able to expect the same benefit levels as previous generations. As a result, careful retirement planning is necessary. Often, management invests time, staff, and money to provide useful information to those approaching retirement. Such assistance can help smooth this major transition in an individual's life.

QUESTIONS FOR REVIEW

1. Distinguish between progressive discipline and discipline without punishment.

2. In progressive disciplinary action, what steps are involved before employee termination?

3. Under a discipline without punishment system, what steps are involved before employee termination?

4. What are the typical steps in handling a grievance under a collective bargaining agreement?

5. Why is arbitration not often used in the settlement of grievances in a unionized firm?

6. How would grievances typically be handled in a nonunion firm? Describe briefly.

7. Define and briefly describe the concept of alternative dispute resolution.

8. Explain the concept of just cause as it pertains to termination.

9. Distinguish between demotions, transfers, and promotions.

10. Why is early retirement used as a substitute for layoffs?

11. Discuss how the surviving employees might feel after a downsizing. What should management do?

DEVELOPING **HRM** SKILLS

An Experiential Exercise

Isadore Lamansky is the manager of the machine tooling operations at Jen Star Industries and has five supervisors who report to him. One of his employees is Susie Canton, a supervisor in maintenance. As Isadore is on his way to work this morning, his thoughts focus on Susie: "Today is the day that I must talk to Susie. I sure hate to do it. I know she is going to take it the wrong way. Ever since Susie was promoted to unit supervisor she has had trouble maintaining discipline. She tries too hard to keep the men in line because she thinks they are continually trying to push her, and she lets the women get away with murder. Well I guess I'll get this over with, since that's what I get paid for."

The grapevine is strong at Jen Star, and it didn't take long for Susie to hear rumours. She thinks, "The word is that old Isadore is going to come down on me. He recommended someone else for my job because he doesn't like women in charge. The reason it is so hard to maintain discipline is that the men I supervise intentionally push me to see what I'll do. The women support me, and they are proud of me; the men just want me gone. He is probably going to dredge up some minor stuff to reprimand me about; we need more women in charge, and the boss will have to accept that I'm here for good!"

Who is right, and who is wrong? Can there be a reasonable solution to these problems? This exercise will require two participants, one to play Susie and the other to play Isadore. All others should observe carefully. Instructors will provide additional information to participants.

HRM INCIDENT

You Know the Policy

Dwayne Alexander was the Halifax-area supervisor for Quik-Stop, a chain of convenience stores. There were seven Quik-Stop stores in Halifax, and Dwayne had full responsibility for managing them. Each store operated with only one person on duty at a time. Although several of the stores stayed open all night, every night, the Centre Street store was open all night Monday through Thursday but only from 6:00 a.m to 10:00 p.m. Friday through Sunday. Because the store was open fewer hours during the weekend, money from sales was kept in the store safe until Monday. The time it took to complete a money count on Monday, therefore, was greater than normal.

The company had a policy that when the safe was being emptied, the manager had to be with the employee on duty, and the employee had to place each $1000 in a brown bag, mark the bag, and leave the bag on the floor next to the safe until the manager verified the amount in each bag.

Anton Janacek worked the Sunday night shift at the Centre Street store and was trying to save the manager time by counting the money prior to his arrival. The store got very busy, and, while bagging a customer's groceries, Anton mistook one of the money bags for a bag containing three sandwiches and put the money bag in with the groceries. Twenty minutes later, the manager arrived, and both men began to search for the money. While they were searching, the customer came back with the bag of money. The company has a policy that anyone violating the money-counting procedure must be fired immediately.

Anton was very upset. "I really need this job," Anton exclaimed. "With the new baby and all the other expenses we've had, I sure can't stand to be out of a job."

"You knew about the policy, Anton," said Dwayne.

"Yes, I did, Dwayne," said Anton, "and I really don't have any excuse. If you don't fire me, though, I promise you that I'll be the best store manager you've got."

While Anton waited on a customer, Dwayne called his boss at the home office in Montreal. With the boss's approval, Dwayne decided not to fire Anton.

Questions

1. Do you agree with Dwayne's decision in view of the text material on progressive discipline? Discuss.

2. How did Dwayne's decision not to fire Anton serve as a motivational force for Anton?

PART SIX   CASE 6

Parma Cycle Company: The Union Organizing Effort

The Digby, Nova Scotia plant of Parma Cycle Company had been open for only six months in March 1999 when the first union organizing attempts became apparent. A known union organizer was in town and pro-union leaflets began to appear around the factory. The human resource director at Digby, Edward Deal, had been expecting this to occur. He knew that the workers brought down from the main plant in Delta, B.C. had a strong union tradition. He also knew that the wage and benefits package at Digby was far less liberal than the one at the B.C. plant. So far, this discrepancy hadn't created a major problem. Most of the workers recruited from the Digby area felt that they were well paid in comparison to others in that area.

In the plant that same day, Janice Snively was thinking about whether or not she should talk to the human resource director. Janice had been hired by Parma two weeks prior to start-up. She had previously worked as a maintenance supervisor at a garment factory about 60 miles from Digby. She had taken a slight pay cut in order to take what she thought would be a better long-term job and to be closer to her family, who lived in Digby.

Janice's crew of 10 machine operators and two parts handlers was among the best in the plant. Janice had made friends with each of them and they obviously respected her. She felt that one reason she was a good leader was her willingness to get her hands dirty. Because of her experience in maintenance she was able to repair the machines herself when they broke down. When an operator was absent, she would take over that machine in order to keep the work flowing.

Lately she had noticed a change. The workers seemed to be shutting her out. In a couple of instances, when several of her crew were congregated at one table in the lunchroom, the conversation stopped as she approached and then awkwardly began again. The change of topic was obvious. For the first time, too, she began to hear complaints. For example, the operator of the cutoff machine, which cuts certain frame members to size, complained of the speed with which the machine operated. "I have less than one second to move the cut-off piece before the tubing feeds through to start another cut. I'll be lucky not to lose an arm," he said. There had been a number of similar complaints (many of them related to safety, some to working conditions), and a number of workers asked about the date of their next raise.

Janice thought that handling these kinds of problems was part of the supervisor's job, so she wasn't too concerned. But now she decided it was time to talk to the human resource director.

Janice walked in as Ed was thinking about the advantages and disadvantages of having a union. "Ed," she said, "I want you to look at this. One of my people gave it to me and asked if it is true. I didn't know how to answer." Janice handed Ed a photocopied sheet. After studying the sheet for a moment Ed said, "It's basically true, but I wish it weren't."

Here is a reproduction of the sheet:

DID YOU KNOW?

- Parma's workers in B.C. do not pay for their dependents' supplemental medical insurance. You do!

- Parma's employees in B.C. have dental insurance. You don't!

- Employees in B.C. have 12 paid holidays. You have only nine.

- Trainees at the B.C. plant get $8.00 per hour. At Digby, they get the minimum wage.

- Senior machine operators in B.C. get $14.00 an hour. Here, they get $10.00 or less.

Questions

1. What do you think caused the union organizing attempt at Parma Cycle's Digby plant?

2. What sequence of events is likely to occur before a union is certified at the Digby plant?

3. Assuming that management wishes to prevent a union from organizing the Digby plant, what can the union and management legally do before and after a union representation election is ordered by the Nova Scotia Labour Board?

PART SIX   CBC 🍁 VIDEO CASE

The New Militants

After the First World War, thousands of returning Canadian soldiers had to find work. There was plenty of work in smokestack industries such as autos and steel, but the pay was low and the hours long. Over time, workers, mostly males, turned to unionism in a collective movement to improve working conditions. Some say that this trend is recurring on a new battlefield: the fast-growing service sector with its low-wage, nonunion jobs.

The young warriors are Generation X-ers, often women like Mary McArthur, who desperately want to improve their pay, working conditions, and dignity. McArthur's struggle began in 1997 when she helped lead a union drive at Wal-Mart's Windsor, Ontario outlet—the first of Wal-Mart's 3000 stores to unionize.

For more than 30 years, the retail giant had staved off unions with the promise of profit sharing, benefits, discounts, and a caring culture. "We feel that if we do a good job taking care of our people, we can provide the kinds of environment that respects them as individuals and that rewards them for their success as Wal-Mart succeeds," said Ed Gould, a Wal-Mart spokesperson. "When you have a third party represent workers, everyone loses." Some workers agreed, and actively campaigned against unionism. But another group of defiant employees felt the Wal-Mart hours and wages didn't add up to a decent standard of living. "I'm afraid of working for $8 an hour for the rest of my life," said McArthur.

Meanwhile, another David and Goliath battle was going on in B.C. The Canadian Auto Workers (CAW) Local 3000 had just signed up eight Starbucks stores. These were the only unionized outlets among the more than 2000 stores in the profitable coffee empire. The union leaders were a group of 20-somethings who got frustrated and then got organized. The issues on the bargaining table were basic: fair wages, earned sick leave, scheduling of work, and training procedures. Like Wal-Mart, Starbucks said it had an employee-friendly company. But the young militants accused the company of forgetting its employees' needs in its rush to expand.

Is militancy spreading? Professor Ann Forrest at the University of Windsor says, "It is certainly arguable that young people as a group will be making demands on employers who in the past have never faced any kind of labour controversy." Joan Pajunen of Retail Consultants Service Dimensions agrees: "I think they are the road warriors. . . . They will not be shunted aside. There will be more unionization simply because it's a way from them to find more control."

These young warriors may be in for a long and bumpy ride. According to a 1999 survey by the Work Research Foundation, some sixty percent of young workers don't believe that union confrontation is necessary. "The hard truth is that most young people don't care about unions," said a frustrated Frank Linhares, a youth activist with the Steelworkers Local 13571. "If they're in a crappy job, they know that they can just walk away from it. Their lives aren't tied up in their jobs. Benefits and pensions aren't such big issues for them." McArthur disagrees: "Young people certainly do care, but you have to get in their face, get out there and get their attention. You have to get them in touch with the realities of the workplace."

If history is any indication, the fight to organize service workers will be long and embittered. According to McArthur, by spring 2000, some three years after certification, unionized workers at the Wal-Mart Windsor outlet were still not working under a labour–management contract. A collective agreement had been signed and ratified, but Wal-Mart had chosen not to honour it, and legal battles continued. About the same time, Starbucks workers at 12 unionized outlets in Vancouver were fighting for a second collective agreement. You could find them on the job defiantly wearing "Warbucks" buttons and T-shirts that read, "I didn't have any sick leave so I phoned in dead. Now my boss wants a Coroner's certificate before I come back to work."

McArthur, who has left Wal-Mart to join a new retail division of the CAW, says, "It's a reality now that there are a lot of people out there who will be stocking shelves and serving coffee for the rest of their lives. They need a decent job and salary to live." Pajunen adds, "The message . . . is that there is a new workforce out there, it is a new time, a different time and people need to be managed in different ways."

Questions

1. What factors led to militant unions at Wal-Mart and Starbucks?

2. About 34 percent of Canadian workers are unionized. Do you expect this percentage to grow or decline? Why?

3. State arguments for and against a unionized service sector.

4. As an HR manager of a unionized company, what strategies would you suggest to reduce confrontation?

Video Resource: "Wal-Mart" (The New Militants), Venture #631 (February 23, 1999)

ENDNOTES

Chapter 1

1. Shari Caudron, "HR Leaders Brainstorm the Profession's Future," *Personnel Journal* 73 (August 1994): 54.

2. The Canadian Council of Human Resources Associations (CCHRA), National Capabilities Project, Phase I: *http:// chrpcanada.com/ncc/html/exec_summary.html*

3. Ibid.

4. P. Wright, J. G. Guidry, and J. Blair, *Opportunities for Vocational Study* (Toronto: University of Toronto Press, 1994): 179–181.

5. Donald V. Brookes, "HR in the '90s: From Tacticians to Strategists," *HR Focus* 71 (September 1994): 12.

6. Rick Spence, *Secrets of Success from Canada's Fastest Growing Companies* (Toronto: John Wiley and Sons Canada, Ltd., 1997): 195.

7. Donald J. McNerney, "Spreading the Wealth," *HR Focus,* 74 (March 1997): 1, 4–5.

8. Jennifer Wunsch, Work Research Foundation "Workers Unions and Choice, a Status Report", 1998: *http://www.interlog.com/ ~wrf/wuc1.htm#Types*

9. B. Downie and M. L. Coates, *The Changing Face of Industrial Relations and Human Resource Management* (Kingston: Industrial Relations Centre, Queen's University, 1993).

10. CCHRA, National Capabilities Project, Phase I.

11. *Restructuring the Human Resources Department,* a report by Saratoga Institute, sponsored by the American Management Association, 1997.

12. Shari Caudron, "HR Leaders Brainstorm the Profession's Future."

13. Donna Keith and Rebecca Hirschfield, "The Benefits of Sharing," *HR Focus* 73 (September 1996): 15.

14. Janet Garry-McLaughlin DeRose, "Outsourcing through Partnerships," *Outsourcing through Partnerships* 49 (October 1995): 51.

15. Jackie Hudson, KPMG Canada: "Actuarial, Benefits & Compensation," *The HumanEdge*, 1996: *http://www.kpmg.ca/ main/mf.htm*

16. John B. Wyatt, "Customer-Driven HR," *HR Focus,* 74 (February 1997): 3.

17. Jackie Hudson, "Actuarial, Benefits & Compensation."

18. James Down, "Human Resources Takes a Strategic Role," *Executive Forum* (March 1997).

19. Shari Caudron, "HR Leaders Brainstorm the Profession's Future."

20. Ibid.

21. Elizabeth Sheley, "Share Your Worth," *HRMagazine* 41 (June 1996): 86.

22. Charlene Marmer Solomon, "Managing the HR Career of the 90's," *Personnel Journal* 73 (June 1994): 62–64.

23. See for example, Industry Canada, *Your Guide to Government of Canada Services and Support for Small Business: Trends and Statistics,* 1996 – 1997, Catalogue No. C1–10/1997E.

24. David Snyder, "The Revolution in the Workplace: What's Happening to Our Jobs?" *Futurist* 30 (March 1996): 8.

25. See, for example, Minister of Supply and Services, *Canada's International Business Strategy*, 1997–1998, Catalogue No. C2-226/1-1998E; and Collin Campbell with Carol Hood, *Where the Jobs Are: Career Survival for Canadians in the New Global Economy*, 2nd ed. (Toronto: Macfarlane Walter & Ross, 1997): 21.

26. P. J. Dowling, R. S. Schuler, and D. E. Welch, *International Dimensions of Human Resource Management* (Belmont: Wadsworth Publishing Co.,1994): VII.

27. P. J. Dowling, R. S. Schuler, and D. E. Welch, *International Dimensions of Human Resource Management*, 5–6.

28. Michael R. Bloom and Kurtis G. Kitagawa, Conference Board of Canada, *Understanding Employability Skills*, 1999, pg. 3.

29. James Down, "Human Resources Takes a Strategic Role," *Executive Forum* (March 1997).

30. CCHRA, National Capabilities Project, Phase I.

31. The Canadian Council of Human Resources Associations (CCHRA): *http://www.chrpcanada.com/*

32. Canadian Compensation Association: *http://www.cca-acr.org/*

33. Canadian Payroll Association: *http://www.payroll.ca/English/ Home/homee.htm*

34. International Foundation of Employee Benefit Plans: *http://www.ifebp.org/cecnhm.html*

35. Bill Leonard, "Business Ethics Touch HR Issues, Survey Finds," *HR News* 10 (June 1991): 13.

36. Patricia Buhler, "How Can We Encourage Ethical Behavior?" *Supervision* 52 (January 1991): 3.

Chapter 2

1. Adapted from Margot Gibb-Clark, "Non–Profit Agencies Must Be Creative to Keep Staff," *The Globe and Mail*, June 8, 1999, B10.

2. See, for example, Statistics Canada, *Perspectives on Labour and Income*, Summer 1999, Cat. No. 75-001-XPE.

3. *The Charter of Rights and Freedoms: A Guide for Canadians* (Ottawa: Minister of Supply and Services Canada, 1992): 15–16. See also: *the Canadian Charter of Rights and Freedoms: http://canada.justice.gc.ca/Loireg/charte/const_en.html*

4. Canadian Human Rights Tribunal: *http://www.chrt-tcdp.gc.ca/ tribunal_contents.htm*

5. KPMG Canada, "Ethics and Integrity": *http://www.kpmg.ca/ ethics/*

6. Kenneth E. Goodpaster and John B. Matthews, Jr., "Can a Corporation Have a Conscience?" *Harvard Business Review* 60 (January-February 1982): 132–141.

7. KPMG Canada: "Ethics and Integrity."

8. B. Downie and M. L. Cootes, *The Changing Face of Industrial Relations and Human Resource Management* (Kingston: Industrial Relations Centre, Queen's University, 1993).

9. Jennifer Wunsch, "Workers, Unions and Choice: a status report": *http://www.interlog.com/~wrf/wuc.htm*

10. Marianne Kolbasuk McGee, "IT Management: Sign-On Bonuses Lure Top IT Talent," *Information Week* (April 12, 1997): 84.

11. See, for example, Human Resources Development Canada, (HRDC) Applied Research Branch "Technological and Organizational Change and Labour Demand: The Canadian Situation:" *http://www.hrdc-drhc.gc.ca/stratpol/arb/publications/research/abr-97-1e.shtml*

12. HRDC, "Technological and Organizational Change and Labour Demand: The Canadian Situation."

13. Statistics Canada, *The Daily*, Tuesday, March 17, 1998: *http://www.statcan.ca/Daily/English/980317/d980317.htm*

14. Industry Canada, "Toward a Society Built on Knowledge": *http://strategis.ic.gc.ca/SSG/ih01639e.html.*

15. Sinclair E. Hugh, "Observations from the Witness Stand," *HRMagazine* 39 (August 1994): 176.

16. Stephanie Overman, "Managing the Diverse Work Force," *HRMagazine* 36 (April 1991): 32.

17. "Managers Must Hit Racial Issue 'Head on,'" *Financial Post Daily* 4, 142, (1991): 35.

18. Mark MacKinnon, "Women Gaining Ground in Work Force," *The Globe and Mail*, April 19, 1999, B1, B4. Reprinted with permission from *The Globe and Mail.*

19. Statistics Canada, 1991–1996 Census, "Labour Force 15 Years and Over by Broad Occupational Categories and Major Groups and Sex, for Canada, Provinces and Territories, 1991 and 1996": *http://www.statcan.ca/english/census96/mar17/occupa/table2/t2p00.htm*

20. Mark MacKinnon, "Women Gaining Ground in Work Force."

21. Statistics Canada, "1996 Census: Aboriginal Data," *The Daily*, Tuesday, January 13, 1998: *http://www.statcan.ca/Daily/English/980113/d980113.htm*

22. Statistics Canada, "1996 Census: Ethnic Origin, Visible Minorities," *The Daily*, Tuesday, February 17, 1998: *http://www.statcan.ca/Daily/English/980217/d980217.*

23. Statistics Canada, *Selected Characteristics of Persons With Disabilities Residing in Households*. Ottawa: Statistics Canada (1994): 82–555.

24. Statistics Canada, *A Portrait of Persons with Disabilities*, 1995, Catalogue 89 – 542E, 5,7.

25. Susan Goff Condon, "Hiring the Handicapped Confronts Cultural Uneasiness," *Personnel Journal* 66 (April 1987): 68.

26. Adapted from "Focus on Ability: Changing the Way Canadians Think about Physical Disability," a special supplement prepared by the Canadian Foundation for Physically Disabled Persons, *The Globe and Mail*, February 12, 1999, 2,11. Reprinted with permission from the Canadian Foundation for Physically Disabled Persons.

27. Statistics Canada, "1996 Census: Mother Tongue, Home Language and Knowledge of Languages," *The Daily*, Tuesday, December 2, 1997: *http://www.statcan.ca/Daily/English/971202/d971202.htm*

28. Margot Gibb-Clark, "Work v. Family: The $2.7 – Billion Crisis," *The Globe and Mail*, June 4, 1999, M1.

29. Amy Saltzman, "A Family Transfer," *U.S. News & World Report* 122 (February 10, 1997): 60–62.

30. Statistics Canada, "Earning Characteristics of two-partner families," *The Daily*, Friday, October 23, 1998: *http://www.statcan.ca/Daily/English/981023/d981023.htm#ART2*

31. Karen Fawcett, "Trailing Spouse Often Must Fend for Self—Herself," *USA Today*, August 9, 1994, 2.

32. Statistics Canada, "1996 Census: Marital Status, Common-Law Unions and Families," *The Daily*, Tuesday, October 14, 1997: Daily *http://www.statcan.ca/Daily/English/971014/d971014.htm*

33. Human Resources Development Canada, "Report of the Advisory Committee on the Changing Workplace," Chapter 4—Serge Brault, 53–54: *http://www.reflection.gc.ca/Report/chap4_e.htm*

34. Joan Hamilton, Stephen Baker, and Bill Vlasic, "The New Workplace," *Business Week*, April 29, 1996, 106.

35. Margot Gibb-Clark, "Non–Profit Agencies Must Be Creative to Keep Staff," *The Globe and Mail*, June 8, 1999, B10.

36. Margot Gibb-Clark, "How a Younger Worker Can Sway Older Colleagues," *The Globe and Mail*, May 11, 1999, B9. Reprinted with permission from *The Globe and Mail.*

37. Mark MacKinnon, "Young Men Facing Tougher Time in Job Race," *The Globe and Mail*, April 19, 1999, B4.

38. Jaclyn Fierman, "The Contingency Workforce," *Fortune* 129 (January 24, 1994): 30; Human Resources Development Canada, Report of the Advisory Committee on the Changing Workplace, Chapter 4.

39. John Ross, "Effective Ways to Hire Contingent Personnel," *HRMagazine* 36 (February 1991): 53.

40. Statistics Canada, "Rising Self–Employment in the Midst of High Unemployment: An Empirical Analysis of Recent Developments in Canada," Research Paper No. 133: *http://www.statcan.ca/english/Vlib/Research/ana133.htm*

41. Perry Pascarella, "Thinking Globally Is 'Sacred' Management Duty," *Management Review* 86 (April 1997): 58–59.

42. Clifford C. Hebard, "Managing Effectively in Asia," *Training & Development* 50 (April 1996): 34.

Chapter 3

1. Connie Freeman, "Strategy: Training HR Pros to Fit Your Culture," HR *Focus* 74 (May 1997): 9.

2. James Down, "From Paper Pushing to Strategic Planning," *Boston Business Journal* 16 (January 24, 1997): 6.

3. Melody Jones, "Four Trends to Reckon With," *HR Focus* 73 (July 1996): 22.

4. Ian Wilson, "The Strategic Management Technology: Corporate Fad or Strategic Necessity," *Long-Range Planning* 19 (1986): 21–22.

5. Margaret Butteriss, *Help Wanted: the Complete Guide to Human Resources for Canadian Entrepreneurs* (Etobicoke: John Wiley & Sons Canada Ltd., 1999): 6.

6. R. Wayne Mondy, Robert M. Noe, and Robert E. Edwards, "What the Staffing Function Entails," *Personnel* 63 (April 1986): 55–56.

7. Paul A. Evans, "Management Development as Glue Technology," *Human Resource Planning* 15 (December 1992): 85–106.

8. James Martin, "HR in the Cybercorp," *HR Focus* 74 (April 1997): 3.

9. Margaret Butteriss, *Help Wanted: the Complete Guide to Human Resources for Canadian Entrepreneurs*, 208–209.

10. Elizabeth Church, "Leadership Crisis Foreseen for Family Firms," *The Globe and Mail*, January 18, 1999, B1.

11. James E. McElwain, "Succession Plans Designed to Manage Change," *HRMagazine* 36 (February 1991): 67.

12. Margaret Butteriss, *Help Wanted: the Complete Guide to Human Resources for Canadian Entrepreneurs*, 209.

13. Kenneth Nowack, "The Secrets of Succession," *Training & Development* 48 (November 1994): 49.

14. R. Wayne Mondy and Harry N. Mills, "Choice Not Chance in Nurse Selection," *Supervisor Nurse* 9 (November 1978): 35–39.

15. Oliver Bertin, "CN Chops 3,000 More Jobs," *The Globe and Mail*, October 21, 1998, A1.

16. Ibid., A1.

17. "Study Finds 'Dim-Witted' Downsizing Sign of Mismanagement," *Ottawa Citizen*, October 26, 1996, D7.

18. Elizabeth Lesly and Larry Light, "When Layoffs Alone Don't Turn the Tide," *Business Week* (December 7, 1992): 100–101.

19. Jaclyn Fierman, "Beating the Midlife Career Crisis," *Fortune* 128 (September 6, 1993): 53.

20. Oliver Bertin, "CN Chops 3,000 More Jobs,", A1.

21. Shari Caudron, "Rebuilding Employee Trust," *Training & Development* 50 (August 1996): 18.

22. Janet Bensu, "Use Your Data Base in New Ways," *HRMagazine* 35 (March 1990): 33–34.

23. Beth Slick, "Technology and the Human Factor (reprinted from *PC Today*)," *Softbase* (April 29, 1996): 10.

24. James L. Wilkerson, "The Future Is Virtual HR," *HR Focus* 74 (March 1997): 15.

25. Ibid.

26. Row Henson, "Globalization: A Human Resources Mandate," *SoftBase* (March 3, 1996): 62–64.

27. Gale Eisenstodt, "Information Power," *Forbes* 151 (June 21, 1993): 44–45.

28. Ibid.

29. Row Henson, "Globalization: A Human Resources Mandate."

30. Ellen Brandt, "Global HR," *Personnel Journal* 70 (March 1991): 38–39.

31. Row Henson, "HRIMS for Dummies: A Practical Guide to Technology Implementation," *HR Focus* 73 (November 1996): 3–6.

Chapter 4

1. James Clifford, "Manage Work Better to Better Manage Human Resources: A Comparative Study of Two Approaches to Job Analysis," *Public Personnel Management* 25 (April 1996): 89.

2. James P. Clifford, "Job Analysis: Why Do It, and How Should It Be Done?" *Public Personnel Management* 23 (Summer 1994): 324.

3. R. Wayne Mondy, Robert M. Noe, and Robert E. Edwards, "What the Staffing Function Entails," *Personnel* 63 (April 1986): 55–58.

4. P. Thériault, *Personal Communication,* March 21, 1995.

5. IBM Human Resources Conference, "IT Should Support HR Changes," October 23, 1996.

6. Mary Molina Fitzer, "Managing from Afar: Performance and Rewards in a Telecommuting Environment," *Compensation & Benefits Review* 29 (January/February 1997): 65–73.

7. N. Fredric Crandall and Marc J. Wallace, Jr., "Inside the Virtual Workplace: Forging a New Deal for Work and Rewards," *Compensation & Benefits Review* 29 (January/February 1997): 27–36.

8. Gilbert B. Siegel, "Job Analysis in the TQM Environment," *Public Personnel Management* 25 (December 1996): 493.

9. Felix M. Lopez, Gerald A. Kesselman, and Felix E. Lopez, "An Empirical Test of a Trait-Oriented Job Analysis Technique," *Personnel Psychology* 35 (August 1981): 480

10. Information for this section was furnished by First Interstate Bancorp.

11. Kaye L. Aho, "Understanding the New Job-Analysis Technology," *Personnel* 66 (January 1989): 38.

12. Donald C. Busi, "The Job Description: More Than Bureaucratic Control," *Supervisory Management* 35 (October 1990): 5.

13. Hubert S. Field and Robert D. Gatewood, "Matching Talent with the Task: To Find the Right People, First Define the Jobs You Want Them to Do," *Personnel Administrator* 32 (April 1987): 113.

14. The following section has been adapted from: *National Occupational Classification*, (Ottawa: Canada Communication Group, 1993).

15. Margaret Butteriss, *Help Wanted: the Complete Guide to Human Resources for Canadian Entrepreneurs* (Etobicoke: John Wiley & Sons Canada Ltd., 1999): 46.

16. Frederick Herzberg, "One More Time: How Do You Motivate Employees?" *Harvard Business Review* 65 (September/October 1987): 109–120.

17. Stephen L. Perlman, "Employees Redesign Their Jobs," *Personnel Journal*, 69 (November 1990): 37–40.

18. Roger J. Plachy, "The Case for Effective Point-Factor Job Evaluation, Viewpoint I," *Personnel* 64 (April 1987): 31.

19. George T. Milkovich and Jerry M. Newman, *Compensation*, 4th ed.: 118.

20. Ibid., 124.

21. Donald L. Caruth, *Compensation Management for Banks* (Boston: Bankers Publishing Company, 1986): 65.

22. William J. Liccione, "Evaluate the Strategic Value of Jobs," *HR Focus* 72 (April 1995): 10.

23. Joseph J. Martocchio, *Strategic Compensation* (Upper Saddle River, NJ: Prentice Hall, 1998).

24. Daniel B. Moskowitz, "How to Cut It Overseas," *International Business* 5 (October 1992): 76–78.

25. Ibid.

Chapter 5

1. "HR-Executive Review: Outsourcing HR Services," *The Conference Board* 1 (1994): 3.

2. Ibid.

3. Statistics Canada, *The Daily*, "1996 Census: Labour Force Activity, Occupation and Industry, Place of Work, Mode of Transportation to Work, Unpaid Work," Tuesday, March 17, 1998: *http://www.statcan.ca/Daily/English/980317/d980317.htm*

4. Cassandra Hayes and Charlene Solomon, "The Lure of Temping," *Black Enterprise 26* (February 1996): 120–122.

5. Allan Harcrow, "The Changing Workforce," *Workforce Tools* (Supplement to the January 1997 Issue, *Workforce*): 5–6.

6. Jay Finegan, "Look Before You Lease," *Inc* 19 (February 1997): 106.

7. Statistics Canada, "The Redistribution of Overtime Hours," *The Daily*, Wednesday, December 10, 1997: *http://www.statcan.ca/Daily/English/971210/d971210.htm#ART1*

8. Martha I. Finney, "Playing a Different Tune: Using the Hidden Assets of Employees," *HRMagazine* 41 (December 1996): 73.

9. Rick Spence, *Secrets of Success from Canada's Fastest Growing Companies*, (Toronto: John Wiley and Sons Canada, Ltd., 1997): 196.

10. Ibid., 197–198.

11. T. Parker, "McCain Foods Appoints New CEO," *The Daily Gleaner*, March 1, 1995, 3.

12. Stephanie Overman, "Myths Hinder Hiring of Older Workers," *HRMagazine* 38 (June 1993): 51.

13. "Don't Put Older Workers out to Pasture." *Daily Commercial News* 65 (122), (1992): 3.

14. "Kenworth's Gray Revolution," *Motor Truck* 61 (10, insert), (1992): 1–3.

15. P. Wright and G.D. Geroy, "Toward a Culturally-Defined Model of Research for Small Business," *Journal of Small Business and Entrepreneurship*, 7(2): 29–37.

16. K. Jensen, personal communication. Mr. Jensen was interviewed on September 20, 1995.

17. *The Definitive Guide to Managing Human Resources for Small Business Owners* (Toronto: Royal Bank of Canada, 1998): 8.

18. G. Donald and P.C. Wright. "Executive Search Firms: A Review and Analysis," (submitted for publication 1995).

19. Bill Leonard, "Resume Databases to Dominate Field," *HRMagazine* 30 (April 1993): 59–60.

20. See, for example, Environment Canada's web site "International Environmental Youth Corps": *http://www.ec.gc.ca/etad/ieyc_e.html*

21. See, for example, the "On Campus" IBM site at: *http://www.can.ibm.com/hr/campus/index.html* or the "Careers" Nortel Networks site at: *http://www.nortelnetworks.com/employment/na/student/index.html*

22. Howard S. Freedman, *How to Get a Headhunter To Call* (New York: John Wiley & Sons, 1989): 60.

23. Ibid., 56.

24. Margaret Butteriss, *Help Wanted: the Complete Guide to Human Resources for Canadian Entrepreneurs* (Etobicoke: John Wiley & Sons Canada Ltd., 1999): 59.

25. David E. Terpstra, "The Search for Effective Methods," *HR Focus* 73 (May 1996): 16.

26. Albert H. McCarthy, "The Human Touch Helps Recruit Quality Workers," *Personnel Journal* 70 (November 1991): 68.

27. Margaret Butteriss, *Help Wanted: the Complete Guide to Human Resources for Canadian Entrepreneurs*, 61.

28. Molly Klimas, "How to Recruit a Smart Team," *Nation's Business* 83 (May 1995): 26.

29. "Recruiting On-Line," HR News Capsules, *HR Focus* 73 (December 1996): 6.

30. "Networking '97: A Research Study on Employment and the Internet," *JWT Specialized Communications* (1997): 4.

31. See, for example, the "On Campus" IBM site at: *http://www.can.ibm.com/hr/campus/index.html*

32. Samantha Drake, "HR Departments Are Exploring the Internet," *HRMagazine* 41 (December 1996): 53–56.

33. Adapted from Lyle M. Spencer, Jr., *Reengineering Human Resources* (New York: Wiley, 1995): 6–7.

34. Bill Leonard, "Resume Databases to Dominate Field," *HRMagazine* 38 (April 1993): 59–60.

35. Barbara Hetzer, "Personal Business: Careers: When the Headhunter Comes Calling," *Business Week* (May 5, 1997): 40.

36. Beth Ashley, "Job Interviews Come to Cyberspace," *USA Today: http://wsf2.usatoday.com/life/cyber/tech/ct351.htm* (May 30 1997).

37. Carrie Mason-Draffen, "Companies Find New Ways to Pay/Workers' Performance Tied to Stock Options, Bonuses, Raises," *Newsday*, January 5, 1997, F08.

38. David E. Terpstra, "The Search for Effective Methods."

39. Gary N. Powell. "The Effects of Sex and Gender on Recruitment," *Academy of Management Review*, 12 (October 1987): 7.

40. Harish C. Jain, "Human Rights: Issues in Employment," in H.C. Jain, C. Hem, and P. Wright, Eds., *Trends and Challenges in Human Resource Management.* (Scarborough: Nelson Canada, 1994): 79.

41. Canadian Human Rights Commission, *Employment: Prohibited Grounds of Discrimination.* (Ottawa: Minister of Supply and Services, 1993). Reproduced with permission of the Minister of Supply and Services Canada, 1993.

42. *Employment Equity: A Guide for Employers* (Ottawa: Employment and Immigration Canada, 1994): 8–9. (Reproduced with permission).

43. Ibid., 13.

44. P. Hartin and P. C. Wright, "Canadian Perspectives on Employment Equity," *Equal Opportunities International.* 13(6/7), (1994): 22–24.

45. Stephanie Overman, "Temporary Services Go Global," *HRMagazine* 38 (August 1993): 72.

46. For example see advertisements in *Training and Development*, 12(10), 52.

47. Stephanie Overman, "Temporary Services Go Global."

48. Hugh Scullion, "Attracting Management Globetrotters," *Personnel Management* (January 1992): 28–32.

Chapter 6

1. Stephen L. Guinn, "Gain Competitive Advantage Through Employment Testing," *HR Focus* 70 (September 1993): 15.

2. Peter F. Drucker, "Getting Things Done: How to Make People Decisions," *Harvard Business Review* 63 (July–August 1985): 22.

3. Donald D. DeCamp, "Are You Hiring the Right People?" *Management Review* 81 (May 1992): 44.

4. Vandra L. Huber, Gregory B. Northcraft, and Margaret A. Neale, "Effects of Decision Strategy and Number of Openings on Employment Selection Decisions," *Organizational Behavior and Human Decisions Processes* 45 (April 1990): 276.

5. G. Lemaitre, G. Picot, and S. Murray, "Employment Flows and Job Tenure in Canada," *The Observer* 5(7), (1992): 4.1–4.13.

6. L. Christofides and C. McKenna, "Employment Flows and Job Tenure in Canada," *Canadian Public Policy*, 19(2) (1993): 157.

7. J. Milne, president of Taylor Enterprises, Willowdale, Ontario, personal communication, April, 11,1995.

8. Edwin N. Walley, "Successful Interviewing Techniques," *The CPA Journal* 63 (September 1993): 70.

9. Jac Fitz-enz, "Getting—and Keeping—Good Employees," *Personnel* 67 (August 1990): 27.

10. Tom Smith, "Resume Help for the Experienced Candidate," *Planning Job Choices*, 37th ed. (Bethlehem, PA: College Placement Council, Inc., 1994): 40–41.

11. T. Tedesco, "Resume Fraud," *The Globe and Mail*, Sept. 30, 1988, B14.

12. Ibid.

13. L. Ramsay, "Tests Help Determine Who's Right for a Job," *The Financial Post*, April 17, 1993, s18.

14. Michael P. Cronin, "Hiring: This is a Test," *Inc.* 15 (August 1993): 64.

15. David E. Terpstra, "The Search for Effective Methods," *HR Focus* 73 (May 1996): 16–17.

16. Ellen Neuborne, "Putting Job Seekers to the Test: Employers Score New Hires," *USA Today,* July 9, 1997, 01B.

17. R.M. Solomon and S.J. Usprich, "Employment Drug Testing," *Business Quarterly* (Winter 1993): 73–78.

18. Ibid., 73.

19. Margot Gibb-Clark, "Staff Reacts Poorly to Co-worker with AIDS," *The Globe and Mail*, May 5, 1998, B16. Reprinted with permission from *The Globe and Mail.*

20. L. Friedenberg, "Testing in Business and Industry" in *Psychological Testing: Design, Analysis and Use* (Toronto: Allyn and Bacon, 1995): 421.

21. L. Brink, "A Discouraging Word Improves Your Interviews," *HRMagazine* 37 (December 1992): 49.

22. Stephen L. Guinn, "Gain Competitive Advantage Through Employment Testing."

23. K. Dunn and E. Dawson. "Right Person for the Job," *Occupational Health and Safety Canada* 10(4) (1994): 28.

24. L. Ramsay, "Tests Help Determine Who's Right for a Job."

25. L. Brink, "A Discouraging Word Improves Your Interviews."

26. *Selection Interviewing for the 1990s* (New York: DBM Publishing, A Division of Drake Beam Morin, Inc., 1993): 28.

27. Timothy A. Judge and Gerald R. Ferris, "The Elusive Criterion of Fit in Human Resources Staffing Decisions," *Human Resources Management: Perspectives, Context, Functions and Outcomes* (Englewood Cliffs, NJ: Prentice Hall, 1995): 217.

28. Mary H. Yarborough, "New Variations on Recruitment Prescreening," *HR Focus* 71 (October 1994): 1.

29. L. Friedenberg, "Testing in Business and Industry."

30. David E. Terpstra, "The Search for Effective Methods."

31. Ken Jordan, "Play Fair and Square When Hiring from Within," *HRMagazine* 42 (January 1997): 49.

Chapter 7

1. Owen Linstein and James Mauro, "Tom Peters . . . and the Healthy Corporation," *Psychology Today* 26 (March/April 1993): 57.

2. G.L. Simpson, "Building Employee Commitment," *The Canadian Manager*, 20 (2) (1995): 24.

3. William Fitzgerald, "Training Versus Development," *Training and Development* 46 (May 1992): 81.

4. Leonard Ackerman, "Whose Ox Is Being Gored?" *HRMagazine* 36 (February 1991): 96.

5. S. Lee, personal communication. Ms. Lee was interviewed in March 1995.

6. Arthur Sharplin, *Strategic Management*, (New York: McGraw-Hill, 1985): 102.

7. Thomas G. Cummings and Christopher G. Worley, *Organization Development and Change*, 5th ed. (Minneapolis/St. Paul: West Publishing Company, 1993): 526.

8. Frank Petrock, "Corporate Culture Enhances Profits," *HRMagazine* 35 (November 1990): 64–66.

9. Brian Dumaine, "Creating a New Company Culture," *Fortune*, 121 (January 15, 1990): 127.

10. D. Shepherdson, *Meeting the Challenge: Managing Change in the Nineties*, Report 130–94 (Ottawa: Conference Board of Canada, 1994).

11. "Going the Distance . . ." *Profit: The Magazine for Canadian Entrepreneurs* 13 (2), (1994): 55–61.

12. "The Heavy Metal Bond . . ." *The Globe and Mail* (September 1, 1992): B18.

13. "Who Wants to Be a Giant," *The Economist* 335 (7920) (1995): 5.

14. "Pumping up the Oil Pot . . ." *The Globe and Mail*, August 25, 1992, B20.

15. N.L. Trainor, "Restructuring: Human Factor Key to Renewal," *Canadian HR Reporter* 8 (1995): 19.

16. P. Wright and K. Kusmonadji, "The Strategic Application of TQM Principles to HRM," *Training for Quality* 1(3) (1993): 5–14.

17. Benson Rosen and Kay Lovelace, "Fitting Square Pegs into Round Holes," *HRMagazine* 39 (January 1994): 86–93.

18. Thomas G. Cummings and Christopher G. Worley, *Organization Development and Change*, 5th ed. (Minneapolis/St. Paul: West Publishing Company, 1993): 2.

19. Ibid., p. 2.

20. D. Shepherdson, *Meeting the Challenge: Managing Change in the Nineties* (Ottawa: The Conference Board of Canada, 1994): 11.

21. N. M. Dixon, *Organizational Learning* (Ottawa: The Conference Board of Canada, 1993): 3–4.

22. Thomas G. Cummings and Christopher G. Worley, *Organization Development and Change*, 5th ed.,136–137.

23. Ibid.,137.

24. The material on transactional analysis in this section is

abridged and adapted from Thomas A. Harris, M.D., *I'm O.K.—You're O.K.* Copyright ®1967, 1968, and 1969 by Thomas A. Harris, M.D.

25. David J. Lill and John T. Rose, "Transactional Analysis and Personal Selling: A Primer for Banks." *Journal of Commercial Bank Lending* 70 (February 1988): 57.

26. Barbara Mandell, "Does a Better Worklife Boost Productivity?" *Personnel*, 66 (October 1989): 49.

27. Ibid., 27.

28. Ibid., 49.

29. James L. Gibson and John M. Ivancevich, *Organizations: Behavior, Structure, Processes*, 4th ed. (Plano, Texas: Business Publications, 1982): 580–581.

30. John P. Campbell and Marvin D. Dunnette, "Effectiveness of T- Group Experiences in Managerial Training and Development," *Psychological Bulletin* 70 (August 1968): 23–104.

31. Irwin L. Goldstein, *Training in Organizations: Needs Assessment, Development, and Evaluation*, 2nd ed. (Monterey, Calif.: Brooks/Cole Publishing Company, 1986): 243.

32. "Buzzword Management: Why Excellence Programs Fail," *B.C. Business Magazine* 22 (11) (1994): 26–37.

33. Michael Hammer and James Champy, *Reengineering the Corporation: A Manifesto for Business Revolution* (New York: HarperCollins, 1993): 32.

34. Michael Hammer and James Champy, "The Malapropian 'R' Word," Industry Forum, prepared by the American Management Association September 1993, 1.

35. Oren Harari, "Why Did Reengineering Die?" *Management Review* 85 (July 1996): 49.

36. Ibid.

37. Stratford Sherman and Eanne C. Lee, "Levi's as Ye Sew, So Shall Ye Reap Vastly Successful, Immensely Rich, a Little Smug: The World's Premier Blue Jeans Maker Has Created a Unique Bond with Employees. Will Layoffs Wreck It?" *Fortune* 135 (May 1997): 104.

38. Edward Shugrue, Joan Berland, and Bob Gonzales, "Case Study: How IBM Reengineered Its Benefits Center into a National HR Service Center," *Compensation & Benefits Review* 29 (March/April 1997): 41–48.

39. "Getting Used to It: The Team Concept . . ." *Canadian Papermaker* 47 (6),(1994): 29–31.

40. Richard Wellins and Jill George, "The Key to Self-Directed Teams," *Training and Development Journal* 45 (April 1991): 27.

41. Shari Caudron, "Are Self-Directed Teams Right for Your Company?" *Personnel Journal* 72 (December 1993): 78.

42. Richard Wellins and Jill George, "The Key to Self-Directed Teams."

43. "How to Make a Small, Smart Factory," *The Globe and Mail*, February 2, 1993, B24.

44. Donna Robbins, "The Dark Side of Team Building," *Training and Development* 47 (December 1993): 17.

45. "Now Everyone Can Be a Boss . . ." *Canadian Business* 67 (5) (1994): 48–50.

46. Wayne F. Cascio and Manuel G. Serapio, Jr., "Human Resources Systems in an International Alliance: The Undoing of a Done Deal?" *Organizational Dynamics* 19 (Winter 1991): 65.

47. R. Chan, personal communication. Mr. Chan was interviewed in Hong Kong in November 1994.

48. Wayne F. Cascio and Manuel G. Serapio, Jr., "Human Resources Systems in an International Alliance," 68.

Chapter 8

1. "CEO: Problems Often Management's Fault," *Canadian Press*, as quoted in the *Daily Gleaner*, April 20, 1995, 20.

2. Ibid.

3. Rick Spence, *Secrets of Success from Canada's Fastest Growing Companies* (Toronto: John Wiley and Sons Canada, Ltd., 1997): 204.

4. D. McIntyre, *Training and Development, 1993: Policies, Practices, and Expenditures* (Ottawa: The Conference Board of Canada, 1994): 7.

5. M. Belcourt and P. Wright, *Managing Performance Through Training and Development* (Scarborough: Nelson, 1996).

6. D. McIntyre, *Training and Development*: 6.

7. Laurie J. Bassi, George Benson, et al., "The Top Ten Trends," *Training & Development* 50 (November 1996): 28.

8. J.J. Phillips, "Measuring the returns on HRD," *Employment Relations Today* 18 (1991): 329–342.

9. R.W. Pace, P.C. Smith and G.E. Mills, *Human Resource Development: The Field* (Englewood Cliffs, N.J.: Prentice Hall, 1991).

10. McIntyre, *Training and Development*, 11–12.

11. P. Sullivan, "Nine best practices," *Executive Excellence* 10 (1993): 3–4.

12. M. Belcourt and P. Wright, *Managing Performance Through Training and Development*.

13. D. McIntyre, *Training and Development*: 13.

14. Ibid., 16.

15. Kenneth N. Wexley and Gary P. Latham, *Developing and Training Human Resources in Organizations*, 2nd ed. (New York: Harper–Collins Publishers, Inc., 1991): 36.

16. C. Knight, "Unions Will Focus on Security . . ." *Canadian HR Reporter* 8(4), (1995:1.

17. Kenneth M. Nowack, "A True Training Needs Analysis," *Training and Development Journal* 45 (April 1991): 69.

18. Ibid.

19. *The Training Plan* (Toronto: Ministry of Skill Development, 1987) A–3, A–4.

20. S. Cunningham, "Coaching today's Executive," *Public Utilities Fortnightly* 128 (1991): 22–25.

21. B. Whittaker, "Shaping the Competitive Organization—Managing or Coaching," *CMA Magazine* 67 (1993): 5.

22. T. Scandura, "Mentorship and Career Mobility: An Empirical Investigation," *Journal of Organizational Behaviour* 13 (1992): 169–174.

23. Don Barner, "What is This Thing Called Mentoring?" *National Underwriter* 94 (May 28, 1990): 9.

24. P. Wright, "The Incident as a Technique for Teaching Undergraduates in Hospitality Management and Food Administration," *Hospitality Education and Research Journal* 12 (1), (1988): 16–28.

25. William M. Fox, "Getting the Most from Behavior Modelling Training," *National Productivity Review* 7 (Summer 1988): 238.

26. Samuel Greengard, "How Technology Is Advancing HR," *Personnel Journal* 72 (September 1993): 81.

27. Ibid.

28. Canadian Tire Corporation Limited, "Company Snapshot" Internet site: *http://investdb.theglobeandmail.com/invest/investSQL/ gx.company_prof?company_in=Canadian+Tire+Corporation*

29. Michael J. Marquardt, "Cyberlearning: New Possibilities for HRD," *Training & Development* 50 (November 1996): 56–57.

30. Martha I. Finney, "Harness the Power Within," *HRMagazine* 42 (January 1997): 66–74.

31. Lyle M. Spencer, Jr., *Reengineering Human Resources* (New York: John Wiley, 1995): 8–9.

32. "Interactive Satellite Learning Improves Training Programs," *Personnel Journal* 72 (September 1993): 86.

33. P. Larson and R. Mimgie, *Leadership for a Changing World* Report 95–92, S (Ottawa: Conference Board of Canada, 1992):5.

34. "Long-time Employers Benefit . . ." *Northern Ontario Business*, 11 (10), (1991): 8.

35. P. Wright, M. Belcourt, and M. Lauri, *Apprenticeship: The Canadian Dilemma* (Working Paper, 95-009), Faculty of Administration, University of New Brunswick, Fredericton, NB, 1995.

36. T. Hrynyshyn, "Siemens Chief Critical of Skilled Labour Shortage," *Computing Canada*, 19 (1993): 1.

37. "Atlantis Simulating Success," *The Globe and Mail* (October 27, 1993): B5.

38. "Training still top priority," *Plant,* 52 (5), (1993): 1.

39. Diana Reed-Mendenhall and C. W. Millard, "Orientation: A Training and Development Tool," *Personnel Administrator*, 25 (August 1980): 42–44.

40. D. Letourneau, "Getting Off to a Safe Start," *Occupational Health and Safety Canada* 8 (1992): 46–50.

41. B. Sebnell, "A Training Management System," *Computerworld*, 23 (1989): 134.

42. Jack Asgar, "Give Me Relevance or Give Me Nothing," *Training*, 27 (July 1990): 49.

43. J. Fitz-Enz, "Yes . . . You Can Weigh Training's Value," *Training*, 7 (July 1994): 54–58.

44. Jack J. Phillips, "ROI: The Search for Best Practices," *Training & Development* 50 (February 1996): 42–47.

45. Leslie E. Overmyer Day, "Benchmarking Training," *Training & Development* 49 (November 1995): 27–30.

46. Mike Fergus, "Employees on the Move," *HRMagazine*, 36 (May 1990): 45.

47. Wayne F. Cascio and Manuel G. Serapio, Jr., "Human Resources Systems in an International Alliance: The Undoing of a Done Deal?" *Organizational Dynamics*, 19 (Winter 1991): 69 .

48. S. Keen, "UK Firms Must Forgo Analytical View of Culture," *People Management* (April 16, 1995): 12.

49. Wayne F. Cascio and Manuel G. Serapio, Jr., "Human Resources Systems in an International Alliance: The Undoing of a Done Deal?" *Organizational Dynamics*, 19 (Winter 1991): 68.

50. Ibid.

Chapter 9

1.Donald J. McNerney, "As HR Changes, So Do HR Career Paths," *HR Focus* 73 (February 1996): 1–4.

2. Jenny C. McCune, "HR's Top Concerns," *HR Focus* 74 (March 1997):6.

3. Barbara Moses, "The Sea Change in Career Planning," *The Globe and Mail* February 1, 1999, B1.

4. Rick Spence, *Secrets of Success from Canada's fastest Growing Companies*, (Toronto: John Wiley and Sons Canada, Ltd., 1997): 207.

5. Keith H. Hammonds, "Social Issues: The Issue Is Employment, not Employability," *Business Week* (June 10, 1996): 64.

6. Janin Friend, "Enterprise: Management: Workforce: 'How Ya Gonna Keep Em?'" *Business Week* (June 3, 1996): 4.

7. Donald J. McNerney,"Life in the Jobless Economy," *HR Focus* 73 (August 1996): 9–10.

8. D. Nye, "Writing off Older Assets," *Across the Board* (September, 1988): 44–52.

9. P.S. Taylor, "Social Studies," *Saturday Night* (June 1995): 18–23.

10. Information for this section was drawn from the research carried out by Edgar Schein, "How 'Career Anchors' Hold Executives to Their Career Paths," *Personnel* 52 (May–June 1975): 11–24; and Barbara Moses, "Just who is and what turns on today's new worker," *The Globe and Mail*, November 9, 1998, B13 and November 10, 1998, B15.

11. Donald J. McNerney, "Trend Analysis: Know What's Happening before It Happens," *HR Focus* 72 (March 1995):1–3.

12. Jaclyn Fierman, "Beating the Midlife Career Crisis," *Fortune* 128 (September 6, 1993): 54.

13. R. Brillinger, "HR Manager's Bookshelf," *Canadian HR Reporter* 8(2), (1995): 14.

14. Lewis Newman, "Career Management Starts with Goals," *Personnel Journal* 68 (April 1989): 91.

15. G. William Dauphnais, "Who's Minding the Middle Manager?" *HR Focus* 73 (October 1996): 12–13.

16. Janin Friend, "Enterprise: Management: Workforce: 'How Ya Gonna Keep Em?'"

17. C. Knight, "Economics of Simplicity," *Canadian HR Reporter* 8(11), (1995): 1,3.

18. Milan Moravec, "A Cost-Effective Career Planning Program Requires A Strategy," *Personnel Administrator* 27 (January 1982): 29.

19. Donald L. Caruth, Robert M. Noe III, and R. Wayne Mondy, *Staffing the Contemporary Organization* (New York: Praeger Publishers, 1990): 253–254.

20. David K. Foot with Daniel Stoffman, *Boom Bust & Echo*, (Macfarlane Walter & Ross, 1996): 62.

21. Barbara Moses, "The sea change in career planning."

22. Brian O'Reilly, "The New Deal: What Companies and Employees Owe One Another," *Fortune,* 129 (June 13, 1994): 44.

23. Louis S. Richman, "How to Get Ahead in America," *Fortune,* 129 (May 14, 1994): 49.

24. Susan Sonnesyn Brooks, "Moving Up is Not the Only Option," *HRMagazine* 39 (March 1994): 79.

25. Zandby B. Leibowitz and Sherry H. Mosley, "Career Development Works Overtime at Corning, Inc.," *Personnel,* 67 (April 1990): 38.

26. Loretta D. Foxman and Walter L. Polsky, "Aid in Employee Career Development," *Personnel Journal* 69 (January 1990): 22.

27. Daniel B. Moskowitz, "How to Cut It Overseas," *International Business* (October, 1992): 76, 78.

28. Ibid.

Chapter 10

1. "The Team Building Tool Kit," *Compensation and Benefits Review* 26 (March/April 1994): 67.

2. Iris Randall, "Performance Appraisal Anxiety," *Black Enterprise* 25 (January 1995): 60.

3. Edward E. Lawler, III, "Performance Management: The Next Generation," *Compensation & Benefits Review* 26 (May/June 1994): 16.

4. Chris Lee, "Performance Appraisal," *Training* 33 (May 1996): 44.

5. Robert B. Campbell and Lynne M. Garfinkel, "Performance Management: Strategies for Success," *HRMagazine* 41 (June 1996): 98.

6. Steven E. Gross, *Compensation for Teams* (New York: American Management Association, 1995): 87.

7. Robert C. Joines, Steve Quisenberry, and Gary W. Sawyer, "Business Strategy Drives Three-Pronged Assessment System," *HRMagazine* 38 (December 1993): 70.

8. Stephen E. Gross, *Compensation for Teams,* 90.

9. Tom Payne, "Management by Behaviors," *Supervision* 57 (June 1996): 8–9.

10. Philip Ricciardi, "Simplify Your Approach to Performance Measurement," *HRMagazine* 41 (March 1996): 99.

11. Margaret Butteriss, *Help Wanted: the Complete Guide to Human Resources for Canadian Entrepreneurs,* (Toronto: John Wiley and Sons Canada, Ltd., 1999): 153.

12. Mathew Budman and Berkeley Rice, "The Rating Game," *Across the Board* 31 (February 1994): 34–38.

13. "The Team Building Tool Kit," 68.

14. James G. Goodale, "Seven Ways to Improve Performance Appraisals," *HRMagazine* 38 (May 1993): 80.

15. Michelle A. Yakovac, "Paying for Satisfaction," *HR Focus* 73 (June 1996): 10–11.

16. Robert Hoffman, "Ten Reasons You Should Be Using 360-Degree Feedback," *HRMagazine* 40 (April 1995): 82.

17. Bob Filipczak, Marc Hequet, Chris Lee, Michele Picard, and David Stamps, "360-Degree Feedback: Will the Circle Be Broken?" *Training* 33 (October 1996): 24.

18. Robert B. Campbell and Lynne M. Garfinkel, "Performance Management: Strategies for Success," *HRMagazine* 41 (June 1996): 102.

19. Michelle Neely Martinez, "Rewards Given the Right Way," *HRMagazine* 42 (May 1997): 116.

20. "Steps to Maximize Consistency," *HRMagazine* http://www.shrm.org/hrmagazine/articles/10steps.html (1 July 1997).

21. Adapted from Richard O'Reilly, "The Cutting Edge: Computing/Technology/Innovation: Employee Review Software," *Los Angeles Times,* June 28, 1995, D-5.

22. Jay T. Knippen, "Boost Performance Through Appraisals," *Business Credit,*92 (November–December 1990): 27.

23. "Research on Performance Appraisals Wins Award," *HR News* 16 (July 1997): 13.

24. Jeffrey S. Kane, H. John Bernardin, Peter Villanova, and Joseph Peyrefitte, "Stability of Rater Leniency: Three Studies," *Academy of Management Journal* 39 (August 1995): 1036–1037.

25. Larry L. Axline, "Ethical Considerations of Performance Appraisals," *Management Review* 83 (March 1994): 62.

26. Margaret Butteriss, *Help Wanted: the Complete Guide to Human Resources for Canadian Entrepreneurs,* 153.

27. William S. Hubbartt, "Bring Performance Appraisal Training to Life," *HRMagazine* 40 (May 1995): 168.

28. K. Gay, "Thorough Probe a Must before Firing," *The Financial Post* 88(42), (October 15, 1994): 510.

29. Margaret Butteriss, *Help Wanted: the Complete Guide to Human Resources for Canadian Entrepreneurs,* 152.

30. Randall Scott Echlin, "Why Firms Need Performance Reviews," *The Globe and Mail,* December 14, 1998, B15.

31. Charles M. Vance, Shirley R. McClaine, David M. Boje, and H. Daniel Stage, "An Examination of Transferability of Traditional Performance Appraisal Principles across Cultural Boundaries," *Management International Review* (Fourth Quarter, 1992): 313–326.

32. Wayne F. Cascio and Manuel G. Serapio, Jr., "HR Systems in an International Alliance: The Undoing of a Done Deal?" *Organizational Dynamics* 19 (Winter 1991): 65.

33. Mark E. Mendenhall and Gary Oddon, "The Overseas Assignment: A Practical Look," *Business Horizons* 31 (September/October 1988): 81.

34. Ibid., 70.

35. Ibid.

Chapter 11

1. Vicki Fuehrer, "Total Reward Strategy: A Prescription for Organizational Survival," *Compensation and Benefits Review,* 26 (January–February 1994): 45.

2. For example, see: "Midland Bosses Reap Rich Rewards: $1M Plus Bonuses for Top Executives . . ." *The Globe and Mail,* March 22, 1994, B11.

3. L. Livingstone, S Roberts, and L. Chinko, "Perceptions of Internal and External Equity . . ." *Journal of Personal Selling and Sales Management,* 15(2), (1995): 33–46.

4. Edward J. Giblin, Geoffrey A. Wiegman, and Frank Sanfilippo, "Bringing Pay Up To Date," *Personnel,* 67 (November 1990): 17.

5. George T. Milkovich and Jerry M. Newman, *Compensation,* 4th ed. (Homewood, Ill.: Richard D. Irwin, Inc., 1993): 3.

6. David W. Belcher and Thomas J. Atchison, *Compensation Administration,* 2nd ed. (Englewood Cliffs, N.J.: Prentice-Hall, 1987): 127.

7. D. Willett, "Promoting Quality through Compensation," *Business Quarterly* 58 (1) (1993): 107–111.

8. Joseph E. McKendrick, Jr., "Salary Surveys: Roadmaps for the Volatile Employment Scene of the 1990s," *Management World* 19 (March–April 1990): 18–20.

9. "AGT's Rate Request Called 'Unconscionable': Citizens Give CRTC Hearing an Earful," *The Globe and Mail*, Aug. 10, 1993, B2.

10 "Slow and Sluggish: . . ." *Canadian Underwriter,* 60 (6) (1993): 10–11.

11. The following sections have been adapted from Human Resources Development Canada, *Employment Standards Legislation* (1995–96 ed., DSS Cat. #631-78/1995 E. (Ottawa: Canada Communications Group); and *http://labour-travail.hrdc-drhc. gc.ca/policy/leg/e/index.html*

12. For example, see "Simple Concept Sparking Heated Debate," *Calgary Herald*, April 25, 1993, A1, A2.

13. Human Resources Development Canada, *Employment Standards Legislation*, 47.

14. M. Campbell and J. Gadd, "Ontario to Scrap Equity Law," *The Globe and Mail,* July 20, 1995, A-1.

15. J.L. Milne, "Hiring Managers . . ." *Canadian Manager* 19 (4) (1994): 5.

16. Shawn Tully, "Your Paycheck Gets Exciting," *Fortune* 126 (November 1, 1993): 96.

17. N. B. Carlyle and W. Payette, *Compensation Planning Outlook 1998*, Conference Board of Canada, October 1997.

18. Ibid.

19. John L. Morris, "Lessons Learned in Skill-Based Pay," *HRMagazine* 41 (June 1996): 137.

20. Rick Spence, *Secrets of Success from Canada's fastest Growing Companies* (Toronto: John Wiley and Sons Canada, Ltd., 1997): 206–207.

21. Steven E. Gross, *Compensation for Teams* (New York: American Management Association) 1995: 47.

22. Rick Spence, *Secrets of Success from Canada's fastest Growing Companies*, 206.

23. Joseph J. Martocchio, *Strategic Compensation* (Upper Saddle River, NJ: Prentice Hall, 1998): 121

24. Jack Stack, "The Problem with Profit Sharing," *Inc* (November 1996): 67.

25. "Profit Sharing Can Help Bottom Line," *The Globe and Mail,* Aug. 3, 1993, B4.

26. John E. Hempstead, "When Employees Want to Buy the Company," *Folio* 25 (October 15, 1996): 132.

27. Rick Spence, *Secrets of Success from Canada's fastest Growing Companies*, 206.

28. Joseph J. Martocchio, *Strategic Compensation*:115.

29. Carrie Mason-Draffen, "Companies Find New Ways to Pay/ Worker's Performance Tied to Stock Options, Bonuses, Raises," *Newsday*, January 5, 1997, F08.

30. James Martin, "HR In The Cybercorp," *HR Focus* 74 (April 1997): 3–4.

31. Rick Spence, *Secrets of Success from Canada's fastest Growing Companies*, 205.

32. "Do Work Teams Need Compensation?" *Supervisory Management* 40 (2) (1995): 12.

33. Susan Haslett, "Broadbanding: A Strategic Tool for Organizational Change," *Compensation & Benefits Review* 27 (November/December 1995): 40–46.

34. Kenan S. Abosch, "The Promise of Broadbanding," *Compensation & Benefits Review* 27 (January/February 1995): 55–56.

35. "Going Global," *HRMagazine* 38 (September 1993): 49.

36. E. Shum, executive director of HRED, personal communication. Dr. Shum was interviewed in November 1994.

37. Wayne F. Cascio and Manuel G. Serapio, Jr., "Human Resources Systems in an International Alliance: The Undoing of a Done Deal?" *Organizational Dynamics* 19 (Winter 1991): 70.

38. Ibid., p. 71.

39. Daniel B. Moskowitz, "How to Cut It Overseas," *International Business* (October, 1992): 76, 78.

Chapter 12

1. Human Resources Development Canada, Applied Research Branch, "Flexible Work Arrangements: Evidence from the 1991 and 1995 Survey of Work Arrangements": *http://www.hrdc-drhc.gc.ca/arb/publications/research/abr-97-10e.shtml*

2. "Employers Favour Work Incentives over Benefits," *The Globe and Mail*, October 22, 1994, B5.

3. Human Resources Development Canada, Income Securities Programs, "Old Age Security Pension": *http://www.hrdc-drhc. gc.ca/isp/oas/ispb185.shtml*

4. Human Resources Development Canada, Income Securities Programs, "General Information About The Canada Pension Plan,": *http://www.hrdc-drhc.gc.ca/isp/cpp/genera_e.shtml*

5. Human Resources Development Canada, "Employment Insurance,": *http://www.hrdc-drhc.gc.ca/dept/guide98/ei.shtml*

6. *Seventy-Fifth Annual Report* (Fredericton: Workers' Compensation Board, 1993).

7. See, for example, "Table of Rates," (Fredericton: Workers' Compensation Board, 1995).

8. R. King, "Medicare—Where Is Its Future?" *Employee Benefits Journal* 20 (1) (1995): 33–35.

9. W. Morneau, "Managing Canadian Health Programs: A Cost-Containment Challenge," *Benefits and Compensation International* 23 (7) (1994): 16–20.

10. A. Downey and R. Kador, "The High Cost of Health," *CMA Magazine,* 69 (3) (1995): 12–14.

11. W. Morneau, "Managing Canadian Health Programs: A Cost-Containment Challenge."

12. Human Resources Development Canada, "Employment Standards Legislation in Canada": *http://labour-travail.hrdc-drhc.gc.ca/policy/leg/e/index.html*

13. Human Resources Development Canada, "General Holidays With Pay,": *http://labour-travail.hrdc-drhc.gc.ca/policy/leg/e/ stand8-e1.html*

14. G. Mitchell, "Strategies for Health Care Cost Containment," *Employee Benefits Journal* 20 (2) (1995), 18–22.

15. "Do-It-Yourself Insurance," *B.C. Business Magazine* 22 (8) (1994): 13.

16. "Visions: Funding Retiree Benefits," *HRMagazine* 36 (February 1991): 87.

17. Royal Bank of Canada, Royal Bank Financial Group, "Retirement Centre Resources": *http://www.royalbank.com/retirement/index.html*

18. Margot Gibb-Clark "AIDS Plays Havoc with Group Insurance: Company Reluctantly Lets Employee Go to Avoid Soaring Cost of Premiums," *The Globe and Mail*, November 15, 1993, B1, B8.

19. "An Investment in Education . . . ." *Oilweek*, 45(39), (1994): 8, 9.

20. C. Philip, "Financial Planning Eases Complications," *Pensions and Investments* 22 (21) (1994): 17, 29.

21. Statistics Canada, "Earnings characteristics of two-partner families, 1996," *The Daily*, Friday, October 23, 1998, *http://www.statcan.ca/Daily/English/981023/d981023.htm#ART2*

22. Julie Cohen Mason, "Whoever Said There Was No Such Thing as a Free Lunch?" *Management Review* 83 (April 1994): 60–62.

23. KPMG Canada, *Twentieth Survey of Employee Benefits Costs in Canada*, "Cost of Individual Employee Benefits Expressed as a Percentage of Gross Annual Payroll," (Toronto: KPMG, 1996).

24. KPMG Canada, Media Release, September 15, 1998, "Demand for Talent and Strong Economy boosts total compensation increases: KPMG,": *http://audit.kpmg.ca/media/releases/m980915.htm*

25. "Employers Favour Work Incentives over Benefits," *The Globe and Mail*, October 22, 1994, B5.

26. "Health Benefits Headed Beyond the Fringe," *The Globe and Mail*, May 10, 1994, C1, C7.

27. "We Can No Longer Take Benefits for Granted," *This Week in Business*, Nov. 15, 1993, C13.

28. "3M's 'Beneflex' Plan Popular with Employees," *Canadian HR Reporter* 8 (4) (1995): 11.

29. William Bridges, "The End of the Job," *Fortune*, September 19, 1994, 62–74.

30. "Cognos Trains Itself to Invest in Employees," *Ottawa Citizen*, February 28, 2000, B1.

31. Human Resources Development Canada, Applied Research Branch, "Flexible Work Arrangements—Gaining Ground," Volume 3, No. 1 (Winter–Spring 1997): *http://www.hrdc-drhc.gc.ca/stratpol/arb/publications/bulletin/vol3n1/v3n1c3e.shtml#tab2*

32. "Flex-Time Schemes Stretch to Fit Needs of Firms, Workers," *Financial Post* 86 (15), April 11/13, 1992, S27.

33. "Bell Workers Can Switch Work Week . . ." *The Globe and Mail*, April 15, 1994, B3.

34. "Board Measures Cost of Worker Absenteeism," *Daily Commercial News* 66(62), (1993): 9, 11.

35. Maureen Minehan, "Consider All Possibilities for Telecommuters," *HRMagazine* 41 (November 1996): 160.

36. Human Resources Development Canada, Applied Research Branch, "Flexible Work Arrangements—Gaining Ground."

37. Robert Brehl, "Study Predicts Telecommuting to Double in the Next 3 Years," *The Ottawa Citizen*, November 9, 1996, E4. This article was based on a 1996 study by the Yankee Group described in their report "Meeting the Telecommuter Challenge," and on several other North American studies.

38. Linda Bennett, "The CBR Advisory Board Comments on: Compensation Fads, Custom Pay Plans, and Team Play," *Compensation & Benefits Review* 28 (March/April 1996): 58–65.

39. "A Flexible Style of Management," *Nation's Business* 81 (December 1993): 70–71.

40. Knight, C. "Saskatchewan Legislation Benefits for Part-Timers." *Canadian HR Reporter* 8 (6) (1995): 1.

41. Joan Szabo, "Severance Plans Shift Away from Cash," *HRMagazine* 41 (July 1996): 104.

42. Gary E. Jenkins, "Beyond the Borders: The Human Resource Professional in a Global Economy," *Employment Benefit Plan Review* (May 1993): 43–44.

43. Cooke, A. and S. Sarouer. "Moving employees into or out of Canada—the pension issues. *Benefits and Compensation International*: 23(9) (1994): 2–7.

44. Neil B. Krupp, "Managing Benefits in Multinational Organizations," *Personnel* 63 (September 1986): 76.

45. Ibid.

Chapter 13

1. K. Palmer, "How Can You Be Sure Your Employees Are Fit to Work?" *People Management*, May 18, 1995: 51.

2. See, for example, Canadian Centre for Occupational Health & Safety, "It might have happened to you," Article 24.9: *http://www.ccohs.ca/NAOSH/ENGLISH/wk24-9en.htm*; and "Compelling Statistics,"Article 26.8: *http://www.ccohs.ca/NAOSH/ENGLISH/w26-8en.htm*

3. Much of the information for this section was drawn from: Canadian Centre for Occupational Health and Safety, "Legislation": *http://www.ccohs.ca/oshanswers/legisl/legislation.htm*

4. Information for this section was drawn from Canadian Centre for Occupational Health and Safety: "What is WHMIS?": *http://www.ccohs.ca/naosh/english/wk23-4en.htm*; "WHMIS—General Information": *http://www.ccohs.ca/oshanswers/legisl/intro_whmis.html*; and Health Canada: "Workplace Hazardous Materials Information Systems (WHMIS)": *http://www.hc-sc.gc.ca/ehp/ehd/psb/whmis.htm*

5. Robert Pater, "Safety Leadership Cuts Costs," *HRMagazine* 35 (November 1990): 46.

6. "To OSHA, 'Workplace Safety Is Good Business,'" *Risk Management* 36 (October 1989): 172.

7. J. Canto-Thaler "Increasing Liability Seen in Workplace Health and Safety," *Canadian HR Reporter* 8(12) (1995): 15.

8. "Safety Motivation Demands an Involved Process," *Iron Age* 8 (2) (1995): 30–31.

9. J.E. Canto-Thaler, "Due Diligence Can Blunt AHSA Prosecution," *Canadian HR Reporter* 8 (1) (1995): 10–11.

10. K.A. Krout, "Supervisory Safety Survey . . ." *Occupational Health and Safety*, 62(5), (1993): 50–51.

11. Ann Flynn, Safety and Training Coordinator for the City of Fredericton, NB, personal communications. Ms. Flynn was interviewed on July 17, 1995.

12. Canadian Centre for Occupational Health and Safety, "How is the effectiveness of OH&S programs evaluated?": *http://www. ccohs.ca/oshanswers/hsprograms/basic.html#_1_21*

13. Canadian Centre for Occupational Health and Safety "Violence in the Workplace": *http://www.ccohs.ca/oshanswers/psychosocial/violence.html*

14. D. Hockley, "Assisting Employees at B.C. Tel.," *Canadian Business Review* 19 (2) (1992): 25–28.

15. Paul Farrell, "Pass or Fail: Managing a Drug and Alcohol Testing Program," *Risk Management* 43 (May 1996): 34.

16. Bill Oliver, "How to Prevent Drug Abuse in Your Workplace," *HRMagazine* 38 (December 1993): 79–80.

17. Health Canada, "AIDS": *http://www.hc-sc.gc.ca/english/aids.htm*

18. Nancy L. Breuer, "Emerging Trends for Managing AIDS in the Workplace," *Personnel Journal* 74 (June 1995).

19. J. Doiron, "Active Living," *The Canadian Manager* 17 (3) (1995): 15.

20. J. Doiron," Active Living," 16.

21. E . Thompson, "Walk the Walk," *Canadian Banker* 101 (1) (1993): 10.

22. Sharon A. Haskins and Brian H. Kleiner, "Employee Assistance Programs Take New Directions," *HR Focus* 71 (January 1994), 16.

23. See, for example, M. Coshan, "An EAP Can Be Part of the Solution," *Canadian Business Review* 19(2) (1992), 28.

24. Peggy Stuart, "Investments in EAPs Pay Off," *Personnel Journal* (February 1993): 54.

25. See, for example, Mark Ralfs and John M. Morley, "Turning Employee Problems into Triumphs," *Training and Development Journal* 44 (November 1990): 73.

26. M.P. Rowan and P.C. Wright,. "Ergonomics is Good for Business," *Facilities* 13 (8) (1995): 18–25.

27 "How to Avoid Burnout," *Training,* 30 (February 1993): 16.

28. M. Coshan "An EAP Can Be Part of the Solution," 22–24.

29. Centers for Disease Control and Prevention, "Is Your Workplace Prepared?": *http://www.brta-lrta.org/start.htm*

30. Wright, P. and W. Nasierowski, "The Expatriate Family Firm and Cross-cultural Management Training . . ." *Human Resource Development Quarterly* 5 (2) (1994): 153–167.

31. M. Swenarchuk, "NAFTA and the Environment," *Canadian Forum* 71 (816) (1993): 13–14.

32. M. Swenarchuk, "Threat to Worker Safety . . ." *Occupational Health and Safety Canada* 9 (5) (1993): 138.

33. Mark C. Butler and Mary B. Teagarden, "Strategic Management of Worker Health, Safety, and Environmental Issues in Mexico's Maquiladora Industry," *Human Resource Management* (Winter 1993): 479–503.

34. Marvina Shilling, "Avoid Expatriate Culture Shock," *HRMagazine* 38 (July 1993): 58.

Chapter 14

1. Jennifer Wunsch, "Workers, Unions and Choice: A Status Report," Work Research Foundation: *http://www.interlog.com/~wrf/wuc.htm*

2. P. Kumar, *From Uniformity to Divergence* (Kingston: IRC Press, 1993).

3. W. Roberts and J. Bullen, "A Heritage of Hope and Struggle: Workers, Unions, and Politics in Canada," In D. J. Bercuson and D. Bright, Eds., *Canadian Labour History*, 2nd ed. (Toronto: Copp Clark Longmans, 1994).

4. D. A. Peach and D. Kuechle, *The Practice of Industrial Relations* (Toronto: McGraw-Hill Ryerson, 1975).

5. D. A. Peach and P. Bergman, *The Practice of Labour Relations*, 3rd ed. (Toronto: McGraw Hill, 1991): 22.

6. F. Kehoe and M. Archer, *Canadian Industrial Relations* (Oakville: Twentieth Century Labour Publications, 1980).

7. A. Craig, *The Systems of Industrial Relations in Canada*, 2nd ed. (Scarborough: Prentice Hall Canada, 1986). See also D. A. Peach and P. Bergman, *The Practice of Labour Relations*.

8. A. Craig, *The System of Industrial Relations in Canada*.

9. Carter, D. D. Collective Bargaining Legislation in Canada, in Anderson, J., M. Gunderson and A. Ponak (eds.). *Union–Management Relations in Canada*, 2nd ed. (Don Mills: Addison-Wesley, 1989): 33.

10. D. A. Peach and P. Bergman, *The Practice of Labour Relations*.

11. Jennifer Wunsch, "Workers, Unions and Choice: A Status Report," Chapter 2.

12. Ibid., Appendix.

13. Ibid., Chapter 2.

14. Human Resources Development Canada, "Canada Labour Code": *http://labour-travail.hrdc-drhc.gc.ca/doc/lab-trav/eng/clc-cct/*

15. See, for example, R. Wright, *Industrial Relations Outlook 1994*, Report 113-94 (Ottawa: Conference Board of Canada): 17.

16. "Living on Mother's Allowance Is No Bed of Roses: Single Mother," *Peterborough Examiner*, July 18, 1987: 8, as quoted in A. Price et al. "Work in the Electronic End," in L.S. MacDowell, and I. Radford, Eds., *Canadian Working Class History* (Toronto: Canadian Scholars Press, 1992): 728.

17. Canadian Labour Congress, "About the CLC": *http://www.clc-ctc.ca/about/index.html*

18. Jennifer Wunsch, "Workers, Unions and Choice: A Status Report," Chapter 1.

19. A. Bernstein, "Busting Unions Can Backfire on the Bottom Line," *Business Week*, March 18, 1991, 108.

20. Wiley I. Beavers, "Employee Relations Without a Union," in Dale Oder and Herbert G. Heneman, Jr., Eds., *ASPA Handbook of Personnel and Industrial Relations: Employee and Labor Relations*, III (Washington, D.C.: The Bureau of National Affairs, 1976): 7–82.

21. Human Resources Development Canada, "Chronological Perspective on Work Stoppages" (work stoppages involving one or more workers, 1990–1999): *http://labour-travail.hrdc-drhc.gc.ca/doc/wid-dimt/eng/ws-at/*

22. P. Kumar, *From Uniformity to Divergence* (Kingston: IRC Press, 1993).

23. N. Winter, "The High Cost of No-Risk Compensation," *Canadian HR Reporter*, June 18, 1992: 13.

24. J. Godard, *Industrial Relations: The Economy and Society*.

25. See, for example, Human Resources Development Canada, "Labour Code Review," Part 1, Chapter 2: *http://labour-travail. hrdc-drhc.gc.ca/labour/labstand/page5.html*

26. H.W. Arthurs, *Labour Law and Industrial Relations in Canada*, 185.

27. B.W. Werther, K. Davis, H. Schwind, and H. Das, *Canadian Human Resource Management*, 3rd ed., (Toronto: McGraw-Hill Ryerson Ltd., 1989): 563.

28. G.T. Milkovich, W.F. Glueck, R.T. Barth, S.L. McShane, *Canadian Personnel/Human Resource Management* (Plano, Texas: Business Publications, Inc., 1988): 611.

29. Reginald W. Bibby, "Canadians and Unions: A National Reading at the Turn of the New Century."

30. Work Research Foundation, "Union Democracy, Freedom of Association and the Injustice of Compulsory Unionism": *http://www.interlog.com/~wrf/uniondmc.htm*

31. J. Godard, *Industrial Relations: The Economy and Society* (Toronto: McGraw Hill Ryerson, 1994).

32. J.D. Reid Jr., "Future Unions," *Industrial Relations*, 31 (Winter 1992): 122–136.

33. Human Resources Development Canada, "Workplace Innovations—Dialogue on Changes in the Workplace,": *http://labour-travail.hrdc-drhc.gc.ca/WIP/english/May95.pdf*

34. B. Downie and M. L. Coates, *The Changing Face of Industrial Relations and Human Resource Management* (Kingston: Industrial Relations Centre, Queen's University, 1993).

35. W.C. Riddell, "Labour-Management Co-operation in Canada," 46. Royal Commission on Economic Union and Development Prospects for Canada, 15 (1986).

36. Reginald W. Bibby, "Canadians and Unions: A National Reading at the Turn of the New Century."

37. Work Research Foundation, "Union Democracy, Freedom of Association and the Injustice of Compulsory Unionism."

38. R. Wright, *Industrial Relations Outlook 1994*, 17.

39. Susan Bourette, "Unions Find the Strike Zone," *The Globe and Mail* (April17, 1999): B4.

40. James Worsham, "Labor Comes Alive," *Nation's Business* 84 (February 1996): 16.

41. Donald W. Nauss, "It's Fun, It's Useful, It's a Mercedes?" *Los Angeles Times*, May 18, 1997: A-1.

42. Ibid.

Chapter 15

1. Human Resources Development Canada, "Calendar of Expiring Major Collective Agreements in 1999": *http://labour-travail.hrdc-drhc.gc.ca/doc/wid-dimt/eng/expreo.cfm*

2. See, for example, Alexandra Dagg, "Worker Representation and Protection in the 'New Economy,'" Report of the Advisory Committee on the Changing Workplace, Human Resources Development Canada, Chapter 5: *http://www.reflection.gc.ca/report/contnt_e.htm*

3. Human Resources Development Canada, "Workplace Innovations Overview—1996," 5: *http://labour-travail.hrdc-drhc.gc.ca/wip/publications.html-ssi*

4. Human Resources Development Canada, "Workplace Innovations—Dialogue on Changes in the Workplace," 1995: *http://labour-travail.hrdc-drhc.gc.ca/WIP/english/June96.pdf*

5. Alexandra Dagg, "Worker Representation and Protection in the 'New Economy,'" Chapter 5: 78.

6. Mark MacKinnon, "Canada Leads G7 in Time Lost to Strikes," *The Globe and Mail*, April 5, 1999, B4.

7. Margot Gibb-Clark, "Key Employees Commanding Top Dollar," *The Globe and Mail*, November 2, 1999, B11.

8. This study was reported in: Alexandra Dagg, "Worker Representation and Protection in the 'New Economy,'" Chapter 5: 84.

9. Margot Gibb-Clark, "Key employees commanding top dollar."

10. Alexandra Dagg, "Worker Representation and Protection in the 'New Economy,'" Chapter 5: 76; and Statistics Canada, "General Social Survey: Time Use" *The Daily*, Tuesday, November 9, 1999: *http://www.statcan.ca/Daily/English/991109/d991109a.htm*

11. Human Resources Development Canada, "Workplace Innovations—Dialogue on Changes in the Workplace," 1995: 1.

12. D. Peach and P. Bergman, *The Practice of Labor Relations*, 3rd ed. (Toronto: McGraw-Hill Ryerson Ltd., 1991). See also A. B. Sloane and F. Witney, *Labor Relations*, 4th ed. (Englewood Cliffs, N.J.: Prentice-Hall, 1981): 28–35.

13. Abby Brown, "An Interview with Fritz Ihrig," *Personnel Management*, 31 (April 1986): 60.

14. H. Levinson, "Stress at the Bargaining Table," in *Labor Relations: Reports From the Firing Line* (Plano, Texas: Business Publications, 1988): 310.

15. *Industrial Relations Act*, RSNB (1973). C.I-4, S.1-100(1). Revised to June, 1994.

16. CAUT Collective Bargaining Cooperative, Collective Bargaining Conference Notes (Val Morin, Quebec), June 1993. Material adapted with permission.

17. Ibid. Material adapted with permission.

18. Canadian Labor Congress—Educational Services (Mimeograph, c. 1992). Adapted with permission.

19. Ibid. Adapted with permission.

20. B.M. Downie, "Third-Party Assistance in Collective Bargaining," in Sethi, A. S., Ed., *Collective Bargaining in Canada* (Scarborough: Nelson Canada, 1989): 153–154.

21. The material that follows was adapted from E.R. Zimmermann, *Manual on Legal Strike Action for Canadian Faculty Associations* (Ottawa: CAUT Collective Bargaining Cooperative, 1990). Adapted with permission.

22. A. MacDonald, "Irving Boycott Taking Its Toll Says Unions," *Halifax Chronicle*, February 11, 1991: C1.

23. The authors are indebted to Mr. Jim Horn, Director, Personnel Services at The University of New Brunswick, who wrote the first draft of this section.

24. N. Fuller, "NHL Owners Authorize a Lockout," *Financial Post Daily*, 7 (1994): 40.

25. G.T. Milkovich, W.F. Gluech, R.T. Barth, S.L. McShane, *Canadian Personnel/Human Resource Management* (Plano, Texas: Business Publications, Inc., 1988): 625.

26. F. Kehoe and M. Archer, *Canadian Industrial Relations* (Oakville: Twentieth Century Publications, 1980): 14.12.

27. Collective Agreement Between the University of New Brunswick and the Association of University of New Brunswick Teachers 1991–1995.

28. J. Gandz and J. Whitehead, "Grievances and Their Resolution," in M. Gunderson et al., Eds.,*Union–Management Relations in Canada*, 2nd ed. (Toronto: Addison-Wesley, 1989).

29. R.C. Basken, "Labor participation key to success," *Canadian Speeches*, 8 (4) (1994): 61–62.

30. Mark MacKinnon, "Canada leads G7 in time lost to strikes:" B4.

31. Information on this report was drawn from: Alexandra Dagg, "Worker Representation and Protection in the 'New Economy,'" Chapter 5: 86.

Chapter 16

1. Arthur R. Pell, "Effective Reprimanding," *Manager's Magazine* 65 (August 1990): 26.

2. David N. Campbell, R.L. Fleming, and Richard C. Grote, "Discipline Without Punishment—At Last," *Harvard Business Review* 63 (July–August 1985): 168.

3. Wallace Wohlking, "Effective Discipline in Employee Relations," *Personnel Journal* 54 (September 1975): 489.

4. Neil W. Chamberlain, *The Labor Sector* (New York: McGraw-Hill, 1985): 240.

5. K.L. Sovereign and Mario Bognanno, "Positive Contract Administration," in Dale Yoder and Herbert G. Heneman, Jr., Eds., *ASPA Handbook of Personnel and Industrial Relations: Employee and Labor Relations*, Vol. III (Washington, D.C.: The Bureau of National Affairs, 1976): 7-161-7-162.

6. Ibid., 7–164.

7. W.J. Alton and N.A. Soloman, *The System of Industrial Relations in Canada*, 5th ed. (Scarborough: Prentice Hall Canada, 1996): 339.

8. W.J. Alton and N. A. Soloman, *The System of Industrial Relations in Canada*: 339–340.

9. Lawrence Stessin, "Expedited Arbitration: Less Grief Over Grievances," *Harvard Business Review* 55 (January–February 1977): 129.

10. "Moving the corporate battle . . ." *The Globe and Mail*, June 21, 1994: B22.

11. Human Resources Development Canada, "Workplace Innovations—Dialogue on Changes in the Workplace": *http://labour-travail.hrdc-drhc.gc.ca/WIP/english/Oct94.pdf*

12. Paula Eubanks, "Employee Grievance Policy: Don't Discourage Complaints," *Hospitals* 64 (December 20, 1990): 36.

13. James P. Swann, Jr., "Formal Grievance Procedures in Non-Union Plants," *Personnel Administrator* 26 (August 1991): 67.

14. Jennifer Laabs, "Remedies for HR's Legal Headache," *Personnel Journal* 73 (December 1994): 69.

15. Edward Baig, "Careers: When It's Time to Do Battle with Your Company," *Business Week* (February 10, 1997): 130.

16. Robert V. Kuenzel, "Alternative Dispute Resolution: Why All the Fuss?" *Compensation & Benefits Review* 28 (July/August 1996): 43.

17. Human Resources Development Canada, "Workplace Innovations—Dialogue on Changes in the Workplace,": *http://labour-travail.hrdc-drhc.gc.ca/WIP/english/Oct94.pdf*

18. This section concerning the psychology of dismissal was written from notes made during a 1998 guest lecture by James Sweet, then manager of employee relations at Moore Business Forms Ltd., based in Toronto, Ontario.

19. Susan Caminiti, "What Happens To Laid-Off Managers," *Fortune,* 129 (June 13, 1994): 69.

20. G. Quill "Fired 'Producer Components' Say CBC Acted Badly," *The Toronto Star*, June 13, 1995, B5.

21. Ontario Ministry of Labour, Employment Standards Fact Sheet, "Termination of Employment,": *http://www.gov.on.ca/LAB/es/terminae.htm*

22. Michael Smith, "Help in Making Those Tough Layoff Decisions," *Supervisory Management* 35 (January 1990): 3.

23. Robert W. Keidel, "Layoffs Take Advance Preparation," *Management Review* 80 (May 1991): 6.

24. D. Lambe, "Downsizing and Workforce Adjustment . . .," Working Paper 94-13 (Faculty of Administration, University of Ottawa, 1994): 1.

25. T. Wagar, "Comparative Systems of Wrongful Dismissal: The Canadian Case," *The Annals of the American Academy of Political and Social Service* (November 1994).

26. E. Mole, *The Wrongful Dismissal Handbook* (Markham: Butterworths, 1990): 1.

27. Ontario Ministry of Labour, Employment Standards Fact Sheet "Termination of Employment,": *http://www.gov.on.ca/LAB/es/terminae.htm*

28. T. Wagar and J. Grant, "Dismissal for Incompetence: . . " *Labor Law Journal,* 44(3) (1993): 66.

29. As usual in Canada, there are exceptions. In three jurisdictions (federal, Quebec, and Nova Scotia) there are provisions for reinstatement through a process similar to arbitration. For example, see *Unjust Dismissal and The Canada Labour Code* (Ottawa: Labour Canada).

30. Randall Scott Echlin, "Courts Apply 'Smell Test' in Judging Contract Workers as Long-Term Employees," *The Globe and Mail* (November 22, 1999): M1.

31. Loretta D. Foxman and Walter L. Polsky, "Outplacement Results in Success," *Personnel Journal* 69 (February 1990): 30.

32. Randall Scott Echlin, "Dismissed, with Career Counselling," *The Globe and Mail*, October 25, 1999, M1.

33. Virginia M. Gibson, "In the Outplacement Door," *Personnel* 68 (October 1991): 3–4.

34. T. Degler, "Employers Continue Interest in EAPs Despite—and Because of—Cutbacks," *Canadian HR Reporter* 7(10) (1994): 10.

35. Joseph R. Rich and Beth C. Florin-Thuma, "Rewarding Employees in an Environment of Fewer Promotions," *Pension World* 26 (November 1990): 16.

36. "How Can We Make Work Rewarding?" *Canadian HR Reporter* 8(12) (1995): 3.

37. R. Degler, "Career Planning Joins Outplacement to Facilitate Employee Transition," *Canadian HR Reporter* 7 (13) (1994): 8.

38. Lin Grensing, "Don't Let Them out the Door without an Exit Interview," *Management World* 19 (March–April 1990): 11.

39. Robert Wolfe, "Most Employers Offer Exit Interviews," *HRNews* 10 (June 1990): 2.

40. Wanda R. Embrey, R. Wayne Mondy, and Robert M. Noe, "Exit Interview: A Tool for Personnel Development," *Personnel Administrator* 24 (May 1979): 46.

41. "Retirement Not an Option," Canadian Press, in *The Daily Gleaner*. July 18, 1995, 31.

42. P. Taylor, "Social Studies," *Saturday Night* (June 1995): 18–23.

43. P. Scherer and P. Statler, "Helping Your Employees Retire," *Canadian HR Reporter* 8(9) (1995): 12.

44. Ellen Brandt, "Global HR," *Personnel Journal* 70 (March 1991): 43.

45. Ibid.

46. Ibid.

SUBJECT INDEX